First published 2025 in Great Britain and the United States by ISTE Ltd and John Wiley & Sons, Inc.

ISTE Ltd
27-37 St George's Road
London SW19 4EU
UK

www.iste.co.uk

John Wiley & Sons, Inc.
111 River Street
Hoboken, NJ 07030
USA

www.wiley.com

Library of Congress Control Number: 2024945128

British Library Cataloguing-in-Publication Data
A CIP record for this book is available from the British Library
ISBN 978-1-78945-214-3

ERC code:
PE6 Computer Science and Informatics
PE6_5 Security, privacy, cryptology, quantum cryptography

Contents

Preface

Emmanuel PROUFF[1], Guénaël RENAULT[2], Matthieu RIVAIN[3] and Colin O'FLYNN[4]

[1] *LIP6, Sorbonne Université, Paris, France*
[2] *Agence nationale de la sécurité des systèmes d'information, Paris, France*
[3] *CryptoExperts, Paris, France*
[4] *Dalhousie University and NewAE Technology Inc, Halifax, Canada*

The idea for this project was born during a discussion with Damien Vergnaud. Damien had been asked to propose a series of volumes covering the different domains of modern cryptography for the SCIENCES series. He offered us the opportunity to take charge of the *Embedded Cryptography* books, which sounded like a great challenge to take on. In particular, we thought it was perfectly timely as the field was gaining increasing importance with the growing development of complex mobile systems and the Internet of Things.

The field of embedded cryptography, as a research domain, was born in the mid-1990s. Until that time, the evaluation of a cryptosystem and the underlying attacker model were usually agnostic of implementation aspects whether the cryptosystem was deployed on a computer or on some embedded hardware like a smart card. Indeed, the attacker was assumed to have no other information than the final results of a computation and, possibly, the corresponding inputs. In this black box context, defining a cryptanalytic attack and evaluating resistance to it essentially consisted of finding flaws in the abstract definition of the cryptosystem.

In the 1990s, teams of researchers published the first academic results, highlighting very effective means of attack against embedded systems. These attacks were based on the observation that a system's behavior during a computation strongly depends on the values of the data manipulated (which was previously known and exploited by intelligence services). Consequently, a device performing

Embedded Cryptography 2,
coordinated by Emmanuel PROUFF, Guénaël RENAULT,
Matthieu RIVAIN and Colin O'FLYNN. © ISTE Ltd 2025.

cryptographic computation does not behave like a black box whose inputs and outputs are the only known factors. The power consumption of the device, its electromagnetic radiation or its running time are indeed other sources that provide the observer with information on the intermediate results of the computation. Teams of researchers have also shown that it was possible to disrupt a computation using external energy sources such as lasers or electromagnetic pulses.

Among these so-called *physical attacks*, two main families emerge. The first gathers the (passive) side-channel attacks, including timing attacks proposed by Kocher in 1996 and power analysis attacks proposed by Kocher et al. in 1999, as well as the microarchitectural attacks which have considerably developed after the publication of the Spectre and Meltdown attacks in 2018. This first family of attacks focuses on the impact that the data manipulated by the system have on measurable physical quantities such as time, current consumption, or energy dissipation related to state changes in memories. The second family gathers the (active) fault injection attacks, whose first principles were introduced by Boneh et al. in 1997. These attacks aim to put the targeted system into an abnormal state of functioning. They consist, for example, of ensuring that certain parts of a code are not executed or that operations are replaced by others. Using attacks from either of these families, an adversary might learn sensitive information by exploiting the physical leakage or the faulted output of the system.

Since their inception, *side-channel attacks* and *fault injection attacks*, along with their countermeasures, have significantly evolved. Initially, the embedded systems industry and a limited number of academic labs responded with ad hoc countermeasures. Given the urgency of responding to the newly published attacks, these countermeasures were reasonably adequate at the time. Subsequently, the invalidation of many of these countermeasures and the increasing sophistication of attack techniques highlighted the need for a more formalized approach to security in embedded cryptography. A community was born from this observation in the late 1990s and gathered around a dedicated conference known as *Cryptographic Hardware and Embedded Systems* (CHES). Since then, the growth of this research domain has been very significant, resulting from the strong stake of the industrial players and the scientific interest of the open security issues. Nowadays, physical attacks involve state-of-the-art equipment capable of targeting nanoscale technologies used in the semiconductor industry. The attackers routinely use advanced statistical analyses or signal processing, while the defenders designing countermeasures calls on concepts from algebra, probability theory, or formal methods. More recently, and notably with the publication of the *Spectre* and *Meltdown* attacks, side-channel attacks have extended to so-called microarchitectural attacks, exploiting very common optimization techniques in modern CPUs such as out-of-order execution or speculative execution. Twenty-five years after the foundational work, there is now a large community of academic and industrial scientists dedicated to these problems. Embedded cryptography has gradually become a classic topic in cryptography and computer security, as illustrated by the increasing importance of this field in major cryptography and security conferences besides CHES, such as CRYPTO, Eurocrypt, Asiacrypt, Usenix Security, IEEE S&P or ACM CCS.

Pedagogical material

For this work, it seemed important to us to have both scientifically ambitious and pedagogical content. We indeed wanted this book to appeal not only to researchers in embedded cryptography but also to Master's students interested in the subject and curious to take their first steps. It was also important to us that the concepts and notions developed in the book be as illustrated as possible and therefore accompanied by a pedagogical base. In addition to the numerous illustrations proposed in the chapters, we have made pedagogical material available (attack scripts, implementation examples, etc.) to test and deepen the various concepts. These can be found on the following GitHub organization: https://github.com/embeddedcryptobook.

Content

This book provides a comprehensive exploration of embedded cryptography. It comprises 40 chapters grouped into nine main parts, and spanning three volumes. The book primarily addresses side-channel and fault injection attacks as well as their countermeasures. Part 1 of Volume 1 is dedicated to *Software Side-Channel Attacks*, namely, timing attacks and microarchitectural attacks, primarily affecting software; whereas Part 2 is dedicated to *Hardware Side-Channel Attacks*, which exploit hardware physical leakages, like power consumption and electromagnetic emanations. Part 3 focuses on the second crucial family of physical attacks against embedded systems, namely, *Fault Injection Attacks*.

A full part of this volume is dedicated to *Masking* in Part 1, which is a widely used countermeasure against side-channel attacks and which has become an important research topic since their introduction in 1999. This part covers a variety of masking techniques, their security proofs and their formal verification. Besides general masking techniques, efficient and secure embedded cryptographic implementations are very dependent on the underlying algorithm. Consequently, Part 2, *Cryptographic Implementations*, is dedicated to the implementation of specific cryptographic algorithm families, namely, AES, RSA, ECC, and post-quantum cryptography. This part also covers hardware acceleration and constant-time implementations. Secure embedded cryptography needs to rely on secure hardware and secure randomness generation. In cases where hardware alone is insufficient for security, we must rely on additional software techniques to protect cryptographic keys. The latter is known as white-box cryptography. The next three parts of the book address those aspects. Part 3 of this current volume, *Hardware Security*, covers invasive attacks, hardware countermeasures and physically unclonable functions (PUF).

Part 1 of Volume 3 is dedicated to *White-Box Cryptography*: it covers general concepts, practical attack tools, automatic (gray-box) attacks and countermeasures as well as code obfuscation, which is often considered as a complementary measure to white-box cryptography. Part 2 of Volume 3 is dedicated to *Randomness and Key Generation* in embedded cryptography. It covers both true and pseudo randomness generation as well as randomness generation for specific cryptographic algorithms (prime numbers for RSA, random nonces for ECC signatures, random errors for post-quantum schemes).

Finally, we wanted to include concrete examples of real world attacks against embedded cryptosystems. The final part of this series of books contains those examples of *Real World Applications and Attacks in the Wild*. While not exhaustive, we selected representative examples illustrating the practical exploitation of the attacks presented in this book, hence demonstrating the necessity of the science of embedded cryptography.

Acknowledgments

This series of books results from a collaborative work and many persons from the embedded cryptography community have contributed to its development. We have tried to cover (as broadly as possible) the field of embedded cryptography and the many research directions related to this field. This has not been an easy task, given the dynamism and growth of the field over the past 25 years. Some experts from the community kindly shared their insights on the preliminary plan of the book, namely, Sonia Belaïd, Pierre-Alain Fouque, Marc Joye, Victor Lomné and Yannick Sierra. We would like to thank them for their insightful comments.

For each of the identified topics we wanted the book to cover, we have called upon expert researchers from the community, who have honored us by joining this project. The essence of this work is theirs. Dear Guillaume Barbu, Lejla Batina, Sonia Belaïd, Davide Bellizia, Florent Bernard, Begül Bilgin, Eleonora Cagli, Łukasz Chmielewski, Jessy Clédière, Brice Colombier, Jean-Sébastien Coron, Jean-Luc Danger, Lauren De Meyer, Cécile Dumas, Jean-Max Dutertre, Viktor Fischer, Pierre Galissant, Benedikt Gierlichs, Louis Goubin, Vincent Grosso, Sylvain Guilley, Patrick Haddad, Laurent Imbert, Ján Jančár, Marc Joye, Matthias Kannwischer, Stefan Katzenbeisser, Victor Lomné, José Lopes-Esteves, Ange Martinelli, Pedro Massolino, Loïc Masure, Nele Mentens, Debdeep Mukhopadhyay, Camille Mutschler, Ruben Niederhagen, Colin O'Flynn, Elisabeth Oswald, Dan Page, Pascal Paillier, Louisa Papachristodoulou, Thomas Peeters, Olivier Peirera, Thomas Pornin, Bart Preneel, Thomas Prest, Jean-René Reinhard, Thomas Roche,

Francisco Rodríguez-Henríquez, Franck Rondepierre, Eyal Ronen, Melissa Rossi, Mylene Rousselet, Sylvain Ruhault, Ulrich Ruhrmair, Sayandeep Saha, Patrick Schaumont, Sebastian Schrittwieser, Peter Schwabe, Richa Singh, Sergei Skorobogatov, François-Xavier Standaert, Petr Svenda, Marek Sys, Akira Takahashi, Abdul Rahman Taleb, Yannick Teglia, Philippe Teuwen, Adrian Thillard, Medhi Tibouchi, Mike Tunstall, Aleksei Udovenko, David Vigilant, Lennert Wouters, Yuval Yarom and Rina Zeitoun: thank you so much for the hard work!

To accompany these authors, we also relied on numerous reviewers who kindly shared their remarks on the preliminary versions of the chapters. Their behind-the-scenes work allowed us to greatly improve the technical and editorial quality of the books. We express our gratitude to them, namely, Davide Alessio, Sébastien Bardin, Sonia Belaïd, Eloi Benoist-Vanderbeken, Gaëtan Cassiers, Jean-Sebastien Coron, Debayan Das, Cécile Dumas, Julien Eynard, Wieland Fischer, Thomas Fuhr, Daniel Genkin, Dahmun Goudarzi, Eliane Jaulmes, Victor Lomné, Loïc Masure, Bart Mennink, Stjepan Picek, Thomas Pornin, Thomas Prest, Jurgen Pulkus, Michaël Quisquater, Thomas Roche, Franck Rondepierre, Franck Salvador, Tobias Schneider, Okan Seker, Pierre-Yves Strub, Akira Takahashi, Abdul Rahman Taleb, Mehdi Tibouchi, Aleksei Udovenko, Gilles Van Assche, Damien Vergnaud, Vincent Verneuil and Gabriel Zaid.

October 2024

Part 1

Masking

1

Introduction to Masking

Ange MARTINELLI and Mélissa ROSSI

Agence nationale de la sécurité des systèmes d'information, Paris, France

1.1. An overview of masking

In order to thwart the menace of passive side-channel attacks such as Differential Power Analysis (DPA) or templates attacks, the most deployed software countermeasure has been masking since its introduction in 1999. The main observation is that side-channel attacks use the relation between intermediates values and leakage traces. Thus, if intermediate values are independent from any secret, no information can be retrieved from the leakage. In a nutshell, masking consists of randomizing the intermediate data, which depend on both the secret values and known variables.

Each secret input x is basically split into $d+1$ variables $(x_i)_{0\leq i\leq d}$ referred as shares: d of them are generated uniformly at random, whereas the last one is computed such that their combination through some defined operation reveals the secret value x. The integer d is called *masking order*.

DEFINITION 1.1.– Sharing: let $\mathcal{E}$ be the finite support of the possible values for a sensitive variable x. Let $\mathsf{F} : \mathcal{E}^{d+1} \rightarrow \mathcal{E}$ be a function. A $(d+1)$-uple $\tilde{x} := (x_0, \ldots, x_d)$ is a *sharing* of x with respect to the recombination function F iff:

1) the distribution of all subsets of $(x_0, \ldots, x_d)$ of size at most d is statistically independent from x;

2) $x = \mathsf{F}(x_0, \ldots, x_d)$.

Embedded Cryptography 2,
coordinated by Emmanuel PROUFF, Guénaël RENAULT,
Matthieu RIVAIN and Colin O'FLYNN. © ISTE Ltd 2025.

The following example gives a method to design a three-sharing of an 8-bit value with respect to the XOR operation $\oplus$.

EXAMPLE 1.1.– *To mask an 8-bit value $x \in \mathbb{Z}_{2^8}$ at order 2 with respect to the recombination function $\mathsf{F}(x_0, x_1, x_2) := x_0 \oplus x_1 \oplus x_2$, we can proceed by generating two values x_0 and x_1 uniformly at random in $\mathbb{Z}_{2^8}$, and next defining $x_2 := x \oplus x_0 \oplus x_1$. That way, the second condition is automatically validated. For the first condition, any set of two values in (x_0, x_1, x_2) is indistinguishable from $\mathcal{U}(\mathbb{Z}_{2^8}) \times \mathcal{U}(\mathbb{Z}_{2^8})$ (where $\mathcal{U}$ denotes the uniform distribution in the given finite set) and the same is verified for singletons. Thus, (x_0, x_1, x_2) is a sharing of x with respect to operation $\oplus$.*

DEFINITION 1.2.– Masked scheme: let C be a circuit implementing a cryptographic scheme; we call *masked scheme* a scheme $\tilde{C}$ that is *functionally equivalent* and where all the sensitive values are manipulated in masked form.

Note that a masked scheme is *not secure by design* and designing a masked scheme could be an error-prone task. Each masked design should be proved in a security model as will be presented later in Chapter 4 of this volume. For this purpose, we also define the notion of *gadget* that corresponds to sub-algorithms.

DEFINITION 1.3.– Gadget: a gadget is a probabilistic algorithm that takes shared and unshared inputs values and returns shared and unshared values.

In practice, while security increases with the masking order, the cost of masking can be quite heavy, both in terms of circuit size and performances and increases with the number of shares; thus, most masked scheme implementations are in first order (i.e. with two shares) or second order (i.e. with three shares).

1.2. The effect of masking on side-channel leakage

In general, if the device leaks information on one manipulated variable at a time, a d-order masking resists to stronger attacks which can combine information on at most d points of measure. In particular, Chari et al. (1999) have shown that the number of measurements required to mount a successful power analysis attack increases exponentially with the number of shares – see higher order attacks in Chapter 7 of Volume 1. Their model was considering the very classical case where each manipulated bit is leaking its noisy value, that is, the sum of its value and a Gaussian noise. Therefore, the masking order represents a trade-off between security and efficiency.

However, the reader may wonder about the precise theoretical link between masking and the potential physical leakages. Indeed, the masking countermeasure protects against an attacker able to obtain at most d intermediate values with exact precision. This attacker model is called the d-probing model. Such a model could be far from the reality where the attacker actually obtains *many noisy intermediate values through measured leakage*. We can thus define various *leakage models* being more realistic, such as the *noisy leakage model*, or in which the security of masking is easier to assess, such as the probing model.

Let us first mention the three prominent leakage models. More details with formal definitions will be provided later in this chapter.

Probing model: in this model, besides the black-box information of the cryptosystem, the attacker is able to obtain the actual value (called "probes") of at most d exact intermediate values of its choice, where d is a parameter. Masking allows us to reach provable security in this model.

Random probing model: in this model, besides the black-box information of the cryptosystem, the attacker has access to *each intermediate value with a certain probability* p, where p is a parameter.

Noisy leakage model: in this model, besides the black-box information of the cryptosystem, the attacker has access to *all intermediate values but they are all noisy*. The standard deviation of the noise level is a parameter of this model.

The precise description and reductions between models will be detailed and proved in Chapter 4 of this volume. A high level idea that outlines the power of provable security of masking is as follows: it is possible to derive bounds on the parameters to move from a model to another. For example, if a scheme is secure in the probing model with a high d, it will be secure in the noisy leakage model with a low level of noise.

1.3. Different types of masking

As seen in our Definition 1.1, masking is a very versatile definition that can be implemented with any recombination function, purposely arbitrarily denoted as F. The choice of this function has strong repercussions on the efficiency and the leakage of the overall implementation. For efficiency matters, an operator that behaves efficiently, typically linearly, when composed with operations on shares is desirable. However, linear operation allows for easy recovery with side-channel information. In particular, the higher the algebraic complexity of the operation, the higher the impact of the noise on the recombining function, thus the higher the concrete security against side-channel attacks. In practice, masking is a costly countermeasure and efficiency matters are prominent. Thus, the vast majority of the masked schemes involve efficient recombination functions when composed of the most numerous operations of the cryptographic algorithm, often linear operations such as XOR, modular additions or multiplications by scalars. In practice, the two foremost maskings are *Boolean masking* and *arithmetic masking*.

Boolean and arithmetic masking: these families of masking provide the best trade-off concerning the efficiency and leakage. Main cryptographic operations are linear with either Boolean or arithmetic maskings. Thus, even if the leakage could be strong in case of low noise, it is sometimes less expensive to increase the masking order than to consider another type of masking with the same order.

DEFINITION 1.4.– Let $\mathcal{E}$ be the support of the possible values for a sensitive variable x. Let $\mathsf{F} : \mathcal{E}^{d+1} \to \mathcal{E}$ be a function and $q \in \mathbb{Z}$ a parameter. A Boolean, respectively, arithmetically, masked value is a sharing as defined in Definition 1.1 with $\mathsf{F}(x_0, \dots, x_d) := x_0 \oplus \dots \oplus x_d$, respectively, $\mathsf{F}(x_0, \dots, x_d) := x_0 + \dots + x_d \mod q$.

Let us remark that the space $\mathcal{E}$ is not necessarily a set of integers, and it can be any set compatible with the recombination function. Commonly, for example, a sharing can be defined over a polynomial ring like $\mathcal{E} = \mathbb{Z}_q[X]/(X^n + 1)$ for $q, n \in \mathbb{Z}$. In that case, an arithmetic masking modulus q is a natural masking solution.

Polynomial masking: this masking leverages the idea behind Lagrange polynomials: let P be a degree $d + 1$ polynomial. The knowledge of $d + 1$ couples $(y_i, \mathsf{P}(y_i))$ for any all distinct $y_0, y_1 ... y_d$ allows us to completely reconstruct the polynomial P. Conversely, the knowledge of strictly less than $d + 1$ couples $(y_i, \mathsf{P}(y_i))$ gives no information on the actual polynomial. The principle for masking a sensible value $x \in \mathcal{E}$ is simple: x is first embedded in a $(d + 1)$-degree polynomial $\mathsf{P} \in \mathcal{E}[X]$, typically x is such that $\mathsf{P}(0) = x$. The shares are therefore defined as $d + 1$ couples $x_i = (y_i, \mathsf{P}(y_i))$, and we choose here $(1, \mathsf{P}(1))$, $(2, \mathsf{P}(2)), \dots, (d + 1, \mathsf{P}(d + 1))$. To recover the polynomial with the knowledge of all the $\mathsf{P}(i)$, we can recover the polynomial through Lagrange's formula:

$$L_{\mathsf{P}(1),\dots,\mathsf{P}(d+1)}(X) := \sum_{i=1}^{d+1} \mathsf{P}(i) \cdot \left(\prod_{j=1, j \neq i}^{j=d+1} \frac{X - j}{i - j} \right)$$

Next, we can recombine the secret with $\mathsf{F}(x_0, \dots, x_d) = L_{\mathsf{P}(1),\dots,\mathsf{P}(d+1)}(0)$.

This type of masking has a quite complex recombination function, thus it intuitively leads to a very low practical leakage while being somehow more expensive in terms of performance. Indeed, few common cryptographic operations are linear with a decomposition on polynomial images.

Multiplicative masking: the multiplicative masking consists of applying $\mathsf{F}(x_0, \dots, x_d) := x_0 \times \dots \times x_d$ in Definition 1.1, where the multiplication is made in the corresponding field $\mathcal{E}$. This type of masking can be very well suited for the SubBytes step of the AES. Indeed, $x \mapsto x^{-1}$ is an endomorphism of $GF(256)^*$.

Practical activity: Algorithm 1.1 is applying this technique for a field inversion after an addition of the key to the plaintext. The inversion is performed in $GF(256)^*$ and it is sequentially applied to every byte of the 128-bit state, denoted as S. For the sake of simplicity and because the XOR operation is outside of the scope of this activity, the masked state $S = (S_0, \dots, S_d)$ given as input of the algorithm is the masked XOR of the key k and the plaintext P. The shares $S_1, \dots S_d$ are generated uniformly at random in $(GF(256)^*)^{16}$ and $S_0 = x \times S_1 \times \cdots \times S_d$. In the additional material, some traces of this algorithm are provided with the corresponding plaintexts. They were derived on a ChipWhisperer-Lite Xmega. A high-order side-channel attack seems tedious; you could exploit a property of multiplicative masking to recover the whole secret k with a simple first-order DPA (see Chapter 4 of Volume 1).

Algorithm 1.1.

Secret : A multiplicative masking $(k_0, \cdots k_4) \in [0, 255]^5$ of a key $k = k_0 \cdot k_1 \cdots k_4 \in [0, 255]$

Input : A multiplicative masking $(S_0, \cdots S_4) \in ([0, 255]^{16})^5$ of a value $P \oplus k$ for a known P

for $b \in [0, 15]$ **do**
  for $i \in [0, 4]$ **do**
    $S_i[b] := (S_i[b])^{254}$
  end
end

Inner-product masking and affine masking: as outlined above, multiplicative masking has some vulnerabilities if not used properly but we can combine it with a Boolean one as follows.

DEFINITION 1.5.– Let $x \in \mathcal{E}$ be a sensitive value, $(v_0, \dots, v_d) \in \mathcal{E}$ be fixed vector and $\langle \cdot, \cdot \rangle$ be a $\oplus$-linear inner product defined on $\mathcal{E}$. An inner product masked value is a masked value as defined in Definition 1.1, with:

$$\mathsf{F}(x_0, \dots, x_d) := \langle (x_0, \dots, x_d), (v_0, \dots, v_d) \rangle.$$

The particular case of $d = 1$ and $v_1 = 1$ is called an *affine masking*.

This masking is slightly less efficient than the Boolean masking because of the extra multiplication operations but it may offer stronger security as the leakage can be better de-correlated from the secret. This kind of masking and the following schemes aim at lowering down the amount of information which can be recovered from the leakage. They can all offer a better security/complexity tradeoff in a specific setup.

Leakage squeezing: this consists of applying a different bijection to each share and proceeds with standard masking – mostly Boolean. The squeezing functions need to be bijective to recover the plain shares during computation and to unmask the output. Eventually, first-order Boolean masking combined with leakage squeezing gives similar security than masking with two to three more shares for a different complexity, more suited in hardware.

DEFINITION 1.6.– Let $x = (x_0, \ldots, x_d) \in \mathcal{E}^{d+1}$ be a masked sensitive value. Let $(B_0, \ldots, B_d)$ be a set of bijections over $\mathcal{E}$. We call leakage squeezing the application of the B_is over x such that the operated circuit works on $\tilde{x} = (B_0(x_0), \ldots, B_d(x_d))$.

Orthogonal direct sum masking: in order to ensure dual security against both passive and active attacks, masking using error correcting codes has been proposed as follows.

DEFINITION 1.7.– Let $x \in \mathcal{E}$ be a sensitive value and $\mathbf{y} \in \mathcal{E}^d$ a vector of masks. Let G and H be generator matrices of two linear codes $\mathcal{C}$ and $\mathcal{D}$ such that $\mathcal{C} \cap \mathcal{D} = \{0\}$ and $\mathcal{C} + \mathcal{D} = \mathcal{E}^{d+1}$. We can define the orthogonal direct sum masking of x as $z = xG \oplus \mathbf{y}H$, where xG denote the scalar–vector product and $\mathbf{y}H$ the vector–matrix product. We can then recover x as $x = zG^T(GG^T)^{-1}$.

1.4. Code-based masking: toward a generic framework

While Boolean and arithmetic masking are the most common choices, a lot of other operations are possible as outlined in section 1.4. Many more masking recombination functions F have been attempted to improve either the security in some settings or to provide a more global theoretical background. In this section, we outline a generalization of the Boolean masking family. Indeed, the Boolean masking can be seen as a sub-case of the inner product masking. This can go further: inner product masking is a sub-case of leakage squeezing (LS), itself generalized as orthogonal direct sum masking. As a side methodology with some intersections, there stands polynomial masking.

As an attempt at uniformization, generalized code-based masking has been introduced to give a common framework to all of these schemes as shown in Figure 1.1. It has been shown that any other masking scheme outlined in section 1.4 can be instantiated using generalized code-based masking.

Generalized code-based masking is similar to orthogonal direct sum masking where $\mathcal{C}$ and $\mathcal{D}$ can be any matrices such that $dim(\mathcal{C}) + dim(\mathcal{D}) \leq d + 1$. Let us define the matrices G and H as generator matrices of the linear codes $\mathcal{C}$ and $\mathcal{D}$, respectively. Let k be the dimension of G and t the dimension of H. Table 1.1 gives an overview of how to parameterize code-based masking to instantiate specific masking.

Scheme	Boolean	IP	LS	ODS	Polynomial	GCB
Conditions	$\mathcal{C} \cap \mathcal{D} = \{0\}$ $\mathcal{C} + \mathcal{D} = \mathcal{E}^{d+1}$	$\mathcal{C} \cap \mathcal{D} = \{0\}$ $\mathcal{C} + \mathcal{D} = \mathcal{E}^{d+1}$	$\mathcal{C} \cap \mathcal{D} = \{0\}$ $\mathcal{C} + \mathcal{D} = \mathcal{E}^{d+1}$	$\mathcal{C} \cap \mathcal{D} = \{0\}$	$\mathcal{C} \cap \mathcal{D} = \{0\}$	$\mathcal{C} \cap \mathcal{D} = \{0\}$
$G \in \mathcal{E}^{k \times d}$	$(1\,0\,0 \cdots 0)$	$(1\,0\,0 \cdots 0)$	$G \in \mathcal{E}^{k \times d}$	$G \in \mathcal{E}^{k \times d}$	$(1\,1 \cdots 1)$	$G \in \mathcal{E}^{k \times d}$
$H \in \mathcal{E}^{t \times d}$	$\begin{pmatrix} 1 & 0 & \cdots & 0 \\ 1 & 1 & \cdots & 0 \\ \vdots & \vdots & \ddots & \vdots \\ 1 & 0 & \cdots & 1 \end{pmatrix}$	$\begin{pmatrix} a_1 & 1 & 0 & \cdots & 0 \\ a_2 & 0 & 1 & \cdots & 0 \\ \vdots & \vdots & \vdots & \ddots & \vdots \\ a_t & 0 & 0 & \cdots & 1 \end{pmatrix}$	$H \in \mathcal{E}^{t \times d}$	$H \in \mathcal{E}^{t \times d}$	$\begin{pmatrix} a_1^1 & a_2^1 & \cdots & a_d^1 \\ a_1^2 & a_2^2 & \cdots & a_d^2 \\ \vdots & \vdots & \ddots & \vdots \\ a_1^t & a_2^t & \cdots & a_d^t \end{pmatrix}$	$H \in \mathcal{E}^{t \times d}$
Parameters	$k = 1, d = t + 1$	$k = 1, d = t + 1$	$d = k + t$	$d = k + t$	$d \geq k + t$	$d \geq k + t$

Table 1.1. *Instantiation of masking schemes through generalized code-based masking*

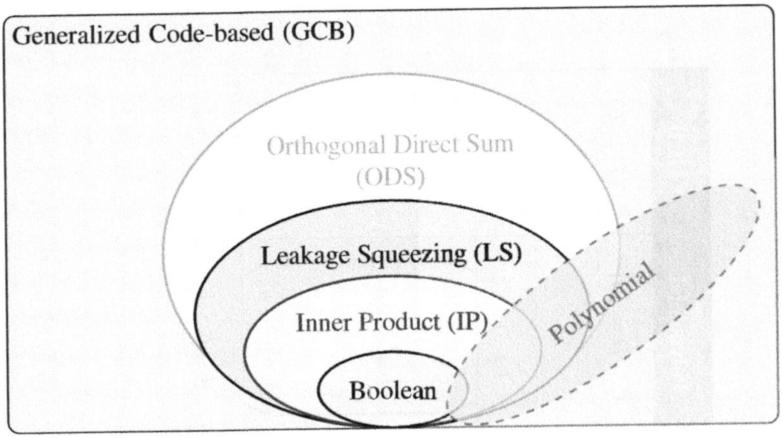

Figure 1.1. *Generalization of masking schemes under code-based masking. For a color version of this figure, see www.iste.co.uk/prouff/cryptography2.zip*

1.5. Hybrid masking

One type of masking is not often suited for a whole cryptographic algorithm. For example, whereas a multiplicative masking can be well suited for a SubBytes application corresponding to $x \mapsto x^{254}$ in $GF(256)$, it is not suited for the addition of the sub-keys in the value (this time linear for $\oplus$). Furthermore, an arithmetic masking could be perfectly suited for addition of polynomials in $\mathbb{Z}_q[X]/(X^n+1)$ for $q, n \in \mathbb{Z}$, but it is not well suited for deriving a masked outcome of a comparison $|p| \geq K$ for p being a polynomial coefficient and K being a constant. These cases are very frequent in cryptographic algorithms. Hence, several types of masking can be necessary for an efficient masked algorithm. In consequence, *conversion algorithms are necessary*. The particularity of these algorithms is the fact that they are functionally equivalent to the identity function; however, they take a masked variable as input and return this same variable but masked with a different type of masking.

There is no generic technique for deriving such algorithms independently of the types of masking. Efficient conversions are sometimes challenging to design in a secure way. The case of Boolean to arithmetic conversions will be depicted later in Chapter 2 of this volume. There also exist less widespread conversions like multiplicative to Boolean. Some additional information on these conversions will be pointed out later in the references.

1.6. Examples of specific maskings

Masking is a very powerful countermeasure and is usually implemented either table-based or directly implementing masked operations. Nevertheless, some algorithms can be efficiently masked with specific methods.

As will be detailed in Chapter 9 of this volume, the RSA algorithm has simple and efficient ways to do exponent *blinding* to protect the exponentiation modulo, the product of two primes. This kind of masking uses a random multiple of the order of the multiplicative group to protect the exponentiation. The eventual output stays unchanged but the actual exponent used in the computation is randomized.

Mini-game: let us try to wear the adversary's shoes. Here are several masked algorithms, and we assume that they are functionally correct, that is, the outputs are correctly computed as functions of the inputs. However, for each algorithm, there is a masking flaw in the probing model (informally defined earlier in this chapter and formally defined later in Chapter 4 of this volume). In a masking context, the goal of an adversary against the masking is to break Definition 1.1. Thus, the goal is to find a subset of less than d variables, which is correlated to the secret.

1) Here, $d = 2$. This algorithm is simply computing an XOR of its inputs. The secret here is a.

Algorithm 1.2.

Input : Boolean masking $(a_0, a_1), (b_0, b_1) \in [0, 255]^2$
Output: Boolean masking $(c_0, c_1) \in [0, 255]^2$

```
c_0 := a_0 ⊕ a_1
c_0 := c_0 ⊕ b_0
c_1 := b_1
return (c_0, c_1)
```

2) Here, $d = 3$. This algorithm is computing the multiplication of two inputs masked in Boolean form. Your goal is to recover a with at most two intermediate values.

3) In this algorithm, $d = 4$. This algorithm generates an arithmetic masking in $\mathbb{Z}/2^{16}\mathbb{Z}$ of a sample whose distribution is centered and has a small standard deviation. Let us define D as a centered discrete Gaussian distribution on $\mathbb{Z}/2^{16}\mathbb{Z}$ with a small standard deviation 0.5. Note that distribution does not correspond to the final one, and the precise description of the final distribution is not necessary for finding flaws in this algorithm. Your goal is to find three intermediate variables that provide some information about the secret, the output c.

Algorithm 1.3.

Input : $(a_0, a_1, a_2), (b_0, b_1, b_2) \in [0, 255]^3$
Output: $(c_0, c_1, c_2) \in [0, 255]^3$

$r_{0,1}, r_{0,2}, r_{1,2} \xleftarrow{\$} [0, 255]$
$r_{1,0} := a_0 b_1 \oplus a_2 b_1$
$r_{2,0} := (r_{0,2} \oplus a_0 b_2) \oplus a_1 b_0$
$r_{2,1} := (r_{0,1} \oplus a_1 b_2) \oplus a_2 b_0$
$c_0 := a_0 b_0 \oplus (r_{0,1} \oplus r_{0,2})$
$c_1 := a_1 b_1 \oplus r_{1,0}$
$c_2 := a_2 b_2 \oplus (r_{2,0} \oplus r_{2,1})$
return (c_0, c_1, c_2)

Algorithm 1.4.

Output: $(c_0, c_1, c_2, c_3) \in \mathbb{Z}/2^{16}\mathbb{Z}$

for $i \in [0, 3]$ **do**
  $r_i \leftarrow D$
  $y_i \xleftarrow{\$} \mathbb{Z}/2^{16}\mathbb{Z}$ /* drawing in $\mathbb{Z}/2^{16}\mathbb{Z}$ uniformly at random */
  $c_i := r_i + y_i$
end
return (c_0, c_1, c_2, c_3)

1.7. Outline of the part

Masking is a very powerful tool to generically protect cryptographic algorithms against side-channel attacks. However, there is an important tradeoff between efficiency and security with many levels, and it will be the main subject of this part.

In Chapter 2, several common cryptographic algorithms and functions will be masked with emphasis on elementary operations.

Chapter 3 of this volume outlines the impact of hardware on masking and the necessity to take into account physical phenomena like glitches in the design of masking implementations. Chapter 4 focuses on the various security models available to prove masking implementations. Eventually, Chapter 5 gives tools to implement masking schemes on specific algorithms and to assess their security.

1.8. Notes and further references

– Section 1.1. The theory of masking has been seminally introduced in Goubin and Patarin (1999); Ishai et al. (2003); Goudarzi and Rivain (2016).

– Section 1.2. For more information about the effect of masking on side-channel leakage, we refer to Chari et al. (1999) and Barthe et al. (2017), and more information on the different models will be presented later in the chapter.

– Section 1.3. For concrete examples of Boolean, arithmetic and multiplicative masking, we refer to Rivain and Prouff (2010) and Genelle et al. (2011).

– Section 1.4. For more information and recent works in the domain of code-based masking, we recommand Bringer et al. (2014); Wang et al. (2020) and Cheng et al. (2021).

1.9. References

Barthe, G., Dupressoir, F., Faust, S., Grégoire, B., Standaert, F.-X., Strub, P.-Y. (2017). Parallel implementations of masking schemes and the bounded moment leakage model. Report 2016/912, Cryptology ePrint Archive [Online]. Available at: https://eprint.iacr.org/2016/912.

Bringer, J., Carlet, C., Chabanne, H., Guilley, S., Maghrebi, H. (2014). Orthogonal direct sum masking: A smartcard friendly computation paradigm in a code, with builtin protection against side-channel and fault attacks. In *WISTP*. Springer, Berlin, Heidelberg.

Chari, S., Jutla, C.S., Rao, J.R., Rohatgi, P. (1999). Towards sound approaches to counteract power-analysis attacks. In *Advances in Cryptology – CRYPTO' 99*, Wiener, M. (ed.). Springer, Berlin, Heidelberg.

Cheng, W., Guilley, S., Carlet, C., Danger, J.-L., Mesnager, S. (2021). Information leakages in code-based masking: A unified quantification approach. *IACR Transactions on Cryptographic Hardware and Embedded Systems*, 3, 465–495.

Genelle, L., Prouff, E., Quisquater, M. (2011). Thwarting higher-order side channel analysis with additive and multiplicative maskings. In *Cryptographic Hardware and Embedded Systems – CHES 2011*, Preneel, B. and Takagi, T. (eds). Springer, Berlin, Heidelberg.

Goubin, L. and Patarin, J. (1999). DES and differential power analysis (the "duplication" method). In *Cryptographic Hardware and Embedded Systems – CHES 1999*, Koç, Ç.K. and Paar, C. (eds). Springer, Berlin, Heidelberg.

Goudarzi, D. and Rivain, M. (2016). On the multiplicative complexity of Boolean functions and bitsliced higher-order masking. In *Cryptographic Hardware and Embedded Systems – CHES 2016*. Springer, Berlin, Heidelberg.

Ishai, Y., Sahai, A., Wagner, D. (2003). Private circuits: Securing hardware against probing attacks. In *Advances in Cryptology – CRYPTO 2003*, Boneh, D. (ed.). Springer, Berlin, Heidelberg.

Rivain, M. and Prouff, E. (2010). Provably secure higher-order masking of AES. In *Cryptographic Hardware and Embedded Systems – CHES 2010*, Mangard, S. and Standaert, F.X. (eds). Springer, Berlin, Heidelberg.

Wang, W., Méaux, P., Cassiers, G., Standaert, F.-X. (2020). Efficient and private computations with code-based masking. *IACR Transactions on Cryptographic Hardware and Embedded Systems*, 2, 128–171.

2

Masking Schemes

Jean-Sébastien CORON[1] and Rina ZEITOUN[2]
[1] *University of Luxembourg, Luxembourg*
[2] *Cryptography & Security Labs, IDEMIA, Courbevoie, France*

2.1. Introduction to masking operations

As we have seen in the previous chapter, the main countermeasure against side-channel attacks is masking. For Boolean masking, it consists of splitting each variable x into n Boolean shares $x = x_1 \oplus x_2 \oplus \cdots \oplus x_n$, with $n > t$ for security against t probes. Initially, the shares are generated uniformly at random under this condition. For example, we can generate $x_1, \ldots, x_{n-1}$ randomly and let $x_n = x \oplus x_1 \oplus \cdots \oplus x_{n-1}$. The shares are then processed separately in masked operations (also called gadgets) that enable us to compute the underlying secret variables in a secure way.

2.2. Classical linear operations

A block-cipher such as AES alternates several rounds, each containing some linear transformations, and some nonlinear transformations. A linear function $y = f(x)$ is easy to mask when x is shared as $x = x_1 \oplus \cdots \oplus x_n$, as we have:

$$y = f(x) = f(x_1 \oplus \cdots \oplus x_n) = f(x_1) \oplus \cdots \oplus f(x_n),$$

so it suffices to compute $y_i = f(x_i)$ separately for every i, so that we eventually get $y = y_1 \oplus \cdots \oplus y_n$ as required. Consider, for example, the squaring operation. Since

Embedded Cryptography 2,
coordinated by Emmanuel PROUFF, Guénaël RENAULT,
Matthieu RIVAIN and Colin O'FLYNN.

squaring is linear in $\mathbb{F}_{2^k}$, given as input the shares x_i of $x = x_1 \oplus \cdots \oplus x_n$, we can compute the shares y_i of $y = x^2 = (x_1 \oplus \cdots \oplus x_n)^2 = x_1^2 \oplus \cdots \oplus x_n^2$ simply by letting $y_i = x_i^2$ for all $1 \leq i \leq n$.

Similarly, processing the xor operation is straightforward. Given as input the shares x_i and y_i of $x = x_1 \oplus \cdots \oplus x_n$ and $y = y_1 \oplus \cdots \oplus y_n$, we can obtain the shares z_i of $z = x \oplus y$ simply by letting $z_i = x_i \oplus y_i$ for all $1 \leq i \leq n$.

2.3. Classical nonlinear operations

As explained above, linear operations are straightforward to mask by performing computations on each share independently. This is however not the case for nonlinear operations, which generally require the processing of all shares together to compute the correct result. To preserve security against t-th order attack in this context, a dedicated method becomes necessary, usually involving additional randomness.

In the following, the crucial problem of masking the AND operation is addressed, as any circuit (at the hardware level) can be implemented using only the linear XOR gate and the nonlinear AND gate. As a second step, we describe mask refreshing techniques, which are frequently required to ensure the security of a full construction when composing many gadgets.

The so-called Ishai, Sahai and Wagner (ISW) scheme securely computes a sharing of $c = a \wedge b$ from two input sharings $(a_1, a_2, \ldots, a_n)$ and $(b_1, b_2, \ldots, b_n)$ of a and b, respectively, by computing all of the cross-products $a_i \wedge b_j$ for $1 \leq i, j \leq n$ based on the following equation:

$$c = ab = \left(\bigoplus_{i=1}^{n} a_i\right) \cdot \left(\bigoplus_{i=1}^{n} b_i\right) = \bigoplus_{1 \leq i,j \leq n} a_i b_j \qquad [2.1]$$

Those n^2 products are then recombined in n new shares $(c_1, c_2, \ldots, c_n)$, including fresh random elements $r_{i,j}$ to ensure security; namely, a straightforward recombination of the cross-products would not achieve security against t probes for any $t < n$.

The ISW scheme is pictured in Algorithm 2.1. It was originally described over $\mathbb{F}_2$. To process an AND gate over $\{0,1\}^k$, the algorithm is adapted as follows: (i) all 1-bit variables defined over $\mathbb{F}_2$ are replaced by k-bit variables defined over $\{0,1\}^k$; (ii) the 1-bit XOR operations are replaced by k-bit XOR operations; and (iii) the 1-bit AND operations are replaced by k-bit AND operations. This extension still preserves the security of the original scheme. In line 8, we use brackets to indicate the order of the operations, as this is mandatory for the security of the scheme. Algorithm 2.1 enables us to securely evaluate the AND operation at the cost of n^2 multiplications (which correspond to the n^2 cross-products), $n(n-1)/2$ random values (which are necessary to perform their secure recombination) and $2n(n-1)$ additions (which allow us to achieve the aforementioned recombination). Its complexity is therefore $\mathcal{O}(n^2)$, with a number of operations $T_{\mathsf{ISW}}(n) = n(7n-5)/2$.

Algorithm 2.1. SecAnd

Input: $k \in \mathbb{N}$, shares $a_i \in \{0,1\}^k$ satisfying $\bigoplus_{i=1}^{n} a_i = a$, shares $b_i \in \{0,1\}^k$ satisfying $\bigoplus_{i=1}^{n} b_i = b$

Output: shares $c_i \in \{0,1\}^k$ satisfying $\bigoplus_{i=1}^{n} c_i = a \wedge b$

for $i = 1$ **to** n **do**
    $c_i \leftarrow a_i \wedge b_i$
end for
for $i = 1$ **to** $n-1$ **do**
    for $j = i+1$ **to** n **do**
        $r \leftarrow \mathbb{F}_{2^k}$ ▷ referred by $r_{i,j}$
        $c_i \leftarrow c_i \oplus r$ ▷ referred by $c_{i,j}$
        $r \leftarrow ((a_i \wedge b_j) \oplus r) \oplus (a_j \wedge b_i)$ ▷ referred by $r_{j,i}$
        $c_j \leftarrow c_j \oplus r$ ▷ referred by $c_{j,i}$
    end for
end for
return $(c_1, \ldots, c_n)$

2.3.1. *Application of ISW algorithm for* $n = 2$ *and* $n = 3$

We illustrate the ISW algorithm for $n = 2$ and $n = 3$.

– For $n = 2$ with input shares (a_1, a_2) and (b_1, b_2), the output shares (c_1, c_2) are given as:

$$c_1 = (a_1 \wedge b_1) \oplus r_{1,2}$$

$$c_2 = (a_2 \wedge b_2) \oplus (((a_1 \wedge b_2) \oplus r_{1,2}) \oplus (a_2 \wedge b_1))$$

– For $n = 3$ with input shares (a_1, a_2, a_3) and (b_1, b_2, b_3), the output shares (c_1, c_2, c_3) are given as:

$$c_1 = ((a_1 \wedge b_1) \oplus r_{1,2}) \oplus r_{1,3}$$

$$c_2 = ((a_2 \wedge b_2) \oplus (((a_1 \wedge b_2) \oplus r_{1,2}) \oplus (a_2 \wedge b_1))) \oplus r_{2,3}$$

$$c_3 = ((a_3 \wedge b_3) \oplus (((a_1 \wedge b_3) \oplus r_{1,3}) \oplus (a_3 \wedge b_1))) \oplus (((a_2 \wedge b_3) \oplus r_{2,3}) \oplus (a_3 \wedge b_2))$$

2.4. Mask refreshing

A mask refreshing algorithm consists of updating a given sharing while encoding the same value. Refreshing algorithms are an essential ingredient for secure masking, as they enable us to securely compose gadgets within a larger circuit. This enables the partitioning of a masked implementation into small components that are easier to analyze in terms of security. A drawback of refreshing algorithms is their randomness cost, which can account for a significant part of the global performance overhead. Three classical refresh masks algorithms are depicted hereafter according to their security level and efficiency.

2.4.1. *Refresh masks with complexity* $\mathcal{O}(n)$

The mask refreshing scheme depicted in Algorithm 2.2 has complexity $\mathcal{O}(n)$, which is quite efficient. However, it is only useful in specific constructions such as the table recomputation countermeasure (see section 2.5). As depicted in Figure 2.1, it simply consists of updating all shares by xoring each of them with a fresh random value, and in accumulating all of those fresh random values into a dedicated share (here the last one c_n) in order to encode the same value (see Figure 2.1 for an illustration). This gives a total number of operations $T_{\mathsf{LinearRefreshMasks}}(n) = 3(n-1)$.

Algorithm 2.2. LinearRefreshMasks

Input: $a_1, \ldots, a_n$

Output: $c_1, \ldots, c_n$ such that $\bigoplus_{i=1}^{n} c_i = \bigoplus_{i=1}^{n} a_i$

$c_n \leftarrow a_n$

for $j = 1$ to $n-1$ **do**

  $r_j \leftarrow \mathbb{F}_{2^k}$

  $c_j \leftarrow a_j \oplus r_j$

  $c_n \leftarrow c_n \oplus r_j$

end for

return $c_1, \ldots, c_n$

2.4.2. *Refresh masks with complexity* $\mathcal{O}(n^2)$

The refresh masks operation depicted in Algorithm 2.3 has complexity $\mathcal{O}(n^2)$, but it enables the secure composability of gadgets in a full construction. The algorithm is a straightforward application of the ISW multiplication scheme by performing a secure multiplication by 1, that is, by using $(1, 0, \ldots, 0)$ as second input of the ISW algorithm. The security and efficiency properties therefore directly follow from ISW. With $(1, 0, \ldots, 0)$ as a multiplicand, the n^2 cross-products do not need to be performed, however, we must still generate $n(n-1)/2$ random values and perform $n(n-1)$ additions, which gives a total number of operations $T_{\mathsf{QuadraticRefreshMasks}}(n) = 3n(n-1)/2$.

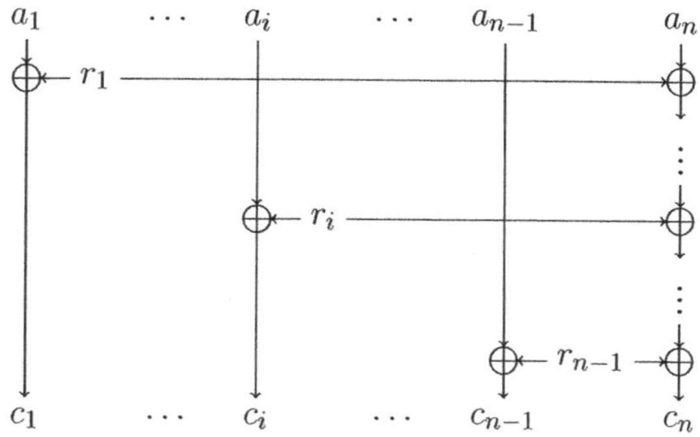

Figure 2.1. *The LinearRefreshMasks algorithm, with the randoms r_i accumulated on the last column*

Algorithm 2.3. QuadraticRefreshMasks

Input: $a_1, \ldots, a_n$

Output: $c_1, \ldots, c_n$ such that $\bigoplus_{i=1}^{n} c_i = \bigoplus_{i=1}^{n} a_i$

for $i = 1$ **to** n **do** $c_i \leftarrow a_i$
for $i = 1$ to $n-1$ **do**
  for $j = i+1$ to n **do**
    $r \leftarrow \mathbb{F}_{2^k}$
    $c_i \leftarrow c_i \oplus r$
    $c_j \leftarrow c_j \oplus r$
  end for
end for
return $c_1, \ldots, c_n$

2.4.3. *Refresh masks with complexity* $\mathcal{O}(n \cdot \log n)$

The QuasiLinearRefreshMasks algorithm depicted in Algorithm 2.4 has complexity $\mathcal{O}(n \cdot \log n)$, instead of $\mathcal{O}(n^2)$ for the previous algorithm, but with the same level of security. That is, it can still ensure secure composition in a full construction. As illustrated in Figure 2.2, the scheme is defined recursively and for simplicity, it is assumed here that n is a power of 2. First, a preprocessing layer L_I is applied on the n input shares a_i, corresponding to lines 5–9 of Algorithm 2.4. Then the refresh masks algorithm is applied recursively on the two halves of the shares. Eventually, a post-processing layer L_O is applied (same as L_I), before outputting the output shares d_i (it corresponds to lines 12–16 in Algorithm 2.4) (see Figure 2.2 for an illustration). The complexity $T(n) = \mathcal{O}(n \cdot \log n)$ comes from the fact that $T(n) \leq 2 \cdot T(n/2) + c \cdot n$ for some constant c, which recursively gives $T(n) \leq 2^i \cdot T(n/2^i) + i \cdot c \cdot n$, implying $T_{\mathsf{QuasiLinearRefreshMasks}}(n) = \mathcal{O}(n \cdot \log n)$.

Algorithm 2.4. QuasiLinearRefreshMasks

Input: $a_1, \ldots, a_n$
Output: $d_1, \ldots, d_n$ such that $\bigoplus_{i=1}^n d_i = \bigoplus_{i=1}^n a_i$

1: **if** $n = 2$ **then**
2: $\quad r \leftarrow \mathbb{F}_{2^k}$
3: $\quad$ **return** $(a_1 \oplus r, a_2 \oplus r)$
4: **end if**
5: **for** $i = 1$ **to** $n/2$ **do**
6: $\quad r_i \leftarrow \mathbb{F}_{2^k}$
7: $\quad b_i \leftarrow a_i \oplus r_i$
8: $\quad b_{i+n/2} \leftarrow a_{i+n/2} \oplus r_i$
9: **end for**
10: $(c_1, \ldots, c_{n/2}) \leftarrow$ QuasiLinearRefreshMasks$(b_1, \ldots, b_{n/2})$
11: $(c_{n/2+1}, \ldots, c_n) \leftarrow$ QuasiLinearRefreshMasks$(b_{n/2+1}, \ldots, b_n)$
12: **for** $i = 1$ **to** $n/2$ **do**
13: $\quad r_i \leftarrow \mathbb{F}_{2^k}$
14: $\quad d_i \leftarrow c_i \oplus r_i$
15: $\quad d_{i+n/2} \leftarrow c_{i+n/2} \oplus r_i$
16: **end for**
17: **return** $(d_1, \ldots, d_n)$

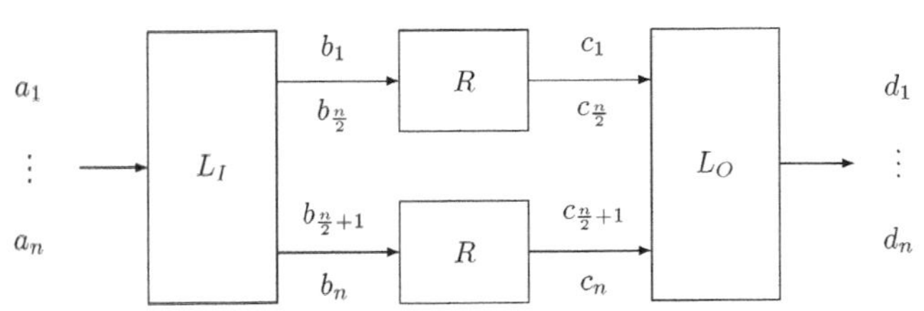

Figure 2.2. *Recursive definition of* QuasiLinearRefreshMasks, *with the preprocessing layer L_I, the two recursive applications of* QuasiLinearRefreshMasks *on the two halves of the shares, and the post-processing layer L_O*

2.5. Masking S-boxes

A block-cipher such as AES alternates several rounds, each containing some linear transformations, and some nonlinear transformations, usually based on S-boxes. In the following, we show how to securely mask such S-boxes at any order.

2.5.1. *The Rivain–Prouff countermeasure for AES*

In order to mask the AES block-cipher, the previous ISW multiplication gadget can be adapted to the AES finite field $\mathbb{F}_{2^8}$ instead of $\mathbb{F}_2$, by replacing the AND operation by a finite field multiplication in $\mathbb{F}_{2^8}$. We describe the corresponding SecMult algorithm in Algorithm 2.5.

Algorithm 2.5. SecMult

Input: shares a_i satisfying $\bigoplus_{i=1}^n a_i = a$, shares b_i satisfying $\bigoplus_{i=1}^n b_i = b$
Output: shares c_i satisfying $\bigoplus_{i=1}^n c_i = a \cdot b$

for $i = 1$ **to** n **do**
  $c_i \leftarrow a_i \cdot b_i$
end for
for $i = 1$ **to** n **do**
  for $j = i + 1$ **to** n **do**
    $r \leftarrow \mathbb{F}_{2^k}$ ▷ referred by $r_{i,j}$
    $c_i \leftarrow c_i \oplus r$ ▷ referred by $c_{i,j}$
    $r \leftarrow (a_i \cdot b_j \oplus r) \oplus a_j \cdot b_i$ ▷ referred by $r_{j,i}$
    $c_j \leftarrow c_j \oplus r$ ▷ referred by $c_{j,i}$
  end for
end for
return $(c_1, \ldots, c_n)$

Moreover, the nonlinear part of the AES S-box can be written as $S(x) = x^{254}$ over $\mathbb{F}_{2^8}$, and can be evaluated as a sequence of nonlinear multiplications and linear squarings, with only four nonlinear multiplications. More precisely, to compute $y = x^{254}$ over $\mathbb{F}_{2^8}$ with four multiplications, we use the sequence of multiplications described in Figure 2.3.

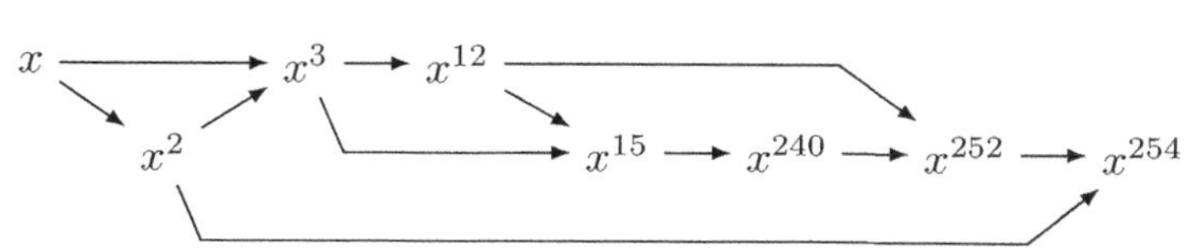

Figure 2.3. *Sequential computation of* x^{254}

Eventually, we obtain the SecExp254 algorithm described in Algorithm 2.6. Thanks to the additional mask refreshing, resistance against an attack of order t is achieved with $n \geq t+1$ shares. The RefreshMasks scheme used in Algorithm 2.6 corresponds to the QuadraticRefreshMasks or QuasiLinearRefreshMasks algorithms described in the previous section.

Algorithm 2.6. SecExp254

```
Input: shares x_1, ..., x_n satisfying x = ⊕_{i=1}^n x_i
Output: shares y_1, ..., y_n such that ⊕_{i=1}^n y_i = x^254
for i = 1 to n do z_i ← x_i^2                                  ▷ ⊕_i z_i = x^2
(z_i)_{1≤i≤n} ← RefreshMasks((z_i)_{1≤i≤n})
(y_i)_{1≤i≤n} ← SecMult((z_i)_{1≤i≤n}, (x_i)_{1≤i≤n})          ▷ ⊕_i y_i = x^3
for i = 1 to n do w_i ← y_i^4                                  ▷ ⊕_i w_i = x^12
(w_i)_{1≤i≤n} ← RefreshMasks((w_i)_{1≤i≤n})
(y_i)_{1≤i≤n} ← SecMult((y_i)_{1≤i≤n}, (w_i)_{1≤i≤n})          ▷ ⊕_i y_i = x^15
for i = 1 to n do y_i ← y_i^16                                 ▷ ⊕_i y_i = x^240
(y_i)_{1≤i≤n} ← SecMult((y_i)_{1≤i≤n}, (w_i)_{1≤i≤n})          ▷ ⊕_i y_i = x^252
(y_i)_{1≤i≤n} ← SecMult((y_i)_{1≤i≤n}, (z_i)_{1≤i≤n})          ▷ ⊕_i y_i = x^254
return y_1, ..., y_n
```

2.5.2. *Extension to any S-box*

The Rivain–Prouff countermeasure can be extended to the high-order computation of any S-box. Namely, any given k-bit S-box can be represented by a polynomial $\sum_{i=0}^{2^k-1} a_i x^i$ over $\mathbb{F}_{2^k}$ using Lagrange's interpolation theorem, and therefore, it can be securely evaluated with a sequence of n-shared additions, squarings and multiplications. Asymptotically, the running time of the countermeasure is dominated by the number of nonlinear multiplications, where each nonlinear multiplication has complexity $\mathcal{O}(n^2)$ for n shares. To minimize the number of such nonlinear multiplications, the authors described a technique called Parity-Split, with a proven complexity of $\mathcal{O}(2^{k/2})$ nonlinear multiplications for evaluating any k-bit S-box.

More precisely, any S-box $S : \mathbb{F}_{2^k} \rightarrow \mathbb{F}_{2^k}$ can be written using Lagrange's interpolation theorem as:

$$S(x) = \sum_{i=0}^{2^k-1} a_i \cdot x^i$$

for coefficients $a_i \in \mathbb{F}_{2^k}$. The naive method to high-order compute $S(x)$ would require $2^k - 2$ multiplications in $\mathbb{F}_{2^k}$. Since squarings are essentially free in $\mathbb{F}_{2^k}$, we can do better using the following simple observation: any polynomial $Q(x)$ of degree t can be written as:

$$Q(x) = Q_1(x^2) + Q_2(x^2) \cdot x$$

where both $Q_1(x)$ and $Q_2(x)$ have degree at most $\lfloor t/2 \rfloor$. Using this relation, we can precompute the set of powers x^{2i} for $1 \leq i \leq 2^{k-1} - 1$, which requires $2^{k-1} - 2$ multiplications. This set of powers is used to evaluate $Q_1(x^2)$ and $Q_2(x^2)$, and the product $Q_2(x^2) \cdot x$ requires one additional multiplication, hence a total of $2^{k-1} - 1$ multiplications (instead of $2^k - 2$). By applying recursively the above relation, we can evaluate $S(x)$ with $\mathcal{O}(2^{k/2})$ multiplications only.

2.5.3. *The randomized table countermeasure*

An alternative countermeasure for S-box computation is based on randomized tables. The simplest case is first-order computation. The first-order countermeasure consists in recomputing in RAM the original S-box S with inputs shifted by some random r and with masked outputs. More precisely, we compute the randomized table:

$$T(u) = S(u \oplus r) \oplus s$$

for all $u \in \{0,1\}^k$, where $r \in \{0,1\}^k$ is the input mask and $s \in \{0,1\}^k$ is the output mask. To evaluate $S(x)$ from the masked value $x' = x \oplus r$, it suffices to compute $y' = T(x')$, which gives $y' = T(x') = S(x' \oplus r) \oplus s = S(x) \oplus s$, and therefore y' is a masked value for $S(x)$.

The first-order countermeasure can be generalized as follows. Every row of the randomized table T now consists of n shares. Given the n input shares x_i such that $x = x_1 \oplus \cdots \oplus x_n$, we start with an n-encoding of each row of the original S-box S, with:

$$T(u) = (S(u), 0, \ldots, 0) \qquad [2.2]$$

for all rows $u \in \{0,1\}^k$, and we progressively shift the table T by the successive input shares $x_1, \ldots, x_{n-1}$. Between every shift, the n-encodings on each row of the table are refreshed. After the last shift by x_{n-1}, the rows of the table have been shifted by $x_1 \oplus \cdots \oplus x_{n-1}$ and therefore the table T satisfies for all $u \in \{0,1\}^k$:

$$\bigoplus_{j=1}^{n} T(u)[j] = S(u \oplus x_1 \oplus \cdots \oplus x_{n-1}) \qquad [2.3]$$

Then it suffices to read the table T at the row $u = x_n$ to get the n output shares y_i corresponding to $y = S(x)$. More precisely, we let $(y_1, \dots, y_n) \leftarrow T(x_n)$, which from [2.3] gives as required:

$$y_1 \oplus \cdots \oplus y_n = S(x_n \oplus x_1 \oplus \cdots \oplus x_{n-1}) = S(x)$$

The high-order randomized countermeasure is described in Algorithm 2.7. The asymptotic complexity of this countermeasure for k-bit S-boxes is $\mathcal{O}(2^k \cdot n^2)$.

Algorithm 2.7. Masked computation of $y = S(x)$

Input: $x_1, \dots, x_n$ such that $x = x_1 \oplus \cdots \oplus x_n$
Output: $y_1, \dots, y_n$ such that $y = S(x) = y_1 \oplus \cdots \oplus y_n$

- **for all** $u \in \{0,1\}^k$ **do**
  - $T(u) \leftarrow (S(u), 0, \dots, 0) \in (\{0,1\}k')^n$ ▷ $\oplus(T(u)) = S(u)$
- **end for**
- **for** $i = 1$ to $n - 1$ **do**
  - **for all** $u \in \{0,1\}^k$ **do**
    - **for** $j = 1$ **to** n **do** $T'(u)[j] \leftarrow T(u \oplus x_i)[j]$ ▷ $T'(u) \leftarrow T(u \oplus x_i)$
  - **end for**
  - **for all** $u \in \{0,1\}^k$ **do**
    - $T(u) \leftarrow \mathsf{LinearRefreshMasks}(T'(u))$ ▷ $\oplus(T(u)) = S(u \oplus x_1 \oplus \cdots \oplus x_i)$
  - **end for**
- **end for** ▷ $\oplus(T(u)) = S(u \oplus x_1 \oplus \cdots \oplus x_{n-1})$
- $(y_1, \dots, y_n) \leftarrow \mathsf{LinearRefreshMasks}(T(x_n))$ ▷ $\oplus(T(x_n)) = S(x)$
- **return** $y_1, \dots, y_n$

2.5.4. *Attacks*

The goal of this section is to illustrate some of the pitfalls of high-order masking. We first describe an attack against a variant of the high-order computation of $y = x^{254}$ (Algorithm 2.6) in which we use the more efficient LinearRefreshMasks algorithm (Algorithm 2.2) for mask refreshing. We also describe an attack against a variant of the randomized table countermeasure in which the same masks are used for every row of the table. These attacks demonstrate the need for provably secure constructions of high-order masking.

2.5.4.1. *Attack against $x \rightarrow x^3$ with ISW and linear mask refreshing*

In this section, we show that if in Algorithm 2.6 we use the LinearRefreshMasks algorithm (Algorithm 2.2) instead of the QuadraticRefreshMasks algorithm

(Algorithm 2.3), then we have an attack that requires the knowledge of fewer than d probes when using $n = d + 1$ shares.

Even though Algorithms 2.5 and 2.2 are both secure against d-th order probing attack when considered separately, we show hereafter that their sequential application, as done in Steps 2–3 and Steps 5–6 of Algorithm 2.6, is not. Namely, we exhibit a tuple of $\lceil d/2 \rceil + 1$ intermediate variables that jointly depend on the sensitive input. Hence, for $d > 1$, this implies that the scheme does not achieve d-th order security.

To exhibit the flaw, we assume that the attacked S-box evaluation procedure contains the following sequence:

$$
\begin{aligned}
&(z_0, z_1, \cdots, z_d) \leftarrow (g(x_0), g(x_1), \ldots, g(x_d)),\\
&(z'_0, z'_1, \cdots, z'_d) \leftarrow \mathsf{RefreshMasks}((z_0, z_1, \cdots, z_d)),\\
&(y_0, y_1, \cdots, y_d) \leftarrow \mathsf{SecMult}((x_0, x_1, \cdots, x_d), (z'_0, z'_1, \cdots, z'_d)),
\end{aligned}
$$

with $(x_i)_i$ being a sharing of some sensitive variable x and with g being some $\mathbb{F}_2$-linear function. Two examples of occurrence of this sequence can be found in Algorithm 2.6: from Steps 1 to 3 (with the function g corresponding to a squaring over $\mathbb{F}_{256}$), and from Steps 4 to 6 (with the function g corresponding to a raising to the 4 over $\mathbb{F}_{256}$).

For the sake of clarity, we only consider the case where d is even (in the odd case an extra intermediate variable would be needed). The flaw arises from a particular intermediate variable of the mask refreshing combined with $d/2$ intermediate variables of the multiplication. Namely, the targeted intermediate variables are:

– the variable z'_0 just after the fourth step during the $(d/2)$-th iteration of the loop in RefreshMasks (Algorithm 2.2), denoted ℓ_0 hereafter, and which satisfies:

$$
\begin{aligned}
\ell_0 &= z_0 \oplus \bigoplus\nolimits_{i=1}^{d/2} r_i\\
&= z \oplus \bigoplus\nolimits_{i=1}^{d} z_i \oplus \bigoplus\nolimits_{i=1}^{d/2} r_i\\
&= z \oplus \bigoplus\nolimits_{i=1}^{d/2} (z_i \oplus r_i \oplus z_{d/2+i})\\
&= g(x) \oplus \bigoplus\nolimits_{i=1}^{d/2} \left(g(x_i) \oplus r_i \oplus g(x_{d/2+i})\right),
\end{aligned}
\qquad [2.4]
$$

– the product $z'_i \cdot x_j$ arising in Step 4 of SecMult (Algorithm 2.5 called on $(x_i)_i$ and $(z'_i)_i$) for every $i \in \{1, 2, \ldots, d/2\}$ and $j = i + d/2$, denoted ℓ_i hereafter, and which satisfies:

$$
\ell_i = z'_i \cdot x_{d/2+i} = (z_i \oplus r_i) \cdot x_{d/2+i} = (g(x_i) \oplus r_i) \cdot x_{d/2+i}\,. \qquad [2.5]
$$

In a nutshell, the intermediate variable $\ell_i = (g(x_i) \oplus r_i) \cdot x_{d/2+i}$ is statistically dependent on the sum $g(x_i) \oplus r_i \oplus g(x_{d/2+i})$ involved to mask $z = g(x)$ in the expression of ℓ_0 (see equation [2.4]). Therefore, the $(d/2)$-tuple $(\ell_i)_i$ defined in equation [2.5] provides information on the $d/2$ masks $g(x_i) \oplus r_i \oplus g(x_{d/2+i})$ and this information can be used to partially unmask ℓ_0. In other terms, the family of $d/2+1$ intermediate variables $\ell_0, \ell_1, \ldots, \ell_{d/2}$ depends on the sensitive variable x.

2.5.4.2. *Attack against the Schramm and Paar countermeasure for LUTs*

We start with the classical randomized table countermeasure, which is secured against first-order attacks only. The S-box table $S(u)$ with k-bit input is first randomized in RAM by letting:

$$T(u) = S(u \oplus r) \oplus s$$

for all $u \in \{0,1\}^k$, where $r \in \{0,1\}^k$ is the input mask and $s \in \{0,1\}^k$ is the output mask[1]. To evaluate $S(x)$ from the masked value $x' = x \oplus r$, it suffices to compute $y' = T(x')$, as we get $y' = T(x') = S(x' \oplus r) \oplus s = S(x) \oplus s$. This shows that y' is indeed a masked value for $S(x)$. In other words, the randomized table countermeasure consists of first recomputing in RAM a temporary table with inputs shifted by r and with masked outputs, so that it can later be evaluated on a masked value $x' = x \oplus r$ to obtain a masked output.

A natural generalization at any order n would be as follows: given as input $x = x_1 \oplus \cdots \oplus x_n$, we would start with a randomized table with inputs shifted by x_1 only and with $n-1$ output masks. We would then incrementally shift the full table by x_2 and so on until x_{n-1}, at which point the table could be evaluated at x_n. More precisely, we would initially define the randomized table:

$$T(u) = S(u \oplus x_1) \oplus s_2 \oplus \cdots \oplus s_n$$

where $s_2, \ldots, s_n$ are the output masks, and then progressively shift the randomized table by letting $T(u) \leftarrow T(u \oplus x_i)$ for all u, iteratively from x_2 until x_{n-1}. Eventually the table would have all of its inputs shifted by $x_1 \oplus \cdots \oplus x_{n-1}$, so as previously we could evaluate $y' = T(x_n)$ and obtain $S(x)$ masked by $s_2, \ldots, s_n$.

What we have described above is essentially the Schramm and Paar countermeasure. However, this countermeasure was later shown to be insecure. Namely consider the table $T(u)$ after the last shift by x_{n-1}. At this point, we have $T(u) = S(u \oplus x_1 \oplus \cdots \oplus x_{n-1}) \oplus s_2 \oplus \cdots \oplus s_n$ for all u. Now assume that we can probe $T(0)$ and $T(1)$: we can then compute $T(0) \oplus T(1) =$

1 We can also take $s = r$. For simplicity, we first assume that the S-box has both k-bit input and k-bit output.

$S(x_1 \oplus \cdots \oplus x_{n-1}) \oplus S(1 \oplus x_1 \oplus \cdots \oplus x_{n-1})$, which only depends on $x_1 \oplus \cdots \oplus x_{n-1}$. Therefore, it suffices to additionally probe x_n to leak information about $x = x_1 \oplus \cdots \oplus x_{n-1} \oplus x_n$. This gives an attack of order 3 only for any value of n and therefore, the countermeasure can only be secure against second-order attacks.

The main issue with the previous countermeasure is that the *same* masks $s_2, \ldots, s_n$ were used to mask all of the $S(u)$ entries, so we can exclusive-or (XOR) any two lines of the randomized table and remove all of the output masks. A natural fix is to use *different* masks for every line $S(u)$ of the table, so we would initially write:

$$T(u) = S(u \oplus x_1) \oplus s_{u,2} \oplus \cdots \oplus s_{u,n}$$

for all $u \in \{0,1\}^k$, and as previously we would have iteratively shifted the table by $x_2, \ldots, x_{n-1}$, and also the masks $s_{u,i}$ separately for each i. The previous attack is thwarted because the lines of $S(u)$ are now masked with different set of masks. Eventually we would read $T(x_n)$, which would give $S(x)$ masked by $s_{x_n,2}, \ldots, s_{x_n,n}$. This is the countermeasure described in Algorithm 2.7.

2.6. Masks conversions

As depicted earlier, Boolean masking is well adapted for algorithms with Boolean operations only, such as the AES block-cipher. However, for algorithms that combine Boolean and arithmetic operations, it can be advantageous to use arithmetic masking to protect the arithmetic operations, and periodically switch between Boolean and arithmetic masking whenever necessary. Obviously, the conversion algorithm itself must be secure against side-channel attacks.

2.6.1. *First-order Boolean to arithmetic masking*

The first and undoubtedly most efficient method for converting between Boolean and arithmetic masking secure against first-order attacks was proposed by Goubin in 2001. Its complexity is in $\mathcal{O}(1)$, that is, independent of the register size k. The method is based on a surprising property of the function $\Psi(x, r) : \mathbb{F}_{2^k} \times \mathbb{F}_{2^k} \rightarrow \mathbb{F}_{2^k}$:

$$\Psi(x, r) = (x \oplus r) - r \pmod{2^k} \quad [2.6]$$

Namely, although it contains an arithmetic operation, the function Ψ is affine in r with respect to the xor. More precisely, we have for any $x, r_1, r_2 \in \mathbb{F}_{2^k}$:

$$\Psi(x, r_1 \oplus r_2) = x \oplus \Psi(x, r_1) \oplus \Psi(x, r_2) \quad [2.7]$$

Hence, given as input the two Boolean shares x_1, x_2 such that $x = x_1 \oplus x_2$, we can write using the definition of the Ψ function and from [2.7]:

$$\begin{aligned} x &= ((x_1 \oplus x_2) - x_2) + x_2 = \Psi(x_1, x_2) + x_2 \\ &= \big[(x_1 \oplus \Psi(x_1, r \oplus x_2)) \oplus \Psi(x_1, r)\big] + x_2 \end{aligned}$$

where $r \leftarrow \{0,1\}^k$ is a randomly generated value. We can therefore compute the arithmetic share:

$$A \leftarrow (x_1 \oplus \Psi(x_1, r \oplus x_2)) \oplus \Psi(x_1, r)$$

which eventually gives two arithmetic shares A and x_2 of x, as required:

$$x = A + x_2 \pmod{2^k}.$$

The complexity in $\mathcal{O}(1)$ follows from the constant number of operations. Indeed, as depicted in Algorithm 2.8, it requires only eight operations. Moreover, it is easy to see that the algorithm is secure against first-order attacks, because the left term $x_1 \oplus \Psi(x_1, r \oplus x_2)$ is independent of x_2 (thanks to the mask r), and the right term $\Psi(x_1, r)$ is also independent from x_2. Eventually, the arithmetic share A is uniformly distributed when x_2 is uniformly distributed.

Algorithm 2.8. Goubin's first order Boolean to arithmetic conversion

Input: $x_1, x_2 \in \{0,1\}^k$
Output: A such that $x_1 \oplus x_2 = A + x_2 \pmod{2^k}$

$r \leftarrow \mathbb{F}_{2^k}$
$T \leftarrow x_1 \oplus r$
$T \leftarrow T - r$
$T \leftarrow T \oplus x_1$
$r \leftarrow r \oplus x_2$
$A \leftarrow x_1 \oplus r$
$A \leftarrow A - r$
$A \leftarrow A \oplus T$
return A

2.6.2. *Generalization to high order for Boolean to arithmetic masking*

A generalization of Goubin's Boolean to arithmetic conversion algorithm to high-order masking was proposed with a complexity $\mathcal{O}(2^n)$, which is still independent of the register size k. While it is exponential in the number of shares n, this method is currently the most efficient one for small orders. The scheme is designed recursively and is based on a function $\mathcal{C}_n$ described in Algorithm 2.10, which takes as input $n+1$ Boolean shares x_i such that $x = x_1 \oplus \cdots \oplus x_{n+1}$ and outputs n arithmetic shares D_i such that $x = D_1 + \cdots + D_n \pmod{2^k}$. Then, to convert from n Boolean shares instead of $n+1$, it suffices to initially let $x_{n+1} = 0$ as depicted in Algorithm 2.9.

The $\mathcal{C}_n$ algorithm is illustrated in Figure 2.4 and works as follows: if $n = 1$, the algorithm takes as input two shares x_1 and x_2 and outputs $D_1 = x_1 \oplus x_2$. For $n \geq 2$, the following steps are performed:

1) A mask refreshing of the $n+1$ shares x_i's is done, so that the following $n+1$ shares are obtained:

$$y_1, \ldots, y_{n+1} \leftarrow \mathsf{RefreshMasks}_{n+1}(x_1, \ldots, x_{n+1})$$

Note that the RefreshMasks algorithm used here corresponds to the LinearRefreshMasks described in Algorithm 2.2, but where the random values are accumulated on the first share instead of the last one. Therefore, the following relations hold:

$$\begin{aligned} x &= y_1 \oplus y_2 \oplus \cdots \oplus y_{n+1} \\ &= y_2 \oplus \cdots \oplus y_{n+1} + (y_1 \oplus \cdots \oplus y_{n+1} - y_2 \oplus \cdots \oplus y_{n+1}) \\ &= y_2 \oplus \cdots \oplus y_{n+1} + \Psi(y_1, y_2 \oplus \cdots \oplus y_{n+1}) \end{aligned}$$

2) Thanks to the affine property of Ψ, this gives:

$$x = y_2 \oplus \cdots \oplus y_{n+1} + (\overline{n \wedge 1}) \cdot y_1 \oplus \Psi(y_1, y_2) \oplus \cdots \oplus \Psi(y_1, y_{n+1})$$

Therefore, by letting $z_1 \leftarrow (\overline{n \wedge 1}) \cdot y_1 \oplus \Psi(y_1, y_2)$ and $z_i \leftarrow \Psi(y_1, y_{i+1})$ for all $2 \leq i \leq n$, this gives:

$$x = y_2 \oplus \cdots \oplus y_{n+1} + z_1 \oplus \cdots \oplus z_n \qquad [2.8]$$

3) Two recursive calls to the Boolean to arithmetic conversion algorithm $\mathcal{C}_{n-1}$ are then performed:

$$\begin{aligned} &A_1, \ldots, A_{n-1} \leftarrow \mathcal{C}_{n-1}(y_2, \ldots, y_{n+1}) \\ &B_1, \ldots, B_{n-1} \leftarrow \mathcal{C}_{n-1}(z_1, \ldots, z_n) \end{aligned}$$

This gives from [2.8]:

$$x = A_1 + \cdots + A_{n-1} + B_1 + \cdots + B_{n-1}$$

4) The number of arithmetic shares are subsequently reduced from $2n - 2$ to n by some additive grouping, letting $D_i \leftarrow A_i + B_i$ for $1 \leq i \leq n-2$ and $D_{n-1} \leftarrow A_{n-1}$ and $D_n \leftarrow B_{n-1}$. This gives as required the n arithmetic shares as output: $x = D_1 + \cdots + D_n \pmod{2^k}$.

Complexity: the number T_n of operations performed within $\mathcal{C}_n$ is recursively defined as $T_n = 2 \cdot T_{n-1} + 6 \cdot n + 1$ where $T_1 = 1$ since $\mathcal{C}_1$ performs a single xor. This gives the complexity $T_n = 10 \cdot 2^n - 6 \cdot n - 13$. Furthermore, the number R_n of random generations performed within $\mathcal{C}_n$ is recursively defined as $R_n = n + 2 \cdot R_{n-1}$ where $R_1 = 0$ since no random value is generated in $\mathcal{C}_1$. This gives the randomness complexity $R_n = (3/2) \cdot 2^n - n - 2$.

Therefore, the complexity of Algorithm 2.9 is exponential in n, but as previously mentioned, it performs in practice about one order of magnitude faster than existing algorithms for small values of n.

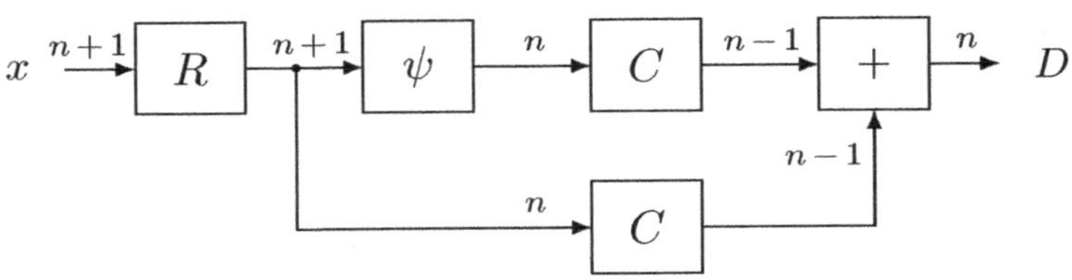

Figure 2.4. *The sequence of gadgets of high order Boolean to arithmetic conversion algorithm $\mathcal{C}_n$*

Algorithm 2.9. High-order Boolean to arithmetic conversion

Input: $x_1, \ldots, x_n$

Output: $D_1, \ldots, D_n$ such that $x_1 \oplus \cdots \oplus x_n = D_1 + \cdots + D_n \pmod{2^k}$

1: $D_1, \ldots, D_n \leftarrow \mathcal{C}_n(x_1, \ldots, x_n, 0)$

2: **return** $D_1, \ldots, D_n$

2.6.3. *High order Boolean to arithmetic and arithmetic to Boolean masking*

The main drawback of the previous algorithm is that its complexity is exponential in the number of shares n. In the following, we describe conversion algorithms with complexity $\mathcal{O}(k \cdot n^2)$ only. We start with the problem of how to apply arithmetic operations directly on Boolean shares and present an algorithm for secure addition modulo 2^k with n shares with complexity $\mathcal{O}(n^2 k)$. Then, we introduce algorithms to convert from Boolean to arithmetic masking and vice versa, again with a complexity of

$\mathcal{O}(n^2k)$ in both directions. These algorithms are proven secure in the ISW framework for private circuits.

Algorithm 2.10. $\mathcal{C}_n$: Recursive high-order Boolean to arithmetic conversion ($n+1 \to n$ shares)

Input: $x_1, \dots, x_{n+1}$
Output: $D_1, \dots, D_n$ such that $x_1 \oplus \dots \oplus x_{n+1} = D_1 + \dots + D_n \pmod{2^k}$
if $n = 1$ **then**
    return $D_1 \leftarrow x_1 \oplus x_2$
end if
$y_1, \dots, y_{n+1} \leftarrow \mathsf{RefreshMasks}(x_1, \dots, x_{n+1})$
$z_1 \leftarrow (\overline{n \wedge 1}) \cdot y_1 \oplus \Psi(y_1, y_2)$
for $i = 2$ to n **do**
    $z_i \leftarrow \Psi(y_1, y_{i+1})$
end for
$A_1, \dots, A_{n-1} \leftarrow \mathcal{C}_{n-1}(y_2, \dots, y_{n+1})$
$B_1, \dots, B_{n-1} \leftarrow \mathcal{C}_{n-1}(z_1, \dots, z_n)$
for $i = 1$ to $n-2$ **do**
    $D_i \leftarrow A_i + B_i$
end for
$D_{n-1} \leftarrow A_{n-1}$
$D_n \leftarrow B_{n-1}$
return $D_1, \dots, D_n$

2.6.3.1. *Secure addition on Boolean shares*

The approach is based on the following recursion formula proposed by Goubin, which uses the relation $x + y = x \oplus y \oplus u_{k-1}$, and:

$$\begin{cases} u_0 = 0 \\ \forall i \geq 0, u_{i+1} = 2[u_i \wedge (x \oplus y) \oplus (x \wedge y)]. \end{cases}$$

Algorithm 2.11 represents the solution based on Goubin's formula to compute the addition. We use the SecAnd algorithm (Algorithm 2.1) to securely compute the And operations in the above recursion formula. The time complexity of Algorithm 2.11 is dominated by the $k-1$ SecAnd performed at line 5 and is therefore $\mathcal{O}(n^2k)$.

2.6.3.2. *Secure conversion from arithmetic to Boolean masking*

We describe an algorithm for converting from arithmetic to Boolean masking with a complexity of $\mathcal{O}(n^2k)$. The algorithm is best described recursively and corresponds to Algorithm 2.12. Assume that we already found an algorithm $\mathcal{A}_{n/2}$ for converting a set of $n/2$ arithmetic shares A_i into $n/2$ Boolean shares x_i such that:

$$A_1 + \dots + A_{n/2} = x_1 \oplus \dots \oplus x_{n/2}.$$

Algorithm 2.11. SecAddGoubin

Input: (x_i) and (y_i) for $1 \le i \le n$

Output: (z_i) for $1 \le i \le n$, with $\bigoplus_{i=1}^{n} z_i = \bigoplus_{i=1}^{n} x_i + \bigoplus_{i=1}^{n} y_i$

$(w_i)_{1\le i\le n} \leftarrow \mathsf{SecAnd}((x_i)_{1\le i\le n}, (y_i)_{1\le i\le n})$ ▷ $\omega = x \wedge y$
$(u_i)_{1\le i\le n} \leftarrow 0$ ▷ Initialize shares of u to zero
$(a_i)_{1\le i\le n} \leftarrow (x_i)_{1\le i\le n} \oplus (y_i)_{1\le i\le n}$ ▷ $a = x \oplus y$
for $j = 1$ to $k-1$ **do**
  $(ua_i)_{1\le i\le n} \leftarrow \mathsf{SecAnd}((u_i)_{1\le i\le n}, (a_i)_{1\le i\le n})$
  $(u_i)_{1\le i\le n} \leftarrow (ua_i)_{1\le i\le n} \oplus (w_i)_{1\le i\le n}$
  $(u_i)_{1\le i\le n} \leftarrow 2(u_i)_{1\le i\le n}$ ▷ $u \leftarrow 2(u \wedge a \oplus \omega)$
end for
$(z_i)_{1\le i\le n} \leftarrow (x_i)_{1\le i\le n} \oplus (y_i)_{1\le i\le n} \oplus (u_i)_{1\le i\le n}$ ▷ $z = x + y = x \oplus y \oplus u$
return $(z_i)_{1\le i\le n}$

Algorithm 2.12. ConvertA→B

Input: (A_i) for $1 \le i \le n$

Output: (z_i) for $1 \le i \le n$, with $\bigoplus_{i=1}^{n} z_i = \sum_{i=1}^{n} A_i$

If $n = 1$ then **return** A_1
$(x_i)_{1\le i\le n/2} \leftarrow \mathsf{ConvertA{\to}B}\left((A_i)_{1\le i\le n/2}\right)$
$(x'_i)_{1\le i\le n} \leftarrow \mathsf{Expand}\left((x_i)_{1\le i\le n/2}\right)$ ▷ $\bigoplus_{i=1}^{n} x'_i = \bigoplus_{i=1}^{n/2} x_i = \sum_{i=1}^{n/2} A_i$
$(y_i)_{1\le i\le n/2} \leftarrow \mathsf{ConvertA{\to}B}\left((A_i)_{n/2+1\le i\le n}\right)$
$(y'_i)_{1\le i\le n} \leftarrow \mathsf{Expand}\left((y_i)_{1\le i\le n/2}\right)$ ▷ $\bigoplus_{i=1}^{n} y'_i = \bigoplus_{i=1}^{n/2} y_i = \sum_{i=n/2+1}^{n} A_i$
$(z_i)_{1\le i\le n} \leftarrow \mathsf{SecAdd}\left((x'_i)_{1\le i\le n}, (y'_i)_{1\le i\le n}\right)$
return $(z_i)_{1\le i\le n}$ ▷ $\bigoplus_{i=1}^{n} z_i = \bigoplus_{i=1}^{n} x'_i + \bigoplus_{i=1}^{n} y'_i = \sum_{i=1}^{n} A_i$

Now, given as input a variable x represented with n arithmetic shares A_i:

$$x = A_1 + \cdots + A_n$$

we first apply algorithm $\mathcal{A}_{n/2}$ separately on the two halves to get:

$$\begin{aligned} x &= (A_1 + \cdots + A_{n/2}) + (A_{n/2+1} + \cdots + A_n) \\ &= (x_1 \oplus \cdots \oplus x_{n/2}) + (y_1 \oplus \cdots \oplus y_{n/2}) \end{aligned}$$

A simple expansion step is then applied, in which the $n/2$ shares x_i and y_i are each expanded to n shares. As depicted in Algorithm 2.13, this can be done by randomly splitting every share x_i into $x_i = x'_{2i-1} \oplus x'_{2i}$ and similarly for $y_i = y'_{2i-1} \oplus y'_{2i}$. We obtain:

$$x = (x'_1 \oplus \cdots \oplus x'_n) + (y'_1 \oplus \cdots \oplus y'_n)$$

Then, the n-Boolean addition circuit SecAddGoubin is applied to obtain x represented with n Boolean shares $x = z_1 \oplus \cdots \oplus z_n$ as required. We can check that the algorithm indeed has complexity $\mathcal{O}(n^2k)$, namely, the SecAdd algorithm at line 6 has complexity $\mathcal{O}(n^2k)$.

Algorithm 2.13. Expand

Input: x_i for $1 \le i \le n$

Output: y_i for $1 \le i \le 2n$ with $\bigoplus_{i=1}^{2n} y_i = \bigoplus_{i=1}^{n} x_i$

$(r_i)_{1 \le i \le n} \leftarrow \mathsf{Rand}(k)$

$(y_{2i})_{1 \le i \le n} \leftarrow (x_i \oplus r_i)_{1 \le i \le n}$

$(y_{2i+1})_{1 \le i \le n} \leftarrow (r_i)_{1 \le i \le n}$

return $(y_i)_{1 \le i \le 2n}$

2.6.3.3. *Conversion from Boolean to arithmetic masking*

We now present an algorithm for converting in the other direction, that is, from Boolean to arithmetic masking, again with a complexity of $\mathcal{O}(n^2k)$. The method is depicted in Algorithm 2.14 and is based on the use of the previous algorithm for converting from arithmetic to Boolean masking (Algorithm 2.12).

More precisely, given as input $x = x_1 \oplus \cdots \oplus x_n$, we write:

$$\begin{aligned} x_1 \oplus \cdots \oplus x_n = x_1 \oplus \cdots \oplus x_n + (-A_1) + \cdots + (-A_{n-1}) \\ + A_1 + \cdots + A_{n-1} \pmod{2^k} \end{aligned}$$

for random elements $A_1, \ldots, A_{n-1} \in \mathbb{Z}_{2^k}$. Using the previous algorithm, we perform an arithmetic to Boolean conversion of $(-A_1, \ldots, -A_{n-1}, 0)$ to obtain:

$$y_1 \oplus \cdots \oplus y_n = (-A_1) + \cdots + (-A_{n-1}) \pmod{2^k}$$

This gives:

$$x_1 \oplus \cdots \oplus x_n = (x_1 \oplus \cdots \oplus x_n + y_1 \oplus \cdots \oplus y_n) + A_1 + \cdots + A_{n-1} \pmod{2^k}$$

We use the SecAdd algorithm to compute:

$$z_1 \oplus \cdots \oplus z_n = x_1 \oplus \cdots \oplus x_n + y_1 \oplus \cdots \oplus y_n \pmod{2^k}$$

We use the FullXor algorithm below to compute:

$$A_n = z_1 \oplus \cdots \oplus z_n$$

without leaking information on the individual shares z_i. Eventually, combining the three previous equations, we obtain as required:

$$x_1 \oplus \cdots \oplus x_n = A_1 + \cdots + A_n \pmod{2^k}$$

The FullXor algorithm used in Algorithm 2.14 is depicted in Algorithm 2.15. It allows us to perform a randomized XOR and it is used to compute $A_n \leftarrow \bigoplus_{i=1}^{n} z_i$.

Algorithm 2.14. Conversion from Boolean to arithmetic masking

Input: (x_i) for $1 \leq i \leq n$

Output: (A_i) for $1 \leq i \leq n$, with $\sum_{i=1}^{n} A_i = \bigoplus_{i=1}^{n} x_i$

1: $(A_i)_{1 \leq i \leq n-1} \leftarrow \mathsf{Rand}(k)$

2: $(A'_i)_{1 \leq i \leq n-1} \leftarrow (-A_i)_{1 \leq i \leq n-1}$, $A'_n \leftarrow 0$

3: $(y_i)_{1 \leq i \leq n} \leftarrow \mathsf{ConvertA{\to}B}\big((A'_i)_{1 \leq i \leq n}\big)$ $\triangleright \bigoplus_{i=1}^{n} y_i = \sum_{i=1}^{n} A'_i = -\sum_{i=1}^{n-1} A_i$

4: $(z_i)_{1 \leq i \leq n} \leftarrow \mathsf{SecAdd}\big((x_i)_{1 \leq i \leq n}, (y_i)_{1 \leq i \leq n}\big)$ $\triangleright \bigoplus_{i=1}^{n} z_i = \bigoplus_{i=1}^{n} x_i + \bigoplus_{i=1}^{n} y_i$

5: $A_n \leftarrow \mathsf{FullXor}\big((z_i)_{1 \leq i \leq n}\big)$ $\triangleright A_n = \bigoplus_{i=1}^{n} z_i = \bigoplus_{i=1}^{n} x_i - \sum_{i=1}^{n-1} A_i$

6: **return** $(A_i)_{1 \leq i \leq n}$. $\triangleright \sum_{i=1}^{n} A_i = \bigoplus_{i=1}^{n} x_i$

Algorithm 2.15. FullXor

Input: $y_1, \ldots, y_n$

Output: y such that $y = y_1 \oplus \cdots \oplus y_n$

1: **for** $i = 1$ **to** n **do** $(y_1, \ldots, y_n) \leftarrow \mathsf{LinearRefreshMasks}(y_1, \ldots, y_n)$

2: **return** $y_1 \oplus \cdots \oplus y_n$

2.7. Notes and further references

– Section 2.3. In 2003, Ishai et al. (2003) initiated the theoretical study of securing circuits against an adversary who can probe a fraction of its wires. They showed how to transform any circuit of size $|C|$ into a circuit of size $\mathcal{O}(|C| \cdot t^2)$ secured against any adversary that can probe at most t wires. To achieve this goal, they designed an algorithm to securely evaluate the AND gate over $\mathbb{F}_2$. Rivain and Prouff (2010) extended this method to securely compute a multiplication over $\mathbb{F}_{2^k}$.

– Section 2.4. The LinearRefreshMasks with complexity $\mathcal{O}(n)$ was initially described in Rivain and Prouff (2010) while using the ISW scheme to secure the AES S-box computation. It was later shown in Coron et al. (2014b) that the use of such a mask-refreshing algorithm introduced a security flaw in the overall masking scheme. The QuadraticRefreshMasks with complexity $\mathcal{O}(n^2)$ was further used in Barthe et al. (2015) to prove the t-SNI security of a full construction. Eventually, the QuasiLinearRefreshMasks with complexity $\mathcal{O}(n \cdot \log n)$ was introduced in Battistello et al. (2016), where it was proven to achieve the same t-SNI security as the QuadraticRefreshMasks algorithm. A generalization to arbitrary n (and not only a power of 2) is also provided in Battistello et al. (2016). Note that a completely different mask-refreshing algorithm is described in Andrychowicz et al. (2016), with complexity only $\mathcal{O}(n)$, but using nontrivial tools such as expander graphs with constant degree.

– Section 2.5. The first provably secure high-order masking scheme for the AES block-cipher was described in Rivain and Prouff (2010), by adapting the ISW multiplication gadget to the AES finite field $\mathbb{F}_{2^8}$ instead of $\mathbb{F}_2$, and evaluating the AES S-box $S(x) = x^{254}$ as a sequence of nonlinear multiplications and linear squarings. Resistance against an attack of order t is achieved with $n \geq 2t + 1$ shares, as in the original ISW multiplication. This was later improved to $n \geq t + 1$ by showing that the ISW multiplication gadget achieves the t-SNI property Barthe et al. (2016). This enables us to use the Rivain–Prouff countermeasure for the full AES with $n = t + 1$ shares only, with some additional mask refreshing. The Rivain–Prouff countermeasure was later extended to any look-up table in Carlet et al. (2012). To minimize the number of such nonlinear multiplications, the authors described a technique called Parity-Split, with a proven complexity of $\mathcal{O}(2^{k/2})$ nonlinear multiplications for evaluating any k-bit S-box. This was further improved in Coron et al. (2014a), with a generic technique for fast polynomial evaluation in $\mathbb{F}_{2^k}$, with heuristic complexity $\mathcal{O}(2^{k/2}/\sqrt{k})$. In summary, the asymptotic running time of the Rivain–Prouff countermeasure for AES is $\mathcal{O}(n^2)$, and for k-bit generic S-boxes the running time is $\mathcal{O}(2^{k/2} \cdot n^2)$ [2].

2 Or $\mathcal{O}(2^{k/2}/\sqrt{k} \cdot n^2)$ using the heuristic technique as in Coron et al. (2014a).

A completely different high-order countermeasure for S-box evaluation was described in Coron (2014) based on table randomization. The countermeasure is an extension of the classical first-order randomized table countermeasure first described in Chari et al. (1999). An attempt to generalize this first-order countermeasure to high-order security was proposed by Schramm and Paar (2006), but a security flaw was shown in Coron et al. (2007). The asymptotic complexity of the secure-randomized countermeasure from Coron (2014) for k-bit S-boxes is $\mathcal{O}(2^k \cdot n^2)$, while the previous CGPQR countermeasure has complexity $\mathcal{O}(2^{k/2} \cdot n^2)$ only. In Coron (2014), a variant countermeasure for processors with large register size is described, with the same time complexity $\mathcal{O}(2^{k/2} \cdot n^2)$ as the CGPQR countermeasure using a similar approach as in Rivain et al. (2008).

– Section 2.6. Goubin (2001) described the first conversion algorithms between Boolean and arithmetic masking secure against first-order attacks. In particular, Goubin's first-order Boolean to arithmetic conversion seems optimal with complexity $\mathcal{O}(1)$ independent of the register size k. The other direction (from arithmetic to Boolean) is less efficient with complexity $\mathcal{O}(k)$. This was later improved by $\mathcal{O}(\log k)$ in Coron et al. (2015). The improvement is based on the Kogge–Stone carry look-ahead adder, which computes the carry signal in $\mathcal{O}(\log k)$ instead of $\mathcal{O}(k)$ for the classical ripple carry adder. However, the $\mathcal{O}(\log k)$ complexity hides a larger constant, and in practice for $k = 32$ the number of operations is similar.

For security against high-order attacks (i.e. with n shares), the first conversion algorithms were described in Coron et al. (2014a), with complexity $\mathcal{O}(n^2 \cdot k)$ for n shares and k-bit addition in both directions, with a proof of security in the ISW model. As in Goubin's first-order case, the complexity can be improved to $\mathcal{O}(n^2 \cdot \log k)$ using the same technique as in Coron et al. (2015). However, for $k = 32$, this does not improve the practical efficiency.

In Coron (2017), an efficient high-order Boolean to arithmetic conversion algorithm was described, with complexity independent of the register size k (as in Goubin's first-order algorithm), following an approach initiated by Hutter and Tunstall (2016). This technique was later improved in Bettale et al. (2018) and corresponds to Algorithm 2.9. The conversion algorithm has a security proof in the ISW model. In contrast, the original algorithm described in Hutter and Tunstall (2016) had no such security proof, and quite unsurprisingly, a third-order attack was described in Coron (2017) for any number of shares n. Although the complexity of the new algorithm is $\mathcal{O}(2^n)$, in practice for small values of n, it is at least one order of magnitude more efficient than Coron et al. (2014a, 2015).

2.8. References

Andrychowicz, M., Dziembowski, S., Faust, S. (2016). Circuit compilers with $O(1/\log(n))$ leakage rate. In *EUROCRYPT 2016*, Fischlin, M. and Coron, J.-S. (eds). Springer, Berlin, Heidelberg.

Barthe, G., Belaïd, S., Dupressoir, F., Fouque, P.-A., Grégoire, B. (2015). Compositional verification of higher-order masking: Application to a verifying masking compiler. Report 2015/506, Cryptology ePrint Archive [Online]. Available at: https://eprint.iacr.org/2015/506.

Barthe, G., Belaïd, S., Dupressoir, F., Fouque, P.-A., Grégoire, B., Strub, P.-Y., Zucchini, R. (2016). Strong non-interference and type-directed higher-order masking. In *ACM CCS 2016*, Weippl, E.R., Katzenbeisser, S., Kruegel, C., Myers, A.C., Halevi, S. (eds). ACM Press, New York.

Battistello, A., Coron, J.-S., Prouff, E., Zeitoun, R. (2016). Horizontal side-channel attacks and countermeasures on the ISW masking scheme. Report 2016/540, Cryptology ePrint Archive [Online]. Available at: https://eprint.iacr.org/2016/540.

Bettale, L., Coron, J.-S., Zeitoun, R. (2018). Improved high-order conversion from Boolean to arithmetic masking. *IACR TCHES*, 2018(2), 22–45.

Carlet, C., Goubin, L., Prouff, E., Quisquater, M., Rivain, M. (2012). Higher-order masking schemes for S-boxes. In *FSE 2012*, Canteaut, A. (ed.). Springer, Berlin, Heidelberg.

Chari, S., Jutla, C.S., Rao, J.R., Rohatgi, P. (1999). Towards sound approaches to counteract power-analysis attacks. In *CRYPTO'99*, Wiener, M.J. (ed.). Springer, Berlin, Heidelberg.

Coron, J.-S. (2014). Higher order masking of look-up tables. In *EUROCRYPT 2014*, Nguyen, P.Q. and Oswald, E. (eds). Springer, Berlin, Heidelberg.

Coron, J.-S. (2017). High-order conversion from Boolean to arithmetic masking. In *CHES 2017*, Fischer, W. and Homma, N. (eds). Springer, Berlin, Heidelberg.

Coron, J.-S., Prouff, E., Rivain, M. (2007). Side channel cryptanalysis of a higher order masking scheme. In *CHES 2007*, Paillier, P. and Verbauwhede, I. (eds). Springer, Berlin, Heidelberg.

Coron, J.-S., Großschädl, J., Vadnala, P.K. (2014a). Secure conversion between Boolean and arithmetic masking of any order. In *CHES 2014*, Batina, L. and Robshaw, M. (eds). Springer, Berlin, Heidelberg.

Coron, J.-S., Prouff, E., Rivain, M., Roche, T. (2014b). Higher-order side channel security and mask refreshing. In *FSE 2013*, Moriai, S. (ed.). Springer, Berlin, Heidelberg.

Coron, J.-S., Großschädl, J., Tibouchi, M., Vadnala, P.K. (2015). Conversion from arithmetic to Boolean masking with logarithmic complexity. In *FSE 2015*, Leander, G. (ed.). Springer, Berlin, Heidelberg.

Goubin, L. (2001). A sound method for switching between Boolean and arithmetic masking. In *CHES 2001*, Çetin Kaya, K., Naccache, D., Paar, C. (eds). Springer, Berlin, Heidelberg.

Hutter, M. and Tunstall, M. (2016). Constant-time higher-order Boolean-to-arithmetic masking. Report 2016/1023, Cryptology ePrint Archive [Online]. Available at: http://eprint.iacr.org/2016/1023.

Ishai, Y., Sahai, A., Wagner, D. (2003). Private circuits: Securing hardware against probing attacks. In *CRYPTO 2003*, Boneh, D. (ed.). Springer, Berlin, Heidelberg.

Rivain, M. and Prouff, E. (2010). Provably secure higher-order masking of AES. In *CHES 2010*, Mangard, S. and Standaert, F.-X. (eds). Springer, Berlin, Heidelberg.

Rivain, M., Dottax, E., Prouff, E. (2008). Block ciphers implementations provably secure against second order side channel analysis. In *FSE 2008*, Nyberg, K. (ed.). Springer, Berlin, Heidelberg.

Schramm, K. and Paar, C. (2006). Higher order masking of the AES. In *CT-RSA 2006*, Pointcheval, D. (ed.). Springer, Berlin, Heidelberg.

3

Hardware Masking

Begül BILGIN[1] and Lauren DE MEYER[2]

[1]*Rambus Cryptography Research, Rotterdam, Netherlands*

[2]*Rambus Cryptography Research, San Francisco, USA*

3.1. Introduction

In the previous chapters, various masking schemes (gadgets) have been discussed that are provably secured in the d-probing model and may offer composability by a refreshing of the output shares. During the security arguments, it is assumed that the order of operations is respected and that the internal state of the device, hence the overall leakage, depends on the noisy leakages coming from each intermediate independently. We call a circuit that satisfies these two assumptions an *ideal circuit*. Unfortunately, these assumptions may not hold in practice.

We start this chapter with an example on hardware where the ideal circuit assumption does not hold, which can cause an undesired leakage. We then provide an abstraction of this behavior, which leads to an extended adversary model. Fortunately, it is possible to create hardware implementations that are also secured under this extended adversary model. We present several secure gadgets and discuss the properties that bring this security.

Note that this chapter focuses mostly on Boolean masking and that the gadgets we provide are not exhaustive. We conclude by looking at trade-offs between area footprint, latency and randomness cost.

Embedded Cryptography 2,
coordinated by Emmanuel PROUFF, Guénaël RENAULT,
Matthieu RIVAIN and Colin O'FLYNN.

3.1.1. *Glitches*

Remember from Chapter 2 that the order of calculation in an ISW multiplication gadget is important. While it may be easy to preserve the order when implementing in software, which inherently stores intermediate variables in registers, it is not trivial to achieve this in hardware, without incurring prohibitive area and latency costs.

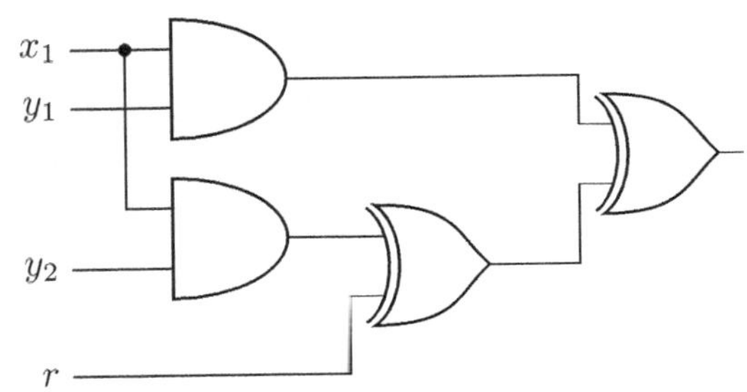

Figure 3.1. *Second output share of ISW with* $n = 2$

Let us look at a naive implementation of ISW with $n = 2$ shares ($x = x_1 \oplus x_2$, $y = y_1 \oplus y_2$), which implements the AND gadget in one cycle, as depicted for one output in Figure 3.1[1]. In order to ensure that the circuit, and hence the order of parenthesis, is maintained exactly, the designer needs to use synthesis constraints. Even then, the circuit is prone to unintended signal transitions, caused by the varying delays of logic gates and routing imbalances. Such a hardware phenomenon (see the bottom signal in Figure 3.2) is called a *glitch*. An adversary in the probing model can obtain information about the value of $y = y_1 \oplus y_2$ by probing a single output share of the ISW AND gate and performing multiple executions with fixed secret y and varying data x. The glitch caused by x_1 arriving late would have a distribution that is dependent on y.

Glitches are difficult to predict, model and control. Therefore, a designer needs to pay attention to the possible intermediate values that can leak. One way to limit glitching is to synchronize certain intermediates by using, for example, registers (or flip-flops at bit level). While registers do not eliminate glitches, they can, if used carefully, limit their adverse affects. In what follows, we denote the synchronization of a variable x with square brackets: $[x]$.

1 Note that Figure 3.1 depicts variables in $\mathbb{F}_2$ for simplicity, but that the gadget and following discussions also apply to variables in $\mathbb{F}_{2^k}$ with multipliers instead of AND gates. Throughout the chapter, we will use xy for such gadgets.

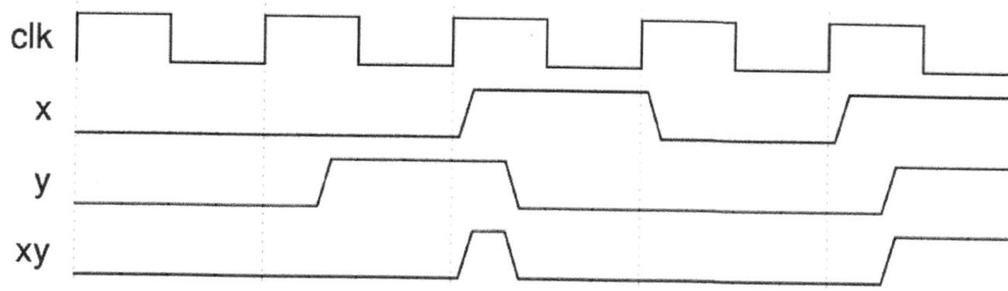

Figure 3.2. *Example of a glitch in the signal xy. For a color version of this figure, see www.iste.co.uk/prouff/cryptography2.zip*

3.1.2. *Glitch-extended probes*

To account for glitches without the need to model them exactly (which would highly depend on the physical characteristics of the hardware), we can use the following simplified adversary model (see also Figure 3.3): for each wire g, we consider a function G that calculates g from stabilized inputs f_i'. When an adversary probes g (or any intermediate of G), we will assume that this probe reveals all inputs f_i' of G up to the last synchronization point (reg_2), but no values from previous synchronization points (reg_1) or intermediates occurring during the calculations of the functions F_i. We call the set $\{f_1', \ldots, f_s'\}$ the *glitch-extended probe* of g. With this set, the adversary can compute any intermediate or output of G (both stable and transient). Therefore, if the glitch-extended probe $\{f_1', \ldots, f_s'\}$ does not reveal sensitive information, then neither can any probe on G, even in the presence of glitches.

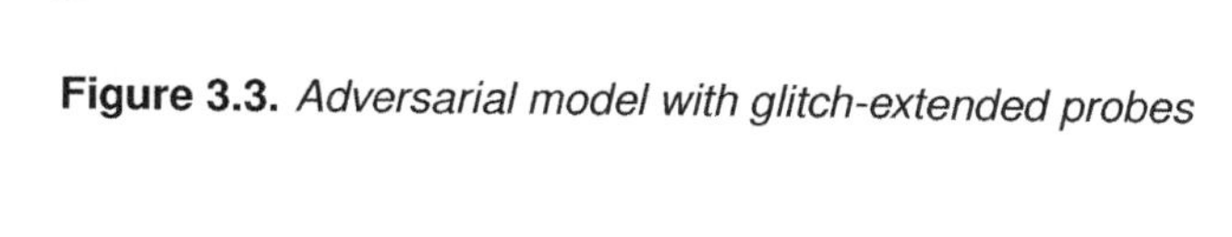

Figure 3.3. *Adversarial model with glitch-extended probes*

3.1.3. *Non-completeness*

In this chapter, we focus on masking schemes with inherent protection against the vulnerabilities arising from glitches. Instead of trying to prevent glitches from happening, the masking schemes we describe ensure that when they do, they cannot reveal any sensitive information. We use an important property, on which many masking schemes rely, to achieve this: non-completeness.

The idea of *non-completeness* is that a potentially glitching function should not depend on the *complete* set of shares of a sensitive value. If it does, as is the case in ISW (see y_1 and y_2 in Figure 3.1), the sensitive value itself is likely to be revealed by the glitch.

DEFINITION 3.1.– *d*th-order non-completeness. Let $\boldsymbol{f} = (f_1, f_2, \ldots)$ be a shared function with component functions f_i such that $\bigoplus f_i = f$. Any combination of up to d component functions f_i of $\boldsymbol{f}$ must be independent of at least one input share of each variable.

The classical approach to share a linear function with $n > d$ shares (see Chapter 1) trivially satisfies the above definition. However, we need to pay more attention to nonlinear gadgets.

3.2. Category I: $td + 1$ masking

It is possible to describe a *d*th-order non-complete sharing of a function in various different ways. In this section, we focus on the case where the component functions are created such that each is independent of the same indexed share(s).

THEOREM 3.1.– There exists a *d*th-order non-complete sharing of a function of degree t with $n \geq td + 1$ input shares.

Proof. Let $k \in \mathbb{N}$. Consider the monomial(s) $x^{j_1}x^{j_2}x^{j_3}\ldots x^{j_t}$ of t variables where $x^j \in \mathbb{F}_{2^k}$. We represent the sharing of each variable x^j as x_i^j where $i \in \{1, ..., n\}$. Then,

$$\begin{aligned} x^{j_1}x^{j_2}x^{j_3}\ldots x^{j_t} &= (x_1^{j_1} \oplus x_2^{j_1} \oplus \ldots \oplus x_n^{j_1})\ldots(x_1^{j_t} \oplus x_2^{j_t} \oplus \ldots \oplus x_n^{j_t}) \\ &= (x_1^{j_1}x_1^{j_2}\ldots x_1^{j_t}) \oplus (x_1^{j_1}x_1^{j_2}\ldots x_2^{j_t}) \oplus \ldots \oplus (x_n^{j_n}x_n^{j_2}\ldots x_n^{j_t}). \end{aligned}$$

Choose t indices from $\{1, ..., n\}$ and place all the terms with those share indices for each monomial in the first component function. Choose another t indices and place all the remaining terms with those share indices in the second component function. Clearly, after $\binom{n}{t}$ iterations, all the terms for each monomial are placed in a component function. Each component function carries information from at most t shares of each input variable. Hence, any combination of up to d component functions carries information from, at most, td shares of an input. To achieve the non-completeness property, $n > td$, which implies the equation $n \geq td + 1$ for the number of input shares. □

While the above theorem and the corresponding proof describe a methodology to generate a dth-order non-complete sharing for any function of algebraic degree t, it does not imply that the number of output shares or the sum of input and output shares are minimum.

In what follows, we first focus on security against first-order ($d = 1$) side-channel analysis (SCA) of a single Boolean function, then discuss the requirements to extend the security to a circuit which consists of multiple such functions. Then, we move to higher-order security.

3.2.1. *First-order security*

Let us generate the sharing such that every component function f_i is independent of share $i - 1$

$$\begin{aligned} z_1 &= f_1(x_{\overline{n}}, y_{\overline{n}}, \ldots) = f_1(x_1, x_2, \ldots x_{n-1}, y_1, y_2, \ldots, y_{n-1}, \ldots) \\ z_2 &= f_2(x_{\overline{1}}, y_{\overline{1}}, \ldots) = f_2(x_2, x_3 \ldots x_n, y_2, y_3, \ldots, y_n, \ldots) \\ &\ldots \\ z_n &= f_n(x_{\overline{n-1}}, y_{\overline{n-1}}, \ldots) = f_n(x_1, \ldots x_{n-2}, x_n, y_1, \ldots, y_{n-2}, y_n \ldots) \end{aligned} \quad [3.1]$$

Clearly such a sharing satisfies the first-order non-completeness property and is inline with Theorem 3.1 with $n \geq t + 1$

THEOREM 3.2.– If the input masking $\boldsymbol{x}$ of the shared function $\boldsymbol{f}$ is a uniform masking and $\boldsymbol{f}$ is first-order non-complete, then a circuit implementing $\boldsymbol{f}$ is first-order secure in the probing model, even if glitches occur in the circuit.

Proof. Since $\boldsymbol{f}$ is non-complete, each glitch extended probe of a component function f_i, as well as the corresponding output share, is independent of at least one input share. The statistical independence of the glitch-extended probe and the output share from the unshared output, and hence security, follows from the uniform input sharing. □

A hardware implementation of a shared circuit that has uniformly shared input and satisfies correctness and non-completeness is called a *threshold implementation* in literature.

EXAMPLE 3.1.– A first-order non-complete sharing of xy using this approach is given as:

$$\begin{aligned} z_1 &= x_1y_1 + x_1y_2 + x_2y_1 \\ z_2 &= x_2y_2 + x_2y_3 + x_3y_2 \\ z_3 &= x_3y_3 + x_3y_1 + x_1y_3 \end{aligned}$$

Given a uniformly distributed input sharing for $\{x, y\} \in \mathbb{F}_2$, the distribution of the output sharing $z \in \mathbb{F}_2$ for the above example is given in Table 3.1. Each table entry records the number of occurrences of a sharing (z_1, z_2, z_3) for z by enumerating every possible sharing (x_1, x_2, x_3) for x and every possible sharing (y_1, y_2, y_3) for y.

	z_1, z_2, z_3							
(x, y)	000	011	101	110	001	010	100	111
$(0, 0)$	7	3	3	3	0	0	0	0
$(0, 1)$	7	3	3	3	0	0	0	0
$(1, 0)$	7	3	3	3	0	0	0	0
$(1, 1)$	0	0	0	0	5	5	5	1

Table 3.1. *Distribution of output sharing for Example 3.1*

Clearly, the output sharing $\boldsymbol{z}$ is not uniformly distributed. Therefore, a trivial composition (i.e. using $\boldsymbol{z}$ as an input to another shared function) may lead to insecure circuits. This is inline with the discussion provided in Chapter 2 in the context of SW masking.

Therefore, the following definition is useful.

DEFINITION 3.2.– Uniformity. Let $Sh(x)$ denote the set of valid sharings $\boldsymbol{x}$. Let $\boldsymbol{f}$ be a circuit that takes n_{in} input shares $\boldsymbol{x}$ and produces n_{out} output shares $\boldsymbol{z}$. The circuit $\boldsymbol{f}$ is uniform if and only if:

$$\forall x \in \mathbb{F}_{2^k}, \forall z \in \mathbb{F}_{2^l} \text{ with } f(x) = z,$$

$$\forall \boldsymbol{z} \in Sh(z) : |\{\boldsymbol{x} \in Sh(x) | \boldsymbol{f}(\boldsymbol{x}) = \boldsymbol{z}\}| = \frac{2^{k(n_{in}-1)}}{2^{l(n_{out}-1)}}$$

3.2.1.1. *Achieving uniformity*

There are different approaches to achieve uniformity. One such method called *refreshing* is already described in Chapter 2. This approach is rather generic as it is independent of the masking and the underlying function, and is applicable here as well.

An alternative method is to increase the number of input shares n_{in}, and if needed, the number of output shares n_{out}. The former increases the amount of entropy in the system and gives flexibility on the construction.

EXAMPLE 3.2.– The following is a correct, non-complete and a uniform sharing of xy where $\{x, y\} \in \mathbb{F}_2$:

$$
\begin{aligned}
z_1 &= (x_2 + x_4)(y_1 + y_4) + x_1 y_2 + x_4 + y_4 \\
z_2 &= (x_2 + x_3 + x_4)(y_2 + y_3) + y_4 \\
z_3 &= (x_1 + x_3)(y_1 + y_4) + x_1 y_3 + x_4
\end{aligned}
$$

Even though we have focused on a multiplication gadget (or an AND gate) so far, it may be beneficial to consider the sharing of a bigger function directly. For example, the following sharing of $z = xy + w$, where the input sharing of w is independent of the sharings of x and y, is also uniform.

$$
\begin{aligned}
z_1 &= x_1 y_1 + x_1 y_2 + x_2 y_1 + w_1 \\
z_2 &= x_2 y_2 + x_2 y_3 + x_3 y_2 + w_2 \\
z_3 &= x_3 y_3 + x_3 y_1 + x_1 y_3 + w_3
\end{aligned}
\qquad [3.2]
$$

Note that the refreshing approach is a special case of the above sharing where $w = 0$.

3.2.1.2. *Vectorial Boolean function*

The nonlinear components of many cryptographic algorithms are represented as a vectorial Boolean function where $f(x^1, x^2, \ldots, x^l) = (z^1, z^2, \ldots z^m)$, where $x^i, z^i \in \mathbb{F}_2$ and:

$$
\begin{aligned}
z^1 &= f^1(x^1, x^2, \ldots, x^l) \\
z^2 &= f^2(x^1, x^2, \ldots, x^l) \\
\ldots \\
z^m &= f^m(x^1, x^2, \ldots, x^l)
\end{aligned}
\qquad [3.3]
$$

In the rest of this section, we will assume $l = m$ and f is invertible for simplicity, that is, f is a *permutation*. In this case, it follows from the uniformity definition that a uniform circuit $\boldsymbol{f}$ with the same number of input and output shares is invertible if and only if f is invertible.

In the case where the algebraic degree of f if high, the sharing $\boldsymbol{f}$ becomes increasingly more expensive. A well-known approach to implement such a permutation is to divide it to lower degree functions first. An example of this for the AES S-box has been provided in Chapter 2. In that case, it is important to ensure uniform sharing of the combined input to a function for security. In some cases, it is possible to divide the high-degree permutation as $f = g_1(g_2(\cdots(g_n)))$. Such a *decomposition* with low-degree g_i is especially useful. On the one hand, the lower degree g_i implies lower complexity for the $\boldsymbol{g_i}$. On the other hand, following the uniformity property, if a uniform sharing $\boldsymbol{g_i}$ exists for all g_is, then first-order security can be achieved without using additional randomness for refreshing.

3.2.2. *Higher-order security*

Note that for $d = 1$, we can have the same number of input and output shares as in the construction in Example 3.1: $n_{in} = n_{out} = td + 1$. However, for $d > 1$ and $n_{in} = td + 1$, we need more output shares: $n_{out} > n_{in}$ (see Example 3.3).

EXAMPLE 3.3.– A second-order non-complete 5-input 10-output sharing of $z = xy$ is as follows:

$$\begin{aligned} z_1 &= x_1y_1 + x_1y_5 + x_5y_1 & z_6 &= x_2y_3 + x_3y_2 \\ z_2 &= x_2y_2 + x_2y_1 + x_1y_2 & z_7 &= x_2y_4 + x_4y_2 \\ z_3 &= x_3y_3 + x_1y_3 + x_3y_1 & z_8 &= x_3y_4 + x_4y_3 \\ z_4 &= x_4y_4 + x_1y_4 + x_4y_1 & z_9 &= x_3y_5 + x_5y_3 \\ z_5 &= x_5y_5 + x_2y_5 + x_5y_2 & z_{10} &= x_4y_5 + x_5y_4 \end{aligned}$$

This increase in the number of output shares brings an interesting challenge in order to avoid excessive increase as multiple functions are composed.

One option to deal with this challenge is to first register the n_{out} shares and then decrease the number of shares by XORing some of them (compression). Note that while this seems trivial, we need to be careful in order to satisfy uniformity. We will discuss such challenges in section 3.3 as there are similarities between the two approaches. Another option is to increase the number of input shares such that n_{in} and n_{out} are equal or very close to each other. Independent of the applied method, unlike the first-order case, uniformity and non-completeness combined is not sufficient to construct higher-order secure implementations. The main reason for this is the possibility of multi-variate attacks, where probes can be placed on intermediates in different cycles.

3.3. Category II: $d + 1$ masking

The threshold implementations described in the previous section achieved d^{th}-order non-completeness by making each set of d component functions independent of *the same share(s) for all inputs* (see equation [3.1]). As a result, at least $td + 1$ shares were required to achieve dth-order non-completeness. However, based on the definition of non-completeness, it is actually sufficient to have each set of d component functions independent of at least one share *of each input*, without restrictions on the share index. This makes it possible to define a masking scheme that satisfies dth-order non-completeness with the minimal number of shares $n = d + 1$.

3.3.1. *General construction*

An established methodology for masking the multiplication of two variables $x, y \in \mathbb{F}_{2^k}$ with d^{th}-order security against SCA can be described in four steps:

1) *Expand* $n = d + 1$ input shares of x and y into n^2 cross products $x_i y_j$.

2) *Refresh* the cross products: $x_i y_j \to z_{ij} = x_i y_j \oplus r_{ij}$ with r_{ij} chosen such that correctness is not affected: $\bigoplus_i \bigoplus_j r_{ij} = 0$.

3) *Synchronize* the refreshed cross products to stop glitches from propagating: $z_{ij} \to [z_{ij}]$ (this step is implicit in software).

4) *Compress* the n^2 shares z_{ij} back into $n = d + 1$ shares $z_i = \bigoplus_j z_{ij}$.

The first two steps are often described in matrix form, as the XOR of a matrix of cross products and a refreshing matrix:

$$\begin{pmatrix} z_{11} & z_{12} & \dots & z_{1n} \\ z_{21} & \ddots & & \vdots \\ \vdots & & \ddots & \vdots \\ z_{n1} & \dots & \dots & z_{nn} \end{pmatrix} = \begin{pmatrix} x_1y_1 & x_1y_2 & \dots & x_1y_n \\ x_2y_1 & \ddots & & \vdots \\ \vdots & & \ddots & \vdots \\ x_ny_1 & \dots & \dots & x_ny_n \end{pmatrix} \oplus \begin{pmatrix} r_{11} & r_{12} & \dots & r_{1n} \\ r_{21} & \ddots & & \vdots \\ \vdots & & \ddots & \vdots \\ r_{n1} & \dots & \dots & r_{nn} \end{pmatrix} \quad [3.4]$$

Variations can be made in the construction of both matrices. The most common type of refreshing is one where only cross products of different shares ($x_i y_j$ for $i \neq j$) need fresh masks (i.e. $r_{ii} = 0$), and where the same mask can be used for cross products $x_i y_j$ and $x_j y_i$ (i.e. the refreshing matrix is symmetric). Such a masking scheme then almost matches that of ISW from the previous chapter.

Independent sharings

In the above scheme, it is essential that the sharings of the inputs are independent. This is a consequence of the fact that we now only require independence of one share of each input, without restrictions on the share index. The following example demonstrates why this matters.

EXAMPLE 3.4.– Consider the cross products in a first-order multiplication when $y = x^2$ with $\boldsymbol{x} = (x_1, x_2)$ and $\boldsymbol{y} = (x_1^2, x_2^2)$:

$$x_1 y_2 = x_1 x_2^2 \quad [3.5]$$

Since both shares of x are combined in a single cross product, non-completeness is clearly not satisfied.

Other types of masking

This generic masking construction is also compatible with other types of masking, such as inner product or polynomial masking. The same four steps can be followed, and the expanded cross product and refreshing matrices differ only by a scaling with public coefficients.

3.3.2. *Security argument*

We can use glitch-extended probes to show why the general masking construction of section 3.3.1 is secure in the presence of glitches. Without loss of generality, we can assume that the refreshing matrix is symmetric. For simplicity, let us consider a three-share multiplication ($d = 2$) as an example:

$$\begin{pmatrix} z_1 \\ z_2 \\ z_3 \end{pmatrix} = \begin{pmatrix} z_{11} & z_{12} & z_{13} \\ z_{21} & z_{22} & z_{23} \\ z_{31} & z_{32} & z_{33} \end{pmatrix} \begin{pmatrix} 1 \\ 1 \\ 1 \end{pmatrix} = \begin{pmatrix} [x_1y_1] \oplus [x_1y_2 \oplus r_{12}] \oplus [x_1y_3 \oplus r_{13}] \\ [x_2y_1 \oplus r_{12}] \oplus [x_2y_2] \oplus [x_2y_3 \oplus r_{23}] \\ [x_3y_1 \oplus r_{13}] \oplus [x_3y_2 \oplus r_{23}] \oplus [x_3y_3] \end{pmatrix} \quad [3.6]$$

Stage 1: Pre-synchronization

The first stage ends with n^2 outputs $z_{ij} = x_iy_j \oplus r_{ij}$. The glitch-extended probe of z_{ij} is $\{x_i, y_j, r_{ij}\}$, so clearly, each output depends on exactly one share of each input, as long as those input shares are independent, that is, $\mathbb{P}[x_i|\boldsymbol{y}] = \mathbb{P}[x_i]$ and $\mathbb{P}[y_j|\boldsymbol{x}] = \mathbb{P}[y_j]$. As a result, any combination of, at most, d probes can reveal, at most, d shares of each input.

Stage 2: Post-synchronization

The second stage has n^2 stable inputs z_{ij} and produces n output shares $z_i = \bigoplus_{j=1}^{n} z_{ij}$. Each output share is the sum of one row of the matrix given in [3.6] (or [3.4]). Hence, the glitch-extended probe of z_i is $\{z_{i1}, z_{i2}, \ldots, z_{in}\}$.

In the $d = 2$ example, it can be verified that any combination of up to $d = 2$ probes does not reveal sensitive information. For example, probing z_1 and z_2 reveals their combined glitch-extended probes: $\{z_{11}, z_{12}, z_{13}, z_{21}, z_{22}, z_{23}\}$. Since z_{11} and z_{22} have not been refreshed, the probes obviously depend on shares 1 and 2 of each input. It remains to be verified that they do not depend on share 3. This is the case since both z_{13} and z_{23} have been refreshed with a uniformly random value that is not used anywhere else in the probe.

Stage 1 + Stage 2

A set of d probes can also consist of probes from different stages. Let us consider the case $d = 2$ as an example again, with one probe in each stage. Let z_{ij} be the probed value in the first stage. In the second stage, we then distinguish two cases. We can probe (1) z_i or z_j, which directly depend on the first probe, or (2) the other output z_k with $k \neq i$ and $k \neq j$. For example, we will use $(i, j) = (1, 2)$, but similar arguments can be made for other indices.

1) The glitch-extended probe for z_{12} and z_1 is $\{x_1, y_2, r_{12}, z_{11}, z_{12}, z_{13}\}$. This probe clearly depends only on share 1 of x. With respect to y, it clearly depends on share 2, as well as on share 1 (since z_{11} is not refreshed). Again, we can claim that the probe does not depend on share 3 of y since z_{13} has been refreshed with r_{13}, which is an independent uniform value.

2) The glitch-extended probe for z_{12} and z_3 is $\{x_1, y_2, r_{12}, z_{31}, z_{32}, z_{33}\}$. This probe clearly depends on shares 1 and 3 of x, and on shares 2 and 3 of y (since z_{33} is not refreshed). It clearly does not depend on share 2 of x, so it remains to be verified that it is independent of y_1. Since z_{31} has been refreshed with independent uniform value r_{31}, this is indeed the case.

3.3.3. Comparing to $td + 1$ masking

Does the $d{+}1$-share construction satisfy the requirements of $td{+}1$-share threshold implementation, non-completeness and uniformity? Compared to first-order threshold implementations with $t + 1$ shares, where a multiplication can be done within a single cycle, the $d + 1$ multiplication consists of two stages, separated by a register. With multiple stages, the intermediates sharings between registers are not necessarily uniform, which means we need more than uniformity and non-completeness to achieve security. The $d + 1$-share construction steps away from the strict $td + 1$ rules, while still adhering to the same principles.

On non-completeness

In the first stage, non-completeness is clearly satisfied, as long as the input shares are independent. Also in the second stage, non-completeness is satisfied, since any set of d outputs will be independent of at least one of the input shares z_{ij}. However, this sharing is not uniform and as such, the uni-variate notion of non-completeness is not enough to achieve probing security, as shown in section 3.2.

We may have noted that the example in section 3.3.2 did still rely on a form of non-completeness, since we constructed glitch-extended probes and verified their independence of at least one share of each input. We thus extended non-completeness to multiple stages, on the one hand, by tracing back each stage to the input sharings of the first stage and, on the other hand, by combining probes in multiple stages.

In fact, if we transformed the non-completeness definition to one where each set of d glitch-extended probes (instead of components) must be independent of at least one share of each input, and we extended it to include probes in different stages (multi-variate), then we would have shown that the $d+1$-share construction satisfies this non-completeness. The non-completeness used by $td+1$ threshold implementations is its uni-variate equivalent, where each set of d glitch-extended probes, taken from within a single stage (i.e. component functions), must be independent of at least one input share. This is why the higher-order threshold implementations from section 3.2.2 do not achieve security against a multi-variate adversary.

Note also that non-completeness is necessary. If any combination of d glitch-extended probes depended on all input shares, it could reveal sensitive information.

On uniformity

Uniformity, on the other hand, is not necessary, as exemplified by the intermediate sharing of z with $(d+1)^2$ shares. In order for an n-share sharing of x to be d^{th}-order probing secure, we require that any set of d shares is jointly independent of x itself. If $n = d+1$, this property is equivalent to uniformity. As such, we still require the input sharings $\boldsymbol{x}$ and $\boldsymbol{y}$ to be uniform. However, when $n > d+1$, it is possible for a non-uniform sharing to satisfy this property. For example, the $(d+1)^2$-sharing of z at the end of stage 1 is dth-order secure because any subset of d shares cannot reveal z itself, nor x and y.

3.3.4. *Higher-degree functions*

We have only considered the multiplication above, which is a function of algebraic degree $t = 2$. The $d+1$-share masking methodology also works for functions of higher algebraic degree. In contrast with $td+1$-TI, the number of shares of the inputs and outputs can remain $d+1$ regardless of the algebraic degree t. However, the number of intermediate shares (or cross products) increases exponentially with t. We will demonstrate it first for simple monomials and then explain how to extend it to generic Boolean functions.

Instead of a multiplication xy, which is a monomial of degree 2, let us consider a monomial $x^1x^2\dots x^t$ of algebraic degree $t > 2$. The masked monomial is similar to that of equation [3.4], but instead of two-dimensional matrices, the cross products extend into more dimensions. If each input has $n = d+1$ shares and there are t inputs in the monomial, there are n^t cross products and thus intermediate shares. These can be refreshed, synchronized and compressed back to $n = d+1$ shares. For example, a first-order ($d = 1$) sharing of a third-degree ($t = 3$) monomial $f(x, y, z) = xyz$ is as follows:

$$\begin{aligned} f_1(\boldsymbol{x},\boldsymbol{y},\boldsymbol{z}) &= [f_{111}] \oplus [f_{112} \oplus r_{112}] \oplus [f_{121} \oplus r_{121}] \oplus [f_{122} \oplus r_{122}] \\ f_2(\boldsymbol{x},\boldsymbol{y},\boldsymbol{z}) &= [f_{222}] \oplus [f_{221} \oplus r_{221}] \oplus [f_{212} \oplus r_{212}] \oplus [f_{211} \oplus r_{211}] \end{aligned} \quad [3.7]$$

with

$$\begin{aligned} f_{111} &= x_1 y_1 z_1 & f_{222} &= x_2 y_2 z_2 \\ f_{112} &= x_1 y_1 z_2 & f_{221} &= x_2 y_2 z_1 \\ f_{121} &= x_1 y_2 z_1 & f_{212} &= x_2 y_1 z_2 \\ f_{122} &= x_1 y_2 z_2 & f_{211} &= x_2 y_1 z_1 \end{aligned} \quad [3.8]$$

Note that $f_{ijk} = f(x_i, y_j, z_k)$.

A generic Boolean function of algebraic degree t consists of m monomials, each with algebraic degree $\leq t$. A naive way to mask the function is to mask each monomial separately, which would mean having $m(d+1)^t$ intermediate shares. It is better to combine the monomials into $k < m$ groups such that we have only $l(d+1)^t$ intermediate shares. Finding a minimal l such that non-completeness is achieved is not always trivial. For any t-degree Boolean function with up to $t+1$ inputs, it is possible to achieve the lower bound $l = 1$. Consider, for example, another third-degree function, this time with four inputs: $f(x, y, z, w) = xyz \oplus yzw \oplus xyw \oplus xzw$. We can still use equation [3.7], but this time with $f_{ijk} = f(x_i, y_j, z_k, w_{i \oplus j \oplus k})$. If there are more inputs, it is possible that we will need $l > 1$.

3.4. Trade-offs

The trade-off between area and latency is one that is known even from unmasked hardware design. However, masking brings several new choices to make in this respect. In addition, a new cost factor in the world of masking is that of randomness. Most masking schemes require a constant supply of fresh random bits during a calculation. In cases where the total number random of bits per cryptographic operation becomes too high, a pseudo-random number generator (PRNG) may be required, operating in parallel to the algorithm and supplying "online" fresh random bits. Hence, the more fresh randomness is needed per cycle, the higher the cost of the implementation.

Serial and round-based architecture

As with unmasked hardware design, one way to trade area and latency is to play with the number of parallel copies of the same block. Different architectures for symmetric cryptography are often distinguished in the number of S-boxes they use. Since the S-box is the only nonlinear component, its area and latency are most impacted by masking. As a result, serial architectures that use only one copy of the S-box for the entire state are quite popular. They are however slow. A round-based design is much faster, but requires enough copies of the S-box to process the entire state in parallel, and this tends to be expensive in area. Also, the more copies of the S-box, the higher the fresh randomness requirement. Hence, round-based architectures are good for the latency, but come with higher area and randomness cost.

3.4.1. *Minimizing area*

Decomposition

Both for $td + 1$ and for $d + 1$ masking, the number of (intermediate) shares increases strongly with the algebraic degree t of a masked function. In practice, in order to avoid the area cost that this entails, it is common to decompose high-degree functions into subfunctions of degree two or sometimes three. Since the masking of each sub-function requires at least one register stage for synchronization, masking in hardware has a large impact on the latency of an implementation.

Sharing hardware

The idea of a serial architecture is that the hardware of a single S-box is used for the entire state. More extreme versions of hardware sharing exist but are not very popular. A bit-serial design tries to further optimize the area of the S-box by processing only one bit per cycle. The resulting benefit in area usually does not weigh up against the enormous latency cost, especially with today's applications where high performance is the main goal, whereas area constraints become less and less tight with Moore's law. Moreover, sharing more hardware often entails a higher security risk. The examples of equation [3.7] showed that hardware can be shared between the calculations of different intermediates shares, but doing so without care could result in non-completeness breaking during a clock transition.

3.4.2. *Minimizing latency*

Unrolling

We talked about decomposition as a way to optimize area. When a function already has a low degree, the opposite can be done to optimize latency. For example, the Keccak function family has a quadratic round function. This design ensures a relatively area-efficient implementation. However, when we want to optimize the latency instead, we could partially unroll and combine two iterations of the round functions into a single masked function of higher degree. This naturally comes at the cost of an increased area footprint.

Single-cycle masking

When registers are required in nonlinear functions (such as S-boxes), it is practically impossible to compute a masked round function in a single cycle. Though not literally impossible, the sacrifices in area and randomness that would result from attempting to do so, make it quite infeasible. Nevertheless, single-cycle masking is an important goal to pursue if we want to minimize the overhead of masking in terms of throughput and latency. Certain techniques such as dual-rail logic with precharging do make it possible to achieve synchronization (or one transition per clock cycle) without registers or flip-flops.

3.4.3. *Minimizing randomness*

The best case for randomness cost is when the masked function requires no "online" randomness at all and only a small number of bits that can be supplied as input. The "changing of the guards" trick is a popular mechanism where these extra bits are processed by only one S-box, which produces new such bits for the next S-box, thereby removing the need for an "online" PRNG. So far, masking without fresh randomness in the model of this chapter has only been achieved for first-order security. For higher orders, advances have been made when considering a more practical adversary with bounded query capabilities and measuring security using techniques from linear cryptanalysis.

3.5. Notes and further references

– Section 3.1. One of the first masked multiplication gadgets was introduced by Trichina (2003). While it was introduced as a hardware gadget, it did rely strongly on the order of operations and would turn out not to be secure in the presence of glitches. Mangard et al. (2005a, 2005b) were the first to demonstrate that these existing schemes (Trichina, ISW, etc.) did not provide the claimed security when implemented in hardware, due to glitches. Reparaz et al. (2015) introduced the adversary model that uses glitch-extended probes. There are alternative models for dealing with glitches, such as the transient model by Bertoni et al. (2017). The concept of non-completeness was introduced by Nikova et al. (2006, 2009) and later extended to higher order non-completeness by Bilgin et al. (2014).

– Section 3.2. Hardware masking as described in this section is initially introduced for first-order security as threshold implementations by Nikova et al. (2006, 2009). The name comes from the similarities with (n, n)-sharing in the multi-party computation context. Another proposal for glitch-resistant masking was made by Prouff and Roche (2011) and was also based on multi-party computation concepts. Bilgin et al. (2014) extended threshold implementations to higher-order security. This scheme has been shown to only provide uni-variate and not multi-variate security by Reparaz (2015). Hardware threshold implementations for various cryptographic algorithms, including AES by Moradi et al. (2011), Present by Poschmann et al. (2011); Katan by Bilgin et al. (2014) and Keccak by Bilgin et al. (2013), can be found in literature. It has also been shown to be useful for SW implementations by Sasdrich et al. (2018). For a detailed compendium on threshold implementations (also known as masking with $td + 1$ input shares), the reader should refer to the PhD thesis of Bilgin (2015).

– Section 3.3. Reparaz et al. (2015) noted that it is possible to achieve dth-order non-completeness with only $d + 1$ shares and demonstrated the similarities of hardware masking schemes with the ISW scheme. Simultaneously, Gross et al. (2017a) introduced domain-oriented masking: a hardware masking scheme with $d + 1$ shares, which significantly resembles the proposal of Reparaz, but has a more efficient randomness matrix. De Cnudde et al. (2016) presented the first application of the masking scheme with $d + 1$ shares to AES, providing both first- and second-order secure implementations. For a chronological overview of the history of hardware masking and its application to the AES cipher, the reader can refer to Chapter 1 of the PhD thesis of De Meyer (2020). Gross et al. (2017b) created higher order implementations of Keccak, but Arribas et al. (2018) found a flaw in their design, resulting from dependent input sharings, a common pitfall. Masking types other than Boolean have not been very common in hardware so far. However, the reader can refer to Chapter 3 of the PhD thesis of De Cnudde (2018) for detailed constructions with inner-product and polynomial masking following the same methodology. Ueno et al. (2017) first applied the $d + 1$ masking methodology to cubic Boolean functions. A general methodology for any algebraic degree and any security order was introduced by De Meyer et al. (2018) and Wegener et al. (2020).

– Section 3.4. The work of De Cnudde et al. (2016) presents a comparison of first- and second-order AES implementations with both $td + 1$ and $d + 1$ shares, which clearly shows a trade-off between area and randomness cost. Bilgin et al. (2012), and later Kutzner et al. (2014), created threshold implementations of all 3- and 4-bit S-boxes by using decomposition into quadratic or cubic components. De Meyer et al. (2018) presented a bit-serial AES for FPGA devices with a very small area footprint, but much increased latency cost compared to byte-serial designs. They also demonstrated how the increased degree of hardware sharing can lead to a transient non-completeness break if not careful. Wegener and Moradi (2018) also demonstrated how to use the same hardware for calculating different shares. Arribas et al. (2018) introduced the loop unrolling technique for decreasing the latency of a masked implementation and applied it to Keccak, which has a quadratic round function. The round function of AES, on the other hand, has algebraic degree 7. A single-cycle masked implementation that is secure in the presence of glitches is therefore not straightforward to obtain. Sasdrich et al. (2020) were the first to succeed thanks to the LUT-based masked dual-rail with precharge logic (LMDPL) technique from Leiserson et al. (2014), which avoids the use of registers for synchronization, and relies instead on dual-rail logic and precharging. The "changing of the guards" trick was introduced by Daemen (2017) and applied to Keccak. It was generalized by Sugawara (2018) to make it applicable to AES as well. These approaches enable first-order masking without the need for an online PRNG.

Beyne et al. (2020) introduced an interesting alternative methodology for optimizing randomness while preserving practical higher-order security.

3.6. References

Arribas, V., Bilgin, B., Petrides, G., Nikova, S., Rijmen, V. (2018). Rhythmic Keccak: SCA security and low latency in HW. *IACR Transactions on Cryptographic Hardware and Embedded Systems*, 2018(1), 269–290.

Bertoni, G., Martinoli, M., Molteni, M.C. (2017). A methodology for the characterisation of leakages in combinatorial logic. *J. Hardw. Syst. Secur.*, 1(3), 269–281. doi: 10.1007/s41635-017-0015-0.

Beyne, T., Dhooghe, S., Zhang, Z. (2020). Cryptanalysis of masked ciphers: A not so random idea. In *Advances in Cryptology – ASIACRYPT 2020*, Moriai, S. and Wang, H. (eds). Springer, Heidelberg.

Bilgin, B. (2015). Threshold implementations: As countermeasure against higher-order differential power analysis. PhD Thesis, University of Twente, Enschede [Online]. Available at: http://purl.utwente.nl/publications/95796.

Bilgin, B., Nikova, S., Nikov, V., Rijmen, V., Stütz, G. (2012). Threshold implementations of all 3×3 and 4×4 S-boxes. In *Cryptographic Hardware and Embedded Systems – CHES 2012*, Prouff, E. and Schaumont, P. (eds). Springer, Heidelberg.

Bilgin, B., Daemen, J., Nikov, V., Nikova, S., Rijmen, V., Assche, G.V. (2013). Efficient and first-order DPA resistant implementations of KECCAK. In *Smart Card Research and Advanced Applications - 12th International Conference, CARDIS 2013*, Francillon, A. and Rohatgi, P. (eds). Springer, Cham. doi: 10.1007/978-3-319-08302-5_13.

Bilgin, B., Gierlichs, B., Nikova, S., Nikov, V., Rijmen, V. (2014). Higher-order threshold implementations. In *Advances in Cryptology – ASIACRYPT 2014*, Sarkar, P. and Iwata, T. (eds). Springer, Heidelberg.

Daemen, J. (2017). Changing of the guards: A simple and efficient method for achieving uniformity in threshold sharing. In *Cryptographic Hardware and Embedded Systems – CHES 2017*, Fischer, W. and Homma, N. (eds). Springer, Heidelberg.

De Cnudde, T. (2018). Cryptography secured against side-channel attacks. PhD Thesis, KU Leuven [Online]. Available at: https://www.esat.kuleuven.be/cosic/publications/thesis-311.pdf.

De Cnudde, T., Reparaz, O., Bilgin, B., Nikova, S., Nikov, V., Rijmen, V. (2016). Masking AES with d+1 shares in hardware. In *Cryptographic Hardware and Embedded Systems – CHES 2016*, Gierlichs, B. and Poschmann, A.Y. (eds). Springer, Heidelberg.

De Meyer, L. (2020). Cryptography in the presence of physical attacks: Design, implementation and analysis. PhD Thesis, KU Leuven [Online]. Available at: https://www.esat.kuleuven.be/cosic/publications/thesis-384.pdf.

De Meyer, L., Moradi, A., Wegener, F. (2018). Spin me right round rotational symmetry for FPGA-specific AES. *IACR Transactions on Cryptographic Hardware and Embedded Systems*, 2018(3), 596–626.

Gross, H., Mangard, S., Korak, T. (2017a). An efficient side-channel protected AES implementation with arbitrary protection order. In *Topics in Cryptology – CT-RSA 2017 – The Cryptographers' Track at the RSA Conference 2017*, Handschuh, H. (ed.). Springer, Cham. doi: 10.1007/978-3-319-52153-4_6.

Gross, H., Schaffenrath, D., Mangard, S. (2017b). Higher-order side-channel protected implementations of Keccak. Report 2017/395, Cryptology ePrint Archive [Online]. Available at: https://eprint.iacr.org/2017/395.

Kutzner, S., Nguyen, P.H., Poschmann, A. (2014). Enabling 3-share threshold implementations for all 4-bit S-boxes. In *ICISC 13: 16th International Conference on Information Security and Cryptology*, Lee, H.-S. and Han, D.-G. (eds). Springer, Heidelberg.

Leiserson, A.J., Marson, M.E., Wachs, M.A. (2014). Gate-level masking under a path-based leakage metric. In *Cryptographic Hardware and Embedded Systems – CHES 2014*, Batina, L. and Robshaw, M. (eds). Springer, Heidelberg.

Mangard, S., Popp, T., Gammel, B.M. (2005a). Side-channel leakage of masked CMOS gates. In *Topics in Cryptology – CT-RSA 2005*, Menezes, A. (ed.). Springer, Heidelberg.

Mangard, S., Pramstaller, N., Oswald, E. (2005b). Successfully attacking masked AES hardware implementations. In *Cryptographic Hardware and Embedded Systems – CHES 2005*, Rao, J.R. and Sunar, B. (eds). Springer, Heidelberg.

Moradi, A., Poschmann, A., Ling, S., Paar, C., Wang, H. (2011). Pushing the limits: A very compact and a threshold implementation of AES. In *Advances in Cryptology – EUROCRYPT 2011*, Paterson, K.G. (ed.). Springer, Heidelberg.

Nikova, S., Rechberger, C., Rijmen, V. (2006). Threshold implementations against side-channel attacks and glitches. In *ICICS 06: 8th International Conference on Information and Communication Security*, Ning, P., Qing, S., Li, N. (eds). Springer, Heidelberg.

Nikova, S., Rijmen, V., Schläffer, M. (2009). Secure hardware implementation of non-linear functions in the presence of glitches. In *ICISC 08: 11th International Conference on Information Security and Cryptology*, Lee, P.J. and Cheon, J.H. (eds). Springer, Heidelberg.

Poschmann, A., Moradi, A., Khoo, K., Lim, C.-W., Wang, H., Ling, S. (2011). Side-channel resistant crypto for less than 2,300 GE. *Journal of Cryptology*, 24(2), 322–345.

Prouff, E. and Roche, T. (2011). Higher-order glitches free implementation of the AES using secure multi-party computation protocols. In *Cryptographic Hardware and Embedded Systems – CHES 2011*, Preneel, B. and Takagi, T. (eds). Springer, Heidelberg.

Reparaz, O. (2015). A note on the security of higher-order threshold implementations. Report 2015/001, Cryptology ePrint Archive [Online]. Availale at: https://eprint.iacr.org/ 2015/001.

Reparaz, O., Bilgin, B., Nikova, S., Gierlichs, B., Verbauwhede, I. (2015). Consolidating masking schemes. In *Advances in Cryptology – CRYPTO 2015*, Gennaro, R. and Robshaw, M.J.B. (eds). Springer, Heidelberg.

Sasdrich, P., Bock, R., Moradi, A. (2018). Threshold implementation in software – Case study of PRESENT. In *COSADE 2018: 9th International Workshop on Constructive Side-Channel Analysis and Secure Design*, Fan, J. and Gierlichs, B. (eds). Springer, Heidelberg.

Sasdrich, P., Bilgin, B., Hutter, M., Marson, M.E. (2020). Low-latency hardware masking with application to AES. *IACR Transactions on Cryptographic Hardware and Embedded Systems*, 2020(2), 300–326.

Sugawara, T. (2018). 3-share threshold implementation of AES s-box without fresh randomness. *IACR Transactions on Cryptographic Hardware and Embedded Systems*, 2019(1), 123–145.

Trichina, E. (2003). Combinational logic design for AES subbyte transformation on masked data. Report 2003/236, Cryptology ePrint Archive [Online]. Available at: https://eprint.iacr.org/2003/236.

Ueno, R., Homma, N., Aoki, T. (2017). Toward more efficient DPA-resistant AES hardware architecture based on threshold implementation. In *COSADE 2017: 8th International Workshop on Constructive Side-Channel Analysis and Secure Design*, Guilley, S. (ed.). Springer, Heidelberg.

Wegener, F. and Moradi, A. (2018). A first-order SCA resistant AES without fresh randomness. In *COSADE 2018: 9th International Workshop on Constructive Side-Channel Analysis and Secure Design*, Fan, J. and Gierlichs, B. (eds). Springer, Heidelberg.

Wegener, F., De Meyer, L., Moradi, A. (2020). Spin me right round rotational symmetry for FPGA-specific AES: Extended version. *Journal of Cryptology*, 33(3), 1114–1155.

4

Masking Security Proofs

Sonia BELAÏD

CryptoExperts, Paris, France

4.1. Introduction

The security of cryptographic implementations can be assessed following two different methods. On the one hand, cryptographic implementations can be confronted with concrete side-channel attacks directly on embedded devices (as presented in previous chapters). While their security would thus be directly evaluated on the target device by exploiting the actual leakage that the attacker will have access to, this approach remains empirical, not portable and does not yield measurable security levels (e.g. attacks might be missing). On the other hand, the security of cryptographic implementations can be formally proven based on abstract leakage models, which aim to define the attacker's capabilities. This second approach advantageously makes it possible to measure concrete security levels. Although the leakage models may be too far removed from reality to yield practical security, the community works on improving them with respect to concrete devices in order to connect both sides. In this chapter, we will investigate the different leakage models and the related masking security proofs.

Several leakage models have been introduced to reason on the security of masked cryptographic implementations against side-channel attacks. In this chapter, we selected four of them which we believe are the most widely used. The *noisy leakage model* is often considered to be the closest to the reality of embedded devices by assuming that the adversary gets a noisy function of each manipulated data.

Embedded Cryptography 2,
coordinated by Emmanuel PROUFF, Guénaël RENAULT,
Matthieu RIVAIN and Colin O'FLYNN. © ISTE Ltd 2025.

Given the difficulty of building security proofs in this model, most masking schemes are proven to be secure in the *probing model*, yet further from reality. Several leakage models stand in the middle. Among them, the *robust probing model* supplements the probing model by additionally considering the leakage of physical defaults and the *random probing model* is closer to the noisy leakage model (with a tight reduction), which makes it possible to build security proofs.

The next section introduces all the prerequisites that we need on circuits, sharings, gadgets and compilers to accurately explain the security proofs in the subsequent parts. Section 4.3 intuitively and formally introduces the probing model. Its extension, the robust probing model, is discussed in section 4.4. The more realistic noisy leakage and random probing models are then defined in section 4.5. Finally, the last section is dedicated to the composition of secure gadgets in these models.

4.2. Preliminaries

In this chapter, $\mathbb{K}$ shall denote a finite field and $\mathbb{F}_q$ the finite field with q elements. Any two probability distributions D_1 and D_2 are said ε-close, denoted $D_1 \approx_\varepsilon D_2$, if their statistical distance is upper bounded by ε, that is

$$\mathtt{SD}(D_1; D_2) := \frac{1}{2}\sum_x |p_{D_1}(x) - p_{D_2}(x)| \leq \varepsilon,$$

where $p_{D_1}(\cdot)$ and $p_{D_2}(\cdot)$ denote the probability mass functions of D_1 and D_2.

4.2.1. *Circuits*

An *arithmetic circuit* over $\mathbb{K}$ is a labeled directed acyclic graph, whose edges are *wires* and vertices are *arithmetic gates* processing operations over $\mathbb{K}$. A *randomized arithmetic circuit* is additionally equipped with random gates of fan-in (i.e. number of inputs) 0 and fan-out (i.e. number of outputs) 1, which output a fresh uniform random value in $\mathbb{K}$. A (randomized) arithmetic circuit is further formally composed of input gates of fan-in 0 and fan-out 1 and output gates of fan-in 1 and fan-out 0.

During the evaluation of a ℓ-input circuit on an input $x \in \mathbb{K}^\ell$, each wire is assigned with a value in $\mathbb{K}$. We denote `AssignWires` the probabilistic algorithm that, given a randomized arithmetic circuit C, an input $x \in \mathbb{K}^\ell$, and a subset $\mathcal{W}$ of wire labels outputs a set of $|\mathcal{W}|$ values corresponding the assignments of the wires of C with label in $\mathcal{W}$ for an evaluation on input x.

4.2.2. *Additive sharings and gadgets*

In this chapter, the *n-additive decoding* mapping, denoted AddDec, refers to the function $\bigcup_n \mathbb{K}^n \to \mathbb{K}$ defined as

$$\mathsf{AddDec} : (x_1, \ldots, x_n) \mapsto x_1 + \cdots + x_n,$$

for every $n \in \mathbb{N}$ and $(x_1, \ldots, x_n) \in \mathbb{K}^n$. We shall further consider that, for every $n, \ell \in \mathbb{N}$, on input $(\widehat{x}_1, \ldots, \widehat{x}_\ell) \in (\mathbb{K}^n)^\ell$ the n-additive decoding mapping acts as

$$\mathsf{AddDec} : (\widehat{x}_1, \ldots, \widehat{x}_\ell) \mapsto (\mathsf{AddDec}(\widehat{x}_1), \ldots, \mathsf{AddDec}(\widehat{x}_\ell)).$$

For some tuple $\widehat{x} = (x_1, \ldots, x_n) \in \mathbb{K}^n$ and for some set $I \subseteq [1; n]$, the tuple $(x_i)_{i \in I}$ is denoted $\widehat{x}|_I$.

DEFINITION 4.1.– Additive Sharing: let $n, \ell \in \mathbb{N}$. For any $x \in \mathbb{K}$, an *n-additive sharing* of x is a random vector $\widehat{x} \in \mathbb{K}^n$ such that $\mathsf{AddDec}(\widehat{x}) = x$. It is said to be *uniform* if for any set $I \subseteq [1; n]$ with $|I| < n$ the tuple $\widehat{x}|_I$ is uniformly distributed over $\mathbb{K}^{|I|}$. An *n-additive encoding* is a probabilistic algorithm AddEnc which on input a tuple $\boldsymbol{x} = (x_1, \ldots, x_\ell) \in \mathbb{K}^\ell$ outputs a tuple $\widehat{\boldsymbol{x}} = (\widehat{x}_1, \ldots, \widehat{x}_\ell) \in (\mathbb{K}^n)^\ell$ such that $\widehat{x}_i$ is a uniform n-sharing of x_i for every $i \in [\ell]$.

We shall call an *(n-share, ℓ-to-m) gadget*, a randomized arithmetic circuit that maps an input $\widehat{\boldsymbol{x}} \in (\mathbb{K}^n)^\ell$ to an output $\widehat{\boldsymbol{y}} \in (\mathbb{K}^n)^m$ such that $\boldsymbol{x} = \mathsf{AddDec}(\widehat{\boldsymbol{x}}) \in \mathbb{K}^\ell$ and $\boldsymbol{y} = \mathsf{AddDec}(\widehat{\boldsymbol{y}}) \in \mathbb{K}^m$ satisfy $\boldsymbol{y} = g(\boldsymbol{x})$ for some function g.

For an (n-share, ℓ-to-m) gadget, if we denote by $\boldsymbol{I}$ a collection of sets $\boldsymbol{I} = (I_1, \ldots, I_\ell)$ with $I_1 \subseteq [1; n]$, ..., $I_\ell \subseteq [1; n]$ where $n \in \mathbb{N}$ refers to the number of shares, for some $\widehat{\boldsymbol{x}} = (\widehat{x}_1, \ldots, \widehat{x}_\ell) \in (\mathbb{K}^n)^\ell$, we denote $\widehat{\boldsymbol{x}}|_{\boldsymbol{I}} = (\widehat{x}_1|_{I_1}, \ldots, \widehat{x}_\ell|_{I_\ell})$ where $\widehat{x}_i|_{I_i} \in \mathbb{K}^{|I_i|}$ is the tuple composed of the coordinates of the sharing $\widehat{x}_i$ of indexes included in I_i.

4.2.3. *Compilers*

DEFINITION 4.2.– Circuit Compiler: a *circuit compiler* is a triplet of algorithms (CC, Enc, Dec) defined as follows:

– CC (circuit compilation) is a deterministic algorithm that takes as input an arithmetic circuit C and outputs a randomized arithmetic circuit $\widehat{C}$.

– Enc (input encoding) is a probabilistic algorithm that maps an input $\boldsymbol{x} \in \mathbb{K}^\ell$ to an encoded input $\widehat{\boldsymbol{x}} \in \mathbb{K}^{\ell'}$.

– Dec (output decoding) is a deterministic algorithm that maps an encoded output $\widehat{\boldsymbol{y}} \in \mathbb{K}^{m'}$ to a plain output $\boldsymbol{y} \in \mathbb{K}^m$.

These three algorithms satisfy the following properties:

– *Correctness*: for every arithmetic circuit C of input length ℓ, and for every $\boldsymbol{x} \in \mathbb{K}^\ell$, we have

$$\Pr\left(\mathsf{Dec}\big(\widehat{C}(\widehat{\boldsymbol{x}})\big) = C(\boldsymbol{x}) \,\big|\, \widehat{\boldsymbol{x}} \leftarrow \mathsf{Enc}(\boldsymbol{x})\right) = 1\ , \text{ where } \widehat{C} = \mathsf{CC}(C).$$

– *Efficiency*: for some security parameter $\lambda \in \mathbb{N}$, the running time of $\mathsf{CC}(C)$ is $\mathrm{poly}(\lambda, |C|)$, the running time of $\mathsf{Enc}(\boldsymbol{x})$ is $\mathrm{poly}(\lambda, |\boldsymbol{x}|)$ and the running time of $\mathsf{Dec}(\widehat{\boldsymbol{y}})$ is $\mathrm{poly}(\lambda, |\widehat{\boldsymbol{y}}|)$, where $\mathrm{poly}(\lambda, q) = O(\lambda^{k_1} q^{k_2})$ for some constants k_1, k_2.

A *standard circuit compiler* with sharing order n and arithmetic base gadgets is a compiler $(\mathsf{CC}, \mathsf{Enc}, \mathsf{Dec})$, which additionally satisfies the following properties:

– the input encoding Enc is an n-additive encoding;

– the output encoding Dec is the n-additive decoding mapping AddDec;

– the circuit compilation CC consists of replacing each gate in the original circuit by an n-share gadget with corresponding functionality, and each wire by a set of n wires carrying an n-additive sharing of the original wire. If the input circuit is a randomized arithmetic circuit, each of its random gates is replaced by n random gates, which duly produce an n-additive sharing of a random value.

For standard circuit compilers, the correctness and efficiency directly hold from the correctness and efficiency of its gadgets.

4.3. Probing model

The *probing model* is one of the most broadly used leakage models. Informally, the t-probing model states that during the evaluation of a circuit C at most t wires (chosen by the adversary) leak the value they carry. The circuit C is thus claimed to be t-probing secure if the exact values of any set of t intermediate variables, which are referred to as *observations* or *probes*, do not reveal any information about its inputs. As in reality, the leakage traces somehow reveal noisy functions of the manipulated data; this model is motivated by the difficulty of learning information from the combination of t variables from their noisy functions in masking schemes (as t grows).

4.3.1. *Formal definition*

We first recall the formal definition of the t-probing security. Intuitively, if a simulator can perfectly simulate any set of t probes without any knowledge of the secret inputs, then an attacker will not learn any sensitive information from any set of t probes.

DEFINITION 4.3.– t-Probing Security: a randomized arithmetic circuit $\widehat{C}$ equipped with an encoding Enc is t-probing secure if there exists a simulator Sim which, for any input $\boldsymbol{x} \in \mathbb{K}^{\ell}$, for every set of wires $\mathcal{W}$ such that $|\mathcal{W}| \leq t$, satisfies:

$$\texttt{Sim}(\widehat{C}, \mathcal{W}) = \texttt{AssignWires}(\widehat{C}, \mathcal{W}, \texttt{Enc}(\boldsymbol{x})).$$

EXAMPLE 4.1.– Let us take a toy example to illustrate this notion. Consider a randomized arithmetic circuit $\widehat{C}$ which implements a second-order multiplication (as given in Algorithm 4.1 and deeply explained in Chapter 2. Basically, from the shared input $\widehat{\boldsymbol{x}} = (\widehat{a}, \widehat{b}) = ((a_0, a_1, a_2), (b_0, b_1, b_2)) \in \mathbb{F}_2^6$, it computes a shared output $\widehat{c} = (c_0, c_1, c_2) \in \mathbb{F}_2^3$ as follows:

$$\begin{aligned}
&c_0 \leftarrow a_0 \cdot b_0 + r_{0,1} + r_{0,2} \\
&c_1 \leftarrow a_1 \cdot b_1 + (r_{0,1} + a_0 \cdot b_1 + a_1 \cdot b_0) + r_{1,2} \\
&c_2 \leftarrow a_2 \cdot b_2 + (r_{0,2} + a_0 \cdot b_2 + a_2 \cdot b_0) + (r_{1,2} + a_1 \cdot b_2 + a_2 \cdot b_1)
\end{aligned}$$

such that $c = c_0 + c_1 + c_2 = a \cdot b = (a_0 + a_1 + a_2) \cdot (b_0 + b_1 + b_2)$. From the probing security definition, $\widehat{C}$ is 2-probing secure if and only if any pair of leaking wires can be perfectly simulated without the knowledge of inputs a or b. Ignoring the copy gates to replicate variables that are to be used more than once, Algorithm 4.1 manipulates 27 intermediate variables; therefore, the dependency of $\binom{27}{2} = 351$ pairs of potential leaking wires with the secrets a and b must be determined to conclude.

Algorithm 4.1. Second-order multiplication

Require: (a_0, a_1, a_2) and (b_0, b_1, b_2)
Ensure: (c_0, c_1, c_2)

$c_0 \leftarrow a_0 \cdot b_0$
$c_0 \leftarrow c_0 + r_{0,1}$
$c_0 \leftarrow c_0 + r_{0,2}$
$t \leftarrow a_0 \cdot b_1$
$u \leftarrow a_1 \cdot b_0$
$v \leftarrow r_{0,1} + t$
$v \leftarrow v + u$
$c_1 \leftarrow a_1 \cdot b_1$
$c_1 \leftarrow c_1 + v$
$c_1 \leftarrow c_1 + r_{1,2}$
$t \leftarrow a_0 \cdot b_2$
$u \leftarrow a_2 \cdot b_0$
$v \leftarrow r_{0,2} + t$
$v \leftarrow v + u$
$c_2 \leftarrow a_2 \cdot b_2$
$c_2 \leftarrow c_2 + v$
$t \leftarrow a_1 \cdot b_2$
$u \leftarrow a_2 \cdot b_1$
$v \leftarrow r_{1,2} + t$
$v \leftarrow v + u$
$c_2 \leftarrow c_2 + v$

4.3.2. *Proofs for small gadgets*

This section describes two widely deployed methods to prove the t-probing security of a circuit, namely, computing the distributions and simulating the values carried by leaking wires with input shares.

4.3.2.1. *Distribution-based proofs*

Determining whether the values carried by t leaking wires are jointly independent from a secret in $\mathbb{K}^\ell$ can be done exactly by computing the distributions. Namely, given a set $\mathcal{W}$ of t leaking wires and a $\mathbb{K}^\ell$-valued random variable $\mathcal{X}$, we must check if the following equality is satisfied:

$$\forall\, \boldsymbol{w} \in \mathbb{K}^t,\ \forall\, \boldsymbol{x} \in \mathbb{K}^\ell, \Pr[\texttt{AssignWires}(\widehat{C}, \mathcal{W}, \mathsf{Enc}(\mathcal{X})) = \boldsymbol{w}]$$
$$= \Pr[\texttt{AssignWires}(\widehat{C}, \mathcal{W}, \mathsf{Enc}(\mathcal{X})) = \boldsymbol{w} | \mathcal{X} = \boldsymbol{x}].$$

This can be done by computing the realizations of $\mathcal{W}$ and $\mathcal{X}$ for all the possible inputs (including all the possible random values involved). Such a method quickly becomes very expensive. Then, it remains to extend the verification to all the possible wire sets $\mathcal{W}$, whose number is exponential in t and in the total number of wires.

EXAMPLE 4.2.– Let us take the example of the randomized arithmetic circuit implementing the second-order multiplication of Algorithm 4.1. Taking $\mathcal{W}$ as the wires carrying variable c_0 as defined at Step 2 (i.e. $a_0 \cdot b_0 + r_{0,1}$) and variable u as defined at Step 12 (i.e. $a_2 \cdot b_0$), the idea is to compute the values taken by $\mathcal{W}$ and $\mathcal{X}$ for all the possible values of the variables involved: a, b, a_0, a_2, b_0 and $r_{0,1}$. We get (e.g. using a truth table) that, for all $\alpha \in \mathbb{F}_2$:

$$\Pr[\texttt{AssignWires}(\widehat{C}, \mathcal{W}, \mathsf{Enc}(\mathcal{X})) = (\alpha, 0)] = 3/8$$
$$\Pr[\texttt{AssignWires}(\widehat{C}, \mathcal{W}, \mathsf{Enc}(\mathcal{X})) = (\alpha, 1)] = 1/8$$

and

$$\forall\, \boldsymbol{x} \in \mathbb{F}_2^2,\ \Pr[\texttt{AssignWires}(\widehat{C}, \mathcal{W}, \mathsf{Enc}(\mathcal{X})) = (\alpha, 0), \mathcal{X} = \boldsymbol{x}] = 3/32$$
$$\forall\, \boldsymbol{x} \in \mathbb{F}_2^2,\ \Pr[\texttt{AssignWires}(\widehat{C}, \mathcal{W}, \mathsf{Enc}(\mathcal{X})) = (\alpha, 1), \mathcal{X} = \boldsymbol{x}] = 1/32.$$

The desired equality directly follows using the Bayes formula. The same computation is then to be performed for the 350 remaining pairs.

4.3.3. *Simulation-based proofs*

A second method to circumvent the heavy computation of distributions relies on simulation-based properties to demonstrate the independence of the leaking wires from the input secrets. Informally, the idea is to perfectly simulate each possible set of leaking wires with the smallest set of input shares. If the latter is independent from the secret, then so is the set of leaking wires. If any set of t leaking wires can be perfectly simulated with at most t shares of each input, then the circuit is said to be *t-non-interferent* (t-NI); and if the input sharing is uniform, it directly implies the t-probing security. The formal definition is recalled hereafter.

DEFINITION 4.4.– t-Non-Interference: a randomized arithmetic circuit $\widehat{C}$ equipped with an encoding Enc is t-NI if there exists a deterministic simulator Sim_1 and a probabilistic simulator Sim_2, such that, for any input $\boldsymbol{x} \in \mathbb{K}^\ell$, for every set of leaking wires $\mathcal{W}$ of size t:

$$(\mathcal{I}_1, \mathcal{I}_2, \ldots, \mathcal{I}_\ell) \leftarrow \mathsf{Sim}_1(\widehat{C}, \mathcal{W}) \quad \text{with } |\mathcal{I}_1|, |\mathcal{I}_2|, \ldots, |\mathcal{I}_\ell| \leq t$$

$$\text{and} \quad \mathsf{Sim}_2(\mathcal{I}_1, \mathcal{I}_2, \ldots, \mathcal{I}_\ell) = \texttt{AssignWires}(\widehat{C}, \mathcal{W}, \mathsf{Enc}(\boldsymbol{x})).$$

Two different types of security proofs can be envisioned to demonstrate that a circuit is t-NI, which we refer to as *exhaustive* proofs and *generic* proofs.

Exhaustive simulation-based proofs simply enumerate all the possible sets of t leaking wires in the circuit and check (for each of them) that the minimal number of input shares that are needed for a perfect simulation is at most equal to t.

EXAMPLE 4.3.– The set $\mathcal{W}$ of two leaking wires carrying the variables $a_0 \cdot b_0 + r_{0,1}$ and $a_2 \cdot b_0$ of our second-order multiplication circuit can be perfectly simulated from the set of input shares (a_2, b_0). Indeed, the second variable is perfectly simulated from the two input shares and the first variable can be generated uniformly as random as its distribution is independent from any input share with the addition of the random value $r_{0,1}$, which is used nowhere else in $\mathcal{W}$.

Such exhaustive simulation-based proofs are implemented in automatic verification tools that take the description of a randomized arithmetic circuit as input and produce either a security proof in the probing model or output a potential attack path. Some of these tools determine the smallest set of input shares required for the simulation from various methods that are more or less efficient and complete. See Chapter 5 for further details on these tools.

Generic NI-based proofs aim to demonstrate the t-non-interference of a circuit masked with n shares (e.g. $n = t + 1$ shares), without instantiating n and t. The main idea is to prove that whatever the set of $t < n$ leaking wires, they can be simulated with at most t shares of each input.

EXAMPLE 4.4.– Consider a very simple sharewise addition gadget masked with n shares such that for any input sharings $\widehat{a} \in \mathbb{K}^n$ and $\widehat{b} \in \mathbb{K}^n$, the output sharing $\widehat{c}$ is defined as follows:

$$c_i \leftarrow a_i + b_i, \quad \forall i \in [1; n].$$

Now, let $\mathcal{W}$ be a set of probes such that $|\mathcal{W}| \leq t < n$. In our example, probes can take the form of a share of $\widehat{a}$, a share of $\widehat{b}$, or a share of $\widehat{c}$. We need to demonstrate that these probes can be perfectly simulated using at most t shares of $\widehat{a}$ and t shares of $\widehat{b}$. To do so, we define two sets I and J that are initially empty and which will represent the indices of the needed shares of $\widehat{a}$ and $\widehat{b}$, respectively. Namely, for each probe p in $\mathcal{W}$, we suggest to fill them as follows:

– we add the index i to I if p corresponds to a_i;

– we add the index i to J if p corresponds to b_i;

– we add the index i to I and the index i to J if p corresponds to c_i.

Doing so, we have covered all the possible probes and we can note that $|I|$ and $|J|$ are both upper bounded by $|\mathcal{W}|$ (since each probe adds at most one index to each set). Now, it remains to show that the shares of $\widehat{a}$ whose indices are in I and the shares of $\widehat{b}$ whose indices are in J are enough to perfectly simulate all the probes in $\mathcal{W}$:

– for any probe p such that $p = a_i$, i is in I and so p can be perfectly simulated from a_i;

– for any probe p such that $p = b_i$, i is in J and so p can be perfectly simulated from b_i;

– for any probe p such that $p = c_i$, i is in $I \cap J$ and so p can be perfectly simulated from a_i and b_i.

We have thus demonstrated that any set $\mathcal{W}$ of at most t probes (with $t < n$) can be perfectly simulated from at most $|\mathcal{W}|$ shares of each input, hence the considered gadget is t-NI.

While this example remains very simple, a very detailed example of such a proof of t non-interference for a more complex gadget is provided in Appendix C of Barthe et al.'s (2016) paper from CCS.

4.3.4. *Limitations*

The probing model is quite convenient for security proofs as it manipulates the exact values carried by the leaking wires. Nevertheless, it fails in precisely reflecting the reality of embedded devices in at least two main aspects.

On the one hand, it does not natively consider physical defaults, like glitches or couplings which can yield leakage on secret values with less observations than expected from the probing security order (see Chapter 3 for more details).

EXAMPLE 4.5.– In order to illustrate the limitations of the probing model with respect to some physical effects, we take a simple example. On many micro-controllers, we observe that the power consumption could strongly depend on the number of bits that are actually modified when adding a new variable in a register. In the example of Algorithm 4.1, if output variables correspond to registers, then we can see that $a_0 \cdot b_2$ (line 11) and $a_1 \cdot b_2$ (line 17) are successively stored in the same register. These successive operations are likely to leak at once the Hamming distance (i.e. the number of ones in the binary expression of the exclusive or) between $a_0 \cdot b_2$ and $a_1 \cdot b_2$. A single observation might reveal information on two shares of input a, and the corresponding gadget made of n-share variables would not be $(n-1)$-NI.

On the other hand, the probing model fails to capture the powerful horizontal attacks, that is, it typically ignores the repeated manipulation of identical sensitive intermediate variables which would average the noise and hence remove uncertainty on secret variables. In practice, if we reasonably assume that each variable concretely leaks a deterministic function of its value plus an independent Gaussian noise with a constant standard deviation, then observing α occurrences of this variable will yield a reduction of the noise by a factor $\sqrt{\alpha}$. In the probing model, such repetitions have no effect on the targeted security order.

4.4. Robust probing model

In the t-probing model, t circuit wires are supposed to leak, independently from each other. However, in practice, physical defaults might generate a leakage of values carried by several wires at once. In that case, the lowest secret-dependent statistical moment of the leakage distribution could be lower than t. The most typical examples of physical defaults include transitions and glitches, and probes can be extended accordingly. For instance, in the presence of glitches, probes (or equivalently observations) might reveal all the variables carried by coming wires up to the last synchronization point. Such probes thus include not only one, but a set of wires (see Chapter 3 for further details). Similarly, pairs of values that are successively stored in the same memory cell may leak at once (when the second variable replaces the first one); therefore, in the presence of transition-based leakage, probes are generally assumed to include specific pairs of wires.

Informally, a circuit is t-robust probing secure if any set of t so-called extended probes is independent from its inputs. The main idea remains similar to that of the probing model with the difficulty of combining several noisy values but the model is now refined by extending the probes that are likely to reveal more information than one single variable at once, following the practical observations on embedded devices.

4.4.1. *Formal definition*

The formal definition of the t-robust probing model directly follows that of the probing model in which wires are replaced by extended probes. The latter may be reduced to sets of wires which simultaneously leak the values they carry. The definition of these sets completely depends on the physical defaults that are captured and on the architecture of the circuit.

DEFINITION 4.5.– t-Robust Probing Security: a randomized arithmetic circuit $\widehat{C}$ equipped with an encoding $\texttt{Enc}$ is t-robust probing secure if there exists a simulator $\texttt{Sim}$ which, for any input $\boldsymbol{x} \in \mathbb{K}^\ell$, for every set of extended probes $\mathcal{P}$ such that $|\mathcal{P}| \leq t$ and pointing to the set of wires $\mathcal{W}$, satisfies:

$$\texttt{Sim}(\widehat{C}, \mathcal{W}) = \texttt{AssignWires}(\widehat{C}, \mathcal{W}, \texttt{Enc}(\boldsymbol{x})).$$

In this definition, a single extended probe in $\mathcal{P}$ potentially represents several wires in $\mathcal{W}$. That is why $|\mathcal{P}| \leq t$ but $\mathcal{W}$ can be larger in size than t.

EXAMPLE 4.6.– Let us consider a randomized arithmetic circuit implementing Algorithm 4.1 such that the three first steps are executed before the variable c_0 is stored in a register. In the presence of glitches, an extended probe on c_0 after these three steps (i.e. $\mathcal{P} = \{c_0\}$) could leak all the variables of coming wires up to the last synchronization point at once, namely, a_0, b_0, $r_{0,1}$ and $r_{0,2}$ (i.e. $\mathcal{W} = \{a_0, b_0, r_{0,1}, r_{0,2}\}$). Four wires could thus be targeted at the cost of a single probe.

Similarly, in case variable u at Step 5 and variable u at Step 12 are stored in the same memory cell consecutively, then a single probe at Step 12 might reveal information on the two variables $a_1 \cdot b_0$ and $a_2 \cdot b_0$ (corresponding to two different wires). In this case, two shares of a would be partly revealed at the cost of a single observation, which would reduce the robust security order to at most 1.

4.4.2. *Proofs for small gadgets*

As in the probing model, the security of small gadgets in the robust probing model can be demonstrated through distribution-based proofs or (exhaustive or generic) simulation-based proofs. The former behave the same as in the probing model but the leaking wire set $\mathcal{W}$ can be of size larger than t with extended probes. Exhaustive simulation-based proofs enumerate all the possible sets of leaking wires corresponding to t extended probes (i.e. sets of leaking wires which are at least of size t) in the circuit and check for each of them that the minimal number of input shares that are needed for a perfect simulation is at most equal to t. Proving that a larger set only depends on t input shares may be more complex but the number of possible sets is very likely to be reduced.

EXAMPLE 4.7.– Let us get back to the example of the second-order multiplication. We rewrite it in Algorithm 4.2 with a careful usage of registers. Namely, the notation "[v]" means that at this step, the output variable of the expression v is stored in a register. We then assume that each intermediate variable leaks all its inputs from their last storage in registers. For instance, the output c_1 (at Step 10) would leak a_1, b_1, $r_{1,2}$ and $v = ((r_{0,1} + a_0 \cdot b_1) + a_1 \cdot b_0)$, making it useless for an attacker to target these variables individually. The leaking sets are then larger but their number is much smaller: $\binom{9}{2} = 36$ compared to $\binom{27}{2} = 351$ in the probing model.

Algorithm 4.2. Second-order multiplication with careful storage in registers

Require: (a_0, a_1, a_2) and (b_0, b_1, b_2)
Ensure: (c_0, c_1, c_2)

1: $c_0 \leftarrow a_0 \cdot b_0$
2: $c_0 \leftarrow c_0 + r_{0,1}$
3: $c_0 \leftarrow c_0 + r_{0,2}$
4: $t \leftarrow a_0 \cdot b_1$
5: $u \leftarrow a_1 \cdot b_0$
6: $v \leftarrow [r_{0,1} + t]$
7: $v \leftarrow [v + u]$
8: $c_1 \leftarrow a_1 \cdot b_1$
9: $c_1 \leftarrow c_1 + v$
10: $c_1 \leftarrow c_1 + r_{1,2}$
11: $t \leftarrow a_0 \cdot b_2$
12: $u \leftarrow a_2 \cdot b_0$
13: $v \leftarrow [r_{0,2} + t]$
14: $v \leftarrow [v + u]$
15: $c_2 \leftarrow a_2 \cdot b_2$
16: $c_2 \leftarrow c_2 + v$
17: $t \leftarrow a_1 \cdot b_2$
18: $u \leftarrow a_2 \cdot b_1$
19: $v \leftarrow [r_{1,2} + t]$
20: $v \leftarrow [v + u]$
21: $c_2 \leftarrow c_2 + v$

Eventually, generic simulation-based proofs are also a bit different. Unlike in the probing model, where t input shares can be used to simulate t leaking wires, we now need t input shares to potentially simulate significantly more.

EXAMPLE 4.8.– Getting back to our example of the n-share sharewise addition gadget, each probe p on an output share c_i (for $1 \leq i \leq n$) would leak information on $c_i = a_i + b_i$, a_i and b_i (instead of only c_i). However, the gadget remains t-NI (for $t < n$) in the robust probing model since each (extended) probe can still be simulated using at most one share of each input. In our example, when $p = c_i$ (for some $1 \leq i \leq n$), all the corresponding leaking wires $c_i = a_i + b_i$, a_i and b_i can be simulated from one share of $\widehat{a}$ (i.e. a_i) and one share of $\widehat{b}$ (i.e. b_i).

4.4.3. *Limitations*

While the robust probing model nicely supplements the probing model by handling physical defaults, it suffers from the same limitations regarding horizontal attacks. Indeed, the robust probing model is similarly based on a fixed number of probes, regardless of their number of occurrences (i.e. usages).

4.5. Random probing model and noisy leakage model

The *noisy leakage model* can be seen as a specialization of the *only computation leaks* model. Informally, a circuit is secure in the noisy leakage model if the adversary cannot recover non-negligible information on the secrets from a noisy function of each intermediate variable of the implementation. Such a noisy function f is said to be δ-noisy if it satisfies $\beta(\mathcal{X}, f(\mathcal{X})) \stackrel{\text{def}}{=} \Delta(\mathcal{X}; (\mathcal{X}|f(\mathcal{X}))) \leq \delta$, where Δ denotes the statistical distance between the laws of $\mathcal{X}$ and $(\mathcal{X}|f(\mathcal{X}))$ over the random distribution of $f(\mathcal{X})$ and for a uniform random variable $\mathcal{X}$. We stress that any power or electromagnetic leakage can be captured by this model.

4.5.1. *Formal definition of the noisy leakage model*

In the noisy leakage model, each wire is assumed to leak a noisy function of the value it carries. Let δ be the corresponding noise parameter. The formal definition follows. Informally, a circuit is secure against noisy leakage if the noisy leakage of each of its wires is not enough to recover non-negligible information on the input secrets.

DEFINITION 4.6.– Security against δ-Noisy Leakage: let $\mathcal{X}$ be a uniform random variable over $\mathbb{K}^\ell$. A randomized arithmetic circuit C with $\ell \cdot n \in \mathbb{N}$ input gates and made of a set $\mathcal{W}$ of wires is ε-secure against δ-*noisy leakage* with respect to encoding Enc if:

$$\beta(\mathcal{X}|f_1(W_1), \ldots, f_{|\mathcal{W}|}(W_{|\mathcal{W}|})) \leq \varepsilon$$

where

$$W_1, \ldots, W_{|\mathcal{W}|} \leftarrow \mathsf{AssignWires}(C, \mathcal{W}, \mathsf{Enc}(\mathcal{X}))$$

for any δ-noisy functions $f_1, \ldots, f_{|\mathcal{W}|}$.

Note that the statistical distance can be based on the L_2 (Euclideans) norm, on the L_1 norm, or even on the relative error.

4.5.2. *Limitations*

The security proofs remain far from convenient and masking schemes continue to be verified in the probing model.

4.5.3. *Reduction to the probing model*

The noisy leakage security can be reduced to the probing security. This reduction relies on an intermediate leakage model, called *random probing model*. Informally in the random probing model, each intermediate variable leaks with some constant leakage probability p. A circuit is secure if there is a negligible probability that these leaking wires actually reveal information about the secrets. The random probing model further encompasses the powerful horizontal attacks that exploit the repeated manipulations of variables in an implementation and also benefits from a tight reduction with the noisy leakage model, which becomes independent of the size of the circuit.

The reduction of the noisy leakage security to the probing security first relies on the fact that, by applying the Chernoff bound, a t-probing secure computation is also p-random probing secure with $p = t/s$, where s denotes the number of gates in the original circuit. The reduction is not tight in this respect (considering a constant number of probes) since the security level decreases as the size of the circuit increases. The second transition and key lemma of the reduction proves that p-random probing security implies δ-noisy leakage security with $\delta = p/|\mathbb{K}|$, where $|\mathbb{K}|$ denotes the cardinal of the base field $\mathbb{K}$. This is because any δ-noisy function f can be written as $f(\cdot) = g \circ \phi(\cdot)$, where g is a randomized function and ϕ is a p-random probing function (i.e. $\phi(x) = x$ with probability p and $\phi(x) = \perp$ otherwise) with $p = \delta \cdot |\mathbb{K}|$.

REMARK 4.1.– Note that the definition of the noisy leakage model can be modified using other metrics than the statistical distance in order to tighten the reduction. For instance, using the average relative error (ARE) from pointwise mutual information would eliminate the multiplicative factor $|\mathbb{K}|$. This is because the statistical distance is an average case metric, while the random probing is a worst-case measurement of the leakage.

4.5.4. *Formal definition of the random probing model*

Let $p \in [0, 1]$ be some constant leakage probability parameter. This parameter is sometimes called *leakage rate* in the literature. Informally, the p-random probing model states that, during the evaluation of a circuit C, each wire leaks its value with probability p (and leaks nothing otherwise), where all the wire leakage events are mutually independent.

In order to formally define the random-probing leakage of a circuit, we shall define an additional *leaking-wires sampler*. This probabilistic algorithm takes as input a randomized arithmetic circuit C and a probability $p \in [0, 1]$, and outputs a set $\mathcal{W}$, denoted as:

$$\mathcal{W} \leftarrow \mathsf{LeakingWires}(C, p) ,$$

where $\mathcal{W}$ is constructed by including each wire label from the circuit C with probability p to $\mathcal{W}$ (where all the probabilities are mutually independent).

DEFINITION 4.7.– (p, ϵ)-Random Probing Security: a randomized arithmetic circuit C with $\ell \cdot n \in \mathbb{N}$ input gates is (p, ϵ)-*random probing secure* with respect to encoding Enc if there exists a simulator Sim such that for every $\boldsymbol{x} \in \mathbb{K}^\ell$:

$$\mathsf{Sim}(C) \approx_\varepsilon \mathsf{AssignWires}(C, \mathsf{LeakingWires}(C, p), \mathsf{Enc}(\boldsymbol{x})).$$

We can further consider a *simulation with abort.* In this approach, the simulator first calls the leaking-wires sampler to get a set $\mathcal{W}$ and then either aborts (or fails) with probability ε or outputs the exact distribution of the wire assignment corresponding to $\mathcal{W}$. Formally, for any leakage probability $p \in [0, 1]$, the simulator Sim is defined as:

$$\mathsf{Sim}(C) = \mathsf{SimAW}(C, \mathsf{LeakingWires}(C, p))$$

where SimAW, the *wire assignment simulator*, either returns $\perp$ (simulation failure, with probability ε) or a perfect simulation of the requested wires. It is not hard to see that if we can construct such a simulator SimAW for a compiled circuit $\widehat{C}$, then this circuit is (p, ε)-random probing secure.

4.5.5. *Proofs in the random probing model*

In this section, we show how to compute the simulation failure probability ε as a function $f(p)$ of the leakage probability p.

We consider a compiled circuit $\widehat{C}$ composed of s wires labeled from 1 to s. The simulation failure probability ε can then be explicitly expressed as a function of p. Namely, we have $\varepsilon = f(p)$ with f defined for every $p \in [0, 1]$ by:

$$f(p) = \sum_{i=1}^{s} c_i \cdot p^i \cdot (1-p)^{s-i}$$

with c_i the number of subsets $\mathcal{W} \subseteq [s]$ of cardinality i for which the simulation fails. For any circuit $\widehat{C}$ achieving t-probing security, the values c_i with $i \leq t$ are equal to zero, which implies the following simplification:

$$f(p) = \sum_{i=t+1}^{s} c_i \cdot p^i \cdot (1-p)^{s-i}. \qquad [4.1]$$

EXAMPLE 4.9.– Evaluating $f(p)$ for the second-order multiplication gadget: getting back to our second-order multiplication gadget from Algorithm 4.1, we can compute the failure function (using automatic tools; see Chapter 5) and display its first coefficients:

$$f : p \mapsto 1\,297 \cdot p^3 + \mathcal{O}(p^4).$$

Note that the three first coefficients are zero, which confirms the second-order probing security of this gadget. Then, $1,297$ triplets of intermediate variables are leaking information on the secret inputs (on $2,925$ triplets in total). Given the level of noise of a chosen underlying platform, the probability p can be defined to evaluate the random probing security parameter $\varepsilon = f(p)$ of this gadget.

4.5.6. *Extension to handle physical defaults*

In a first attempt, the random probing model assumes that all the wires in a circuit are leaking independently with the same probability p. In practice, in presence of physical defaults, this assumption may be too strong. First, different wires may leak with different probabilities (i.e. different signal-to-noise ratios). Second, dependencies might occur between the leakage of different wires.

In the first scenario, more accurate probabilities can be computed from the signal-to-noise ratios. From independent probabilities for each wire, it is easy (but much less efficient) to compute the failure function f. Unlike the formula from equation [4.1], sets of wires cannot be jointly evaluated based on their size as they would not share the same probability to leak anymore. The probability that a tuple $(x_1, x_2, \ldots, x_\alpha)$ of *at least* α wires jointly leaks is then:

$$p_{x_1} \cdot p_{x_2} \cdot \cdots \cdot p_{x_\alpha}.$$

The probability that a tuple $(x_1, x_2, \ldots, x_\alpha)$ of *only* α wires among $\beta > \alpha$ wires leaks is then:

$$p_{x_1} \cdot p_{x_2} \cdot \cdots \cdot p_{x_\alpha} \cdot (1 - p_{x_{\alpha+1}}) \cdot (1 - p_{x_{\alpha+2}}) \cdot \cdots \cdot (1 - p_{x_\beta}).$$

If all the probabilities are different, then all the tuples must be individually considered in the computation of the failure function.

The presence of physical defaults like glitches breaks the independence between the leaking probabilities of different variables. In particular, wires that carry variables in the same computation between two synchronization points are likely to leak simultaneously. The computation of the failure function then depends on the dependencies between the leaking wires.

4.6. Composition

As explained in the previous sections, exhaustive or generic proofs can be built to demonstrate the security of small gadgets implementing atomic operations (e.g. additions and multiplications). One step further, building security proofs for complex circuits was shown to be either error prone for hand-made proofs or computationally impossible with automatic verification tools. Hence, the need to split big circuits into smaller blocks that can be proven secure and then safely combine them with well-defined composition rules (see Figure 4.1 for an illustration).

In the following, we will recall the main composition rules for the aforementioned models and explain how to use them to safely compose small secure gadgets.

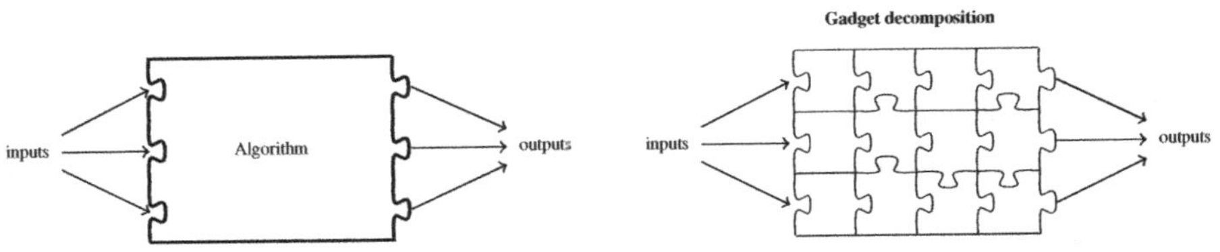

Figure 4.1. *Illustration of (de)composition*

4.6.1. *Composition in the probing model*

The two main composition techniques to achieve global probing security are described hereafter.

4.6.1.1. *Doubling the Number of Shares*

A simple method to build secure masked schemes for Boolean circuits is based on the use of two specific gadgets and the doubling of the number of shares. Concretely, any Boolean circuit can be decomposed into and and `not` gates only:

– Each and gate can be replaced by the $(n = 2t + 1)$-share ISW multiplication gadget recalled in Chapter 2.

– Each `not` gate can be replaced by a $(n = 2t + 1)$-share gadget applying a `not` gate to one single share only.

Then, it can be easily shown that any wire among these gadgets in a Boolean circuit can be perfectly simulated from at most the same two shares i and j at input/output of all the circuit's gadgets. Therefore, any set of t probes can trivially be simulated from at most $2 \cdot t$ shares of all the manipulated data in the circuit and the whole Boolean circuit is thus t-probing secure.

Although this method can be used to safely mask any Boolean circuit in the probing model, the doubling of the number of shares makes it quite expensive.

4.6.1.2. *Non-interference-based proofs*

Relying on simulation-based properties, it is possible to achieve a tighter composition with gadgets with the optimal number of $n = t + 1$ shares, at the cost of stronger security properties. Indeed, directly composing any gadget of $n = t + 1$ shares does not always yield t-probing security, due to the dependency between some gadgets' inputs.

EXAMPLE 4.10.– See, for instance, the masking scheme that takes a $(n = t + 1)$-sharing $\boldsymbol{a}$ and that computes $g_2(\boldsymbol{a}, g_1(\boldsymbol{a}))$ using two t-NI gadgets g_1 and g_2 (see Definition 4.4), illustrated in Figure 4.2.

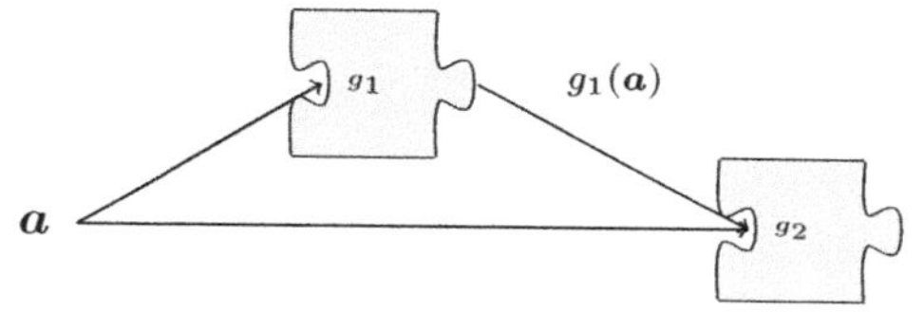

Figure 4.2. *Composition of two t-NI gadgets. For a color version of this figure, see www.iste.co.uk/prouff/cryptography2.zip*

A t-probing adversary can observe t_0 input shares of $\boldsymbol{a}$, t_1 intermediate variables on g_1 and t_2 intermediate variables on g_2 as soon as $t_0 + t_1 + t_2 \leq t$. From the t-NI property of g_2, all its t_2 probes can be perfectly simulated from t_2 shares of $\boldsymbol{a}$ and t_2 output shares of g_1. The t_1 probes of g_1 together with the t_2 output shares required to simulate g_2's probes can themselves be perfectly simulated from $t_1 + t_2$ input shares of g_1, that is, shares of $\boldsymbol{a}$. At the end, all the probes can be simulated from $t_0 + t_1 + 2 \cdot t_2$ shares of $\boldsymbol{a}$, which can be higher than t. The proof therefore cannot be completed; hence the need for stronger properties[1].

An example of a stronger property is the *strong non-interference*. This benefits from stopping the propagation of the probes between the output and the input shares and additionally trivially implies t-NI. Intuitively, a circuit is t-strong non-interferent (t-SNI) if and only if any set of at most t intermediate variables whose t_{int} on internal variables and t_{out} on the output shares can be perfectly simulated with at most t_{int} shares of each input.

DEFINITION 4.8.– t-Strong Non-Interference: a randomized arithmetic circuit $\widehat{C}$ equipped with an encoding Enc is t-SNI if there exists a deterministic simulator Sim_1 and a probabilistic simulator Sim_2, such that, for any input $\boldsymbol{x} \in \mathbb{K}^\ell$, for every set of

1 In practice, such a structure indeed yields concrete probing attacks for specific choices of gadgets g_1 and g_2.

internal leaking wires $\mathcal{W}_i$ of size t_i and output leaking wires $\mathcal{W}_o$ of size t_o such that $t_i + t_o \leq t$:

$$(\mathcal{I}_1, \mathcal{I}_2, \ldots, \mathcal{I}_\ell) \leftarrow \mathsf{Sim}_1(\widehat{C}, \mathcal{W}_i, \mathcal{W}_o) \quad \text{with } |\mathcal{I}_1|, |\mathcal{I}_2|, \ldots, |\mathcal{I}_\ell| \leq t_i$$

$$\text{and} \quad \mathsf{Sim}_2(\mathcal{I}_1, \mathcal{I}_2, \ldots, \mathcal{I}_\ell) = \texttt{AssignWires}(\widehat{C}, \mathcal{W}_i \cup \mathcal{W}_o, \mathsf{Enc}(\boldsymbol{x})).$$

EXAMPLE 4.11.– Getting back to our example, let us assume now that g_1 is t-SNI, as illustrated in Figure 4.3. A t-probing adversary can still observe t_0 input shares of $\boldsymbol{a}$, t_1 intermediate variables on g_1 and t_2 intermediate variables on g_2 (which is t-NI) as soon as $t_0 + t_1 + t_2 \leq t$.

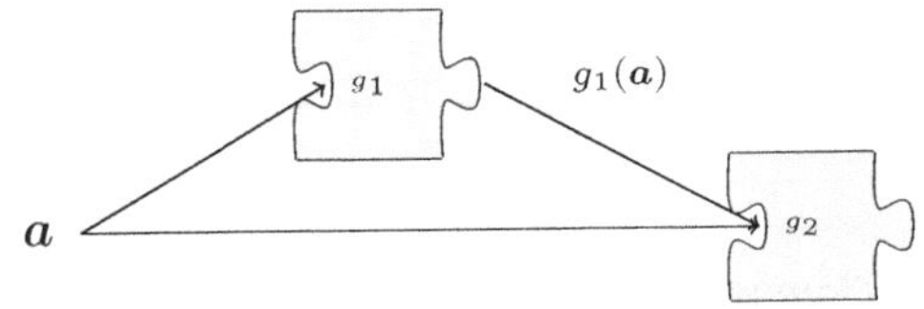

Figure 4.3. *Composition of a t-SNI gadget and a t-NI gadget. For a color version of this figure, see www.iste.co.uk/prouff/cryptography2.zip*

From the t-NI property of g_2, all its t_2 probes can be perfectly simulated from t_2 shares of $\boldsymbol{a}$ and t_2 output shares of g_1. Then, the t_1 probes of g_1 together with the t_2 output shares required to simulate g_2's probes can themselves be perfectly simulated from only t_1 input shares of g_1, thanks to the t-SNI property (and because $t_1 + t_2 \leq t$). At the end, all the probes of the circuit can be simulated from $t_0 + t_1 + t_2$ shares of $\boldsymbol{a}$ which is always lower or equal to t, which is enough to conclude that the circuit is t-NI, hence t-probing secure.

REMARK 4.2.– Many other properties based on the non-interference notions can be used to build tighter compositions with lower complexity and/or better security levels; in particular, the probe isolating non-interference (PINI) property reasons on the dependency between a probe and the index of the share of input it can be simulated from, rather than the number of probes and input shares.

In case a circuit misses gadgets with strong properties to achieve composition, a common practice is to add so-called *refresh gadgets*. The latter are functionally equivalent to the identity function but refresh the sharing with new random values to break the dependencies between the old input sharing and the new one. Note that inserting t-SNI refresh gadgets at careful locations is enough to make a randomized arithmetic circuit made of t-NI secure gadgets globally t-probing secure.

4.6.1.3. *Extension in the glitch robust probing model*

Intuitively, the simulation strategy used in the probing model to securely compose probing gadgets can directly be applied to the glitch robust probing model when there are no glitches on the inputs. Also, it is actually proven to be true in the latter scenario. Namely, we can build a global simulator from glitch-robust probing simulators on each individual gadget which take and produce extended probes.

4.6.2. *Composition in the random probing model*

Probing-secure schemes are also secure in the random probing model, but the tolerated leakage probability might not be constant, which is not satisfactory from a practical viewpoint. Indeed, in practice, the side-channel noise may not be customizable by the implementer.

In this section, we describe two methods to safely compose gadgets and build schemes that are secure in the random probing model.

4.6.2.1. *Simulation based on the number of shares*

The first method relies on the *random probing composability* notion for a gadget. Informally and similarly to the non-interference property in the probing model, this notion relies on the capability for a gadget to tolerate a certain number of probes on its output and a certain number of probes on its intermediate variables. All these probes must additionally be (almost perfectly) simulated by a fixed set of input shares to ensure the composition with prior gadgets.

DEFINITION 4.9.– Random Probing Composability: let $n, \ell, m \in \mathbb{N}$. An ($n$-share, ℓ-to-m) gadget $G : (\mathbb{K}^n)^\ell \to (\mathbb{K}^n)^m$ is (t, p, ε)-*random probing composable (RPC)* for some $t \in \mathbb{N}$ and $p, \varepsilon \in [0, 1]$ if there exists a deterministic algorithm Sim_1^G and a probabilistic algorithm Sim_2^G such that for every input $\widehat{\boldsymbol{x}} \in (\mathbb{K}^n)^\ell$ and for every set collection $J_1 \subseteq [1; n]$, ..., $J_m \subseteq [1; n]$ of cardinals $|J_1| \leq t$, ..., $|J_m| \leq t$, the random experiment:

$$\mathcal{W} \leftarrow \mathsf{LeakingWires}(G, p)$$

$$\boldsymbol{I} \leftarrow \mathsf{Sim}_1^G(\mathcal{W}, \boldsymbol{J})$$

$$out \leftarrow \mathsf{Sim}_2^G(\widehat{\boldsymbol{x}}|_{\boldsymbol{I}})$$

yields

$$\Pr\big((|I_1| > t) \vee \ldots \vee (|I_\ell| > t)\big) \leq \varepsilon \qquad [4.2]$$

and

$$out \overset{\text{id}}{=} \big(\mathsf{AssignWires}(G, \mathcal{W}, \widehat{\boldsymbol{x}})\ ,\ \widehat{\boldsymbol{y}}|_{\boldsymbol{J}}\big)$$

where $\boldsymbol{J} = (J_1, \ldots, J_m)$ and $\widehat{\boldsymbol{y}} = G(\widehat{\boldsymbol{x}})$. Let $f : \mathbb{R} \to \mathbb{R}$. The gadget G is (t, f)-RPC if it is $(t, p, f(p))$-RPC for every $p \in [0, 1]$.

In the above definition, the first-pass simulator Sim_1^G determines the necessary input shares (through the returned collection of sets $\boldsymbol{I}$) for the second-pass simulator Sim_2^G to produce a perfect simulation of the leaking wires defined by the set $\mathcal{W}$, together with the output shares defined by the collection of sets $\boldsymbol{J}$. Note that there always exists such a collection of sets $\boldsymbol{I}$ since $\boldsymbol{I} = ([1; n], \ldots, [1; n])$ trivially allows a perfect simulation, whatever $\mathcal{W}$ and $\boldsymbol{J}$. However, the goal of Sim_1^G is to return a collection of sets $\boldsymbol{I}$ with cardinals at most t. The idea behind this constraint is to keep the following composition invariant: for each gadget, we can achieve a perfect simulation of the leaking wires plus t shares of each output sharing from t shares of each input sharing. We shall call *failure event* the event that at least one of the sets I_1, ..., I_ℓ output of Sim_1^G has cardinality greater than t. When (t, p, ε)-RPC is achieved, the failure event probability is upper bounded by ε according to equation [4.2]. A failure event occurs whenever Sim_2^G requires more than t shares of one input sharing to be able to produce a perfect simulation of the leaking wires (i.e. the wires with label in $\mathcal{W}$), together with the output shares in $\widehat{\boldsymbol{y}}|_{\boldsymbol{J}}$. Whenever such a failure occurs, the composition invariant is broken. In the absence of a failure event, the RPC notion implies that a perfect simulation can be achieved for the full circuit composed of RPC gadgets. This is formally stated in the next theorem.

THEOREM 4.1.– Composition: let $t \in \mathbb{N}$, $p, \varepsilon \in [0, 1]$, and CC be a standard circuit compiler with (t, p, ε)-RPC base gadgets. For every (randomized) arithmetic circuit C composed of $|C|$ gadgets, the compiled circuit $\mathsf{CC}(C)$ is $(p, |C| \cdot \varepsilon)$-random probing secure.

4.6.2.2. *Simulation based on the set of shares*

The first method relies on the number of leaking wires at the input and output of each composable gadget. By preserving the same number of leaking wires at the input and output, the security of each gadget can be easily considered separately and the composition can be efficiently evaluated. Nevertheless, the security of the composition can be tighter by further considering specific sets of leaking inputs and outputs rather than their number.

This second method therefore relies on so-called (two-entry) *probe distribution tables* (PDT). Informally, for some gadget $\mathcal{G}$, its PDT provides, for a set of input shares I and a set of output shares O, the probability that a simulator exactly needs I to simulate the leaking wires in $\mathcal{G}$ (i.e. from $\mathsf{LeakingWires}(G, p)$) and the output shares O. Contrary to the first method, which records the number of required input and output shares, the PDT records the exact input and output sets of shares.

DEFINITION 4.10.– Probe Distribution Table: let $p \in [0, 1]$ be some constant leakage probability parameter. Let G be an (n-share, ℓ-to-m) gadget with a set of input wires

$\boldsymbol{I} = (I_1, \ldots, I_\ell)$ and a set of output wires $\boldsymbol{O} = (O_1, \ldots, O_m)$. The PDT of G is a $[0,1]^{2^{\ell \cdot n} \times 2^{m \cdot n}}$ matrix such that $\text{PDT}_G[\boldsymbol{I'}, \boldsymbol{O'}]$ is the probability for $\boldsymbol{I'}$ to be the smaller set that is enough to simulate the leaking wires from LeakingWires(G, p) together with $\boldsymbol{O'}$.

EXAMPLE 4.12.– Let us take the very simple example of a (1-share, 2-to-1) gadget as an `xor` gate, as represented in Figure 4.4.

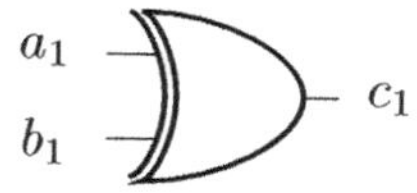

Figure 4.4. `xor` *gate with a single share for each input*

If we assume that each internal wire leaks with probability p, then its PDT table is given by:

	$O' = \emptyset$	$O' = \{c_1\}$
$\boldsymbol{I'} = \emptyset$	$1 - p^2$	0
$\boldsymbol{I'} = \{\{a_1\}\}$	$p \cdot (1-p)$	0
$\boldsymbol{I'} = \{\{b_1\}\}$	$p \cdot (1-p)$	0
$\boldsymbol{I'} = \{\{a_1\}, \{b_1\}\}$	p^2	1

For instance, the probability for $\boldsymbol{I'} = \{\{a_1\}\}$ to be the smallest set that is enough to simulate the leaking wires from LeakingWires(G, p) is computed from the probability that exactly a_1 is leaking (and not b_1, otherwise we would need b_1 as well), which is $p \cdot (1-p)$. Furthermore, if O' is not empty, that is, $O' = \{c_1\}$, then we need both input shares to simulate it, that is, $\boldsymbol{I'} = \{\{a_1\}, \{b_1\}\}$, hence the second column.

Note that $\text{PDT}_G[\boldsymbol{I'}, \boldsymbol{O'}] = \sum_{i=1}^{s} c_i \cdot p^i \cdot (1-p)^{s-i}$ is similar to the failure function from equation [4.1] but where c_i denotes the number of leaking sets of size i that exactly requires the input shares $\boldsymbol{I'}$ to be simulated together with $\boldsymbol{O'}$.

One step further, there is a direct relation between the probe distribution table and the random probing security: a gadget G with a single input (whose sharing is indexed by I) and a PDT PDT_G is $(p, \text{PDT}_G[I, \emptyset])$-random probing secure. The relation can be extended to multiple-input gadgets by considering the sum $\sum_{I'} \text{PDT}_G[I', \emptyset]$ for all I' that cover at least one input. A partial order can be defined on PDT so that for two gadgets G_1 and G_2:

$$\text{PDT}_{G_1} \leq \text{PDT}_{G_2}$$

means that the amount of information leaked in G_1 is less than or equal to the information leaked in G_2. Using this partial order, composition of gadgets can be built directly from their PDTs. We recall two main composition theorems to handle the two scenarios of parallel composition and sequential composition (see Figure 4.5).

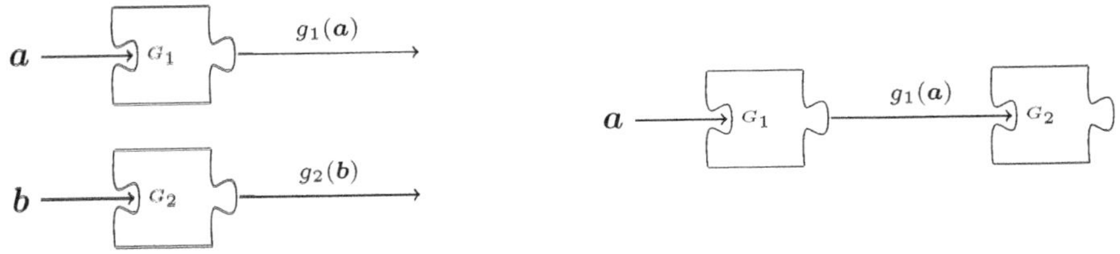

Figure 4.5. *Parallel (left) and sequential (right) composition of two gadgets*

THEOREM 4.2.– Parallel Composition: let G_1 and G_2 be two gadgets and let $\texttt{PDT}_{G_1}$ and $\texttt{PDT}_{G_2}$ be their respective probe distribution tables. The probe distribution table $\texttt{PDT}_G$ of gadget $G = G_1 \| G_2$ can be computed as follows:

$$\texttt{PDT}_G = \texttt{PDT}_{G_1} \otimes \texttt{PDT}_{G_2}$$

where $\otimes$ denotes the Kronecker product between matrices.

THEOREM 4.3.– Sequential Composition: let G_1 be an (ℓ_1-to-m) gadget and let G_2 be an (m-to-ℓ_2) gadget. Let $\texttt{PDT}_{G_1}$ and $\texttt{PDT}_{G_2}$ be their respective probe distribution tables. The probe distribution table $\texttt{PDT}_G$ of gadget $G = G_2 \circ G_1$ is bounded as follows:

$$\texttt{PDT}_G \leq \texttt{PDT}_{G_1} \cdot \texttt{PDT}_{G_2}$$

where $\cdot$ denotes the standard matrix multiplication.

The global composition theorem is stated below.

THEOREM 4.4.– Composition: let $p, \varepsilon \in [0,1]$. Let C be a (n-share, ℓ-input) randomized arithmetic circuit of input sharings indexed by $\boldsymbol{I}$ made of gadgets $G_1, \ldots, G_m$. Then, the PDT of C is upper bounded by a composition f of the PDTs of $G_1, \ldots, G_m$, which directly depends on the circuit's structure:

$$\texttt{PDT}_C \leq f(\texttt{PDT}_{G_1}, \ldots, \texttt{PDT}_{G_m}).$$

C is then (p, $\sum_{\boldsymbol{I}'} \texttt{PDT}_C[\boldsymbol{I}', \emptyset]$)-random probing secure for all the sets $\boldsymbol{I}'$ that cover at least one input of C. While this method yields tighter security parameters, it is also more expensive to evaluate. Hybrid methods can be exhibited with different trade-offs in terms of complexity and security evaluation.

4.7. Conclusion

This chapter has introduced several leakage models that are commonly used to model the attacker's observations on masking schemes during a side-channel attack. Different methods have been discussed depending on these leakage models to prove the security of the underlying masking schemes. Some of these apply directly to individual gadgets and can then be extended with composition techniques to prove the security of larger circuits.

The next chapter will present verification techniques to automatically prove the security of individual gadgets in the different leakage models, following the security notions introduced in this chapter.

4.8. Notes and further references

The second-order multiplication example was introduced by Ishai et al. (2003).

– Section 4.3. The probing model was introduced by Ishai et al. (2003).

– Section 4.5. The noisy leakage model was inspired from Chari et al. (1999) and formalized by Rivain and Prouff (2010) and then by Prest et al. (2019). The random probing model was first used in Ishai et al. (2003); Ajtai (2011), and then formalized in Duc et al. (2014).

– Section 4.6. Puzzles are largely inspired from figures in Rossi (2020). Doubling the number of shares was suggested by Ishai et al. (2003). NI and SNI were introduced in Barthe et al. (2016) and PINI was introduced in Cassiers and Standaert (2020). Random probing composability was defined in Belaïd et al. (2020) and further refined in Belaïd et al. (2021a).

4.9. References

Ajtai, M. (2011). Secure computation with information leaking to an adversary. In *43rd ACM STOC*, Fortnow, L. and Vadhan, S.P. (eds). ACM Press, New York.

Barthe, G., Belaïd, S., Dupressoir, F., Fouque, P.-A., Grégoire, B., Strub, P.-Y., Zucchini, R. (2016). Strong non-interference and type-directed higher-order masking. In *ACM CCS 2016*, Weippl, E.R., Katzenbeisser, S., Kruegel, C., Myers, A.C., Halevi, S. (eds). ACM Press, New York.

Belaïd, S., Coron, J.-S., Prouff, E., Rivain, M., Taleb, A.R. (2020). Random probing security: Verification, composition, expansion and new constructions. In *CRYPTO 2020*, Micciancio, D. and Ristenpart, T. (eds). Springer, Heidelberg.

Belaïd, S., Rivain, M., Taleb, A.R. (2021a). On the power of expansion: More efficient constructions in the random probing model. In *EUROCRYPT 2021*, Canteaut, A. and Standaert, F.-X. (eds). Springer, Heidelberg.

Belaïd, S., Rivain, M., Taleb, A.R., Vergnaud, D. (2021b). Dynamic random probing expansion with quasi linear asymptotic complexity. In *ASIACRYPT 2021*, Tibouchi, M. and Wang, H. (eds). Springer, Heidelberg.

Cassiers, G. and Standaert, F. (2020). Trivially and efficiently composing masked gadgets with probe isolating non-interference. *IEEE Trans. Inf. Forensics Secur.*, 15, 2542–2555. doi: 10.1109/TIFS.2020.2971153.

Cassiers, G., Faust, S., Orlt, M., Standaert, F.-X. (2021). Towards tight random probing security. In *CRYPTO 2021*, Malkin, T. and Peikert, C. (eds). Springer, Heidelberg.

Chari, S., Jutla, C.S., Rao, J.R., Rohatgi, P. (1999). Towards sound approaches to counteract power-analysis attacks. In *CRYPTO'99*, Wiener, M.J. (ed.). Springer, Heidelberg.

Duc, A., Dziembowski, S., Faust, S. (2014). Unifying leakage models: From probing attacks to noisy leakage. In *EUROCRYPT 2014*, Nguyen, P.Q. and Oswald, E. (eds). Springer, Heidelberg.

Ishai, Y., Sahai, A., Wagner, D. (2003). Private circuits: Securing hardware against probing attacks. In *CRYPTO 2003*, Boneh, D. (ed.). Springer, Heidelberg.

Prest, T., Goudarzi, D., Martinelli, A., Passelègue, A. (2019). Unifying leakage models on a Rényi day. In *CRYPTO 2019*, Boldyreva, A. and Micciancio, D. (eds). Springer, Heidelberg.

Rivain, M. and Prouff, E. (2010). Provably secure higher-order masking of AES. In *CHES 2010*, Mangard, S. and Standaert, F.-X. (eds). Springer, Heidelberg.

Rossi, M. (2020). Extended security of lattice-based cryptography (Sécurité étendue de la cryptographie fondée sur les réseaux euclidiens). PhD Thesis, Paris Sciences et Lettres University [Online]. Available at: https://tel.archives-ouvertes.fr/tel-02946399.

5

Masking Verification

Abdul Rahman TALEB
CryptoExperts, Paris, France

5.1. Introduction

Chapter 4 formally discussed proving the security of masked implementations in different leakage models. The main leakage models introduced are the noisy leakage model, the (robust) random probing model and the (robust) probing model. While the noisy leakage model best describes the reality of physical leakage, it remains challenging to establish security proofs in this model. Meanwhile, thanks to the security reduction in the noisy model with regard to the probing model, going through the intermediate random probing model, it remains interesting to construct masked circuits that are proven secure in the latter two models. Hence, this chapter focuses on verifying security properties in the probing and random probing models.

There are mainly two types of proofs for security in the (random) probing models, as presented in Chapter 4, distribution-based proofs and (exhaustive or generic) simulation-based proofs. Generic simulation-based proofs are handmade, which makes them very error prone, even at small masking orders. For this reason, automatic tools are built to apply exhaustive simulation (or distribution) based verification. The goal is to explore all possible sets of observations on the circuit up to a specific size defined by the security order and check the desired property. In the context of distribution-based verification, the distribution of each set of observations must be independent of the secret inputs. For simulation-based verification, each set must be perfectly simulatable using only a subset of the input shares to the circuit.

Embedded Cryptography 2,
coordinated by Emmanuel PROUFF, Guénaël RENAULT,
Matthieu RIVAIN and Colin O'FLYNN.

The bound on the size of the subsets is defined by the property (e.g. t-NI, t-SNI, etc.). These verification techniques extend to the random probing model. In this case, we consider all possible sets of observations on the circuit without an upper bound on the size to approximate the failure probability function $f(p)$.

In this chapter, we will discuss how automatic verification tools work. Section 5.2 starts by presenting the general verification procedure that any automatic tool applies. It mainly consists of an exploration algorithm to enumerate sets of variables on the circuit and a verification algorithm called on each set to check the desired property. Then, sections 5.3 and 5.4 introduce different instantiations of the verification and exploration algorithms, respectively. While the goal is not to exhaust all existing automatic verification techniques, we will present some important ones relevant to understanding the main idea and show the diversity of the techniques in the field.

We encourage the reader to read Chapter 4 first, as in the following, we use the same notations and formalism and suppose that the notions of leakage models are acquired. Also, all circuits and operations are defined over the field $\mathbb{K} = \mathbb{F}_2$. We point out, for each described algorithm, when it can be easily extended to larger fields. When we describe a circuit, we define the intermediate variables with respect to the order of the operations. The latter is the standard order of operations in an algebraic expression. For example, to compute the variable $c = a \cdot b + \big((d + e) + f\big)$, we get the intermediate results $a \cdot b$, $d + e$ and $(d + e) + f$.

5.2. General procedure

Automatic verification tools consist of two main algorithms: *exploration* and *verification*. Given a randomized arithmetic circuit $\widehat{C}$ and a property to check, the *exploration* algorithm goes through all possible sets of variables (or probes) on the circuit up to a size imposed by the property. Then, the *verification* algorithm is executed on each of the enumerated sets to check if the property is satisfied. For instance, Algorithm 5.1 illustrates this procedure for checking the t-NI property on an ℓ-to-m n-share circuit $\widehat{C}$ with $t < n$. We recall that a circuit is t-NI if any set $\mathcal{W}$ of at most t probes on $\widehat{C}$ can be perfectly simulated using at most t input shares of each of the ℓ input sharings.

Algorithm 5.1, which we call `Explore`, is a simple instantiation of the exploration algorithm, which enumerates all possible sets of at most t variables. We will see later that different optimizations can be applied to `Explore` to avoid checking all sets. Then, `Explore` calls the verification algorithm `Verify` on each enumerated set, taking as additional input the description of the circuit and the property to verify. `Verify` then verifies that the set of variables given as input satisfies the t-NI property. Otherwise, it returns *False*, ending the execution and meaning that the circuit is not t-NI. Such a set that does not respect the property is generally called a *failure set*.

Algorithm 5.1. `Explore` for t-NI

Require: n-share ℓ-to-m circuit $\widehat{C}$
Ensure: *True* if $\widehat{C}$ is t-NI, *False* otherwise

$V \leftarrow$ set of all variables on $\widehat{C}$
$S \leftarrow$ set of all subsets $\mathcal{W}$ of V such that $|\mathcal{W}| \leq t$
while $S \neq \emptyset$ **do**
  $\mathcal{W} \leftarrow$ a set from S
  $S \leftarrow S \setminus \{\mathcal{W}\}$
  if not `Verify`$(\widehat{C}, \mathcal{W}, t\text{-NI})$ **then**
    return *False*
  end if
end while
return *True*

EXAMPLE 5.1.– Consider a randomized arithmetic circuit $\widehat{C}$ that implements the following first-order multiplication on shared input $\widehat{\boldsymbol{x}} = (\widehat{a}, \widehat{b}) = ((a_0, a_1), (b_0, b_1)) \in \mathbb{F}_2^4$:

$$c_0 \leftarrow a_0 \cdot b_0 + r_{0,1}$$

$$c_1 \leftarrow a_1 \cdot b_1 + \big((r_{0,1} + a_0 \cdot b_1) + a_1 \cdot b_0\big)$$

such that $c = c_0 + c_1 = a \cdot b = (a_0 + a_1) \cdot (b_0 + b_1)$. We can execute Algorithm 5.1 on this circuit to check if it is 1-NI. We first get the set V, as described in the algorithm, of 13 variables:

$$V = \{a_0,\ a_1,\ b_0,\ b_1,\ r_{0,1},$$
$$a_0 \cdot b_0,\ a_0 \cdot b_1,\ a_1 \cdot b_0,\ a_1 \cdot b_1,$$
$$(r_{0,1} + a_0 \cdot b_1),\ \big((r_{0,1} + a_0 \cdot b_1) + a_1 \cdot b_0\big),\ c_0,\ c_1\}.$$

Then, for the 1-NI property, we consider subsets of V formed of a single variable. A simple implementation of `Explore` and `Verify` would be to go through all of the 13 subsets and check that each variable contains in its expression at most one share of $\widehat{a}$ and one share of $\widehat{b}$ or a fresh additive random value (since the random value can then be used to mask the expression and break the dependence with any input share, considering that it is uniformly generated, as explained in the previous chapter). Namely, each variable of the form a_i, b_j, $a_i \cdot b_j$ for $0 \leq i, j \leq 1$ contains at most one input share of each input sharing in its expression. Then, the intermediate variables which contain an additive random value in their expressions are c_0, $(r_{0,1} + a_0 \cdot b_1)$,

$\big((r_{0,1}+a_0\cdot b_1)+a_1\cdot b_0\big)$ and c_1. Considering each of these variables independently, its distribution is independent of any input share with the addition of the random value, which is used nowhere else (this can be checked by computing the truth table). The algorithm finally outputs that $\widehat{C}$ is 1-NI.

Notice that the instantiation of `Verify` in the above example is simulation-based. We only suppose that the random values used by the circuit are generated uniformly at random and do not assume the same on the input sharings. In fact, the definition of t-NI does not suppose the uniformity of the input sharings. Whenever an input share appears in the expression of a variable and is not masked by a uniform random value, we consider that it is needed to produce a perfect simulation of the variable. Indeed, as explained in Chapter 4, the additional uniformity constraint on the input sharings directly implies probing security.

As we saw, verifying basic probing-like properties on first-order implementations can sometimes be manageable with simple exploration and verification algorithms. However, such simple procedures do not scale well when considering larger sets of variables. Such scenarios occur when considering, for example, higher order implementations or robust probing properties and (robust) random probing properties. In this case, determining the number of input shares necessary for a perfect simulation can be difficult, depending on the number of variables to consider and the complexity of their expressions. Recall that an algorithm must do this in an automated fashion.

EXAMPLE 5.2.– Consider a two-share randomized arithmetic circuit $\widehat{C}$ with input $\widehat{\boldsymbol{x}} = (\widehat{a}) = (a_0, a_1) \in \mathbb{F}_2^2$. Suppose the following variables occur in the circuit:

$$\mathcal{W} = \{\Big(\big((a_0 + r_0) + a_1\big) + r_1\Big),\ \Big(\big((a_0 + r_0) + a_1\big) + r_1\Big) + r_2,\ r_0 + r_2\}$$

where $r_0, r_1, r_2 \in \mathbb{F}_2^3$ are uniform random variables. Observe that all of the shares of the input $\widehat{a}$ appear in $\mathcal{W}$. Also, no random variable appears only once in the set $\mathcal{W}$, meaning no random value can mask any expression in $\mathcal{W}$. However, an automatic verification algorithm must still be able to judge that no input shares are necessary to simulate the variables perfectly. We can rewrite the expressions in the set $\mathcal{W}$ as:

$$\mathcal{W} = \{w_1 = \Big(\big((a_0 + r_0) + a_1\big) + r_1\Big),\ w_2 = w_1 + r_2,\ w_3 = r_0 + r_2\}$$

and check that $\mathcal{W}$ is equivalent to the following set of variables:

$$\mathcal{W}' = \{w_1 = \Big(\big((a_0 + r_0) + a_1\big) + r_1\Big),\ w_2 + w_1 = r_2,\ w_3 = r_0 + r_2\}.$$

Indeed, if we can perfectly simulate the variables in $\mathcal{W}'$ (respectively, $\mathcal{W}$), then we can also perfectly simulate the variables in $\mathcal{W}$ (respectively, $\mathcal{W}'$) with some substitutions. Now, the random value r_1 only appears in the expression of w_1 in $\mathcal{W}'$, which means that it can be used to mask the expression of w_1 as a uniform random value. Finally, we can check that perfectly simulating $\mathcal{W}'$ is equivalent to perfectly simulating the set $\{r_1,\ r_2,\ r_0 + r_2\}$, which does not involve any input share. We can check by some distribution computation that all three sets have identical distributions conditioned on any realization of the input a and the corresponding shares (a_0, a_1).

All of this raises the need for efficient verification algorithms. Many instantiations of `Verify` exist in the literature. Some are distribution-based, while others are simulation-based. In the next section, we will see some important instantiations widely used by the community. Then, section 5.4 discusses instantiations of `Explore` to explore all sets of variables, taking into account the underlying leakage model and the property to be verified. We will discuss the advantages and disadvantages of each algorithm along the way.

5.3. `Verify`: verification mechanisms for a set of variables

This section will first revisit the distribution-based technique to instantiate `Verify`. Indeed, it has already been shown in some examples in Chapter 4 that it becomes quickly exponential as the number of involved variables grows. The goal is to present some optimizations to show how distribution-based techniques can verify security notions such as composition. Then, we will mainly focus on widely used simulation-based techniques which manipulate the variables' symbolic expressions and have proven more efficient than the former distribution techniques. We insist that whatever the instantiation of `Verify`, an exponential cost is still present in `Explore` when we need to iterate over subsets of variables on the circuit. Nevertheless, with a sufficiently efficient `Verify` algorithm and optimizations on `Explore`, we can check the security of circuits and gadgets of reasonable sizes for concrete implementations.

5.3.1. *Distribution-based* `Verify`

Given an n-share ℓ-to-m circuit $\widehat{C}$, and a set of variables $\mathcal{W}$ on the circuit and a $\mathbb{K}^\ell$-valued random variable $\mathcal{X}$, distribution-based procedures essentially verify the statistical independence between $\texttt{AssignWires}(\widehat{C}, \mathcal{W}, \mathsf{Enc}(\mathcal{X}))$ and $\mathcal{X}$ (recall that Enc is an n-additive encoding producing a uniform sharing of each of the ℓ inputs). A direct approach to check this independence is by verifying that the following equality holds $\forall\, \boldsymbol{w} \in \mathbb{K}^{|\mathcal{W}|}$, $\forall\, \boldsymbol{x} \in \mathbb{K}^\ell$:

$$\Pr[\texttt{AssignWires}(\widehat{C}, \mathcal{W}, \mathsf{Enc}(\mathcal{X})) = \boldsymbol{w}\ ,\ \mathcal{X} = \boldsymbol{x}]$$

$$= \Pr[\texttt{AssignWires}(\widehat{C}, \mathcal{W}, \mathsf{Enc}(\mathcal{X})) = \boldsymbol{w}] \cdot \Pr[\mathcal{X} = \boldsymbol{x}].$$

Note that this verification is done to prove probing security. In other words, to prove t-probing security, `Explore` iterates on all sets $\mathcal{W}$ of at most t probes and then calls `Verify` on each to verify the above equality. We can extend this verification to other simulation-based notions, which require the set of probes to be perfectly simulated using only a subset of the input shares. For instance, in the context of t-NI, each set $\mathcal{W}$ of at most t probes must be perfectly simulated using at most t shares of each input sharing. Then, if we suppose that the input sharings are independent and uniform, there must exist a collection of sets $\boldsymbol{I} = (I_1, \ldots, I_\ell)$ such that $\forall i \in [1;\ell], |I_i| \leq t$ and the following holds $\forall\, \boldsymbol{w} \in \mathbb{K}^t,\ \forall\, \boldsymbol{x} \in \mathbb{K}^\ell,\ \forall\, \widehat{\boldsymbol{x}} = \mathsf{Enc}(\boldsymbol{x}) \in \mathbb{K}^{n\cdot\ell}$:

$$\begin{aligned}&\Pr[\texttt{AssignWires}(\widehat{C}, \mathcal{W}, \mathsf{Enc}(\mathcal{X})) = \boldsymbol{w} \mid \mathsf{Enc}(\mathcal{X}) = \widehat{\boldsymbol{x}}]\\&= \Pr[\texttt{AssignWires}(\widehat{C}, \mathcal{W}, \mathsf{Enc}(\mathcal{X})) = \boldsymbol{w} \mid \mathsf{Enc}(\mathcal{X})|_{\boldsymbol{I}} = \widehat{\boldsymbol{x}}|_{\boldsymbol{I}}].\end{aligned} \qquad [5.1]$$

Observe that knowing that $\mathsf{Enc}(\mathcal{X}) = \widehat{\boldsymbol{x}}$ directly gives $\mathcal{X} = \boldsymbol{x}$. This ensures that a simulator can use the shares $\widehat{\boldsymbol{x}}|_{\boldsymbol{I}}$ to perfectly simulate $\mathcal{W}$, exactly like in the case where it would have access to the complete sharing $\widehat{\boldsymbol{x}}$. While the original non-interference notion does not suppose the input sharings to be independent and uniform, proving t-NI using distributions of variables requires it (generally, t-probing security can be seen as a specialization of t-NI with independent and uniform input sharings). Once equation [5.1] is defined, it can be adapted to other notions. For t-SNI, for example, we restrict the sizes of $|I_i|$ to t_1 for all $i \in [1;\ell]$, the number of intermediate variables in $\mathcal{W}$.

Since we suppose that all input sharings are uniform, testing equation [5.1] amounts to checking that $\forall\, \boldsymbol{w} \in \mathbb{K}^t,\ \forall\, \boldsymbol{x} \in \mathbb{K}^\ell,\ \forall\, \widehat{\boldsymbol{x}} = \mathsf{Enc}(\boldsymbol{x}) \in \mathbb{K}^{n\cdot\ell}$:

$$\begin{aligned}&\Pr[\texttt{AssignWires}(\widehat{C}, \mathcal{W}, \mathsf{Enc}(\mathcal{X})) = \boldsymbol{w},\ \mathsf{Enc}(\mathcal{X}) = \widehat{\boldsymbol{x}}]\\&= \Pr[\texttt{AssignWires}(\widehat{C}, \mathcal{W}, \mathsf{Enc}(\mathcal{X})) = \boldsymbol{w},\ \mathsf{Enc}(\mathcal{X})|_{\boldsymbol{I}} = \widehat{\boldsymbol{x}}|_{\boldsymbol{I}}]\cdot\\&\Pr[\mathsf{Enc}(\mathcal{X})|_{\bar{\boldsymbol{I}}} = \widehat{\boldsymbol{x}}|_{\bar{\boldsymbol{I}}}].\end{aligned} \qquad [5.2]$$

where $\bar{\boldsymbol{I}} = ([1;n] \setminus I_1, \ldots, [1;n] \setminus I_\ell)$.

In this case, an instantiation of `Verify` tries to find the collection of sets $\boldsymbol{I}$ of the right size such that equation [5.2] holds, depending on the considered property. For instance, checking that the equation holds can be done by computing truth tables for all possible realizations of the involved variables. Since we are working on $\mathbb{K} = \mathbb{F}_2$, some optimizations can be applied to reduce the complexity. Namely, we can use the following proven result.

THEOREM 5.1.– Let $\mathcal{X}$, $\mathcal{Y}$ be two sets of binary random variables. Then $\mathcal{X}$ and $\mathcal{Y}$ are statistically independent, if and only if $\forall \mathcal{X}' \subseteq \mathcal{X},\ \mathcal{Y}' \subseteq \mathcal{Y}$, we have:

$$\Pr[\mathcal{X}' = \boldsymbol{x}, \mathcal{Y}' = \boldsymbol{y}] = \Pr[\mathcal{X}' = \boldsymbol{x}'] \cdot \Pr[\mathcal{Y}' = \boldsymbol{y}']$$

for any fixed set of values $\boldsymbol{x} \in \mathbb{F}_2^{|\mathcal{X}'|}, \boldsymbol{y} \in \mathbb{F}_2^{|\mathcal{Y}'|}$

Theorem 5.1 implies that it is necessary and sufficient to verify that equation [5.2] holds for one fixed realization, for example, $\boldsymbol{w} = \mathbf{1}, \widehat{\boldsymbol{x}} = \mathbf{1}$, instead of trying all combinations of realizations. On the other hand, we must compute this for all subsets of $\mathcal{W}$ and I_i for $i \in [1; n]$.

EXAMPLE 5.3.– Consider a 3-share randomized arithmetic circuit $\widehat{C}$ with input $\widehat{\boldsymbol{x}} = (\widehat{a}, \widehat{b}) = ((a_0, a_1, a_2), (b_0, b_1, b_2)) \in \mathbb{F}_2^6$ such that $\widehat{a}, \widehat{b}$ are uniform and independent sharings. Suppose that we want to check if a set of probes $\mathcal{W} = \{w_1, w_2\}$ on $\widehat{C}$ is perfectly simulatable with $\boldsymbol{I} = (\{0,1\}, \{2\})$. Then, we need to check the following equalities:

$$\begin{aligned}
\Pr[w_1 = 1,\ a_0 = 1,\ a_1 = 1,\ a_2 = 1] &= \Pr[w_1 = 1] \cdot \Pr[a_0 = 1,\ a_1 = 1,\ a_2 = 1],\\
\Pr[w_1 = 1,\ a_0 = 1,\ a_1 = 1,\ a_2 = 1] &= \Pr[w_1 = 1,\ a_0 = 1] \cdot \Pr[a_1 = 1,\ a_2 = 1],\\
\Pr[w_1 = 1,\ a_0 = 1,\ a_1 = 1,\ a_2 = 1] &= \Pr[w_1 = 1,\ a_1 = 1] \cdot \Pr[a_0 = 1,\ a_2 = 1],\\
\Pr[w_1 = 1,\ a_0 = 1,\ a_1 = 1,\ a_2 = 1] &= \Pr[w_1 = 1,\ a_0 = 1,\ a_1 = 1] \cdot \Pr[a_2 = 1],\\
\Pr[w_1 = 1,\ b_0 = 1,\ b_1 = 1,\ b_2 = 1] &= \Pr[w_1 = 1] \cdot \Pr[b_0 = 1,\ b_1 = 1,\ b_2 = 1],\\
\Pr[w_1 = 1,\ b_0 = 1,\ b_1 = 1,\ b_2 = 1] &= \Pr[w_1 = 1,\ b_2 = 1] \cdot \Pr[b_0 = 1,\ b_1 = 1].
\end{aligned}$$

In addition, we also need to consider eight more equations with combinations of both secrets. Finally, we need to check the same set of 14 equations when considering the realization of the probe $w_2 = 1$, then both $w_1 = 1$ and $w_2 = 1$, for a total of 42 equalities to check.

Note that to compute the realization of a set of binary variables to $\mathbf{1}$, we can use *Reduced Order Binary Decision Diagrams* (ROBDD). In a nutshell, the goal is to represent each variable in the circuit by a corresponding ROBDD using the inputs to the circuit (including random variables) to make the computation of the probabilities more efficient.

This verification method remains heavy and does not scale well when the number of shares and the size of the circuit grow. Meanwhile, the main advantage of this method is that it is *complete*. We call an implementation of `Verify` *complete* when a set of wires $\mathcal{W}$ is considered a *failure set* by `Verify` if and only if it is a failure set for the desired property. We will see later in the chapter that some methods are more efficient at the expense of being slightly less *complete*. When a set $\mathcal{W}$ is considered a *failure set* by a verification algorithm without actually being a failure for the desired property, we call it a *false positive*.

Another novel approach for testing the independence of probed variables from the secrets over $\mathbb{F}_2$ was introduced in the literature using the *Fourier expansion* of Boolean functions. The method considers uniform input sharings. On a first-order (i.e. 2-share) example, an input secret a has a sharing $\widehat{a} = (r, a \oplus r)$, where r is a uniform random value and $\oplus$ is the XOR operation. This technique consists of computing each gate's Fourier expansion in the circuit and checking that no coefficient containing only the secret value a appears in the expansion without any uniform random variable, directly implying that the gate is statistically independent of the secret a. For instance, a XOR gate taking as input the secret a and a uniform random value r' has the Fourier expansion $F(a \oplus r') = a \cdot r'$, where a only appears in a coefficient with a random masking value. Hence, the gate is independent of the secret. Meanwhile, an AND gate taking as input a and r' has the Fourier expansion $F(a \wedge r') = \frac{1}{2} + \frac{1}{2}a + \frac{1}{2}r' - \frac{1}{2}ar'$, where a appears in a coefficient without any random mask, so the gate is not statistically independent of the secret. We can check the statistical independence by computing the expansion of each gate in the circuit using the input shares and random values, and this method is *complete*. Meanwhile, extending the verification to check composition notions such as SNI and PINI is not trivial. Moreover, for higher-order implementations, we need to check several combinations of gates and compute the Fourier expansion of the combinations, which becomes very expensive. Some methods exist to approximate the Fourier expansion faster, making the verification possible but not *complete* anymore.

5.3.2. *Simulation-based* `Verify`

Simulation-based instantiations of `Verify` manipulate the symbolic expressions of the variables to conclude the simulatability of a set of probes for the property. In the following, we present a substitution- and transformation-based method that works on any gadget or circuit structure but is only sometimes *complete*. Then, we present a *complete* method restricted to specific gadget structures covering most of the widely used constructions in the literature. Both techniques can be generalized to any field $\mathbb{K}$. However, we assume $\mathbb{K} = \mathbb{F}_2$ for simplicity of presentation.

5.3.2.1. *Substitution rules algorithm*

Given a set of probes $\mathcal{W}$, a first approach is to apply a certain number of transformations on the probes' symbolic expressions until we can precisely determine the input shares necessary to produce a perfect simulation. The procedure relies on three main rules. Algorithm 5.2 gives the instantiation to check t-SNI, which can be adapted to any other property. We can see in the algorithm that each rule is applied a certain number of times until no more transformations can be done on the expressions, in which case, we have no choice but to use the input shares appearing in the expressions.

Algorithm 5.2. `Verify` as described in section 5.3.2.1 for t-SNI

Require: n-share ℓ-to-m circuit $\widehat{C}$, a set of t probes $\mathcal{W}$, k number of iterations on **Rule 3**.

Ensure: *True* if $\mathcal{W}$ satisfies t-SNI, *False* if $\mathcal{W}$ is a failure set

1: $t_1 \leftarrow$ number of probes on internal variables to $\widehat{C}$
2: **do**
3:     **do**
4:         $(I_1, \dots I_\ell) \leftarrow$ **Rule 1** executed on $\mathcal{W}$
5:         **if** $|I_i| \leq t_1$ for each $i \in [1;\ell]$ **then**
6:             **return** *True*
7:         **end if**
8:         $\mathcal{W}' \leftarrow \mathcal{W}$
9:         $\mathcal{W} \leftarrow$ **Rule 2** executed on $\mathcal{W}'$
10:     **while** $\mathcal{W}' \neq \mathcal{W}$
11:     **for** $i = 1$ **to** k **do**
12:         $\mathcal{W} \leftarrow$ **Rule 3** executed on $\mathcal{W}$
13:     **end for**
14: **while** $\mathcal{W}' \neq \mathcal{W}$
15: **return** *False*

Rule 1: the first rule is to extract the input shares that appear in all of the symbolic expressions in $\mathcal{W}$, outputting $(I_1, \dots, I_\ell)$ as shown on line 4 of Algorithm 5.2. Indeed, a trivial way of perfectly simulating these probes is to give all of the input shares involved to the simulator. Then, if the sizes of the sets $I_1, \dots, I_\ell$ already satisfy the desired property, we can stop the verification and consider the set a success case.

Otherwise, we can apply additional rules to try and reduce the sizes of the sets of shares necessary until we can satisfy the property (or not, which leads to a *failure*). We can use the observation already presented in Chapter 4, where we say that an additive random value to a symbolic expression appearing only once in the set $\mathcal{W}$ can mask this expression. This transformation is performed by **Rule 2** to output a new equivalent set of expressions on Line 9 of the algorithm.

Rule 2: for each expression $w_i \in \mathcal{W}$, if $w_i = A + r$ where $r \in \mathbb{F}_2$ is a uniform random value and does not appear in any expression in $\mathcal{W} \setminus \{w_i\}$, nor in A, then replace $\mathcal{W}$ by an equivalent set:

$$\mathcal{W}' = \{r\} \cup (\mathcal{W} \setminus \{w_i\})$$

We have previously seen that perfectly simulating $\mathcal{W}$ is equivalent to perfectly simulating the output of **Rule 2** on $\mathcal{W}$, and that both sets have identical distributions. Then, we can loop on **Rule 2** and **Rule 1** as long as we find new random values that can mask other expressions or until **Rule 1** exits with success. This loop is executed on Lines 3 through 10 of Algorithm 5.2. Note that looping on **Rule 2** is sometimes necessary as masking an expression can make new random values appear only once in other expressions, which can then be seen as masks.

At the end of the loop on the first two rules, if `Verify` did not return *True*, the set $\mathcal{W}$ is considered a potential failure set. Precisely, no more random values can be used as masks, and too many input shares are necessary for a perfect simulation. Meanwhile, we can still apply another rule by observing that probing $\{w_1, w_1 + w_2\}$ is equivalent to probing $\{w_1, w_2\}$, as in the following example.

EXAMPLE 5.4.– Let $\widehat{C}$ be a randomized circuit with input $\widehat{x} = (\widehat{a}, \widehat{b}) = ((a_0, a_1), (b_0, b_1)) \in \mathbb{F}_2^4$. Let $\mathcal{W} = \{w_1 = a_0 + b_0 + r_0 + a_1, w_2 = a_0 + b_0 + r_0\}$ a set of probes on $\widehat{C}$, where $r_0 \in \mathbb{F}_2$ is a uniform random value. Suppose that we are checking 1-NI. Applying **Rule 2** on $\mathcal{W}$ will not perform any transformations because r_0 appears twice. Since both input shares of $\widehat{a}$ appear in the expressions in $\mathcal{W}$, `Verify` concludes that $\mathcal{W}$ is a failure set. Meanwhile, we can see that $w_1 = w_2 + a_1$, i.e. w_2 is a subexpression of w_1. Hence, a simulator that can perfectly simulate $\mathcal{W}$ is equivalent to a simulator that can perfectly simulate $\mathcal{W}' = \{a_1, w_2\}$, up to some linear transformations on the expressions. Now the random value r_0 only appears once in $w_2 \in \mathcal{W}'$, so it can be used to mask the expression of w_2. We conclude that $\mathcal{W}'$ is equivalent to $\mathcal{W}'' = \{a_1, r_0\}$, where only one share of $\widehat{a}$ is necessary for a perfect simulation.

We generalize the above example to the following rule (**Rule 3**), executed by `Verify` whenever **Rule 1** and **Rule 2** are not enough to conclude. On Lines 11 through 13 of Algorithm 5.2, we execute this rule k times, where k is given as input to the algorithm.

Rule 3: for each $(w_i, w_j) \in \mathcal{W}$, if the number of variables in the expression of $w_i + w_j$ is less than the number of variables in the expression of w_i, then replace $\mathcal{W}$ by an equivalent set:

$$\mathcal{W}' = \{w_i + w_j\} \cup (\mathcal{W} \setminus \{w_i\}).$$

Otherwise, if the number of variables in the expression of $w_i + w_j$ is less than the number of variables in the expression of w_j, then replace $\mathcal{W}$ by an equivalent set:

$$\mathcal{W}' = \{w_i + w_j\} \cup (\mathcal{W} \setminus \{w_j\}).$$

Stop when all couples of expressions in $\mathcal{W}$ are visited.

After executing **Rule 3**, we go back to looping on **Rule 1** and **Rule 2** again to check if we can use any random value to mask new expressions. We get to the final main loop of the algorithm on Lines 2 through 14. The termination condition of applying the different steps is when no more transformations can be applied to the initial set of wires. If we never output *True* in the main loop, the algorithm eventually returns *False*, meaning that too many input shares are involved in the variables' expressions to satisfy the property.

We can see that such implementation of `Verify` is sometimes not *complete*. Nevertheless, it detects all possible attacks, so it is conservative. Further optimizations and elimination techniques are implemented in recent verification tools to avoid *false positives* as much as possible. For instance, we can execute **Rule 3** indeterminately if we modify $\mathcal{W}$. Since the criterion is to replace an expression w with another w' with fewer variables in the expression, we are sure that the rule terminates. This induces an execution time overhead. Many tools try to find trade-offs between execution time and completeness.

EXERCISE 5.1.– Consider some randomized arithmetic circuit $\widehat{C}$ with input $\widehat{\boldsymbol{x}} = (\widehat{a}, \widehat{b}) = ((a_0, a_1, a_2, a_3), (b_0, b_1, b_2, b3)) \in \mathbb{F}_2^8$. Now, let $\mathcal{W}$ be a set of probes on $\widehat{C}$ with $\mathcal{W} = \{a_0 \cdot b_0 + (a_0 \cdot b_1 + r_{0,1}) + (a_0 \cdot b_2 + r_{0,2}) + (a_0 \cdot b_3 + r_{0,3}) + r_{1,0} + r_{2,0} + r_{3,0}, r_{1,0} + r_{2,0} + r_{3,0},\ r_{0,1} + r_{2,1} + r_{3,1},\ r_{0,2} + r_{1,2} + r_{3,2},\ r_{0,3} + r_{1,3} + r_{2,3},\ r_{0,2} + r_{1,2},\ r_{0,3} + r_{1,3},\ r_{0,1} + r_{2,1} + r_{3,1},\ a_0 \cdot b_0 + (a_0 \cdot b_1 + r_{0,1}) + (a_0 \cdot b_2 + r_{0,2}) + (a_0 \cdot b_3 + r_{0,3})\}$. How many input shares of $\widehat{a}$ and $\widehat{b}$ are needed to produce a perfect simulation of $\mathcal{W}$ after running the three rules of the verification? Can we reduce further these numbers of shares?

Now let us consider another randomized arithmetic circuit $\widehat{C}'$ with the same inputs and a set of probes $\mathcal{W}' = \{a_0 \cdot b_0 + r_{0,1} + b_0 \cdot r_0 + b_0 \cdot r_1,\ a_1 \cdot b_1 + r_{1,1} + b_1 \cdot r_1 + b_1 \cdot r_2,\ r_{0,1},\ r_{1,1},\ r_0\}$. How many input shares of $\widehat{a}$ and $\widehat{b}$ are needed to produce a perfect simulation of $\mathcal{W}'$ after running the three rules of the verification? Can we further reduce these numbers of shares?

Finally, if we want to check properties under the hypothesis of input sharings uniformity (e.g. t-probing security), we can apply the following trick without changing the verification procedure. For each secret input a to the circuit, we compute its sharing as $\widehat{a} = (r_0, \ldots, r_{n-1}, a + r_0 + \ldots + r_{n-1})$, where $r_0, \ldots, r_{n-1}$ are now internal random values to the circuit, but we allow no probes to the internal computation of $a + r_0 + \ldots + r_{n-1}$. Then, the failure condition for t-probing security would be that the secret input a is required by a simulator to produce a perfect simulation of a given set of probes.

5.3.2.2. *Linear algebra algorithm*

In the following, we discuss another instantiation of `Verify` based on an algebraic characterization of the variables. This characterization introduces a *complete* and efficient verification method. It restricts the types of circuits as input but covers most masking gadgets for standard operations such as addition, multiplication and refreshing. Covering these gadgets is satisfying in composition, where we construct big, secure circuits from smaller secure gadgets.

To this purpose, we slightly modify the notations in this section. For an n-share ℓ-to-m gadget, we denote its input and output sharings as column vectors $(\overrightarrow{x_1}, \ldots, \overrightarrow{x_\ell}) \in \left(\mathbb{F}_2^n\right)^\ell$, $(\overrightarrow{y_1}, \ldots, \overrightarrow{y_m}) \in \left(\mathbb{F}_2^n\right)^m$, respectively. We also group all the gadget's random variables in a column vector $\overrightarrow{r} \in \mathbb{F}_2^\rho$ of uniformly and independently drawn random values. We finally consider "vectors" of probes $\overrightarrow{\mathcal{W}}$ instead of "sets" of probes.

Given a vector of probes $\overrightarrow{\mathcal{W}}$, our goal is to precisely determine the expressions that uniform random values can mask. The strategy from section 5.3.2.1 applies a set of rules in the hope of masking additional input shares. In this section, we provide a linear algebra-based method that determines the exact expressions which can be masked by random values and those that cannot. Then, the idea is to provide the remaining input shares to the simulator as they are potentially needed for a perfect simulation. We focus on gadgets where all random values are additive to the variables. In other words, we write the output vectors $(\overrightarrow{y_1}, \ldots, \overrightarrow{y_m})$ as:

$$(\overrightarrow{y_1}, \ldots, \overrightarrow{y_m}) = R\big(F(\overrightarrow{x_1}, \ldots, \overrightarrow{x_\ell}), \overrightarrow{r}\big) ,$$

where F is an arbitrary arithmetic circuit (composed of addition and multiplication gates over $\mathbb{F}_2$) and R is a linear arithmetic circuit (composed of addition gates over $\mathbb{F}_2$). With this definition of the gadget's outputs, we can write the expression of any internal wire w of the gadget as:

$$w = f_w(\overrightarrow{x_1}, \ldots, \overrightarrow{x_\ell}) + \overrightarrow{r}^T \cdot \overrightarrow{s_w} \qquad [5.3]$$

for some arithmetic function $f_w : (\mathbb{F}_2^n)^\ell \to \mathbb{F}_2$ and some constant vector $\overrightarrow{s_w} \in \mathbb{F}_2^\rho$.

To determine the random variables that can be used for masking, we use a strategy based on Gaussian elimination. Let $\overrightarrow{\mathcal{W}} = (w_1, \ldots, w_t)$ be a vector of t probes.

Since each expression w_i can be written as in equation [5.3], we can construct the following matrix $S \in \mathbb{F}_2^{t \times \rho}$:

$$S = \begin{pmatrix} \overrightarrow{s_{w_1}}^T \\ \vdots \\ \overrightarrow{s_{w_t}}^T \end{pmatrix},$$

where the ith row of S is the vector $\overrightarrow{s_{w_i}}^T$ representing the dependence of w_i on the corresponding random values of the gadget. To check that a random r_j for $1 \leq j \leq \rho$ appears only once in all the expressions in $\overrightarrow{W}$, we can easily check that the jth column in S has a single non-zero value. By applying a row reduction algorithm on S, we obtain its row-reduced echelon matrix S', which up to some permutations is equal to:

$$S' = \begin{pmatrix} I_{k,k} & T_{k,\rho-k} \\ 0_{t-k,k} & 0_{t-k,\rho-k} \end{pmatrix}$$

with $S' = N \cdot S$ where $N \in \mathbb{F}_2^{t \times t}$ is an invertible matrix, $I_{k,k} \in \mathbb{F}_2^{k \times k}$ is the identity matrix, $0_{t-k,k} \in \mathbb{F}_2^{(t-k) \times k}$ and $0_{t-k,\rho-k} \in \mathbb{F}_2^{(t-k) \times (\rho-k)}$ are the matrices with zero coefficients, and $T_{k,\rho-k} \in \mathbb{F}_2^{k \times (\rho-k)}$ is a matrix with any coefficients. We can apply the same transformations to $\overrightarrow{W}$ using N to get $\overrightarrow{W}'$ defined as:

$$\overrightarrow{W}'^T = N \cdot \overrightarrow{W} = (w'_1, \ldots, w'_k, w'_{k+1}, \ldots, w'_t).$$

The transformations applied to expressions in $\overrightarrow{W}$ are linear and equivalent to the ones applied during **Rule 3** of Algorithm 5.2. Since N is invertible, and the operations performed on rows of S are linear, then perfectly simulating $\overrightarrow{W}$ is equivalent to perfectly simulating $\overrightarrow{W}'$ ($\overrightarrow{W}'$ is obtained as $N \cdot \overrightarrow{W}$ and $\overrightarrow{W}$ is obtained as $N^{-1} \cdot \overrightarrow{W}'$). By closely looking at the expressions in $\overrightarrow{W}'$, we can check that the first k rows in S' correspond to the random dependence of the first k expressions in $\overrightarrow{W}'$. In other words, for each $1 \leq i \leq k$, we can write w'_i as:

$$w'_i = f_{w'_i}(\overrightarrow{x_1}, \ldots, \overrightarrow{x_\ell}) + \overrightarrow{r}^T \cdot \overrightarrow{s_{w'_i}}$$

for some arithmetic function $f_{w'_i} : (\mathbb{F}_2^n)^\ell \rightarrow \mathbb{F}_2$ and $\overrightarrow{s_{w'_i}} \in \mathbb{F}_2^\rho$ is the jth row vector of S'. Since S' is in row-reduced form and thanks to the identity matrix $I_{k,k}$, each such vector $\overrightarrow{s_{w'_i}}$ has its leading coefficient non-zero on the ith column and all other coefficients of S' on the same column are zeros. Therefore, we are sure that the random value corresponding to column i appears only in the expression of w'_i

among expressions in $\overrightarrow{W}'$ and is additive. Therefore, we can use this random to mask the expression of w'_i, and its distribution is thus independent of any input share and mutually independent of the other expressions w'_j for $j \in [1;t] \setminus \{i\}$.

Similarly, for each row $k+1 \leq j \leq t$, we can write w'_j as:

$$w'_j = f_{w'_j}(\overrightarrow{x_1}, \ldots, \overrightarrow{x_\ell}) + \overrightarrow{r}^T \cdot \overrightarrow{0} = f_{w'_j}(\overrightarrow{x_1}, \ldots, \overrightarrow{x_\ell})$$

for some arithmetic function $f_{w'_j} : (\mathbb{F}_2^n)^\ell \to \mathbb{F}_2$ and $\overrightarrow{0} \in \mathbb{F}_2^\varrho$ the vector with zero coefficients. This means that each such expression w'_j contains no random value and cannot be masked. A perfect simulation of w'_j eventually requires all of the input shares appearing in $f_{w'_j}(\overrightarrow{x_1}, \ldots, \overrightarrow{x_\ell})$. As a result, we conclude that the input shares needed to perfectly simulate $\overrightarrow{W}'$ are exactly the ones appearing in the expressions of $(w'_{k+1}, \ldots, w'_t)$. Thanks to the exactness of the row reduction, we are sure that the sets of input shares are of minimal sizes.

EXAMPLE 5.5.– Let us take a toy example to apply this technique. Consider the vector of expressions $\overrightarrow{W}^T = (w_1, w_2, w_3, w_4) = (a_0 \cdot b_0 + r_1 + r_2,\ a_1 \cdot b_1 + r_2 + r_1,\ a_2 \cdot b_2 + r_3 + r_4,\ a_3 \cdot b_3 + r_3)$ on a gadget with input $\widehat{x} = (\widehat{a}, \widehat{b}) = ((a_0, a_1, a_2, a_3), (b_0, b_1, b_2, b_3)) \in \mathbb{F}_2^8$. The vector of randoms used by the gadget is $\overrightarrow{r}^T = (r_1, r_2, r_3, r_4)$. Let us now construct the matrix S as explained above.

$$S = \begin{pmatrix} \overrightarrow{s_{w_1}}^T \\ \overrightarrow{s_{w_2}}^T \\ \overrightarrow{s_{w_3}}^T \\ \overrightarrow{s_{w_4}}^T \end{pmatrix} = \begin{pmatrix} 1\,1\,0\,0 \\ 1\,1\,0\,0 \\ 0\,0\,1\,1 \\ 0\,0\,1\,0 \end{pmatrix}$$

By performing row reduction on S, we obtain:

$$S' = \begin{pmatrix} 1\,1\,0\,0 \\ 0\,0\,0\,0 \\ 0\,0\,1\,0 \\ 0\,0\,0\,1 \end{pmatrix} \quad \text{with} \quad N = \begin{pmatrix} 1\,0\,0\,0 \\ 1\,1\,0\,0 \\ 0\,0\,1\,0 \\ 0\,0\,1\,1 \end{pmatrix}.$$

Using N, we can construct the vector of expressions $\overrightarrow{W}'$ equivalent to $\overrightarrow{W}$ such that:

$$\overrightarrow{W}' = (w'_1, w'_2, w'_3, w'_4) = (a_0 \cdot b_0 + r_1 + r_2,\ a_0 \cdot b_0 + a_1 \cdot b_1,\ a_3 \cdot b_3 + r_3,\ a_2 \cdot b_2 + a_3 \cdot b_3 + r_4).$$

We can see that the only expression in $\overrightarrow{W}'$ that does not contain any random value is $w'_2 = a_0 \cdot b_0 + a_1 \cdot b_1$, and each of the other expressions contains a random value that is additive and does not appear anywhere else in $\overrightarrow{W}'$. Precisely, w'_1 is masked by r_1 or r_2, w'_3 is masked by r_3 and w'_4 is masked by r_4. Consequently, perfectly simulating $\overrightarrow{W}'$ requires the input shares that only appear in the expression of w'_2, which are a_0, b_0, a_1 and b_1. By perfectly simulating $\overrightarrow{W}'$ using these input shares, we can also perfectly simulate $\overrightarrow{W}$ using the same input shares by first simulating $\overrightarrow{W}'$ and then computing $\overrightarrow{W}$ as $N^{-1} \cdot \overrightarrow{W}'$. We could have permuted some rows of S' to place the zero rows at the bottom, as described above. However, this additional step was only necessary for the clarity of the presentation.

The `Verify` instantiation method described in this section is *complete* because it determines the minimal sets of input shares necessary for a perfect simulation. In addition, its complexity is exactly the complexity of performing row reduction on the vectors of randomness, which can be estimated to $\mathcal{O}(t^2 \cdot \rho)$ if we use a simple row reduction algorithm.

Meanwhile, it is restricted to specific types of constructions, where all random variables are additive to the wires of the gadget. The literature extended this technique to support limited nonlinear operations between input shares and random values. In a nutshell, on a 2-to-1 n-share gadget, for instance, the output must be expressed as $R(F(R_1(\overrightarrow{x_1}, \overrightarrow{r_1}), R_1(\overrightarrow{x_2}, \overrightarrow{r_2})), \overrightarrow{r})$, where $\overrightarrow{r_1}, \overrightarrow{r_2}, \overrightarrow{r}$ are distinct random vectors used by the gadget. This construction covers composed gadgets such as a multiplication gadget, which first starts by refreshing both inputs. Finally, if we want to check properties under the hypothesis of input sharings uniformity, we can apply the same trick discussed at the end of section 5.3.2.1.

5.4. `Explore`: exploration mechanisms for all sets of variables

In section 5.3, we described different ways of defining the procedure `Verify` to judge if a given set of probes or variables represents a failure for the checked property. We now discuss the next main algorithm of any automatic verification tool, `Explore`, which explores all the possible sets of variables of the circuit and passes each as input to `Verify` (as described in Algorithm 5.1). Indeed, scanning all possible sets of variables of a given size on a circuit has inevitable exponential complexity. In this section, we describe different optimizations leading to a practical speed-up to test circuits and gadgets of reasonable sizes. We first show tricks specific to the probing model, then move on to exploration in the random probing model. Finally, we end with a discussion about exploring sets of variables, while taking physical defaults into account.

5.4.1. *Probing model*

Security properties in the probing model are easier to verify than in the random probing model. Given a security parameter t, we need to call `Verify` on all possible sets of at most t variables, where $t \leq n - 1$. For a gadget or circuit of s wires, this amounts to enumerating at most the following number of sets:

$$\binom{s}{0} + \ldots + \binom{s}{t} \qquad [5.4]$$

When checking a property in the probing model, it suffices to encounter one set representing a failure. The rest of this section exhibits two essential optimizations that reduce the number of sets to consider for the verification.

5.4.1.1. *Considering larger sets*

The first optimization comes from the fact that if a set of probes $\mathcal{W}'$ is a failure for the property, we can always find a set $\mathcal{W}$ such that $\mathcal{W}' \subseteq \mathcal{W}$, which is also a failure. Let us take the example for t-SNI with $t < n$ and a n-share 2-to-m circuit $\widehat{C}$ with input $\widehat{x} = (\widehat{a}, \widehat{b})$ (we can also generalize to ℓ inputs), which is not t-SNI for $t < n$. Suppose now that there exists a set $\mathcal{W}'$ of t_1 internal probes and t_2 output probes such that $t_1 + t_2 < t$ and a perfect simulation of probes in $\mathcal{W}'$ requires sets of input shares (I_1, I_2) such that $|I_1| > t_1$ or $|I_2| > t_1$. Without loss of generality, let $|I_1| > t_1$. Now let I_1' be any subset of $[1; n] \setminus I_1$ such that $|I_1'| = t - |\mathcal{W}'|$, and let $\mathcal{W} = \mathcal{W}' \cup \{\widehat{a}|_{I_1'}\}$. Observe that $|\mathcal{W}| = t$ with t_2 output probes and $t_1 + |I_1'|$ internal probes. Since $I_1 \cap I_1' = \emptyset$, a perfect simulation of probes in $\mathcal{W}$ will require sets $(I_1 \cup I_1', I_2)$ (the set I_2 does not change since we only add probes from input shares of $\widehat{a}$). We now have $|I_1 \cup I_1'| \geq t_1 + |I_1'| + 1$. Thus, $\mathcal{W}$ is also a failure set for t-SNI.

Hence, to check if a given circuit is t-SNI, we only need to check if sets of exactly t probes satisfy the property instead of checking all sets of $\leq t$ probes. If no such set is a failure for t-SNI, then we are sure that all sets of smaller size also satisfy the property. The total number of sets to check in equation [5.4] is reduced to $\binom{s}{t}$ sets. Note that this can be generalized to any property in the probing model.

At this point, `Explore` iterates over all sets of probes of size exactly t and then calls `Verify` on each of them. For each such set $\mathcal{W}$, `Verify` determines the sets of input shares $(I_1, \ldots, I_\ell)$ necessary to perfectly simulate $\mathcal{W}$ and checks if the size of these sets respects the property. Let us suppose that $\mathcal{W}$ is not a failure set, meaning that $(I_1, \ldots, I_\ell)$ are authorized for a perfect simulation. Now, we can construct a set $\mathcal{W}'$ such that $\mathcal{W} \subset \mathcal{W}'$ and a perfect simulation of $\mathcal{W}'$ requires the same sets of input shares $(I_1, \ldots, I_\ell)$. If we can construct $\mathcal{W}'$, then `Explore` can eliminate all subsets of $\mathcal{W}'$ from the verification since we are sure they will not be failure sets.

EXAMPLE 5.6.– Let us consider the randomized arithmetic circuit $\widehat{C}$, which implements the second-order multiplication from Chapter 4. We recall the expressions of the output sharing (the full description is given in the chapter):

$$
\begin{aligned}
c_0 &\leftarrow a_0 \cdot b_0 + r_{0,1} + r_{0,2}\\
c_1 &\leftarrow a_1 \cdot b_1 + (r_{0,1} + a_0 \cdot b_1 + a_1 \cdot b_0) + r_{1,2}\\
c_2 &\leftarrow a_2 \cdot b_2 + (r_{0,2} + a_0 \cdot b_2 + a_2 \cdot b_0) + (r_{1,2} + a_1 \cdot b_2 + a_2 \cdot b_1).
\end{aligned}
$$

To check 2-NI, we need to consider $\binom{27}{2} = 351$ pairs of potential probes. Let us start for instance with $\mathcal{W} = \{a_0 \cdot b_0 + r_{0,1},\ r_{0,1}\}$, which requires the sets of input shares $I_1 = I_2 = \{0\}$ for a perfect simulation (determined using any instantiation of `Verify` from section 5.3.2). This is not a failure set for 2-NI. Now, let

$$
\mathcal{W}' = \{a_0 \cdot b_0 + r_{0,1},\ r_{0,1},\ a_0,\ b_0,\ r_{0,2},\ a_1 \cdot b_2 + r_{1,2}\}
$$

of six potential probes. We can verify that $\mathcal{W}'$ requires the same sets of input shares I_1, I_2 for a perfect simulation, so it is not a failure set either. Thus, we are sure any subset of $\mathcal{W}'$ is not a failure set. We can immediately eliminate the remaining $\binom{6}{2} - 1 = 14$ subsets of $\mathcal{W}'$ from the verification.

The example above demonstrates that we can eliminate many sets of probes from the verification with a single set. The extension of the set of probes with additional probes must be carefully done in order to reduce the complexity of the verification. Moreover, the implementation of `Verify` must allow quick checking if a superset of a previous set would require the same sets of input shares. If done correctly, `Explore` needs only to iterate a few of the $\binom{s}{t}$ sets to conclude on all sets. Current implementations in the automatic verification field show that such optimization on the exploration algorithm drastically reduces the practical complexity.

5.4.1.2. *Eliminating* weaker *observations*

In simulation-based proofs, we consider that variables which contain "more" input shares in their expressions are more advantageous for an attacker. For example, for a 3-share circuit with input $\widehat{a} = (a_0, a_1, a_2)$, if an attacker can probe either a_0 or $a_0 + a_1$, they will indeed choose to probe the second variable, which involves two input shares. In fact, by probing $a_0 + a_1$, only another probe a_2 is needed to retrieve the secret input a. We can apply a preprocessing phase to the input circuit variables to eliminate such *weaker* observations and reduce the total number of wires before enumerating the sets with `Explore`. In Algorithm 5.3, we present a preprocessing algorithm that eliminates different types of weak observations on a circuit with two inputs. It can be generalized to circuits with more inputs.

Algorithm 5.3. Preprocessing to be executed at the beginning of `Explore`

Require: n-share 2-to-m circuit $\widehat{C}$ with input $\widehat{\boldsymbol{x}} = (\widehat{a}, \widehat{b}) \in \mathbb{F}_2^{2 \cdot n}$

Ensure: Processed set of variables V on $\widehat{C}$

1: $V \leftarrow$ set of all variables of $\widehat{C}$

2: $V \leftarrow V \setminus \{a_i\}_{0 \leq i < n}$

3: $V \leftarrow V \setminus \{b_i\}_{0 \leq i < n}$

4: $V \leftarrow V \setminus \{a_i \cdot b_j\}_{0 \leq i,j < n}$

5: **for each** $w \in V$ **do**

6:     $(I_1, I_2) \leftarrow$ sets of input shares appearing in the expression of w

7:     **for each** $w' \in V \setminus \{w\}$ **do**

8:         $(I'_1, I'_2) \leftarrow$ sets of input shares appearing in the expression of w'

9:         $w'' \leftarrow w + w'$

10:         $R'' \leftarrow$ set of random values appearing in the expression of w''

11:         **if** $I'_1 \subseteq I_1$ **and** $I'_2 \subseteq I_2$ **and** $R'' = \emptyset$ **then**

12:             $V \leftarrow V \setminus \{w'\}$

13:         **end if**

14:     **end for**

15: **end for**

16: **return** V

First, on Lines 2, 3 and 4, we remove input shares and products of input shares called *elementary deterministic probes*. If a set of probes $\mathcal{W}$ functionally depends on t input shares, we can always make it depend on $t+t_0$ input shares by adding elementary deterministic probes. For example, if $\mathcal{W}$ does not depend on the input share a_0, then the set $\mathcal{W}' = \mathcal{W} \cup \{a_0\}$ and any set of the form $\mathcal{W}' = \mathcal{W} \cup \{a_0 \cdot b_i\}$ do. With this optimization, the definition of a failure set slightly changes for some properties. In the case of t-NI, a failure set $\mathcal{W}$ such that $|\mathcal{W}| \leq t$ is one where at least $|\mathcal{W}| + 1$ shares (instead of $t+1$) of any of the inputs are needed for a perfect simulation. Indeed, if $\mathcal{W}$ needs $|\mathcal{W}| + 1$ shares, then we can construct a failure for t-NI by completing $\mathcal{W}$ with additional input shares as above.

It is similarly the case for t-probing security. The definition meanwhile remains the same in the case of t-SNI and t-PINI, since we already reason on the number of intermediate probes in the set we consider.

EXAMPLE 5.7.– Let us consider a circuit $\widehat{C}$ with input $\widehat{\boldsymbol{x}} = (\widehat{a}, \widehat{b}) = ((a_0, a_1, a_2, a_3), (b_0, b_1, b_2, b_3)) \in \mathbb{F}_2^8$. Suppose that we would like to check 3-NI and let:

$$\mathcal{W} = \{a_0 + b_0,\ a_1 + a_2\}$$

be a set of potential observations. In order to perfectly simulate this set for 3-NI, `Verify` concludes that the sets of input shares needed are $I_1 = \{0,\ 1,\ 2\}$ and $I_2 = \{0\}$. We can construct a failure for 3-NI from this set by considering, for example, $\mathcal{W}'' = \mathcal{W} \cup \{a_3\}$, where $4 > t$ shares of $\widehat{a}$ are required for a perfect simulation of only three probes.

Next, the goal of the loop on all variables from Lines 5 to 15 of the algorithm is to keep in V the variables that contain the most input shares, on the condition that the same random values are used.

EXAMPLE 5.8.– Let $\widehat{C}$ be some circuit with input $\widehat{\boldsymbol{x}} = (\widehat{a}, \widehat{b}) = ((a_0, a_1), (b_0, b_1)) \in \mathbb{F}_2^4$. Let $w_1 = a_0 \cdot b_1 + r_0$ and $w_2 = a_0 \cdot b_1 + r_0 + a_1 \cdot b_0 = w_1 + a_1 \cdot b_0$ be intermediate variables of $\widehat{C}$ for some uniform random value r_0. For the set $\mathcal{W} = \{w_1, r_0\}$, a perfect simulation requires the input shares a_0 and b_1. Meanwhile, a perfect simulation of $\mathcal{W}' = \{w_2, r_0\}$ requires both shares of both inputs. Hence, instead of calling `Verify` on both sets $\mathcal{W}$ and $\mathcal{W}'$, we can consider $\mathcal{W}'$ where more input shares are required for perfect simulation.

We can generalize the above example as depicted in Algorithm 5.3. Namely, if two variables $w,\ w' \in V$ use the same random values, while w' contains more input shares than w, we can remove w from V. It is proven that a failure set for a property occurs when considering $V \setminus \{w\}$ if and only if it occurs when considering V.

EXAMPLE 5.9.– If we apply Algorithm 5.3 to the second-order multiplication discussed earlier, and in Chapter 4, which initially contains 27 variables, we end up with only seven variables. Precisely, we first remove variables $\{a_0, a_1, a_2, b_0, b_1, b_2\}$, then products of input shares $\{a_i \cdot b_j\}_{\forall 0 \leq i,j \leq 2}$. Finally, with the last step of the algorithm, we can check that the following variables are also eliminated from the set: $\{r_{0,1} + a_0 \cdot b_1,\ r_{0,1} + a_0 \cdot b_1 + a_1 \cdot b_0,\ r_{0,2} + a_0 \cdot b_2,\ r_{0,2} + a_0 \cdot b_2 + a_2 \cdot b_0,\ r_{1,2} + a_1 \cdot b_2\}$.

REMARK 5.1.– For the optimization described in this section, we suppose that `Explore` enumerates all sets of at most t probes. If we want to merge this optimization with the one presented in section 5.4.1.1, where we only consider sets of exactly t probes, we must keep the input shares in the set of variables. In the case of Algorithm 5.3, the variables $\{a_i, b_i\}_{0 \leq i < n}$ must be kept in the set V. This is because of the result presented at the beginning of section 5.4.1.1, where we use such input shares to construct failure sets of size t.

5.4.2. *Random probing model*

In the probing model, it is sufficient to find one failure set to conclude that the circuit is insecure. As discussed in the previous section, many optimizations can be applied to find one as soon as possible or eliminate unnecessary verification. Meanwhile, verifying a security property in the random probing model amounts to finding *all failure sets* to compute the failure probability ε since each variable can leak independently with probability $p \in [0, 1]$. Recall from Chapter 4 that ε can be expressed as a function $f(p)$.

For example, to determine the $(p, \varepsilon = f(p))$-*random probing security* of an n-share ℓ-to-m circuit $\widehat{C}$ with a total of s internal wires, we need to compute:

$$\varepsilon = f(p) = \sum_{i=0}^{s} c_i \cdot p^i \cdot (1-p)^{s-i}. \qquad [5.5]$$

The coefficient c_i is equal to the number of sets $\mathcal{W}$ of exactly i wires that are not independent of the secret inputs. In other words, c_i sets of i wires are considered failures by `Verify`. Similarly to proofs in the probing model, we can use the simulation-based definition to check that a perfect simulation of such a set $\mathcal{W}$ requires at most $n - 1$ shares of each input sharing, directly implying the independence of the secret when the sharings are uniformly and independently generated. The exploration algorithm then needs to enumerate a total of $\binom{s}{0} + \ldots + \binom{s}{s} = 2^s$ sets. We insist that in the random probing model, the s wires include the different copies of the same variable produced using copy gates, contrary to proofs in the probing model, where we do not need to consider the copies. An instantiation of `Explore` for (p, ε)-random probing security is described in Algorithm 5.4. The procedure then returns the list of coefficients for $f(p)$.

In the case of $(t, p, f(p))$-*random probing composability* for a circuit $\widehat{C}$ with input $\widehat{\boldsymbol{x}} \in (\mathbb{K}^n)^\ell$ and output $\widehat{\boldsymbol{y}} \in (\mathbb{K}^n)^m$, a set of internal wires $\mathcal{W}$ (i.e. without output shares) fails if there exists a collection of sets $\boldsymbol{J} = (J_1, \ldots, J_m)$ such that $\forall i \in [1; m]$, $|J_i| \leq t$, and a perfect simulation of $\mathcal{W} \cup \{\widehat{\boldsymbol{y}}|_{\boldsymbol{J}}\}$ requires more than t shares of any of the ℓ input sharings. In order to compute $f(p)$ in this case, we need to consider each possible set of t output shares of each output sharing and check if $\mathcal{W}$ along with any of these sets represent a failure. In other words, for each possible collection of sets $\boldsymbol{J}$ as described above, we compute a list of coefficients $(c_0^{\boldsymbol{J}}, \ldots, c_s^{\boldsymbol{J}})$ as described in Algorithm 5.4, with the condition that at most, t shares of each input are required to perfectly simulate each set of probes along with $\widehat{\boldsymbol{y}}|_{\boldsymbol{J}}$. After computing these coefficients for each possible $\boldsymbol{J}$, the final coefficients for $f(p)$ would be equal to:

$$(c_0, \ldots, c_s) = (\max_{\boldsymbol{J}} c_0^{\boldsymbol{J}}, \ldots, \max_{\boldsymbol{J}} c_s^{\boldsymbol{J}}).$$

Algorithm 5.4. `Explore` for $(p, f(p))$-random probing security

Require: n-share ℓ-to-m circuit $\widehat{C}$ of s internal wires
Ensure: $(c_0, \ldots, c_s)$ coefficients of $f(p)$

$(c_0, \ldots, c_s) \leftarrow (0, \ldots, 0)$
$V \leftarrow$ set of all variables on $\widehat{C}$
for $i = 0$ **to** s **do**
    $S \leftarrow$ set of all subsets $\mathcal{W}$ of V such that $|\mathcal{W}| = i$
    while $S \neq \emptyset$ **do**
        $\mathcal{W} \leftarrow$ a set from S
        $S \leftarrow S \setminus \{\mathcal{W}\}$
        if not `Verify`$(\widehat{C}, \mathcal{W}, (p, \varepsilon)$-random probing security) **then**
            $c_i \leftarrow c_i + 1$
        end if
    end while
end for
return $(c_0, \ldots, c_s)$

The total number of calls to `Verify` is larger than in the case of random probing security for a total of:

$$\binom{n}{t}^m \cdot 2^s, \qquad [5.6]$$

where the factor $\binom{n}{t}^m$ is due to the number of sets containing t shares of each of the m outputs.

In the same context of composition, we can also compute a circuit's probe distribution table (PDT). Each entry of the table is a different function $f_{\boldsymbol{I},\boldsymbol{J}}(p)$ indexed by sets of input shares $\boldsymbol{I}$ and output shares $\boldsymbol{J}$, instead of the number of shares as in the previous properties. Computing the PDT is similar to verifying random probing composability. In other words, we have to consider all possible collections of sets $\boldsymbol{J} = (J_1, \ldots, J_m)$ such that $\forall i \in [1; m],\ |J_i| \leq t$. Then, for each set of internal wires $\mathcal{W}$, instead of checking if it is a failure as in random probing composability, we determine the sets of input shares $\boldsymbol{I} = (I_1, \ldots, I_\ell)$ necessary to produce a perfect simulation of $\mathcal{W} \cup \{\widehat{\boldsymbol{y}}|_{\boldsymbol{J}}\}$, and then we increment the coefficient $c_{|\mathcal{W}|}$ of the corresponding function $f_{\boldsymbol{I},\boldsymbol{J}}(p)$. A complete instantiation is described in

Algorithm 5.5. In this case, we call the function `SIS` (for Sets of Input Shares) instead of `Verify`, which outputs the sets of input shares necessary for a perfect simulation instead of checking if the set represents a failure for the property. Note that both functions are similar; `Verify` and `SIS` can be instantiated in the same way with simulation-based approaches, but `SIS` stops at the step of determining the sets of input shares, while `Verify` additionally tests if their sizes respect the property. The number of calls to `SIS` is the most expensive compared to other properties since we need to consider $2^{n \cdot m + s}$ sets.

Algorithm 5.5. `Explore` for computing the probe distribution table

Require: n-share ℓ-to-m circuit $\widehat{C}$ of s internal wires, with input $\widehat{\boldsymbol{x}}$ and output $\widehat{\boldsymbol{y}}$

Ensure: Probe Distribution Table (PDT) of $\widehat{C}$

PDT $\leftarrow$ table of $2^{n \cdot m} \times 2^{n \cdot \ell}$ entries. Each entry is a list of $s + 1$ coefficients all set to zero.
$V \leftarrow$ set of all intermediate variables on $\widehat{C}$
$JT \leftarrow$ set of the $2^{n \cdot m}$ possible collection of sets $\boldsymbol{J} = (J_1, \ldots, J_m)$
for $i = 0$ **to** s **do**
    $S \leftarrow$ set of all subsets $\mathcal{W}$ of V such that $|\mathcal{W}| = i$
    while $S \neq \emptyset$ **do**
        $\mathcal{W} \leftarrow$ a set from S
        $S \leftarrow S \setminus \{\mathcal{W}\}$
        for each $\boldsymbol{J} \in JT$ **do**
            $\mathcal{W}' \leftarrow W \cup \{\widehat{\boldsymbol{y}}|_{\boldsymbol{J}}\}$
            $\boldsymbol{I} \leftarrow \texttt{SIS}(\widehat{C}, \mathcal{W}')$
            $c_i \leftarrow i^{\text{th}}$ coefficient of PDT[$\boldsymbol{I}$][$\boldsymbol{J}$]
            $c_i \leftarrow c_i + 1$
        end for
    end while
end for
return PDT

For any of the above properties, we can see that computing the failure functions is very costly since we need to enumerate all sets of wires without an upper bound on the size to consider. In addition, specific optimizations of eliminating sets of wires from the verification in the probing model cannot be used in this case. It is generally infeasible to compute all the coefficients, even for small four-share circuits. The rest of this section will discuss some optimizations applicable to the random probing model, which can help accelerate the verification.

5.4.2.1. *Incompressible failure sets*

An *incompressible failure set* $\mathcal{W}$ is a set that is considered a *failure set* for the checked property, and such that none of the subsets of $\mathcal{W}$ are also failures (i.e. $\nexists \mathcal{W}' \subset \mathcal{W}$ such that $\mathcal{W}'$ is also a failure set). Then, all supersets of an *incompressible failure set* are failures. The proof of this property is very similar to the one exhibited at the beginning of section 5.4.1.1 for using larger sets in the probing model. The goal is to avoid enumerating sets containing *incompressible failure sets*. When computing the failure function $f(p)$, `Explore` iterates on sets of wires of size 0 to s. We can benefit from this increasing size to store at each step the set of *incompressible failure sets*. Then, we will have two kinds of failure sets in the next step: ones containing incompressible failure sets and ones deemed failures after calling `Verify`. In Algorithm 5.6, we exhibit this optimization on the verification of $(p, f(p))$-random probing security. Note that the efficiency of this optimization depends on the data structure used to implement the set of incompressible sets `Inc`. For instance, if we implement `Inc` as a list, testing if any set in the list is a subset of $\mathcal{W}$ becomes expensive as the list size grows. Other, more efficient structures include hash tables where the keys are the sets of variables or *tries* (i.e. prefix trees) for the variables (testing membership of a set $\mathcal{W}$ of size k inside a trie has complexity $\theta(k)$). The benefits of this approach generally depend on the size of the circuit and the sets, since when `Inc` becomes very big (i.e. a lot of failures are found within the circuit), then the speed-up becomes close to enumerating all sets. Also, note that this optimization is not directly applicable in the case of PDT computation.

EXAMPLE 5.10.– Let us consider a randomized circuit $\widehat{C}$ with input sharing $\widehat{\boldsymbol{x}} = (\widehat{a}, \widehat{b}) = ((a_0, a_1), (b_0, b_1)) \in \mathbb{F}_2^4$ of s internal wires. Suppose that we would like to check $(p, f(p))$-random probing security and let $\mathcal{W} = \{a_0 + a_1 + r_0,\ r_0\}$, where r_0 is a uniform random value. Calling `Verify` on $\mathcal{W}$ outputs a failure since both shares of $\widehat{a}$ are needed to simulate $\mathcal{W}$ perfectly. Using this conclusion, we can notice that all the supersets of $\mathcal{W}$ will also constitute a failure. When enumerating all sets of size $i \geq 2$ to compute coefficient c_i of $f(p)$, we will call `Verify` on $\binom{s}{i} - \binom{s-2}{i-2}$ instead of $\binom{s}{i}$ sets. If looking for an incompressible set is done with an adapted data structure, this can lead to a significant speedup.

5.4.2.2. *Grouping wires with same expressions*

In most circuits, several wires have the same value assigned to their expressions. It is especially the case in the random probing model, where we also consider copies of variables. Unlike the probing model, where a variable used several times is probed only once, a variable used k times in the random probing model passes through $k - 1$ copy gates of a single input and two outputs, and thus occurs $2 \cdot k - 1$ times in the circuit. Grouping those variables allows us to reduce the number of wires to consider.

Each variable is then represented by (w_i, nb_i) where w_i is its expression and nb_i is the number of its occurrences in the circuit.

Algorithm 5.6. `Explore` for $(p, f(p))$-random probing security with incompressible sets

Require: n-share ℓ-to-m circuit $\widehat{C}$ of s internal wires
Ensure: $(c_0, \dots, c_s)$ coefficients of $f(p)$

$(c_0, \dots, c_s) \leftarrow (0, \dots, 0)$
$V \leftarrow$ set of all variables on $\widehat{C}$
`Inc` $\leftarrow \emptyset$
for $i = 0$ **to** s **do**
  $S \leftarrow$ set of all subsets $\mathcal{W}$ of V such that $|\mathcal{W}| = i$
  while $S \neq \emptyset$ **do**
    $\mathcal{W} \leftarrow$ a set from S
    $S \leftarrow S \setminus \{\mathcal{W}\}$
    if $\exists\, \mathcal{W}' \in$ `Inc` such that $\mathcal{W}' \subseteq \mathcal{W}$ **then**
      $c_i \leftarrow c_i + 1$
    else
      if not `Verify`$(\widehat{C}, \mathcal{W}, (p, \varepsilon)$-random probing security$)$ **then**
        $c_i \leftarrow c_i + 1$
        `Inc` $\leftarrow$ `Inc` $\cup \{\mathcal{W}\}$
      end if
    end if
  end while
end for
return $(c_0, \dots, c_s)$

EXAMPLE 5.11.– Consider the randomized circuit $\widehat{C}$ which implements the first-order multiplication from the first example in section 5.2. We can enumerate all variables as $V = \{(a_0, 3), (a_1, 3), (b_0, 3), (b_1, 3), (r_{0,1}, 3), (a_0 \cdot b_0, 1), (a_0 \cdot b_1, 1), (a_1 \cdot b_0, 1), (a_1 \cdot b_1, 1), (r_{0,1} + a_0 \cdot b_1, 1), ((r_{0,1} + a_0 \cdot b_1) + a_1 \cdot b_0, 1), (c_0, 1), (c_1, 1)\}$. The total number of couples is equal to $|V| = 13$, while the actual number of wires used in $\widehat{C}$ is equal to 23.

Then, we can directly apply `Explore` to the shortened list of wires. The single main difference is that we need to consider the number of occurrences of the variable when updating the coefficients c_i. Instead of the instruction $c_i \leftarrow c_i + 1$, we replace it by $(c_i, \ldots, c_s) \leftarrow$ `updateCoeffs`$((c_i, \ldots, c_s), \mathcal{W})$, where `updateCoeffs` updates several coefficients at a time using the number of occurrences of the variables in $\mathcal{W}$. It can be efficiently implemented as a recursive function that consumes the number of occurrences of the variables to construct the different failure sets from $\mathcal{W}$. Note that this optimization can also be used in the case of PDT computation.

EXAMPLE 5.12.– Consider the same randomized circuit $\widehat{C}$ as in the above example for the first-order multiplication, where we need to compute the failure function $f(p)$ for random probing security. Let $\mathcal{W} = \{(a_1, 3),\ (r_{0,1} + a_0 \cdot b_1, 1),\ (r_{0,1}, 3)\}$. Calling `Verify` on $\mathcal{W}$ will output that both shares of $\widehat{a}$ and a single share of $\widehat{b}$ are needed to simulate $\mathcal{W}$ perfectly. Hence, $\mathcal{W}$ is a failure set. From $\mathcal{W}$, the function `updateCoeffs` needs to update $c_3 \leftarrow c_3 + 9$ because we can add any of the copies of a_1 and any of the copies of $r_{0,1}$ to construct the same failure set. Then, `updateCoeffs` must also update $c_4 \leftarrow c_4 + 18$, $c_5 \leftarrow c_5 + 15$, $c_6 \leftarrow c_6 + 6$, $c_7 \leftarrow c_7 + 1$. The biggest failure set we can construct from $\mathcal{W}$ is of size 7, where we add all copies of the variables.

Even with these optimizations, computing all coefficients of the failure function remains very expensive. An instantiation of `Explore` for random probing-like properties usually takes as input an upper bound $\beta \leq s$ on the coefficients of $f(p)$ to compute in a reasonable execution time. Instead of computing $(c_0, \ldots, c_s)$, `Explore` computes $(c_0, \ldots, c_\beta)$ and potentially a few more coefficients since `updateCoeffs` allows us to update several coefficients at a time. When `Explore` cannot compute all coefficients, it outputs upper and lower bounds on the list of coefficients for $f(p)$. In other words, let $\gamma \leq s$ such that $c_\gamma \neq 0$ and $c_i = 0,\ \forall\, i > \gamma$ (i.e. c_γ is the highest non-zero coefficient in the list $(c_0, \ldots, c_s)$). The lower bound output by `Explore` is the list $(c_0, \ldots, c_\gamma, 0, \ldots, 0)$, while an upper bound is $(c_0, \ldots, c_\gamma, \binom{s}{\gamma+1}, \ldots, \binom{s}{s})$, since we can have at most $\binom{s}{i}$ sets of i variables. Such bounds are sometimes tight enough to have a clear idea of the behavior of the function $f(p)$ without needing to compute all of the coefficients. Other approximations include using Monte Carlo techniques for probability bounding, especially in the case of PDT computation, where many functions $f(p)$ have to be computed.

5.4.3. *Handling physical defaults*

As discussed in Chapter 4, physical defaults (such as glitches and transitions) generate a leakage of several values from a single wire. In the case of glitches, a variable stored in a register resulting from the combination of several operands reveals all of its operands (e.g. an observation on variable $c = a + b$ reveals a and b). In the case of transitions, two values successively stored in the same memory cell may leak at once (e.g. an observation on $c = e + d$ preceded by the instruction $c = a + b$ reveals $e + d$ and $a + b$). In an automatic verification tool, taking physical defaults into account changes how we enumerate the different sets of wires. Typically, a set of t observations $\mathcal{W}$ may leak more than t wires simultaneously. Each wire w is then replaced by a set of wires which leak if w is probed. Some countermeasures can then be added to the description of the circuit to reduce the leakage due to physical defaults (e.g. storing an intermediate result in a register). Nevertheless, the same techniques for `Verify` and optimizations for `Explore` can be applied in this context.

In the case of the robust probing model, we can further eliminate weak observations with Algorithm 5.3 from section 5.4.1.2. We can observe that when a single probed wire w leads to the leakage of several wires $\{w_1, \ldots, w_k\}$, an attacker has more advantage in probing w than each of the wires independently. Hence, we can eliminate $w_1, \ldots, w_k$ from the set of variables V. We can easily prove that if an attack does not occur by considering $V \setminus \{w_1, \ldots, w_k\}$, then no attack occurs by considering V. In the case of t-NI, only t input shares must be enough to simulate potentially more than t leaking wires.

In the case of the robust random probing model, we can also apply the optimizations discussed in section 5.4.2. The main difference is that, as introduced in Chapter 4, the leakage probability of the different variables is not independent in the presence of physical defaults. Computing the failure function then changes with the dependencies between the leaking wires.

5.5. Conclusion

This chapter shows how an automatic verification tool works with `Verify` and `Explore` algorithms. We discussed some of the most deployed techniques to instantiate the `Verify` algorithm and optimizations that can be applied to `Explore` to reduce the verification complexity. While the chapter was not exhaustive on all existing techniques, its goal was to gently introduce the concept of automatic verification of security properties in the probing and random probing models. Note that such verification tools work with software-level and hardware-level implementations. Indeed, the exploration algorithm differs when considering the former or the latter. Some automatic verification tools also take into account models of processors and memory management issues to translate physical defaults and limitations into the verification.

Finally, the field of formal verification is vibrant, and many tools implementing different techniques and use-cases exist in the literature. Once we construct a circuit, define how it will be implemented, and the hypotheses on the surrounding leakage environment, we can choose the tool that best suits our needs.

5.6. Notes and further references

The first-order and second-order multiplication examples were introduced in Ishai et al. (2003).

– Section 5.3. The distribution-based verification technique from section 5.3.1 was introduced and implemented in the tool SILVER in Knichel et al. (2020). The fourier expansion technique at the end of section 5.3.1 was introduced and implemented in the tool Rebecca in Bloem et al. (2018).

The substitution and simulation-based technique from section 5.3.2.1 was introduced and implemented in the tool maskVerif in Barthe et al. (2015).

The linear algebra technique with row reduction from section 5.3.2.2 was introduced and implemented in the tool IronMask in Belaïd et al. (2022).

– Section 5.4. The optimization in the probing model by considering larger sets from section 5.4.1.1 was first introduced in Barthe et al. (2015) with the tool maskVerif.

The optimization in the probing model by eliminating weak observations from section 5.4.1.2 was first introduced in Bordes and Karpman (2021) with the tool matverif.

The exploration algorithms and optimizations in the random probing model from section 5.4.2 were first introduced in Belaïd et al. (2020) with the verification tool VRAPS, and later revisited in Belaïd et al. (2022) with IronMask.

The PDT computation algorithm (i.e. Algorithm 5.5) and using Monte-Carlo techniques for probability bounding in the context of verification were implemented in the verification tool STRAPS in Cassiers et al. (2021).

5.7. Solution to Exercise 5.1

Let us consider the randomized arithmetic circuit $\widehat{C}$ with input $\widehat{\boldsymbol{x}} = (\widehat{a}, \widehat{b}) = ((a_0, a_1, a_2, a_3), (b_0, b_1, b_2, b3)) \in \mathbb{F}_2^8$. and the first set of probes $\mathcal{W} = \{a_0 \cdot b_0 + (a_0 \cdot b_1 + r_{0,1}) + (a_0 \cdot b_2 + r_{0,2}) + (a_0 \cdot b_3 + r_{0,3}) + r_{1,0} + r_{2,0} + r_{3,0},\ r_{1,0} + r_{2,0} + r_{3,0},\ r_{0,1} + r_{2,1} + r_{3,1},\ r_{0,2} + r_{1,2} + r_{3,2},\ r_{0,3} + r_{1,3} + r_{2,3},\ r_{0,2} + r_{1,2},\ r_{0,3} + r_{1,3},\ r_{0,1} + r_{2,1} + r_{3,1},\ a_0 \cdot b_0 + (a_0 \cdot b_1 + r_{0,1}) + (a_0 \cdot b_2 + r_{0,2}) + (a_0 \cdot b_3 + r_{0,3})\}$.

We can rename the expression in $\mathcal{W}$ as follows:

– $w_1 = a_0 \cdot b_0 + (a_0 \cdot b_1 + r_{0,1}) + (a_0 \cdot b_2 + r_{0,2}) + (a_0 \cdot b_3 + r_{0,3}) + r_{1,0} + r_{2,0} + r_{3,0}$;

– $w_2 = r_{1,0} + r_{2,0} + r_{3,0}$;

– $w_3 = r_{0,1} + r_{2,1} + r_{3,1}$;

– $w_4 = r_{0,2} + r_{1,2} + r_{3,2}$;

– $w_5 = r_{0,3} + r_{1,3} + r_{2,3}$;

– $w_6 = r_{0,2} + r_{1,2}$;

– $w_7 = r_{0,3} + r_{1,3}$;

– $w_8 = r_{0,1} + r_{2,1} + r_{3,1}$;

– $w_9 = a_0 \cdot b_0 + (a_0 \cdot b_1 + r_{0,1}) + (a_0 \cdot b_2 + r_{0,2}) + (a_0 \cdot b_3 + r_{0,3})$.

While this is a big set of expressions, the simplification rules from section 5.3.2.1 allow us to easily conclude on the input shares necessary for a perfect simulation of $\mathcal{W}$. **Rule 1** cannot conclude immediately since all shares of input $\widehat{a}$ appear in the expressions in $\mathcal{W}$. However, by iterating on the three verification rules, we observe that $w_1 = w_9 + w_2$, $w_3 = w_8$, $w_4 = w_6 + r_{3,2}$, and $w_5 = w_7 + r_{2,3}$. Then, we can check that perfectly simulation $\mathcal{W}$ is equivalent to perfectly simulating $\mathcal{W}_1 = \{0,\ r_{1,0}+r_{2,0}+r_{3,0},\ r_{0,1}+r_{2,1}+r_{3,1}\ r_{3,2},\ r_{2,3},\ r_{0,2}+r_{1,2},\ r_{0,3}+r_{1,3},\ 0,\ a_0 \cdot b_0 + (a_0 \cdot b_1 + r_{0,1}) + (a_0 \cdot b_2 + r_{0,2}) + (a_0 \cdot b_3 + r_{0,3})\}$. Finally, we can apply **Rule 2** to mask some expressions by random values to obtain the following equivalent set $\mathcal{W}_2 = \{0,\ r_{1,0},\ r_{2,1},\ r_{3,2},\ r_{2,3},\ r_{0,2},\ r_{0,3},\ 0,\ r_{0,1}\}$, where no input shares appear anymore in the expressions. Hence, no input shares are required to simulate the set $\mathcal{W}_2$ perfectly and, equivalently, the set $\mathcal{W}$.

Now let us consider the second example with the set of probes $\mathcal{W}' = \{a_0 \cdot b_0 + r_{0,1} + b_0 \cdot r_0 + b_0 \cdot r_1,\ a_1 \cdot b_1 + r_{1,1} + b_1 \cdot r_1 + b_1 \cdot r_2,\ r_{0,1},\ r_{1,1},\ r_0\}$. After applying the three rules on $\mathcal{W}'$, we end up with the equivalent set $\mathcal{W}_1' = \{a_0 \cdot b_0 + b_0 \cdot r_0 + b_0 \cdot r_1,\ a_1 \cdot b_1 + b_1 \cdot r_1 + b_1 \cdot r_2,\ r_{0,1},\ r_{1,1},\ r_0\}$, where the first two expressions involve two shares of both inputs $\widehat{a}$ and $\widehat{b}$. No more simplifications can be done on $\mathcal{W}_1'$ with additional applications of the rules, which means that a perfect simulation of $\mathcal{W}$ potentially requires the knowledge of the first and second shares of both inputs. Meanwhile, we can observe that $\mathcal{W}_1'$ can be rewritten as $\mathcal{W}_1' = \{(a_0+r_0+r_1)\cdot b_0,\ (a_1+r_1+r_2)\cdot b_1,\ r_{0,1},\ r_{1,1},\ r_0\}$, where r_0, r_1 and r_2 are additive to the shares of input $\widehat{a}$. Since r_2 appears only once in $\mathcal{W}_1'$, we can use it to mask the expression of $(a_1+r_1+r_2)$, which then enables us to use r_1 to mask the expression of $(a_0+r_0+r_1)$. Finally, we can check that $\mathcal{W}_2' = \{r_1 \cdot b_0,\ r_2 \cdot b_1,\ r_{0,1},\ r_{1,1},\ r_0\}$ has an identical distribution as $\mathcal{W}'$ and $\mathcal{W}_1'$. In this new set $\mathcal{W}_2'$, no shares of input $\widehat{a}$ are required to produce a perfect simulation, only b_0 and b_1, shares of $\widehat{b}$. Hence, this is also the case for the set $\mathcal{W}'$. This example shows us that we can add another simplification step to the previously defined steps, where we try to factorize the expressions and check if any random values are additive on the input shares in the different factors.

5.8. References

Barthe, G., Belaïd, S., Dupressoir, F., Fouque, P.-A., Grégoire, B., Strub, P.-Y. (2015). Verified proofs of higher-order masking. In *EUROCRYPT 2015*, Oswald, E. and Fischlin, M. (eds). Springer, Heidelberg.

Belaïd, S., Coron, J.-S., Prouff, E., Rivain, M., Taleb, A.R. (2020). Random probing security: Verification, composition, expansion and new constructions. In *CRYPTO 2020*, Micciancio, D. and Ristenpart, T. (eds). Springer, Heidelberg.

Belaïd, S., Mercadier, D., Rivain, M., Taleb, A.R. (2022). Ironmask: Versatile verification of masking security. In *43rd IEEE Symposium on Security and Privacy, SP 2022*. San Francisco. doi: 10.1109/SP46214.2022.9833600.

Bloem, R., Groß, H., Iusupov, R., Könighofer, B., Mangard, S., Winter, J. (2018). Formal verification of masked hardware implementations in the presence of glitches. In *EUROCRYPT 2018*, Nielsen, J.B. and Rijmen, V. (eds). Springer, Heidelberg.

Bordes, N. and Karpman, P. (2021). Fast verification of masking schemes in characteristic two. In *EUROCRYPT 2021*, Canteaut, A. and Standaert, F.-X. (eds). Springer, Heidelberg.

Cassiers, G., Faust, S., Orlt, M., Standaert, F.-X. (2021). Towards tight random probing security. In *CRYPTO 2021*, Malkin, T. and Peikert, C. (eds). Springer, Heidelberg.

Ishai, Y., Sahai, A., Wagner, D. (2003). Private circuits: Securing hardware against probing attacks. In *CRYPTO 2003*, Boneh, D. (ed.). Springer, Heidelberg.

Knichel, D., Sasdrich, P., Moradi, A. (2020). SILVER – Statistical independence and leakage verification. In *ASIACRYPT 2020*, Moriai, S. and Wang, H. (eds). Springer, Heidelberg.

PART 2

Cryptographic Implementations

6

Hardware Acceleration of Cryptographic Algorithms

Lejla BATINA,[1] Pedro Maat COSTA MASSOLINO[2] and Nele MENTENS[3,4]

[1] *Radboud University, Nijmegen, Netherlands*
[2] *PQShield, Oxford, United Kingdom*
[3] *Leiden University, Netherlands*
[4] *KU Leuven, Belgium*

6.1. Introduction

In this chapter, we discuss the use of hardware platforms for the implementation of cryptographic algorithms. While most traditional cryptographic algorithms can be implemented in software on general-purpose microprocessors, there are applications that require cryptographic algorithms to be implemented in hardware. Depending on the specific application, there are several reasons for moving to hardware. The first reason is that hardware platforms are typically more energy efficient than software platforms. Energy efficiency is important in applications that are battery-powered or relying on energy-harvesting. The second reason is that hardware implementations can typically achieve a higher performance than software implementations. This is important for applications that require a low latency or a high throughput. The third reason why a hardware implementation is preferred over a software implementation is that it is typically more difficult to tamper with hardware than with software, that is, an adversary can more easily modify the software of a system than the hardware.

Embedded Cryptography 2,
coordinated by Emmanuel PROUFF, Guénaël RENAULT,
Matthieu RIVAIN and Colin O'FLYNN.

There is also a downside to implementing cryptographic algorithms in hardware, and this has to do with flexibility. Software can be modified after deployment, while hardware cannot. When we look at the whole spectrum of implementation platforms that we refer to as hardware, however, there also exist hardware platforms that are programmable like software. The most popular programmable hardware platform is a field-programmable gate array (FPGA). As opposed to an application-specific integrated circuit (ASIC), which is a fixed chip, an FPGA is a regular structure of configurable cells with configurable routing in between the cells. In the past decades, FPGAs have moved from mainly homogeneous systems to more heterogeneous systems with dedicated building blocks for specific applications, in addition to the regular configurable cells. Given that FPGAs are produced in high volumes, it is feasible for commercial vendors to follow the latest technology nodes. For that reason, and thanks to the availability of application-specific dedicated building blocks, FPGAs are very attractive implementation platforms. They combine the energy-efficiency and the performance of hardware with the flexibility of software. In Figure 6.1, the properties of ASICs, FPGAs and general-purpose microprocessors are summarized.

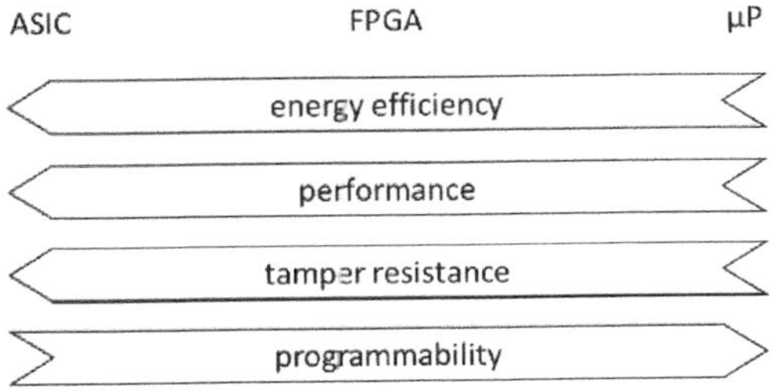

Figure 6.1. *Comparison of the implementation properties of ASICs (application-specific integrated circuits), FPGAs (field-programmable gate arrays) and μPs (general-purpose microprocessors)*

6.2. Hardware optimization of symmetric-key cryptography

While software implementations concentrate on optimally executing algorithms in chunks of 8, 16, 32 or 64 bits, depending on the datapath width of the processor, hardware implementations are capable of processing all bits in parallel. The following operations are commonly used in symmetric-key cryptographic algorithms: shift operations, logical operations (XOR, AND, etc.), additions modulo 2^n and substitution boxes (with a typical input/output size between 3 and 8 bits). The most intensively studied components, with the largest range of optimization possibilities, are substitution boxes or S-boxes. The example we use in this section to illustrate the hardware implementation of S-boxes is the S-box in the Advanced Encryption Standard (AES).

6.2.1. *Hardware implementation of the AES S-box*

The S-box appears 16 times in each round of AES. In the key schedule, the S-box is also used four times for the calculation of each round key. This leads to a total of 200, 240 and 280 S-box computations in one AES encryption, for key lengths of 128, 192 or 256 bits, respectively. As a result, improving the efficiency of one S-box has a significant effect on the efficiency of the overall AES encryption. The implementation approaches of the AES S-box can be divided into three categories:

– look-up table (LUT)-based implementation in logic;

– LUT-based implementation in embedded memory;

– composite field based implementation in logic.

In the first option, the 8-bit S-box is implemented as a LUT using logic gates, typically in a structure with a logical depth equal to two. This approach leads to the fastest implementation, but consumes a lot of resources. For FPGA implementations, a more suitable solution relies on the use of embedded memory blocks, like Block RAM (BRAM). Because a lot of BRAM is available on the FPGA anyway, this saves area in the configurable part of the FPGA. However, the hardware architecture has to be redesigned in order to be able to address the BRAM and to cope with the one-cycle delay for reading values from the RAM. Another solution, which is more compact than the LUT approach and can also be implemented with logical gates, takes advantage of the arithmetic structure of the S-box by using composite field arithmetic. We elaborate on this option in the next paragraph.

6.2.2. *Composite field based implementation of the AES S-box*

The AES standard describes the S-box computation as a sequence of two operations:

1) a multiplicative inverse in the Galois field $GF(2^8)$, where the byte consisting of all zero-bits is mapped to itself;

2) an affine transformation, represented as:

$$\begin{bmatrix} c_0 \\ c_1 \\ c_2 \\ c_3 \\ c_4 \\ c_5 \\ c_6 \\ c_7 \end{bmatrix} = \begin{bmatrix} 1\,0\,0\,0\,1\,1\,1\,1 \\ 1\,1\,0\,0\,0\,1\,1\,1 \\ 1\,1\,1\,0\,0\,0\,1\,1 \\ 1\,1\,1\,1\,0\,0\,0\,1 \\ 1\,1\,1\,1\,1\,0\,0\,0 \\ 0\,1\,1\,1\,1\,1\,0\,0 \\ 0\,0\,1\,1\,1\,1\,1\,0 \\ 0\,0\,0\,1\,1\,1\,1\,1 \end{bmatrix} \begin{bmatrix} b_0 \\ b_1 \\ b_2 \\ b_3 \\ b_4 \\ b_5 \\ b_6 \\ b_7 \end{bmatrix} + \begin{bmatrix} 1 \\ 1 \\ 0 \\ 0 \\ 0 \\ 1 \\ 1 \\ 0 \end{bmatrix},$$

in which $B = [b_0, b_1, b_2, b_3, b_4, b_5, b_6, b_7]^T$ and $C = [c_0, c_1, c_2, c_3, c_4, c_5, c_6, c_7]^T$ are the inputs and outputs of the affine transformation.

The irreducible polynomial $m(x) = x^8 + x^4 + x^3 + x + 1$ defines the field $\mathrm{GF}(2^8)$. An element of the field is represented by a polynomial of degree 7: $A(x) = a_7x^7 + a_6x^6 + a_5x^5 + a_4x^4 + a_3x^3 + a_2x^2 + a_1x + a_0$. In order to compute $B(x)$, the inverse of $A(x)$, the equation $A(x) \cdot B(x) \equiv 1 \mod m(x)$ needs to be satisfied.

Calculating an inverse in $\mathrm{GF}(2^8)$ is done through the use of composite field arithmetic for field extensions of degree 2. $\mathrm{GF}((2^4)^2)$ can be viewed as a field extension of degree 2 over $\mathrm{GF}(2^4)$. An irreducible polynomial $f(x) = x^2 + \alpha x + \beta$, with $\alpha, \beta \in \mathrm{GF}(2^4)$, is used to generate the field $\mathrm{GF}((2^4)^2)$ as an extension of $\mathrm{GF}(2^4)$. The extension field $\mathrm{GF}((2^4)^2)$ is a two-dimensional vector space over $\mathrm{GF}(2^4)$. An element $\Delta \in \mathrm{GF}((2^4)^2)$ can be written as $\Delta = \delta_1 x + \delta_0$, with $\delta_1, \delta_0 \in \mathrm{GF}(2^4)$. The inversion can be calculated as follows using operations in the subfield $\mathrm{GF}(2^4)$:

$$\Delta^{-1} = \delta_1(\delta_1^2\beta + \delta_1\delta_0\alpha + \delta_0^2)^{-1}x + (\delta_0 + \delta_1\alpha)(\delta_1^2\beta + \delta_1\delta_0\alpha + \delta_0^2)^{-1}. \quad [6.1]$$

When using extensions fields for the inversion in the AES S-box, there are two implementation options. Either the subfield operations are directly performed in $\mathrm{GF}(2^4)$ or the equation can be applied recursively by using the tower field $\mathrm{GF}(((2^2)^2)^2)$. In any case, the transformation from $\mathrm{GF}(2^8)$ to $\mathrm{GF}((2^4)^2)$ or $\mathrm{GF}(((2^2)^2)^2)$ needs to be done, as well as the inverse transformation. The latter can be combined with the affine transformation that follows the finite field inversion in the AES S-box. In order to optimize the implementation of the AES S-box in hardware, the coefficients of the irreducible polynomials are chosen in such a way that circuit area of the transformation matrices and the computations in the subfields is minimized. Other work also proposes the use of normal bases instead of only polynomial bases to achieve the smallest reported circuit area.

6.3. Modular arithmetic for hardware implementations

In this section, we turn our attention to implementations of the most frequently used public-key cryptosystems such as RSA and elliptic curve cryptography (ECC). To this end, we focus on the most critical operations that are modular exponentiation and accordingly modular multiplication.

Modular exponentiation is executed via repeated modular multiplication, which is the core operation of the RSA cryptosystem. It is also present in many other cryptographic algorithms including those based on ECC and other curve-based cryptosystems, such as hyperelliptic-curve crypto algorithms, isogeny-based cryptosystems, etc. In particular, the main building block in ECC-based cryptosystems is scalar multiplication. This operation requires multiplying a point on a curve with a large scalar and this is done via repeated group operations in the elliptic curve group. This group consists of all points on the elliptic curve, together with the point at infinity that serves as the "zero" in this group, and the addition operation (the group operations, that is, point additions and doublings are implemented as sequences of instructions in the underlying field (GF(p) or GF(2^n))). Of all finite field arithmetic operations, the most critical one is modular multiplication where different approaches can be used.

6.3.1. *Montgomery's arithmetic*

The most popular algorithm for modular multiplication is the Montgomery's multiplication method. The approach of Montgomery avoids the time-consuming trial division that is the common bottleneck of other algorithms. His method is proven to be very efficient, especially in hardware. We give here the details for all of the Montgomery's arithmetic.

Let N be an RSA modulus. For a word base $b = 2^\alpha$, the Montgomery radix (or parameter) R is typically chosen such that $R = 2^r = (2^\alpha)^n > N$. Let x be an odd integer represented by its radix b representation $x = \sum_{i=0}^{n-1} x_i b_i$. There is a one-to-one correspondence between each element $x \in \mathbb{Z}_N$ and its representation $X = xR \pmod N$. This representation is usually referred to as the Montgomery representation. Addition and subtraction of two elements in Montgomery representation is again an element in Montgomery representation. This fact is also used for efficient implementations of RSA and ECC over $\mathbb{F}_p$.

For efficient implementation of modular multiplication, the crucial operation is modular reduction, which is computed as follows. Let N and R be as above, so $R > N$ and $gcd(N; R) = 1$ and let T be an integer such that $0 \leq T < NR$. A method to compute $TR^{-1} \bmod N$ is called the Montgomery reduction.

To compute Montgomery's modular multiplication (MMM), we proceed as follows. We consider the Montgomery's product of two elements X and Y that are written in the Montgomery representation. The product of X and Y is the element Z for which $z = (xy) \pmod N$. More precisely, for $X = xR \pmod N$ and $Y = yR \pmod N$, the following holds: $Z = zR \pmod N = [(xy) \pmod N]R \pmod N = (xR \pmod N)(yR \pmod N) = XYR^{-1} \pmod N$. The computation is executed as in Algorithm 6.1 due to Peter Montgomery from 1985.

Algorithm 6.1. Montgomery's multiplication algorithm

Require: Integers $N = (N_{n-1}, \ldots, N_1, N_0)_b, x = (x_{n-1}, \ldots, x_1, x_0)_b, y = (y_{n-1}, \ldots, y_1, y_0)_b$, with $0 \leq x, y < N$ and $gcd(N, b) = 1$, $R = b^n$ and $N' = -N^{-1} \pmod b$

Ensure: $xyR^{-1} \pmod N$

1: $T \leftarrow 0$ (Notation $(T = (t_l, t_{l-1}, \ldots, t_1, t_0)_b)$.)
2: **for** $i = 0, \ldots, n-1$ **do**
3: $\quad m \leftarrow (t_0 + x_i y_0)N' \pmod b$
4: $\quad T \leftarrow (T + x_i y + m_i N)/b$
5: **end for**
6: **if** $T \geq N$ **then**
7: $\quad T \leftarrow T - N$
8: **end if**
9: **return** T

In this original version of Montgomery's multiplication algorithm, a reduction was needed after each multiplication (Step 6 in Algorithm 6.1). The input had the restriction $X, Y < N$ and the output T was bounded by $T < 2N$. Hence, if $T > N$, N must be subtracted so that the output can be used as the input of the next multiplication. This step then not only slows down the algorithm, but more importantly introduces a vulnerability to side-channel attacks. To overcome this issue, another bound was proposed. For example, when $X, Y < 2N$ and $R > 4N$, it can be shown that the result of a Montgomery multiplication remains within the input bound $2N$ so $XYR^{-1} \pmod N < 2N$. In this way, the exponentiation using MMM can complete without any conditional subtraction. As the final step, the Montgomery multiplication function applied to T and 1 maps the final result back to the integers domain.

Instead of executing a Montgomery multiplication, it is also possible to perform an integer multiplication followed by a Montgomery reduction. Montgomery reduction is shown in Algorithm 6.2.

6.3.2. *Barret reduction*

Another modular reduction method is Barrett reduction shown in Algorithm 6.3. This version of the algorithm is not the same as seen in Barrett original publication, but a more generalized version. Barrett's reduction operates through approximation of the quotient computed in $\hat{q} = \lfloor((\lfloor x/2^{n+\beta}\rfloor) \cdot (\lfloor 2^{n+\alpha}/N\rfloor))/b^{\alpha-\beta}\rfloor$. The approximated quotient $\hat{q}$ requires the computation of the constant $\mu = (\lfloor b^{2n}/N\rfloor)$ which only varies with the modulus N. The value of μ can be deployed as constant in the case of ECC or lattice cryptosystems, however in the case of RSA the value has to be computed during the key generation.

Algorithm 6.2. Montgomery's reduction algorithm

Require: Integers $N = (N_{n-1}, \ldots, N_1, N_0)_b, x = (x_{2n-1}, \ldots, x_1, x_0)_b$, with $gcd(N, b) = 1$, $R = b^n$, $N' = -N^{-1} \pmod{b}$ and $x \leq NR$

Ensure: $xR^{-1} \pmod{N}$

$T \leftarrow x$ (Notation $(T = (t_{2n-1}, t_{2n-2}, \ldots, t_1, t_0)_b)$.)
for $i = 0, \ldots, n-1$ **do**
  $m_i \leftarrow t_i N' \pmod{b}$
  $T \leftarrow T + m_i N b^i$
end for
$T \leftarrow T/b^n$
if $T \geq N$ **then**
  $T \leftarrow T - N$
end if
return T

Algorithm 6.3. Barrett's reduction algorithm

Require: Integers $N = (N_{n-1}, \ldots, N_1, N_0)_2, x = (x_{n+\gamma-1}, \ldots, x_1, x_0)_2$, with $0 \leq x, \gamma \leq n, \alpha \geq \gamma + 1, \beta \leq -2, \mu = \lfloor 2^{n+\alpha}/N \rfloor, N_{n-1} \neq 0$.

Ensure: $T = x \pmod{N}$

$\hat{q} \leftarrow \lfloor x/2^{n+\beta} \rfloor$
$\hat{q} \leftarrow \hat{q}\mu$
$\hat{q} \leftarrow \lfloor \hat{q}/2^{\alpha-\beta} \rfloor$
$T \leftarrow x - \hat{q}N$
if $T \geq N$ **then**
  $T \leftarrow T - N$
end if
return T

When comparing Montgomery reduction and Barret reduction, Montgomery is much faster when using multi-words arithmetic, even though Barrett does not require values to be converted like Montgomery reduction. However, when using single-word arithmetic, such as done in post-quantum lattices schemes, Barrett's reduction can be faster than Montgomery reduction.

6.3.3. *Implementations using residue number system*

Residue number system (RNS) is a special representation of an integer by its residues in a given base of co-prime numbers. RNS is advantageous for parallelism in computations and thus can speed up public-key cryptographic implementations.

In cryptographic applications of public-key cryptography, the recommended bit length varies between 256 bits (for ECC) to 3,072 bits (for RSA). RNS-based implementations offer the possibility to perform the required modular operations on smaller numbers, that is, residues, so similar to the idea behind the Chinese remainder theorem (CRT). Similarly, RNS computations can be executed independently for each residue, boosting performance through parallelization of the computation.

In RNS, an integer X is represented by a set of individual n moduli x_i ($x \overset{RNS}{\rightarrow} X : (x_1, x_2, ...x_n)$) of a given RNS basis $B : (m_1, m_2, ...m_n)$ as long as $0 \leq x < M$ where $M = \prod_{i=1}^{n} m_i$ is the RNS dynamic range and all m_i are pair-wise relatively prime. The elements of the RNS basis need to be co-prime in order to uniquely reconstruct X.

We remind the reader here that CRT states the following: we consider a n-tuple of coprime numbers $(m_1, m_2, \ldots, m_n)$. We note $M = \prod_{i=1}^{n} m_i$. If we consider the n-tuple $(x_1, x_2, \ldots, x_n)$ of integers such that $x_i < m_i$, then there exists a unique X, such that $0 \leq X < M$ and $x_i = X \pmod{m}_i = |X|_{m_i}$ for $1 \leq i \leq n$.

It is evident that RNS is based on the CRT. Each x_i in an RNS basis can be derived from X by calculating $x_i = \langle x \rangle_{m_i} = x \ mod \ m_i$.

Assuming that we have two integers a and d represented in RNS as $A : (a_1, a_2, ...a_n)$ and $D : (d_1, d_2, ...d_n)$, we can obtain addition, subtraction and multiplication in RNS as $A \oslash D = (\langle a_1 \oslash d_1 \rangle_{m_1}, ... \langle a_n \oslash d_n \rangle_{m_n})$, where $\oslash : (+, -, \times)$. Exact division by D coprime with M is equivalent to multiplying by the inverse $\langle D^{-1} \rangle_M$. Since RNS is a non-positional representation, comparisons, divisions and modular reductions are complex operations, which are performed either by converting the number from RNS to binary representation or by using base extension algorithms.

Binary reconstruction from RNS representation can be done either by using CRT or through a mixed radix system (MRS) transformation. Using CRT, an integer x can be written as $x = \left\langle \sum_{i=1}^{n} \left\langle x_i \cdot M_i^{-1} \right\rangle_{m_i} \cdot M_i \right\rangle_M$, where $M_i = \frac{M}{m_i}$ and M_i^{-1} is the multiplicative inverse of M_i modulo m_i. As the modular inverse is computationally demanding, it is typically computed by introducing a correction factor w, where $x = \sum_{i=1}^{n} \left\langle x_i \cdot M_i^{-1} \right\rangle_{m_i} \cdot M_i - w \cdot M$. Using the MRS approach, this correction factor can be avoided but RNS numbers need to be transformed into MRS representation (so-called a weighted moduli RNS variant) and then from this representation to binary numbers. This technique will be explained in the next section.

For elliptic curves defined over $\mathbb{F}_p$, all $\mathbb{F}_p$ operations (addition, subtraction, multiplication) are modular operations. The RNS modular multiplication over $\mathbb{F}_p$ is a computationally difficult operation, which can be realized through the RNS Montgomery multiplication algorithm that avoids modular inversions, but includes base extension operations instead.

6.4. RSA implementations

In this section, we revisit the critical issues to address when implementing the two traditional public-key cryptosystems: RSA and ECC. As explained above, one of the most important contribution to efficient hardware implementations was the modular multiplication according to Montgomery. Until today, this method remains as a predominant choice in hardware design solutions for the public-key cryptosystems. In addition, in the late 1990s after the invention of side-channel attacks and seeing the impact they can have on cryptographic implementations, a lot of work was completed on revisiting the existing algorithms and modifying them to become less vulnerable to side-channel attacks. Basically, the challenge lies in dealing with the intrinsically nonconstant time computation for modular arithmetic. The improvements and new proposals include new bounds for the Montgomery's algorithms, revisiting the original versions of RNS and CRT and other parameter- or platform-specific solutions.

At the time of writing this chapter, RSA and ECC are the still the most commonly used public-key cryptosystems in real-world applications. Typically, ECC is predominantly used for constrained platforms and embedded systems such as smart cards, passports and other small gadgets, for example, crypto wallets and secure tokens. Implementations options vary from software running on microcontrollers or dedicated hardware such as ASIC cores and FPGAs. Here, we focus on hardware implementations' aspects. Below we mention some relevant contributions to both types of hardware implementations.

6.4.1. *Previous works on RSA implementations*

By means of the CRT, the speed for the RSA decryption scheme can be increased up to four times. This possibility is very attractive for practical applications and is hence predominantly present in the RSA deployments in the real world. However, it includes some pitfalls on security, so it has to be carefully implemented.

There is a long history of RSA hardware implementations. The first RSA chip design was conceptualized by the RSA inventors Rivest, Shamir and Adleman in 1980. In contained approximately 40,000 transistors but failed to work reliably. The challenge of implementing modular reduction efficiently in hardware resulted several methods being proposed in the 1980s, most notable ones are due to Montgomery and Barrett.

In 1985, Kochanski proposed an RSA chip in which the modular exponentiation operation was divided between a CMOS array and a microprocessor. A full length modular multiplication took place in the CMOS array by the commands from a microcontroller. The complete modular exponentiation was performed by microcontroller. In 1986, Rankine introduced an implementation of a 512-bit modulus exponentiator for RSA applications. As a result, a wide range of applications including smart cards was claimed. This device was able to execute a 512-bit exponentiation in < 1 s.

The work of Tenca and Koç (1999) defines precisely the notion of scalable hardware. They have introduced a pipelined Montgomery multiplier, which has the ability to work on any given operand precision and is adjustable to the available area and/or performance. This work was later extended to the higher radix algorithms in another paper by Tenca et al. (2001).

6.4.2. *ECC implementations over prime fields*

Most of the work on hardware implementations of ECC is for binary fields as the arithmetic in this case is easier to implement and area and power consumption are smaller than in the case of prime fields. However, for platforms where specialized arithmetic co-processors for finite field arithmetic are available, there is an advantage in using prime fields. It is this not surprising than some authors considered a single platform for both cryptosystems, RSA and ECC over prime field, with the scalability feature as critical.

The first documented ECC processor for prime fields was proposed by Orlando and Paar (2001). This so-called elliptic curve processor (ECP) is scalable in terms of area and speed and especially suited for FPGAs. The work of Batina et al. (2004) introduced a unique hardware module, that is, a scalable Montgomery multiplication-based module, that can be used for both ECC and RSA with different parameters and implementation options (e.g. with or without CRT).

Later works were mainly focusing on compactness and the challenge to get ECC ready for constrained environments, including RFID tags and sensor nodes.

With this goal in mind and the fact that the power and energy budgets are extremely low, the only feasible choice was to use binary fields ECC.

6.5. Post-quantum cryptography

Hardware implementations of post-quantum cryptosystems are generally more complex than traditional ECC and RSA implementations, because of the different types of operations applied. When designing hardware circuits for RSA and ECC, designers focus on implementing the basis operations such as modular arithmetic for integers bigger than 16 bytes or modular exponentiation for RSA or elliptic curve point addition or scalar multiplication. However, post-quantum primitives employ a much smaller arithmetic that can fit around one to four bytes and have a lot of unique procedures that are used to compute the entire algorithm. For example, in the case of the cryptosystem Kyber, the encryption procedure requires sampling, NTT, inverse of NTT, convolution, compression, decompression, decoding and encoding. Implementing a separate custom hardware circuit for each operation would be costly in terms of hardware resources, verification and maintainability, therefore most designers have opted to some operations in hardware, while others in software. In the example of Kyber, designers mostly focus the hardware resources on the NTT, the inverse of the NTT and the hash function used during the sampling, while the other operations are done in software. Therefore, post-quantum primitives are more complex than RSA and ECC because they apply different types of operations, which all have to be implemented. This increase of complexity has, as a consequence, increased the number of hardware and software co-designs in the hardware implementations literature.

The underlying arithmetic of lattice-based cryptosystems for key encapsulation such as Crystals-Kyber, Saber, NTRU and NTRU Prime is based on polynomials and matrices with coefficients smaller than 16-bits. Unlike, previous cryptosystems based on large integer but few operands, these schemes operate with small integers and many operands. This change from few bigger operands to many small operands pushes the optimization to not only the base arithmetic, but also on the higher level functions. One of the main operations that needs such optimization is a multiplication between polynomials or a matrix vector multiplication. In the case of Crystals-Kyber, the polynomial multiplication is done by using polynomials in the NTT domain, then performing the convolution, and if required the removal of the NTT domain. In the case of other schemes, like Saber or NTRU Prime, the polynomial multiplication can be done through the NTT+convolution+inverse NTT, but also through Karatsuba or Toom-Cook. While the polynomial multiplications in Crystals-Kyber can also be computed with Karatsuba or Toom-Cook, the scheme requires that some of the messages to be in the NTT domain, therefore implementations that do not use the convolution are slower than the ones that use it.

Code-based cryptosystems employ more than one type of underlying arithmetic. The KEM's Classic McEliece, BIKE and HQC employ arrays and matrices over binary fields during the public-key operations. However, during the private-key operations, Classic McEliece and HQC require binary extensions field arithmetic, and BIKE still does use a binary field plus some integer arithmetic. This difference between private and public-key operations is because the code structure is hidden during the public-key operations and it is assumed to be a linear block code with a binary field. When generating or using the private keys, it will use the arithmetic of the underlying error-correcting code, which in the case of Classic McEliece are binary Goppa codes and HQC is Reed-Solommon codes. BIKE uses MDPC codes, which also uses a binary field during it is private key operations, but the underlying decoder requires some counting, which is why it requires some basic integer arithmetic. In the case of the Classic McEliece, the decoder for binary Goppa codes may use some complex arithmetic, since it can be done through the use of the Fourier transform.

Multivariate quadratics signatures schemes, like Rainbow, require a binary extensions field that is smaller or equal to 8-bits, as well as being arranged on matrix and vector operations. Therefore, the optimization on those schemes have been focused on fast matrix and vector operations, such as multiplication and row reduction.

In the case of SIKE or other cryptosystem based on isogenies between supersingular elliptic curves, the arithmetic is based on big integers, like in those of discrete logarithm in prime-based elliptic curves, therefore several known techniques to accelerate and implement them can be applied. However, there are some differences that needs to be taken into account in order to accelerate even further, such as the use of quadratic extensions fields and integers ranging from around 400 to 800 bits.

Finally, the signature schemes based on hashes and multiparty computation of block ciphers require the underlying primitive to be as much optimized as possible.

6.6. Conclusion

Implementing algorithms in hardware always leads to a trade-off between performance, energy consumption and area overhead. Each specific application or product is constrained with respect to these nonfunctional properties. When it comes to cryptographic hardware, the security strength of the resulting implementation has to be taken into account additionally, which makes the trade-off even more complex. Therefore, accelerating cryptographic algorithms through hardware implementation is never exclusively oriented towards a performance boost only, but should always take into account all other constraints of the system.

6.7. Notes and further references

The AES algorithm referred to in section 6.2.1 is described in Daemen and Rijmen (2002).

The equation, shown in section 6.2.2 to compute the multiplicative inverse in $GF(2^8)$ using operations in the subfield $GF(2^4)$ is based on observations made in Paar (1994) and Guajardo and Paar (1997).

Rudra et al. (2001) elaborate on the use of the composite field $GF((2^4)^2)$ for the AES S-box inversion, but no hardware implementation is presented. Wolkerstorfer et al. (2002) applied the idea to make a compact implementation of the AES S-box.

Satoh et al. (2001) work in the tower field $GF(((2^2)^2)^2)$, where they make fixed choices for the coefficients of the irreducible polynomials. Mentens et al. (2005) explore the design space for $GF(((2^2)^2)^2)$ based S-boxes in polynomial bases to reduce the circuit area. David Canright proposes the use of normal bases and manages to reduce the circuit area even further Canright (2005).

– Section 6.3.1. More on the Montgomery's parameter bound adjustment can be found in the paper of Walter (2001) and Batina and Muurling (2002). The work of Walter offers many other useful results for Montgomery's arithmetic in implementations.

– Section 6.3.2. More information on Barret reduction can be found in Barrett (1987), Knezevic et al. (2010) and Dhem (1998). One work that compares Montgomery and Barret reduction algorithms is by Bosselaers et al. (1994).

– Section 6.3.3. The earliest known statement of the CRT theorem was by the Chinese mathematician Sunzi in the third-century CE.

Binary reconstruction from RNS representation can be done with the concept of Cox and Rower as introduced in Nozaki et al. (2001).

Some recent result that demonstrates how to benefit from the parallelism of RNS for hardware implementations of public-key cryptosystems can be found in the works of Bajard et al. (2001, 2004).

The RNS Montgomery multiplication algorithm that avoids modular inversions, but requires base extension operations is described in Bajard et al. (1997, 2001); Fournaris et al. (2016); Fournaris (2017).

– Section 6.4.1. The two most well-known methods for modular reduction are due to Montgomery and Barrett Großschädl (2000) and Barrett (1987). Starting from the first RSA chip design, by the RSA inventors Rivest (1982) many other proposal follows and interested reader is pointed to the following papers: Kochanski (1986) and Rankine (1987).

The works on efficient implementation of a Montgomery multiplier for PKC featuring scalability were done by Tenca and Koç (1999); Tenca et al. (2001).

– Section 6.4.2. More recent works on implementations on programmable hardware such as FPGAs include Orlando and Paar (2001); Güneysu and Paar (2008).

A proposal for a single scalable module performing Montgomery arithmetic for RSA and ECC is described in Batina et al. (2004).

– Section 6.5. Examples of a few hardware implementations of KEMs and signatures cryptosystems based on lattices have been presented as a pure hardware solution (Zhao et al. 2022; Xing and Li 2021; Land et al. 2021; Imran et al. 2021; Marotzke 2020; Howe et al. 2018), or a CPU with special instructions (Alkim et al. 2020; Fritzmann et al. 2020), or only with a few operations/accelerators done in hardware (Banerjee et al. 2019; Dang et al. 2019). Code-based cryptography has been implemented as a pure hardware solution (Wang et al. 2018; Hu et al. 2020; Eisenbarth et al. 2009; Richter-Brockmann et al. 2022) or as a hardware/software co-design (Ghosh et al. 2012). In the case of signatures, cryptosystems based on multivariate quadratics have been done mostly as a pure hardware solution (Balasubramanian et al. 2008; Tang et al. 2011; Ferozpuri and Gaj 2018). There is also implementation for signature cryptosystems based on hash functions and zero-knowledge computations of block ciphers as a pure hardware solution (Amiet et al. 2020; Kales et al. 2020), or as hardware/software co-design (Wang et al. 2019). Finally, implementations of cryptosystems based on isogenies of supersingular elliptic curves with a hardware/software co-design are from Massolino et al. (2020); Longa et al. (2021) and Roy et al. (2020), and as a pure hardware solution from Liu et al. (2020) and Farzam et al. (2021).

6.8. References

Alkim, E., Evkan, H., Lahr, N., Niederhagen, R., Petri, R. (2020). ISA extensions for finite field arithmetic. *IACR TCHES*, 2020(3), 219–242.

Amiet, D., Leuenberger, L., Curiger, A., Zbinden, P. (2020). Fpga-based sphincs$^+$ implementations: Mind the glitch. In *23rd Euromicro Conference on Digital System Design*, August 26–28. IEEE, Kranj. doi: 10.1109/DSD51259.2020.00046.

Bajard, J., Didier, L., Kornerup, P. (1997). An RNS Montgomery modular multiplication algorithm. In *Proceedings 13th IEEE Symp. on Comp. Arithmetic*, Asilomar.

Bajard, J., Didier, L., Kornerup, P. (2001). Modular multiplication and base extensions in residue number systems. In *Proceedings 15th IEEE Symposium on Computer Arithmetic, ARITH-15 2001*, Vail.

Bajard, J.-C., Imbert, L., Liardet, P.-Y., Teglia, Y. (2004). Leak resistant arithmetic. In *CHES 2004*, Joye, M. and Quisquater, J.-J. (eds). Springer, Berlin, Heidelberg.

Balasubramanian, S., Bogdanov, A., Rupp, A., Ding, J., Carter, H.W. (2008). Fast multivariate signature generation in hardware: The case of rainbow. In *16th IEEE International Symposium on Field-Programmable Custom Computing Machines, FCCM 2008*, 14–15 April, Stanford. doi: 10.1109/ FCCM.2008.52.

Banerjee, U., Ukyab, T.S., Chandrakasan, A.P. (2019). Sapphire: A configurable crypto-processor for post-quantum lattice-based protocols. *IACR TCHES*, 2019(4), 17–61.

Barrett, P. (1987). Implementing the Rivest Shamir and Adleman public key encryption algorithm on a standard digital signal processor. In *CRYPTO'86*, Odlyzko, A.M. (ed.). Springer, Berlin, Heidelberg.

Batina, L. and Muurling, G. (2002). Montgomery in practice: How to do it more efficiently in hardware. In *Topics in Cryptology – CT-RSA 2002, The Cryptographer's Track at the RSA Conference*, Preneel, B. (ed.). Springer, Berlin, Heidelberg. doi: 10.1007/3-540-45760-7_4.

Batina, L., Bruin-Muurling, G., Örs, S.B. (2004). Flexible hardware design for RSA and elliptic curve cryptosystems. In *Topics in Cryptology – CT-RSA 2004, The Cryptographers' Track at the RSA Conference 2004*, Okamoto, T. (ed.). Springer, Berlin, Heidelberg. doi: 10.1007/978-3-540-24660-2_20.

Bosselaers, A., Govaerts, R., Vandewalle, J. (1994). Comparison of three modular reduction functions. In *CRYPTO'93*, Stinson, D.R. (ed.). Springer, Berlin, Heidelberg.

Canright, D. (2005). A very compact s-box for AES. In *International Workshop on Cryptographic Hardware and Embedded Systems*. Springer, Berlin, Heidelberg.

Daemen, J. and Rijmen, V. (2002). *The Design of Rijndael*. Springer, Berlin, Heidelberg.

Dang, V.B., Farahmand, F., Andrzejczak, M., Gaj, K. (2019). Implementing and benchmarking three lattice-based post-quantum cryptography algorithms using software/hardware codesign. In *International Conference on Field-Programmable Technology, FPT 2019*, December 9–13. IEEE, Tianjin. doi: 10.1109/ICFPT47387.2019.00032.

Dhem, J.-F. (1998). Design of an efficient public-key cryptographic library for RISC-based smart cards. PhD Thesis, UCLouvain, Leuven.

Eisenbarth, T., Güneysu, T., Heyse, S., Paar, C. (2009). MicroEliece: McEliece for embedded devices. In *CHES 2009*, Clavier, C. and Gaj, K. (eds). Springer, Berlin, Heidelberg.

Farzam, M.H., Sarmadi, S.B., Mosanaei-Boorani, H., Alivand, A. (2021). Hardware architecture for supersingular isogeny Diffie-Hellman and key encapsulation using a fast Montgomery multiplier. *IEEE Trans. Circuits Syst. I Regul. Pap.*, 68(5), 2042–2050. doi: 10.1109/TCSI.2021.3062871.

Ferozpuri, A. and Gaj, K. (2018). High-speed FPGA implementation of the NIST round 1 rainbow signature scheme. In *2018 International Conference on ReConFigurable Computing and FPGAs*, December 3–5. IEEE, Cancun. doi: 10.1109/RECONFIG.2018.8641734.

Fournaris, A.P. (2017). *Fault and Power Analysis Attack Protection Techniques for Standardized Public Key Cryptosystems*. Springer, Cham.

Fournaris, A.P., Papachristodoulou, L., Batina, L., Sklavos, N. (2016). Residue number system as a side channel and fault injection attack countermeasure in elliptic curve cryptography. In *2016 International Conference on Design and Technology of Integrated Systems in Nanoscale Era (DTIS)*. IEEE, Istanbul.

Fritzmann, T., Sigl, G., Sepúlveda, J. (2020). RISQ-V: Tightly coupled accelerators for post-quantum cryptography. *IACR TCHES*, 2020(4), 239–280.

Ghosh, S., Delvaux, J., Uhsadel, L., Verbauwhede, I. (2012). A speed area optimized embedded co-processor for McEliece cryptosystem. In *23rd IEEE International Conference on Application-Specific Systems, Architectures and Processors*, July 9–11, Delft. doi: 10.1109/ASAP.2012.16.

Großschädl, J. (2000). High-speed RSA hardware based on Barret's modular reduction method. In *CHES 2000*, Çetin Kaya, K. and Paar, C. (eds). Springer, Berlin, Heidelberg.

Guajardo, J. and Paar, C. (1997). Efficient algorithms for elliptic curve cryptosystems. In *Annual International Cryptology Conference*, Kaliski, B.S. (ed.). Springer, Berlin, Heidelberg.

Güneysu, T. and Paar, C. (2008). Ultra high performance ECC over NIST primes on commercial FPGAs. In *CHES 2008*, Oswald, E. and Rohatgi, P. (eds). Springer, Berlin, Heidelberg.

Howe, J., Oder, T., Krausz, M., Güneysu, T. (2018). Standard lattice-based key encapsulation on embedded devices. *IACR TCHES*, 2018(3), 372–393.

Hu, J., Baldi, M., Santini, P., Zeng, N., Ling, S., Wang, H. (2020). Lightweight key encapsulation using LDPC codes on FPGAs. *IEEE Trans. Computers*, 69(3), 327–341. doi: 10.1109/TC.2019.2948323.

Imran, M., Almeida, F., Raik, J., Basso, A., Roy, S.S., Pagliarini, S. (2021). Design space exploration of SABER in 65 nm ASIC. In *ASHES@CCS 2021: Proceedings of the 5th Workshop on Attacks and Solutions in Hardware Security, Virtual Event, Republic of Korea*, Chang, C., Rührmair, U., Katzenbeisser, S., Mukhopadhyay, D. (eds). ACM, New York. doi: 10.1145/3474376.3487278.

Kales, D., Ramacher, S., Rechberger, C., Walch, R., Werner, M. (2020). Efficient FPGA implementations of LowMC and Picnic. In *CT-RSA 2020*, Jarecki, S. (ed.). Springer, Berlin, Heidelberg.

Knezevic, M., Vercauteren, F., Verbauwhede, I. (2010). Faster interleaved modular multiplication based on Barrett and Montgomery reduction methods. *IEEE Trans. Computers*, 59(12), 1715–1721. doi: 10.1109/TC.2010.93.

Kochanski, M. (1986). Developing an RSA chip. In *CRYPTO'85*, Williams, H.C. (ed.). Springer, Berlin, Heidelberg.

Land, G., Sasdrich, P., Güneysu, T. (2021). A hard crystal – Implementing dilithium on reconfigurable hardware. Report 2021/355, Cryptology ePrint Archive [Online]. Available at: https://eprint.iacr.org/2021/355.

Liu, W., Ni, Z., Ni, J., Rafferty, C., O'Neill, M. (2020). High performance modular multiplication for SIDH. *IEEE Trans. Comput. Aided Des. Integr. Circuits Syst.*, 39(10), 3118–3122. doi: 10.1109/TCAD.2019.2960330.

Longa, P., Wang, W., Szefer, J. (2021). The cost to break SIKE: A comparative hardware-based analysis with AES and SHA-3. In *CRYPTO 2021*, Malkin, T. and Peikert, C. (eds). Springer, Berlin, Heidelberg.

Marotzke, A. (2020). A constant time full hardware implementation of streamlined NTRU prime. In *Smart Card Research and Advanced Applications*, Liardet, P. and Mentens, N. (eds). Springer, Cham. doi: 10.1007/978-3-030-68487-7_1.

Massolino, P.M.C., Longa, P., Renes, J., Batina, L. (2020). A compact and scalable hardware/software co-design of SIKE. *IACR TCHES*, 2020(2), 245–271.

Mentens, N., Batina, L., Preneel, B., Verbauwhede, I. (2005). A systematic evaluation of compact hardware implementations for the Rijndael S-Box. In *Cryptographers' Track at the RSA Conference*. Springer, Berlin, Heidelberg.

Nozaki, H., Motoyama, M., Shimbo, A., Kawamura, S. (2001). Implementation of RSA algorithm based on RNS Montgomery multiplication. In *CHES 2001*, Çetin Kaya, K., Naccache, D., Paar, C. (eds). Springer, Berlin, Heidelberg.

Orlando, G. and Paar, C. (2001). A scalable GF(p) elliptic curve processor architecture for programmable hardware. In *CHES 2001*, Çetin Kaya, K., Naccache, D., Paar, C. (eds). Springer, Berlin, Heidelberg.

Paar, C. (1994). Efficient VLSI architectures for bit-parallel computation in Galois fields. PhD Thesis, University of Duisburg-Essen, Duisburg and Essen.

Rankine, G. (1987). THOMAS – A complete single chip RSA device (informal contribution). In *CRYPTO'86*, Odlyzko, A.M. (ed.). Springer, Berlin, Heidelberg.

Richter-Brockmann, J., Chen, M., Ghosh, S., Güneysu, T. (2022). Racing BIKE: Improved polynomial multiplication and inversion in hardware. *IACR Trans. Cryptogr. Hardw. Embed. Syst.*, 2022(1), 557–588. doi: 10.46586/tches.v2022.i1.557-588.

Rivest, R.L. (1982). A short report on the RSA chip. In *CRYPTO'82*, Chaum, D., Rivest, R.L., Sherman, A.T. (eds). Plenum Press, New York.

Roy, D.B., Fritzmann, T., Sigl, G. (2020). Efficient hardware/software co-design for post-quantum crypto algorithm SIKE on ARM and RISC-V based microcontrollers. In *IEEE/ACM International Conference On Computer Aided Design*. IEEE, San Diego. doi: 10.1145/3400302.3415728.

Rudra, A., Dubey, P.K., Jutla, C.S., Kumar, V., Rao, J.R., Rohatgi, P. (2001). Efficient Rijndael encryption implementation with composite field arithmetic. In *International Workshop on Cryptographic Hardware and Embedded Systems*, Koç, Ç.K., Naccache, D., Paar, C. (eds). Springer, Berlin, Heidelberg.

Satoh, A., Morioka, S., Takano, K., Munetoh, S. (2001). A compact Rijndael hardware architecture with B-box optimization. In *International Conference on the Theory and Application of Cryptology and Information Security*, Boyd, C. (ed.). Springer, Berlin, Heidelberg.

Tang, S., Yi, H., Ding, J., Chen, H., Chen, G. (2011). High-speed hardware implementation of Rainbow signature on FPGAs. In *Post-Quantum Cryptography – 4th International Workshop, PQCrypto 2011*, Yang, B.-Y. (ed.). Springer, Berlin, Heidelberg.

Tenca, A.F. and Koç, Ç. (1999). A scalable architecture for Montgomery multiplication. In *CHES'99*, Çetin Kaya, K. and Paar, C. (eds). Springer, Berlin, Heidelberg.

Tenca, A.F., Todorov, G., Koç, Ç. (2001). High-radix design of a scalable modular multiplier. In *CHES 2001*, Çetin Kaya, K., Naccache, D., Paar, C. (eds). Springer, Berlin, Heidelberg.

Walter, C.D. (2001). Sliding windows succumbs to Big Mac attack. In *CHES 2001*, Çetin Kaya, K., Naccache, D., Paar, C. (eds). Springer, Berlin, Heidelberg.

Wang, W., Szefer, J., Niederhagen, R. (2018). FPGA-based Niederreiter cryptosystem using binary Goppa codes. In *Post-Quantum Cryptography – 9th International Conference, PQCrypto 2018*, Lange, T. and Steinwandt, R. (eds). Springer, Berlin, Heidelberg.

Wang, W., Jungk, B., Wälde, J., Deng, S., Gupta, N., Szefer, J., Niederhagen, R. (2019). XMSS and embedded systems. In *SAC 2019*, Paterson, K.G. and Stebila, D. (eds). Springer, Berlin, Heidelberg.

Wolkerstorfer, J., Oswald, E., Lamberger, M. (2002). An ASIC implementation of the AES SBoxes. In *Cryptographers' Track at the RSA Conference*, Preneel, B. (ed.). Springer, Berlin, Heidelberg.

Xing, Y. and Li, S. (2021). A compact hardware implementation of CCA-secure key exchange mechanism CRYSTALS-KYBER on FPGA. *IACR TCHES*, 2021(2), 328–356.

Zhao, C., Zhang, N., Wang, H., Yang, B., Zhu, W., Li, Z., Zhu, M., Yin, S., Wei, S., Liu, L. (2022). A compact and high-performance hardware architecture for crystals-dilithium. *IACR Trans. Cryptogr. Hardw. Embed. Syst.*, 2022(1), 270–295.

7

Constant-Time Implementations

Thomas Pornin
NCC Group, Canada

7.1. What does constant-time mean?

7.1.1. *Timing attacks*

Timing attacks are a class of side-channel attacks that rely on time measurements. They were first described by Kocher (1996), in the context of asymmetric algorithms using modular arithmetics, and especially modular exponentiation, on big integers (RSA, Diffie–Hellman, etc.). In this context, an implementation would exhibit a total execution time correlated with some part of the secret elements. The attacker would measure the total execution time of the implementation over various known inputs, and use the bias to infer information on the private key bits.

This first class of timing-based side-channels was later expanded to cover, more generally, all side-channels that can be detected through timing measurements, not only the execution time of the attacked system itself. For instance, the layout of data in cache memory left after execution of the implementation can be obtained by measuring the time needed for access to various data elements, even though the attacked system has already completed execution at this point. A particular implementation of an algorithm is said to be *constant-time* if it is inherently immune to timing attacks in that extended meaning.

Embedded Cryptography 2,
coordinated by Emmanuel Prouff, Guénaël Renault,
Matthieu Rivain and Colin O'Flynn. © ISTE Ltd 2025.

The expression "constant-time" is somewhat misleading:

– A constant-time implementation does not necessarily execute in a constant amount of time. Timing attacks try to recover secret information (in particular private keys); if variations in execution time do not depend on secret data, or cannot be practically correlated with secret data, then a non-constant execution time does not prevent the implementation from being constant-time.

– A contrario, a constant execution time does not guarantee an implementation to be constant-time. Indeed, the system state left after execution of the implementation may have secret-dependent characteristics that can potentially be measured by the attacker through timings. Contents of cache memory, keeping a partial trace of the memory access pattern of the implementation, are a prime target for such attacks.

The salient points of the definition of constant-time code are as follows:

– *Inherent immunity*: constant-time implementation is about using code techniques that *cannot* be exploited through timing attacks. The attacker is supposed to be able to perform precise measurements with no noise on any specific instruction. There are possible mitigations against some timing attacks, for example, random masking, cache line pre-filling, or adding some random delays, but their effectiveness relies on specific assumptions on how the attack itself is implemented; as such, these mitigations are not considered to be part of the concept of "constant-time".

– *Hardware dependence*: an implementation can be said to be constant-time only relatively to a specific model of the hardware on which the code executes. This model is, mostly, a definite set of assumptions on the timing behavior of individual operations, and what secret-dependent state variations may be detected through timing measurements.

We specifically do not address random blinding and masking, which are common defenses against a range of side-channel attacks (see Chapter 1). Such operations would nominally fall under the definition above, in that any information on the masked values, leaked through timing measurements, would be inexploitable by attackers; however, the mask generation itself, as well as its application on the data and ulterior removal, would still need to be constant-time in the sense developed in this chapter.

7.1.2. *Applicability and importance*

It is reasonable to ask why, among all possible side-channels, timing-related attacks deserve a special treatment, so that most general-purpose cryptographic libraries focus on having constant-time implementations but not, for instance, implementations protected against differential power analysis. One main reason is that timing attacks can sometimes be exercised remotely. For most side-channel attacks, the attacker must bring some dedicated measuring apparatus into the physical vicinity of the attacked system, for example, an oscilloscope plugged into the power lines of the target device. However, in the case of timing attacks:

– Modern communication hardware, optimized to have the lowest possible latency, allows for precise remote measurements, especially when trying to pinpoint slight differences between two similar experiments. Sub-microsecond precision can be achieved from several hundreds of miles away, over standard optic fiber networks.

– Measuring timing differences only requires a precise clock, and such a clock is a standard issue in general-purpose hardware, since all modern CPUs now include simple cycle counters. No dedicated apparatus is necessary; a simple shell account on a virtual machine in a cloud is enough to begin attempting timing attacks on neighboring servers.

Thus, contrary to most side-channel attacks, timing attacks cannot be fully mitigated by local physical actions such as shielding or secure premises. It can be hard to assess whether some mitigations are really effective at preventing timing attacks with unknown characteristics. Constant-time implementations, on the other hand, nominally provide immunity to the whole class of timing attacks.

Another reason for the focus on timing attacks is that defending against them is possible in a generic way. Preventing side-channel attacks requires first establishing a model of the side-channel, and that depends heavily on the involved hardware. In the case of timing attacks, though, it is possible to use a generic model that applies to most CPUs, from small embedded systems to large servers. As will be detailed in section 7.2, timing-related side-channels in current CPUs boil down to a few opcodes with a variable execution time, and memory access patterns (the latter covers both data accesses and conditional jumps, since a conditional jump changes the sequence of instruction addresses that the CPU fetches during execution). It is therefore possible to make an implementation of an algorithm that will defeat timing attacks on at least most systems, regardless of usage context; this is what constant-time implementations are about. In constrast, differential power analysis cannot really be prevented abstractly for all possible hardware on which a given implementation may run.

7.1.3. *Example: rejection sampling*

To illustrate the subtleties of the definition of "constant-time", consider the following piece of C code that generates a random integer d modulo, with another integer q provided as parameter; this integer could be, for instance, a private key for ECDSA when working with a curve of order q:

```
void generate_key(uint8_t *d, const uint8_t *q, size_t len)
{
    for (;;) {
        randombytes(d, len);
        for (int i = len - 1; i >= 0; i --) {
```

```
                if (d[i] > q[i]) {
                    break;
                }
                if (d[i] < q[i]) {
                    return;
                }
            }
        }
    }
```

In this code, integers are represented as byte sequences in little-endian order. The outer `for` loop implements rejection sampling in order to generate an integer uniformly distributed modulo q: random bytes are obtained from a PRNG and then interpreted as an integer value; if the value is lower than the modulus, then it is returned, otherwise the process loops. The inner `for` loop is the comparison between the candidate d and the modulus, proceeding byte by byte in most-to-least significant order.

In this code there are two conditional jumps that operate on secret data (the elements of `d[]`). A conditional jump leaks information through timing since the overall execution time, as well as the memory access pattern, will depend on whether the jump was taken or not.

Thus, conditional jumps on secret data usually mean that the implementation is not constant-time. However, in this example, only the second test (`d[i] < q[i]`) breaks constant-time discipline; the first one does not.

The first test can still be considered constant-time because the test will match only for candidates who are rejected, and a rejected candidate is not, in fact, secret. For the actually returned secret key, this test was necessarily never matched (otherwise the key would not have been returned), and thus the matching or non-matching of that test yields no information whatsoever on the returned key.

The second test, however, is not constant-time. Indeed, it will return the value d as soon as it can be decided that the candidate d is in the proper range, without inspecting the lower order bytes. Thus, the number of iterations of the inner loop, and therefore the execution time and the memory access pattern will depend on how many of the top bytes of the returned d are equal to the top bytes of q.

A constant-time version of this function is as follows:

```
void generate_key(uint8_t *d, const uint8_t *q, size_t len)
{
    for (;;) {
        randombytes(d, len);
        unsigned cc = 0;
        for (int i = len - 1; i >= 0; i --) {
            cc = d[i] - q[i] - cc;
            cc = (cc >> 8) & 1;
        }
        if (cc) {
            return;
        }
    }
}
```

In this version, the comparison is performed by computing the subtraction $d - q$. The computation proceeds from low to high order bytes, and the variable `cc` contains the running borrow. The result of the subtraction is not kept, but the borrow will be non-zero if and only if the result is negative, that is, $d < q$. It is easily seen that the inner loop will always have exactly `len` iterations, and will access bytes in an order that does not depend on the value of d. A final conditional jump remains: this is the test corresponding to rejection sampling, and, as explained above, it does not break constant-time discipline.

A few points are noteworthy in that example:

– A conditional jump on secret data does not *necessarily* imply that the implementation is not constant-time. Analysis may show that the information leak cannot be exploited, as shown above in the case of rejection sampling. Interestingly, when a value d is rejected, that value *was* secret and sensitive at the time the test was performed; but the fact that the test matched turned that d into a non-secret.

– The example above used bytes (`uint8_t` type in C), but a similar implementation could be made with larger words. If 32-bit words were used, then the potential information leak would be rarer, to the extent that it may evade detection by generic testing processes. This highlights the importance of analyzing the source code itself, not just relying on sample measurements, when writing constant-time code. A contrario, if using large enough words (e.g. 64 bits), then the potential information leak could be argued to become rare enough that it cannot be exploited in practice, thereby restoring security, even with a nominally non-constant-time implementation. Note that event rarity can be, in general, hard to guarantee in cryptographic implementations, when working over attacker-provided data: the attacker may choose data that specifically exercises edge cases; however, in this example, the `randombytes()` function is not attacker-controlled.

– Implicit in this analysis is that the source PRNG (the `randombytes()` function) is cryptographically secure. When a candidate is rejected, this inherently leaks the information that the PRNG produced a value that was not lower than q. If the PRNG is assumed to be secure, then this yields no usable information on subsequent outputs from the same PRNG. If the source PRNG were not that secure (e.g. if the PRNG was seeded on a low entropy password, susceptible to dictionary attacks), then the analysis would not hold, and rejection sampling would not be constant-time.

A case can be made that any system using cryptography necessarily includes a formally non-constant-time processing step. For instance, when verifying a MAC on some data, the outcome (accept or reject), and thus the subsequent behavior of the application, depends on the value of the secret key. More generally, we can classify every data element within a running implementation as "secret" or "non-secret", such that any operation that involves some secret input produces a secret output, potentially subject to side-channel leakage. However, there will be a few "exit points" in which secret data are converted into non-secret, because the properties of the involved cryptographic algorithms provide us such guarantees: when encrypting secret data, the ciphertext is non-secret, because that is the whole point of encrypting the data! A practical approach to constant-time implementations is thus to "follow the secrets" throughout the execution, taking care to only apply operations that do not leak usable information through timing-based side-channels, until the secret reaches one of these exit points for which cryptographic analysis tells us that the conversion from secret to non-secret classification is safe.

7.2. Low-level issues

7.2.1. *CPU execution pipeline*

There is a large variety of hardware architectures, covering the whole range from the smallest embedded CPUs (e.g. in smartcards) to large multicore processors running in powerful servers. However, some CPU characteristics are now almost universal due to the wide adoption of RISC architectural design elements, in particular; we review here a few key concepts that are needed to properly assess whether a given implementation is constant-time (see Chapter 2 of Volume 1 for a more detailed discussion of program execution in modern CPUs).

Modern CPUs tend to execute instructions in the following way:

1) Instructions are decoded from their in-memory representation. For large CPUs with CISC-like instructions (especially x86), this decoding is a full translation layer that breaks down instructions into a stream of simpler, RISC-like instructions (called

micro-operations or μops in Intel terminology); smaller CPUs (e.g. embedded ARM CPUs) will usually stick to a RISC-like instruction set, making this translation layer mostly trivial.

2) The μops are processed over a pipeline which handles dependencies between instructions, and decides when an instruction processing can start. Each instruction may execute over several cycles (sometimes more than a dozen), but most hardware units allow a new instruction to start before the previous one has finished executing. Such overlapping execution between two instructions is feasible as long as the second instruction does not need the output of the first as an input operand. If the pipeline detects such a dependency, then a pipeline stall may occur.

3) To help with breaking false dependencies, registers may be renamed. The programming model may offer a number of named registers to hold data (e.g. `eax` on x86 CPUs), but these get translated into internal registers at execution time, with dynamic allocation. For instance, if an instruction reads register `eax`, then a later instruction writes into the same `eax`, the two instructions do not depend on each other, and the second instruction may start executing before the first has completed, even though they apparently work over the same resource (the register `eax`). The register renaming unit will allocate two separate internal registers in that case.

4) Large CPUs may feature out-of-order execution: if two instructions do not depend on each other, then the second one may be executed before the first one; if the first instruction is waiting for some input, while the second is already ready to start. The range over which the CPU may pick candidates for out-of-order execution is the *pipeline depth* and exceeds 100 instructions in modern CPUs.

5) Execution can be *speculative*: some instructions may be executed out-of-order under some heuristic assumption; the instruction output will be committed when these assumptions can be verified, or discarded if the assumptions turn out not to be fulfilled. These assumptions can be of many types, but typically include branch prediction (see section 7.2.4) and memory independence (a read from RAM at a dynamically computed address is often assumed not to be at the same address as a write to RAM that occurred in the few previous instructions).

6) Exceptional conditions may interrupt the pipeline execution. The pipeline may stall while the CPU switches to an internal routine made of μops that handle a special case; this is called *microcode*. Microcode is used for all "complex" operations (e.g. related to change of privilege level or hypervisor management), but may also be triggered by some instructions with rare edge cases (typically floating-point operations).

7) Memory accesses are performed both for instruction fetching, and for data reading and writing. Complex hierarchies of caches are used to heuristically reduce access latency.

The exact details vary a lot between CPU architectures but also CPU models. Roughly speaking, deep pipelines and out-of-order speculative execution are found mostly on the larger processors, but basic pipelined execution is used even in the smallest embedded CPUs. Pipeline depth and management are rarely fully documented, and may differ between any two versions of the same CPU core. For the purpose of writing constant-time implementations of cryptographic algorithms, the main points to remember are as follows:

– When exactly instructions will execute cannot be truly predicted by the developer. This is handled by the CPU using scheduling techniques that are hidden from the programmer's model, poorly documented, and subject to change.

– Instruction scheduling works by maintaining *data dependencies*, but does not (normally) depend on data contents. When an instruction executes, and possible pipeline stalls, depend on, for instance, which register is used or which memory slot is accessed, but not on the contents of the said register or memory slot.

– Exceptional cases that interrupt processing may depend on the values which are processed, and pipeline flushing may have a relatively high cost (several dozens of cycles) that could be leveraged for a timing attack.

The impossibility to reliably predict execution scheduling implies that many cheap mitigations for timing attacks lose effectiveness on newer CPU designs. For instance, following the first publications of cache attacks, some table-based AES implementations tried to make "safe" accesses to tables (at secret-dependent addresses) by adding a few extra reads, so that all cache lines corresponding to the table were touched; however, in newer CPU designs, these extra accesses tend to be executed much earlier than the actual secret accesses, because the latter must wait for the secret index to be computed, while the extra accesses used indexes that could be computed dozens of cycles in advance by the CPU.

In practice, instructions that may lead to timing-based side-channels fall into three categories, which we will now detail: instructions with a variable execution time, memory accesses at secret addresses, and conditional and indirect jumps.

7.2.2. *Variable time instructions*

In modern CPUs, instructions tend to be implemented with a fixed non-iterative circuit, since this is what most benefits performance: in a fixed loop-less circuit, one execution can be started every cycle, even if the computation requires several cycles to complete. Moreover, handling potential early availability of results, for circuits that can do so, consumes some extra silicon resources, and is therefore done only for instructions for which an actual performance benefit can be extracted in that way. Thus, in practice, only a few purely computational instructions (without memory accesses) may exhibit a variable execution time.

7.2.2.1. *Integer division*

Integer division opcodes typically exhibit a high execution latency, moreover variable depending on inputs. For instance, an ARM Cortex M4 CPU has signed and unsigned 32-bit division opcodes (`idiv` and `udiv`) that complete in 2–12 cycles. The exact conditions for early termination are rarely documented (e.g. the M4 technical reference manual only says that the division operation terminates "when the divide calculation completes"). Execution time is typically roughly proportional to the difference in sizes of the dividend and divisor, with possible shortcuts when the divisor is a power of two, but no general rule can be reliably inferred.

Some CPUs lack a division opcode (especially the small embedded CPUs, such as the ARM Cortex M0+), in which case any integer division will be implemented by an ad hoc routine provided with the compiler for the programming language used. Whether this routine is constant-time depends on that compiler (it rarely is in practice).

7.2.2.2. *Integer multiplication*

In recent CPU designs, integer multiplication is generally implemented with an optimized circuit that has constant-time behavior. However, older CPUs, and CPUs for small embedded systems, may still have multiplication opcodes with a varying execution time. The most frequently encountered CPUs of that category include the following:

– The PowerPC cores of the 6xx, 7xx (G3) and 74xx (G4) lines implement early returns in some cases, mostly when one operand is short (with signed or unsigned interpretation). These cores have been reused in many embedded CPUs, under various names (e.g. the radiation-shielded RAD750, popular in aerospace systems, uses a G3 core).

– The ARM Cortex M3, which follows the ARMv7m architecture, has a constant-time $32 \times 32 \rightarrow 32$ multiplication opcode, but also signed and unsigned $32 \times 32 \rightarrow 64$ multiplication opcodes which are *not* constant-time, taking between three and five cycles. There are variants of the M3 core meant for security applications (e.g. the SC300), which can optionally be synthesized with a constant-time multiplier, for a lower average performance (since the multiplier always has the highest possible cost) but no timing-based side-channel on multiplications.

– The ARM Cortex M0+, a very low-power core, has a constant-time $32\times32 \rightarrow 32$ opcode, but no $32 \times 32 \rightarrow 64$ opcode at all. The latter is thus implemented with a compiler-provided routine, which may or may not be constant-time.

Varying-time integer multiplications are the most vexing issue for constant-time implementations, because multiplications are extensively used in most asymmetric cryptographic algorithms, and mitigations to obtain constant-time behavior are very expensive. Most nominally "constant-time" implementations include a documented caveat that the execution platform is assumed to provide constant-time multiplications.

7.2.2.3. *Shift and rotation*

Logical and arithmetic shifts, and bit rotation opcodes, have in some CPUs a variable execution time. A constant-time optimized shift circuit is known as a *barrel shifter*, which is efficient but relatively expensive in terms of silicon area and gates (the barrel shifter is, more or less, a selection tree for each output bit). Some old designs forgo that cost and use an iterated algorithm for these operations, leading to an execution time that depends on the shift count. Note that the instructions are still constant-time with regard to the value which is shifted or rotated; impacted algorithms are those that use secret values as shift counts. Such algorithms are rare, but include the symmetric block cipher RC5, and also software implementations of floating-point operations.

In the Intel x86 line, only the early Pentium IV (Willamette and Northwood cores) lacked a barrel shifter, while all of the others (since the 80386) had constant-time shifts. ARM CPUs traditionally had barrel shifters.

Importantly, we are talking here only about instructions for shifting a single register. Shifts that operate on larger values (typically when shifting a 64-bit value on a 32-bit machine) may involve a compiler-generated routine that, again, may not be constant-time with regard to the shift count.

7.2.2.4. *Floating-point*

Floating-point values use a mantissa+exponent representation. The representation format also supports denormalized values (for values very close to zero, at the bottom of the exponent range), infinites and not-a-number (NaN) placeholders. Additions and subtractions involve normalizing the two operands under a common exponent, a process which is akin to a shift with a variable, potentially secret shift count; all operation outputs also need to be normalized, again with a shift count that depends on the value. While the situation varies a lot depending on the involved hardware, a few general rules can be made:

– Special values (denormalized values, infinites and NaNs) are never constant-time. When such a value is encountered (whether as input or as output), a pipeline stall occurs, with moderate (a dozen cycles) or heavy cost (several hundred cycles, as is typical of Intel CPUs). In some CPUs, the hardware is unable to handle special cases, and a CPU exception is thrown; the handler for that exception in the operating system is then supposed to perform the computation.

– In recent, large CPUs, additions, subtractions and multiplications are constant-time as long as only normal values are involved, both as input and as output. Multiplication by zero may exhibit an early result, although usually not in the case of CPUs with SIMD units (because it is quite rare that all parallel multiplications can be optimized that way simultaneously). Divisions are *mostly* constant-time, but usually have shortcuts when the dividend is zero, the divisor is a power of two, or the divisor is zero (in the latter case, the result is a special infinite value). Similarly, square roots are mostly constant-time, except for powers of four.

– Slightly older CPUs with floating-point support will typically not have constant-time behavior for any operation. This is the common case of embedded systems.

In general, it is best not to use floating-point types and operations in cryptographic implementations.

7.2.3. *Memory and caches*

Apart from inherently non-constant-time instructions, the main source of timing-based side-channels in a software implementation is the memory access pattern, specifically the *addresses* at which accesses are performed, because that pattern influences the contents of caches, in ways that can be detected with timing measurements, during or even after the execution of the attacked code.

In a typical computer system, RAM is much slower than the main CPU, especially with regard to latency: when a specific byte is requested at a given address, the value may be available only dozens or even hundreds of cycles afterward. To avoid severe performance degradation, CPUs commonly contain caches that keep copies of parts of the RAM under the heuristic assumption that most memory read accesses in a typical application are for data which were relatively recently read or written. One or several nested layers of caches are maintained, of increasing size and access latency. Each layer is usually organized as follows:

– The address space is split into elements called *cache lines* with a fixed size (often 32 or 64 bytes).

– Each given cache line may be stored in a specific set of line slots inside the cache. The number of slots in each set is called the cache associativity. Larger associativity increases the flexibility of the cache, but also its hardware complexity. Associativity of innermost cache layers in modern CPUs often lies between 2 and 8.

– When a new line must be cached, one of the slots must be evicted, which may entail writing it into the next layer (or main RAM), if that line was modified and the modification was not yet propagated. The policy used to choose that eviction target depends on the CPU and is rarely documented, though innermost layers tend to use a simple least-recently-used policy, since these layers strive for minimal access latency and thus do not have time to implement more complex policies.

From this description, one may assume that cache granularity is that of a line, and the exact byte within a given line that is accessed cannot leak through side-channels. This is unfortunately not true. In particular, modern CPUs often run several threads concurrently on the same core, and these threads may access the cache within the same cycle, but may incur detectable time penalties when the concurrent accesses conflict in some way. In particular, on Intel CPUs, accesses within the same "bank" (a 16-byte subdivision of the cache line), even if targeting different lines, may incur that penalty and this has been used to demonstrate a timing attack on a cryptographic application. Thus, the actual granularity of memory accesses, with regard to timing-based information leaks, can be lower than that of the cache line, and, again, in ways that are not documented, and can change without notice in subsequent variants of a given CPU. The only reliably safe way to organize constant-time code is to ensure that the memory access pattern is truly independent of secret data.

Cache-related leaks are only about the *address* of each access; cache management does not normally depend in any way on the *values* of bytes which are read from and stored to RAM. Most constant-time implementations are built on that assumption. It is, in practice, *mostly* true; some high-end Intel CPUs have been found to optimize long sequences of memory writes by omitting cache flushes for a write of an all-zeros line over a line which was already all-zeros. This specific instance was reported as a potential security risk, and the optimization was disabled in a CPU firmware update; however, this example illustrates that security is at odds with some ongoing work on improving performance in CPUs, and other similar features may show up in later CPUs. Constant-time implementations should be understood as a best effort mitigation that protects against timing attacks under a given model of the hardware behavior. If that model is inaccurate in a given CPU, then protection against timing-based side-channels requires extra measures akin to those used against power analysis attacks, following a deeper analysis which is specific to the hardware model involved.

The caches on main RAM are not the only CPU feature that can exhibit cache-like characteristics and be a source of timing-based side-channels. Other relevant features in most modern CPUs include at least the following:

– The *translation look-aside buffer* is a dedicated cache structure for the mapping of memory pages from the virtual to the physical address space.

– The *write buffer* transiently contains very recently written data elements that have not yet been sent to the innermost cache, but may still be used to execute read accesses.

– Jump prediction uses its own cache that records the previous target or branch of some jump opcodes (see section 7.2.4).

In all these features, the independence of cache behavior from memory contents is maintained, thus not requiring any extra mitigation.

The layered cache hierarchy outlined above is found in "large systems" like smartphones, laptops or servers. Small embedded systems, using microcontrollers that integrate a CPU core, RAM and ROM/Flash, often have somewhat different characteristics:

– RAM is usually an SRAM block that can be accessed from the CPU with minimal latency, requiring no cache.

– ROM/Flash may have higher access latency, with occasional extra delays for some addresses (e.g. at the start of a Flash block). The microcontroller may have an extra cache between the CPU and ROM; that cache may or may not have separate structures for instruction fetching and for data.

– Such embedded systems often support direct access from peripherals to RAM. An interconnection matrix arbitrates between concurrent accesses, and may induce extra delays upon apparent conflicts; conflict detection may be based on parts of the target addresses.

The overall conclusion is similar to the case of large systems: any access to RAM or ROM at secret-dependent addresses *may* be vulnerable to timing attacks and should be shunned in a truly constant-time implementation. A few existing specialized implementations of cryptographic primitives for some embedded CPUs assume that accesses to RAM (not ROM) at secret-dependent addresses are safe, but this is a fragile property that is hard to ascertain in any given hardware instance. In particular, the CPU core itself is cache-less; any cache, and the interconnection matrix, are added during integration within a microcontroller, and thus not documented in the CPU technical reference manual itself.

7.2.4. *Jumps and jump prediction*

Jump instructions direct instruction fetching to a distinct address. Some jumps have a data-dependent behavior:

– *Conditional jumps* are taken only if a specific, dynamically evaluated condition is true.

– *Indirect jumps* are always taken, but fall at an address that is dynamically evaluated. They are mostly encountered in support of function pointers, virtual object method invocation and return from function calls.

If the condition for a conditional jump depends on secret data, then the memory access pattern for instruction fetching will be modified depending on the condition value. Similarly, if an indirect jump target address depends on secret data, then again the memory access pattern will vary in ways correlated with the secret data. Thus, nominally, conditional and indirect jumps are covered by the same proscription against memory access patterns that depend on secret information. They are still treated specially because in the programming model, such jumps correspond to syntactic structures that are quite unlike data accesses. Moreover, caches may be specialized for instruction fetching, thus changing the details of potential exploits; some CPUs cache decoded μops instead of encoded machine instructions.

Jump prediction is a mechanism by which the CPU tries to predict whether conditional jumps will be taken, and where indirect jumps will fall, in order to keep the pipeline fed and avoid stalls. Large CPUs often feature dynamic jump prediction, which leverages a dedicated cache-like structure that records past behavior of recently encountered jump opcodes. These caches do not induce an extra vulnerability, in that jump instructions that are subject to such caches are still the conditional and indirect jumps, but they offer an extra avenue, beyond instruction fetches, through which timing attacks may be performed. This is helped by the fact that a mispredicted jump implies a pipeline flush, often leading to a substantial penalty (a dozen or more cycles), especially on high-performance large CPUs for which processing of any given instruction spreads over many cycles. Thus, we cannot really hope for inner instructions caches (or even caches over decoded μops) to mitigate timing attacks on tight loops that use conditional or indirect jumps.

7.3. Primitive implementation techniques

Any constant-time implementation will rely on elementary constructs that implement some primitive operations in a constant-time way. As we saw previously, some basic arithmetic and logic operations directly map to CPU opcodes with constant-time behavior (e.g. adding two integers); here, we detail how some other commonly used primitives can be implemented.

7.3.1. *Compiler issues and Booleans*

As a rule, a developer almost never deals with raw machine instructions; most software is written in a programming language that gets translated into instructions in some way. We traditionally distinguish between *interpretation* and *compilation*, but the boundary between these two concepts is a bit fuzzy; for example, many efficient interpreters actually generate a compact form known as *threaded code*, in which some chunks of raw opcodes can be inserted, leading to a continuum between interpretation and compilation. Here, we will use the term "compilation" exclusively.

There are many modes of compilation. *Ahead-of-time* (AoT) compilation is done once, usually on the developer's system, and outputs the translated instructions into an executable form that is stored; this is the classic mode associated with programming languages such as C or Rust. *Just-in-time* (JiT) compilation is dynamically performed whenever the piece of software is executed; this is how Javascript is usually processed. Some programming languages combine both, with an initial AoT pass that produces an intermediate format known as *bytecode* that will be subject to JiT compilation when executed; this is how Java or C# software is normally used. A developer can, nominally, inspect the output of an AoT compiler to verify how a given piece of code was translated, and thus check whether only constant-time instructions were used, whereas JiT compilers are not as easily controlled, since they operate in other systems, and are subject to change. However, the hope that pure AoT compilation allows the developer to *ascertain* that the output is constant-time is an illusion; indeed, some CPUs include an additional JiT compilation directly inside the hardware, using the provided machine instructions as a sort of source code, which is compiled to internal instructions which are not available to the developer, and rarely documented. This kind of "hardware JiT" is encountered mostly in CPUs meant for mobile applications such as smartphones: the CPU offers an high-power execution engine, but also a distinct low-power engine that takes over when the device is idle, with a simpler, slower, and less energy-intensive execution model. In that case, the low-power execution engine will usually be a simplified RISC-like system, and the hardware JiT processes the provided machine instructions.

Since later (JiT) compilation may thus always happen, most of the effort on the developer's side relies on making sure that the source code will be translated into a constant-time instruction sequence by any *possible* compilation process. Looking at what an actual AoT compiler outputs is instructive, but certainly not enough to provide any sort of guarantee. It is thus important to understand how compilers process the source code and infer what values may actually be present in the variables the code handles. The main issue we are trying to avoid is related to Boolean values. Consider, for instance, the following piece of C code:

```
#include <stdbool.h>

void bar(void);

void foo(bool a, bool b, bool c)
{
    if (a & b & c) {
        bar();
    }
}
```

In this example, we assume that a cryptographic analysis shows that the Boolean values `a`, `b` and `c` are individually secret, but that their conjunction is not; in other words, it is not a problem if outsiders learn that one of these three values was `false`, but they must not learn which one was `false`. The `if` clause leads to a conditional jump (indeed, the `bar()` function is invoked only if all three Booleans are `true`) but, per our assumptions, this does not lead to an exploitable information leak. What matters for constant-time implementation, here, is that the logical conjunction "`a & b & c`" is computed in a pure constant-time fashion. This is why we use the `&` operator, and not the `&&` operator, because the latter, in C, is defined to use shortcut semantics (its right operand is evaluated only if the left operand is `true`), while `&` is defined to always evaluate its two operands.

Does it actually work? Let us look at the assembly output produced by the compiler (using Clang, version 10.0.0, with optimization level `-O3` on a 64-bit x86 system):

```
foo:
        testb   %dil, %dil
        je      .LBB0_3
        testb   %sil, %sil
        je      .LBB0_3
        testb   %dl, %dl
        je      .LBB0_3
        jmp     bar
.LBB0_3:
        retq
```

We see that the compiler produced *three* conditional jumps ("`je`" opcodes, meaning "jump-if-equal"). The compiler leveraged its knowledge that the operands are indeed Booleans, and helpfully optimized the code by noticing that if the first Boolean (`a`) is `false`, then it is not needed to compute the conjunction of `b` and `c`, since that would not impact the final outcome. This applies shortcut semantics, the very thing we wanted to avoid. Still, this is not a compiler bug: the compiler is perfectly allowed to perform that "optimization" since it does not change the abstract outcome of the execution. This highlights that the timing behavior of the code is *not* part of the properties that a standard-compliant C compiler is supposed to maintain. The whole difficulty of constant-time implementation lies there.

In this example, we can modify the `foo()` function into this:

```
void foo(int a, int b, int c)
{
    if (a & b & c) {
        bar();
    }
}
```

We replaced the `bool` parameters with `int` parameters. Now, the compiler produces a constant-time output:

```
foo:
        andl    %esi, %edi
        testl   %edx, %edi
        je      .LBB1_1
```

```
        jmp     bar
.LBB1_1:
        retq
```

When the parameters have type `int`, they may have many different values, and the compiler can no longer assume that each of them will be equal to 0 or 1, even if we, as developers, will call the `foo()` function only with 0 or 1 parameter values. This leads the compiler to perform the two conjunctions (the second one is combined with the test itself, in the `testl` opcode), and the result is constant-time (it does not leak which one of `a`, `b` and `c` was `false`).

Take care that even in that case, the non-constant-time instruction sequence may reappear if the compiler can notice that we indeed always call the `foo()` function with values which are, in fact, Booleans. This may happen if we make that function local (`static`, in C terminology), in which case it can be called only from the same file, and the compiler will thus see all possible calls to that function and thus use that information to work out the "best" instruction sequence (with its own notion of "best", which, as we see, does not necessarily match our goals). A constant-time compilation output is achieved here only insofar as we can successfully *hide* from the compiler the fact that the apparent integer parameters are really Booleans in disguise. This is not a comfortable position; this hiding may be defeated in later compiler versions (or later JiT execution engines or CPUs), especially when using *link-time optimizations*, in which a compiler observes a complete program in one pass and thus gains global knowledge on how any given function is called and what kind of parameters it may receive in practice.

A reasonable, best-effort rule for constant-time implementations is to avoid all Boolean types. Whenever a Boolean value is needed, it should be represented as an integer type, for example, `int` in the C language. This will be enough, provided that the compiler does not notice that such values really behave like Booleans. In practice, compilers usually apply *range analysis* on integer values to infer a minimum and a maximum bound on the value; this range analysis is especially important in languages that check bounds on array accesses (e.g. Java or Rust, unlike C), because that analysis can often work out that some array accesses are necessarily in-range, allowing the bounds checking to be removed from the compiled output. A compiler using range analysis *may* infer that if the range is "0 to 1", then the value really is a Boolean. Subsequent trouble can be avoided by using unsigned types and a 0/-1 duality: store a Boolean in a fixed-width unsigned integer (e.g. `uint32_t` in C), with the convention that an all-zeros value (0) means `false`, while an all-ones value (e.g. `0xffffffff` for a 32-bit integer) means `true`. This rule will, in practice, avoid Boolean-related "optimizations" by compilers; it is also convenient for implementing some primitive operations with bitwise Boolean logic.

7.3.2. *Bitwise Boolean logic*

We present here some constant-time implementations of a few elementary operations that occur in cryptographic algorithms. We use here the C programming language, but the techniques can be applied to about any other language.

7.3.2.1. *Sign extension*

In two's complement representation, an n-bit signed integer type can hold values in the -2^{n-1} to $+2^{n-1}-1$ range; non-negative values have the same representation as they would have in an unsigned integer type, while negative values x use the unsigned representation of $x + 2^n$. Thus, the most significant bit (of rank $n-1$) is the *sign bit*: it has value 0 for non-negative integers (0 or positive), or value 1 for negative integers. *Sign extension* corresponds to storing that value into a larger m-bit slot, with $m > n$. In practice, this means duplicating the value of the sign bit (bit $n-1$) into the upper bits (n to $m-1$).

When n and m correspond to native sizes of types in the used language (e.g. $n = 32$ and $m = 64$), then the language normally offers a corresponding construction as a "type cast" (e.g. from `int32_t` to `int64_t` in C). However, this sign extension is not necessarily performed in constant-time by the compiler; it depends on the abilities of the underlying hardware. If the hardware system does not offer an adequate sign extension opcode, then the compiler may decide to extract the source sign bit, then use a jump conditional to its value. To avoid this situation, and to also handle cases when n is not a natural integer type size, we need to perform the sign extension with specific code. For instance, if we have to sign-extend a 24-bit value to 32 bits, then it can be done as follows:

```
uint32_t sign_extend_24(uint32_t x)
{
    return x | -(x & ~(uint32_t)0x007fffff);
}
```

Here, the constant `0x007fffff` is $2^{23}-1$; by reversing its bits (`~` operator) then a bitwise AND (`&`) with `x`, we isolate the sign bit: the value will be equal to 2^{23} if `x` is negative, and to zero otherwise. The unary negation (`-`) then sign-extends that bit properly: if `x` was negative, then we get `0xff800000`; otherwise, we still have zero. The final bitwise OR (`|`) puts these extended bits back into the output.

7.3.2.2. *Multiplexers*

A *multiplexer* chooses between two values `x` and `y`, using a third one (`c`) as a control: if the control is `true`, then the result is `x`, otherwise it is `y`. In languages such as C, this corresponds to the ternary choice operator (`c ? x : y`). Many CPUs offer a "conditional move" instruction that allows easy and efficient constant-time implementation; however, some CPUs do not have that instruction (in the Intel x86 line, the cmov instruction was added in the Pentium Pro, previous CPUs did not have it) and use of the ternary choice operator may lead to a conditional jump. CPU vendors also rarely guarantee that a conditional move is constant-time and will never be, for instance, subject to speculated execution. Moreover, as explained above, we would prefer never to have to use expressions that the compiler will interpret as Booleans.

A constant-time choice between two integer values can be implemented with a few bitwise operators:

```
uint32_t choose(uint32_t x, uint32_t y, uint32_t c)
{
    return y ^ (c & (x ^ y));
}
```

If c is zero, then the AND will yield zero, and the output of the outer XOR will be the value of y. If c is all-ones, then the expression will compute y ^ (x ^ y), and the two y values will cancel each other out, yielding the expected output x. We note here the convenience of representing the Boolean true with -1 instead of 1.

This multiplexer is used as a building component in many other primitives, and we will encounter it again.

7.3.2.3. *Comparisons*

An integer value can be compared with zero with the following:

```
uint32_t is_nonzero(uint32_t x)
{
    return -((x | -x) >> 31);
}

#define is_zero(x)   (~is_nonzero(x))
```

This relies on the following fact: if x is zero, then -x will also be zero. Otherwise, at least one of x and -x will have its sign bit equal to 1 (the sign bit may be 1 in both if the value x is exactly 2^{31}). The bitwise OR output will thus have its high bit set to 1 if and only if x is non-zero. The right shift yields the result as a 0 or 1 value; the final negation transforms that into a 0 or -1 value, following the convention we previously set for representing Booleans. From is_nonzero(), which returns 0 for a zero input, and -1 for all other values, we can define is_zero() (to get -1 for a zero) with a simple macro that applies the bitwise negation operation (~).

The right-shift and negation can be combined into a single arithmetic shift, but, in C, this requires using signed integer types, which is somewhat uncomfortable:

```
uint32_t is_nonzero(uint32_t x)
{
    uint32_t y = x | -x;
    return (uint32_t)(*(int32_t *)&y >> 31);
}
```

The trouble here is inherent to the C language: as per the C standard, a conversion from an unsigned type to a signed type triggers an "implementation-defined" behavior if the source unsigned value does not fit in the formal range of the destination signed type. This is not exactly an "undefined behavior" (in which basically anything goes), but the standard still allows the compiler to produce an arbitrary result, or to raise a signal, the latter often implying an application crash. As with all implementation-defined behaviors, the C compiler is supposed to explicitly document how it handles such cases; not all compilers have complete and up-to-date documentation. To avoid relying on this implementation-defined behavior, we use a pointer (`&y`), cast the pointer and then dereference it; this should yield the expected result in all cases, thanks to the guarantees of the C standard for exact-width integer types such as `int32_t` (this would *not* reliably work to cast between non-exact-width type such as `int` or `unsigned long`, though). The C compiler will still note that the construction is a value cast and will not actually write the value to RAM, get the address, and follow the pointer, so the output will be efficient. Meanwhile, the right-shift is then performed on a signed integer, and it will perform the needed sign extension. Formally, the C standard states that right-shifting a signed negative value also yields an implementation-defined result; contrary to the case of a type conversion, compilers are not allowed to raise a signal in that situation, and in practice all C compilers use an arithmetic shift.

This description shows that the C language in particular has a complicated relationship with signed integers; computations with unsigned types are much more preferable, since they allow for simpler and more robust implementations that do not rely on non-portable assumptions. Most other languages (e.g. Go, C# or Rust) have more precisely defined semantics and avoid such issues. Here, we will stick to C for examples, but use only unsigned integer types.

We can extend the `is_zero()` function into a generic equality comparison by noticing that two values are equal if and only if their bitwise XOR is zero:

```
#define equals(x, y)   is_zero((x) ^ (y))
```

For *ordering* comparisons, we can use the following:

```
uint32_t is_greater(uint32_t x, uint32_t y)
{
    uint32_t z = y - x;
    return -((z ^ ((x ^ y) & (x ^ z))) >> 31);
}
```

This function relies on the following:

– If x and y are both lower than 2^{31}, then $y - x$ (i.e. the variable z) will have its highest bit set to 1 if and only if $x > y$.

– Otherwise, if either x or y is at least 2^{31} (but not both), then the result is the highest bit of x.

– Otherwise, if both x and y are at least 2^{31}, then the comparison between x and y should yield the same result as the comparison between $x - 2^{31}$ and $y - 2^{31}$, and $y - x = (y - 2^{31}) - (x - 2^{31})$, which brings us back to the first case.

Therefore, we need to keep the high bit of z if x and y have the same high bit value (i.e. the highest bit of `x ^ y` is 0), or the high bit of x otherwise. The expression is really a multiplexer between x and z, using the value of `x ^ y` as control. Finally, the right shift and negation extract and sign-extend the high bit to yield the result (as with `is_nonzero()`, an arithmetic right shift could be used for the sign extension, which may be slightly faster in some cases).

Using a "greater than" comparison, we can easily implement the "greater or equal", "lower than" and "lower or equal":

```
#define is_greater_or_equal(x, y)    (~is_greater(y, x))
#define is_lower(x, y)               (is_greater(y, x))
#define is_lower_or_equal(x, y)      (~is_greater(x, y))
```

The comparison above is for *unsigned* integers. Sometimes, we need a *signed* comparison that uses the highest bit as a sign bit, even if the values are held inside variables with unsigned integer types. A signed 32-bit comparison can be implemented as follows:

```
uint32_t is_greater_signed(uint32_t x, uint32_t y)
{
    uint32_t z = y - x;
    return -((z ^ ((x ^ y) & (y ^ z))) >> 31);
}
```

This is almost the same code as previously, except that y was used instead of x in the rightmost XOR: all the analysis on the high bits remains valid, except that if x and y have different values in their top bits, then the result should be the top bit of y.

7.3.2.4. *Bit length*

The *bit length* of an integer is the minimal size of its binary representation; in other words, it is the number of bits that remain after you have removed all leading zeros ("leading" in the big-endian convention, where most significant bits are written first). Extracting the bit length without leaking information on how many leading bits were indeed zero is needed in some operations, fo example, in some implementations of the extended binary GCD to compute modular inverses. The dual of the bit length is the count of leading zeros (if working with n-bit values, and the bit length of a value is k, then its number of leading zeros is $n - k$, and vice versa).

Some CPU architectures offer an opcode to count leading zeros (`lzcnt` in recent enough x86 CPUs, `clz` on ARMv7-M CPUs such as the ARM Cortex M4), but many others do not. A portable, constant-time bit length measurement function is as follows:

```
uint32_t bit_length(uint32_t x)
{
        uint32_t m = 30, c = 0;
        c = ((x >> 16) - 1) >> 31;
        m -= (c << 4);
        x ^= (c - 1) & (x ^ (x >> 16));
        c = ((x >> 8) - 1) >> 31;
        m -= (c << 3);
        x ^= (c - 1) & (x ^ (x >> 8));
        c = ((x >> 4) - 1) >> 31;
        m -= (c << 2);
        x ^= (c - 1) & (x ^ (x >> 4));
        c = ((x >> 2) - 1) >> 31;
        m -= (c << 1);
        x ^= (c - 1) & (x ^ (x >> 2));
        return m + x - (x & (x >> 1));
}
```

In this function, m accumulates the count of bits. The first group of three expressions does the following: if x fits on 16 bits, then c has value 1 and we substract 16 from the current bit count (m); otherwise, c has value 0, m is unchanged, and x is replaced with its value right-shifted by 16 bits. In other words, if x did not fit on 16 bits, then its bit length should be 16 plus the bit length of its high half. In all cases, x necessarily fits on 16 bits after executing these three expressions. The next nine lines of code apply the same process three other times to reduce the size of x to

8, 4 and then 2 bits. Finally, when we reach the `return` clause, the value of `x` is either 0, 1, 2 or 3 (it is a value of at most two bits in length), and the length of the original value is the sum of the value `m` (which is in the 0–30 range), and the length of the current value of `x`. Since 0, 1, 2 and 3 have bit length 0, 1, 2 and 2, respectively, we just have to add `x` to `m`, and make a small correction in case `x` is equal to 3 (that is the "`x & (x >> 1)`" expression).

This function can be extended to larger register sizes at moderate cost; indeed, it can process an n-bit register with $O(\log n)$ expressions. However, this low complexity can be maintained only as long as operations on registers, such as a shift or a subtraction, have unit cost. A constant-time bit length function on a big integer, represented as a potentially large array of limbs in some basis, will necessarily involve a linear search for the highest non-zero limb, with a cost proportional to the number of limbs.

7.3.2.5. *Arrays*

Array accesses are a prime target for cache attacks, in case the index of the accessed slot is secret. Traditional AES implementations, for instance, are typically used for the S-box (combined with some subsequent linear transforms), a lookup table with 256 entries of 32 bits. Another situation with accesses at secret addresses is window optimizations for modular exponentiation with a secret exponent, as part of RSA (or, similarly, for point multiplication in an elliptic curve). Such accesses leak information about the address through the effect on caches, which can be measured during or after execution of the cryptographic algorithm through timing of accesses.

It is possible to perform a constant-time array access, albeit with a much higher cost than the non-constant-time access. For instance, reading the byte of index `k` in an array of size `n` can be done as follows (using the `equals()` function defined earlier):

```
uint32_t read_byte(const uint8_t *a, uint32_t k, uint32_t n)
{
        uint32_t x = 0;
        for (uint32_t u = 0; u < n; u ++) {
                x |= equals(u, k) & a[u];
        }
        return x;
}
```

Here, all bytes are read. The exact order in which bytes are accessed depends on the vagaries of the CPU pipeline and current cache state, but, crucially, it will not depend on the value of the secret index `k`. For a write access, the implementation would be:

```
void set_byte(uint8_t *a, uint32_t x, uint32_t k, uint32_t n)
{
    for (uint32_t u = 0; u < n; u ++) {
        a[u] = choose(x, a[u], equals(u, k));
    }
}
```

using the previously defined multiplexer function `choose()`. Note that, in that case, all bytes of the array are both read and written back. Notably, if the array was not explicitly initialized, then its previous contents would be undefined. Accessing nominally undefined byte values can lead to various issues in the C language, at the very least, some warnings from static analysis tools, even though the access is formally safe when the array elements use one of the exact-width types (the values may be undefined, but they are not "trap representations"). This is, again, an issue specific to C and does not impact other languages with more precise defined semantics, where arrays are typically initialized to zero.

Another common array-related task is an equality check: the contents of two arrays should be compared for equality. A typical case is verifying a password hash, or a MAC value. Common comparison functions, such as `memcmp()` in C, look at the values to compare in increasing addresses, and stop at the first divergence; while this is conceptually faster than always looking at all source bytes, this is also non-constant-time, and an attacker leveraging a timing-based side-channel may mount a byte-by-byte guessing attack, each time retaining the one byte value that makes the comparison access further bytes. The attack can be difficult to exploit in practice if the comparison function accesses source elements by large chunks of 32 or 64 bits at a time; conversely, it is hard to ascertain that the given usage context makes exploitation impossible. It is therefore recommended to stick to a pure constant-time implementation, such as this one:

```
uint32_t equals_array(const uint8_t *a,
                      const uint8_t *b, size_t len)
{
    uint32_t r = 0;
    for (size_t u = 0; u < len; u ++) {
        r |= a[u] ^ b[u];
    }
    return is_zero(r);
}
```

If the source arrays indeed have equal contents, then all XOR outputs are zero, and the final value of `r` is zero; otherwise, at least one of the XOR outputs is non-zero, and since these values are combined with a bitwise OR, the final `r` will be non-zero. A few points here are noteworthy:

– This function is expressed for bytes (`uint8_t`), but can be easily extended to any other type as long as constant-time XOR and OR are available.

– Since we do not need to perform constant-time operations on the indexes, we can use the natural C type of indexes, which is `size_t`. In `read_byte()`, we had to use the `uint32_t` type for indexes since we had to perform constant-time comparisons between index values.

– The final comparison of `r` with zero uses our `is_zero()` function, in case the final outcome is secret. In many cases, the index of first divergence between inputs is secret, but the final equality verdict is not (e.g. when comparing MAC values, a failed MAC verification usually leads to observable consequences such as dropping a connection); in such cases, this `is_zero()` call can be replaced with a simple `r == 0`, which is (potentially) not constant-time since it outputs a Boolean. This situation is an "exit point" in the sense explained in section 7.1.3.

– This constant-time implementation *concentrates* the equality result into a single word value (here, the `r` variable) and a single comparison. It can be argued that such concentration increases the vulnerability to fault attacks by providing a single point of failure (see Chapters 9 to 12 of Volume 1). It must be remembered that while constant-time implementations are, in general, necessary to avoid secret information leakage, they are not sufficient to ensure protection against all kinds of side-channel attacks.

Another array operation which is sometimes encountered is *array rotation*: for an array of n elements, and a rotation count k such that $0 \leq k < n$, we want to store at each index i the value which is previously at index $i + k \bmod n$. If k is not secret then this can be done with a few block copies, but if k is secret this is a more complicated task. A simple implementation would simply use `read_byte()` repeatedly to extract the correct element $i + k \bmod n$ for all destination indexes i; however, each `read_byte()` has cost $O(n)$ (it must read and process the whole source array) and the overall rotation cost would be in $O(n^2)$, which can be prohibitive if n is large. A faster method, implemented below, has cost $O(n \log n)$:

```
void rotate_array(uint8_t *a, uint32_t k, uint32_t n,
                  uint8_t *tmp)
{
    for (uint32_t rc = 1; rc < n; rc <<= 1) {
        uint32_t c = -(k & 1);
        for (uint32_t u = 0, v = rc; u < n; u ++) {
            tmp[u] = choose(a[v], a[u], c);
            v ++;
            if (v == n) {
```

```
                v = 0;
            }
        }
        memcpy(a, tmp, n);
        k >>= 1;
    }
}
```

This function performs the rotation by k slots as the combination of elementary rotations by 2^j slots; the value `rc` contains 2^j for each iteration of the outer loop, and the inner loop performs that rotation, conditionally on the jth bit of k (stored in `c` with our 0/-1 convention). It can easily be seen that none of the memory accesses depend on the secret value: the `k` parameter is used only to compute `c`, which is itself used only for the `choose()` call. In this implementation, an extra temporary array (`tmp`), disjoint from the array `a`, is used; it is possible to make a different implementation that does not need such a temporary array, but it would require accessing the array `a` in steps of `rc` slots, with an extra loop in case `rc` is not relatively prime to `n`.

Array rotation appears in constant-time implementations of CBC+HMAC encryption of records in the SSL/TLS protocols (TLS-1.3 fortunately removed support for this particular mode of encryption). The MAC-then-encrypt construction was used: CBC encryption is applied on the concatenation of the plaintext, a MAC value computed over the plaintext, some padding bytes and a single byte that contains the length of the padding:

plaintext || MAC || padding || padding_length

An attack may try to leverage a padding oracle attack, submitting maliciously crafted ciphertext and trying to obtain the corresponding padding length. To prevent this attack, all operations between CBC decryption and final MAC verification must happen in constant-time, hiding the padding length. One of these operations is the extraction of the MAC value; this can be done with the following code chunk:

```
uint32_t k = 0;
memset(mac, 0, mac_len);
uint32_t len_withmac = len_pt + mac_len;
for (uint32_t u = len1, v = 0; u < len2; u ++) {
    mac[v] |= choose(src[u], 0x00,
        is_greater_or_equal(u, len_pt)
        | is_lower(u, len_withmac));
    k = choose(v, k, equals(u, len_pt));
    v ++;
```

```
        if (v == mac_len) {
            v = 0;
        }
    }
    rotate_array(mac, k, mac_len, tmp);
```

This code expects that the minimum and maximum possible lengths of the plaintext (as can be inferred from the total size of the record, the known length of the MAC value (`mac_len`), and the fact that the padding length is necessarily between 0 and 255) are in `len1` and `len2`, respectively; these are public values. The actual plaintext length, which is secret, is in `len_pt`. The code extracts the correct MAC value by reading bytes whose index indeed falls within the MAC, using zero otherwise, and combining them (with bitwise OR) into the `mac[]` buffer, whose size is that of the MAC output. While a single pass is needed to get the MAC, the obtained value is, indeed, "rotated" (the first MAC byte is at offset `k` in the `mac[]` array); this is why a call to our `rotate_array()` function is needed.

7.3.2.6. *Bitslicing*

Bitslicing is the traditional name of a technique also known as *data orthogonalization*. The principle is to "spread" the bits of a value over many variables, and to implement the computation as a circuit of Boolean gates. For instance, suppose that an algorithm calls for computing a XOR of two 32-bit values. A straightforward implementation would store the values in two CPU registers, and use a XOR opcode. In a bitslice implementation, each bit of each value would be stored in the lowest bit of a register, thus splitting the input values over 64 registers; the XOR would be done bit by bit, hence requiring 32 CPU instructions; the output would also be obtained as 32 separate registers. The core observation of data orthogonalization is that when doing each individual XOR to combine two 1-bit values, stored in the least significant of two registers, the CPU also performs a XOR over all other bits of the involved registers. More generally, on a hardware system with n-bit registers, when a given circuit of Boolean gates is evaluated in a bitslice way on data spread over as many registers as input bits, n parallel evaluations of the circuit are performed simultaneously for the same price, for all bit ranks from 0 to $n - 1$.

Bitslicing has several performance-related benefits:

– The CPU's abilities at computing Boolean bitwise operations are maximized, especially when registers are larger than the natural data value width in the implemented algorithm. In the example above, the 32 XOR operations on registers collectively compute $32n$ elementary XOR gates; in large CPUs, registers of 256 or even 512 bits are available, making the bitslice computation up to 16 times more efficient than the straightforward code that would only use 32 bits per register and discard the rest.

– Any bit permutation, which may involve considerable shifting and masking when done in a straightforward implementation, becomes in bitslice mode a mere problem of using the right register for the next post-permutation gate. This is a data routing issue solved at compile-time, with no runtime cost.

Historically, bitslicing was first applied in cryptography for attack purposes in order to break password hashes that used the traditional DES-derived Unix `crypt()` function. DES was designed to be amenable to efficient low-area hardware circuits, and thus most suited to bitslice implementations, that mimic a circuit layout; notably, DES contains several complex bit permutations that are expensive in traditional software implementations, but mostly free in bitslicing. Password breaking is also an extremely parallel task, thereby easily leveraging the parallelism of bitslicing. However, bitslicing was later applied for constructive purposes, because of its potential performance benefits, but also because a bitsliced implementation is inherently constant-time: the execution path and the memory access pattern cannot depend on the processed data, since n instances of the algorithm are executed at the same time, on n distinct sets of input values.

While immunity to timing-based side-channels is an alluring property, bitslice implementations have their own challenges, in particular, the following:

– *Parallelism*: the high performance of bitslicing is achievable only if enough instances of the algorithm can be executed in parallel. For instance, in the context of symmetric encryption with a block cipher, CBC *encryption* is not parallelizable, since the input to each block cipher invocation requires the output of the previous block; on the other hand, CBC *decryption* can benefit from parallelism.

– *Large state*: since n instances are executed in parallel, this requires handling the state values of these n instances. For instance, in a full bitslice AES implementation, the running block value is 128 bits, and each subkey is also 128 bits, thus nominally requiring 256 registers. The CPU does not offer 256 registers, neither at the programming level, nor even internally in the register renaming unit. Thus, some amount of extra data movement will be needed. The developer writes bitslice code in a language such as C with as many variables as required for the bitslice representation; the compiler will map these variables to available registers and add memory reads and writes to flush data to RAM and read it back, thus managing the registers like a cache on the state, and the CPU pipeline will try to perform these reads and writes at opportune times. On large CPUs, with a superscalar architecture, the extra reads and writes can *usually* be done with low overhead, in parallel with the bitwise Boolean computations; on small embedded systems, though, these extra reads incur runtime overhead and significantly decrease performance.

– *Code footprint*: bitslice code is often large, since each wordwise operation is translated to many bitwise instructions. Small embedded systems are often constrained in available space for code, and a fully bitslice implementation can be prohibitively large. Large systems such as smartphones or servers are usually less constrained, but a large chunk of code representing a fully unrolled circuit may exceed the size of the internal cache for code, which leads to performance degradation through cache misses, as well as instruction decoding bottlenecks in CPUs whose cache for code operates over μops.

– *Operation types*: since bitslicing emulates a hardware circuit, it is well suited to Boolean gates such as XOR or AND, but much less to arithmetic operations. A bitslice addition of 32-bit words, as is commonly used in software-oriented symmetric primitives, requires performing carry propagation with a full-adder circuit (five gates) per input bit, which lowers the performance benefits and also induces a large latency, since the processing of each bit in a word then depends on the output of the processing of the previous bit. Integer multiplications are too expensive to envision. In practice, this limits the use of bitslicing to algorithms that do not use such arithmetics operations, for example, AES, SHA-3/SHAKE, or possibly asymmetric cryptography using elliptic curves in binary fields; for software-oriented algorithms such as the stream cipher ChaCha20, the hash function BLAKE2, or most algebraic asymmetric cryptography (RSA, Diffie-Hellman, elliptic curves in prime fields, etc.), bitslicing is usually considered not to be a worthwhile implementation technique.

Look-up tables are challenging elements for bitslice implementations. A general process for converting an $n \rightarrow m$ table (a table with an n-bit entry and an m-bit output, i.e. 2^n table elements of m bits each) into a circuit amenable to a bitslice implementation is as follows:

1) Split the table into m equivalent $n \rightarrow 1$ tables, each computing one bit of output.

2) Convert an $n \rightarrow 1$ table into a tree of multiplexers of depth n that selects the output from 2^n leaves. The leaves are the possible outputs of the table, and each row in the tree uses one of the n table input bits. Provided that the leaves are adjusted accordingly, each multiplexer can be converted into a two-gate cirtuit "a XOR (b AND c)" that selects between a and a XOR b depending on the value of the bit c.

3) Optimize the tree. In particular, every multiplexer in the lowest row of the tree can be replaced with either a constant bit (0 or 1), the entry bit for that row, or the opposite of that entry bit. There may also be parts shareable between the m trees, since they operate on the same n input bits, though with distinct leaves.

The goal of the optimization is to minimize the total number of gates in the circuit to reduce both the CPU cost and the code footprint; if the target architecture can execute many operations in parallel, then reducing the circuit depth may also be important for performance. There is no known practical process for obtaining an optimal circuit; exhaustive searching on possible circuits is too expensive except for the smallest tables.

We will now consider the case of AES implementations exclusively, though the techniques used may be applicable to other algorithms. AES uses 10–14 rounds (depending on key size), and each round includes some linear operations (XOR with a subkey, ShiftRows, MixColumns) and an application of the "AES S-box", an $8 \rightarrow 8$ table on each of the 16 bytes that constitute the running round state. This S-box has an algebraic structure: it consists of an inversion in the finite field $\mathbb{F}_{256}$, followed by an affine transform in the vector space $\mathbb{F}_2^8$. This structure has been leveraged to find optimized circuits, with the help of some heuristic search algorithms for additional cost savings. In 2009, an AES table circuit with 117 gates was published, for the whole table (Boyar and Peralta 2009).

Since AES is a block cipher, it may be used in the reverse direction, using the inverse table; inversion in $\mathbb{F}_{256}$ being an involution, that specific piece of the circuit is potentially shareable between the S-box and inverse S-box implementations, though this may prevent some of the optimizations that lead to the lowest gate count. Another approach for the inverse S-box is to use the forward S-box in a wrapper: if the affine transform is A and inversion in $\mathbb{F}_{256}$ is denoted I, then the S-box is computed as $S(x) = A(I(x))$, and we can compute the inverse S-box as $S^{-1}(x) = A^{-1}(S(A^{-1}(x)))$. This yields lower performance for the inverse S-box than a dedicated circuit, but it also minimizes code footprint if both AES directions must be implemented, without altering the performance of the forward direction of AES. We may note that, for instance, some encryption modes such as GCM or EAX use only the forward direction of AES, and also that in CBC mode, encryption is not parallel but decryption is parallel, thereby making optimization of the encryption direction more important than that of the decryption direction.

Since the high parallelism and large state often make fully bitsliced implementations impractical on embedded systems, alternate strategies that use only *partial* bitslicing have been employed, especially with the AES block cipher. In AES, an $8 \rightarrow 8$ table is used (the "AES S-box"); in each round, 16 instances of the S-box are evaluated in parallel on the current 16 state bytes. It is thus possible to perform the 16 instances at the same time with a bitslice AES S-box circuit, even though they all relate to the same AES block evaluation. If using, for instance, 32-bit registers, then this strategy would mean that only two instances of AES are performed in parallel, and each register contains 16 state bits for each instance. This *semi-bitslice* architecture has some advantages, especially on small microcontrollers:

– The complete state of the evaluated AES instances will fit on only eight registers, minimizing the need for extra traffic between CPU registers and RAM, thereby promoting execution speed and reducing code footprint and transient RAM usage.

– The implementation performance can be tolerable even for non-parallel workloads such as encryption in CBC mode. With 32-bit registers, using a non-parallel mode means that only half of the computing power is used, which lowers performance compared with fully parallel tasks (e.g. *decryption* in CBC mode), but much less so than the $1/32$ factor that would be obtained with a fully bitsliced implementation.

On the other hand, the fact that bits relevant to a single AES instance may now appear on various ranks in a register implies that data movements such as permutations of bits are no longer a mere routing problem entirely solved at compile-time. The MixColumns and ShiftRows operations of AES now involve extra computations, whose cost depends on the exact location of the data bits among the registers. There are many opportunities for additional optimizations, and this is an area of active research.

7.4. Constant-time algorithms

In the previous sections, we described implementation techniques for some primitive operations. We now explore some classic algorithms that use these techniques to provide constant-time functionalities.

7.4.1. *Modular integers*

Modular integers are used in many asymmetric algorithms based on algebraic structures, in particular, RSA, Diffie–Hellman and elliptic curve cryptography; modular integers are also found in most lattice-based algorithms, though in that case the modulus is often much shorter and values fit in a single machine register.

Initial implementations of many of these algorithms were designed before side-channel attacks were even considered, and usually worked over a generic "big integer" library. When aiming for constant-time implementations, using big integers is an essentially hopeless strategy: a big integer is represented as an array of *limbs* (i.e. digits in some basis, usually 2^w on a machine using w-bit registers), and the length of that array depends on the value itself: big integers grow and shrink as needed for the computation. This variable length implies a memory access pattern that depends on the numerical values of the integers, thus an inherently non-constant-time construct. Efforts at coercing a big integer library into constant-time behavior lead to, at best, fragile implementations with a complex API. What is really needed is a library for big *modular* integers, that is, integers that work modulo a given integer m, and that are aware of the size of m; with modular integers, the array of limbs can have a fixed size (which is the size that would be needed to store m itself) and a memory access pattern that depends only on that size, not on the value. Note that here we are assuming that the size of the modulus m is public, even if the value of m itself is not.

The most commonly used technique for computations on modular integers is the *Montgomery representation*. This representation works as long as the modulus m is an odd integer (it does not require m to be prime, but it must be odd). We suppose that values are represented as arrays of k limbs in basis 2^w (this implies that $m < 2^{kw}$).

Let $R = 2^{kw} \bmod m$. The Montgomery representation of x modulo m is the value $xR \bmod m$, represented as an integer in the 0 to $m-1$ range. This representation is compatible with additions and subtractions, since $(x+y)R = xR+yR$ for all integers x and y. The process to perform a modular addition in constant-time is as follows:

1) Add the two operands x and y limb by limb in the least to most significant order. Each addition receives a carry (0 or 1) from the previous addition, and outputs a carry. The value $x + y$ is stored in a temporary array t_1. The last carry is retained in a local variable c.

2) Subtract m from the result of the addition. Subtraction is also performed limb by limb, and a borrow (0 or 1) is similarly propagated. The subtraction output is written into another temporary t_2, and the borrow is stored in b.

3) If the final borrow equals the carry retained from the initial addition (i.e. b XOR $c = 0$), then the integer $x + y - m$ is non-negative; it is also less than m, since x and y were assumed to be less than m on entry. Thus, in that case, the proper result is in t_2. Otherwise, if the borrow is distinct from the carry (b XOR $c = 1$), then $x + y - m < 0$, and the correct result is in t_1. The modular addition routine thus ends with a constant-time selection process that copies into the destination array the value of either t_1 or t_2, depending on the value of b XOR c.

Montgomery multiplication is the reason we use the Montgomery representation: it is an operation which is related to modular multiplication, but easily amenable to constant-time implementations. The Montgomery multiplication of x and y computes $xy/R \bmod m$; thus, applying the Montgomery multiplication on $xR \bmod m$ and $yR \bmod m$ (the Montgomery representations of x and y modulo m, respectively) yields $(xR)(yR)/R = (xy)/R \bmod m$, that is, the Montgomery representation of the product xy modulo m. This leads to the following overall implementation strategy: input values are converted to the Montgomery representation, all operations are then performed in the Montgomery representation, and only the final output (e.g. right before encoding into bytes for I/O purposes) is converted back to the normal representation. Conversion *to* the Montgomery representation is done by doing a Montgomery multiplication of the input with the value $R^2 \bmod m$, which can be precomputed if m is known in advance, or otherwise computed once for each modulus m; conversion *from* the Montgomery representation back to the normal representation similarly uses a Montgomery multiplication with 1. Thus, all we need is an efficient constant-time implementation of the Montgomery multiplication itself.

Montgomery multiplication works as follows:

– Given inputs x and y, compute $z = xy$ as an integer. Since x and y use k limbs each, the product z may use as much as $2k$ limbs. We number limbs z_i in least to most significant order, starting at z_0.

– We set the n low limbs of z to zero as follows. For $i = 0$ to $k - 1$:

- compute $f_i = -z_i/m_0 \bmod 2^w$. This involves only register-sized integers (w bits);

- add $2^{wi} f_i m$ to z. This leaves the limbs 0 to $i-1$ of z undisturbed, and on output z_i, they are now zero as well.

– We now have $z = xy + fm$ for some integer f. Since the k low limbs of z are now all zeros, z is a non-modular multiple of 2^{kw}, and we can divide it by R by simply right-shifting the whole value by k limbs.

– Analysis shows that the value of z at this point is equal to $xy/R \bmod m$, and, as an integer, lies between 0 and $2m-1$. It suffices to perform a conditional subtraction of m to obtain the result (subtract m, and keep the result if and only if the final borrow from the subtraction is 0).

There are various ways to organize this process in order to minimize RAM usage or data movement, for example, by interleaving the initial computation of xy (as integers) with the addition of the $f_i m$ values and right shifting. The division by $-m_0$ modulo 2^w can be performed with a single integer multiplication instruction, as long as the value $-1/m_0 \bmod 2^w$ is precomputed; this can be done at development time if the modulus is known a priori, but it can also be efficiently computed at runtime by noticing that if a is an inverse of b modulo 2^t, then $a(2-ab)$ is an inverse of b modulo 2^{2t} (this is a subcase of Hensel's lifting lemma). This leads to the following routine to compute $-1/m_0 \bmod 2^{32}$:

```
uint32_t neginvert32(uint32_t m0)
{
        uint32_t t = 2 - m0;
        t *= 2 - t * m0;
        t *= 2 - t * m0;
        t *= 2 - t * m0;
        t *= 2 - t * m0;
        return -t;
}
```

Normally, we choose k to be of minimal size, since Montgomery multiplication has cost $O(k^2)$. However, in some situations, it can be worthwhile to add an extra limb, and allow input operands to slightly exceed m. Indeed, suppose that $m \leq 2^{(k-1)w} - 2^{(k-2)w}$ (i.e. m fits on $k-1$ limbs, and its top limb is not $2^w - 1$). Then, we allow operands x and y to slightly exceed m, as long as they also fit on $k-1$ limbs (i.e. $x, y \leq 2^{(k-1)w} - 1$). Then, the value z computed after k rounds of Montgomery reduction, right before the division (right shift) by R, is such that:

$$
\begin{aligned}
z &= xy + fm \\
&\leq (2^{(k-1)w} - 1)^2 + (2^{kw} - 1)(2^{(k-1)w} - 2^{(k-2)w}) \\
&< 2^{kw}(2^{(k-1)w} - 1)
\end{aligned}
$$

Thus, after the right shift, the result already fits on $k - 1$ limbs, and the conditional subtraction of m is no longer needed. For large moduli, this trick does not bring substantial improvements, since the cost of conditional subtraction is much smaller than that of the multiplication; however, it can be worthwhile for small moduli, especially in the extreme situation where the modulus is smaller than a single register, as is typically the case for lattice-based cryptography. For instance, if the modulus is lower than 2^{16} on a 32-bit system, then using $R = 2^{32}$ instead of $R = 2^{16}$ can leverage this kind of optimization. Careful analysis or exhaustive tests are required to make sure that the computed output is correct in all cases. Note that allowing elements to exceed the modulus in their representation means that some normalization will be needed at some point, for example, before encoding, but also when performing equality comparisons.

While the Montgomery representation works for any odd modulus, some situations allow using a modulus with a special format that allows for faster reduction. This is, in particular, the case for many elliptic curves, where the base field modulus is chosen a priori and is fixed. For instance, the well-known Curve25519 has coordinates in the field of integers modulo $p = 2^{255} - 19$; in that case, a value x larger than p (e.g. the result of an integer multiplication) can be split into a low and high halves as $x = x_0 + 2^{255}x_1$ (with $x_0 < 2^{255}$) that allows an efficient partial reduction modulo p as $x = x_0 + 19x_1 \bmod p$, since $2^{255} = 19 \bmod p$. Fast implementations typically use limbs slightly shorter than a machine register to allow delaying carry propagation by accumulating some extra bits in each limb. The main implementation difficulty is ensuring that no internal value overflows its storage slot, that is, that sufficient carry propagation is performed as appropriate. This is related to constant-time issues in the following sense: in a constant-time implementation, we cannot test at runtime whether more propagation or reduction effort is needed; thus, a thorough mathematical analysis must be performed to guarantee that in all possible situations, all internal values have their expected range. In particular, edge cases that make some incorrect implementations fail are often rare, and thus not detected with randomized procedures such as Monte Carlo tests.

7.4.2. *Modular exponentiation*

Modular exponentiation is the expensive core of the classic asymmetric cryptographic algorithms RSA and Diffie–Hellman. The operation consists of computing $y = x^d \bmod m$. The exponent d is large (possible as large as m) and secret; the input x or the output y may also be secret; in the case of RSA, where private key operations typically use the Chinese remainder theorem to work modulo each of the private factors, the modulus m is also secret, even though the length of the modulus is not. We assume that arithmetic operations modulo m are implemented in a constant-time manner, for instance, using the Montgomery representation, as described above.

The base algorithm is the “square-and-multiply”, which is classically described as follows (we assume that $x \neq 0$):

1) Start with $y = 1$.

2) For each bit d_i of d, in most-to-least significant order:

- compute: $y \leftarrow y^2 \bmod m$;
- if $d_i = 1$, then compute: $y \leftarrow xy \bmod m$.

If the exponent has length k bits, then this process entails k squarings (we can avoid the very first squaring, since at that point y is necessarily equal to 1) and on average $k/2$ multiplications, depending on how many bits of d are equal to 1. This is, of course, not constant-time, for two reasons:

– The total number of iterations depends on the length of the exponent d, which is secret.

– The multiplications by x are performed conditionally on the bits of d, leading to a memory access pattern and a total execution time that depend on these secret values.

Other side-channels (e.g. power analysis) may also reveal whether individual multiplications by x are performed or not; the constant-time techniques described below can help with defending against such non-timing-based side-channels.

These two issues can be addressed in a simple way, although at a cost. To hide the length of d, the trick is to pad the exponent with as many zero bits as needed to reach a publicly known maximum size of the exponent; for instance, if working modulo a 1024-bit prime p, then the exponent can always fit in a 1024-bit integer (since we can use d modulo $p - 1$), and thus perform exactly 1024 iterations of the loop, even though the first few of them may be mathematically useless (value y will remain 1 until the first non-zero bit of d is reached). The conditional execution of multiplications must also be converted into an *unconditional* execution: the multiplication is always performed, but a constant-time multiplexer is used to either keep or discard the result, depending on the value of the bit d_i.

These modifications make the exponentiation constant-time, but also substantially increase the cost, since we now perform k squarings and k multiplications. The number of multiplications can be reduced by using a *window optimization*, in which bits of the exponents are processed in chunks of w bits. We suppose here (for simplicity) that the length of d is k bits (possibly with padding, i.e. the top few bits of d may be zero) and is a multiple of w. The algorithm becomes the following:

1) Compute values $t_j = x^j \bmod m$ for all integers j from 0 to $2^w - 1$, and keep them in a table of length 2^w.

2) Set $y = 1$.

3) For $i = k/w - 1$ down to 0:

- compute $y \leftarrow y^{2^w} \bmod m$ with m successive squarings;

- using $n = \sum_{j=0}^{w-1} d_{iw+j}2^j$ (i.e. the value of the ith chunk of w bits of the exponent), compute: $y \leftarrow yt_n \bmod m$.

This algorithm is constant-time provided that:

– the lookup process, to retrieve value t_n from the table, is constant-time. This is done similarly to the `read_byte()` function described previously, but with larger elements;

– the lookup and the multiplication are always done, even if n is zero for an iteration, and the value t_n is then equal to 1. We must not "optimize" that case away.

This process does not change the cost of the squarings of y (there are still k squarings, although we can statically avoid the first w of them). The number of multiplications in the main loop is now k/w, which is quite lower than k, and gets even lower with a larger window w; on the other hand, a larger w implies more work to build the window ($2^w - 2$ multiplications), higher temporary storage costs (the table has size 2^w elements) and a more expensive lookup process in the table (the lookup must read all 2^w elements and select the correct one). There is thus an optimal value of w that depends on the usage context (typical values range from 2 to 6).

There is another classic optimization known as w-NAF (non-adjacent form). This method can be understood as a refinement over the window optimization: the algorithm above performs one multiplication every w squarings, but if the multiplication was for a value x^n with an even value of n, then it could have been replaced with a multiplication with $x^{n/2}$ performed one squaring earlier: $y^2x^n = (yx^{n/2})^2$. This can be leveraged into an algorithm that performs fewer multiplications (one every $w + 1$ squarings on average, instead of one every w squarings), and the table size and construction cost are halved (we only need x^n for odd integers n). However, an inherent consequence of that algorithm is that multiplications occur at varying times that depend on the values of the exponent bits. Therefore, a w-NAF optimization *cannot* be constant-time, and it *must not* be used when the exponent d is secret.

7.4.3. *Modular inversion*

Modular inversion consists of computing $1/x \bmod m$, given x and m. This operation is used in various algorithms, in particular in elliptic curve computations, where fractional coordinate systems are often used, requiring an inversion in the field to convert back points to affine coordinates.

When the modulus m is prime, a simple method is to use Fermat's Little Theorem: $1/x = x^{m-2} \bmod m$; thus, a modular exponentiation is sufficient. Moreover, if the prime modulus is also public (as is common in elliptic curve implementations), then the exponent $m - 2$ is non-secret, and some further optimizations such as w-NAF can be safely used. In the extreme case, a carefully tuned addition chain on the exponent is employed to make the number of extra multiplications as low as possible in a fully unrolled implementation (the number of squarings, though, does not change).

However, this method cannot be readily used when m is not prime; moreover, the cost of the modular exponentiation is usually cubic in the size of the modulus (for a modulus of k bits, it entails $O(k)$ squarings and multiplications, which have cost $O(k^2)$ with classic implementations such as Montgomery multiplication). It is possible to compute an inversion modulo an odd integer m (not necessarily prime) in quadratic cost with variants of the extended Euclidean GCD algorithm. In its initial formulation, the extended GCD requires integer divisions and remainders, which will not be constant-time; but the *binary GCD* is amenable to constant-time implementations. One formal description of the binary GCD is as follows:

1) Set: $(a, b, u, v) \leftarrow (x, m, 1, 0)$.

2) While $a \neq 0$:
   if a is even, then:
   $$(a, u) \leftarrow (a/2, u/2 \bmod m);$$
   otherwise:
   If $a < b$, then: $(a, u, b, v) \leftarrow (b, v, a, u)$
   $$(a, u) \leftarrow ((a - b)/2, (u - v)/2 \bmod m).$$

3) If $b = 1$, then return v. Otherwise, x was not invertible modulo m.

This algorithm can be implemented in constant-time in the following way:

– It can be shown that if m has size k bits, then, at most, $2k - 1$ iterations are needed. Moreover, when a reaches zero, then extra iterations do not change the value of v and are thus harmless. We can therefore systematically run $2k - 1$ iterations, removing the conditional test on a in the "while" loop.

– At each iteration, two Boolean elements can be computed: a_0 is the least significant bit of a (0 if a is even, 1 otherwise), and c is the borrow resulting from the integer subtraction $a - b$. Then the three following operations are performed, in that order:

- (a, u) and (b, v) can be exchanged conditionally on the bit a_0 AND c;
- (b, v) are subtracted from (a, u) conditionally on the bit a_0;
- $(a, u) \leftarrow (a/2, u/2 \bmod m)$.

Provided that the conditional operations above are performed in a constant-time way, that is, always computed but conditionally retained with multiplexers, then each iteration is constant-time.

– The final test on b should also be made in constant-time. In some cases, it can be omitted; for instance, if the modulus is prime, then a non-invertible x may happen only if $x = 0$, in which case the final values of b and v are both zero. Depending on usage context, it may be appropriate to return a value of zero when trying to invert zero.

The binary GCD has quadratic complexity, but works on a bit-by-bit basis and thus tends to be somewhat slow with practical moduli sizes. Variants of this algorithm can be optimized, though, leading to implementations which are not only constant-time, but also even faster than Fermat's Little Theorem, even when working modulo a small prime with a special format that favors fast multiplications. The core observation is that in the binary GCD, decisions are made based both on the low bits (test on whether a is even or odd) and on the high bits (test on whether a is lower than b), so that each iteration needs to update the full values of a and b. However, we can make several iterations by only looking at small portions of the values, using an approximation of the real a and b:

– If using registers of size w bits, then we can extract the top $w/2 + 1$ bits of a and b (adjusted on the top non-zero bit of a or of b, whichever is highest) and the bottom $w/2 - 1$ bits of both to obtain approximate values a' and b' on which to run $w/2 - 1$ iterations. After this inner loop, modifications to the full-size a, b, u and v are performed in a single pass, and a potential sign adjustment is performed (Pornin 2020).

– Instead of the actual values of a and b, an approximation of the difference of their sizes can be maintained in a small integer variable. Iterations can then proceed looking only at the low bits of a and b, again propagating updates to the full-size a and b only once every w iterations (when using w-bit registers). More than $2k - 1$ iterations are then needed to always reach the result, but individual iterations are faster (Bernstein and Yang 2019).

If the modulus is even, then the binary GCD shown above cannot be used as is. We can extract the even part of m by writing $m = 2^s m'$ for some integer s and an odd m'; the input value x can then be inverted modulo 2^s and modulo m', separately, and recombined with the Chinese remainder theorem (for the inversion modulo 2^s, see the `neginvert32()` function above, the same principle can be applied for any size s). From a constant-time point of view, this will leak through side-channels, the number s of trailing zero bits of m, which may or may not be an issue in any specific context. One such case is when doing RSA key pair generation: the secret primes p and q are chosen randomly, and the public exponent e is inverted modulo $p - 1$ and $q - 1$; both $p - 1$ and $q - 1$ are even integers. A simple solution here is to choose p and q as Blum primes, that is, equal to 3 modulo 4, which implies that $(p - 1)/2$ and $(q - 1)/2$ are both odd. This makes the CRT reassembly easy and efficient: for a given e (odd), the inverse of e modulo 2 is 1; if the inverse of e modulo $(p - 1)/2$ is d', then the inverse of e modulo $p - 1$ is d' itself if the least significant bit of d' is 1, or $d' + (p - 1)/2$ if the least significant bit of d' is 0.

7.4.4. *Elliptic curves*

Elliptic curves are groups adequate for some cryptographic operations, in particular, key exchange (ECDH) and signatures (ECDSA, or variants of Schnorr signatures). The group is defined as points (x, y), whose two coordinates are elements of a finite field (usually integers modulo a given prime) that fulfill the curve equation, which is a polynomial in x and y of degree 3 (or 4, in some cases). Two points can be added together with a group law that can be expressed geometrically or analytically, and an extra formal point called the "point at infinity", with no defined coordinates, serves as neutral element in the group.

7.4.4.1. *Formula completeness*

The analytic expression of the point addition uses formulas over the source point coordinates that depend on the exact form of curve equation; although all curves can be expressed, with isomorphic changes of variables, into a *short Weierstraß* equation ($y^2 = x^3 + ax + b$, for two constants a and b, for finite fields of characteristic 5 or more), other equations can be used for *some* curves, and lead to distinct formulas. Obtained formulas, expressed in affine coordinates (x and y themselves), invariably involve at least one division in the field, which is expensive. Better performance is obtained by switching to a fractional coordinate system, in which both x and y are expressed as fractions, thus allowing most computations to use only additions, subtractions and multiplications in the field, and requiring only a single inversion at the end of a complex computation, such as multiplying a curve point by a scalar. Several such coordinate systems have been proposed (projective, Jacobian, etc.), leading to a large number of combinations of coordinate systems and curve equations, and so many resulting formulas for point addition.

All these formulas differ from each other in terms of performance and *completeness*. Completeness expresses whether formulas have special edge cases that require special handling. The following terminology is used, when adding points P_1 and P_2 together:

– *Incomplete formulas* have special cases when P_1 and P_2 are the same point, when P_1 and P_2 are opposite to each other (i.e. their sum is the point-at-infinity $\mathcal{O}$), and when either P_1 or P_2 (or both) are equal to $\mathcal{O}$.

– *Unified formulas* do not have a special case when $P_1 = P_2$. They still have edge cases for operations involving $\mathcal{O}$ as input or output operand.

– *Complete formulas* do not have any special case; they can handle all combinations of input points, including the point-at-infinity.

When making a constant-time implementation, involving secret point values, incomplete formulas are problematic, because the straightforward handling of special cases is with a conditional test that detects and handles special cases separately; the fact that a special case was encountered thus becomes detectable through timing-based side-channels, and that can leak information on the involved points and scalars. To avoid this problem, a *complete routine* for point addition is convenient. Complete formulas naturally lead to a complete routine. Unified formulas can be implemented in a complete routine by adjoining to the point representation a flag that marks the point as being equal to $\mathcal{O}$; the routine then uses the normal formulas, but also uses the flag to efficiently handle the formula edge cases as a corrective action. If working with incomplete formulas, then the same principle can be used, but at a substantially higher cost because of the doubling case ($P_1 = P_2$): a complete routine built upon incomplete formulas must usually compute both the normal point addition formulas and the specific point doubling formulas, and select the appropriate result in a constant-time way.

Therefore, it is possible to make a complete routine out of any formulas, but for improved performance, it is better to start with at least unified formulas. Unified and complete formulas exist for all curves, but with various costs, and some non-negligible savings can sometimes be achieved for some curves by using incomplete formulas in cases where it can be shown a priori that edge cases are not encountered.

7.4.4.2. *Point multiplication*

Point multiplication is about computing the point dP for a source point P and an integer d. The multiplier is often called a *scalar* to distinguish it from the field in which point coordinates are expressed; scalars are integers modulo the order of the curve (or of a subgroup of the curve of which the provided point P is part); here, we will use q to denote the (sub)group order. Formally, this operation should be described as "multiplication of a point by a scalar", since we are not multiplying two points together. The expression "point multiplication" is thus an abuse of terminology, but has become a de facto accepted expression through widespread usage.

Point multiplication can be treated in about the same way as modular exponentiation. Since the curve group law is traditionally called an "addition", point addition is the equivalent of multiplication of modular integers, and the square-and-multiply algorithm is now called a double-and-add algorithm. This is, however, the same structure, and window optimizations apply. As in the case of modular exponentiation, w-NAF optimizations *must not* be used in constant-time implementations that handle secret scalars. Two issues specific to elliptic curves must still be discussed, about *signed windows*, and about incomplete formulas.

Signed windows are an additional optimization over the window optimizations. In the description of the modular exponentiation, the window contained values x^j for j ranging from 0 to $2^w - 1$. With elliptic curves, we can halve the table size by storing points jP for j ranging from 1 to 2^{w-1} instead. The idea is that given the point $Q = (x, y)$, the opposite $-Q$ can normally be computed very efficiently (with a short Weierstraß curve, $-Q = (x, -y)$). Thus, given the table of points jP for $j = 1$ to

2^{w-1}, we can easily obtain the points $-jP$. This allows a modified double-and-add algorithm with window optimization with the following characteristics:

– The scalar d is split into *signed* chunks d_i, each in the -2^{w-1} to $+2^{w-1}$ range, with the following process: using a carry bit c (initialized to 0) and processing the bits of e in chunks of w bits in least-to-most significant order, we consider the value $v + c$ for a chunk of value v:

- if $v + c \leq 2^{w-1}$, then emit $d_i = v + c$ and set c to 0;
- otherwise, emit $d_i = v + c - 2^w$ and set c to 1.

If the (public) maximum length of d is k bits, then $\lceil (k + 1)/w \rceil$ signed chunks d_i must be produced to ensure that the final carry value is zero.

– Only the points P to $2^{w-1}P$ are computed and stored in the table.

– During the double-and-add algorithm, whenever the point d_iP must be obtained from the table, the constant-time lookup is performed on index $|d_i|$, and a constant-time conditional negation is used to compute $-|d_i|P$ from the point looked up from the table in case $d_i < 0$; similar constant-time code is used to substitute the point-at-infinity in case $d_i = 0$.

Since signed windows halve the size of the window, hence also its cost of construction, and the cost of each lookup, they allow the use of larger windows, thereby improving performance.

Incomplete formulas, as pointed out previously, are inconvenient for constant-time implementations, but they can to some extent be used for point multiplication. Indeed, if both following conditions hold:

– the source point P is guaranteed to be part of a subgroup of prime order q, and is not $\mathcal{O}$;

– the scalar d is in the 0 to $q - 1$ range.

Then it can be shown that none of the point additions in the double-and-add algorithm with signed windows, except in the last iteration, may involve the special case of a point added to itself. In other words, we do not have to worry about additions being in fact doublings in disguise, and incomplete formulas can thus be used. Note, however, that we still need to maintain "neutral" flags to handle cases where either the current intermediate result or the point looked up from the table is the neutral $\mathcal{O}$; these operations are not expensive, but they must not be omitted. Also, the last iteration *must* use a complete routine: that last iteration may indeed really be a point doubling, for a specific scalar value. Finally, note the importance of the conditions expressed above: if the scalar is not lower than the point order, or if the point order is not prime (e.g. it is not part of the expected subgroup), then the use of incomplete formulas may fail and produce wrong values.

Some widespread elliptic curves use the short Weierstraß equation; this is the case, in particular, for the NIST curves P-256, P-384 and P-521, as well as the well-known secp256k1 curve. When implementing support for such curves, it is *recommended* that complete formulas be used (Renes et al. 2016). If, in a given situation, you are desperate for performance, then the trick with incomplete formulas described above can be used, because these standard curves also have prime order, and thus validate that an incoming point fulfilling the curve equation is enough to guarantee that the point is in the proper prime-order group; this, however, entails some more code complexity than the direct use of complete formulas, and is thus not recommended in general.

7.4.4.3. *Montgomery Ladder*

The *Montgomery Ladder* is based on the remark that in some curve equations, the x coordinate of point dP depends only on the scalar d and the x coordinate of P, not on the y coordinate of P (in other words, dP and $-dP$ have the same x coordinate). Thus, it is possible to make an x-only point multiplication algorithm. The algorithm, at any point, maintains the x coordinates of points nP and $(n+1)P$ for some integer n; then, at each iteration:

– the points nP and $(n+1)P$ are added together, yielding the x coordinate of $(2n+1)P$. The formulas leverage the fact that $(n+1)P - nP$ is the known point P to avoid using the y coordinate of any point, which can remain implicit;

– one of the points nP and $(n+1)P$ is doubled, yielding the x coordinate of either $2nP$ or $(2n+2)P$.

Thus, with a single conditional swap of the two points nP and $(n+1)P$, the iteration produces the x coordinates of either $(2nP, (2n+1)P)$ or $((2n+1)P, (2n+2)P)$. Using the bits of the scalar e as control for this swap operation, the algorithm finally yields the x coordinates of dP and $(d+1)P$. The x coordinate of dP is enough for some protocols (e.g. ECDH, where the obtained shared secret is indeed defined as the x coordinate of the point). Moreover, if the y coordinate of P is also known, then the y coordinate of dP can be computed at moderate cost from the x coordinates of dP and $(d+1)P$.

The Montgomery Ladder eschews the use of window optimizations. However, each iteration is especially efficient when the used curve is a Montgomery curve (the equation is $By^2 = x^3 + Ax^2 + x$ for two constants A and B), thus allowing very good performance for point multiplication by a scalar, with a very simple and size-efficient implementation (both in terms of code footprint and transient RAM usage). For other curves, similar x-only ladder formulas exist, but with higher costs (up to about 1.6 times the cost of a Montgomery curve implementation).

If code compactness and low RAM usage are high-priority goals, then the use of an x-only ladder is a convenient way to compute point multiplications; the involved formulas are complete, and a constant-time implementation is easily achieved with a single primitive (a constant-time swap of two values), provided that the underlying field operations are themselves implemented in a constant-time way.

7.5. References

Bernstein, D.J. and Yang, B.-Y. (2019). Fast constant-time GCD computation and modular inversion. Report 2019/266, Cryptology ePrint Archive [Online]. Available at: https://eprint.iacr.org/2019/266.

Boyar, J. and Peralta, R. (2009). New logic minimization techniques with applications to cryptology. Report 2009/191, Cryptology ePrint Archive [Online]. Available at: https://eprint.iacr.org/2009/191.

Kocher, P.C. (1996). Timing attacks on implementations of Diffie-Hellman, RSA, DSS, and other systems. In *CRYPTO'96*, Koblitz, N. (ed.). Springer, Heidelberg.

Pornin, T. (2020). Optimized binary GCD for modular inversion. Report 2020/972, Cryptology ePrint Archive [Online]. Available at: https://eprint.iacr.org/2020/972.

Renes, J., Costello, C., Batina, L. (2016). Complete addition formulas for prime order elliptic curves. In *EUROCRYPT 2016*, Fischlin, M. and Coron, J.-S. (eds). Springer, Heidelberg.

8

Protected AES Implementations

Franck RONDEPIERRE
Agence nationale de la sécurité des systèmes d'information, Paris, France

AES stands for Advanced Encryption Standard and was the algorithm selected in 2000 after an international competition organized by the American Institute for Standardization (NIST). The algorithm is designed to encrypt or decrypt blocks of fixed size (of 16 bytes) with one of three security levels: 128, 192 or 256 bits. It is very efficient in ensuring confidentiality and integrity of large amount of data. It can also be used as a key derivation or a hash function. Due to its efficiency and its robustness, the AES is probably the most used algorithm for symmetric cryptography nowadays.

We give hereafter a short overview of the encryption in Algorithm 8.1. Details will be given in the following sections.

The AES function is a bit faster than its inverse[1] and hence has been selected for encryption, but it can also be used for decryption. It all depends on the context, such as if we want to speed up the evaluation of encryptions or decryptions. For instance, if we want to keep data encrypted which we will often access, we can use the inverse function to "encrypt" it and the AES function to "decrypt" it.

We will look at the possible ways to implement the AES cryptosystem while taking into account the running time, the memory footprint and the security against side-channel attacks.

1 The inverse of the MixColumn and the key scheduling are slower.

Embedded Cryptography 2,
coordinated by Emmanuel PROUFF, Guénaël RENAULT,
Matthieu RIVAIN and Colin O'FLYNN.

Algorithm 8.1. AES function

Require: key k, block b
Ensure: block c, the encryption of b

```
state = State(b)
n ∈ {10, 12, 14}, depending on keylength
state = state ⊕ RoundKey(k, 0)
for i from 1 to n − 1 do
    state = SubByte(state)
    state = ShiftRow(state)
    state = MixColumn(state)
    state = state ⊕ RoundKey(k, i)
end for
state = SubByte(state)
state = ShiftRow(state)
state = state ⊕ RoundKey(k, n)
c = UnState(state)
```

8.1. Generic countermeasures

8.1.1. *1 among N*

In order to increase the security of an implementation of a block-cipher, we can hide the real computation among dummy processes, with a total of N process. Each process consists of the whole computation with either a dummy key or the real key. This generic method always applies and is especially interesting if we cannot access the AES implementation itself, such as when driving a hardware AES. It also applies, of course, for both encryption and decryption. In the context of a very fast AES execution combined with a low probability to mount a successful attack, this countermeasure can be the most efficient one.

8.1.1.1. *Secure "if"*

The selection of the correct key shall not leak through the execution, otherwise an attacker can select the correct process with a post-execution analysis or, even worse, they may achieve the detection during the execution with a module that recognizes the leakage. In Algorithm 8.2, we can see a way to securely implement this selection. Note that the presented solution requires a bit table s whose memory cost depends on N. How to efficiently implement this table or how to generate the same bit of information without a table is generally dependent on the instruction set of the processor. It may also happen that the hardware module for the AES already implements this countermeasure and we only have to select the value of N according to our needs.

8.1.1.2. *Values of N*

In practice, the size and the form of the value N matters. For instance, we can restrict N to be a power of 2 (i.e. $N = 2^a$) in order to improve the generation of r in Algorithm 8.2 (only select a random bits). If N is not a power of 2, we will have to draw and discard (if $r \geq N$) in order to avoid any bias. For high values of N, it is probably best to remove the restriction about power of 2, since in this case, the cost needed to generate r will be negligible against the cost of all AES executions.

Besides, we will often want the loop to support the trivial case $N = 1$. Indeed, having N as an input parameter instead of a constant offers two advantages: the same function can be used for several contexts, and for a given context, we can adapt the security during the lifetime of a product.

Algorithm 8.2. 1 among N with secure if

Require: Key k, block b, N
Ensure: block c, the encryption of b
  Generate k' a dummy key with same length as k
  Draw a random value $0 \leq r < N$
  Generate a select table: $\forall i \neq r, s[i] = 0; s[r] = 1$
  Two address tables K and C: $K[0] = @k', K[1] = @k, C[0] = @c', C[1] = @c$
  for i **from** 0 to $N - 1$ **do**
    $C[s[i]] = \text{AES}(K[s[i]], b)$
  end for

8.1.2. *Integrity*

We have to check the integrity of the key and the encrypted/decrypted block after an AES computation. Indeed, many attacks rely on disturbing the chip in order to get a modified intermediate state for a given static key. The more controlled the fault is, the more information is retrieved about the key. Detecting each perturbation greatly limits the power of the attacker if we implement a deadlock mechanism, which accepts only a given number of detected faults. Due to calibration and low reproductibility of perturbations, many faults are needed in practice to mount a successful attack. Hence, even if some perturbations are not detected (like ineffective or safe errors), we will thwart attacks in practice.

8.1.2.1. *Result integrity*

This check allows us to detect ephemeral faults. There are two generic methods to check the integrity of the computed block: compare the results of two identical executions ($E_1(x) = E_2(x)$) or compare the input block with the result of one execution and its inverse ($x = E^{-1}(E(x))$). However, if an attacker is able to inject the same fault twice with good temporal precision, they will defeat the first countermeasure by disturbing the same operation in E_1 and E_2, whereas the inversion E^{-1} should be different enough from the direct function E to prevent this attack.

Besides, the more executions, the harder it is to mount an attack. For instance, you can triple executions (and combine double execution with inverse computation) with two comparisons or you can also check the integrity of all (dummy) computed blocks when combined with the "1 among N" countermeasure.

8.1.2.2. *Key integrity*

It is possible to detect (semi-)permanent faults applied to the key. Once a key K has been generated, we compute a constant checksum value $c_K = C(K)$ and store it with the key. After the computation of one (or several) block(s) with the key K, we are now able to detect that a fault occurred if the values c_K and $C(K)$ are different. We may instantiate the function C with a CRC (polynomial division), a hash function or the AES encryption/decryption of a constant message. In case of hardware implementation of the AES, this latter case is likely the best option if we do not need to reload the key. In case of software implementation, it is also possible to store both the first round key and the last one. In case we limit the RAM consumption to only one round key, this will speed up the decryption and we will be able to check the key scheduling by comparing the round key used for the final xor with the round key stored.

8.1.2.3. *Overall integrity*

If we are able to compute several blocks with a unique sequence of operations, we can use one of these blocks as an integrity block control. For instance, this is the case with the so-called bitslice implementation where two (or even four) blocks are simultaneously computed. We can lose some performance and use one block (out of two or four) for an integrity check.

After the generation of a key K, we have to compute both values $c_{\text{enc}} = \text{AES}(K, m_{\text{enc}})$ and $c_{\text{dec}} = \text{AES}^{-1}(K, m_{\text{dec}})$ for given values m_{enc} and m_{dec}. The encryption e_b of a block b is hence computed as $(e_b, c) = \text{AES}(K, b, m_{\text{enc}})$, where c is the check value computed for this block. The integrity of e_b and K is ensured if we have the equality $c = c_{\text{enc}}$.

8.2. Secure evaluation of the SubByte function

Many operations of the AES are performed in the field $\mathbb{F}_{2^8}$. An element a can be represented as a polynomial $a = a_7 \cdot X^7 + a_6 \cdot X^6 + a_5 \cdot X^5 + a_4 \cdot X^4 + a_3 \cdot X^3 + a_2 \cdot X^2 + a_1 \cdot X^1 + a_0$ with $a_i \in \{0, 1\}$. Hence, an element a can be represented as a byte: $a_7 \cdot 2^7 + a_6 \cdot 2^6 + a_5 \cdot 2^5 + a_4 \cdot 2^4 + a_3 \cdot 2^3 + a_2 \cdot 2^2 + a_1 \cdot 2^1 + a_0$. For example, the byte 2 stands for the element X. For the AES, this field is defined over $\mathbb{F}_2$ with the irreducible polynomial[2] $X^8 + X^4 + X^3 + X + 1$.

With such a representation, the addition of two elements a and b is performed with an exclusive-or: $a + b = a \oplus b$. The multiplication $a \cdot X$ (or $a \cdot 2$) is:

$$a_7 \cdot (X^4 + X^3 + X + 1) + a_6 \cdot X^7 + a_5 \cdot X^6 + a_4 \cdot X^5 + \\ a_3 \cdot X^4 + a_2 \cdot X^3 + a_1 \cdot X^2 + a_0 \cdot X^1$$

The multiplication of two elements a and b is:

$$a \cdot b = \sum_{i=0}^{7} b_i \cdot (a \cdot X^i) = \sum_{i=0}^{7} a_i \cdot (b \cdot X^i).$$

and the inverse of a is the element b such that $a \cdot b = 1$.

EXERCISE 8.1.– Compute the result of $\left(X^6 + X^5 + X + 1\right) \cdot \left(X^2 + X + 1\right)$.

EXERCISE 8.2.– Perform the Euclidean division of $\left(X^5 + X^4 + X\right)$ by $\left(X^2 + X + 1\right)$.

EXERCISE 8.3.– The following sequence is the application of the Euclidean algorithm to compute the greatest common divisor (gcd) of 0x11b and 0x63:

$$\begin{aligned} \texttt{0x11b} &= \texttt{7} \cdot \texttt{0x63} + \texttt{0x32} \\ \texttt{0x63} &= \texttt{2} \cdot \texttt{0x32} + \texttt{7} \\ \texttt{0x32} &= \texttt{0xb} \cdot \texttt{7} + \texttt{3} \\ \texttt{7} &= \texttt{2} \cdot \texttt{3} + \texttt{1} \end{aligned}$$

Deduce from this sequence the inverse of 0x63 in the AES field.

8.2.1. *S-box and inverse S-box*

The SubByte function is the most critical part of an AES implementation for the security and the performances.

2 If you know the complex numbers, $\mathbb{C}$ is built over $\mathbb{R}$ with the irreducible polynomial $X^2 + 1$.

8.2.1.1. *Definition*

This function is defined as the application of the same nonlinear function to each byte of the state. This function is generally represented as a table, the so-called S-box, and is defined as:

$$S[x] = A[x^{-1}] \oplus \texttt{0x63}$$

The inverse is taken in $\mathbb{F}_{2^8}^*$ (by convention $0^{-1} = 0$), and the $\mathbb{F}_2$ linear function A is defined as:

$$A[x]_i = x_i \oplus x_{i+4 \mod 8} \oplus x_{i+5 \mod 8} \oplus x_{i+6 \mod 8} \oplus x_{i+7 \mod 8}.$$

The inverse B of A is defined as:

$$B[x]_i = x_{i+2 \mod 8} \oplus x_{i+5 \mod 8} \oplus x_{i+7 \mod 8}.$$

Let T denote the inverse of S, i.e. $T[x] = (B[x \oplus \texttt{0x63}])^{-1}$. We also have:

$$T[x] = B[S[B[x \oplus \texttt{0x63}]] \oplus \texttt{0x63}].$$

So, we are now able to evaluate the T-box by reusing the code for the S-box at the expense of some extra xors. This will be useful for section 8.2.6.

8.2.2. *Security*

The first operation of the AES consists of combining (xoring) a secret key and the input block. The AES state after this operation is a sensitive value, which can be the target of side-channel attacks. In order to thwart these attacks, sensitive values are split in several shares; the more shares, the better the security. The order t of protection of an implementation refers here to a number $t+1$ of shares. A sensitive value a is noted in lowercase, the shared variable A is noted in uppercase and denotes the vector of shares a_i. We have:

$$A = (a_0, \ldots, a_t)$$

$$a = \bigoplus_i a_i$$

We will discuss how to evaluate $S[x]$ when x is represented as a shared variable. We can note that for a function f which is $\mathbb{F}_2$ linear, $(f(a_0), \ldots, f(a_t))$ is a sharing of $f(a)$. Hence, we will focus on the inversion that is not $\mathbb{F}_2$ linear.

8.2.3. *Secure table lookup*

We will look at generic methods to securely evaluate the S-box.

8.2.3.1. *S-box*

Any S-box can be protected with table recomputations. When targeting only the first order of protection, the table can be computed once for a whole AES execution, for constant masks m drawn for this execution:

$$\forall x, S'[x] = S[x \oplus m] \oplus m.$$

We can either only compute the table corresponding to the mask m or store all the 256 tables in non-volatile memory for a total cost of 65,536 bytes, though this latter solution is a bit overkill. We can note that the mask m is combined with a potentially known value x when computing the table S'. Besides, we have at most 252 evaluations of the S-box S' for one AES execution (in case of AES 256), which should not be enough to allow a successful attack to recover the mask m in practice.

When targeting higher orders of protection, the table shall be refreshed before each evaluation that heavily impacts performances.

8.2.3.2. *White box*

White box cryptography relies on lookup tables, although it has its own attacker model. In particular, the key shall be concealed even for the owner of the storage device. Before any SubByte evaluation, one round key is added (xored) to the state. Hence, we can merge this addition with the S-box evaluation. For instance, let $k_{i,j}$ denote the jth byte of the ith round key. Then the stored tables would look like:

$$S_{i,j}[x] = S[x \oplus k_{i,j}].$$

Hence, the 128-bit subkey is no more stored as 128-bit value, but its information is split between several tables, and tables are very convenient to implement any function or function composition (on the respective input/output domains). This principle also applies to different expressions of the S-box. It is especially used with a sequence of Boolean expressions equivalent to the S-box. Indeed, when tabulating functions, the smaller the inputs the less memory consuming. See section 8.2.6 for such sequences.

White box cryptography also relies on many more techniques to increase the obfuscation.

8.2.4. *Evaluation in* $\mathbb{F}_{2^8}$

In this section, we will use the definition of the S-box to securely compute its evaluation. In $\mathbb{F}_{2^8}$, we have $x^{-1} = x^{254}$. There are several ways to evaluate this exponentiation. For instance, we have:

$$x^{254} = \left(\left(x \cdot x^2\right)^4 \cdot x^3\right)^{16} \cdot \left(x^{12} \cdot x^2\right)$$
$$= \left(x^{16} \cdot x\right)^{(4+1)\cdot 2+4} \cdot x^{16}$$

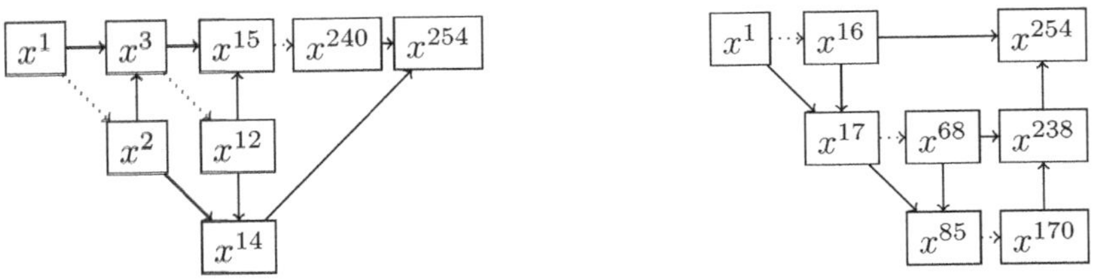

Both sequences require four multiplications in $\mathbb{F}_{2^8}$ and three evaluations of x^{2^n}. Depending on how the multiplication is implemented, it can be of interest to have in the sequence pairs of multiplications with the format $a \cdot b$, $a \cdot c$.

Since the Frobenius is a linear application (i.e. we have $(x+y)^{2^n} = x^{2^n} + y^{2^n}$), it can be efficiently applied to masked variables. We shall use an ISW algorithm to secure the multiplication $a \cdot b$ in $\mathbb{F}_{2^8}$.

8.2.4.1. *ISW multiplication*

Algorithm 8.3 describes the multiplication of two shared variables A and B. This algorithm implies $(t+1)^2$ multiplications and $\frac{t(t+1)}{2}$ draws of random values.

Secure usage of the ISW multiplication $a \cdot b$ requires that the shares of A and B are independent. A mask refreshing is equivalent to an ISW multiplication by the neutral element 1 (seen as shared value) and allows us to get new independent shares. No multiplication between shares is required for a mask refreshing, but we still have to draw as many random values.

8.2.4.2. *Multiplication in* $\mathbb{F}_{2^8}$

We can first evaluate the multiplication $\mathbb{F}_{2^8} \times \mathbb{F}_{2^8} \mapsto \mathbb{F}_{2^8}$ with a lookup table. This solution offers fast evaluation but the table requires a significant amount of memory to be stored: 65,536 bytes. We can also split values in $\mathbb{F}_{2^8}$ as the sum of two 4-bit elements. For instance, let $a = \left(a_1 \cdot X^4 + a_0\right)$, the product of $a, b \in \mathbb{F}_{2^8}$ becomes:

$$a \cdot b = (a_1 \cdot b_1)\, X^8 + ((a_0 + a_1) \cdot (b_0 + b_1) + a_1 \cdot b_1 + a_0 \cdot b_0)\, X^4 + (a_0 \cdot b_0).$$

Algorithm 8.3. ISW multiplication

Require: Shared variables $A = (a_0, \ldots, a_t)$, $B = (b_0, \ldots, b_t)$ such that $a = \bigoplus a_i$, $b = \bigoplus b_i$
Ensure: Shared variable C such that $c = a \cdot b$
  for i **from** 0 to t **do**
    $c_i \leftarrow a_i \cdot b_i$
  end for
  for i **from** 0 to $t-1$ **do**
    for j **from** $i+1$ to t **do**
      Draw random value r
      $c_i \leftarrow (r \oplus c_i) \oplus a_i \cdot b_j$
      $c_j \leftarrow (r \oplus c_j) \oplus a_j \cdot b_i$
    end for
  end for

We can use three tables of 256 bytes each to evaluate the products $m \cdot n$, $m \cdot X^4$, $m \cdot X^8$ with $m, n \in \mathbb{F}_{2^4}$.

We can also select a generator α of $\mathbb{F}_{2^8}$ and use two tables E and L: $E[i] = \alpha^i$, $L[\alpha^i] = i$.

With these tables, a multiplication is actually transformed into an addition modulo 255. For $a, b \in \mathbb{F}^*_{2^8}$, we have $a \cdot b = E[L[a] + L[b] \mod 255]$. As you may have noticed, the multiplication by zero requires a dedicated process which should not leak through side-channels. We can use another dedicated table D for this process:

$$D[i] = \begin{cases} 0 & \text{if } i = 0 \\ 255 & \text{otherwise} \end{cases}$$

and eventually, we have our multiplication for $a, b \in \mathbb{F}_{2^8}$:

$$a \cdot b = D[a] \& D[b] \& E[L[a] + L[b] \mod 255]$$

EXERCISE 8.4.– Find a generator α and generate corresponding tables E and L.

EXERCISE 8.5.– Find an algorithm to efficiently reduce modulo $2^n - 1$.

8.2.4.3. *Frobenius in* $\mathbb{F}_{2^8}$

In order to evaluate the Frobenius x^{2^n}, we can either store a dedicated table for every value $n \in \{1, 2, 4\}$ or we can use the same tables E, L and D as for the multiplication:

$$x^{2^n} = D[x] \& E[L[x] \cdot 2^n \mod 255]$$

8.2.4.4. *Multiplication* $x \cdot x^{2^n}$

There are two ways to consider the evaluation of $x \cdot x^{2^n}$: either as one multiplication or as one function of x.

After the Frobenius application, shares of x and x^{2^n} are not independent. Hence, actually one ISW multiplication and a mask refreshing shall be performed for the first consideration:

$$x \cdot \left(x^{2^n} \cdot 1\right).$$

For $n > 0$, let $h(x) = x \cdot x^{2^n}$ and let $f(x, y) = x \cdot y^{2^n} \oplus y \cdot x^{2^n}$. For $x, y, r \in \mathbb{F}_{2^8}$, we have:

$$f(x, y) = h(x \oplus y \oplus r) \oplus h(x \oplus r) \oplus h(y \oplus r) \oplus h(r).$$

By using a lookup table to evaluate h, we can speed up the secure multiplication $x \cdot x^{2^n}$. Only four table lookups are required in the ISW loop (see Algorithm 8.4) instead of the two multiplications $a_i \cdot a_j^{2^n}$ and $a_j \cdot a_i^{2^n}$. Note that overall the same amount of random values are needed in both cases ($t(t+1)$).

Algorithm 8.4. ISW for the special case $x \cdot x^{2^n}$

Require: Shared variable $A = (a_0, \ldots, a_t)$ such that $a = \bigoplus a_i$, table $h(x) = x \cdot x^{2^n}$
Ensure: Shared variable C such that $c = a \cdot a^{2^n}$

```
for i from 0 to t do
    c_i ← h(a_i)
end for
for i from 0 to t − 1 do
    for j from i + 1 to t do
        Draw two random values r, r'
        c_i ← c_i ⊕ r'
        c_j ← c_j ⊕ r'
        c_i ← c_i ⊕ h(r)
        c_i ← c_i ⊕ h(a_i ⊕ r)
        c_i ← c_i ⊕ h(a_j ⊕ r)
        c_i ← c_i ⊕ h((a_j ⊕ r) ⊕ a_i)
    end for
end for
```

8.2.5. *Tower field*

They are many equivalent representations of $\mathbb{F}_{2^8}$. Canright (2005) and Boyar and Peralta (2009) use the following constructions:

– $\mathbb{F}_{2^2}$ is defined over $\mathbb{F}_2$ with the polynomial $X^2 + X + 1$ and a root α.

– $\mathbb{F}_{4^2}$ is defined over $\mathbb{F}_4$ with the polynomial $X^2 + X + \alpha^2$ and a root β.

– $\mathbb{F}_{16^2}$ is defined over $\mathbb{F}_{16}$ with the polynomial $X^2 + X + \lambda$ and a root γ, $\lambda = \alpha\beta$.

Kim et al. (2011) use slightly different polynomials ($X^2+X+\alpha$ and $\lambda = (\alpha+1)\beta$) and they actually only need $\mathbb{F}_{16}$. In both cases, the idea is to compute in practice the inversion in $\mathbb{F}_{16}$. Indeed, for $x \in \mathbb{F}_{2^8}$, we have $c = x^{17} \in \mathbb{F}_{16}$ (since $c^{16} = c$) and then $x^{-1} = c^{-1} \cdot x^{16}$.

8.2.5.1. *Tower field down to* $\mathbb{F}_{16}$

Let $a = a_h\gamma + a_\ell$ be an element of $\mathbb{F}_{16^2}$, with $a_h, a_\ell \in \mathbb{F}_{16}$. We have:

$$a^{16} = a_h\gamma + (a_h + a_\ell)$$

$$a^{17} = \lambda a_h^2 + (a_h + a_\ell) \cdot a_\ell$$

$$c^{-1} = (c^2 \cdot c)^4 \cdot c^2$$

If we list the operations in $\mathbb{F}_{16}$, we have one addition, one square, one λ product, three multiplications and one inversion (can cost two multiplications, one square and one fourth power). Elements are small enough to allow evaluations of these operations through look-up tables. Especially for the multiplication $\mathbb{F}_{16} \times \mathbb{F}_{16} \mapsto \mathbb{F}_{16}$, we can store the operation in only one table of 256 elements (either 256 bytes, or 128 bytes if we compress the table).

Besides, two isomorphisms δ and δ^{-1} are needed to map elements back and forth between $\mathbb{F}_{2^8}$ and $\mathbb{F}_{16^2}$. These mappings are $\mathbb{F}_2$ linear and can be merged with the linear part of the S-box.

If we compare with what is done in $\mathbb{F}_{2^8}$, we have to evaluate one more (ISW) multiplication, but each ($\mathbb{F}_{16}$) multiplication can be computed more efficiently.

8.2.5.2. *Tower field down to* $\mathbb{F}_2$

As per Boyar and Peralta (2009), we represent $\mathbb{F}_{2^2}$ using the basis (α, α^2), $\mathbb{F}_{(2^2)^2}$ using the basis (β^2, β^8) and $\mathbb{F}_{((2^2)^2)^2}$ using the basis (γ, γ^{16}). Let $a = a_h\gamma^{16} + a_\ell\gamma$ be an element of $\mathbb{F}_{((2^2)^2)^2}$. We have:

$$a^{16} = a_\ell\gamma^{16} + a_h\gamma$$

$$a^{17} = \lambda(a_h + a_\ell)^2 + a_h \cdot a_\ell$$

Let m, n be two elements of $\mathbb{F}_{(2^2)^2}$ ($m = m_h\beta^8 + m_\ell\beta^2$; $m_t = m_h + m_\ell$) and u, v two elements of $\mathbb{F}_{2^2}$ ($u = u_h\alpha^2 + u_\ell\alpha$; $u_t = u_h + u_\ell$). Karatsuba leads to:

$$u \cdot \alpha = u_t\alpha^2 + u_h\alpha$$

$$u \cdot \alpha^2 = u_\ell\alpha^2 + u_t\alpha$$

$$u \cdot v = (u_t \cdot v_t + u_h \cdot v_h)\,\alpha^2 + (u_t \cdot v_t + u_\ell \cdot v_\ell)\,\alpha$$

$$m \cdot n = \left(o^{(\ell)}\alpha^2 + o^{(h)}\alpha\right)\beta^8 + \left((m_\ell \cdot n_\ell)\alpha^2 + (o^{(\ell)})\alpha\right)\beta^2$$

where $o^{(h)} = m_t \cdot n_t + m_h \cdot n_h$ and $o^{(h)} = m_t \cdot n_t + m_\ell \cdot n_\ell$. By noting that a multiplication (respectively an addition) in $\mathbb{F}_2$ is a logical AND (respectively an XOR), we can count the number of binary operations needed for the multiplication in $\mathbb{F}_{(2^2)^2}$: 9 AND, 26 XOR.

Besides, Boyar and Peralta (2009) found a heuristic to compute an inversion in $\mathbb{F}_{(2^2)^2}$ with only five AND and 11 XOR. Since an inversion in $\mathbb{F}_{((2^2)^2)^2}$ requires three multiplications and an inversion in $\mathbb{F}_{(2^2)^2}$, at least 32 AND are needed so far for the whole inversion.

8.2.6. *Bitslice S-box*

The AES S-box applies to one byte at a time, which means we can only evaluate one byte per CPU instruction with a straightforward implementation. However, modern processors can process more bits per instruction (typically 32 or 64 bits) and hence processing only 8 bits for the S-box evaluation is not always optimal.

One solution could be to store a huge table of $2^{32} \cdot 4$ bytes (16 gigabytes) for 32-bit processors (to evaluate 4 bytes with one table lookup). However, this solution is too expensive in memory and does not work for 64-bit processors.

8.2.6.1. *Boolean sequence*

Finding an equivalent Boolean expression to the S-box S (see section 8.2.5) allows us to achieve bitslice implementation. Given an input byte $I = (I_7, I_6, I_5, I_4, I_3, I_2, I_1, I_0)_2$, we look for a sequence of binary operations that allows us to compute the bits O_i from the bits I_i such that $O = S[I]$ (with $O = (O_7, O_6, O_5, O_4, O_3, O_2, O_1, O_0)_2$). Such sequences have been first designed to generate hardware evaluations of the S-box. Among all the existing sequences, we are looking for the ones minimizing the number of AND. Indeed, the secure evaluation of an AND is quadratic in the secure order, whereas the secure evaluation of a XOR is linear (see Chapter 1 of this volume). We also need a sequence for both the S-box S and its inverse T. However, as shown in section 8.2.1, both sequences can have the same number of nonlinear operations. Figure 8.1 describes a sequence credited to Çağdaş Çalik, whereas Figure 8.2 gives a sequence for the inverse S-box.

8.2.6.2. *Bitsliced word*

The optimal size of the word is determined by the size of the processor, but it also determines the number of bytes which shall be processed. Indeed, one AES state only contains 16 bytes, hence we have to combine several states to efficiently compute on 32-bit or 64-bit processors. The S-box is also applied on only 4 bytes while computing the round keys; and in this case, we should not apply the bitslice technique.

Besides, the organization inside each word is determined by several factors: the orthogonalization function, and other functions (like ShiftRow and MixColumn) if you keep the state orthogonalized (see section 8.3.8).

8.2.7. *How to select the S-box implementation*

We have covered several techniques to securely evaluate the AES S-box. We will briefly discuss in which context each technique applies.

8.2.7.1. *No masking or only one mask*

Before considering this case, you should verify twice if this security level fits your context. If it does, the lookup table is the easiest to implement, and it is probably the most efficient choice (especially on 8-bit CPU). On highend CPU, the bitslice implementation might provide the best performances when several blocks are processed in parallel.

8.2.7.2. *Constrained CPU or few S-box computations*

We will have to process in the field $\mathbb{F}_{2^8}$ when parallel computations are not interesting. This is the case when computing the AES round keys. Indeed, the S-box applies only on 4 bytes out of 16 and we have to wait for the computation of a whole round key before computing the next one. This may also correspond to the case where you can only compute one AES block at a time (for instance, when using CBC). Besides, if the CPU is limited in memory access to fetch only bytes or has a small number of registers when compared to the size of an AES state, then the bitslice technique will not improve the performances.

8.2.7.3. *Highend CPU and S-box computations in parallel*

If the CPU can process on a large amount of bits, you should use the bitslice implementation in order to achieve high performances. To store the AES state, at least eight words are required (one for each bit of the S-box input). It means that these words can contain one (respectively, 2, 4) AES state if the bitsize of a word is 16 (respectively, 32, 64). Hence, most modern CPU will be able to process several blocks of AES at a time. This can be used to speed up the encryption of a large sequence of blocks or to increase the integrity of the result (see section 8.1.2).

$$\begin{aligned}
B_8 &= B_4 \oplus B_2 \\
B_9 &= B_7 \oplus B_1 \\
B_{10} &= B_7 \oplus B_4 \\
B_{11} &= B_7 \oplus B_2 \\
B_{12} &= B_6 \oplus B_5 \\
B_5 &= B_{12} \oplus B_0 \\
B_{13} &= B_5 \oplus B_4 \\
B_4 &= B_9 \oplus B_8 \\
B_{14} &= B_5 \oplus B_7 \\
B_{15} &= B_5 \oplus B_1 \\
B_1 &= B_{15} \oplus B_{11} \\
B_{16} &= B_3 \oplus B_4 \\
B_3 &= B_{16} \oplus B_2 \\
B_2 &= B_{16} \oplus B_6 \\
B_6 &= B_3 \oplus B_0 \\
B_{16} &= B_3 \oplus B_{12} \\
B_{17} &= B_2 \oplus B_{10} \\
B_{18} &= B_0 \oplus B_{17} \\
B_{19} &= B_{16} \oplus B_{17} \\
B_{20} &= B_{16} \oplus B_{11} \\
B_{21} &= B_{12} \oplus B_{17} \\
B_{12} &= B_9 \oplus B_{21} \\
B_{22} &= B_7 \oplus B_{21} \\
B_7 &= B_4 \cdot B_3 \\
B_{23} &= B_1 \cdot B_6 \\
B_{24} &= B_{23} \oplus B_7 \\
B_{23} &= B_{13} \cdot B_0 \\
B_{25} &= B_{23} \oplus B_7 \\
B_7 &= B_9 \cdot B_{21}
\end{aligned}$$

$$\begin{aligned}
B_{23} &= B_{15} \cdot B_5 \\
B_{26} &= B_{23} \oplus B_7 \\
B_{23} &= B_{14} \cdot B_{18} \\
B_{27} &= B_{23} \oplus B_7 \\
B_7 &= B_{10} \cdot B_{17} \\
B_{23} &= B_8 \cdot B_{19} \\
B_{28} &= B_{23} \oplus B_7 \\
B_{23} &= B_{11} \cdot B_{16} \\
B_{29} &= B_{23} \oplus B_7 \\
B_7 &= B_{24} \oplus B_2 \\
B_2 &= B_{25} \oplus B_{29} \\
B_{23} &= B_{26} \oplus B_{28} \\
B_{24} &= B_{27} \oplus B_{29} \\
B_{25} &= B_7 \oplus B_{28} \\
B_7 &= B_2 \oplus B_{20} \\
B_2 &= B_{23} \oplus B_{12} \\
B_{12} &= B_{24} \oplus B_{22} \\
B_{20} &= B_{25} \oplus B_7 \\
B_{22} &= B_{25} \cdot B_2 \\
B_{23} &= B_{12} \oplus B_{22} \\
B_{24} &= B_{20} \cdot B_{23} \\
B_{25} &= B_{24} \oplus B_7 \\
B_{24} &= B_2 \oplus B_{12} \\
B_{26} &= B_7 \oplus B_{22} \\
B_7 &= B_{26} \cdot B_{24} \\
B_{22} &= B_7 \oplus B_{12} \\
B_7 &= B_2 \oplus B_{22} \\
B_2 &= B_{23} \oplus B_{22} \\
B_{24} &= B_{12} \cdot B_2
\end{aligned}$$

$$\begin{aligned}
B_{26} &= B_{24} \oplus B_7 \\
B_2 &= B_{23} \oplus B_{24} \\
B_7 &= B_{25} \cdot B_2 \\
B_{12} &= B_{20} \oplus B_7 \\
B_2 &= B_{12} \oplus B_{26} \\
B_7 &= B_{25} \oplus B_{22} \\
B_{20} &= B_{25} \oplus B_{12} \\
B_{23} &= B_{22} \oplus B_{26} \\
B_{24} &= B_7 \oplus B_2 \\
B_{27} &= B_{23} \cdot B_3 \\
B_{28} &= B_{26} \cdot B_6 \\
B_3 &= B_{22} \cdot B_0 \\
B_6 &= B_{20} \cdot B_{21} \\
B_0 &= B_{12} \cdot B_5 \\
B_{21} &= B_{25} \cdot B_{18} \\
B_5 &= B_7 \cdot B_{17} \\
B_{18} &= B_{24} \cdot B_{19} \\
B_{17} &= B_2 \cdot B_{16} \\
B_{19} &= B_{23} \cdot B_4 \\
B_{16} &= B_{26} \cdot B_1 \\
B_{23} &= B_{22} \cdot B_{13} \\
B_1 &= B_{20} \cdot B_9 \\
B_4 &= B_{12} \cdot B_{15} \\
B_9 &= B_{25} \cdot B_{14} \\
B_{12} &= B_7 \cdot B_{10} \\
B_{13} &= B_{24} \cdot B_8 \\
B_{10} &= B_2 \cdot B_{11} \\
B_7 &= B_{12} \oplus B_{13} \\
B_2 &= B_{16} \oplus B_7
\end{aligned}$$

$$\begin{aligned}
B_8 &= B_{19} \oplus B_2 \\
B_{11} &= B_{27} \oplus B_3 \\
B_3 &= B_{28} \oplus B_{27} \\
B_{13} &= B_6 \oplus B_0 \\
B_0 &= B_1 \oplus B_{11} \\
B_{14} &= B_{18} \oplus B_{13} \\
B_{15} &= B_{17} \oplus B_0 \\
B_{16} &= B_{14} \oplus B_{15} \\
B_0 &= B_{13} \oplus B_3 \\
B_3 &= B_6 \oplus B_{21} \\
B_6 &= B_4 \oplus B_7 \\
B_{13} &= B_{11} \oplus B_3 \\
B_4 &= B_8 \oplus B_0 \\
B_{11} &= B_5 \oplus B_{14} \\
B_{14} &= B_9 \oplus B_{16} \\
B_3 &= B_6 \oplus B_{13} \\
B_0 &= \overline{B_1 \oplus B_3} \\
B_5 &= B_{12} \oplus B_{11} \\
B_9 &= B_2 \oplus B_{23} \\
B_7 &= B_8 \oplus B_{11} \\
B_1 &= \overline{B_{16} \oplus B_3} \\
B_3 &= B_{13} \oplus B_4 \\
B_6 &= \overline{B_4 \oplus B_{11}} \\
B_2 &= B_{14} \oplus B_5 \\
B_5 &= \overline{B_2 \oplus B_{10}} \\
B_2 &= B_9 \oplus B_{14}
\end{aligned}$$

Figure 8.1. *Bit-sliced AES S-box where* $(B_7, B_6, B_5, B_4, B_3, B_2, B_1, B_0)_2$ *is the input/output*

However, the random number generator can severely limit the benefits from parallel computations. Indeed, when targeting security higher than first order, we have to generate many random values in order to securely evaluate AND functions. This generation is expensive (and soon to become the main task of the AES process) and will be generated at a rate different from the CPU performances to process logical functions.

$$
\begin{aligned}
B_0 &= \overline{B_0} \\
B_1 &= \overline{B_1} \\
B_5 &= \overline{B_5} \\
B_6 &= \overline{B_6} \\
B_8 &= B_3 \oplus B_4 \\
B_3 &= B_6 \oplus B_7 \\
B_6 &= B_8 \oplus B_3 \\
B_9 &= B_3 \oplus B_4 \\
B_{10} &= B_0 \oplus B_1 \\
B_{11} &= B_{10} \oplus B_8 \\
B_{12} &= B_7 \oplus B_9 \\
B_{13} &= B_4 \oplus B_7 \\
B_{14} &= B_0 \oplus B_8 \\
B_0 &= B_{10} \oplus B_{12} \\
B_{15} &= B_{10} \oplus B_3 \\
B_{10} &= B_4 \oplus B_{14} \\
B_4 &= B_{10} \oplus B_3 \\
B_{16} &= B_8 \oplus B_0 \\
B_{17} &= B_2 \oplus B_5 \\
B_2 &= B_0 \oplus B_5 \\
B_{18} &= B_{17} \oplus B_7 \\
B_7 &= B_2 \oplus B_1 \\
B_1 &= B_{17} \oplus B_{12} \\
B_{17} &= B_8 \oplus B_5 \\
B_5 &= B_{18} \oplus B_2 \\
B_{19} &= B_7 \oplus B_{11} \\
B_{20} &= B_8 \oplus B_5 \\
B_{21} &= B_4 \oplus B_5 \\
B_{22} &= B_{15} \cdot B_1 \\
B_{23} &= B_{13} \cdot B_9 \\
B_{24} &= B_{23} \oplus B_{22} \\
B_{23} &= B_0 \cdot B_{18}
\end{aligned}
$$

$$
\begin{aligned}
B_{25} &= B_{23} \oplus B_{22} \\
B_{22} &= B_{11} \cdot B_{19} \\
B_{23} &= B_{12} \cdot B_{14} \\
B_{26} &= B_{23} \oplus B_{22} \\
B_{23} &= B_{16} \cdot B_2 \\
B_{27} &= B_{23} \oplus B_{22} \\
B_{22} &= B_8 \cdot B_5 \\
B_{23} &= B_6 \cdot B_{21} \\
B_{28} &= B_{23} \oplus B_{22} \\
B_{23} &= B_3 \cdot B_4 \\
B_{29} &= B_{23} \oplus B_{22} \\
B_{22} &= B_{24} \oplus B_{20} \\
B_{20} &= B_{25} \oplus B_{29} \\
B_{23} &= B_{26} \oplus B_{28} \\
B_{24} &= B_{27} \oplus B_{29} \\
B_{25} &= B_{22} \oplus B_{28} \\
B_{22} &= B_{20} \oplus B_{10} \\
B_{10} &= B_{23} \oplus B_7 \\
B_7 &= B_{24} \oplus B_{17} \\
B_{17} &= B_{25} \oplus B_{22} \\
B_{20} &= B_{25} \cdot B_{10} \\
B_{23} &= B_7 \oplus B_{20} \\
B_{24} &= B_{17} \cdot B_{23} \\
B_{25} &= B_{24} \oplus B_{22} \\
B_{24} &= B_{10} \oplus B_7 \\
B_{26} &= B_{22} \oplus B_{20} \\
B_{20} &= B_{26} \cdot B_{24} \\
B_{22} &= B_{20} \oplus B_7 \\
B_{20} &= B_{10} \oplus B_{22} \\
B_{10} &= B_{23} \oplus B_{22} \\
B_{24} &= B_7 \cdot B_{10} \\
B_{26} &= B_{24} \oplus B_{20}
\end{aligned}
$$

$$
\begin{aligned}
B_7 &= B_{23} \oplus B_{24} \\
B_{10} &= B_{25} \cdot B_7 \\
B_{20} &= B_{17} \oplus B_{10} \\
B_7 &= B_{20} \oplus B_{26} \\
B_{10} &= B_{25} \oplus B_{22} \\
B_{17} &= B_{25} \oplus B_{20} \\
B_{23} &= B_{22} \oplus B_{26} \\
B_{24} &= B_{10} \oplus B_7 \\
B_{27} &= B_{23} \cdot B_1 \\
B_{28} &= B_{26} \cdot B_9 \\
B_{29} &= B_{22} \cdot B_{18} \\
B_9 &= B_{17} \cdot B_{19} \\
B_{18} &= B_{20} \cdot B_{14} \\
B_{19} &= B_{25} \cdot B_2 \\
B_1 &= B_{10} \cdot B_5 \\
B_{14} &= B_{24} \cdot B_{21} \\
B_5 &= B_7 \cdot B_4 \\
B_2 &= B_{23} \cdot B_{15} \\
B_{21} &= B_{26} \cdot B_{13} \\
B_{15} &= B_{22} \cdot B_0 \\
B_{13} &= B_{17} \cdot B_{11} \\
B_{22} &= B_{20} \cdot B_{12} \\
B_{11} &= B_{25} \cdot B_{16} \\
B_0 &= B_{10} \cdot B_8 \\
B_{12} &= B_{24} \cdot B_6 \\
B_8 &= B_7 \cdot B_3 \\
B_4 &= B_1 \oplus B_0 \\
B_1 &= B_{13} \oplus B_4 \\
B_6 &= B_2 \oplus B_8 \\
B_2 &= B_6 \oplus B_0 \\
B_0 &= B_2 \oplus B_{15} \\
B_2 &= B_{22} \oplus B_1
\end{aligned}
$$

$$
\begin{aligned}
B_3 &= B_{18} \oplus B_2 \\
B_4 &= B_3 \oplus B_{12} \\
B_7 &= B_4 \oplus B_9 \\
B_1 &= B_7 \oplus B_{14} \\
B_{10} &= B_{28} \oplus B_5 \\
B_{16} &= B_{19} \oplus B_{27} \\
B_{17} &= B_{16} \oplus B_{10} \\
B_2 &= B_4 \oplus B_{17} \\
B_4 &= B_7 \oplus B_{18} \\
B_{17} &= B_4 \oplus B_5 \\
B_7 &= B_{17} \oplus B_{19} \\
B_4 &= B_{29} \oplus B_9 \\
B_5 &= B_{17} \oplus B_4 \\
B_4 &= B_5 \oplus B_{27} \\
B_5 &= B_{29} \oplus B_{21} \\
B_{17} &= B_5 \oplus B_3 \\
B_3 &= B_{17} \oplus B_{16} \\
B_5 &= B_3 \oplus B_{14} \\
B_3 &= B_5 \oplus B_{15} \\
B_3 &= B_3 \oplus B_8 \\
B_5 &= B_{17} \oplus B_9 \\
B_8 &= B_5 \oplus B_{11} \\
B_5 &= B_8 \oplus B_{10} \\
B_8 &= B_5 \oplus B_6 \\
B_6 &= B_8 \oplus B_{13} \\
B_8 &= B_5 \oplus B_{22} \\
B_9 &= B_8 \oplus B_{15} \\
B_5 &= B_9 \oplus B_{12}
\end{aligned}
$$

Figure 8.2. *Bit-sliced AES inv S-box where* $(B_7, B_6, B_5, B_4, B_3, B_2, B_1, B_0)_2$ *is the input/output*

8.2.7.4. *Hardware design*

The bitslice technique is well suited for the hardware context since it requires only Boolean functions. The leakage model is different in this case due to propagation delays and the permanent evaluation of the functions. The number of shares and the global design shall take this reality into account.

8.3. Other functions of AES

8.3.1. *State*

From an input block of 16 bytes $S = (S_0, S_1, \ldots, S_{14}, S_{15})$, the AES state is internally viewed as a 4×4 matrix:

$$S = \begin{pmatrix} S_0 & S_4 & S_8 & S_{12} \\ S_1 & S_5 & S_9 & S_{13} \\ S_2 & S_6 & S_{10} & S_{14} \\ S_3 & S_7 & S_{11} & S_{15} \end{pmatrix}$$

Each byte is considered as an element of $\mathbb{F}_{2^8}$ as defined in section 8.2.

8.3.2. *ShiftRow*

The ShiftRow function rotates the rows of the internal state:

$$\begin{pmatrix} S_0 & S_4 & S_8 & S_{12} \\ S_1 & S_5 & S_9 & S_{13} \\ S_2 & S_6 & S_{10} & S_{14} \\ S_3 & S_7 & S_{11} & S_{15} \end{pmatrix} \mapsto \begin{pmatrix} S_0 & S_4 & S_8 & S_{12} \\ S_5 & S_9 & S_{13} & S_1 \\ S_{10} & S_{14} & S_2 & S_6 \\ S_{15} & S_3 & S_7 & S_{11} \end{pmatrix}$$

and its inverse is just the reverse rotation.

8.3.3. *MixColumn*

The MixColumn function modifies to the bytes of a column. Each new byte will depend on all the input bytes of the column. The same transformation is applied to the four columns. Operations are performed over $\mathbb{F}_{2^8}$. From the input state, we get for the first column:

$$\begin{pmatrix} S_0 \\ S_1 \\ S_2 \\ S_3 \end{pmatrix} \mapsto \begin{pmatrix} S_0 \cdot 2 + S_1 \cdot 3 - S_2 + S_3 \\ S_0 + S_1 \cdot 2 - S_2 \cdot 3 + S_3 \\ S_0 + S_1 + S_2 \cdot 2 + S_3 \cdot 3 \\ S_0 \cdot 3 + S_1 + S_2 + S_3 \cdot 2 \end{pmatrix}$$

The inverse is:

$$\begin{pmatrix} S_0 \\ S_1 \\ S_2 \\ S_3 \end{pmatrix} \mapsto \begin{pmatrix} S_0 \cdot \mathtt{e} + S_1 \cdot \mathtt{b} + S_2 \cdot \mathtt{d} + S_3 \cdot 9 \\ S_0 \cdot 9 + S_1 \cdot \mathtt{e} + S_2 \cdot \mathtt{b} + S_3 \cdot \mathtt{d} \\ S_0 \cdot \mathtt{d} + S_1 \cdot 9 + S_2 \cdot \mathtt{e} + S_3 \cdot \mathtt{b} \\ S_0 \cdot \mathtt{b} + S_1 \cdot \mathtt{d} + S_2 \cdot 9 + S_3 \cdot \mathtt{e} \end{pmatrix}$$

In order to minimize the computations, we can write the MixColumn as:

$$\begin{pmatrix}(S_0+S_1)\cdot 2+(S_1+S_2)+S_3\\(S_1+S_2)\cdot 2+(S_2+S_3)+S_0\\(S_2+S_3)\cdot 2+(S_3+S_0)+S_1\\(S_3+S_0)\cdot 2+(S_0+S_1)+S_2\end{pmatrix}$$

and its inverse as:

$$\begin{pmatrix}(S_0+S_1+S_2+S_3)\cdot 8+(S_0+S_2)\cdot 4+(S_0+S_1)\cdot 2+(S_1+S_2)+S_3\\(S_0+S_1+S_2+S_3)\cdot 8+(S_1+S_3)\cdot 4+(S_1+S_2)\cdot 2+(S_2+S_3)+S_0\\(S_0+S_1+S_2+S_3)\cdot 8+(S_0+S_2)\cdot 4+(S_2+S_3)\cdot 2+(S_3+S_0)+S_1\\(S_0+S_1+S_2+S_3)\cdot 8+(S_1+S_3)\cdot 4+(S_3+S_0)\cdot 2+(S_0+S_1)+S_2\end{pmatrix}$$

When using lookup tables for the S-box implementation, we can mix both functions. While encrypting (respectively, decrypting, see section 8.3.5) a block, the table stores:

$$\begin{array}{llll}S[x]\cdot 2 & S[x] & S[x] & S[x]\cdot 3\\T[x]\cdot \mathtt{e} & T[x]\cdot 9 & T[x]\cdot \mathtt{b} & T[x]\cdot \mathtt{d}\end{array}$$

8.3.4. *KeyScheduling*

A round key $k^{(u)}$ is a sequence of sixteen bytes, or better, a sequence of four 32-bit words: $k^{(u)} = (w_{4u}, w_{4u+1}, w_{4u+2}, w_{4u+3})$. The key derivation and the number of round keys depend on the size of the AES key k (128, 192 or 256 bits). The words are defined as follows, where k_j denotes the jth word of k and m (4,6,8) is the key size divided by 32.

$$w_j = \begin{cases} k_j & \text{if } j < m \\ w_{j-m} \oplus \mathrm{SubByte}(\mathrm{Rot}(w_{j-1})) \oplus R_{\frac{j}{m}} & \text{if } j \geq m \text{and } m|j \\ w_{j-m} \oplus \mathrm{SubByte}(w_{j-1}) & \text{if } j \geq m,\, m = 8 \text{and } m|(j-4) \\ w_{j-m} \oplus w_{j-1} & \text{otherwise} \end{cases}$$

Rot denotes a left rotation of the bytes in a word: $\mathrm{Rot}(S_3, S_2, S_1, S_0) = (S_2, S_1, S_0, S_3)$. SubByte of a word is simply the application of the S-box on the bytes of the word. The constant R_i is a word $(c_i, 0, 0, 0)$, where $c_i \in \mathbb{F}_{2^8}$ and $c_i = 2^{i-1}$ ($c_9 =$ `0x1b` and $c_{10} =$ `0x36`). Since $k^{(0)}$ is the first round key used for encryption, if only k is stored in NVM, then we will have to compute all the round keys before starting a decryption.

EXERCISE 8.6.– Write an algorithm that computes all the words and taking as input the last m words. For instance, if the AES key has 192 bits, the algorithm computes w_j for all $j < 48$ if given words w_i with $48 \leq i < 54$. The same question if the words w_i given as input have indexes $46 \leq i < 52$.

8.3.5. *AES inverse function*

Algorithm 8.5 shows how to invert the AES function. All steps of the AES are taken in reverse order and each step is reversed. The AES specification mentions the possibility to keep the sequence InvSubByte, InvShiftRow, InvMixColumn in the inverse function. Indeed, the composition of the functions InvShiftRow and InvSubByte is commutative. Besides, by linearity, we have $\text{InvMixColumn}(a \oplus b) = \text{InvMixColumn}(a) \oplus \text{InvMixColumn}(b)$. Hence, we can perform the InvMixColumn before adding the round key, if the added round key is: $\text{InvMixColumn}(\text{RoundKey}(k, i))$. This equivalent inverse is interesting when the S-box is evaluated through table lookup since it allows us to also precompute the multiplication needed for the InvMixColumn: for a byte x, the table returns the sequence $(T[x] \cdot \mathtt{e}, T[x] \cdot \mathtt{9}, T[x] \cdot \mathtt{b}, T[x] \cdot \mathtt{d})$.

Algorithm 8.5. AES Inverse Function

Require: Key k, block b
Ensure: block c, the decryption of b

```
state = State(b)
n ∈ {10, 12, 14}, depending on keylength
state = state ⊕ RoundKey(k, n)
state = InvShiftRow(state)
state = InvSubByte(state)
for i from n − 1 to 1 do
    state = state ⊕ RoundKey(k, i)
    state = InvMixColumn(state)
    state = InvShiftRow(state)
    state = InvSubByte(state)
end for
state = state ⊕ RoundKey(k, 0)
c = UnState(state)
```

8.3.6. *Key generation*

Generating the plain value of a key and then masking the key is a possibility. But, instead, we can generate random values that will be the shares of a key, whose plain value is never explicitly stored in memory. Once the shares are generated, you should compute a constant value to preserve the key integrity against fault attacks (see section 8.1.2). Keys shall be generated using True Random Generators (see Chapter 5 of Volume 3).

All the round keys can also be generated during the key generation and then stored in memory. It will save some time during the execution at the expense of memory. This is especially true for decryption.

8.3.7. *Interface*

The computation of one block is probably not what you are looking for. Hence, you should design an interface that will be responsible to handle the load of the key, the chaining of the blocks according to the block-cipher mode and the integrity checks (see section 8.1.2). In case of integrity check failure, the interface returns the appropriate error. Some countermeasures shall be applied at the block cipher mode level (see Chapter 8 of Volume 1).

8.3.8. *Bitsliced state example*

Let $b_{i,j}$ denote the *j*th bit of the state byte S_i : $b_{i,j} = (S_i/2^j)\&1$. After orthogonalization, the words of the state can be organized as:

$$W_j = (b_{15}, b_{11}, b_7, b_3, b_{14}, b_{10}, b_6, b_2, b_{13}, b_9, b_5, b_1, b_{12}, b_8, b_4, b_0)_2$$

where we put all the *j*th bits in word W_j (we omit to precise the j index for the bits). This orthogonalization keeps the rows and columns of the AES state and hence allows efficient implementation of the ShiftRow and MixColumn functions.

In order to efficiently get this orthogonalization, it is convenient to arrange order of the input block like this:

$$(S_0, S_1, \ldots, S_{14}, S_{15}) \mapsto \begin{pmatrix} W_0 = S_2 \cdot 2^8 + S_0 \\ W_1 = S_6 \cdot 2^8 + S_4 \\ W_2 = S_{10} \cdot 2^8 + S_8 \\ W_3 = S_{14} \cdot 2^8 + S_{12} \\ W_4 = S_3 \cdot 2^8 + S_1 \\ W_5 = S_7 \cdot 2^8 + S_5 \\ W_6 = S_{11} \cdot 2^8 + S_9 \\ W_7 = S_{15} \cdot 2^8 + S_{13} \end{pmatrix}$$

By using bit twiddling hacks, we have our orthogonalization. Let (x, y) denote the result of a function $\text{Swap}_s(a, b)$ applied on 16-bit values, such that:

$$m_l = \sum_{j=0}^{8/s-1} \sum_{i=2js}^{(2j+1)s-1} 2^i \qquad m_h = \sum_{j=0}^{8/s-1} \sum_{i=(2j+1)s}^{(2j+2)s-1} 2^i$$

$$x = (a\&m_l) \oplus (b\&m_l) \cdot 2^s \qquad y = (b\&m_h) \oplus (a\&m_h) \cdot 2^{-s}$$

The words shall be updated pairwise by processing all Swap_s at each step:

$$\begin{array}{lll}
(W_0, W_1) \leftarrow \text{Swap}_1(W_0, W_1) & (W_0, W_2) \leftarrow \text{Swap}_2(W_0, W_2) & (W_0, W_4) \leftarrow \text{Swap}_4(W_0, W_4) \\
(W_2, W_3) \leftarrow \text{Swap}_1(W_2, W_3) & (W_1, W_3) \leftarrow \text{Swap}_2(W_1, W_3) & (W_1, W_5) \leftarrow \text{Swap}_4(W_1, W_5) \\
(W_4, W_5) \leftarrow \text{Swap}_1(W_4, W_5) & (W_4, W_6) \leftarrow \text{Swap}_2(W_4, W_6) & (W_2, W_6) \leftarrow \text{Swap}_4(W_2, W_6) \\
(W_6, W_7) \leftarrow \text{Swap}_1(W_6, W_7) & (W_5, W_7) \leftarrow \text{Swap}_2(W_5, W_7) & (W_3, W_7) \leftarrow \text{Swap}_4(W_3, W_7)
\end{array}$$

The same sequence of operations allows us to convert back from the bitsliced state.

EXERCISE 8.7.– Write the orthogonalization for the case of 32-bit CPU where registers store the states of two blocks.

EXERCISE 8.8.– Write the functions ShitRow and InvShiftRow.

8.3.8.1. *MixColumn*

The MixColumn function can be written as (see section 8.3.3):

$$(S_i \oplus S_{i+1 \mod 4}) \times 2 \oplus S_{i+1 \mod 4} \oplus (S_{i+2 \mod 4} \oplus S_{i+3 \mod 4})$$

which means that two consecutive rows shall be xored. Thanks to our bitslice construction, a rotation on a word W_j by α (where α is four times the number of blocks) allows us to rotate the rows of each column. Thanks to this rotation, we can compute the column S_1 from S_0 and the column $S_2 \oplus S_3$ from $S_0 \oplus S_1$.

In $\mathbb{F}_{2^8}$, the multiplication of the byte $(b_7, b_6, b_5, b_4, b_3, b_2, b_1, b_0)_2$ by 2 (see section 8.2) is the byte:

$$(b_6, b_5, b_4, b_3, b_2, b_1, b_0, b_7)_2 \ominus (0, 0, 0, b_7, b_7, 0, b_7, 0)_2$$

So, let $R_j = \text{rotr}\alpha(W_j), T_j = W_j \oplus R_j, U_j = \text{rotr}2\alpha(T_j)$, the whole MixColumn is computed as:

$$W'_j = \begin{cases} T_{j-1 \mod 8} \oplus R_j \oplus U_j \oplus T_7 & \text{if } j \in \{1, 3, 4\} \\ T_{j-1 \mod 8} \oplus R_j \oplus U_j & \text{otherwise} \end{cases}$$

8.3.8.2. *InvMixColumn*

The InvMixColumn function can be written as:

$$(S_i \oplus S_{i+1 \mod 4}) \times 2 \oplus S_{i+1 \mod 4} \oplus (S_{i+2 \mod 4} \oplus S_{i+3 \mod 4}) \oplus$$
$$(S_i \oplus S_{i+2 \mod 4}) \times 4 \oplus (S_i \oplus S_{i+1 \mod 4} \oplus S_{i+2 \mod 4} \oplus S_{i+3 \mod 4}) \times 8$$

In $\mathbb{F}_{2^8}$, the multiplication of the byte $(b_7, b_6, b_5, b_4, b_3, b_2, b_1, b_0)_2$ by 4 is the byte:

$$(b_5, b_4, b_3, b_2, b_1, b_0, b_7, b_6)_2 \oplus (0, 0, b_7, b_7 \oplus b_6, b_6, b_7, b_6, 0)_2$$

The multiplication of the byte $(b_7, b_6, b_5, b_4, b_3, b_2, b_1, b_0)_2$ by 8 is the byte:

$$(b_4, b_3, b_2, b_1, b_0, b_7, b_6, b_5)_2 \oplus (0, b_7, b_7 \oplus b_6, b_6 \oplus b_5, b_7 \oplus b_5, b_6, b_5, 0)_2$$

When looking at the whole InvMixColumn operation, it is possible to save some additions. For instance, in the addition $S_i \times 2 \oplus S_i \times 4 \oplus S_i \times 8$, the "carry" vector is $(0, b_7, b_6, b_5, b_5, b_6, b_5, 0)_2$.

Let $R_j = \text{rotr}\alpha(W_j)$, $S_j = \text{rotr}2\alpha(W_j)$, $Q_j = \text{rotl}\alpha(W_j)$, $T_j = W_j \oplus R_j$, $U_j = \text{rotr}2\alpha(T_j)$, the whole InvMixColumn is computed as:

$$W'_0 = T_7 \oplus R_0 \oplus U_0 \oplus W_6 \oplus S_6 \oplus T_5 \oplus U_5$$
$$W'_1 = T_0 \oplus R_1 \oplus U_1 \oplus R_7 \oplus S_7 \oplus T_5 \oplus U_5 \oplus R_6 \oplus Q_6$$
$$W'_2 = T_1 \oplus R_2 \oplus U_2 \oplus W_0 \oplus S_0 \oplus T_6 \oplus U_6 \oplus R_7 \oplus Q_7$$
$$W'_3 = T_2 \oplus R_3 \oplus U_3 \oplus W_1 \oplus S_1 \oplus T_5 \oplus U_5 \oplus T_0 \oplus U_0 \oplus U_7 \oplus W_6 \oplus S_6$$
$$W'_4 = T_3 \oplus R_4 \oplus U_4 \oplus W_2 \oplus S_2 \oplus T_5 \oplus U_5 \oplus T_1 \oplus U_1 \oplus R_7 \oplus S_7 \oplus R_6 \oplus Q_6$$
$$W'_5 = T_4 \oplus R_5 \oplus U_5 \oplus W_3 \oplus S_3 \oplus T_6 \oplus U_6 \oplus T_2 \oplus U_2 \oplus R_7 \oplus Q_7$$
$$W'_6 = T_5 \oplus R_6 \oplus U_6 \oplus W_4 \oplus S_4 \oplus T_7 \oplus U_7 \oplus T_3 \oplus U_3$$
$$W'_7 = T_6 \oplus R_7 \oplus U_7 \oplus W_5 \oplus S_5 \oplus T_4 \oplus U_4$$

8.4. Notes and further references

Details of the algorithm can also be found in the FIPS 197 standard publication (NIST 2001). The cost of drawing random shares is often underestimated, although it may be the most time-consuming part of an implementation protected against high orders. Some shares can be used to mask several variables as shown in Coron et al. (2016). Besides, shares from one variable can mask other variables with the technique of changing the guards Daemen (2016) used for the AES in Sugawara (2018) and Askeland et al. (2021).

– Section 8.1.2. Look at Chapter 10 of Volume 1 for examples of fault attacks on AES.

– Section 8.2. Look at Chapters 1 and 4 of Volume 3 for more information about white-box implementations. Coron (2014) published a secured algorithm to evaluate a table at any order. Mask refreshing can be done with a complexity $\mathcal{O}(t\log(t))$ as shown in Battistello et al. (2016), which can be of interest for high orders. Carlet et al. (2015) actually proved that ISW applies to any $\mathbb{F}_2$ bilinear function. Peralta gathered some circuit references in his homepage (Peralta n.d.). Hardware implementations have to take into account glitches, for instance, with threshold implementation (see Chapter 3 of this volume). S-box implementations process the sensitive value/key by chunks of 8 bits, which is helpful to mount side-channel attacks as the principle is to bruteforce chunks of the secrets with the help of leakages. Bitslice implementations are based on the bit size of the CPU registers and process bigger chunks of sensitive values (16, 32, 64 or even 128 bits).

– Section 8.3.8. Most optimizations are taken from Bear SSL Pornin (n.d.), which implements the bitsliced representation of Käsper and Schwabe (2009).

8.5. References

Askeland, A., Dhooghe, S., Nikova, S., Rijmen, V., Zhang, Z. (2021). Guarding the first order: The rise of AES maskings. Report 2021/734, Cryptology ePrint Archive [Online]. Available at: https://eprint.iacr.org/2021/734.

Battistello, A., Coron, J.-S., Prouff, E., Zeitoun, R. (2016). Horizontal side-channel attacks and countermeasures on the ISW masking scheme. In *CHES 2016*, Gierlichs, B. and Poschmann, A.Y. (eds). Springer, Heidelberg.

Boyar, J. and Peralta, R. (2009). New logic minimization techniques with applications to cryptology. Report 2009/191, Cryptology ePrint Archive [Online]. Available at: https://eprint.iacr.org/2009/191.

Canright, D. (2005). A very compact S-box for AES. In *CHES 2005*, Rao J.R. and Sunar, B. (eds). Springer, Heidelberg.

Carlet, C., Prouff, E., Rivain, M., Roche, T. (2015). Algebraic decomposition for probing security. In *CRYPTO 2015*, Gennaro, R. and Robshaw, M.J.B. (eds). Springer, Heidelberg.

Coron, J.-S. (2014). Higher order masking of look-up tables. In *EUROCRYPT 2014*, Nguyen, P.Q. and Oswald, E. (eds). Springer, Heidelberg.

Coron, J.-S., Greuet, A., Prouff, E., Zeitoun, R. (2016). Faster evaluation of SBoxes via common shares. In *CHES 2016*, Gierlichs, B. and Poschmann, A.Y. (eds). Springer, Heidelberg.

Daemen, J. (2016). Changing of the guards: A simple and efficient method for achieving uniformity in threshold sharing. Report 2016/1061, Cryptology ePrint Archive [Online]. Available at: https://eprint.iacr.org/2016/1061.

Ishai, Y., Sahai, A., Wagner, D. (2003). Private circuits: Securing hardware against probing attacks. In *CRYPTO 2003*, Boneh, D. (ed.). Springer, Heidelberg.

Käsper, E. and Schwabe, P. (2009). Faster and timing-attack resistant AES-GCM. In *CHES 2009*, Clavier, C. and Gaj, K. (eds). Springer, Heidelberg.

Kim, H., Hong, S., Lim, J. (2011). A fast and provably secure higher-order masking of AES S-box. In *CHES 2011*, Preneel, B. and Takagi, T. (eds). Springer, Heidelberg.

NIST (2001). FIPS 197, Advanced Encryption Standard (AES). National Institute of Standards and Technology, U.S. Department of Commerce.

Peralta, R. (n.d.). Circuit minimization work [Online]. Available at: http://www.cs.yale.edu/homes/peralta/CircuitStuff/CMT.html.

Pornin, T. (n.d.). Bear SSL [Online]. Avaiable at: https://bearssl.org/index.html.

Rivain, M. and Prouff, E. (2010). Provably secure higher-order masking of AES. In *CHES 2010*, Mangard, S. and Standaert, F.-X. (eds). Springer, Heidelberg.

Sugawara, T. (2018). 3-share threshold implementation of AES s-box without fresh randomness. *IACR TCHES*, 1, 123–145.

9
Protected RSA Implementations

Mylène ROUSSELLET, Yannick TEGLIA and David VIGILANT
Thales DIS, France

9.1. Introduction

9.1.1. *The RSA cryptosystem*

RSA is the famous public key cryptosystem that takes its name from its inventors Ron Rivest, Adi Shamir and Leonard Adleman. Since its introduction in 1977, RSA has become a gold standard for asymmetric encryption and digital signature in SSL/TLS certificates, crypto currencies and email encryption. In parallel to its massive deployment, the crypto community has been regularly publishing new attacks against implementations exploiting timing, fault and side channel. Building a resistant RSA implementation is still a practical challenge when considering skilled experts in labs applying all state-of-the-art attack techniques.

9.1.2. *RSA and security recommendations*

The best known method to solve the RSA problem is the factorization of the RSA public modulus, which is the product of two large secret prime numbers. As no quantum computer is available yet, it provides sufficient practical security today if RSA keys are large enough and generated carefully. The security may totally decrease if the prime generation method showed some bias. Additionally, RSA keys must satisfy some properties in order to guarantee an optimal security level. Several recommendations (length of each prime number, difference between the two primes,

Embedded Cryptography 2,
coordinated by Emmanuel PROUFF, Guénaël RENAULT,
Matthieu RIVAIN and Colin O'FLYNN. © ISTE Ltd 2025.

length of public and private exponents, etc.) must be followed carefully during key generation in order to guarantee a good cryptanalytic resistance of the crypto system. Moreover, several constructions of RSA have been shown to be insecure. For instance, RSA without padding (plain RSA) as well as some padding methods like PKCS#1 v1.5 have been shown to be vulnerable to adaptive inputs attacks. Only robust padding methods must be used. All of these recommendations can be found in guidance published by national certification authorities and must be strictly followed. Before adding countermeasures to an RSA signature implementation, the starting point of designing a secure device executing RSA signature is to use recommended methods and recommended parameters.

9.1.3. *RSA-CRT and straightforward mode*

RSA was introduced in 1977 in its so-called straightforward mode. (N, e) is the RSA public key and (N, d) the RSA private key such that $N = pq$, where p and q are large prime integers, $\gcd((p-1), e) = \gcd((q-1), e) = 1$ and $d = e^{-1} \bmod \operatorname{lcm}((p-1),(q-1))$. The RSA signature of a message $m < N$ is given by $S = m^d \bmod N$ (m represents the padded message).

Main known drawbacks of RSA signature are its relative slowness and its large key material. 2K RSA is now a standard functionality, and 3K is recommended by national certification authorities at mid-term. It may be a strong constraint on embedded devices where few RAM memory is available and where processors have a clock frequency of only a few tens of megahertz. RSA is more efficient in Chinese remainder theorem mode (RSA-CRT) than in straightforward mode. As for straightforward RSA, (N, e) is the public key. Here, the RSA private key is (p, q, d_p, d_q, i_q) where $d_p = e^{-1} \bmod (p-1)$, $d_q = e^{-1} \bmod (q-1)$ and $i_q = q^{-1} \bmod p$. RSA-CRT handles data with half the RSA modulus size and is theoretically about four times faster. Therefore, it is better suited to embedded devices. The RSA signature in CRT mode is described step by step in Figure 9.1.

Input: message $m < N$
Output: signature $m^d \in \mathbb{Z}_N$

1) Get key (p, q, d_p, d_q, i_q)
2) $m_p = m \bmod p$, $m_q = m \bmod q$
3) $S_p = m_p^{d_p} \bmod p$, $S_q = m_q^{d_q} \bmod q$
4) $S = S_q + q \cdot (i_q \cdot (S_p - S_q) \bmod p)$
5) RETURN(S)

Figure 9.1. *RSA-CRT pseudo-code*

9.1.4. *Toward a device product embedding RSA-CRT*

The way toward a secure device embedding RSA-CRT signature requires some formalization at the device interface level. Common Criteria (CC) documentation gives a complete framework to build a secure device from specification to manufacturing. For instance, regarding devices implementing crypto services, the process of CC certification has already been applied to the smart card industry for decades. One first step is the identification of the security functional requirements (SFRs) at the user level, for example, authentication through RSA-PSS digital signature. Then, the developer shall build the system and show evidence that there is no implementation attack that allows for the bypassing of these SFRs. For instance, implementation attacks (through side channel leakages or perturbation) may allow for breaking the confidentiality of cryptographic keys.

For example, for smart cards and related secure cryptographic implementations, certification authorities provide the mandated evaluators with an up-to-date list of relevant attack paths published in books and proceedings of conferences. From this list and from the complete access to the device architecture, the evaluator is able to perform practical tests on the most relevant potential vulnerabilities. CC also specifies a comprehensive way of rating attacks. This allows us to evaluate the resistance level of a product, assuming that no attack below a defined rating exists.

Concerning RSA signature, several protected implementations have already been published in conference proceedings, often assuming a context and an attacker power as a starting point. When designing and developing a secure embedded RSA-CRT signature, having this CC framework and approach in mind may be very useful. Indeed, it could ensure that original assumptions about the context and the attacker power are correct.

The asset considered here will be the confidentiality of the RSA-CRT private key against side channel and fault attacks. We first gathered the main related implementation attacks, which have been published for several decades, and then proposed to review a list of some of the published countermeasures with their rationale. By parsing the successive steps of the RSA-CRT pseudo-code in Figure 9.1, and by reviewing some of the main implementation attacks at each step, this chapter aims to provide a path toward a secure RSA-CRT signature implementation.

9.2. Building a protected RSA implementation step by step

The RSA-CRT pseudo-code in Figure 9.1 represents the naive RSA-CRT. This section will relate a selection of attacks for each step. Examples of published countermeasures will be proposed in order to break attack paths, up until the complete secure RSA-CRT signature pseudo-code.

9.2.1. *Loading RSA-CRT key parameter – Step 1*

9.2.1.1. *Considering profiling attacks*

Usually the preliminary step of the RSA-CRT signature is to copy the key elements from nonvolatile memory to a working space in RAM. During this transfer, an attacker can run a profiling attack in order to recover the private key elements. This type of profiling attack requires the ability for the hacker to set many varying keys in an open sample to build templates, train a neural network or use any supervised learning algorithm. Then, the results of this training phase will be used to attack a device with unknown keys and recover the private elements.

To prevent profiling attacks, the key elements must be manipulated in a secure way [CM1]. They may be shared in random parts so that the relation between the data manipulated and the secret key elements is broken. The random shares must be manipulated carefully to avoid any involuntary unmasking.

Another extra barrier could be the manipulation of key bytes or key words in a random order (shuffling), different for each execution. Even if this countermeasure does not thwart the attack in theory, it will increase the required number of acquisitions, and would make the side channel analysis too costly or even no longer feasible, for instance, when only a limited number of executions with the same key is allowed.

9.2.1.2. *Considering fault injection on key parameters*

Let $S = m^d \bmod N$ be the correct signature obtained when signing message m. During a RSA-CRT computation, an attacker could inject a fault in the computation of S in order to obtain a faulty signature $\tilde{S}$, which is faulty (either only modulo p or only modulo q). Then, by computing $gcd(S - \tilde{S}, N)$ the prime number p or q can be recovered. When the input message m is known, this attack was shown applicable with only one faulty signature by computing $gcd(m - \tilde{S}^e \bmod N, N)$.

The initialization of the key and more globally all manipulations of the key parameters in the RSA-CRT signature are also particularly sensitive to a *Bellcore* attack.

A simple way to prevent this attack is to verify the result before sending it back as the attacker needs the faulty result to perform his attack. This is done simply by checking if S^e actually equals to m [CM5]. This then costs a verification, usually a few multiplications, but requires to own the public exponent e which is not always available depending on the API, as, for instance, in Javacard. Other examples of countermeasures against *Bellcore* are also cited later in section 9.2.5.

Additionally, the security of RSA must not be downgraded by using weak parameters (small modulus, non-prime elements p or q, ...). Some attacks target the modulus N. Faulting some bits of the modulus N can lead to recover information on private exponent d. Even if this kind of attack mainly targets the straightforward implementation of RSA, the integrity of all parameters must be guaranteed in RSA-CRT implementation. To ensure that the parameters are correct, an integrity value must be associated to each key element [CM2]. This integrity can be verified whenever in the algorithm to make sure the data used are still the correct ones.

9.2.2. *Message reductions – Step 2*

9.2.2.1. *Considering side channel analysis*

In RSA-CRT, the second step consists of reducing the message m modulo the primes p and q.

If an attacker is able to choose the input message, the primes p and/or q may be inferred just by analyzing side channel during the reduction step. In fact, if the message is already lower that p (respectively, q), in a naive implementation, the reduction is not performed, while it is computed when the message is greater than p (respectively, q). This results in a difference in the execution time. So by testing several messages, an attacker can reduce the interval containing p (resp q) and find the value of p (respectively, q). A simple division of N by p will give q.

It is also possible to conduct some statistical attacks like DPA or CPA during the reduction step. The attacker collects series of traces for signature of chosen messages that are equidistant: series k are obtained from messages $m_i = m - i * 256^k$, k being the byte length of the prime. The DPA attack targets the remainder r after reduction step. A gcd computed over the k DPA results will give the prime value.

To prevent these side channel attacks, two countermeasures can be implemented. The randomization of prime numbers p and q makes any statistical attack on several executions unfeasible. Let small random numbers r_p and r_q and compute new moduli $p' = r_p \cdot p$ and $q' = r_q \cdot q$ [CM3]. Usually, random values are small (32, 64 or 128 bits) leading to an additional cost reasonable for this step. The message reduction must be computed whatever the value of the message. To enforce this reduction, the message may be randomized in order to have the same size as N: for a random value r_m, compute $m' = m + r_m \cdot N$ [CM4]. Then the randomized message m' is reduced modulo p and q. In RSA-CRT, the modulus N may be not provided by the application but can be computed from p and q. The random value r_m is usually small as well (32, 64 or 128 bits). The overhead of this countermeasure is then a large multiplication, a small multiplication and an addition.

9.2.2.2. *Considering faults either mod p or mod q*

Injecting a fault in either m_p (respectively, m_q) would allow us to obtain a faulty value for S_p (respectively, S_q). A *Bellcore* attack should be taken into account during the reduction of the input message. We will refer to the countermeasures cited in section 9.2.5 to prevent the *Bellcore* attack.

9.2.3. *Exponentiations – Step 3*

Exponentiations are the core operations in the RSA signature. In order to compute m_p to the power d_p modulo p (respectively, m_q to the d_q mod q), the algorithm scans the exponent from right to left, or from left to right. Exponentiation algorithms execute modular multiplications and modular squarings, and the values of the temporary variables involved in those operations depend on the private exponent bit values. As treating exponent by very small chunk (per bit, or per small window of bits), exponentiations are particularly subject to implementation attacks.

9.2.3.1. *Considering timing and simple side channel analysis*

Timing and simple side channel analysis have been the first published threats targeting exponentiations. They were introduced from the late 1990s.

These attacks exploit every slight differences in the flow that could allow us to find information about the exponent bits. For instance, squarings can be implemented in a different (and more effective) way than multiplications when implemented as multi-precision algorithm entirely in software. On the one hand, it may allow for a better performance to be achieved. On the other hand, this would give clear hints to an attacker about the exponent value when analyzing the timing, or even the actual value through a simple power analysis of the exponentiation.

Cryptographers have introduced the notion of *atomicity* in exponentiations. This formalizes the idea that the developers should use side channel equivalent blocks of instructions. This makes the execution of one block or the other indistinguishable from the attacker, whatever the value of the processed bit of exponent.

From this notion of *atomicity*, several exponentiation algorithms have been published with various complexities and intrinsic resistance, for example, *Atomic Square and Multiply*, *Square and Multiply Always*, *Montgomery Powering Ladder* and *Squaring Always*.

Exponentiation *atomicity* [CM6] needs to be applied when designing the source code. Ideally from the highest level view (e.g. modular operations), down to the lowest level view (e.g. CPU assembly selection of exponent bit), without forgetting intermediary levels (e.g. final subtraction in Montgomery reduction algorithm). Achieving *atomicity* may be challenging and should be verified practically. Differences may not be visible at source code, but may appear at the execution, due to external events (e.g. compilation optimizations and cache effects). The overhead added by this countermeasure depends on the chosen algorithm. *Square and Multiply*

Always or *Montgomery Powering Ladder* for example imply two modular multiplications per bits of exponent, while the original *Square and Multiply* implies about 1.5. This means a significant overhead of around 33%.

Even if ever only a very small part of the exponent bits is recovered over a single execution, due to some noise in the acquisition signal, an attacker may try to target several different chunks of the exponent successively over several executions. This may be repeated until recovering a sufficient part for brute-force, or more sophisticated attacks. Thus it can also be useful to randomize the exponent as a preventive barrier. For the straightforward RSA signature, the exponent d is transformed into d' such that $d' = d + r_d \cdot \phi(N)$ and ϕ is Euler's totient function. r_d is a random number drawn from a uniform distribution at each signature. In practice for the RSA-CRT, $d'_p = d_p + r_{d_p} \cdot (p-1)$, respectively, $d'_q = d_q + r_{d_q} \cdot (q-1)$ [CM7]. Recovering the whole key over multiple acquisitions can be made rather impossible by this simple countermeasure, given that a sufficient large length is chosen for the random number. For this countermeasure, the addition executed during exponent randomization should be implemented carefully, especially if the single precision of the adder is small. Indeed, some attacks may exploit the carry leakage during this step. Assuming that the exponentiations represent 90% of the execution process, the overhead of exponent randomization is exactly $0.9 \cdot \frac{|r_{d_p}|}{|d_p|}$.

Additionally, when the message can be freely chosen by the attacker, the randomization of the exponent has been shown to be insufficient for some specific input. Moreover, it may sometimes be not possible to guarantee the *atomicity* of the Barret or Montgomery modular multiplication (e.g. when provided by a hardware accelerator and therefore out of control of the software developer). In such cases, both the message and the modulus randomization would help in achieving a sufficient security level. The randomization of the message m_p is such that $m'_p = m_p + r_{m_p} \cdot p \bmod p'$, with $p' = r_p \cdot p$ (respectively, $m'_q = m_q + r_{m_q} \cdot q \bmod q'$, with $q' = r_q \cdot q$). The exponentiation is then performed modulo p' (respectively, q'). Assuming that the exponentiations represent 90% of the execution process, the overhead of this countermeasure is theoretically about $0.9 \cdot \left(\left(\frac{|p'|}{|p|}\right)^3 - 1\right)$.

9.2.3.2. *Considering side-channel analysis of intermediate values*

By using statistical side channel analysis, and from hypothesis regarding the exponent bits, an attacker could attempt to correlate some intermediary values in the exponentiation. For instance, Messerges et al. (1999) proposed the so-called *ZEMD* attack based on the DPA introduced by Kocher et al. (1996). The principle of the *ZEMD* attack is to confirm or infirm the hypothesis of exponent bit per bit by classifying intermediate powers of m according to their high or low hamming weight. This could have been exploited through CPA too. However, this attack may be complicated to mount in practice for the specific case of RSA-CRT, since the modulus used in the modular exponentiation is unknown to the attacker. Hence, intermediate powers of m cannot be guessed unless no modular reduction is applied. However, it could be applied for the very first bits until the index j of an L-bit exponent d with small messages, while intermediate powers of $m^{\Sigma_{i=0}^{j} 2^{j-i} d_{L-1-i}}$ are smaller than the modulus.

Another attack targeting intermediate values in the exponentiation is the so-called doubling attack. For this attack, it is assumed that it is possible to run successively an exponentiation with a message m and then m^a, for example, with $a = 2$. Finally, information about exponent bits can be recovered from the correlation of the same intermediate value appearing at two different indexes in the two exponentiations.

The attacks of this section can be covered by the same randomization techniques as for timing and simple side-channel analysis: the randomization of the exponent and the randomization of the message. Again, some of these attacks may be harder to mount in practice when the attacker cannot choose or know completely the input message.

9.2.3.3. *Considering safe error*

Fault injection attacks have immediately been seen as a threat as they allow for the recovery of secrets using faulty intermediate variables (either semipermanent or permanent faults) or faulty data flow (transient faults). While the countermeasures certainly have a cost, they are pretty easy to figure out and to implement.

It is usually a matter of redundancy for the variables, the computation or both. This can happen time-wise, by doing the computation several times in a sequential order or space-wise by doing the computation in several units at the same time. Safe error attacks are far more difficult to identify and solve. They consist of injecting an effective fault that has no outcome on the final result and then deduce part of the secret from it.

For instance, in the *Square and Multiply Always*, the *else* branch is a SPA countermeasure that actually has no effect on the computation. Hence, if an attacker succeeds in faulting this useless computation (sometimes called *dummy*), the final result is still correct and they thereby know that they were faulting the *else* branch and then the value of the secret bit. By performing several attacks (up to the number of bits of the secret exponent), they can recover the whole secret.

A countermeasure could then require that each and every variable is actually involved in the computation so that any error yields an erroneous result, allowing then to apply the regular countermeasures against fault injections.

Other countermeasures exist as the *exponent blinding*: $d' = d + r_d \cdot \phi(N)$ [CM7], where r_d is a random number drawn from a uniform distribution at each new usage of the secret key d. Doing so will not prevent the attacker to fault the *dummy* branch of the *Square and Multiply Always* but it will remove the possibility to discover the exponent bit by bit as each fault will require a new exponentiation that will in turn yield a new exponent d' due to the countermeasure.

Please note that while clever and elegant, this attack is not the easiest to perform as the attacker shall know that their attack on the *dummy* variable or *dummy* computation actually occurred and was effective and thereby the lack of error in the final computation is indeed linked to this *dummy* target. Said differently, the attacker has to be able to link the absence of an erroneous result to an effective successful fault on the *dummy* computation or variable, which may not be easy from a practical standpoint.

9.2.3.4. *Considering combined attacks*

Combined attacks is a class of attack that involves a fault injection to trigger a side-channel vulnerability. Hence such attacks are particularly suited for breaking algorithms that are protected against side channel. Even if the algorithm also embeds protection against fault injection, the latter would be useless as it arrives too late in the processing since the fault injection already had the opportunity to leak some secret data through the side-channel medium.

Countermeasures against side-channel attacks and against fault injection must then be considered as a single one. For instance, we can modify the parameters of the exponentiation using randomization in a specific way where a further fault injection will yield computing on garbage data. Such a technique is called *poisoning* as not only it modifies the asset but it also embeds a payload that needs at some point be canceled out. If a fault injection occurs in between the cancellation does not match the seminal modification and the final data is garbage.

9.2.3.5. *Considering horizontal attacks*

Horizontal attack is a class of side-channel attacks that considers only one execution of the algorithm, here the exponentiation. The goal is to recover the private exponent from the most significant bit to the least significant bit by analyzing each modular multiplication separately. It differs from the classical vertical mode which targets several execution of an algorithm to recover the secret key.

The first horizontal attack, named the *Big Mac* attack, is a collision analysis in one trace. Using the Euclidean distance, the attacker compares each modular multiplication with a reference to determine if it is a square of a multiplication by m and recovers the private exponent from most significant bit to least significant bit. The reference is usually the first multiplication by m.

The *Big Mac* attack can be improved by using the correlation analysis on the *Atomic Square and Multiply* method. A modular multiplication of $x \cdot y$ is split into subparts, each corresponding to smaller multiplications $x_i \cdot y_j$. Then the attacker computes the correlation between sub-traces and messages words. A high level of correlation indicates that the operation is a multiplication with the message m, otherwise it is a square. The message randomization [CM4] is a good countermeasure against this attack. Another way to protect the long integer multiplication itself consists of randomizing the data inside the multiplication and/or randomizing the execution order of the internal loops. It appeared that only a fully randomized execution order of the long integer multiplication algorithm is efficient. We must note that the randomization of long integer multiplication would be an effective but costly countermeasure. Even if the number of small multiplications remains the same, there are additional manipulation of data and it needs further storage area.

The *Square and Multiply Always* algorithm is not sensitive to these attacks as the message is always manipulated, whatever the exponent bit. It is however sensitive to a cross-correlation attack. The goal is to identify when two consecutive modular multiplications involve the same operand to determine if the multiplication with message m was a true or dummy one.

Another way to attack an RSA exponentiation in a single trace is to use clustering algorithms. Each exponentiation trace is split into single operations and a clustering algorithm, such as K-means, tries to classify these operations into two classes (one for bit 0 and the other for bit 1). When a correct partition is found the attacker just has to assign label 0 or 1 to the two classes to recover the secret exponent.

To improve the clustering algorithm's efficiency, it was proposed to combine several measurements (obtained with different probe positions, for example).

There is no algorithmic countermeasure to theoretically prevent all horizontal attacks. All of the methods that would reduce the signal-to-noise ratio, will make the attack more difficult. Generally, from feedback with practical testings, these are the skills of developers and designers that will avoid horizontal attacks.

9.2.3.6. *Considering faults either mod p or mod q*

The exponentiations mod p and mod q are also the target of faults attack. Whatever the fault injected during one of the two exponentiations, an attacker can recover p or q by conducting a *Bellcore* attack. As mentioned previously, this attack can be prevented by a systematic signature verification before returning the result. Other countermeasures are discussed in section 9.2.5.

To prevent fault attacks on exponentiations, several countermeasures have been proposed in the literature. A first family of countermeasures is based on extending the modulus by a multiplication with a small random number. Then from the computation modulo the extended modulus, there must remain an invariant that can be verified modulo the random number. Let us choose a random integer t to compute

$S_{pt} = m^d \bmod p \cdot t$ and $S_{qt} = m^d \bmod q \cdot t$. Then we just have to verify the equality $S_{pt} = S_{qt} \bmod t$ in order to be sure that no fault has been injected during the exponentiations. This technique has inspired several publications.

Another way to protect exponentiations against fault attacks is to use a self-secure algorithm. The use of the *Montgomery Powering Ladder* exponentiation algorithm allows us to prevent fault attacks. Indeed, at each step of this exponentiation algorithm the couple (a_0, a_1) is of the form $(m^\alpha, m^{\alpha+1})$. Then we just have to test if $m \cdot a_0 = a_1 \bmod N$ at the end of the exponentiation to make sure that no fault has been injected. This invariant between the two outputs has been exploited in some published countermeasures in order to protect exponentiations against fault attacks, and more generally to protect RSA-CRT without the extra verification step using public exponent e.

Other published propositions were based on double addition chains. The idea consists of processing a double exponentiation to compute the pair $(m^d, m^{\phi(N)-d}) \bmod N$ by using addition chains for exponents. The consistency of the exponentiation can be verified by computing $m^d \cdot m^{\phi(N)-d} \stackrel{?}{=} 1 \bmod N$.

9.2.4. *Recombination – Step 4*

9.2.4.1. *Considering side-channel analysis*

Attacking the recombination using side-channel analysis will leverage macroscopic consumption or EM pattern that may result from this very step.

First, we can think of a coarse grained attack using a SPA for targeting macroscopic consumption or EM patterns. A good candidate is, for instance, the inner multiplication of $(S_p - S_q)$ by i_q. If at some point, one of those quantities equals *0*, then the further multiplication will be done by a null operand which triggers the biggest Hamming difference in the registers containing the result as half of the bits will flip. This will happen if S_p equals S_q for some reason for instance. The attacker then needs to craft specific messages to reach this goal.

Another finer-grained possibility would be to look at a CPA like attack on the same step of the algorithm by noticing that it can be transformed from $S = S_q + q \cdot (i_q \cdot (S_p - S_q) \bmod p) \iff S = q \cdot x + S_q$ into $x = S \cdot q^{-1}$ as S_q is only half the size of S.

In a regular CPA, the attacker needs to be able to exhibit a relationship between a known variable and the secret quantity that will yield an intermediate value producing a side-channel effect. Here as S is known, the attacker can setup q which are the hypotheses on the secret value q to mount a CPA-like attack where x is the intermediate value. Please note that since q is too large to exhaust all of the possible hypotheses, the attacker will need to adopt a divide-and-conquer approach by breaking it into smaller chunks.

9.2.4.2. *Considering faults either mod p or mod q*

The recombination is also a window sensitive to fault attacks. Whatever the injected fault, an attacker can recover p or q by conducting a *Bellcore* attack. As mentioned previously this attack can be prevented by a systematic signature verification before returning the result. Other countermeasures are discussed in section 9.2.5.

9.2.5. *Return S*

As already discussed, S should be returned only if it is guaranteed that there was no perturbation, at least no perturbation only modulo p or only modulo q.

The verification $S^e \stackrel{?}{=} m$ after the signature implies only a few modular multiplications. This countermeasure avoids the attack path while being negligible in terms of overhead. But it requires the public exponent e to be available, which is not always the case depending on the API. For example, in the Javacard API, only private elements are given in the interface for the private operation (signature or decryption).

Several papers proposing a global alternative to verification have been published when public exponent is not available.

These methods have been described in more details in section 9.2.3.6. Some methods are based on modulus extension combined with consistency verification in the small ring. Some others would exploit relations that are inherent to a given exponentiation algorithm.

Protecting RSA exponentiations is important. But it must be guaranteed that all steps of the RSA-CRT signature are covered by a global fault detection mechanism, so that no exploitable faulty signature is returned to an attacker.

9.2.6. *Protected RSA-CRT pseudo-code*

Bringing together all countermeasures discussed in the previous sections, Figure 9.2 presents an example of protected RSA-CRT pseudo-code. Simple side-channel, horizontal and combined attacks on exponentiations have to be tackled by the developer. The related countermeasures are not explicitly mentioned here in the pseudo-code.

Input: message $m < N$
Output: signature $S = m^d \in \mathbb{Z}_N^*$

1) Get key $(p, q, d_p, d_q, i_q, e, N)$ (protection in confidentiality and integrity)

[CM1], [CM2]

2) Generate uniform random numbers $(r_p, r_q, r_{m_p}, r_{m_q}, r_{d_p}, r_{d_q})$
3) Mask moduli $p' = p \cdot r_p \;,\; q' = q \cdot r_q$

[CM3]

4) Mask messages $m'_p = m + r_{m_p} \cdot p \bmod p' \;,\; m'_q = m + r_{m_q} \cdot q \bmod q'$

[CM4]

5) Mask exponents $d'_p = d_p + r_{d_p} \cdot (p-1) \;,\; d'_q = d_q + r_{d_q} \cdot (q-1)$

[CM7]

6) $S'_p = m_p'^{d'_p} \bmod p' \;,\; S'_q = m_q'^{d'_q} \bmod q'$ (Atomic- and Fault-protected exponentiations)

[CM6], [CM8]

7) $S' = S'_q + q \cdot (i_q \cdot (S'_p - S'_q) \bmod p')$

[CM3]

8) Check key integrity and : $S'^e \bmod N = m$

[CM5]

9) RETURN($S' \bmod N$) if no alarm

Figure 9.2. *Protected RSA-CRT pseudo-code*

9.3. Remarks and open discussion

9.3.1. *Security resistance consideration*

This chapter aims to review the way up to a protected RSA implementation. By starting from a selection of attacks, the RSA-CRT signature pseudo-code has been scanned step by step, and countermeasures have been presented for each phase. Applying this methodology has implied a subjective choice at the starting point regarding what are the considered attacks. We have selected a considerable list that sounded reasonable to us. Extra attacks (or fewer) could have been taken into account as a starting point, resulting to another protected pseudo-code.

Some concepts have been reviewed at relative high level. For instance, the timing, simple side channel, horizontal analysis and combined attacks on exponentiations have been discussed, but the related practical resistance remains challenging, and based on the developer's and the evaluator's expertise.

In the same way, some main types of published countermeasures have been discussed. But there exists a variety of details and configurations that is left to the developers. This can be configured depending on the context of the final use case (e.g. RSA modes to be supported, unavailability of some public key material, limitation regarding the number of possible signatures, etc.), depending on the hardware platform (e.g. resource and inherent resistance against attacks) and depending on expected performance (e.g. transaction timing limit). All of these constraints are specific to the user context, and this makes a generic definition of a protected implementation barely impossible.

A complete methodology to build a protected RSA could also comprise a formal verification phase. Formal verification could theoretically give an entire confidence about the security level of an implementation. However, the related abstraction level is often subject to trade-off when coming to engineering. On the one hand, the formal verification at assembly level gives assurance that a given binary is secure on a specific chip. But applying formal proof at assembly level with a huge number of lines of code can represent a prohibitive effort. On the other hand, proving formally the resistance at pseudo-code level is portable and allows us to validate countermeasures with reasonable workload, but it does not give the full guarantee that no vulnerability has been introduced from the pseudo-code to the execution of the binary on the hardware platform.

9.4. Notes and further references

– Section 9.1.1. The concept of asymmetric cryptosystem was already introduced by Diffie and Hellman but in the context of key exchange. RSA inventors published the first asymmetric cryptosystem for public key encryption/signature in Rivest et al. (1978). In the late 1990s, the British Government Communication Headquarter (GCHQ) declassified some research documents where the same idea was discussed already from 1973.

– Section 9.1.2. Special care has to be taken when generating RSA keys. Cryptanalysis exist when RSA keys do not respect some recommendations regarding distance between primes, length of private and public exponents. For instance, Boneh (1999) gives a list of main known cryptanalysis. Additionally, some bias in the prime generation algorithm leading to a complete secret recovery were highlighted by researchers in Bernstein et al. (2013) and Nemec et al. (2017). A complete key generation algorithm, which is considered without bias, is specified in NIST (2013). Other additional recommendations regarding key lengths for example are given by national certification authorities in NIST (2013); ANSSI (2020); BSI (2021). Because of its multiplicative relations (e.g. $m_1^e m_2^e = (m_1 m_2)^e$), RSA without padding is known to be vulnerable against chosen input attacks. RSA laboratories specified padding schemes to be applied to the input before encryption or signature.

RSA Paddings PKCS#1 v1.5 were introduced by RSA laboratories, which was supposed to make RSA semantically secure and protected against chosen input attacks. Unfortunately, these versions of padding schemes were demonstrated insufficient for some adaptative input attacks Bleichenbacher et al. (1997); Brier et al. (2001); Coron et al. (2009). It is now recommended to use RSA with Optimal Asymmetric Encryption Padding (OAEP) or Probabilistic Signature Scheme (PSS) specified in PKCS#1 v2.1 Jonsson and Kaliski (2003).

– Section 9.1.4. JIL (2020) provides a comprehensive way to rate attacks, from objective success requirements in several categories: knowledge of the product, expertise of the attacker, elapsed time, equipment, access to one or more devices, etc.). The more requirements for the attacks, the biggest score given by category. Scores by category are agreed and updated regularly in subgroups bringing together mandated labs, certification authorities and industry vendors. The sum of all scores gives the attack rating. Several thresholds are specified for several security levels, and the product cannot claim a corresponding security level if a successful attack performed by a mandated labs with a rating below this threshold exists.

For example, Shamir (1997); Blömer et al. (2003); Giraud (2006); Kim and Quisquater (2007); Courrege et al. (2010) proposed complete protected RSA signature algorithms, all assuming an attacker power and an execution context (memory footprint, available parameters, etc.).

– Section 9.2.1. Before real fault injection on RSA cryptosystems becomes reality, Boneh et al. (1997) proposed a theoretical way to inject faults in the RSA-CRT signature, called a *Bellcore* attack, from the name of the company where the authors worked. The idea is to exploit an injection of fault in the signature either only modulo p or only modulo q. To reach this effect, the attacker can target the key parameters during the initialization, but also any step of the RSA-CRT signature. They showed that with only two RSA-CRT signatures they can recover p or q and factorize N. In Joye (1999), the authors shown that the attack is also applicable with only one faulty signature when the message is known.

Some attacks, introduced by Seifert (2005), aim at modifying the public modulus N during verification in order to obtain a prime number. Then the attacker is able to compute $\tilde{d}$ from modified $\tilde{N}$ and e to initiate fraudulent signatures.

The most natural way to protect signature against fault injection could be to perform a verification just after the signature by using the public key. It can be checked. However, in some context, it may be not so easy to access the public key. Indeed, interface is sometimes specified very strictly for inter-operability reasons. For example, the Java card 3.1 documentation (Oracle 2019) specifies the RSA-CRT private key (p, q, d_p, d_q, i_q) and the RSA-CRT public key (N, e). Moreover, it is specified that when performing a private operation (signature or deciphering), the caller could access only the private key buffer. This means that the public exponent may be not available for the implementation of a countermeasure based on the verification of the signature.

– Section 9.2.2. Boer et al. (2003) presented a variant of the DPA attack named *MRED* in 2002 which targets the message reduction modulo p or q. The attack must have the possibility to choose the message which is not necessary the case in many applications. Later, Amiel et al. (2007) suggested an improvement by using CPA to recover p or q with just the knowledge of the message (no need to choose it anymore).

– Section 9.2.3.1. Timing and simple side channel analysis have been the first published threats targeting exponentiations. The first timing attack on RSA was introduced from the late nineties by Kocher (1996). Schindler also proposed a timing attack on exponentiations for the RSA-CRT later in Schindler (2000) by analyzing the timing leakages in Montgomery's algorithm for modular operations.

Chevallier-Mamès et al. (2003) introduced the concept of side channel *atomicity* in exponentiation in 2003. The idea consists of finding a common block of instructions (potentially including dummy instructions) such that all of the processes using this common block are indistinguishable through side-channel analysis. In RSA, the *atomicity* in exponentiations were applied to several algorithms: *Atomic Square and Multiply* (Joye 2002; Chevallier-Mames et al. 2003); *Square and Multiply Always* (Coron 1999); *Montgomery Powering Ladder* (Joye and Yen 2003); *Squaring Always* (Clavier et al. 2011). Heninger and Shacham (2009) proposed an algorithm to reconstruct RSA private keys from a minimum of 27% of known bits.

Randomization of the exponent was first introduced by Kocher (1996) and extended to elliptic curves by Coron (1999). For the size of the random integer used when blinding the exponent, Schindler and Itoh (2011) and Schindler and Wiemers (2014) published several studies about the minimum size to be chosen depending how far the attacker is able to get partial leakage over several executions. Additionally, when the message can be freely chosen by the attacker, the randomization of the exponent has been shown to be insufficient for some specific input (Courrege et al. 2010; Schindler and Itoh 2011). In such cases, both the message and the modulus randomization would help achieving a sufficient security level (Mittmann and Schindler 2021; Dugardin et al. 2021).

Fouque et al. (2008) showed that the randomization operation itself may leak statistical information about d when studying the propagation of carry bits during the addition operation ($d' = d + r_d \cdot \phi(N)$).

– Section 9.2.3.2. Messerges et al. (1999) presented several statistical analyses on RSA. Depending on the possibility given to the attacker to choose/know several exponents or data, different DPA can be applied. Among them, the *ZEMD*

(*Zero-Exponent Multiple-Data*) allows for the recovery of the private exponent bit per bit. Later Fouque and Valette (2003) published the doubling attack. First, proposed on elliptic-curve scalar multiplication, this attack is easily application to RSA exponentiation.

– Section 9.2.3.3. Safe error attacks on modular exponentiation have been tacked first, which was illustrated by Joye and Yen (2003) and denoted as *M-safe error attack*, where they showed that having a *dummy* variable might yield an attacker to recover the secret. They solved it by proposing a countermeasure where each and every variable as actually a functional purpose and whose faulting will result in an actual error that can be caught by regular means as redundancy. Please note that their first counter-measure against *M-safe error attacks* was also error-prone, as it was possible to mount a clever yet realistic attack to overcome the protection. This resulted in a *C-safe error attack* for which a counter-measure has also been presented and known as the final version of the *Montgomery Powering Ladder*.

– Section 9.2.3.4. Combined attacks have been described in Amiel et al. (2007) such as *PACA* (*Passive and Active Combined Attacks*). The targeted algorithm was protected against side channel attack using message randomization and *atomicity*, but also against fault injection by performing the verification using the public exponent. Such a combination of countermeasures may seem strong at the first glance, yet the authors have found a flaw.

Their attack consists of faulting the randomization in the initialization of one intermediate variable, expecting a partial set to 0, so that the intermediate computation will have a characteristic power consumption profile, revealing by SPA the location of the multiplications by the faulted parameters in the signal and thereby the secret bits of the exponent. They then proposed a set of countermeasures that aim at poisoning the computation in case of fault injection, yielding then no specific pattern in the power consumption trace that would reveal the secret. Hence as soon as a fault is injected, it will turn in performing a modular exponentiation with a faulty private key whose recovering by SPA will not bring any knowledge about the actual private key.

– Section 9.2.3.5. The *Big Mac* attack was presented by Walter in 2001 (Woodruff and Zhou 2022). It is an horizontal collision attack targeting the *Square and Multiply* exponentiation with unknown message. Each modular multiplication is made of elementary operations $x_i \cdot y_j$. The attack consists in computing the Euclidean Distance between two sets of elementary operations to differentiate when common operands are involved in two multiplications. This allows for the distinction between square and multiplication and the recovery of the exponent bits. Then the concept of horizontal attacks was generalized by Clavier et al. (2010) and formalized in Bauer et al. (2013).

The *Square and Multiply Always* algorithm was the target of a cross-correlation attack detailed in Witteman et al. (2011). Contrary to the *Square and Multiply*, the correlation is computed between a multiplication and the following square. When a same operand is shared by these two operations, the multiplication was a dummy one and the exponent bit a 0.

Many clustering attacks on RSA were published Heyszl et al. (2013); Specht et al. (2015); Perin et al. (2014) and Perin and Chmielewski (2015).

– Section 9.2.3.6. A first family of countermeasures against the injection of a fault in the exponentiations either modulo p or modulo q has been introduced by Shamir (1997). This method is based on the extension of the modulus by a multiplication by a small random number. This solution assumed that d is available in the key buffer, which is not always the case. Its recomputation could be costly in some cases. This technique has inspired several publications, such as Aumüller et al. (2003); Blömer et al. (2003); Ciet and Joye (2005); Coron et al. (2010), based on modulus extension as well.

Several researchers have exploited specific exponentiation algorithms that can output several results, coming a given mathematical relation between them. This allows to perform multiple recombinations and checking whether mathematical relation still holds. For example, the property of *Montgomery Powering Ladder* has been exploited in Giraud (2006). The *Montgomery Powering Ladder* computes both (m^d, m^{d+1}). By performing two recombinations, one with expected outputs (m^{d_p}, m^{d_q}) giving the expected signature S, the other with the extra outputs (m^{d_p+1}, m^{d_q+1}) giving an extra signature S^*, it is possible to verify at the end that $S^* = m \cdot S$. Boscher et al. (2009) also proposed another secure RSA-CRT implementation based on a specific *left-to-right* exponentiation algorithm. Rivain (2009) proposed a solution based on double addition chains. The idea consists of processing a double exponentiation to compute the pair $(m^d, m^{\phi(N)-d}) \bmod N$ by using addition chains for exponents. The consistency of the exponentiation can be verified by computing $m^d \cdot m^{\phi(N)-d} \stackrel{?}{=} 1 \bmod N$.

– Section 9.2.4.1. Novak (2002) proposed a clever adaptive chosen plaintexts SPA attack on the RSA-CRT. Instead of simply looking at the raw traces, he rather took advantage of the recombination step, namely, $S = S_q + q \cdot (i_q \cdot (S_p - S_q) \bmod p)$, searching for a specific behavior.

As such, he targeted the case where S_p is equal to S_q to generate a 0 in the subsequent multiplication by i_q thus yielding a characteristic pattern in the signal, as all intermediate bits will be equal to 0. This is made possible by crafting inputs M_i so that:

$$S_p - S_q = 0 \iff S_p = S_q \iff M_i^{d_p} \bmod p = M_i^{d_q} \bmod q$$

Knowing that $(M^d)^e = M$, the attacker will then craft inputs $M = X^e$ to remove the contribution of the private exponent. This hence yields:

$$(X_i^e)^{d_p} \bmod p = (X_i^e)^{d_q} \bmod q \iff X_i \bmod p = X_i \bmod q$$

The equality will occur as soon as the modular reductions do not operate, namely when X_i is smaller than the both moduli. Starting with $X_0 = \sqrt{N}$ and going left toward 1 or right toward N using a dichotomic approach allows an adaptive attack using the feedback of whether or not $S_p = S_q$ when looking at the trace, thus disclosing a bit of p at each step. Afterwards, q is recovered by simply dividing N by p.

A regular way to prevent this attack is to randomize the both moduli p and q with $p' = p \cdot r_p$, $q' = q \cdot r_q$ [CM3], where r_p and r_q are two random numbers that shall follow a uniform distribution to avoid weaknesses. Afterward, the contribution of the random numbers has to be removed to recover a computationally correct result. The countermeasure comes then at the cost of two additional modular multiplications and three additional modular reductions, hence five modular multiplications overall.

Another attack on the RSA-CRT has been illustrated by Witteman (2009). As previously, this is the recombination step which is targeted:

$$S = S_q + q \cdot (i_q \cdot (S_p - S_q) \bmod p) \iff S = q \cdot x + S_q$$

Witteman (2009) further noted that actually: $S \approx x \cdot q$ as S_q is only half the size of S, yielding $x = S \cdot q^{-1}$

As x is an intermediate value, he further performed a CPA by making hypotheses on the least significant bit of q, as S is assumed to be known. He was then able to iteratively recover q.

This is a powerful attack that could be thwarted by using the same countermeasure used for the previous SPA attack by Novak (2002).

– Section 9.3.1. Several attempts of using formal methods in order to get a proof of resistance against a *Bellcore* attack for a given RSA-CRT implementation have been published by researchers Christofi et al. (2013); Rauzy and Guilley (2014); Kiss et al. (2016). The starting point for this verification is an implementation in a given programming language (compatible with the formal tool that checks mathematical properties) and a given fault model (possible fault injections). The property to be formally verified in general is "the faulty result is not exploitable", meaning "the signature is never faulty only modulo p or only modulo q". The formal tools allow us to automatically inject all possible faults exhaustively while checking whether the required property is still met, leading to a formal proof. Recently, promising methodologies and tools for proving the resistance of implementations against side-channel attacks have also been published, but still mainly practically tested on symmetric cryptography (Bloem et al. 2018; Meunier et al. 2021).

9.5. References

Amiel, F., Feix, B., Villegas, K. (2007). Power analysis for secret recovering and reverse engineering of public key algorithms. In *SAC 2007*, Adams, C.M., Miri, A., Wiener, M.J. (eds). Springer, Berlin, Heidelberg.

ANSSI (2020). Règles et recommandations concernant le choix et le dimensionnement des mécanismes cryptographiques Document, ANSSI-PG-083 [Online]. Available at: https://www.ssi.gouv.fr/uploads/2021/03/anssi-guide-mecanismes_crypto-2.04.pdf.

Aumüller, C., Bier, P., Fischer, W., Hofreiter, P., Seifert, J.-P. (2003). Fault attacks on RSA with CRT: Concrete results and practical countermeasures. In *CHES 2002*, Kaliski Jr., B.S., Koç, Ç.K., Paar, C. (eds). Springer, Berlin, Heidelberg.

Bauer, A., Jaulmes, É., Prouff, E., Wild, J. (2013). Horizontal and vertical side-channel attacks against secure RSA implementations. In *CT-RSA 2013*, Dawson, E. (ed.). Springer, Berlin, Heidelberg.

Bernstein, D.J., Chang, Y.-A., Cheng, C.-M., Chou, L.-P., Heninger, N., Lange, T., van Someren, N. (2013). Factoring RSA keys from certified smart cards: Coppersmith in the wild. In *ASIACRYPT 2013*, Sako, K. and Sarkar, P. (eds). Springer, Berlin, Heidelberg.

Bleichenbacher, D., Joye, M., Quisquater, J.-J. (1997). A new and optimal chosen-message attack on RSA-type cryptosystems. In *ICICS 97*, Han, Y., Okamoto, T., Qing, S. (eds). Springer, Berlin, Heidelberg.

Bloem, R., Iusupov, R., Krenn, M., Mangard, S. (2018). Sharing independence & relabeling: Efficient formal verification of higher-order masking. Report 2018/1031, Cryptology ePrint Archive [Online]. Available at: https://eprint.iacr.org/2018/1031.

Blömer, J., Otto, M., Seifert, J.-P. (2003). A new CRT-RSA algorithm secure against Bellcore attacks. In *ACM CCS 2003*, Jajodia, S., Atluri, V., Jaeger, T. (eds). ACM Press, New York. doi: 10.1145/948109.948151.

den Boer, B., Lemke, K., Wicke, G. (2003). A DPA attack against the modular reduction within a CRT implementation of RSA. In *CHES 2002*, Kaliski Jr., B.S., Koç, Ç.K., Paar, C. (eds). Springer, Berlin, Heidelberg.

Boneh, D. (1999). Twenty years of attacks on the RSA cryptosystem. *Notices of the AMS*, 46, 203–213.

Boneh, D., DeMillo, R.A., Lipton, R.J. (1997). On the importance of checking cryptographic protocols for faults (extended abstract). In *EUROCRYPT'97*, Fumy, W. (ed.). Springer, Berlin, Heidelberg.

Boscher, A., Handschuh, H., Trichina, E. (2009). Blinded fault resistant exponentiation revisited. In *Sixth International Workshop on Fault Diagnosis and Tolerance in Cryptography, FDTC 2009*, Breveglieri, L., Koren, I., Naccache, D., Oswald, E., Seifert, J. (eds). IEEE, Lausanne. doi: 10.1109/FDTC.2009.31.

Brier, E., Clavier, C., Coron, J.-S., Naccache, D. (2001). Cryptanalysis of RSA signatures with fixed-pattern padding. In *Advances in Cryptology – CRYPTO 2001*, Kilian, J. (ed.). Springer, Berlin, Heidelberg.

BSI (2021). BSI TR-02102-1: "Cryptographic Mechanisms: Recommendations and Key Lengths" Version: 2021-1. Technical Guideline [Online]. Available at: https://www.bsi.bund.de/SharedDocs/Downloads/EN/BSI/Publications/TechGuidelines/TG02102/BSI-TR-02102-1.html.

Chevallier-Mames, B., Ciet, M., Joye, M. (2003). Low-cost solutions for preventing simple side-channel analysis: Side-channel atomicity. Report 2003/237, Cryptology ePrint Archive [Online]. Available at: https://eprint.iacr.org/2003/237.

Christofi, M., Chetali, B., Goubin, L., Vigilant, D. (2013). Formal verification of a CRT-RSA implementation against fault attacks. *Journal of Cryptographic Engineering*, 3(3), 157–167.

Ciet, M. and Joye, M. (2005). Practical fault countermeasures for Chinese remaindering based RSA (extended abstract). In *PROC. FDTC'05*, 16196472 [Online]. Available at: https://marcjoye.github.io/papers/CJ05fdtc.pdf.

Clavier, C., Feix, B., Gagnerot, G., Roussellet, M., Verneuil, V. (2010). Horizontal correlation analysis on exponentiation. In *ICICS 10*, Soriano, M., Qing, S., López, J. (eds). Springer, Berlin, Heidelberg.

Clavier, C., Feix, B., Gagnerot, G., Roussellet, M., Verneuil, V. (2011). Square always exponentiation. In *INDOCRYPT 2011*, Bernstein, D.J. and Chatterjee, S. (eds). Springer, Berlin, Heidelberg.

Coron, J.-S. (1999). Resistance against differential power analysis for elliptic curve cryptosystems. In *CHES'99*, Koç, Ç.K. and Paar, C. (eds). Springer, Berlin, Heidelberg.

Coron, J.-S., Naccache, D., Tibouchi, M., Weinmann, R.-P. (2009). Practical cryptanalysis of ISO/IEC 9796–2 and EMV signatures. In *CRYPTO 2009*, Halevi, S. (ed.). Springer, Berlin, Heidelberg.

Coron, J-J., Giraud, G., Morin, N., Piret, G., Vigilant, G., (2010). Fault attacks and countermeasures on vigilant's RSA-CRT algorithm. In *2010 Workshop on Fault Diagnosis and Tolerance in Cryptography*, 89–96. IEEE, Santa Barbara.

Courrege, J.-C., Feix, B., Roussellet, M. (2010). Simple power analysis on exponentiation revisited. In *CARDIS 2010*, Gollman, D. and Lanet, J.-L. (eds). Springer, Berlin, Heidelberg.

Dugardin, M., Schindler, W., Guilley, S. (2021). Stochastic methods defeat regular RSA exponentiation algorithms with combined blinding methods. *J. Math. Cryptol.*, 15(1), 408–433. doi: 10.1515/jmc-2020-0010.

Fouque, P.-A. and Valette, F. (2003). The doubling attack – Why upwards is better than downwards. In *CHES 2003*, Walter, C.D., Koç, Ç.K., Paar, C. (eds). Springer, Berlin, Heidelberg.

Fouque, P.-A., Réal, D., Valette, F., Drissi, M. (2008). The carry leakage on the randomized exponent countermeasure. In *CHES 2008*, Oswald, E. and Rohatgi, P. (eds). Springer, Berlin, Heidelberg.

Giraud, C. (2006). An RSA implementation resistant to fault attacks and to simple power analysis. *IEEE Trans. Computers*, 55(9), 1116–1120.

Heninger, N. and Shacham, H. (2009). Reconstructing RSA private keys from random key bits. In *CRYPTO 2009*, Halevi, S. (ed.). Springer, Berlin, Heidelberg. doi: 10.1007/978-3-642-03356-8_1.

Heyszl, J., Ibing, A., Mangard, S., De Santis, F., Sigl, G. (2013). Clustering algorithms for non-profiled single-execution attacks on exponentiations. Report 2013/438, Cryptology ePrint Archive [Online]. Available at: https://eprint.iacr.org/2013/438.

JIL (2020). Application of attack potential to smartcards and similar devices version 3.1. Document, Joint Interpretation Library [Online]. Available at: https://www.sogis.eu/documents/cc/domains/sc/JIL-Application-of-Attack-Potential-to-Smartcards-v3-1.pdf.

Jonsson, J. and Kaliski, B. (2003). Public-key cryptography standards (PKCS) 1: RSA cryptography specifications version 2.1. Standard, RFC3447, The Internet Society [Online]. Available at: https://datatracker.ietf.org/ doc/html/rfc3447.

Joye, M. (2002). Recovering lost efficiency of exponentiation algorithms on smart cards. *Electronics Letters*, 38, 200–2.

Joye, M. and Yen, S.-M. (2003). The Montgomery powering ladder. In *CHES 2002*, Kaliski Jr., B.S., Koç, Ç.K., Paar, C. (eds). Springer, Berlin, Heidelberg. doi: 10.1007/3-540-36400-5_22.

Joye, M., Lenstra, A.K., Quisquater, J-J. (1999). Chinese remaindering based cryptosystems in the presence of faults. *J. Cryptol.*, 12(4), 241–245. doi: 10.1007/s001459900055.

Kim, C.H. and Quisquater, J.-J. (2007). How can we overcome both side channel analysis and fault attacks on rsa-crt? In *Workshop on Fault Diagnosis and Tolerance in Cryptography*. IEEE, Vienna.

Kiss, Á., Krämer, J., Rauzy, P., Seifert, J.-P. (2016). Algorithmic countermeasures against fault attacks and power analysis for RSA-CRT. In *COSADE 2016*, Standaert, F.-X. and Oswald, E. (eds). Springer, Heidelberg.

Kocher, P.C. (1996). Timing attacks on implementations of Diffie-Hellman, RSA, DSS, and other systems. In *CRYPTO'96*, Koblitz, N. (ed.). Springer, Berlin, Heidelberg.

Messerges, T.S., Dabbish, E.A., Sloan, R.H. (1999). Power analysis attacks of modular exponentiation in smartcards. In *CHES'99*, Koç, Ç.K. and Paar, C. (eds). Springer, Berlin, Heidelberg.

Meunier, Q.L., Pons, E., Heydemann, K. (2021). LeakageVerif: Scalable and efficient leakage verification in symbolic expressions. Report 2021/1468, Cryptology ePrint Archive [Online]. Available at: https://eprint.iacr.org/2021/1468.

Mittmann, J. and Schindler, W. (2021). Timing attacks and local timing attacks against Barrett's modular multiplication algorithm. *Journal of Cryptographic Engineering*, 11(4), 369–397.

Nemec, M., Sýs, M., Svenda, P., Klinec, D., Matyas, V. (2017). The return of coppersmith's attack: Practical factorization of widely used RSA moduli. In *ACM CCS 2017*, Thuraisingham, B.M., Evans, D., Malkin, T., Xu, D. (eds). ACM Press, New York.

NIST (2013). FIPS 186-4, Digital Signature Standard (DSS). Standard, National Institute of Standards and Technology, Gaithersburg. doi: 10.6028/NIST.FIPS.186-4.

Novak, R. (2002). SPA-based adaptive chosen-ciphertext attack on RSA implementation. In *PKC 2002*, Naccache, D. and Paillier, P. (eds). Springer, Berlin, Heidelberg.

Oracle (2019). Java card 3.1 documentation [Online]. Available at: https://docs.oracle.com/en/java/javacard/3.1/.

Perin, G. and Chmielewski, L. (2015). A semi-parametric approach for side-channel attacks on protected RSA implementations. In *CARDIS*, Homma, N. and Medwed, M. (eds). Springer, Cham.

Perin, G., Imbert, L., Torres, L., Maurine, P. (2014). Attacking randomized exponentiations using unsupervised learning. In *COSADE 2014*, Prouff, E. (ed.). Springer, Berlin, Heidelberg.

Rauzy, P. and Guilley, S. (2014). A formal proof of countermeasures against fault injection attacks on CRT-RSA. *Journal of Cryptographic Engineering*, 4(3), 173–185.

Rivain, M. (2009). Securing RSA against fault analysis by double addition chain exponentiation. In *CT-RSA*, Fischlin, M. (ed.). Springer, Berlin, Heidelberg.

Rivest, R.L., Shamir, A., Adleman, L. (1978). A method for obtaining digital signatures and public-key cryptosystems. *Communications of the ACM*, 21(2), 120–126.

Schindler, W. (2000). A timing attack against RSA with the Chinese remainder theorem. In *CHES 2000*, Koç, Ç.K. and Paar, C. (eds). Springer, Berlin, Heidelberg.

Schindler, W. and Itoh, K. (2011). Exponent blinding does not always lift (partial) spa resistance to higher-level security. In *ACNS 11*, Lopez, J. and Tsudik, G. (eds). Springer, Berlin, Heidelberg.

Schindler, W. and Wiemers, A. (2014). Power attacks in the presence of exponent blinding. *Journal of Cryptographic Engineering*, 4(4), 213–236.

Seifert, J.-P. (2005). On authenticated computing and RSA-based authentication. In *ACM CCS 2005*, Atluri, V., Meadows, C., Juels, A. (eds). ACM Press, New York.

Shamir, A. (1997). Method and apparatus for protecting public key schemes from timing and fault attacks. United States Patent 5,991,415 [Online]. Available at: https://www.torsten-schuetze.de/sommerakademie2009/papers/Shamir_US_Patent_1999.pdf.

Specht, R., Heyszl, J., Kleinsteuber, M., Sigl, G. (2015). Improving non-profiled attacks on exponentiations based on clustering and extracting leakage from multi-channel high-resolution EM measurements. In *COSADE 2015*, Mangard, S. and Poschmann, A.Y. (eds). Springer, Berlin, Heidelberg.

Witteman, M.F. (2009). A DPA attack on RSA in CRT mode. Riscure Technical Report [Online]. Available at: http://www.cadshop.ru/articles/3.pdf.

Witteman, M.F., van Woudenberg, J.G.J., Menarini, F. (2011). Defeating RSA multiply-always and message blinding countermeasures. In *CT-RSA 2011*, Kiayias, A. (ed.). Springer, Berlin, Heidelberg.

Woodruff, D.P. and Zhou, S. (2022). Tight bounds for adversarially robust streams and sliding windows via difference estimators. In *2021 IEEE 62nd Annual Symposium on Foundations of Computer Science (FOCS)*. Denver.

10

Protected ECC Implementations

Łukasz CHMIELEWSKI[1,2] and Louiza PAPACHRISTODOULOU[3]

[1]Radboud University, Nijmegen, Netherlands

[2]Masaryk University, Czechia

[3]Fontys University of Applied Sciences, Eindhoven, Netherlands

10.1. Introduction

This chapter considers various techniques for protecting implementations based on elliptic curve cryptosystems against side-channel and fault injection attacks.

Elliptic curve cryptography (ECC) is broadly used in security products for digital signatures (ECDSA) and for the establishment of a common secret key (ECDH). Sometimes, ECC is also used for encryption (EC-ElGamal), but this is not common, since symmetric algorithms are much faster. ECC consists of algorithms and protocols with small key lengths and memory requirements compared to equivalent RSA implementations. Therefore, ECC offers suitable implementation options for embedded devices, where the resources in terms of memory and power are limited. The security of elliptic curve cryptosystems relies on the difficulty of solving the discrete logarithm problem on elliptic curves defined over finite fields of large characteristic or binary fields. The focus, from a security point of view, is on scalar multiplication because this is the operation that involves the manipulation of the secret in an ECC protocol. For digital signature protocols using elliptic curves, there are also other operations that need to be protected. Essentially, all values that allow the private key recovery need to be protected. For instance, not only does the scalar multiplication need to be protected but also modular multiplication involves the private key. We do not discuss this topic in this chapter since this operation can be

Embedded Cryptography 2,
coordinated by Emmanuel PROUFF, Guénaël RENAULT,
Matthieu RIVAIN and Colin O'FLYNN.

protected with multiplicative masking, which is not specific to ECC. Another example is generating the cryptographically secure and random scalar nonce used in ECDSA signature generation; this number can be random or deterministic but must be unique for every signature, otherwise a nonce leakage attack can lead to signature forgery[1].

There are various ways to implement ECC algorithms in a secure way in embedded devices, and in principle, the following techniques are used:

– constant time and/or regular scalar multiplication algorithm;

– masked (or blinded) implementations;

– randomization of scalar and/or point coordinates.

In real-world applications that require security against SCA, for example, payment, these techniques are used, but are not always implemented correctly, making the end product vulnerable to various types of implementation attacks, such as simple power analysis (SPA), differential power analysis (DPA), template attacks (TA) and fault analysis (FA)[2].

In the rest of this chapter, we analyze five techniques and provide algorithmic countermeasures, in a step-by-step, incremental approach. We start with the most basic countermeasures that protect against SPA in sections 10.2.1 and 10.2.2. We move to countermeasures that protect against DPA and TA in sections 10.2.3 and 10.2.4 and then we present protected algorithms against more sophisticated attacks, such as the conditional swap (see section 10.2.6.1) and address-bit side-channel attacks (see section 10.2.6).

The aforementioned side-channel techniques are described in Part 1 and 2. In particular, the unsupervised approaches, such as SPA and DPA, are described in Chapter 4, while the supervised approaches, such as TA, are described in Chapter 5. Even more advanced attacks, mostly supervised ones, are covered in Chapter 7.

Part 3 covers fault injection and FA. In particular, generic fault injection techniques are described in Chapter 9. The FA on public key cryptographic algorithms, including ECC, is described in Chapter 11 and advanced fault injection attacks are described in Chapter 12.

10.2. Protecting ECC implementations and countermeasures

In this section, we give a step-by-step approach of how to develop a secure ECC implementation against SCA and FA. The methodology and countermeasures described here can be followed in order to derive a protected ECC implementation.

---

1 Similarly to protecting modular multiplication, secure random generation is out of the scope of this chapter.

2 The attacks based on fault analysis are also often called *fault injection* attacks.

First of all, we start with the selection of a curve that is approved by several standards for use in ECC.

Organization and practical examples

In this section, we also present practical examples for described countermeasures. The examples come from a library available at the following open-access repository: https://github.com/sca-secure-library-sca25519/sca25519. This repository contains a library that provides three implementations computing the X25519 key-exchange protocol on the ARM Cortex-M4 micro-controller; their functionalities are equivalent, but differ in the degree of the employed side-channel and fault injection countermeasures.

We distinguish between unprotected X25519 (called *STM32F407-unprotected* in the repository), X25519 with ephemeral keys (called *STM32F407-ephemeral*) and X25519 with static keys (called *STM32F407-static*). The unprotected implementation includes only basic countermeasures (e.g. constant time operations), while the ephemeral implementation increases the number of countermeasures to protect the ephemeral key. The static implementation adds further countermeasures to protect the static key since it can be used multiple times, contrary to the ephemeral case. As expected, the extra security comes at the cost of computational overhead.

10.2.1. *Unified arithmetic and complete formulae*

Elliptic curves used in cryptography must use unified and complete formulae without exceptional cases for protection against several types of attacks and in particular, SCA. An elliptic curve addition law is *complete* if it correctly computes the sum of any two points in the group without exceptions. The addition law is *unified* if the addition and doubling of points can be computed by the same formulae.

Weierstrass curves are widely used in cryptography and they are standardized by several organizations. However, they had a main drawback regarding their side channel resistance; namely, their addition formulae were incomplete and not unified. Since 2016, there have been complete addition formulae for prime order elliptic curves defined over a finite field $E/\mathbb{F}_q : y^2 = x^3 + ax + b$ with $q \geq 5$ ($\mathbb{F}_q$ is a finite field of q elements, where q is a power of a prime number p), which is an important step toward SCA resistance of Weierstrass curves.

Edwards curves were the first curves shown to have a complete addition law. The completeness property of the addition law offers the possibility to secure ECC implementations against attacks that take advantage of the different patterns between addition and multiplication, such as TA, for example. By removing the "branching" to handle exceptional cases, some side-channel attack vulnerabilities caused by handling these cases can be prevented. It is trickier, but still possible, to also achieve secure ECC implementations without complete addition formulae, but the difference between addition and doubling operations should be handled carefully. The way the multiplication is handled in the underlying field operations, and more specifically the handling of carries, can cause side-channel leakages that can be exploited by, for example, carry-based attacks.

Example

The arithmetic employed in the repository uses unified and complete formulae on Curve25519. For all three implementations, the code implementing this arithmetic is located in the `crypto/numerics` folder and in the `curve25519_ladderstep` function in the `crypto/scalarmult/scalarmult_25519.c` file. Since we concentrate on describing the countermeasures here, we do not delve into the details of that arithmetic implementation. For more details on how arithmetic is used, we refer the reader to the example in section 10.2.3.

10.2.2. *Constant-time scalar multiplication*

As previously mentioned, scalar multiplication is the most critical operation in ECC implementations, since it manipulates the secret key. The straightforward implementation of scalar multiplication on an elliptic curve involves repeated doubling and addition operations, which is known as the *double-and-add algorithm*. When the bit of the scalar is 0, a doubling is performed, and when the bit is 1, a doubling is followed by an addition.

Algorithm 10.1. Left-to-right double-and-add algorithm

Input: P, $k = (k_{n-1}, k_{n-2}, \dots, k_0)_2$
Output: $Q = [k]P$

$R_0 \leftarrow O$
for $i \leftarrow n-1$ **down to** *0* **do**
  $R_0 \leftarrow 2R_0$
  if $k_i = 1$ **then**
    $R_0 \leftarrow R_0 + P$
  end if
end for
return R_0

This is an efficient algorithm since it performs the addition only if the current bit is 1; otherwise, it performs only one doubling. However, it is vulnerable to SPA since distinct patterns can be exploited in the execution of the algorithm. In a non-protected implementation like Algorithm 10.1, the sequence of point additions and point doublings can reveal the bits of the secret scalar k. When two operations are performed, this is obvious in a single power analysis leakage trace, and in this way, we can recover the current bit in each round of the computation.

Protecting this algorithm from SPA leakage can be done in two ways. The first approach is called *atomicity*, in which individual operations are implemented in such a way that they have an identical side-channel profile (e.g. for any branch and any key-bit related subroutine). In particular, both operations (doubling and addition) should not be recognizable from each other, using for example, unified formulae. However, this approach has a serious drawback: the amount of ones in the scalar simply leaks in timing.

The second, in our opinion more secure approach, requires making the point operations independent of the secret key. Making this algorithm regular can be done by avoiding the `if-then` statement and performing a dummy group addition, when the current bit k_i is 0. Line 4 can be replaced by $\boldsymbol{R}_{1-k_i} \leftarrow \boldsymbol{R}_{1-k_i} + \boldsymbol{P}$ as seen in Algorithm 10.2. However, in this way, the algorithm becomes vulnerable to fault attacks. If the attacker is able to induce a fault during the evaluation of $\boldsymbol{R}_{1-k_i} \leftarrow \boldsymbol{R}_{1-k_i} + \boldsymbol{P}$, they will be able to understand if the current bit is 0, since in that case the evaluation $\boldsymbol{R}_1 + \boldsymbol{P}$ is written in register $\boldsymbol{R}_1$; and as this register is not needed, the final output of the algorithm will not be affected. Therefore, the algorithm is vulnerable to a fault injection attack called *safe-error attack*.

Algorithm 10.2. Left-to-right double-and-always-add algorithm

Input: $\boldsymbol{P}$, $k = (k_{n-1}, k_{n-2}, \ldots, k_0)_2$
Output: $\boldsymbol{Q} = [k]\boldsymbol{P}$

1 $\boldsymbol{R}_0 \leftarrow \boldsymbol{O}, \boldsymbol{R}_1 \leftarrow \boldsymbol{O}$
2 **for** $i \leftarrow n-1$ **down to** *0* **do**
3 $\quad \boldsymbol{R}_0 \leftarrow 2\boldsymbol{R}_0$
4 $\quad \boldsymbol{R}_{1-k_i} \leftarrow \boldsymbol{R}_{1-k_i} + \boldsymbol{P}$
5 **end for**
6 **return** $\boldsymbol{R}_0$

Example

The scalar multiplication algorithm is implemented constant-time for the unprotected implementation in the `crypto/scalarmult/scalarmult_25519.c` file in the function `crypto_scalarmult_curve25519`[3]. We describe this algorithm in detail in the example in section 10.2.3.

10.2.3. *Elimination of if-statements even dummy ones*

As explained previously, eliminating `if`-statements can protect against SPA attacks, but using dummy operations in an algorithm can make it still vulnerable to FA attacks. Therefore, we need a regular algorithm that also does not have dummy operations. The double-and-add-always algorithm was initially proposed as a first attempt to avoid `if`-statements and therefore prevent the identification of different operations. The algorithm performs a point doubling, followed by a point addition in a `for`-loop, scanning the scalar bits from the most significant to the least significant one. Both operations are performed in every loop iteration and according to the key bit, the final assignment to $\boldsymbol{R}_0$ will be either $\boldsymbol{R}_0$ or $\boldsymbol{R}_1$. There are no conditional statements in the algorithm, but there is one key-dependent assignment, which can leak secret information either with DPA or with TA. Another important remark is that $\boldsymbol{R}_0$ is initialized by $\boldsymbol{P}$ instead of $\mathcal{O}$, in order to avoid exceptional cases given by the point at infinity. When this is used, the MSB of the scalar is considered to be equal to 1 and the `for`-loop needs to start from $n-2$.

Algorithm 10.3. Left-to-right double-and-add-always algorithm (Coron 1999)

Input: P, $k = (k_{n-1}, k_{n-2}, \ldots, k_0)_2$
Output: $Q = [k]P$

$\boldsymbol{R}_0 \leftarrow \boldsymbol{P}$
for $i \leftarrow n-2$ **down to** 0 **do**
  $\boldsymbol{R}_0 \leftarrow 2\boldsymbol{R}_0$
  $\boldsymbol{R}_1 \leftarrow \boldsymbol{R}_0 + \boldsymbol{P}$
  $\boldsymbol{R}_0 \leftarrow \boldsymbol{R}_{k_i}$
end for
return $\boldsymbol{R}_0$

The Montgomery Power Ladder (MPL) is one of the most secure algorithms, since it is not only protected against simple side-channel analysis due to its natural regularity of operations, but it is also protected against safe-error attacks since there are no dummy operations. This algorithm is used as the primary secure and efficient choice for resource-constrained devices. The MPL is described in Algorithm 10.4.

3 For the ephemeral and static implementations, the scalar multiplication is additionally randomized and we will explain these randomizations later on, when describing more complex countermeasures.

The regularity of the algorithm makes it intrinsically secure against a large variety of implementation attacks (SPA, some fault attacks, etc.).

Furthermore, for the sake of efficiency, often the ECC operations in the ladder step, the addition and the doubling, are combined into a single operation on the curve.

Algorithm 10.4. The Montgomery Ladder

```
Input: P, k = (k_{n-1}, k_{n-2}, ..., k_0)_2
Output: Q = [k]P
R_0 ← O
R_1 ← P
for i ← n − 1 down to 0 do
    b ← 1 − k_i
    R_b ← R_0 + R_1
    R_{k_i} ← 2 · R_{k_i}
end for
return R_0
```

Combining the above-mentioned regular algorithms with scalar and/or point randomization make ECC implementations secure against various types of attacks. Therefore, in the next sections, we will provide a description of these techniques.

Example

Our example protected ECC library, which implements the X25519 elliptic-curve key exchange, is based on arithmetic on the elliptic curve in Montgomery form $E : y^2 = x^3 + 486,662x^2 + x$ over the finite field $\mathbb{F}_p$ with $p = 2^{255} - 19$. This is essentially a specific version of the Algorithm 10.4 oriented at efficiency and that assures constant-timeness.

The group of $\mathbb{F}_p$-rational points on E has order $8 \cdot \ell$, where ℓ is a 252-bit prime. The central operation is scalar multiplication $\mathsf{smult}(k, x_P)$, which receives as input two 32-byte arrays k and x_P. Each of those arrays is interpreted as a 256-bit integer in little-endian encoding; the integer x_P is further interpreted as an element of $\mathbb{F}_p$. The smult routine first sets the most significant bit of x_P to zero (ensuring that $x_P \in \{0, \ldots, 2^{255} - 1\}$) and sets the least significant 3 bits of k and the most significant bit of k to zero, and the second-most significant bit of k to one (ensuring that $k \in 8 \cdot \{2^{251}, \ldots, 2^{252} - 1\}$). This operation on bits of the input k is often referred to as "clamping"; in our pseudo-code, we denote it by clamp. Subsequently, smult outputs the x-coordinate $x_{[k]P}$ of the point $[k]P$, where P is one of the two points with x-coordinate x_P on E (if there are such points) or the quadratic twist of E (otherwise), and where $[k]$ denotes scalar multiplication by k. The smult operation is commonly implemented using the Montgomery Ladder and a projective representation $(X : Z)$ of an x-coordinate $x = X/Y$. Pseudocode for this ladder is given in Algorithm 10.5 and is implemented in the `crypto/scalarmult/scalarmult_25519.c` file in the function `crypto_scalarmult_curve25519` for the unprotected implementation.

Algorithm 10.5. The Montgomery Ladder for x-coordinate-based X25519 scalar multiplication on $E : y^2 = x^3 + 486662x^2 + x$

Input: $k \in \{0, \ldots, 2^{255} - 1\}$ and the x-coordinate x_P of a point P
Output: $x_{[k]P}$, the x-coordinate of $[k]P$

```
X_1 ← 1, Z_1 ← 0
X_2 ← x_P, Z_2 ← 1
p ← 0
for i ← 254 down to 0 do
    c ← k_i ⊕ p
    p ← k_i
    (X_1, X_2) ← cswap(X_1, X_2, c); (Z_1, Z_2) ← cswap(Z_1, Z_2, c)
    (X_1, Z_1, X_2, Z_2) ← ladderstep(x_P, X_1, Z_1, X_2, Z_2)
end for
(X_1, X_2) ← cswap(X_1, X_2, p); (Z_1, Z_2) ← cswap(Z_1, Z_2, p)
return (X_1, Z_1)
```

This algorithm uses two sub-routines cswap and ladderstep. The cswap ("conditional swap") routine swaps the first two inputs if and only if the last input is 1. For two 32-bit values v_1 and v_2 and the condition bit s, cswap is usually implemented in the following three ways:

$$v_2 = v_2 + s \times (v_1 - v_2), \qquad v_1 = v_1 - s \times (v_1 - v_2), \tag{10.1}$$

$$v_2 = (s - 1) \times v_2 + s \times v_1, \qquad v_1 = (s - 1) \times v_1 + s \times v_2, \tag{10.2}$$

or:

$$v_2 = v_2 \oplus s \wedge (v_1 \oplus v_2), \qquad v_1 = v_1 \oplus s \wedge (v_1 \oplus v_2). \tag{10.3}$$

For the unprotected implementation, the cswap routine is implemented using the last method (from equation [10.3]) in the `crypto/numerics/fe25519.c` file in the `fe25519_cswap` function. The C code implementing this function is presented in Listing 10.1[4].

```
void fe25519_cswap(fe25519* in1, fe25519* in2, int condition) {
    int32_t mask = condition;
    uint32_t ctr;

    mask = -mask;

    for (ctr = 0; ctr < 8; ctr++) {
        uint32_t val1 = in1->as_uint32_t[ctr];
        uint32_t val2 = in2->as_uint32_t[ctr];
        uint32_t temp = val1;

        val1 ^= mask & (val2 ^ val1);
        val2 ^= mask & (val2 ^ temp);

        in1->as_uint32_t[ctr] = val1;
        in2->as_uint32_t[ctr] = val2;
    }
}
```

Listing 10.1. *fe25519_cswap function*

As shown in the listing, the `fe25519_cswap` function uses only arithmetic operations to swap the coordinates. This way, the implementation achieves constant time and eliminates if-statements. Moreover, due to the use of the Montgomery Ladder, dummy operations are not used.

Note that the Montgomery Ladder can be implemented also using scalar-dependent memory access like in Algorithm 10.4. The problem with that approach is that memory accesses might not be constant time if the targeted platform includes, for example, caches.

For the ephemeral static implementation, we use a randomized version of cswap called cswaprr, which provides an extra ladder state randomization (for details on that function, please see the example in section 10.2.5).

The ladderstep computes $(X_{[2]P}, Z_{[2]P}, X_{P+Q}, Z_{P+Q})$ on input coordinates $x_{Q-P}, X_P, Z_P, X_Q, Z_Q$. It is implemented in the `curve25519_ladderstep` function in the `crypto/scalarmult/scalarmult_25519.c` file for all three implementations. Since we concentrate on the countermeasures, we do not delve here into the details of that arithmetic implementation.

4 The code in the repository contains more newlines. In the listing, we slightly compressed that code for the sake of presentation.

The key-exchange protocol uses the smult function and the fixed basepoint $x_B = [9, 0, \ldots, 0]$ and proceeds with straightforward elliptic-curve Diffie–Hellman.

10.2.4. *Scalar randomization*

The correlation between the power consumption/EM emanations and the instructions or the data that are manipulated during the cryptographic operation can be thwarted by randomizing the secret key bits. In the case of ECC implementations, randomization is possible either for the scalar or for the coordinates of the point on the curve, which are involved in the crucial computation of the scalar multiplication[5].

Randomizing the scalar results in getting traces with $[k']P$ instead of $[k]P$, with k' the randomized scalar defined for many different cases below. The randomizations of the scalar are always done modulo q, which is the order of the curve. The different techniques for scalar randomization are:

1) $[k]\boldsymbol{P} = [k-r]\boldsymbol{P} + [r]\boldsymbol{P}$, two scalar multiplications are computed $\boldsymbol{Q} = [k-r]\boldsymbol{P}$ and $\boldsymbol{R} = [r]\boldsymbol{P}$;

2) $[k]\boldsymbol{P} = [r]([k \times r^{-1}]\boldsymbol{P})$, two scalar multiplications are computed $\boldsymbol{Q} = [k \times r^{-1}]\boldsymbol{P}$ and $\boldsymbol{R} = [r]\boldsymbol{Q}$;

3) $[k]\boldsymbol{P} = [k \mod r]\boldsymbol{P} + [\lfloor \frac{k}{r} \rfloor]([r]\boldsymbol{P})$, three scalar multiplications are computed $\boldsymbol{Q} = [k \mod r]\boldsymbol{P}$, $\boldsymbol{R} = [r]\boldsymbol{P}$ and $\boldsymbol{S} = [\lfloor \frac{k}{r} \rfloor]\boldsymbol{R}$;

4) $[k]\boldsymbol{P} = [k]\boldsymbol{P} + [rq]\boldsymbol{P}$, where q is the order of the curve and $k + rq$ is the randomized scalar. Thus, $[rq]\boldsymbol{P} = \mathcal{O}$ the neutral element on $\mathcal{E}$.

Scalar randomization is an effective countermeasure against certain types of attacks, such as SPA, DPA and TA. However, single-trace SPA and template attacks are still possible against ECC implementations protected only with this countermeasure. The important property that thwarts scalar randomization is the fact that we need only one target trace, which is taken using the same randomized k' that is manipulated throughout the attack. For the template traces, we always need the first part of the trace, which corresponds to the beginning of the scalar multiplication algorithm running with input point a multiple m of P. This part of the trace is not affected by scalar randomization.

5 There are also other options for randomization, for instance, randomizing the base field arithmetic by using the residue number system (RNS) representation. In RNS, a number is represented as a set of smaller numbers, where each one is the result of the modular reduction with a smaller modulo basis; these modulo bases can be randomized to protect against SCA and FA. RNS was shown to provide secure ECC implementations, but we do not dive into details in this chapter.

For scalar multiplication over certain cryptographic elliptic curves, typically those over a prime field $\mathbb{F}_p$ where p is a generalized Mersenne number, adding a random multiple of the group order does not hide all the bits of scalar k because the group order q is relatively close to the power of two. In such cases, multiplying random r by q works more like a left binary shift and if the size of r is significantly smaller than q (e.g. q is 512 bits and r is 64 bits), then not all bits of the scalar k are blinded.

For all these four randomization techniques mentioned above, a type of SCA called online template attacks (OTA) can be applied. Roughly speaking, OTA works as follows: the attacker first collects a single trace, a so-called *target trace*. The goal is to recover the scalar iteratively from the target trace, starting from the first iteration and going to the last. Second, the attacker obtains traces with carefully crafted inputs, so-called *(online) template traces*, in order to find similarities with the first iteration of the target trace. By carefully analyzing such similarities, the attacker recovers the first scalar bit. Based on that, the attacker collects new template traces targeting the next iteration and the attack continues until all scalar bits are recovered. The OTA works against all scalar randomization techniques because it simply requires one target trace and the original scalar can be recovered from the randomized ones. The interested reader can find more references about OTA in the notes at the end of the chapter.

Remark on the size of the randomness

For all the randomizations and blindings in this chapter, the natural question is how many bits of entropy they need to have. It is comfortable to think that r is just a random element in the given group but that is too inefficient. In usual practice, it is assumed that the entropy should be big enough so brute-force is not possible. Therefore, as also presented in the example below, it is commonly assumed that 64-bit per one randomization or blinding should be sufficient. Unless stated otherwise, this also applies to the other form of randomizations described in this chapter, including coordinate and point randomizations, among others.

Observe that, as mentioned above, scalar randomization 4 requires more entropy to be secure.

Example

Scalar randomizations are only implemented for the static implementation[6]. In particular, the aforementioned multiplicative scalar multiplication [2] $[k]\boldsymbol{P} = [r]([k \times r^{-1}]\boldsymbol{P})$, where r is a 64-bit random value, is implemented to protect the execution of the scalar multiplication. The function first generates random r and then computes $r^{-1}, \boldsymbol{Q} = [k \times r^{-1}]\boldsymbol{P}$, and $\boldsymbol{R} = [r]\boldsymbol{Q}$.

However, this is not the only scalar randomization included in the static implementation. The scalar in the static library is also protected with static masks,

6 The unprotected and ephemeral implementations do not include any scalar randomizations.

including a blinding factor; there are other masks too and they are described in the example in section 10.2.5. It means that the scalar is not stored in plaintext and the masked scalar is stored together with the blinding factor. Then the blinded scalar and the blinding are automatically updated during scalar-multiplication executions and they should not be modified (or accessed) by the user before the next execution[7]. This static blinding is performed in the following way: a 64-bit blinding factor f and a blinded scalar $k_{f^{-1}} = k \cdot f^{-1}$, such that $f \times k_{f^{-1}} = k$, are stored together.

Both of these countermeasures are implemented in the function `crypto_scalarmult_curve25519`. Note that the scalar k is never accessed in plaintext. The masking f^{-1} is removed from $k_{f^{-1}}$ only after it is multiplied by r^{-1}: $(k_{f^{-1}} \times r^{-1}) \times f$. Moreover, inversions of r and the blinding factor are masked multiplicatively[8] to protect the scalar r used in the second scalar multiplication. An example of such an operation is computing the inverse of r. Finally, the static blinding of the scalar is updated with new random values after the scalar multiplications are finished in `crypto_scalarmult_curve25519` by calling the function `update_static_key_curve25519`. This function first updates the masks that are mentioned in the next section and then performs the following:

1) generates new blinding factor nB and computes nB^{-1} in a multiplicatively masked way;

2) computes $t = (k_{f^{-1}} \times nB^{-1})$;

3) computes $k_{nB^{-1}} = t \times f = k \times nB^{-1}$ and stores $k_{nB^{-1}}$ and nB as a new blinded scalar to be used in the next scalar multiplication.

This way, the scalar k even if it is used multiple times is never accessed in the same way multiple times. This countermeasure heavily hinders attacks oriented on key transfer.

10.2.5. *Coordinate and point randomizations*

For ECC implementations, the choice of point representation is very crucial, as it is shown that it can reveal information about the underlying discrete logarithms. More precisely, it is shown that projective coordinates leak when applied, for example, at Schnorr Signatures, by recovering a few bits of the scalar k at each iteration[9].

---

7 The main idea is that if possible they should be stored in the memory isolated from the user. However, such a feature is not offered by the library platform.

8 Inversions can be masked multiplicatively in an easy way: a value to be inverted is first multiplied by a new fresh mask m. Then, the inversion is a computer and the result is multiplied by m. This way, the result is correct but the power consumption is randomized.

9 The interested reader can find references in the notes at the end of the chapter.

Randomizing the point representation of the scalar multiplication state is commonly done by either coordinate or point randomization. Randomizing the homogeneous projective coordinates involves choosing a random number λ and replacing (X, Y, Z) with $\lambda X, \lambda Y, \lambda Z$. In this way, the leaking of additional information can be prevented. Since usually $Z = 1$, this randomization costs only two finite field multiplications. The Jacobian representation can be randomized similarly: it consists of selecting a random r in the finite field $\mathbb{F}_q$, and computing: $(X, Y, Z) \mapsto (r^2 \times X, r^3 \times Y, r \times Z)$. In most cases, the input point is in affine coordinates and $Z = 1$, so the randomization of the point is reduced to: $(x, y) \mapsto (r^2 \times x, r^3 \times y, r)$. The supplementary cost of this countermeasure is four finite field multiplications. For comparison, the cost of one scalar multiplication using a 256-bit scalar with a regular algorithm such as double-and-add-always is 5,100 multiplications.

As shown above, coordinate randomization is efficient. However, it has a drawback: while the non-zero coordinates are randomized, the 0 values remain unchanged. This leakage can be used by so-called zero-value attacks. This problem is avoided by randomizing the point on the curve: the idea is that before the scalar multiplication, we add a random blinding point to the input point, and then perform the scalar multiplication with the new input. Then, the scalar multiplication is performed a second time with the blinding random point as the input, and finally, the result is subtracted from the result of the first multiplication. This way, the result is correct and the execution is randomized at a twofold cost; how to perform point randomization in a more efficient way is described below in the example section.

The aforementioned countermeasures work well against TA (including OTA) since they do not allow for the prediction of intermediate values of the calculation and prevent the construction of template traces in a deterministic way. Coordinate blinding is implemented in some cryptographic libraries, like MbedTLS [10], and it should be used when the device under attack has a random generator.

Example

Since the scalar multiplication in the library uses the (X, Z) representation, the ephemeral and the static implementation fully randomize the Z coordinate before the Montgomery Ladder is executed. This is done in the function `crypto_scalarmult_curve25519`.

Additionally, re-randomizing the projective representation in the cswaprr procedure is implemented. The strategy of cswaprr, which merges conditional swaps with projective re-randomization, takes into account that memory access leaks significantly more than register operations. Therefore, the ephemeral and the static

10 MbedTLS also implements scalar blinding.

implementations fetch input words from memory, conditionally swap and randomize in registers and then store the results back. Randomization here means multiplying both the X and the Z coordinate by a 29-bit random value. This is implemented in the assembly in the procedure `cSwapAndRandomize_asm` in the file `crypto/asm/cortex_m4_cSwapAndRandomize.S`. This re-randomization protects the implementations against cross-correlation attacks.

Furthermore, to protect against attacks that use special points as input, the static implementation use static random points R and S for input point blinding, where $S = [-k]R$. Initially, R is added to the input point and after scalar multiplication ladders, S is added to the result. This is implemented in `crypto_scalarmult_curve25519` for the static implementation. The points R and S are always securely re-randomized at the end of scalar multiplication (together with the blinded scalar; see section 10.2.4 for details) in the function `update_static_key_curve25519`. They should also be stored securely.

10.2.6. *Protection against address-bit side-channel attacks*

Address-bit side-channel attacks, and the specific countermeasures, have received relatively little attention in the literature since blinding methods typically randomize the bitwise representation of a scalar, and therefore the accessed addresses. However, only randomizing the scalar does not remove the address-bit leakage and does not prevent single-trace attacks: the attacker can still perform a single-trace attack to recover the randomized scalar and then re-compute the original secret. This is even more important since, as mentioned before, for scalar multiplication over certain cryptographic elliptic curves adding a random multiple of the group order does not hide all the bits of scalar k. In this section, we investigate the countermeasure that makes such a single-trace attack harder or even impossible. We do not present them in section 10.2.4 since this method can be either combined or added on top of any scalar randomization.

A typical countermeasure against side-channel attacks consists of masking the intermediate values with a random number. In symmetric cryptographic algorithms, Boolean shares of the secret are typically used, whether in asymmetric algorithms, the secret exponent/scalar is masked using group arithmetic properties. This section presents a recent scalar splitting technique with minimal impact on performance based on Boolean shares, analogous to the countermeasures that we would use for an implementation of a block cipher and similar to the countermeasures used to prevent address-bit side-channel attacks. More precisely, Algorithm 10.6 shows how an exponent can be efficiently split into two shares, where the exponent is the exclusive OR (XOR) sum of the two shares, typically requiring only an extra register and a few registers copies per bit. Scalar multiplication algorithms can be randomized for every execution and combined with other blinding techniques, maintaining at the same time the regularity feature. In this way, both the scalar and the intermediate values can be protected against a broad range of side-channel attacks.

Algorithm 10.6 shows how the MPL can be implemented with the XOR-split scalar during a scalar multiplication on a curve $\mathcal{E}$. Initially, we split the scalar κ into two Boolean shares A and B, which are $n-$bit integers, with n equal to the scalar number bits. During the execution of the algorithm, one share a_i is used to indicate the address accessed, and the other acts as a scalar. Whenever both values a_i, b_i appear in a computation, they are always XOR-ed with a random value b' so that there is no leakage of the current scalar bit at any point of the implementation. This is shown in Line 6 of Algorithm 10.6, where the assignment of the values is randomized according to the random bit b'. This is the main point that prevents address-bit side-channel attacks. This technique can be applied also in exponentiation, in order to blind the secret exponent.

The main advantage of scalar multiplication (or exponentiation) algorithms using this technique, is that the adversary needs a combination of leakages to recover the scalar. For instance, a single trace attack targeting one intermediate value would not be able to succeed, but a combination of TA with a higher-order DPA might work. Of course, the corresponding implementation should be done in a specific way, so that other leakages are prevented. For instance, we need to make sure that during the computation of $\boldsymbol{R}_{(b_i \oplus b') \oplus a_i}$ the operations happen in this order in the compiler and the values a_i, b_i during the computation of $a_i \oplus b_i$ are never stored in a single register together.

Algorithm 10.6. MPL with XOR-Split Scalar on an EC

Input: $\mathcal{E}, \mathbb{F}_q, \boldsymbol{P} \in \mathcal{E}$, n-bit integers $A = \sum_{i=0}^{n-1} a_i\, 2^i, B = \sum_{i=0}^{n-1} b_i\, 2^i$
Output: $\boldsymbol{Q} = [\kappa]\boldsymbol{P}$ where $\kappa = A \oplus B$

1 $\boldsymbol{R}_0 \leftarrow \boldsymbol{P}\,; \boldsymbol{R}_1 \leftarrow \boldsymbol{P}\,; \boldsymbol{R}_2 \leftarrow \boldsymbol{P}$
2 $b' \xleftarrow{R} \{0,1\}$
3 $\boldsymbol{R}_{\neg b'} \leftarrow 2\boldsymbol{P}$
4 **for** $i = n-2$ **down to** 0 **do**
5 $\quad \boldsymbol{R}_2 \leftarrow \boldsymbol{R}_{a_i} + \boldsymbol{R}_{\neg a_i}$
6 $\quad \boldsymbol{R}_{a_i} \leftarrow 2\boldsymbol{R}_{(b_i \oplus b') \oplus a_i}$
7 $\quad \boldsymbol{R}_{\neg a_i} \leftarrow \boldsymbol{R}_2$
8 $\quad b' \leftarrow b_i$
9 **end for**
10 **return** $\boldsymbol{R}_{b'}$

10.2.6.1. *Protection against attacks on conditional swap*

Many software libraries implement MPL without the usage of memory-dependent memory accesses to avoid timing leakage, which might happen in the presence of, for example, caching. In such cases, usually the cswap is used. However, the cswap was shown to leak the information about the scalar bits, by employing for example TS. This leakage although data-based is very similar to address-bit leakage and can be exploited in the same way. Fortunately, the countermeasure from Algorithm 10.6 can be applied in this context as well; the Montgomery Ladder from Algorithm 10.5 can be protected with XOR-Split as presented in Algorithm 10.7. This countermeasure adds additional random cswap executions to make the cswap sequence in the scalar multiplication independent from the scalar itself.

Algorithm 10.7. The Montgomery Ladder for X25519 with XOR-Split Scalar

Input: $k \in \{0, \ldots, 2^{255} - 1\}$ and the x-coordinate x_P of a point P
Output: $x_{[k]P}$, the x-coordinate of $[k]P$

$a \xleftarrow{R} \{0, \ldots, 2^{255} - 1\}$
$X_1 \leftarrow 1, Z_1 \leftarrow 0$
$X_2 \leftarrow x_P, Z_2 \leftarrow 1$
$c \leftarrow k \oplus 2k \oplus 2a$ `// mult. by 2 shifts vectors to the left by 1 position`
$(X_1, X_2) \leftarrow \text{cswap}(X_1, X_2, a_{254})$; $(Z_1, Z_2) \leftarrow \text{cswap}(Z_1, Z_2, a_{254})$
for $i \leftarrow 255$ **down to** *0* **do**
  $(X_1, X_2) \leftarrow \text{cswap}(X_1, X_2, c_i)$;$(Z_1, Z_2) \leftarrow \text{cswap}(Z_1, Z_2, c_i)$
  if $i \geq 1$ **then**
    $(X_1, Z_1, X_2, Z_2) \leftarrow \text{ladderstep}(x_P, X_1, Z_1, X_2, Z_2)$
    $(X_1, X_2) \leftarrow \text{cswap}(X_1, X_2, a_i)$;$(Z_1, Z_2) \leftarrow \text{cswap}(Z_1, Z_2, a_i)$
end for
return (X_1, Z_1)

Another approach for protecting cswap is to protect the operation itself. In particular, equation [10.2] can be randomized in the following way to limit dependence on the cswap condition bit s:

$$\begin{aligned} v_2 &= (s + r_0) \times v_1 + (1 - (s - r_1)) \times v_2 - r_0 \times v_1 - r_1 \times v_2, \\ v_1 &= (s + r_0) \times v_2 + (1 - (s - r_1)) \times v_1 - r_0 \times v_2 - r_1 \times v_1, \end{aligned} \quad [10.4]$$

where r_0 and r_1 are random variables.

With equation [10.2], the result of the operation that manipulates the bit s was 0 or a 32-bit input value. With the new implementation, 0 is never used for multiplications and the leakage is avoided. The overhead due to the countermeasure is negligible, but some small leakage is still present since the plaintext bit s is accessed directly, even twice. Therefore, we conclude that this countermeasure is not perfect, but the leakage is expected to be significantly decreased.

Example

The example static implementation employs the countermeasure from Algorithm 10.7 for the blinded scalar and the randomized value r.

10.2.7. *Additional fault injection protections*

The goal of a fault injections' attacker against ECC is to learn the secret; in the case of the key exchange, it is to learn the shared secret. This goal can be achieved either by learning the secret scalar or by influencing the scalar multiplication through fault injection during both key generation and shared-key computation (and scalar multiplication is the main part of those) to an easily guessable value.

Classical fault attacks on ECC aim at introducing faults in the scalar multiplication computation to obtain faulty results. Then from the inputs, the correct results, and these faulty results, the adversary is able to recover information about the secret scalar based on the mathematical properties of ECC. Observe that such attacks are thwarted by the combination of scalar and point/coordinate randomizations, because then the relation between the inputs and the faulty result is broken: the faulty results are not only incorrect but also heavily randomized.

In this section, we describe additional fault injection countermeasures that can be implemented, mostly to protect against fixing the shared secret to predictable values. There are various generic fault injection protections that should be considered, for example, redundancy. In the redundancy case, security-relevant operations are implemented twice and their results are compared. If there is a difference, then the execution stops; otherwise, it continues. Additionally, the implementation can check the input and output on the elliptic curve; however, this check on its own is not sufficient since it does not stop safe-error attacks, even if we consider single-fault attacks.

In the example library of the ephemeral and static implementations, other countermeasures against fault injection are implemented. First, the implementation employs a flow-counter countermeasure: they use a single counter monotonously incremented throughout the scalar multiplication to detect changes in the execution flow. If the counter value does not match the expected constant at the end of the computation, then we return a random value. This countermeasure helps to protect against, for example, loop-abort attacks. The second extra countermeasure is against an attacker that aims to set the output of the scalar multiplication to a predictable value. To stop that threat, the implementation initializes the output buffer with random bytes, in order to make it impossible for the adversary to set the output to a predictable value by skipping most of the operations using fault injection.

10.3. Conclusion

In this chapter, we presented various techniques for protecting implementations based on elliptic curve cryptographic schemes against side-channel and fault injection attacks. We analyzed five techniques and we provided algorithmic countermeasures, in a step-by-step, incremental approach. We started with the most basic countermeasures that protect against SPA and then we moved to countermeasures that protect against DPA and TA. Finally, we presented protected algorithms against more sophisticated attacks, such as conditional swap and address-bit side-channel attacks.

10.4. Notes and further references

There are several survey papers and two relevant Ph.D. theses by Chmielewski (2019) and Papachristodoulou (2019) analyzing efficient countermeasures for ECC implementations. Abarzúa et al. (2019) analyze the state-of-the-art of several proposals of algorithmic countermeasures to prevent passive SCA on ECC defined over prime fields for applications on embedded devices, which can be used in the Internet of Things. Fan and Verbauwhede (2012) review the state of the art and various countermeasures. Although this paper is from 2012, it is still a good starting point for implementing protected ECC.

There are also other survey papers that can be checked (Fan et al. 2010; Danger et al. 2013; Abarzúa et al. 2019). The German Federal Office for Information Security (BSI) also published a document "ECC-guide: Minimal Requirements for Evaluating Side-Channel attack resistance of Elliptic Curve Implementations" by Feldhusen et al. (2016) that contains a survey on SCA and FA attacks on ECC.

The example implementations used in this chapter come from the paper "SoK:SCA-secure ECC in software – mission impossible?" by Batina et al. (2022) and are accessible in an open-access repository[11]. The starting point of these implementations is the library by Haase and Labrique (2019); the main difference is that these implementations by Batina et al. (2021) add many side-channel and fault injection countermeasures. The paper by Batina et al. (2022) also includes an overview of side-channel and fault-injection attacks on ECC scalar multiplication.

– Section 10.1. Over the years, there have been many papers published related to nonce leaks in ECDSA; an interesting attack using Bleichenbacher's solution to the hidden number problem to attack nonce leaks in 384-Bit ECDSA is given by De Mulder et al. (2013). A DPA attack against modular multiplication used in ECDSA is presented in Hutter et al. (2009).

11 Available at: https://github.com/sca-secure-library-sca25519/sca25519.

– Section 10.2. There are several standards recommending how to use elliptic curve cryptography in a secure way (ANSI 1998; Lochter et al. 2014; National Institute of Standards and Technology (NIST) 2009; BSI 2011). We can use ECC for digital signatures and for key establishment schemes, and we must follow these standards since it is critical to use secure implementations with stronger cryptography requirements as we migrate to higher security strengths. An extensive analysis of safe curves, fulfilling certain criteria, is given by Bernstein and Lange (n.d.).

In FIPS 186-4, NIST recommends fifteen elliptic curves of varying security levels for use in these elliptic curve cryptographic standards. However, more than fifteen years have passed since these curves were first developed, and the community now knows more about the security of elliptic curve cryptography and practical implementation issues. Advances within the cryptographic community have led to the development of new elliptic curves and algorithms, whose designers claim to offer better performance and are easier to implement in a secure manner. An updated standard FIPS 186-5 by NIST proposes the adoption of two new elliptic curves, Ed25519 and Ed448, for use with EdDSA and the removal of the standard DSA for generating secure signatures.

– Section 10.2.1. Edwards (2007) introduced Edwards curves. Applications of Edwards and twisted Edwards curves (Bernstein et al. 2008) in cryptography are extensively studied by Bernstein and Lange (2007, 2009) and Hisil et al. (2008). The cost of addition and doubling on Edwards curves depends on the form of the curve and the coordinates chosen by the developer. An overview of all types of curves and coordinates is given in the Explicit Formulas Database (Bernstein and Lange n.d.).

Regarding the complete formulas for Weierstrass curves, we note here that Bosma and Lenstra (1995) presented complete formulae for Weierstrass curves, which had an exceptional case for the pair of points (P, Q) if and only if $P - Q$ is a point of order two. Renes et al. (2016) presented complete addition formulae for prime order elliptic curves $E/\mathbb{F}_q : y^2 = x^3 + \alpha x + b$ with $q \geq 5$.

Fouque et al. (2008) introduced so-called carry-based attacks, which are a type of SCA that do not attack the scalar multiplication itself but its countermeasures. They rely on the carry propagation occurring when long-integer additions are performed as repeated sub-word additions.

– Section 10.2.2. The observation about the vulnerability of the algorithm to *safe-error attacks* was made by Joye (2007).

Side-channel atomicity is a countermeasure proposed by Chevallier-Mames et al. (2003).

– Section 10.2.3. The Montgomery Power Ladder is initially presented by Montgomery (1987) as a way to speed up scalar multiplication on elliptic curves. A comprehensive security analysis of the MPL, given by Joye and Yen (2003), showed the regularity of this algorithm and its protection against various side-channel attacks. For a specific choice of projective coordinates, as described by Stam (2003), we can do computations with only X and Z coordinates, which makes this option more memory efficient than other algorithms.

– Section 10.2.4. The double-and-add-always algorithm was initially proposed by Coron (1999), who also proposed three countermeasures that can prevent SCA and they are based on introducing random numbers during the scalar multiplication $Q = [k]P$. Online TA are presented by Batina et al. (2019), who showed that scalar randomization is not an efficient countermeasure against this type of attack.

Application of RNS to protecting ECC was presented by Fournaris et al. (2017) and by Papachristodoulou et al. (2018).

Details about the insecurity of randomizing scalar by adding a random multiple of the group order for elliptic curves with special group order are presented by Schindler and Wiemers (2015). A more detailed analysis of such scalar blinding, including an attack, even for elliptic curves without a special group order is presented in Roche et al. (2019).

– Section 10.2.5. Point blinding and projective coordinate randomization was proposed by Coron (1999) and coordinate re-randomization by Nascimento et al. (2015). Naccache et al. (2004) showed that projective coordinates leak, when applied at Schnorr Signatures, by recovering a few bits of the scalar k at each iteration.

– Section 10.2.6. Tunstall et al. (2021) presented the exponent/scalar XOR-split countermeasure. In their work, 14 algorithms for the exponent and scalar protection are presented and thoroughly analyzed. They performed a security evaluation of those algorithms using simulations based on the mutual information framework and formally verified that they are secure against first-order attacks. The resistance of the proposed algorithms against side-channel attacks is practically verified with test vector leakage assessment (TVLA) by Goodwill et al. (2011) performed on Xilinx's Zynq zc702 evaluation board. A security evaluation using the information-theoretic framework of Standaert et al. (2009) is also performed. Examples of attacks on randomized exponent/scalar include analyzing a single trace (from SPA, Kocher et al. (1999) to collisions in manipulated values, Kim et al. (2010); Witteman et al. (2011); Hanley et al. (2015)) or attempting to find collisions in the random values used to then derive a (blinded) exponent (Schindler and Itoh 2011). This countermeasure is particularly important to prevent address-bit side-channel attacks (Messerges et al. 1999; Itoh et al. 2002). The interested reader can also refer to the PhD thesis by Papachristodoulou (2019) for a detailed analysis of this technique.

– Section 10.2.6.1. There were several attacks published against conditional swaps, even if scalar and point randomization are enabled, in particular, a template attack (Nascimento et al. 2016), a clustering attack (Nascimento and Chmielewski 2017) and deep learning attacks (Weissbart et al. 2020; Perin et al. 2021). Note that since both point and scalar randomizations were used, all these approaches target single traces during the attack and were shown to recover the whole scalar with a few errors.

– Section 10.2.7. An analysis of fault attacks applicability on ECC with respect to side-channel countermeasures is presented by Batina et al. (2022).

Various generic software fault injection (and side-channel) countermeasures, including the flow-counter countermeasure, are described by Witteman (2018). We refer an interested reader to that work for generic countermeasures.

Attacks that insert faults with the aim of abruptly halting the normal functionality of a cryptographic algorithm were proposed by Boneh et al. (2001).

10.5. References

Abarzúa, R., Valencia, C., López, J. (2019). Survey for performance & security problems of passive side-channel attacks countermeasures in ECC. Report 2019/010, Cryptology ePrint Archive [Online]. Available at: https://eprint.iacr.org/2019/010.

ANSI (1998). ANSI-X9.62: Public key cryptography for the financial services industry: The Elliptic Curve Digital Signature Algorithm (ECDSA). Technical Report, American National Standards Institute.

Batina, L., Chmielewski, L., Papachristodoulou, L., Schwabe, P., Tunstall, M. (2019). Online template attacks. *Journal of Cryptographic Engineering*, 9(1), 21–36.

Batina, L., Chmielewski, L., Haase, B., Samwel, N., Schwabe, P. (2021). SCA-secure ECC in software – Mission impossible? Report 2021/1003, Cryptology ePrint Archive [Online]. Available at: https://eprint.iacr.org/2021/1003.

Batina, L., Chmielewski, L., Haase, B., Samwel, N., Schwabe, P. (2022). SoK: SCA-secure ECC in software – Mission impossible? *IACR Transactions on Cryptographic Hardware and Embedded Systems*, 2023(1), 557–589.

Bernstein, D.J. and Lange, T. (n.d.). Explicit formulas database [Online]. Available at: http://www.hyperelliptic.org/EFD/.

Bernstein, D.J. and Lange, T. (2007). Faster addition and doubling on elliptic curves. In *ASIACRYPT 2007*, Kurosawa, K. (ed.). Springer, Heidelberg.

Bernstein, D.J. and Lange, T. (2009). A complete set of addition laws for incomplete Edwards curves. Report 2009/580, Cryptology ePrint Archive [Online]. Available at: https://eprint.iacr.org/2009/580.

Bernstein, D.J., Birkner, P., Joye, M., Lange, T., Peters, C. (2008). Twisted Edwards curves. In *AFRICACRYPT 08*, Vaudenay, S. (ed.). Springer, Heidelberg.

Boneh, D., DeMillo, R.A., Lipton, R.J. (2001). On the importance of eliminating errors in cryptographic computations. *Journal of Cryptology*, 14(2), 101–119.

Bosma, W. and Lenstra, H.W. (1995). Complete systems of two addition laws for elliptic curves. *Journal of Number Theory*, 53(2), 229 – 240.

BSI (2011). AIS46: Minimum requirements for evaluating side-channel attack resistance of elliptic curve implementations. Technical Report, Bundesamt für Sicherheit in der Informationstechnik (BSI).

Chevallier-Mames, B., Ciet, M., Joye, M. (2003). Low-cost solutions for preventing simple side-channel analysis: Side-channel atomicity. Report 2003/237, Cryptology ePrint Archive [Online]. Available at: https://eprint.iacr.org/2003/237.

Chmielewski, L. (2019). Exploiting horizontal leakage in public key cryptosystems. PhD Thesis, Radboud University Nijmegen, Nijmegen.

Coron, J.-S. (1999). Resistance against differential power analysis for elliptic curve cryptosystems. In *CHES'99*, Koç, Ç.K. and Paar, C. (eds). Springer, Heidelberg.

Danger, J.-L., Guilley, S., Hoogvorst, P., Murdica, C., Naccache, D. (2013). A synthesis of side-channel attacks on elliptic curve cryptography in smart-cards. *Journal of Cryptographic Engineering*, 3(4), 241–265.

De Mulder, E., Hutter, M., Marson, M.E., Pearson, P. (2013). Using Bleichenbacher's solution to the hidden number problem to attack nonce leaks in 384-bit ECDSA. In *Cryptographic Hardware and Embedded Systems – CHES 2013*, Bertoni, G. and Coron, J.-S. (eds). Springer, Heidelberg.

Edwards, H.M. (2007). A normal form for elliptic curves. In *Bulletin of the American Mathematical Society*, 44(3), 393–422 [Online]. Available at: http://www.ams.org/journals/bull/2007-44-03/S0273-0979-07-01153-6/home.html.

Fan, J. and Verbauwhede, I. (2012). An updated survey on secure ECC implementations: Attacks, countermeasures and cost. In *Cryptography and Security: From Theory to Applications*, Naccache, D. (ed.). Springer, Heidelberg.

Fan, J., Guo, X., Mulder, E.D., Schaumont, P., Preneel, B., Verbauwhede, I. (2010). State-of-the-art of secure ECC implementations: A survey on known side-channel attacks and countermeasures. In *2010 IEEE International Symposium on Hardware-Oriented Security and Trust (HOST)*.

Feldhusen, D., Gebhardt, M., Illies, G., Kasper, M., Lochter, M., Petri, R., Stein, O., Thumser, W., Wicke, G. (2016). ECC-guide: Minimal requirements for evaluating side-channel attack resistance of elliptic curve implementations. Second draft, Fraunhofer-Gesellschaft.

Fouque, P.-A., Réal, D., Valette, F., Drissi, M. (2008). The carry leakage on the randomized exponent countermeasure. In *CHES 2008*, Oswald E. and Rohatgi, P. (eds). Springer, Heidelberg.

Fournaris, A.P., Papachristodoulou, L., Sklavos, N. (2017). Secure and efficient rns software implementation for elliptic curve cryptography. In *2017 IEEE European Symposium on Security and Privacy Workshops (EuroS&PW)*, Paris.

Goodwill, G., Jun, B., Jaffe, J., Rohatgi, P. (2011). A testing methodology for side-channel resistance validation. Non-Invasive Attack Testing Workshop, NIST, Gaithersburg.

Haase, B. and Labrique, B. (2019). AuCPace: Efficient verifier-based PAKE protocol tailored for the IIoT. *IACR TCHES*, 2019(2), 1–48.

Hanley, N., Kim, H., Tunstall, M. (2015). Exploiting collisions in addition chain-based exponentiation algorithms using a single trace. In *CT-RSA 2015*, Nyberg, K. (ed.). Springer, Heidelberg.

Hisil, H., Wong, K.K.-H., Carter, G., Dawson, E. (2008). Twisted Edwards curves revisited. In *ASIACRYPT 2008*, Pieprzyk, J. (ed.). Springer, Heidelberg.

Hutter, M., Medwed, M., Hein, D., Wolkerstorfer, J. (2009). Attacking ECDSA-enabled RFID devices. In *ACNS 09*, Abdalla, M., Pointcheval, D., Fouque, P.-A., Vergnaud, D. (eds). Springer, Heidelberg.

Itoh, K., Izu, T., Takenada, M. (2002). Address-bit differential power analysis of cryptographic schemes OK-ECDH and OK-ECDSA. In *CHES 2002*, Kaliski Jr., B.S. Koç, Ç.K., Paar, C. (eds). Springer, Heidelberg.

Joye, M. (2007). Highly regular right-to-left algorithms for scalar multiplication. In *CHES 2007*, Paillier, P. and Verbauwhede, I. (eds). Springer, Heidelberg.

Joye, M. and Yen, S.-M. (2003). The Montgomery powering ladder. In *Cryptographic Hardware and Embedded Systems - CHES 2002*, Kaliski Jr., B.S., Koç, Ç.K., Paar, C. (eds). Springer, Heidelberg.

Kim, H., Kim, T.H., Yoon, J.C., Hong, S. (2010). Practical second-order correlation power analysis on the message blinding method and its novel countermeasure for RSA. *ETRI Journal*, 32(1), 102–111.

Kocher, P.C., Jaffe, J., Jun, B. (1999). Differential power analysis. In *Advances in Cryptology – CRYPTO' 99*, Wiener, M.J. (ed.). Springer, Heidelberg.

Lochter, M., Merkle, J., Schmidt, J.-M., Shültze, T. (2014). Requirements for standard elliptic curves [Online]. Available at: http://www.ecc-brainpool.org/.

Messerges, T.S., Dabbish, E.A., Sloan, R.H. (1999). Power analysis attacks of modular exponentiation in smartcards. In *Cryptographic Hardware and Embedded Systems, First International Workshop, CHES'99*, Koç, Ç.K. and Paar, C. (eds). Springer, Heidelberg.

Montgomery, P.L. (1987). Speeding the Pollard and elliptic curve methods of factorization. *Mathematics of Computation*, 48(177), 243–264.

Naccache, D., Smart, N.P., Stern, J. (2004). Projective coordinates leak. In *EUROCRYPT 2004*, Cachin, C. and Camenisch, J. (eds). Springer, Heidelberg.

Nascimento, E. and Chmielewski, L. (2017). Applying horizontal clustering side-channel attacks on embedded ECC implementations. In *Smart Card Research and Advanced Applications*, Eisenbarth, T. and Teglia, Y. (eds). Springer, Cham.

Nascimento, E., López, J., Dahab, R. (2015). Efficient and secure elliptic curve cryptography for 8-bit AVR microcontrollers. In *Proceedings of the 5th International Conference on Security, Privacy, and Applied Cryptography Engineering*. Springer-Verlag, Heidelberg. doi: 10.1007/978-3-319-24126-5_17.

Nascimento, E., Chmielewski, L., Oswald, D., Schwabe, P. (2016). Attacking embedded ECC implementations through CMOV side channels. In *SAC 2016*, Avanzi, R. and Heys, H.M. (eds). Springer, Heidelberg.

National Institute of Standards and Technology (NIST) (2009). Recommended elliptic curves for federal government use. In *Appendix of FIPS 186-3* [Online]. Available at: http://csrc.nist.gov/publications/fips/fips186-3/fips186-3.pdf.

Papachristodoulou, L. (2019). Masking curves: Side-channel attacks on elliptic curve cryptography and countermeasures. Thesis, Radbooud University, Nijmegen [Online]. Available at: https://hdl.handle.net/ 2066/201163.

Papachristodoulou, L., Fournaris, A.P., Papagiannopoulos, K., Batina, L. (2018). Practical evaluation of protected residue number system scalar multiplication. *IACR TCHES*, 2019(1), 259–282.

Perin, G., Chmielewski, L., Batina, L., Picek, S. (2021). Keep it unsupervised: Horizontal attacks meet deep learning. *IACR TCHES*, 2021(1), 343–372.

Renes, J., Costello, C., Batina, L. (2016). Complete addition formulas for prime order elliptic curves. In *EUROCRYPT 2016*, Fischlin, M. and Coron, J.-S. (eds). Springer, Heidelberg.

Roche, T., Imbert, L., Lomné, V. (2019). Side-channel attacks on blinded scalar multiplications revisited. Report 2019/1220, Cryptology ePrint Archive [Online]. Available at: https://eprint.iacr.org/2019/1220.

Schindler, W. and Itoh, K. (2011). Exponent blinding does not always lift (partial) SPA resistance to higher-level security. In *ACNS 11*, Lopez, J. and Tsudik, G. (eds). Springer, Heidelberg.

Schindler, W. and Wiemers, A. (2015). Efficient side-channel attacks on scalar blinding on elliptic curves with special structure. NIST Workshop on ECC Standards [Online]. Available at: https://csrc.nist.gov/csrc/media/events/workshop-on-elliptic-curve-cryptography-standards/documents/papers/session6-schindler-werner.pdf.

Stam, M. (2003). On Montgomery-like representations for elliptic curves over GF(2k). In *Public Key Cryptography – PKC 2003: 6th International Workshop on Practice and Theory in Public Key Cryptography Miami*, Desmedt, Y.G. (ed.). Springer, Heidelberg.

Standaert, F.-X., Malkin, T., Yung, M. (2009). A unified framework for the analysis of side-channel key recovery attacks. In *EUROCRYPT 2009*, Joux, A. (ed.). Springer, Heidelberg.

Tunstall, M., Papachristodoulou, L., Papagiannopoulos, K. (2021). Boolean exponent splitting. In *Proceedings of the 18th International Conference on Security and Cryptography, SECRYPT 2021*, di Vimercati, S.D.C. and Samarati, P. (eds). SCITEPRESS. doi: 10.5220/0010570903210332.

Weissbart, L., Chmielewski, L., Picek, S., Batina, L. (2020). Systematic side-channel analysis of curve25519 with machine learning. *Journal of Hardware and Systems Security*, 4, 1–15.

Witteman, M.F. (2018). Secure application programming in the presence of side channel attacks, Riscure, Technical Report [Online]. Available at: https://www.riscure.com/uploads/2018/11/201708RiscureWhitepaperSideChannelPatterns.pdf.

Witteman, M.F., van Woudenberg, J.G.J., Menarini, F. (2011). Defeating RSA multiply-always and message blinding countermeasures. In *CT-RSA 2011*, Kiayias, A. (ed.). Springer, Heidelberg.

11

Post-Quantum Implementations

Matthias J. KANNWISCHER[1], Ruben NIEDERHAGEN[2,3], Francisco RODRÍGUEZ-HENRÍQUEZ[4] and Peter SCHWABE[5,6]

[1] *Chelpis Quantum Corp, Taipei, Taiwan*
[2] *Academia Sinica, Taipei, Taiwan*
[3] *University of Southern Denmark, Odense, Denmark*
[4] *Cryptography Research Center, Technology Innovation Institute, Abu Dhabi, United Arab Emirates*
[5] *Max Planck Institute for Security and Privacy, Bochum, Germany*
[6] *Radboud University, Nijmegen, Netherlands*

11.1. Introduction

In this chapter, we give an overview of techniques for secure and efficient implementation of so-called post-quantum cryptography, the anticipated next generation of asymmetric cryptography. Today, most cryptographic systems deployed in the real world use asymmetric primitives that rely on the hardness of factoring (most notably RSA public-key encryption and signatures), or the (elliptic-curve) discrete-logarithm problem (see Chapter 10 of this volume). While those systems, with suitably chosen parameters, are believed to resist attacks by classical computers, it has been known since Shor's seminal 1994 paper, that a large universal quantum computer will be able to solve both factoring and discrete logarithms in polynomial time.

Luckily, even if a sufficiently large quantum computer becomes a reality, this does not mean the end of efficient public-key cryptography. There exist various approaches for constructing public-key encryption or key-encapsulation mechanisms

Embedded Cryptography 2,
coordinated by Emmanuel PROUFF, Guénaël RENAULT,
Matthieu RIVAIN and Colin O'FLYNN.

(KEMs) and signatures that – as far as we know – resist attacks even by large universal quantum computers. There are five main approaches to construct such post-quantum asymmetric schemes:

– Problems related to finding short vectors in high-dimensional lattices can be used to construct both efficient key-encapsulation schemes and efficient signatures.

– Hard problems in coding theory are mostly used to construct efficient public-key encryption or key-encapsulation schemes.

– The problem of solving large systems of multivariate quadratic equations is mostly useful to construct signature schemes.

– Cryptographic signatures can be built just from cryptographic hash functions.

– Finally, there are schemes based on the hardness of finding high-degree isogenies between supersingular elliptic curves.

The first schemes of these families reach as far back as the 1970s and the research field of post-quantum cryptography was explicitly established in the early 2000s. However, research into post-quantum cryptography, in particular concrete instantiations of schemes and implementations, received a huge boost in early 2016, when the US-American National Institute of Standards and Technology (NIST) announced that they would launch an effort of evaluating and eventually standardizing such schemes. NIST issued a public call for proposals in late 2016 with a deadline for submissions in November 2017.

At the time of writing this chapter, in early 2023, NIST's post-quantum project had just reached a major milestone with the announcement of the first batch of algorithms NIST are planning to standardize: the lattice-based signature schemes CRYSTALS-Dilithium and Falcon, the hash-based signature scheme SPHINCS$^+$, and the lattice-based key-encapsulation mechanism CRYSTALS-Kyber. However, post-quantum schemes are still far less well understood than the cryptographic schemes considered in the other chapters of this book. The NIST standardization effort continued with multiple KEMs forwarded to another round of evaluation and a renewed call for signature proposals with a submission deadline in June 2023. Consequently, the state of the art in scheme design, cryptanalysis, and techniques for secure implementation is still very actively researched and thus likely to change in the near future.

In order to provide a snapshot of the current state of the art, we take the following approach: we pick one example scheme for lattice-based, one for code-based, and one for isogeny-based key agreement and one example scheme for lattice-based signatures, for multivariate signatures, and for hash-based signatures. Where possible, we focus on schemes that are likely to be relevant for real-world deployments, i.e. schemes that have been selected by NIST for standardization, are still considered for standardization in the NIST competition, or are going to be submitted to the upcoming on-ramp for signatures. In our description of these schemes, we focus on the essentials of the construction and aspects that are particularly relevant for efficient and secure implementation. We omit details that are less relevant here, for example, data serialization or compression routines. We provide references to the full specifications at the end of this chapter.

In the sections explaining secure implementation techniques, we will typically start by discussing "constant-time" implementations of the respective primitive. We use this term to refer to (software) implementations that systematically avoid data flow from secret inputs into branch conditions, memory addresses, and variable-time arithmetic instructions. Together, this ensures protection against classical timing attacks, i.e. timing attacks against sequential execution of the program at a fixed clock frequency. Systematic protection against more advanced microarchitectural attacks that exploit, for example, transient execution or data-dependent dynamic frequency scaling is still mostly unresolved, not just for post-quantum cryptography.

11.2. Post-quantum encryption and key encapsulation

Most current systems are using some variant of the Diffie–Hellman (DH) protocol for key exchange and in some cases, with static keys, also for authentication. The most common instantiation is elliptic-curve DH (see Chapter 10 of this volume). We do not know any post-quantum scheme that we could use as a drop-in replacement for DH, at least not without massively impacting system performance. The abstract primitive that comes closest to DH are KEMs. In many contexts, KEMs *can* be used to straight-forwardly replace DH, and they have been used as a very flexible building block in the construction of multiple post-quantum cryptographic protocols.

Consequently, most proposals aiming at post-quantum confidentiality build a KEM; for scenarios where a public-key encryption (PKE) scheme is needed, we can build such a PKE from a KEM efficiently and generically. Most post-quantum KEMs are constructed by first building a passively secure PKE scheme and then using a generic transform on top to obtain a KEM that is secure against active, that is, chosen-ciphertext, attackers. We thus first consider the construction of passively secure lattice-based PKEs (section 11.2.1), code-based PKEs (section 11.2.2) and isogeny-based PKEs (section 11.2.3), and then look into transforms to actively secure KEMs in section 11.2.4.

11.2.1. *Lattice-based KEMs – Kyber*

Most lattice-based PKE schemes and KEMs are based on variants of the learning-with-errors (LWE) or learning-with-rounding (LWR) problems. The scheme that we are considering as an example in this section is the NIST PQC finalist Kyber. As outlined above, in this section, we will focus on a simplified version of the passively secure PKE underlying Kyber.

Kyber relies on the hardness of the module-learning-with-errors (MLWE) problem. Consider the ring $\mathcal{R}_q = \mathbb{Z}_q[X]/(X^n + 1)$, where $\mathbb{Z}_q$ is the ring of integers modulo q and n is a positive integer; in the case of Kyber, we have $q = 3329$ and $n = 256$. Consider further a positive integer k; in Kyber, we have $k \in \{2, 3, 4\}$, depending on the security level. The search version of the MLWE problem is to find $\mathbf{s} \in \mathcal{R}_q^k$, given samples $(\mathbf{A}, \mathbf{A}\mathbf{s} + \mathbf{e})$, where $\mathbf{A} \in \mathcal{R}_q^{k \times k}$ is sampled uniformly at random and $\mathbf{e} \in \mathcal{R}_q^k$ is sampled from a so-called *noise distribution* ψ. The decisional version of the problem is to distinguish such samples from values $(\mathbf{U}, \mathbf{v})$, sampled uniformly at random from $\mathcal{R}_q^{k \times k} \times \mathcal{R}_q^k$. In the original definition of these problems, also $\mathbf{s}$ was assumed to be sampled uniformly at random, but later results showed that the problem remains hard if s is sampled from other distributions, most importantly, if $\mathbf{s}$ is sampled from the noise distribution ψ.

The noise distribution outputs "small" values in $\mathbb{Z}_q$ centered around zero. For example, in Kyber, the noise distribution is generating polynomial coefficients in $\mathbb{Z}_q$ from the set $\{-\eta, \dots, \eta\}$. More concretely, each coefficient c is obtained from a centered binomial distribution as $c = \sum_{i=1}^{\eta}(a_i - b_i)$ for bits a_i, b_i that are the output of a PRF, that is, that are assumed to be indistinguishable from uniformly random bits. Most parameter sets of Kyber use the parameter $\eta = 2$.

11.2.1.1. *Scheme definition*

Let us take a closer look at a simplified version of the public-key encryption scheme underlying Kyber. We will omit details about encoding and decoding of keys and the ciphertext. Note, however, that the complete picture involves lossy compression of the ciphertext.

Key generation of the PKE underlying Kyber consists of the following steps:

1) Sample a public 32-byte string ρ uniformly at random.

2) Sample a secret 32-byte string σ uniformly at random.

3) Expand ρ through an extendable output function (XOF) and run rejection sampling on the output to obtain a matrix $\mathbf{A} \in \mathcal{R}_q^{k \times k}$ that "looks uniformly random".

4) Use the output of a PRF with key σ to obtain $\mathbf{s} \in \mathcal{R}_q^k$ and $\mathbf{e} \in \mathcal{R}_q^k$ with coefficients from the noise distribution (see above).

5) Compute $\mathbf{t} = \mathbf{A}\mathbf{s} + \mathbf{e}$.

6) Return secret key $\mathsf{sk} = \mathbf{s}$ and public key $(\mathbf{t}, \rho)$.

Encryption takes as input a public key $\mathsf{pk} = (\mathbf{t}, \rho)$, a 32-byte message m, and a 32-byte string r of random coins. It then proceeds as follows:

1) Expand ρ to obtain the same matrix $\mathbf{A}$ that was generated in key generation.

2) Use the output of a PRF with key r to obtain $\mathbf{r} \in \mathcal{R}_q^k$, $\mathbf{e}_1 \in \mathcal{R}_q^k$, and $e_2 \in \mathcal{R}_q$ with coefficients from the noise distribution (see above).

3) Compute $\mathbf{u} = \mathbf{A}^T \mathbf{r} + \mathbf{e}_1$.

4) Compute $v = \mathbf{t}^T \mathbf{r} + e_2 + \mathsf{MapToPoly}(m)$.

5) Return ciphertext $c = (\mathbf{u}, v)$.

In this encryption routine, the MapToPoly function maps each bit of the message m to one coefficient of a polynomial in $\mathcal{R}_q$. A zero bit is mapped to 0; a one bit is mapped to $\lceil q/2 \rfloor$.

Decryption takes as input a ciphertext $c = (\mathbf{u}, v)$ and a secret key $\mathbf{s}$ and recovers a message m' as $m' = \mathsf{MapFromPoly}(v - \mathbf{s}^T \mathbf{u})$. Here, the MapFromPoly function maps each coefficient of a polynomial in $\mathcal{R}_q$ to a single bit; a full polynomial is thus mapped to a string of 256 bits or 32 bytes. A coefficient in $\mathbb{Z}_q$ is mapped to 1, if it is in $\{\lceil q/4 \rceil, \ldots, \lfloor 3q/4 \rfloor\}$, otherwise it is mapped to 0.

With very high probability, decryption will succeed and recover the original message, that is, $m' = m$. Let us understand why this is the case: During encryption we add $\mathbf{t}^T \mathbf{r} + e_2$ to $\mathsf{MapToPoly}(m)$ to obtain v. In decryption we subtract $\mathbf{s}^T \mathbf{u}$ from v and use MapFromPoly to obtain m'. The difference of the two terms is:

$$
\begin{aligned}
&\mathbf{t}^T \mathbf{r} - \mathbf{s}^T \mathbf{u} \\
&= (\mathbf{A}\mathbf{s} + \mathbf{e})^T \mathbf{r} + e_2 - \mathbf{s}^T (\mathbf{A}^T \mathbf{r} + \mathbf{e}_1) \\
&= \mathbf{s}^T \mathbf{A}^T \mathbf{r} + \mathbf{e}^T \mathbf{r} + e_2 - \mathbf{s}^T \mathbf{A}^T \mathbf{r} + \mathbf{s}^T \mathbf{e}_1 \\
&= \mathbf{e}^T \mathbf{r} + e_2 + \mathbf{s}^T \mathbf{e}_1
\end{aligned}
$$

As all the coefficients in $\mathbf{s}$, $\mathbf{r}$, $\mathbf{e}$, $\mathbf{e}_1$, and e_2 are small and centered around zero, the coefficients of the difference are also expected to be relatively small. This means that MapFromPoly in decryption receives as input a noisy version of the output of MapToPoly in encryption; as long as this noise has all coefficients smaller than $\lfloor q/4 \rfloor$, decryption will succeed.

11.2.1.2. *Techniques for efficient implementation*

The core operation of Kyber as well as for most other lattice-based KEMs is polynomial multiplication. Specifically, Kyber requires us to multiply polynomials in $\mathcal{R}_q = \mathbb{Z}_q[X]/(X^n + 1)$. Kyber's ring is chosen in a way that allows fast polynomial multiplication using the number-theoretic transform (NTT). The idea of NTT-based polynomial multiplication is to transform the inputs into a different domain (called "NTT domain" or "frequency domain") in which multiplication is cheap (i.e. has linear complexity). The result is then transformed back to "normal domain" (or "time domain"). To obtain the product ab with $a, b \in \mathcal{R}_q$, we compute:

$$ab = \mathtt{NTT}^{-1}(\mathtt{NTT}(a) \circ \mathtt{NTT}(b))$$

where $\mathtt{NTT}$ and $\mathtt{NTT}^{-1}$ are the transformations to and from NTT domain, and $\circ$ is the multiplication in NTT domain. These transformations are particularly fast for power-of-two n. At the core of any (radix-2), NTT is the following ring isomorphism:

$$\mathbb{Z}_q[x]/(X^{2n} - c^2) \cong \mathbb{Z}_q[X]/(X^n - c) \times \mathbb{Z}_q[x]/(X^n + c);$$
$$\sum_{i=0}^{2n-1} f_i X^i \leftrightarrow \left(\sum_{i=0}^{n-1} (f_i + c f_{n+i}) X^i, \sum_{i=0}^{n-1} (f_i - c f_{n+i}) X^i \right).$$

It allows us to split a polynomial $f \in \mathbb{Z}_q[x]/(X^{2n} - c^2)$ into two half-sized polynomials modulo $X^n + c$ and modulo $X^n - c$. The inverse can be computed by applying the Chinese remainder theorem on the two elements in $\mathbb{Z}_q[X]/(X^n - c)$ and $\mathbb{Z}_q[x]/(X^n + c)$ to obtain the element in $\mathbb{Z}_q[x]/(X^{2n} - c^2)$. In the case of $\mathcal{R}_q$, this only works if a c exists, such that $1 \equiv -c^2 \mod q$, that is, we require a fourth primitive root of unity. Note that both the splitting and re-combining only requires us to work on two coefficients of the inputs at a time, which is commonly referred to as a butterfly operation. Both the forward and the inverse transformations require $n/2$ multiplications by c (or $c^{-1}/2$), $n/2$ additions and $n/2$ subtractions. Note that since straightforward polynomial multiplications requires n^2 multiplications, the multiplication of half-sized polynomials is about four times faster than multiplication of full-sized polynomials. Hence, the splitting does result in a net speed-up for larger n. For smaller n (e.g. $n = 2$), the additions and subtractions outweigh the performance improvement.

This trick can be applied recursively to further split the resulting polynomials into halves. However, it requires the existence of the corresponding roots of unity. The splitting is usually referred to as an NTT layer. For a k-layer NTT starting from $\mathcal{R}_q$, one requires a 2^{k+1}-th primitive root of unity. In case one splits all the way down to degree-0 polynomials, it is called a "complete" NTT, otherwise it is called an "incomplete" NTT. In case of a complete NTT, $\circ$ becomes a coefficient-wise (or point-wise) multiplication of the inputs. In case of an incomplete NTT, $\circ$ multiplies 2^k polynomials with $n/2^k$ coefficients. $\circ$ is usually referred to as base multiplication in this case. For the Kyber $\mathcal{R}_q$, a complete NTT would require a 512-th primitive root of unity which does not exist modulo $q = 3329$. Hence, Kyber uses an incomplete seven-layer NTT.

Due to the use of NTTs, Kyber is particularly suitable for vectorized implementations (e.g. using AVX2 or Arm Neon). In each NTT layer, each coefficient is used in exactly one butterfly with one other coefficient. By loading multiple coefficients into one vector register, we can compute multiple butterflies in parallel. This works straightforwardly while polynomials have more coefficients than fit into one register, that is, in the first NTT layers. Once polynomials are split into polynomials of smaller size, we have to shuffle the registers, such that the coefficients involved in one butterfly are in separate registers.

For implementing the modular coefficient multiplications within the NTT, a commonly used technique is Montgomery multiplication. Montgomery's reduction approach is to replace expensive division by odd q with a cheap division by a power of two $R = 2^l$. Assume we have computed the product $c = ab$ of two coefficients. When reducing a value c ($< qR$), which coincidentally is a multiple of $R > q$, we can simply store c/R which reduces the size of c by l bits and is cheaply computed. Montgomery's idea is to make sure that c is a multiple of R by introducing a correction step, that is, we want to find a value t, such that $c - tq$ is divisible by R. Montgomery computes t as $cq^{-1} \mod R$, such that $c - aq^{-1}q \mod R = 0$. Note that the result of the reduction is then $abR^{-1} \mod q$. To obtain the correct result, we have to multiply by R again (or by $R^2 \mod q$ when using Montgomery multiplication). If one of the multiplicands is a constant, we may pre-compute aR mod q. The result of the Montgomery multiplication is then $abRR^{-1} \equiv ab \mod q$. This is commonly used in the NTT.

It is important to note that while polynomial arithmetic accounts for a large fraction of the Kyber run-time, another building block is often even more dominating: hashing based on the Keccak permutation (including both SHA-3 and SHAKE). A hardware-accelerated Keccak implementation or, alternatively, a heavily optimized Keccak software implementation vastly benefits Kyber implementations. Due to the module structure, Kyber implementations can make good use of vectorized Keccak implementations running multiple permutations simultaneously (e.g. 4 for AVX2, or 2 for Arm Neon).

11.2.1.3. *Techniques for secure implementation*

Kyber is very easy to implement following the constant-time paradigm. In fact, the passively secure PKE underlying Kyber is designed in such a way that even a straightforward implementation that simply follows the specification will be free of secret-dependent branches and memory addresses, as long as reductions modulo q do not employ any conditional branches.

There are some common sub-routines in other lattice-based PKE schemes and KEMs that require a bit more care for constant-time implementations. Most notably, some schemes use noise from a fixed-weight distribution, for example, polynomials with a fixed number of coefficients that are 1, a fixed number of coefficients that are -1, and all other entries equal to zero. The standard way to sample a random polynomial satisfying this property is to start with a fixed polynomial with the prescribed number of 1 and -1 coefficients and then randomly shuffle the coefficients. Performing this random shuffling in constant time is not straightforward; standard algorithms like Fisher–Yates shuffle are not constant time. Secure implementations typically use permutation networks like the Benes network or sorting networks like Batcher sort. Furthermore, some schemes involve multiplication of a random polynomial by a polynomial s with coefficients in $\{-1, 0, 1\}$. It is tempting to implement such a multiplication through a sequence of conditional additions and subtractions, but straightforward implementations of this approach will leak information about s.

To protect against side-channel attacks beyond timing attacks, implementations of lattice-based KEMs typically use arithmetic masking, that is, sharing each secret element s of $\mathbb{Z}_q$ in d shares $s_0, \ldots, s_{d-1}$, such that $s = \sum_{i=0}^{d-1} s_i \mod q$. The core arithmetic operations are, from a masking perspective, linear and thus very cheap to mask. Clearly, this is the case for addition of noise polynomials. It also holds for matrix-vector multiplications of the form **As**, because **A** is public and therefore unmasked.

What makes masking of lattice-based KEMs costly is switching between Boolean masking used inside the PRF and arithmetic masking used for arithmetic on polynomials over $\mathbb{Z}_q$, and operations in the CCA transform (see section 11.2.4).

Another generic side-channel countermeasure that has been implemented to protect lattice-based PKE and KEMs is shuffling, that is, executing operations in a randomized order. This is fairly easy and efficient to do for polynomial addition, subtraction, compression and decompression by processing coefficients in a randomized order. Also, the NTT can be efficiently shuffled by randomizing the order of butterflies in each layer.

11.2.2. *Code-based KEMs – Classic McEliece*

Code-based cryptography is almost as old as RSA: it was introduced by McEliece in 1978. The basic idea of code-based public key encryption (PKE) schemes is to use a secret code $\mathcal{G}$ with a code length n and a code rank k that can correct up to t errors as private key and its garbled generator matrix $G \in \mathbb{F}_2^{k \times n}$ as public key. The sender encodes a message into a binary vector $v \in \mathbb{F}_2^k$ and encrypts it to the ciphertext $c \in \mathbb{F}_2^n$ by computing $c = vG + e$ using an error vector $e \in \mathbb{F}_2^n$ of weight t. The receiver uses the secret code $\mathcal{G}$ to obtain $vG = c - e$ by correcting the t bit errors and decodes vG back to v.

A dual-variant to the McEliece cryptosystem was proposed by Niederreiter (1986). Instead of a generator matrix G, he uses a parity-check matrix $H \in \mathbb{F}_2^{(n-k) \times n}$ as public key. The sender then encodes the message as error vector $e \in \mathbb{F}_2^n$ and encrypts it to a ciphertext $c \in \mathbb{F}_2^{n-k}$ as syndrome $c = He$. As in the McEliece cryptosystem, the receiver uses the secret code $\mathcal{G}$ to find the error positions and hence recovers the message. The dual-variant by Niederreiter is equivalent to the McEliece cryptosystem in terms of security.

A common tweak to reduce the size of the public key in the McEliece and Niederreiter cryptosystems is to compute the systematic form of H, that is, apply row operations to transform H into $(I_{n-k}|T)$, where I_{n-k} is an identity matrix of $n - k$ rows and columns. Thus, only T needs to be communicated and stored and the front identity matrix can be regenerated when needed (this, however, requires a semantically secure conversion for the McEliece cryptosystem, which nowadays is state-of-the-art, to ensure that the first $n-k$ bits of the plaintext are not revealed).

The choice of the code family is crucial for the security of code-based cryptosystems. McEliece proposed to use binary Goppa codes, which is still considered secure. Binary Goppa codes are defined by a support $\alpha \in \mathbb{F}_{2^m}^n$ for a small $m \in \mathbb{N}$ and a Goppa polynomial g of degree t. Niederreiter proposed to use a different code family in his dual-variant, which later was broken. However, Niederreiter's dual-variant also remains secure when using, for example, binary Goppa codes. Recent proposals for code-based systems are using either McEliece's or Niederreiter's variant and quasi-cyclic codes or rank metric to further reduce the size of the public key matrices.

11.2.2.1. *Scheme definition*

Classic McEliece is the only code-based third-round finalist in the NIST standardization process. While honoring the founder of code-based cryptography in its name, Classic McEliece is using the Niederreiter variant with binary Goppa codes in its construction. Its parameter sets aiming at NIST security levels 1, 3, and 5 are using $m \in \{12, 13\}$, $n \in \{3488, 4608, 6688, 6960, 8192\}$, $k \in \{2720, 3360, 5024, 5283, 6528\}$, and $t \in \{64, 96, 119, 128\}$.

The secret key is a random seed δ, an irreducible Goppa polynomial g of degree t, the support $\alpha \in \mathbb{F}_{2^m}^n$ and a random bit string s. The public key is computed by generating the $t \times n$ matrix $\tilde{H} = \{h_{i,j}\}$, where $h_{i,j} = \alpha_j^{i-1}/g(\alpha_j)$ for $i = 1, \ldots, t$ and $j = 1, \ldots, n$. Then $\tilde{H}$ is converted to the $(n-k) \times n$ matrix $\hat{H}$ by expanding each $\mathbb{F}_{2^m}$ entry of $\tilde{H}$ into a column of m bits. Finally, $\hat{H}$ is reduced to systematic form $(I_{n-k}|T)$ and T is used as public key.

For encapsulation, a random vector $e \in \mathbb{F}_2^n$ of weight t is encoded to $C_0 = (I_{n-k}|T)e \in \mathbb{F}_2^{n-k}$. The error vector e is hashed to obtain C_1 to obtain the ciphertext $C = (C_0, C_1)$. Finally, C is hashed together with e to obtain the session key K.

For decapsulation, the ciphertext C is split into C_0 and C_1 and C_0 is decoded to e' using the private key. If the weight of e' is t and if $C_0 = (I_{n-k}|T)e$, C_1' is computed by hashing e'. The check of $C_0 = (I_{n-k}|T)e$ is required to achieve CCA security. If $C_1' = C_1$, then $e' = e$ and the session key is computed by hashing e and C. Otherwise, decoding has failed and a false session key is computed by hashing s and C.

11.2.2.2. *Techniques for efficient implementation*

The most time-consuming operation in the key generation of Classic McEliece is the "systemization" of $\hat{H}$, that is, the computation of the systematic form of $\hat{H}$, which usually is done using Gaussian elimination. With a relatively high probability, $\hat{H}$ does not have a systematic form. Therefore, Classic McEliece specifies two variants of the key-generation algorithm: for the systematic variant, the systemization is aborted in case of failure and a new private key is computed. For the semi-systematic variant, an alternative algorithm is specified that allows us to swap columns (in constant-time) such that a systematic public-key can be obtained without repeating key generation.

Efficient implementations of the systematic variant split $\hat{H}$ into a $(n-k) \times (n-k)$ matrix M and a $(n-k) \times k$ matrix $\hat{T}$ such that $\hat{H} = (M|\hat{T})$ and $(I_{n-k}|T) = M^{-1}\hat{H}$ and first operate on M to check if $\hat{H}$ has full rank. During this computation, an LUP-decomposition of M with $PM = LU$ is computed such that T can be efficiently obtained as $T = (U^{-1}L^{-1}P)\hat{T}$ if $\hat{H}$ has full rank. This reduces the cost of repeatedly computing on a $(n-k) \times n$, matrix to only computing on a $(n-k) \times (n-k)$ matrix, plus a final matrix multiplication once a public key with systematic form has been found.

There are several decoding algorithms for binary Goppa codes. Here, we introduce the use of the Berlekamp–Massey algorithm as implemented in the Classic McEliece reference implantation. Due to the error-correction capabilities of this decoding algorithm, first a double-size $2t \times n$ parity-check matrix $\tilde{H}^{(2)} = \{h_{i,j}^{(2)}\}$, where $h_{i,j}^{(2)} = \alpha_j^{i-1}/g^2(\alpha_j)$ for $i = 1, \ldots, 2t$ and $j = 1, \ldots, n$ and a double syndrome $s^{(2)} = \tilde{H}^{(2)}(C_0|0)$ is computed. Then the Berlekamp–Massey algorithm is used to compute an error-locator polynomial σ from $s^{(2)}$. The error positions are then determined by evaluating σ at $\alpha = \{\alpha_1, \ldots, \alpha_n\}$. Instead of re-encrypting the obtained error vector e' using H, the double syndrome $s'^{(2)}$ of the error vector can be computed as $s'^{(2)} = \tilde{H}^{(2)}e'$ and compared with $s^{(2)}$: If $s^{(2)} = s'^{(2)}$ then also $C_0 = (I_{n-k}|T)e'$ and hence $e = e'$. Therefore, the large public key is not required for re-encryption during decapsulation and hence the public key does not need to be stored alongside the private key.

For computing $\hat{H}$ during key generation as well as for computing $\tilde{H}^{(2)}$ and for obtaining the error positions from the error-locator polynomial during decapsulation, a polynomial needs to be evaluated for all $\alpha = \{\alpha_1, \ldots, \alpha_n\}$. Since α contains most of the elements in $\mathbb{F}_{2^m}$ for most parameter sets of Classic McEliece, this can efficiently be accomplished using the additive FFT algorithm by Gao and Mateer. The syndrome computation can be efficiently performed using a transposed FFT.

Classic McEliece requires efficient sorting algorithms for the computation of a random permutation of field elements in $\mathbb{F}_{2^m}$ for obtaining α as well as for computing a random error vector of weight t. Furthermore, the specification of Classic McEliece requires that the support $\alpha = \{\alpha_1, \ldots, \alpha_n\}$ is not stored as a list of elements in $\mathbb{F}_2$ but as $(2m-1)2^{m-4}$ control bits for a Beneš network, which can be obtained using an efficient sorting algorithm. Arithmetic in $\mathbb{F}_{2^m}$ typically can be parallelized and hence is suitable for bitslicing (see Chapter 7 of this volume).

11.2.2.3. *Techniques for secure implementation*

The specification of Classic McEliece is designed to support constant-time implementations as much as possible. The rationale for storing the control bits of a Beneš network as part of the secret key is that, on the one hand, the storage requirements for the private key are significantly reduced and, on the other hand, the correct values for α can be obtained after the evaluation of a polynomial using an additive FFT (which operates on the natural order of field elements) securely in constant time by applying the Beneš network with the stored control bits to the output of the additive FFT. The computation of a (transposed) additive FFT, the Berlekamp–Massey algorithm, as well as sorting algorithms lend themselves for a straightforward constant-time implementation.

Special care needs to be taken for the encoding routine: both the generation of a weight-t error vector e as well as the computation of $C_0 = He$ might leak timing information. A constant-time implementation of the decoding operation can be achieved quite easily, as long as a transposed FFT is used for the re-encryption based on the double syndrome. Otherwise, caution is required when multiplying the parity-check matrix with e'.

During key generation, the Gaussian elimination on $\hat{H}$ for computing the systematic parity-check matrix $(I_{n-k}|T)$ must be performed in constant time. Here, an early abort in case $\hat{H}$ cannot be systemized does not leak timing information since then key generation is restarted with a fresh seed. The irreducible Goppa polynomial can be computed using Gaussian elimination on a matrix over $\mathbb{F}_{2^m}$ or using the Berlekamp–Massey algorithm, which must be implemented in constant time as well.

There is not much work on exploiting other side channels than timing for code-based systems. A general recommendation is to mask the use of the private key. There are message-recovery attacks against (Classic) McEliece, for example, single-trace attacks on encapsulation and differential attacks on decapsulation which exploit power side channels. More research on effective side-channel attacks and countermeasures for such attacks is required.

11.2.3. *Isogeny-based KEMs*

Isogeny-based cryptography was proposed by Couveignes (2006) in "Hard Homogeneous Spaces", whose material was first presented during a seminar held in the mid-1990s. One decade after, Rostovtsev and Stolbunov (2006) independently proposed a public-key cryptosystem based on isogenies of ordinary elliptic curves. That same year, Charles et al. (2009), proposed a hash function whose collision resistance was provably guaranteed by the isogeny problem defined over supersingular elliptic curves.

Let E and E' be two supersingular isogenous elliptic curves defined over a finite field $\mathbb{F}_q$, with q a power of a large prime p. Computing an isogeny map between E and E' is widely believed to be a hard computational problem in the classical and the quantum settings. It is known as the supersingular isogeny path problem. In many scenarios, this isogeny is of known degree ℓ^e for some small prime ℓ and we refer to this variant as the supersingular fixed-degree isogeny path (*SIPFD*) problem. An isogeny graph is a graph that represents the relationships between different elliptic curves that are related to each other by isogenies. The vertices of the graph represent elliptic curves which are determined by their j-invariant, which classify elliptic curves in equivalence classes defined up to endomorphisms. The edges of the graph represent isogenies between the curves.

Variants of the *SIPFD* problem form the basis of several isogeny-based signatures, including the Short Quaternion and Isogeny Signature (SQISign), which was proposed by De Feo et al. (2020). This problem also provides the security guarantees of the Commutative Supersingular Isogeny-based Diffie-Hellman (CSIDH) key exchange scheme, which was introduced by Castryck et al. (2018).

Jao and De Feo (2011) proposed the Supersingular Isogeny-based Diffie-Hellman key exchange protocol (SIDH). Apart from disclosing the degree of its secret isogeny, SIDH also reveals the evaluation of its secret isogenies at a large torsion subgroup. This weaker variant of *SIPFD* was dubbed by the authors as the *Computational Supersingular Isogeny* (CSSI) problem. SIKE, which is a variant of SIDH equipped with a key encapsulation mechanism, was one of the few schemes that made it to the fourth round of the NIST PQC standardization effort as an alternate KEM candidate.

For over a decade, the best-known algorithms for breaking SIDH or SIKE had an exponential time complexity in both classical and quantum settings. However, a recent polynomial-time attack by Castryck and Decru (2022) that was quickly followed by two other variants, ingeniously exploited the auxiliary information leaked in SIDH and SIKE to completely break their security, and in the process, easily breaking and claiming a bounty for an isogeny challenge proposed by Microsoft Research.

11.2.3.1. *Schemes definitions*

SIKE was the solely isogeny-based fourth-round scheme in the NIST standardization process. The official SIKE proposal presented four parameter sets, namely, SIKEp434, SIKEp503, SIKEp610 and SIKEp751, achieving NIST security levels 1, 2, 3 and 5, respectively. The notation used for these instantiations alludes to the bitlength of the underlying prime field characteristic.

SIKE operates on Montgomery supersingular elliptic curves defined over $\mathbb{F}_{p^2}$, where p is a large prime number of the form $p = 2^{e_2}3^{e_3} - 1$. The exponents e_2 and e_3 are chosen such that $2^{e_2} \approx 3^{e_3}$. The public parameters of SIKE are given by a supersingular starting curve $E_0/\mathbb{F}_{p^2} : y^2 = x^3 + 6x^2 + x$, and a set of six x-coordinates corresponding to the basis points $P_2, Q_2, P_3, Q_3 \in E_0$ of order 2^{e_2} and 3^{e_3}, respectively. Additionally, the protocol also uses the auxiliary public points $D_2 = P_2 - Q_2$ and $D_3 = P_3 - Q_3$. SIKE comprises three main algorithms: key generation, encapsulation and decapsulation (which are usually called KeyGen, Encaps and Decaps).

In KeyGen, Bob's public and private key $\{pk_3, (s, sk_3)\}$ are computed by performing the following steps. Bob's private key sk_3, is a uniformly chosen integer in the range $[\![1 \,..\, 2^{e_3-1} - 1]\!]$. Then, Bob computes the 3^{e_3}-isogeny ϕ_3 generated by the kernel point $R_3 = P_3 + [sk_3]Q_3$, obtaining his public key as the tuple of image points, $pk_3 = (\phi_3(P_2), \phi_3(Q_2), \phi_3(D_2))$, along with a randomly selected n-bit string s.

SIKE's encapsulation algorithm computes Alice's public and private key (pk_2, sk_2) using an analogous procedure as the one described above. Alice then uses a key derivation procedure to compute a secret j, which corresponds to the j-invariant of the image supersingular elliptic curve $\phi_3(\phi_2(E_0))$. This algorithm outputs Alice's public key along with the encryption of an n-bit random message m XOR'ed with $F(j)$, where F is a hash function that maps j to bitstrings.

SIKE's Decapsulation algorithm recovers the secret j' corresponding to the j-invariant of the image supersingular elliptic curve $\phi_2(\phi_3(E_0))$. The value j' is then used for finding Alice's private key and from it, her public key. If the received public key is identical to the one recovered, this procedure returns as the shared secret the hash of the secret key and the encapsulation output. Otherwise, it returns a random string.

The main computation of CSIDH consists of the evaluation of its class group action, which takes as input an elliptic curve E_0, represented by its A-coefficient, and an ideal class $\mathfrak{a} = \prod_{i=1}^{n} \mathfrak{l}_i^{e_i}$, represented by its list of exponents $(e_i, \ldots, e_n) \in [\![-m \,..\, m]\!]^n$. This list of exponents is the CSIDH secret key. The output of the class group action is the A-coefficient of the elliptic curve E_A defined as:

$$E_A = a{*}E_0 = \mathfrak{l}_1^{e_1} * \cdots * \mathfrak{l}_n^{e_n} * E_0.$$

One remarkable feature of the CSIDH group action is its commutative property. This allows us to apply the group action directly to the key exchange between two parties by mimicking the DH protocol. Having agreed upon using a starting elliptic curve E_0, Alice and Bob choose a secret key a and b, respectively. Then, they can produce their corresponding public keys by computing the group actions $E_A = a * E_0$ and $E_B = b * E_0$. After exchanging these public keys, Alice and Bob can obtain a common secret by computing:

$$a * E_B = (a \cdot b) * E_0 = (b \cdot a) * E_0 = b * E_A.$$

11.2.3.2. *Techniques for efficient implementation*

The two most expensive computational tasks of SIKE are the computation of large smooth-degree isogenies of supersingular elliptic curves along with the evaluation of the image of elliptic curve points in those isogenies and elliptic curve scalar multiplication computations via three-point Montgomery Ladder procedures. In their 2014 SIDH paper, De Feo et al. (2014) presented optimal computation of large degree isogenies. The cost of optimal strategies for computing a degree-ℓ^e isogeny is of about $\frac{e}{2}\log_2 e$ point multiplications by ℓ, $\frac{e}{2}\log_2 e$ degree-ℓ isogeny evaluations, and e constructions of degree-ℓ isogenous curves. Optimal strategies have also been applied to achieve faster implementations of CSIDH.

Montgomery curves is the preferred curve model for SIKE and CSIDH, since they enable the usage of x-only point arithmetic. This can be advantageously used for performing scalar multiplications with x-coordinates that always lie in the base prime field $\mathbb{F}_p$. The Montgomery model is also useful for computing close to optimal isogeny evaluations.

For practical implementations of CSIDH, constructing and evaluating n degree-ℓ_i isogenies, plus $O(n^2)$ scalar multiplications by the prime factors ℓ_i, overwhelmingly dominate its computational cost. CSIDH uses a prime p such that $p + 1 = 4\prod_{i=1}^{n} \ell_i$, where $\ell_1, \ldots, \ell_n$ are small odd primes. This choice permits us to compute efficiently the degree-ℓ_i isogenies corresponding to the group action of the ideal $\mathfrak{l}_i$ of norm ℓ_i.

Vélu's formulas have been profusely used in the last 50 years for constructing and evaluating degree-ℓ isogenies by performing three main algorithms known as `KPS`, `xISOG` and `xEVAL`. `KPS` computes the first ℓ multiples of the kernel point P, namely, the set $\{P, [2]P, \ldots, [\ell]P = \infty\}$. The calculations done in `KPS` are then used as pre-computation database for `xISOG` and `xEVAL`. `xISOG` and `xEVAL` find the constants $A' \in \mathbb{F}_p$ that determine the codomain curve E', and the x-coordinate $\phi_x(\alpha)$ of the image point Q, respectively. The computational cost associated with Vélu's formulas is of $O(\ell)$ operations. Bernstein et al. (2020) presented a breakthrough approach for constructing and evaluating degree-ℓ isogenies at a combined cost of just $O(\sqrt{\ell})$ operations. This approach has been referred to as square-root Vélu.

11.2.3.3. *Techniques for secure implementation*

In July 2022, Castryck and Decru presented a devastating attack against SIKE. This attack can heuristically solve the CSSI problem in polynomial time, as it was convincingly shown by an accompanying Magma script, which breaks in a matter of hours, random SIKE instances that were once aimed for achieving NIST levels 1, 2, 3 and 5. This original attack was soon improved to break all SIKE instances in a matter of minutes.

The Castryck and Decru attack relies on the knowledge of three crucial pieces of information, namely, (i) the degree of the isogeny ϕ_2, (ii) the ring endomorphism of SIKE's starting curve E_0 and (iii) the images $\phi_3(P_2), \phi_3(Q_2)$ of Alice's generator points $\langle P_2, Q_2 \rangle = E[2^{e_2}]$, where the prime $p = 2^{e_2}3^{e_3} - 1$ is the underlying prime used by SIKE instantiations. We stress here that (ii) and (iii) are only known in the specific case of the CSSI problem, but not in the more general case of the *SIPFD* problem. Furthermore, another attack by Maino and Martindale and yet another one by Robert quickly followed. Maino and Martindale's attack does not require knowledge of the endomorphism ring associated with the base curve. Robert's attack can also break SIDH in polynomial time for any random initial supersingular elliptic curve E_0.

Since the publication of the Castryck and Decru attack, several countermeasures have already been proposed by trying to hide the degree of the isogeny or the images of the torsion points. These solutions are considerably less efficient and practical than the original construction.

On the other hand, CSIDH does not leak any auxiliary information and, for a sensitive choice of parameters, remains secure against all known classical and quantum attacks. Despite its low performance, CSIDH has the smallest public keys of all post-quantum key exchange schemes and is the only one that is commutative. Furthermore, CSIDH admits an efficient public key validation procedure, a feature that permits its usage in the static-dynamic and static-static key exchange settings.

The security guarantees of CSIDH (and its variant CTIDH) rest on an analogue of the discrete logarithm problem: given the base elliptic curve E_0 and the public-key elliptic curve $E_A = \mathfrak{a} * E_0$, we deduced the ideal class $\mathfrak{a}$. Hence, the classical security of CSIDH lies in the problem of finding an isogeny path from the isogenous supersingular elliptic curves E_0 and E_A. From a quantum setting perspective, the best-known attack is Kuperberg's procedure, which has a quantum time and space sub-exponential complexity of $\exp\left(O(\sqrt{\log p})\right)$.

11.2.4. *IND-CCA2 security*

Most post-quantum key-encapsulation mechanisms have in common that the core constructions only achieve chosen-plaintext attack (CPA) security, that is, they are only secure in the presence of a passive adversary that cannot perform chosen-ciphertext attacks (CCA). While in some cases, CPA security may be sufficient (e.g. when secret keys are only used once), many protocols do require CCA security, that is, assuming an active adversary that can manipulate ciphertexts. As it is preferable to standardize and deploy as few cryptographic systems as possible, we commonly focus on CCA-secure schemes. We distinguish between IND-CCA1 and IND-CCA2 security. For the former, the adversary can query arbitrary ciphertexts from a decryption oracle only before receiving the ciphertext they want to attack, while for IND-CCA2, the attacker can perform oracle queries before and after receiving the target ciphertext. In practice, we want to achieve IND-CCA2 security.

Fortunately, generic transformations from CPA security to IND-CCA2 security exist, such as the Fujisaki–Okamoto transform for probabilistic PKEs, which is used in Kyber, and Dent's variant for deterministic cases, which is used in Classic McEliece (see decapsulation in section 11.2.2.1).

11.2.4.1. *The Fujisaki–Okamoto transform*

The general idea of CCA transforms is simple: we have to ensure that a given ciphertext was honestly generated before revealing the decryption. The Fujisaki–Okamoto achieves this by re-encrypting the decrypted plaintext and then comparing the re-encryption to the ciphertext. In case the re-encryption matches the ciphertext, the ciphertext was generated honestly. If there is a mismatch, this indicates that the input ciphertext was faulty and possibly malicious. In that case, the plaintext must not be revealed, but instead either a random value (implicit rejection) or an error message (explicit rejection) needs to be returned.

For allowing the re-encryption to produce the same ciphertext, the encryption procedure requires to be fully deterministic, which is achieved by generating all required randomness pseudo-randomly from the (random) message. In its simplest form, the FO transform constructs an IND-CCA2-secure KEM from a CPA public-key encryption system consisting of the algorithms `CPA.KeyGen()`, `CPA.Encrypt(pk, m, coins)`, and `CPA.Decrypt(sk, c)` (with `coins` corresponding to the required randomness) using a hash-function $\mathcal{H}$ in the following way:

– `CCA.KeyGen()`:

  - `pk,sk` ← `CPA.KeyGen()`

– `CCA.Encaps(pk)`:

  - `x` ← $\{0,1\}^{256}$

  - `k, coins` ← $\mathcal{H}$(`x`)

  - `c` ← `CPA.Encrypt(pk, x, coins)`

– `CCA.Decaps(sk, c)`:

  - `x'` ← `CPA.Decrypt(sk, c)`

  - `k, coins'` ← $\mathcal{H}$(`x'`)

- `c' ←CPA.Encrypt(pk, x', coins')`
- verify that `c' = c`

Variants of the FO transform (as for example used by Kyber) additionally apply two tweaks to this construction: first, the shared secret is derived from the so-called pre-key `k` by hashing it together with the ciphertext `c`. Second, the public key gets added as input to the hash deriving `coins` for protecting against multi-target attacks and turning the construction into a contributory KEM.

11.2.4.2. *Secure implementation*

Implementing the FO transform securely is an astonishingly hard problem that has not been entirely solved in the literature so far. For passive side-channel attacks, this is primarily caused by the much larger attack surface. The processed plaintext has to be considered secret, requiring the entire FO re-encryption to be protected against side-channel attacks. Furthermore, it is often sufficient to distinguish if two ciphertexts decrypt to the same plaintext or not to mount so-called plaintext-checking oracle (PC oracle) attacks. PC-oracle attacks have been demonstrated for code-based KEMs exploiting tiny timing differences in the re-encryption, depending on the plaintext. While these timing-based PC-oracle attacks can be thwarted by ensuring that no timing leakage occurs in re-encryption revealing information about the processed plaintext, protection is much harder when considering more powerful side-channel attacks. When using masking as a countermeasure against power-consumption-based side-channel attacks, this primarily requires to use a much higher masking order than commonly used on other cryptography. For example, while cryptography without the FO transformation may be sufficiently secure at masking order 2 or 3, post-quantum schemes require much higher masking order with some literature showing that even fifth-order masking is insufficient.

The FO transform can also be attacked using fault injection attacks. In the most-straightforward attack, the attacker simply skips the comparison of the ciphertext and the re-encryption, hence completely disabling the purpose of the FO. Another attack avenue is to transmit a faulty ciphertext and to use fault injection to fault the ciphertext back to the original ciphertext, causing the FO to accept the faulty ciphertext in case it decrypts to the same message, that is, providing a PC oracle to the attacker. Countermeasures against fault attacks on the FO are thus far limited to generic countermeasures like fault detection using redundant computation or shuffling computations to increase the attack complexity. The efficacy of such countermeasures is not yet well understood.

11.3. Post-quantum signatures

Just like for KEMs, also post-quantum signature schemes are constructed for a variety of underlying assumptions. The first batch of signatures that will be standardized by NIST includes two lattice-based schemes and one hash-based scheme. In addition, schemes based on the hardness of solving large multivariate systems of equations were prominently represented in the first three rounds of the NIST competition, and we expect that more schemes following this approach will be submitted to the upcoming NIST call for additional post-quantum signatures. Also, multiple signature schemes based on isogenies of elliptic curves (see section 11.2.3) have been proposed in the last couple of years and are likely to enter the NIST competition for additional signatures.

Unlike KEMs, post-quantum signatures are diverse also from a different point of view: while all CCA-secure KEMs follow the approach of first constructing a passively secure PKE and then using some generic transform to construct a CCA-secure KEM, signature schemes are built using very different "templates": Dilithium is using Fiat-Shamir, Falcon is using a hash-and-sign approach and hash-based signatures like SPHINCS$^+$ are typically constructed using Merkle trees; yet other schemes (like the round 3 alternate scheme Picnic) use multiparty computation in the head.

11.3.1. *Lattice-based signatures – Dilithium*

Lattice-based signatures are divided into two major families, either following the hash-and-sign paradigm or the Fiat–Shamir-with-aborts approach. Hash-and-sign schemes are represented in the NIST competition by Falcon and date back to 2003 when Hoffstein et al. (2003) introduced NTRUSign. Fiat–Shamir-with-aborts signatures date back to work by Lyubashevsky (2009). The corresponding finalist in the NIST competition is Dilithium. In the following, we focus on the Fiat–Shamir-with-aborts signatures and Dilithium.

Dilithium relies on the hardness of the MLWE problem (as introduced in section 11.2.1) and the module-short-integer-solutions (MSIS) problem. The MSIS problem is to find a "short" $\mathbf{v} \in \mathcal{R}_q$, given a matrix $\mathbf{A} \in \mathcal{R}_q^{k\times\ell}$, such that $\mathbf{Av} \equiv 0 \mod q$. In particular, Dilithium requires a variant of MSIS called SelfTargetMSIS, which asks to find a vector $\begin{bmatrix}\mathbf{z} \; c \; \mathbf{v}\end{bmatrix}^\mathsf{T}$ with small coefficients and a hash of a message μ, such that:

$$H\left(\mu || [\mathbf{A}|\mathbf{t}|\mathbf{I}] \cdot \begin{bmatrix}\mathbf{z} \\ c \\ \mathbf{v}\end{bmatrix}\right) = c$$

with H a random oracle, $\mathbf{A} \in \mathcal{R}_q^{k\times\ell}$ and $\mathbf{t} \in \mathcal{R}_q^k$ uniformly random and $\mathbf{I}$ the identity matrix.

11.3.1.1. *Scheme definition*

Dilithium is one of the two lattice-based signature finalists in the NIST standardization process. It consists of three parameter sets aiming at the security levels 2, 3 and 5. Across all parameter sets, the same polynomial ring $\mathcal{R}_q = \mathbb{Z}_q[X]/(X^n + 1)$ with $n = 256$ and $q = 2^{23} - 2^{13} + 1$ is used, allowing efficient polynomial multiplication using NTTs. The core differences for each security level are the dimensions of the matrix $(k \times \ell)$, the range of the masking vector (γ_1) and the range of the secret key (η). The parameters $(k, \ell, \gamma_1, \eta)$ are $(4, 4, 2^{17}, 2)$ for security level 2, $(6, 5, 2^{19}, 4)$ for security level 3 and $(8, 7, 2^{19}, 2)$ for security level 5. The remaining parameters $(d, \tau, \gamma_2, \omega)$ are chosen accordingly.

We describe a simplified form of Dilithium without public key compression and deterministic signing. The public key is $(\rho, \mathbf{t})$ consisting of the seed ρ used to pseudo-randomly sample the uniform matrix $\mathbf{A} \in \mathcal{R}_q^{k \times \ell}$ and $\mathbf{t} = \mathbf{A}\mathbf{s}_1 + \mathbf{s}_2$. The private key is $(\rho, \mathbf{t}, \mathbf{s}_1, \mathbf{s}_2)$ consisting of the public key, and the two secret vectors $\mathbf{s}_1$ and $\mathbf{s}_2$.

To sign a hash M of a message, a uniformly random masking vector $\mathbf{y} \in \mathcal{R}_q^{\ell}$ with coefficients in $[-\gamma_1, \gamma_1]$ is sampled. The signer then computes $\mathbf{w} = \mathbf{A}\mathbf{y}$ and computes the high bits of $\mathbf{w}$ (referred to as $\mathbf{w}_1$), such that $\mathbf{w} = 2\gamma_2\mathbf{w}_1 + \mathbf{w}_0$. The challenge polynomial c is derived from the hash $H(M\|\mathbf{w}_1)$. Here, $H()$ is a special hash function that outputs a "short" polynomial which has a small number of coefficients (τ) set to -1 or 1. A potential signature is computed as $\mathbf{z} = \mathbf{y} + c\mathbf{s}_1$. Outputting this signature directly would potentially leak information about the secret $\mathbf{s}_1$ and, hence, rejection sampling has to be used. If a signature is rejected, the signer starts with a fresh masking vector $\mathbf{y}$ and tries again. The signer rejects $\mathbf{z}$ if any coefficient of $\mathbf{z}$ is larger than $\gamma_1 - \tau\eta$. Additionally, the signer rejects if the lower bits of $\mathbf{A}\mathbf{y} - c\mathbf{s}_2$ are larger than $\gamma_2 - \tau\eta$ as this would result in a carry from the lower bits into the higher bits of $\mathbf{w}$ during verification and, consequently, an invalid signature. The signature then consists of $(\mathbf{z}, c)$.

To check a signature $(\mathbf{z}, c)$, the verifier re-computes the high bits of $\mathbf{w}$ as $\mathbf{w}_1' = \mathbf{A}\mathbf{z} - c\mathbf{t}$. They can then check that $c = H(M\|\mathbf{w}_1')$. We also need to verify that $\mathbf{z}$ does not contain any coefficients larger than $\gamma_1 - \tau\eta$.

There are two main differences between the simplified version of Dilithium above compared to the specification submitted to NIST. A major difference is that Dilithium uses compressed public keys, that is, only the high bits $\mathbf{t}_1$ of $\mathbf{t} = 2^d\mathbf{t}_1 + \mathbf{t}_0$ are stored in the public key. While this reduces public key size, it also slightly complicates the scheme as the verifier is no longer able to reliably compute $\mathbf{w}_1$ from $\mathbf{z}$, c, and $\mathbf{t}_1$. This is due to the carries introduced by $c\mathbf{t}_0$ from the lower part to the higher part of $\mathbf{w}_1$. This is resolved by adding a hint vector $\mathbf{h}$ containing the position of said carries to the signature. Another difference is that Dilithium is deterministic rather than the probabilistic scheme presented above. Instead of sampling $\mathbf{y}$ at random,

Dilithium derives it pseudo-randomly from a seed K (part of the secret key), the hash of the message M, a hash of the public key tr (precomputed as a part of the secret key) and a counter that is incremented in case of rejections. This results in a deterministic signature scheme, which is needed by some of the security proofs and is also preferable in case no good randomness source is available.

11.3.1.2. *Techniques for efficient implementation*

Similar to Kyber, the core arithmetic operation is polynomial multiplication and $\mathcal{R}_q$ is chosen, such that fast NTTs can be used. Dilithium uses a modulus q for which 512-th roots of unity exist and, hence, a complete NTT is used. The implementation techniques for NTTs described in section 11.2.1 carry over to Dilithium. The core difference to the Kyber NTTs is the much larger q. As the modulus is 23 bits, the natural size of coefficients in software implementations is 32 bits.

The large modulus, however, presents a challenge for some architectures as a long 32×32-bit constant-time multiplier is not always available. For example, the Arm Cortex-M3 only has a variable-time long-multiply instruction which cannot be safely used for computing 32-bit NTTs on secret inputs. Note that not all NTTs in Dilithium are operating on secret inputs. For example, all NTTs in verifications as well as the NTT of c and $\mathbf{t}_0$ may be performed using variable-time instructions. Another challenge is that, for example, AVX2 does not have a high-multiply for 32-bit inputs, but only for 16-bit inputs. However, such an instruction is needed for fast Montgomery multiplications. This results in a much slower implementation as we have to fall back to widening multiplications.

11.3.1.3. *Techniques for secure implementation*

For Dilithium implementations protected from timing side-channel attacks, we have to slightly deviate from the standard definition of constant-time implementations. Usually, a constant-time implementation is defined as not having any data flow from secret data into branching conditions, memory addresses, or into instructions that have data-dependent timing. However, Dilithium does have data flow from the secret key to the signature, which is used in a branching condition in the rejection sampling. However, since the (candidate) signature is public according to the security proof, this does not present any problem. When using standard tools for finding timing leaks in Dilithium implementations, this branch will likely be found as a false positive.

Protecting Dilithium from other side-channel attacks proves to be significantly harder than for lattice-based encryption. The polynomial arithmetic itself is easily masked using arithmetic masking. However, the remainder of the scheme is much harder to mask. In particular, the sampling of $\mathbf{y}$ and the rejection sampling are best implemented using Boolean masking, requiring a conversion between arithmetic and Boolean masking. As of today, there is no fully masked implementation of Dilithium available. The available masked implementations either implement the predecessor

GLP or modify Dilithium to use a power-of-two modulus allowing for more efficient masking.

Differential fault attacks present a serious threat to Dilithium. When using the deterministic variant of Dilithium, an adversary can inject a fault into the computation of c. The faulty c' is then used to compute a faulty signature $\mathbf{z}' = \mathbf{y} + c'\mathbf{s}_1$. By subtracting the faulty signature from a valid signature $\mathbf{z} = \mathbf{y} + c\mathbf{s}_1$, it is easy to compute $\mathbf{s}_1$. To prevent this attack, we should use the randomized variant of Dilithium whenever fault attacks present a viable attack vector. For protecting against weak randomness, Dilithium derives the masking vector from a secret seed K, the hash of the message M, the hash of the public key tr and a random value ρ'. If ρ' is weak, the resulting scheme is still secure.

11.3.2. *Multivariate-quadratic-based signatures – UOV*

Multivariate cryptography is based on the NP-hardness of solving a system of multivariate polynomials. The public key is a multivariate polynomial system $\mathcal{P}:\mathbb{F}^n \mapsto \mathbb{F}^m$ over some finite field $\mathbb{F}$, while the private key is a trapdoor secret that allows the owner of the key to invert the multivariate system and to compute $\mathcal{P}^{-1}$. For a multivariate encryption scheme, the ciphertext c is obtained by evaluating the system for the plain text m as $c = \mathcal{P}(m)$. In order to decrypt, the receiver computes $m = \mathcal{P}^{-1}(c)$ using the trapdoor secret. A signature scheme is constructed correspondingly by computing the signature s as $s = \mathcal{P}^{-1}(m)$. This signature can be verified by evaluating the public map $m' = \mathcal{P}(s)$ and by verifying that $m = m'$.

The first multivariate-quadratic (MQ) signature scheme called C* was proposed by Matsumoto and Imai (1988). However, C* was later found to insecure by Patarin (1995). Shortly after, in 1996, Patarin introduced an improved cryptosystem following the idea of Matsumoto and Imai called hidden field equations (HFE). While HFE in general remains unbroken up until today, all efficient instantiation have been shown to be insecure. Besides the HFE proposals, there have been a number of proposals based on the "Oil and Vinegar" scheme proposed by Patarin (1997). Soon after, the original OV was shown to be insecure by Kipnis and Shamir (1998). However, another year later, Kipnis et al. (1999) proposed an improved cryptosystem called "Unbalanced oil and vinegar" (UOV). In the third round of the NIST PQC competition, there were two schemes based on MQ: the finalist Rainbow and the alternate GeMSS. Rainbow is an extension of UOV, while GeMSS is based on HFE. In addition, there was a third MQ-based scheme in the second round of the NIST PQC competition called MQDSS, neither based on UOV nor HFE. Unfortunately, all three have suffered severe attacks in the process of the NIST PQC competition. We restrict this chapter to the original UOV, which remains unbroken up until today.

11.3.2.1. *Scheme definition*

The core construction of all MQ schemes is similar: Let $\mathbb{F}_q$ be a finite field. A common choice is $\mathbb{F}_{2^k}$, for example, $\mathbb{F}_{16}$ or $\mathbb{F}_{256}$. A MQ scheme has a public map $\mathcal{P} = \mathcal{S} \circ \mathcal{Q} \circ \mathcal{T} : \mathbb{F}_q^n \to \mathbb{F}_q^m$ where $\mathcal{S} : \mathbb{F}_q^m \to \mathbb{F}_q^m$ and $\mathcal{T} : \mathbb{F}_q^n \to \mathbb{F}_q^n$ are randomly chosen affine and easy to invert maps, that is, $\mathcal{S} : w \mapsto x = M_{\mathcal{S}} w + v_{\mathcal{S}}$ and $\mathcal{T} : y \mapsto z = M_{\mathcal{T}} y + v_{\mathcal{T}}$. The central map $\mathcal{Q} : x \mapsto y$, however, is quadratic and easy to invert. For UOV, the map $\mathcal{S}$ may be omitted, and hence, $\mathcal{P} = \mathcal{Q} \circ \mathcal{T}$. This is, however, not the case for more advanced schemes like Rainbow and HFE.

Key generation consists of choosing $\mathcal{S}$, $\mathcal{Q}$, and $\mathcal{T}$, and computing $\mathcal{P}$. To sign (a hash of) a message $w \in \mathbb{F}_q^m$, we apply the inverse of $\mathcal{S}$, $\mathcal{Q}$ and $\mathcal{T}$ to obtain the signature $z \in \mathbb{F}_q^n$. To verify a signature $z \in \mathbb{F}_q^n$, we check if (the hash of) the message w' is equal to $\mathcal{P}(z)$. For an MQ scheme to be secure, $\mathcal{P}$ must be hard to invert without the knowledge of $\mathcal{S}$, $\mathcal{Q}$ or $\mathcal{T}$.

The security of any MQ scheme stems from the construction of the central map $\mathcal{Q}$. For UOV, $\mathcal{Q}$ consists of m quadratic equations of the form:

$$y_k = \sum_{i=1}^{v} \sum_{j=1}^{v} \alpha_{ij}^{(k)} x_i x_j + \sum_{i=1}^{v} \sum_{j=v+1}^{n} \beta_{ij}^{(k)} x_i x_j + \sum_{i=1}^{n} \gamma_i^{(k)} x_i + \delta^{(k)}$$

with v being the number of vinegar variables (x_i for $1 \leq i \leq v$) and n being g the total number of variables. It is easy to see that the $o = n - v$ oil variables are not combined with other oil variables in the quadratic terms. Without a loss of security, the linear and constant terms can be left out, that is, $\gamma_i^{(k)} = 0$ and $\delta^{(k)} = 0$. To compute the inverse of $\mathcal{Q}$, we choose the vinegar variables at random which turns the quadratic equations into a linear system of equations which can be solved for the oil variables (x_i for $v < i \leq n$). In case no solution exists, we restart with another set of randomly chosen vinegar variables.

A common optimization that does not affect the security is to restrict the map $\mathcal{T}$ to linear maps, that is, $v_{\mathcal{T}} = 0$. Another optimization is to choose $\mathcal{T}$ to have a special structure:

$$\mathcal{T} = \begin{bmatrix} I_{v \times v} T_{v \times o}^{(1)} \\ 0_{o \times v} I_{o \times o} \end{bmatrix}.$$

This optimization does not impact the security of the schemes as for any public key $\mathcal{P}$, there exists a $\mathcal{T}$ and $\mathcal{Q}$ and finding any pair $\mathcal{T}, \mathcal{Q}$, such that $\mathcal{P} = \mathcal{Q} \circ \mathcal{T}$ breaks the security of the scheme.

The public key consists of the m polynomials in $\mathcal{P}(z)$. Each polynomial has $\frac{n \cdot (n+1)}{2}$ coefficients corresponding to $z_i z_j$ for $1 \leq i \leq j \leq n$. For efficient implementation, we represent these polynomials as a Macauley matrix with m rows and $\frac{n \cdot (n+1)}{2}$ columns. The columns are ordered, such that they correspond to the monomials $z_i z_j$ in lexicographic order. The matrix is stored in a column-major form.

11.3.2.2. *Techniques for efficient implementation*

Throughout key generation, signing and verification, we need efficient $\mathbb{F}_q$ arithmetic. We restrict the following to the most common case where $q = 2^k$. For other choices (e.g. the popular choice $q = 31$), other techniques are used. While addition is trivial for $\mathbb{F}_{2^k}$, multiplication and inversion require more attention. Multiplication is much more dominant than inversion. It benefits well from vectorization as one always operated on many field elements in parallel. If available, specialized instructions for $\mathbb{F}_{2^k}$ should be used. For example, Intel's Galois Field New Instructions (GFNI) and Arm's binary polynomial multiplication instructions can be beneficial with the former being much more powerful than the latter. Alternatively, in-register table lookups (e.g. Arm Neon's VTBL or Intel AVX2's VPSHUFB) should be used if supported by the platform. On platforms without either of the above, bitslicing is the preferred approach for implementing $\mathbb{F}_{2^k}$ multiplication. On platforms without a cache, we may want to consider using table look-ups from memory.

During signing, the most time-consuming operation is the inversion of the central map $\mathcal{Q}$, which requires us to solve a linear system of equation. This is achieved using constant-time Gaussian elimination. It proceeds as normal Gauss elimination, except when making sure that the pivot element is non-zero, we have to conditionally add all the subsequent rows instead of just one. In case the system of linear equations does not have a solution, we may abort early as we have to start with a fresh set of vinegar variables.

For verification, the only operation besides hashing of the message is the evaluation of the public map. This consists of the computation of all monomials $z_i z_j$ for $1 \leq i \leq j \leq n$ followed by a multiplication of the product with the corresponding column in the Macauley matrix. The products are then accumulated. Since multiplication is much more expensive than accumulation, it is beneficial to minimize the number of field multiplications. This can be done by using one accumulator for each possible value of $z_i z_j \neq 0$, that is, 15 accumulators for $\mathbb{F}_{16}$. For $\mathbb{F}_{256}$, we can use two sets of accumulators for the lower and higher nibble of $z_i z_j$ separately, that is, we require 2×15 accumulators. Note that this results in a signature-dependent memory access pattern, which can only be used if the signature is considered public or memory access is constant time.

11.3.2.3. *Techniques for secure implementation*

Work on protecting UOV or Rainbow from other side-channel attacks other than timing attacks is very limited. For Rainbow, the straightforward target for DPA during the signing operation is to attack the $\mathcal{T}^{-1}$ computation, which processes the secret key $\mathcal{T}^{-1}$ and the known input w. In UOV, the knowledge of $\mathcal{T}^{-1}$ is sufficient to forge signatures. In Rainbow, we additionally need to recover $\mathcal{S}^{-1}$, which can either be done using algebraic attacks or by another side-channel attack. The side-channel attack is possible since the signature z is known and $\mathcal{S}^{-1}$ has a special sparse structure allowing for a full recovery using CPA. Protection against CPA is not sufficiently studied yet and up until today no masked implementations of either UOV or Rainbow are available.

11.3.3. *Hash-based signatures – XMSS and SPHINCS$^+$*

Hash-based signature schemes go back to the work by Lamport (1979) on one-time signature schemes constructed from a one-way function. The basic idea is to use a secret bit string as private key and its hash value as public key. The most basic construction is a one-time one-bit signature scheme: Alice generates two secret strings s_0 and s_1 and publishes their hash values $h_0 = \mathrm{h}(s_0)$ and $h_1 = \mathrm{h}(s_1)$ as public verification key. Since Alice is using a cryptographically secure hash function h(), nobody can obtain s_0 and s_1 from h_0 and h_1. If later, Alice wants to sign the one-bit message m, she releases the secret string s_m alongside m. Anyone that earlier obtained the public key (h_0, h_1) from Alice can now verify that $h_m = \mathrm{h}(s_m)$. Since previously, only Alice knew s_0 and s_1, the one-bit message m must be from Alice. However, since Alice released part of the secret information, she cannot use this private-public key pair again. Hence, this simple scheme is a one-bit one-time signature scheme.

To construct signature schemes for longer messages, more hash values can be published as public key: to sign a 256-bit message, we could generate 2×256 hash values, using one pair to sign each bit of a 256-bit message. More efficiently, hash chains can be used instead: Winternitz proposed to split a message of n bit into $l_0 = n/w$ words of w bits and to concatenate the message with its check sum computed over the message words, also split into l_1 words of w bits. The Winternitz one-time signature scheme (WOTS) then uses $l = l_0 + l_1$ hash chains, each of length 2^w steps. To generate a public key, Alice starts out with l secret bit strings $r_{i,0}$ with $0 \leq i < l$, she hashes these strings 2^w times such that $r_{i,j+1} = \mathrm{h}(r_{i,j})$ for $0 < i \leq 2^w$, and publishes $r_{i,2^w}$ as public key. To sign, she takes the ith w-bit word of the message for $0 \leq i < l$, treats the w-bit word as an integer M_i and recomputes the M_ith chain step r_{i,M_i} of the ith hash chain. The corresponding elements of all chains are then the signature. For verification, Bob, for all $0 \leq i < l$ also takes the ith w-bit word of the message and treats it as an integer M_i. He then hashes the signature element r_{i,M_i} another $2^w - M_i$ times and verifies that he reaches the public key element $r_{i,2^w}$. If that is the case for all l w-bit words of the message, the signature is successfully verified. This gives us a fairly efficient arbitrary-length one-time signature scheme.

To get from arbitrary-length one-time signature schemes to arbitrary-length many-time signature schemes, we can use binary Merkle trees as proposed by Merkle (1990). The leaf nodes of the Merkle tree are (a hash of) the public keys of one-time signature schemes. The leaf nodes are pairwise hashed over several layers of a binary tree until a single root node is computed. The value of this root node is the public key. For generating a signature in a Merkle tree, a verification path needs to be provided, that is, the pair-nodes on the layers of the Merkle tree that are required to reach the root node from a given leaf node such that for verification, the verifier can re-compute the root node from a leaf node and compare it to the public key. Using many arbitrary-length one-time signature schemes as leaf nodes of a binary Merkle hash-tree, we obtain a arbitrary-length many-time signature scheme. Observe that the number of possible signatures per signature key pair is limited by the height of the Merkle tree and hence needs to be decided and fixed at key-generation time.

11.3.3.1. *Scheme definition*

Common hash-based signature schemes are the stateful signature schemes XMSS and LMS as well as the stateless signature scheme SPHINCS$^+$. In stateful signature schemes, information needs to be stored at the signers side which one-time signature schemes at the leaves of the Merkle tree have already been used; in stateless signature scheme, such a state does not need to be maintained.

Both XMSS and LMS work as described above: they are using variants of WOTS at the leaves of a binary Merkle tree. There are multi-tree versions of XMSS and LMS where a leaf node on one tree is used to sign a root node of another tree, which provides a trade-off between computation time (key generation and signing) as well as the signature length.

As mentioned above, SPHINCS$^+$ is a stateless signature scheme. This is achieved by on the one hand using many layers in a multi-tree setting and on the other hand few-time signature schemes at the highest tree level such that the probability is negligible that a randomly selected leaf is used more often than the few-time signature scheme tolerates.

Both XMSS and SPHINCS$^+$ are using masks as well as keyed hash-functions to ward off multi-target attacks and provide strong security proofs, while the construction of LMS is slightly simpler and cheaper at the cost of reduced security guarantees.

11.3.3.2. *Techniques for efficient implementation*

The main cost factor of hash-based signature schemes is the computation of a hash function with small inputs and small outputs many times. Hence, any optimization that is applied to the hash function directly translates into a speed-up of key generation, signing, and verification. Common techniques for accelerating hash functions are to provide hardware accelerators or instruction set extensions. Since many of the hash operations are independent (e.g. hashing in the different WOTS chains), vectorization and SIMD parallelization can be used.

Depending on the hash function and the parameter set, some prefixes in the hash inputs may be repeated frequently during the hash computations. If these common prefixes fit into one hash block, the resulting intermediate state can be stored and restored instead of repeating corresponding hash computations.

For signing of stateful hash-based signature schemes, the Merkle trees are traversed in order. Hence, some of the computations and some parts of the signature can be shared between consecutive signing operations. Such information can be cached and elaborate tree-traversal algorithms can be used to balance computational cost and storage requirements for efficient signing operations. Such approaches typically are less helpful for stateless signature schemes, since the Merkle trees here are not traversed in-order but the starting leaves are selected randomly between consecutive signature operations.

11.3.3.3. *Techniques for secure implementation*

The attack surface for side-channel attacks on hash-based signature schemes is small. The majority of the computation occur in the Merkle trees, which only consist of public data and are, hence, not relevant for passive side-channel attacks. The only place where secret data is processed is the hash chains of the WOTS signatures and, for SPHINCS$^+$, the few-time signatures. However, these are only processing the secret key and no other variable data known to the attacker. Hence, differential attacks (e.g. CPA) are not possible. The only viable attack type for these schemes appears to be single-trace attacks. Another target is the generation of the secret keys. Those are expanded from a seed together with the address of the corresponding secret key in the tree using a pseudo-random function. As the seed is global for the entire (hyper-)tree, it is called many times with different addresses within a single signature generation. As the address is known to the attacker, it allows attacking the seed in multiple invocations of the pseudo-random function in a differential attack. Hence, the pseudo-random function needs to be protected against side-channel attacks.

Fault attacks present a much larger threat for hash-based signatures, in particular if they are stateless. The multi-tree structure of SPHINCS+ works and is secure, despite the use of one-time signatures at the leaves of the inner trees, because the entire structure is deterministically defined: whenever the same inner leaf node is visited during a signing operation, then the same three nodes of the next higher tree is being signed – hence, the same chain nodes of the one-time signature scheme are computed and released as part of the signature. If, however, a fault is introduced randomly at any time during the signing process (e.g. during the pair-wise hashing in one of the Merkle trees), then with high probability, the root node of the corresponding tree is going to be different than in a non-faulted signature generation. Therefore, a different root node is signed by the next lower one-time signature scheme. Signing different messages with the same one-time signature scheme breaks its security. Hence, if an attacker can inject different faults during the computation of a specific sub-tree, an alternative private key for the following one-time signature scheme can be derived, allowing the attacker to sign arbitrary messages. A signature that has been faulted as described above still verifies correctly (as long as the lowest tree is not affected by the fault). Therefore, such a faulty signature cannot simply be detected by verification. This puts SPHINCS+ (and other hash-based signature schemes using a multi-tree structure such as XMSS-MT) into significant risk in scenarios where an attacker can inject faults during signature generation. For stateful schemes, this can be prevented by caching intermediate signatures, which is usually done to improve performance anyway.

11.4. Notes and further references

– Section 11.2.1. Lattice-based public-key encryption and key encapsulation goes back to the NTRU scheme by Hoffstein et al. (1998). The public-key encryption scheme used in Kyber was introduced by Lyubashevsky et al. (2010, 2013) and goes back to the work by Regev (2005, 2009). Kyber was introduced in Bos et al. (2018); the latest version of the specification is in Schwabe et al. (2022). It also draws many ideas, in particular with regard to a design enabling efficient and secure implementations from the NewHope scheme from Alkim et al. (2016). The other two lattice-based KEM finalist schemes in the NIST PQC project were NTRU (Chen et al. 2020) and Saber (D'Anvers et al. 2020).

Over the last decade, many works improved the performance of multiplication in polynomial rings that are used by lattice-based encryption schemes and KEMs. Some of these works such as Bernstein et al. (2017), Karmakar et al. (2018), and Kannwischer et al. (2019) employ Karatsuba or Toom techniques, but most recent works focus on NTT-based multiplication in NTT-friendly rings (see for example Alkim et al. (2020); Becker et al. (2021); Abdulrahman et al. (2022)) and also in NTT-unfriendly rings (see for example Alkim et al. (2021) and Chung et al. (2021)). Another recent direction of work on implementations of lattice-based crypto is formally verifying correctness of arithmetic (e.g. Hwang et al. 2022) or full schemes (e.g. Almeida et al. 2023).

Various papers present masked implementations of lattice-based public-key encryption schemes and KEMs (see for example Oder et al. (2018); Beirendonck et al. (2021); Bos et al. (2021); Heinz et al. (2022); Kamucheka et al. (2022); Kundu et al. (2022)) and building blocks (such as D'Anvers et al. 2023). Combined countermeasures against side-channel and fault analysis are presented in Heinz and Pöppelmann (2022); these are based on a redundant representation of coefficients in $\mathbb{Z}_q$ and adding a sort of "checksum computations" through a CRT-based technique. A survey of side-channel protections of lattice-based schemes is given in Ravi et al. (2022).

Even more papers present side-channel and fault attacks against lattice-based KEMs, some also against protected implementations (see, for example, Hamburg et al. (2021); Delvaux and Merino Del Pozo (2021); Ngo et al. (2021, 2022); Backlund et al. (2022); Dubrova et al. (2022)). Another class of attack papers considers chosen-ciphertext attacks against the passively secure PKE schemes that are typically underlying CCA-secure KEMs (see, for example, Fluhrer (2016); Bauer et al. (2019); Qin et al. (2021)).Although these attacks do not violate any security claims of the schemes, they become relevant in a scenario where the information hidden by the FO transform (i.e. the information if decryption succeeded) can be recovered from side-channel information.

– Section 11.2.2. The McEliece cryptosystem has been introduced in McEliece (1978) and its dual variant by Niederreiter (1986). The third-round specification of Classic McEliece can be found in Albrecht et al. (2020). Implementation tricks using additive FFT and transpose FFT as well as a Beneš network are explained in Chou (2017). Further implementation tweaks can be found in Chen and Chou (2021). The hardware implementations accompanying the Classic McEliece submission is described in Wang et al. (2017, 2018).

Code-based alternative candidates in the third round of the NIST standardization process are BIKE (Aragon et al. 2020) and HQC (Aguilar Melchor et al. 2020). Since both BIKE and HQC are using quasi-cyclic codes, their implementation requires efficient polynomial arithmetic. BIKE is using a bit-flipping decoder while HQC uses the Berlekamp–Massey algorithm.

Another interesting code-family for the use in code-based cryptography are rank codes. Low Rank Parity Check (LRPC) cods are used, for example, for the round-1 schemes Ouroboros-R (Aguilar Melchor et al. 2017), LAKE (Aragon et al. 2017a) and LOCKER (Aragon et al. 2017b). These schemes have been joined to ROLLO in round 2 (Aragon et al. 2019) and strongly depend on efficient Gaussian reduction for rank computations during decapsulation.

Besides cryptanalytic attacks that attempt to exploit the code structure of a code-based scheme, Information Set Decoding (ISD) is the most relevant generic attack. ISD goes back to Prange (1962) and has been improved over time (for example, by Lee and Brickell 1988; Stern 1988; Finiasz and Sendrier 2009; Becker et al. 2012). Security analyses of code-based schemes can be found in, for example, Baldi et al. (2019) and Esser and Bellini (2021).

– Section 11.2.3. In a seminar held in 1997, Couveignes proposed an isogeny-based scheme for mimicking the Diffie-Hellman key exchange protocol. Couveignes notes were later posted in Couveignes (2006). The first concrete isogeny-based cryptographic primitive was presented by Charles et al. (2009), where the authors proposed a hash function whose collision resistance was extracted from the problem of path-finding in supersingular isogeny graphs. As early as 2006, Rostovtsev and Stolbunov (2006) introduced isogeny-based cryptographic schemes, proposing a Diffie–Hellman-like protocol whose security guarantees were based on the difficulty of finding smooth-degree isogenies between ordinary elliptic curves. While the best classical algorithm by Galbraith and Stolbunov solves this problem in full exponential time, Childs et al. (2014) a quantum algorithm computing such isogenies in subexponential time. Jao and De Feo (2011) proposed a Diffie–Hellman key-exchange scheme, this time relying on the difficulty of constructing isogenies between supersingular elliptic curves. Since the endomorphism ring of a supersingular elliptic curve is no longer commutative, the underlying isogeny problem was, for more than a decade, supposed to be much more difficult to solve. Within the context of the NIST standardization process, it was proposed in Jao et al. (2020) a SIDH variant equipped with a key encapsulation mechanism called SIKE. SIKE was selected as one of the fourth-round alternate KEM candidates of the NIST contest. Castryck and Decru (2022) presented in July 2022 a devastating attack against SIKE that was quickly followed by Maino and Martindale (2022) and Robert (2022). Quickly after that, the authors of SIKE officially withdrawn their NIST submission.

– Section 11.2.4. The Fujisaki–Okamoto transform was introduced in Fujisaki and Okamoto (1999). The security as part of post-quantum constructions was extensively studied in Hofheinz et al. (2017). Higher order masking of the FO transform within lattice-based cryptography is covered in Bos et al. (2021). PC oracle attacks were introduced and analyzed in D'Anvers et al. (2019) and Guo et al. (2022). Fault attacks on CCA-secure lattice schemes was first studied in Hermelink et al. (2021) and Pessl and Prokop (2021).

– Section 11.3.1. Lattice-based signatures have a rather young history and date back to NTRUSign in Hoffstein et al. (2003). The NIST finalist Falcon by Prest et al. (2020) is based on NTRUSign. However, Dilithium (see Ducas et al. 2018; Lyubashevsky et al. 2020) is unrelated to NTRUSign and instead is based on FiatÐShamir-with-aborts (see Lyubashevsky 2009). Efficient implementations of Dilithium are described in Seiler (2018) for AVX2 and in Greconici et al. (2021) for Cortex-M4. Fault attacks on Dilithium have been studied in Bruinderink and Pessl (2018). In Barthe et al. (2018), masking of the scheme GLP by Güneysu et al. (2012) is studied. Masking Dilithium was studied in Migliore et al. (2019).

– Section 11.3.2. Multivariate-quadratic signature date back to Matsumoto and Imai (1988). However, their original proposal C* got broken in Patarin (1995). Later proposals include HFE (Patarin 1996) and OV (Patarin 1997). While the original OV parameters got broken in Kipnis and Shamir (1998), the variation UOV described in Kipnis et al. (1999) remains unbroken up until today. Rainbow was proposed in Ding and Schmidt (2005) and uses multiple layers of the UOV scheme. It was shown in Ding et al. (2008), that it can only be secured with at most two layers.

Rainbow is also a third-round finalist in the NIST PQC project. The specification can be found in Ding et al. (2020). Other proposals in the NIST PQC competition include GeMSS (specified in Casanova et al. (2020)), LUOV (specified in Beullens et al. (2019)) and MQDSS (specified in Samardjiska et al. (2019)). However, all three have been shown to be not secure in Tao et al. (2021), Ding et al. (2021) and Kales and Zaverucha (2020), respectively. Rainbow also suffered numerous attacks (Baena et al. 2022; Beullens 2021, 2022). The most serious attack by Beullens in 2022 vastly reduces the security of Rainbow, essentially breaking the level 1 parameter sets. The use of GFNI for Rainbow was studied in Drucker and Gueron (2020). Rainbow implementations on x86 were studied in Chen et al. (2009). Bitsliced implementations of Rainbow on the Cortex-M4 were studied in Chou et al. (2021). Constant-time Gauss elimination was first described in Bernstein et al. (2013). The only work studying side-channel attacks on Rainbow is Park et al. (2018). Fault attacks on Rainbow and UOV were studied in Krämer and Loiero (2019).

– Section 11.3.3. The initial work on hash-based signatures by Lamport is described in Lamport (1979) and the following constructions by Winternitz and Merkle in Merkle (1990). The stateful signature schemes XMSS and LMS have been introduced in Buchmann et al. (2011) and Leighton and Micali (1995), and specified in IETF RFC 8391 (Hülsing et al. 2018) and RFC 8554 (McGrew et al. 2019). The NIST PQC submission SPHINCS+ is specified in Hülsing et al. (2020). Parallelized vector implementations are described in, for example, Kölbl (2018) and Becker and Kannwischer (2022). Embedded and hardware implementations of hash-based schemes are provided in, for example, Wang et al. (2019) and Campos et al. (2020). Side-channel analysis of hash-based schemes is described in, for example, Kannwischer et al. (2018). Fault-attacks are described in Castelnovi et al. (2018) and Genêt et al. (2018).

11.5. References

Abdulrahman, A., Hwang, V., Kannwischer, M.J., Sprenkels, D. (2022). Faster Kyber and Dilithium on the Cortex-M4. In *ACNS 22: 20th International Conference on Applied Cryptography and Network Security*, Ateniese, G. and Venturi, D. (eds). Springer, Heidelberg.

Aguilar Melchor, C., Aragon, N., Bettaieb, S., Bidoux, L., Blazy, O., Deneuville, J.-C., Gaborit, P., Hauteville, A., Zémor, G. (2017). Ouroboros-R. Technical Report, National Institute of Standards and Technology [Online]. Available at: https://csrc.nist.gov/projects/post-quantum-cryptography/round-1-submissions.

Aguilar Melchor, C., Aragon, N., Bettaieb, S., Bidoux, L., Blazy, O., Deneuville, J.-C., Gaborit, P., Persichetti, E., Zémor, G., Bos, J. (2020). HQC. Technical Report, National Institute of Standards and Technology [Online]. Available at: https://csrc.nist.gov/projects/post-quantum-cryptography/round-3-submissions.

Albrecht, M.R., Bernstein, D.J., Chou, T., Cid, C., Gilcher, J., Lange, T., Maram, V., von Maurich, I., Misoczki, R., Niederhagen, R. et al. (2020). Classic McEliece. Technical Report, National Institute of Standards and Technology [Online]. Available at: https://csrc.nist.gov/projects/post-quantum-cryptography/ round-3-submissions.

Alkim, E., Ducas, L., Pöppelmann, T., Schwabe, P. (2016). Post-quantum key exchange: A new hope. In *USENIX Security 2016: 25th USENIX Security Symposium*, Holz, T. and Savage, S. (eds). USENIX Association, Austin, Texas.

Alkim, E., Bilgin, Y.A., Cenk, M., Gérard, F. (2020). Cortex-M4 optimizations for {R,M}LWE schemes. *IACR Transactions on Cryptographic Hardware and Embedded Systems*, 2020(3), 336–357.

Alkim, E., Cheng, D.Y.-L., Chung, C.-M.M., Evkan, H., Huang, L.W.-L., Hwang, V., Li, C.-L.T., Niederhagen, R., Shih, C.-J., Wälde, J. et al. (2021). Polynomial multiplication in NTRU prime. *IACR Transactions on Cryptographic Hardware and Embedded Systems*, 2021(1), 217–238.

Almeida, J.B., Barbosa, M., Barthe, G., Grégoire, B., Laporte, V., Léchenet, J.-C., Oliveira, T., Pacheco, H., Quaresma, M., Schwabe, P. et al. (2023). Formally verifying Kyber part I: Implementation correctness. Paper 2023/215, Cryptology ePrint Archive [Online]. Available at: https://eprint.iacr.org/2023/215.

Aragon, N., Blazy, O., Deneuville, J.-C., Gaborit, P., Hauteville, A., Ruatta, O., Tillich, J.-P., Zémor, G. (2017a). LAKE. Technical Report, National Institute of Standards and Technology [Online]. Available at: https://csrc.nist.gov/projects/post-quantum-cryptography/round-1-submissions.

Aragon, N., Blazy, O., Deneuville, J.-C., Gaborit, P., Hauteville, A., Ruatta, O., Tillich, J.-P., Zémor, G. (2017b). LOCKER. Technical Report, National Institute of Standards and Technology [Online]. Available at: https://csrc.nist.gov/projects/post-quantum-cryptography/round-1-submissions.

Aragon, N., Blazy, O., Deneuville, J.-C., Gaborit, P., Hauteville, A., Ruatta, O., Tillich, J.-P., Zémor, G., Aguilar Melchor, C., Bettaieb, S. et al. (2019). ROLLO. Technical Report, National Institute of Standards and Technology [Online]. Available at: https://csrc.nist.gov/projects/post-quantum-cryptography/round-2-submissions.

Aragon, N., Barreto, P., Bettaieb, S., Bidoux, L., Blazy, O., Deneuville, J.-C., Gaborit, P., Gueron, S., Guneysu, T., Aguilar Melchor, C. et al. (2020). BIKE. Technical Report, National Institute of Standards and Technology. Available at: https://csrc.nist.gov/projects/post-quantum-cryptography/round-3-submissions.

Backlund, L., Ngo, K., Gürtner, J., Dubrova, E. (2022). Secret key recovery attacks on masked and shuffled implementations of CRYSTALS-Kyber and Saber. Report 2022/1692, Cryptology ePrint Archive [Online]. Available at: https://eprint.iacr.org/2022/1692.

Baena, J., Briaud, P., Cabarcas, D., Perlner, R.A., Smith-Tone, D., Verbel, J.A. (2022). Improving support-minors rank attacks: Applications to GeMSS and Rainbow. In *Advances in Cryptology – CRYPTO 2022*, Dodis, Y. and Shrimpton, T. (eds). Springer, Heidelberg.

Baldi, M., Barenghi, A., Chiaraluce, F., Pelosi, G., Santini, P. (2019). A finite regime analysis of information set decoding algorithms. *Algorithms*, 12(10). doi: 10.3390/a12100209.

Barthe, G., Belaïd, S., Espitau, T., Fouque, P.-A., Grégoire, B., Rossi, M., Tibouchi, M. (2018). Masking the GLP lattice-based signature scheme at any order. In *Advances in Cryptology – EUROCRYPT 2018*, Nielsen, J.B. and Rijmen, V. (eds). Springer, Heidelberg.

Bauer, A., Gilbert, H., Renault, G., Rossi, M. (2019). Assessment of the key-reuse resilience of NewHope. In *Topics in Cryptology – CT-RSA 2019*, Matsui, M. (ed.). Springer, Heidelberg.

Becker, H. and Kannwischer, M.J. (2022). Hybrid scalar/vector implementations of Keccak and SPHINCS$^+$ on AArch64. In *Progress in Cryptology - INDOCRYPT 2022*, Isobe, T. and Sarkar, S. (eds). Springer, Heidelberg.

Becker, A., Joux, A., May, A., Meurer, A. (2012). Decoding random binary linear codes in $2^{n/20}$: How 1 + 1 = 0 improves information set decoding. In *Advances in Cryptology – EUROCRYPT 2012*, Pointcheval, D. and Johansson, T. (eds). Springer, Heidelberg.

Becker, H., Hwang, V., Kannwischer, M.J., Yang, B.-Y., Yang, S.-Y. (2021). Neon NTT: Faster Dilithium, Kyber, and Saber on Cortex-a72 and Apple M1. *IACR Transactions on Cryptographic Hardware and Embedded Systems*, 2022(1), 221–244 [Online]. Available at: https://tches.iacr.org/index.php/TCHES/article/view/929.

Beirendonck, M.V., D'Anvers, J., Karmakar, A., Balasch, J., Verbauwhede, I. (2021). A side-channel-resistant implementation of SABER. *ACM J. Emerg. Technol. Comput. Syst.*, 17(2), 10:1–10:26.

Bernstein, D.J., Chou, T., Schwabe, P. (2013). McBits: Fast constant-time code-based cryptography. In *Cryptographic Hardware and Embedded Systems – CHES 2013*, Bertoni, G. and Coron, J.-S. (eds). Springer, Heidelberg.

Bernstein, D.J., Chuengsatiansup, C., Lange, T., van Vredendaal, C. (2017). NTRU Prime: Reducing attack surface at low cost. In *SAC 2017: 24th Annual International Workshop on Selected Areas in Cryptography*, Adams, C. and Camenisch, J. (eds). Springer, Heidelberg.

Bernstein, D.J., De Feo, L., Leroux, A., Smith, S. (2020). Faster computation of isogenies of large prime degree. *ANTS*, 4(1), 39–55.

Beullens, W. (2021). Improved cryptanalysis of UOV and Rainbow. In *Advances in Cryptology – EUROCRYPT 2021*, Canteaut, A. and Standaert, F.-X. (eds). Springer, Heidelberg.

Beullens, W. (2022). Breaking Rainbow takes a weekend on a laptop. In *Advances in Cryptology – CRYPTO 2022*, Dodis, Y. and Shrimpton, T. (eds). Springer, Heidelberg.

Beullens, W., Preneel, B., Szepieniec, A., Vercauteren, F. (2019). LUOV. Technical Report. National Institute of Standards and Technology [Online]. Available at: https://csrc.nist.gov/projects/post-quantum-cryptography/round-2-submissions.

Bos, J., Ducas, L., Kiltz, E., Lepoint, T., Lyubashevsky, V., Schanck, J.M., Schwabe, P., Stehlé, D. (2018). CRYSTALS – Kyber: A CCA-secure module-lattice-based KEM. In *2018 IEEE European Symposium on Security and Privacy, EuroS&P 2018*.

Bos, J.W., Gourjon, M., Renes, J., Schneider, T., van Vredendaal, C. (2021). Masking Kyber: First- and higher-order implementations. *IACR Transactions on Cryptographic Hardware and Embedded Systems*, 2021(4), 173–214.

Bruinderink, L.G. and Pessl, P. (2018). Differential fault attacks on deterministic lattice signatures. *IACR Transactions on Cryptographic Hardware and Embedded Systems*, 2018(3), 21–43.

Buchmann, J.A., Dahmen, E., Hülsing, A. (2011). XMSS – A practical forward secure signature scheme based on minimal security assumptions. In *Post-Quantum Cryptography – 4th International Workshop, PQCrypto 2011*, Yang, B.-Y. (ed.). Springer, Heidelberg.

Campos, F., Kohlstadt, T., Reith, S., Stöttinger, M. (2020). LMS vs XMSS: Comparison of stateful hash-based signature schemes on ARM Cortex-M4. In *AFRICACRYPT 20: 12th International Conference on Cryptology in Africa*, Nitaj, A. and Youssef, A.M. (eds). Springer, Heidelberg.

Casanova, A., Faugère, J.-C., Macario-Rat, G., Patarin, J., Perret, L., Ryckeghem, J. (2020). GeMSS. Technical Report, National Institute of Standards and Technology [Online]. Available at: https://csrc.nist.gov/projects/post-quantum-cryptography/round-3-submissions.

Castelnovi, L., Martinelli, A., Prest, T. (2018). Grafting trees: A fault attack against the SPHINCS framework. In *Post-Quantum Cryptography – 9th International Conference, PQCrypto 2018*, Lange, T. and Steinwandt, R. (eds). Springer, Heidelberg.

Castryck, W. and Decru, T. (2022). An efficient key recovery attack on SIDH (preliminary version). Report 2022/975, Cryptology ePrint Archive [Online]. Available at: https://eprint.iacr.org/2022/975.

Castryck, W., Lange, T., Martindale, C., Panny, L., Renes, J. (2018). CSIDH: An efficient post-quantum commutative group action. *ASIACRYPT*, 3, 395–427.

Charles, D.X., Lauter, K.E., Goren, E.Z. (2009). Cryptographic hash functions from expander graphs. *Journal of Cryptology*, 22(1), 93–113.

Chen, M.-S. and Chou, T. (2021). Classic McEliece on the ARM Cortex-M4. Report 2021/492, Cryptology ePrint Archive [Online]. Available at: https://eprint.iacr.org/2021/492.

Chen, A.I.-T., Chen, M.-S., Chen, T.-R., Cheng, C.-M., Ding, J., Kuo, E.L.-H., Lee, F.Y.-S., Yang, B.-Y. (2009). SSE implementation of multivariate PKCs on modern x86 CPUs. In *Cryptographic Hardware and Embedded Systems – CHES 2009*, Clavier, C. and Gaj, K. (eds). Springer, Heidelberg.

Chen, C., Danba, O., Hoffstein, J., Hülsing, A., Rijneveld, J., Schanck, J.M., Schwabe, P., Whyte, W., Zhang, Z., Saito, T. et al. (2020). NTRU. Technical Report, National Institute of Standards and Technology [Online]. Available at: https://csrc.nist.gov/projects/post-quantum-cryptography/round-3-submissions.

Childs, A., Jao, D., Soukharev, V. (2014). Constructing elliptic curve isogenies in quantum subexponential time. *Journal of Mathematical Cryptology*, 8(1), 1–29. doi: 10.1515/jmc-2012-0016.

Chou, T. (2017). McBits revisited. In *Cryptographic Hardware and Embedded Systems – CHES 2017*, Fischer, W. and Homma, N. (eds). Springer, Heidelberg.

Chou, T., Kannwischer, M.J., Yang, B.-Y. (2021). Rainbow on Cortex-M4. *IACR Transactions on Cryptographic Hardware and Embedded Systems*, 2021(4), 650–675.

Chung, C.-M.M., Hwang, V., Kannwischer, M.J., Seiler, G., Shih, C.-J., Yang, B.-Y. (2021). NTT multiplication for NTT-unfriendly rings. *IACR Transactions on Cryptographic Hardware and Embedded Systems*, 2021(2), 159–188.

Couveignes, J.-M. (2006). Hard homogeneous spaces. Report 2006/291, Cryptology ePrint Archive [Online]. Available at: https://eprint.iacr.org/2006/291.

D'Anvers, J.-P., Tiepelt, M., Vercauteren, F., Verbauwhede, I. (2019). Timing attacks on error correcting codes in post-quantum schemes. In *Proceedings of ACM Workshop on Theory of Implementation Security*, Bilgin, B., Petkova-Nikova, S., Rijmen, V. (eds). ACM, New York.

D'Anvers, J.-P., Karmakar, A., Roy, S.S., Vercauteren, F., Mera, J.M.B., Beirendonck, M.V., Basso, A. (2020). SABER. Technical Report, National Institute of Standards and Technology [Online]. Available at: https://csrc.nist.gov/projects/post-quantum-cryptography/round-3-submissions.

D'Anvers, J.-P., Van Beirendonck, M., Verbauwhede, I. (2023). Revisiting higher-order masked comparison for lattice-based cryptography: Algorithms and bit-sliced implementations. *IEEE Transactions on Computers*, 72(2), 321–332.

De Feo, L., Jao, D., Plût, J. (2014). Towards quantum-resistant cryptosystems from supersingular elliptic curve isogenies. *J. Math. Cryptol.* 8(3), 209–247.

De Feo, L., Kohel, D., Leroux, A., Petit, C., Wesolowski, B. (2020). SQISign: Compact post-quantum signatures from quaternions and isogenies. *ASIACRYPT*, 1, 64–93.

Delvaux, J. and Merino Del Pozo, S. (2021). Roulette: Breaking Kyber with diverse fault injection setups. Report 2021/1622, Cryptology ePrint Archive [Online]. Available at: https://eprint.iacr.org/2021/1622.

Ding, J. and Schmidt, D. (2005). Rainbow, a new multivariable polynomial signature scheme. In *ACNS 05: 3rd International Conference on Applied Cryptography and Network Security*, Ioannidis, J., Keromytis, A., Yung, M. (eds). Springer, Heidelberg.

Ding, J., Yang, B.-Y., Chen, C.-H. O., Chen, M.-S., Cheng, C.-M. (2008). New differential-algebraic attacks and reparametrization of Rainbow. In *ACNS 08: 6th International Conference on Applied Cryptography and Network Security*, Bellovin, S.M., Gennaro, R., Keromytis, A.D., Yung, M. (eds). Springer, Heidelberg.

Ding, J., Chen, M.-S., Petzoldt, A., Schmidt, D., Yang, B.-Y., Kannwischer, M., Patarin, J. (2020). Rainbow. Technical Report, National Institute of Standards and Technology [Online]. Available at: https://csrc.nist.gov/projects/post-quantum-cryptography/round-3-submissions.

Ding, J., Deaton, J., Vishakha, Yang, B.-Y. (2021). The nested subset differential attack – A practical direct attack against LUOV which forges a signature within 210 minutes. In *Advances in Cryptology – EUROCRYPT 2021*, Canteaut, A. and Standaert, F.-X. (eds). Springer, Heidelberg.

Drucker, N. and Gueron, S. (2020). Speed up over the Rainbow. Report 2020/408, Cryptology ePrint Archive [Online]. Available at: https://eprint.iacr.org/2020/408.

Dubrova, E., Ngo, K., Gärtner, J. (2022). Breaking a fifth-order masked implementation of CRYSTALS-Kyber by copy-paste. *IACR Cryptol. ePrint Arch.* [Online]. Available at: https://eprint.iacr.org/2022/1713.

Ducas, L., Kiltz, E., Lepoint, T., Lyubashevsky, V., Schwabe, P., Seiler, G., Stehlé, D. (2018). CRYSTALS-Dilithium: A lattice-based digital signature scheme. *IACR Transactions on Cryptographic Hardware and Embedded Systems*, 2018(1), 238–268.

Esser, A. and Bellini, E. (2021). Syndrome decoding estimator. Report 2021/1243, Cryptology ePrint Archive [Online]. Available at: https://eprint.iacr.org/2021/1243.

Finiasz, M. and Sendrier, N. (2009). Security bounds for the design of code-based cryptosystems. In *Advances in Cryptology – ASIACRYPT 2009*, Matsui, M. (ed.). Springer, Heidelberg.

Fluhrer, S. (2016). Cryptanalysis of ring-LWE based key exchange with key share reuse. Report 2016/085, Cryptology ePrint Archive [Online]. Available at: https://eprint.iacr.org/2016/085.

Fujisaki, E. and Okamoto, T. (1999). Secure integration of asymmetric and symmetric encryption schemes. In *Advances in Cryptology – CRYPTO'99*, Wiener, M.J. (ed.). Springer, Heidelberg.

Genêt, A., Kannwischer, M.J., Pelletier, H., McLauchlan, A. (2018). Practical fault injection attacks on SPHINCS. Report 2018/674, Cryptology ePrint Archive [Online]. Available at: https://eprint.iacr.org/2018/674.

Greconici, D.O.C., Kannwischer, M.J., Sprenkels, D. (2021). Compact Dilithium implementations on Cortex-M3 and Cortex-M4. *IACR Transactions on Cryptographic Hardware and Embedded Systems*, 2021(1), 1–24.

Güneysu, T., Lyubashevsky, V., Pöppelmann, T. (2012). Practical lattice-based cryptography: A signature scheme for embedded systems. In *Cryptographic Hardware and Embedded Systems – CHES 2012*, Prouff, E. and Schaumont, P. (eds). Springer, Heidelberg.

Guo, Q., Hlauschek, C., Johansson, T., Lahr, N., Nilsson, A., Schröder, R.L. (2022). Don't reject this: Key-recovery timing attacks due to rejection-sampling in HQC and BIKE. *IACR Trans. Cryptogr. Hardw. Embed. Syst.*, 2022(3), 223–263.

Hamburg, M., Hermelink, J., Primas, R., Samardjiska, S., Schamberger, T., Streit, S., Strieder, E., van Vredendaal, C. (2021). Chosen ciphertext k-trace attacks on masked CCA2 secure Kyber. *IACR Transactions on Cryptographic Hardware and Embedded Systems*, 2021(4), 88–113.

Heinz, D. and Pöppelmann, T. (2022). Combined fault and DPA protection for lattice-based cryptography. *IEEE Transactions on Computers*, 72(4), 1055–1066.

Heinz, D., Kannwischer, M.J., Land, G., Pöppelmann, T., Schwabe, P., Sprenkels, D. (2022). First-order masked Kyber on ARM Cortex-M4. Report 2022/058, Cryptology ePrint Archive [Online]. Available at: https://eprint.iacr.org/2022/058.

Hermelink, J., Pessl, P., Pöppelmann, T. (2021). Fault-enabled chosen-ciphertext attacks on Kyber. In *Progress in Cryptology – INDOCRYPT 2021 – 22nd International Conference on Cryptology*, Adhikari, A., Küsters, R., Preneel, B. (eds). Springer, Cham.

Hoffstein, J., Pipher, J., Silverman, J.H. (1998). NTRU: A ring-based public key cryptosystem. In *Third Algorithmic Number Theory Symposium (ANTS)*. Springer, Heidelberg.

Hoffstein, J., Howgrave-Graham, N., Pipher, J., Silverman, J.H., Whyte, W. (2003). NTRUSIGN: Digital signatures using the NTRU lattice. In *Topics in Cryptology – CT-RSA 2003*, Joye, M. (ed.). Springer, Heidelberg.

Hofheinz, D., Hövelmanns, K., Kiltz, E. (2017). A modular analysis of the Fujisaki–Okamoto transformation. In *TCC 2017: 15th Theory of Cryptography Conference*, Kalai, Y. and Reyzin, L. (eds). Springer, Heidelberg.

Hülsing, A., Butin, D., Gazdag, S.-L., Rijneveld, J., Mohaisen, A. (2018). XMSS: eXtended Merkle Signature Scheme. RFC 8391. Internet Research Task Force (IRTF) [Online]. Available at: https://www.rfc-editor.org/ info/rfc8391.

Hülsing, A., Bernstein, D.J., Dobraunig, C., Eichlseder, M., Fluhrer, S., Gazdag, S.-L., Kampanakis, P., Kolbl, S., Lange, T., Lauridsen, M.M. et al. (2020). SPHINCS+. Technical Report, National Institute of Standards and Technology [Online]. Available at: https://csrc.nist.gov/projects/post-quantum-cryptography/round-3-submissions.

Hwang, V., Liu, J., Seiler, G., Shi, X., Tsai, M.-H., Wang, B.-Y., Yang, B.-Y. (2022). Verified NTT multiplications for NISTPQC KEM lattice finalists: Kyber, SABER, and NTRU. *IACR Transactions on Cryptographic Hardware and Embedded Systems*, 2022(4), 718–750.

Jao, D. and De Feo, L. (2011). Towards quantum-resistant cryptosystems from supersingular elliptic curve isogenies. In *Post-Quantum Cryptography – 4th International Workshop, PQCrypto 2011*, Yang, B.-Y. (ed.). Springer, Heidelberg.

Jao, D., Azarderakhsh, R., Campagna, M., Costello, C., De Feo, L., Hess, B., Jalali, A., Koziel, B., LaMacchia, B., Longa, P. et al. (2020). SIKE. Technical Report, National Institute of Standards and Technology [Online]. Available at: https://csrc.nist.gov/projects/post-quantum-cryptography/round-3-submissions.

Kales, D. and Zaverucha, G. (2020). An attack on some signature schemes constructed from five-pass identification schemes. In *CANS 20: 19th International Conference on Cryptology and Network Security*, Krenn, S., Shulman, H., Vaudenay, S. (eds). Springer, Heidelberg.

Kamucheka, T., Nelson, A., Andrews, D., Huang, M. (2022). A masked pure-hardware implementation of Kyber cryptographic algorithm. Report 2022/1547, Cryptology ePrint Archive [Online]. Available at: https://eprint.iacr.org/2022/1547.

Kannwischer, M.J., Genêt, A., Butin, D., Krämer, J., Buchmann, J. (2018). Differential power analysis of XMSS and SPHINCS. In *COSADE 2018: 9th International Workshop on Constructive Side-Channel Analysis and Secure Design*, Fan, J. and Gierlichs, B. (eds). Springer, Heidelberg.

Kannwischer, M.J., Rijneveld, J., Schwabe, P. (2019). Faster multiplication in $\mathbb{Z}_{2^m}[x]$ on Cortex-M4 to speed up NIST PQC candidates. In *ACNS 19: 17th International Conference on Applied Cryptography and Network Security*, Deng, R.H. Gauthier-Umaña, V., Ochoa, M., Yung, M. (eds). Springer, Heidelberg.

Karmakar, A., Mera, J.M.B., Roy, S.S., Verbauwhede, I. (2018). Saber on ARM. *IACR Transactions on Cryptographic Hardware and Embedded Systems*, 2018(3), 243–266.

Kipnis, A. and Shamir, A. (1998). Cryptanalysis of the oil & vinegar signature scheme. In *Advances in Cryptology – CRYPTO'98*, Krawczyk, H. (ed.). Springer, Heidelberg.

Kipnis, A., Patarin, J., Goubin, L. (1999). Unbalanced oil and vinegar signature schemes. In *Advances in Cryptology – EUROCRYPT'99*, Stern, J. (ed.). Springer, Heidelberg.

Kölbl, S. (2018). Putting wings on SPHINCS. In *Post-Quantum Cryptography – 9th International Conference, PQCrypto 2018*, Lange, T. and Steinwandt, R. (eds). Springer, Heidelberg.

Krämer, J. and Loiero, M. (2019). Fault attacks on UOV and Rainbow. In *COSADE 2019: 10th International Workshop on Constructive Side-Channel Analysis and Secure Design*, Polian, I. and Stöttinger, M. (eds). Springer, Heidelberg.

Kundu, S., D'Anvers, J., Beirendonck, M.V., Karmakar, A., Verbauwhede, I. (2022). Higher-order masked Saber. In *Security and Cryptography for Networks – 13th International Conference, SCN 2022*, Galdi, C. and Jarecki, S. (eds). Springer, Cham. doi: 10.1007/978-3-031-14791-3_5.

Lamport, L. (1979). Constructing digital signatures from a one-way function. Technical Report, SRI-CSL-98. SRI International Computer Science Laboratory, California.

Lee, P.J. and Brickell, E.F. (1988). An observation on the security of McEliece's public-key cryptosystem. In *Advances in Cryptology – EUROCRYPT'88*, Günther, C.G. (ed.). Springer, Heidelberg.

Leighton, F.T. and Micali, S. (1995). Large provably fast and secure digital signature schemes based on secure hash functions. U.S. Patent 5,432,852.

Lyubashevsky, V. (2009). Fiat-Shamir with aborts: Applications to lattice and factoring-based signatures. In *Advances in Cryptology – ASIACRYPT 2009*, Matsui, M. (ed.). Springer, Heidelberg.

Lyubashevsky, V., Peikert, C., Regev, O. (2010). On ideal lattices and learning with errors over rings. In *Advances in Cryptology – EUROCRYPT 2010*, Gilbert, H. (ed.). Springer, Heidelberg.

Lyubashevsky, V., Peikert, C., Regev, O. (2013). On ideal lattices and learning with errors over rings. *Journal of the ACM*, 60(6), 43:1–43:35.

Lyubashevsky, V., Ducas, L., Kiltz, E., Lepoint, T., Schwabe, P., Seiler, G., Stehlé, D., Bai, S. (2020). CRYSTALS-DILITHIUM. Technical Report, National Institute of Standards and Technology [Online]. Available at: https://csrc.nist.gov/projects/post-quantum-cryptography/round-3-submissions.

Maino, L. and Martindale, C. (2022). An attack on SIDH with arbitrary starting curve. Report 2022/1026, Cryptology ePrint Archive [Online]. Available at: https://eprint.iacr.org/2022/1026.

Matsumoto, T. and Imai, H. (1988). Public quadratic polynominal-tuples for efficient signature-verification and message-encryption. In *Advances in Cryptology – EUROCRYPT'88*, Günther, C.G. (ed.). Springer, Heidelberg.

McEliece, R.J. (1978). A public-key cryptosystem based on algebraic coding theory. Progress Report 42-44, Jet Propulsion Laboratory, California Institute of Technology [Online]. Available at: https://ipnpr.jpl.nasa.gov/progressReport2/ 42-44/44N.PDF.

McGrew, D., Curcio, M., Fluhrer, S. (2019). Leighton-Micali hash-based signatures. RFC Editor, 8554 [Online]. Available at: https://www.rfc-editor.org/info/rfc8554.

Merkle, R.C. (1990). A certified digital signature. In *Advances in Cryptology – CRYPTO'89*, Brassard, G. (ed.). Springer, Heidelberg.

Migliore, V., Gérard, B., Tibouchi, M., Fouque, P.-A. (2019). Masking Dilithium: Efficient implementation and side-channel evaluation. Report 2019/394, Cryptology ePrint Archive [Online]. Available at: https://eprint.iacr.org/2019/394.

Ngo, K., Dubrova, E., Guo, Q., Johansson, T. (2021). A side-channel attack on a masked IND-CCA secure Saber KEM implementation. *IACR Transactions on Cryptographic Hardware and Embedded Systems*, 2021(4), 676–707.

Ngo, K., Wang, R., Dubrova, E., Paulsrud, N. (2022). Side-channel attacks on lattice-based KEMs are not prevented by higher-order masking. Report 2022/919, Cryptology ePrint Archive [Online]. Available at: https://eprint.iacr.org/2022/919.

Niederreiter, H. (1986). Knapsack-type cryptosystems and algebraic coding theory. *Problems of Control and Information Theory*, 15(2), 159–166.

Oder, T., Schneider, T., Pöppelmann, T., Güneysu, T. (2018). Practical CCA2-secure masked Ring-LWE implementations. *IACR Transactions on Cryptographic Hardware and Embedded Systems*, 2018(1), 142–174.

Park, A., Shim, K.-A., Koo, N., Han, D.-G. (2018). Side-channel attacks on post-quantum signature schemes based on multivariate quadratic equations. *IACR Transactions on Cryptographic Hardware and Embedded Systems*, 2018(3), 500–523.

Patarin, J. (1995). Cryptanalysis of the Matsumoto and Imai public key scheme of eurocrypt'88. In *Advances in Cryptology – CRYPTO'95*, Coppersmith, D. (ed.). Springer, Heidelberg.

Patarin, J. (1996). Hidden fields equations (HFE) and isomorphisms of polynomials (IP): Two new families of asymmetric algorithms. In *Advances in Cryptology – EUROCRYPT'96*, Maurer, U.M. (ed.). Springer, Heidelberg.

Patarin, J. (1997). The oil and vinegar algorithm for signatures. Dagstuhl Workshop on Cryptography.

Pessl, P. and Prokop, L. (2021). Fault attacks on CCA-secure lattice KEMs. *IACR Transactions on Cryptographic Hardware and Embedded Systems*, 2021(2), 37–60.

Prange, E. (1962). The use of information sets in decoding cyclic codes. *IRE Transactions on Information Theory*, 8(5), 5–9.

Prest, T., Fouque, P.-A., Hoffstein, J., Kirchner, P., Lyubashevsky, V., Pornin, T., Ricosset, T., Seiler, G., Whyte, W., Zhang, Z. (2020). FALCON. Technical Report, National Institute of Standards and Technology [Online]. Available at: https://csrc.nist.gov/projects/post-quantum-cryptography/round-3-submissions.

Qin, Y., Cheng, C., Zhang, X., Pan, Y., Hu, L., Ding, J. (2021). A systematic approach and analysis of key mismatch attacks on lattice-based NIST candidate KEMs. In *Advances in Cryptology – ASIACRYPT 2021*, Tibouchi, M. and Wang, H. (eds). Springer, Heidelberg.

Ravi, P., Chattopadhyay, A., Baksi, A. (2022). Side-channel and fault-injection attacks over lattice-based post-quantum schemes (Kyber, Dilithium): Survey and new results. Report 2022/737, Cryptology ePrint Archive [Online]. Available at: https://eprint.iacr.org/2022/737.

Regev, O. (2005). On lattices, learning with errors, random linear codes, and cryptography. In *37th Annual ACM Symposium on Theory of Computing*, Gabow, H.N. and Fagin, R. (eds). ACM Press, Baltimore.

Regev, O. (2009). On lattices, learning with errors, random linear codes, and cryptography. *Journal of the ACM*, 56(6), 34.

Robert, D. (2022). Breaking SIDH in polynomial time. Report 2022/1038, Cryptology ePrint Archive [Online]. Available at: https://eprint.iacr.org/2022/1038.

Rostovtsev, A. and Stolbunov, A. (2006). Public-key cryptosystem based on isogenies. Report 2006/145, Cryptology ePrint Archive [Online]. Available at: https://eprint.iacr.org/2006/145.

Samardjiska, S., Chen, M.-S., Hülsing, A., Rijneveld, J., Schwabe, P. (2019). MQDSS. Technical Report, National Institute of Standards and Technology [Online]. Available at: https://csrc.nist.gov/projects/post-quantum-cryptography/round-2-submissions.

Schwabe, P., Avanzi, R., Bos, J., Ducas, L., Kiltz, E., Lepoint, T., Lyubashevsky, V., Schanck, J.M., Seiler, G., Stehlé, D. et al. (2022). CRYSTALS-KYBER. Technical Report, National Institute of Standards and Technology [Online]. Available at: https://csrc.nist.gov/Projects/ post-quantum-cryptography/selected-algorithms-2022.

Seiler, G. (2018). Faster AVX2 optimized NTT multiplication for ring-LWE lattice cryptography. Report 2018/039, Cryptology ePrint Archive [Online]. Available at: https://eprint.iacr.org/2018/039.

Stern, J. (1988). A method for finding codewords of small weight. In *Coding Theory and Applications, 3rd International Colloquium*, Cohen, G.D. and Wolfmann, J. (eds). Springer, Heidelberg.

Tao, C., Petzoldt, A., Ding, J. (2021). Efficient key recovery for all HFE signature variants. In *Advances in Cryptology – CRYPTO 2021*, Malkin, T. and Peikert, C. (eds). Springer, Heidelberg.

Wang, W., Szefer, J., Niederhagen, R. (2017). FPGA-based key generator for the Niederreiter cryptosystem using binary Goppa codes. In *Cryptographic Hardware and Embedded Systems – CHES 2017*, Fischer, W. and Homma, N. (eds). Springer, Heidelberg.

Wang, W., Szefer, J., Niederhagen, R. (2018). FPGA-based Niederreiter cryptosystem using binary Goppa codes. In *Post-Quantum Cryptography – 9th International Conference, PQCrypto 2018*, Lange, T. and Steinwandt, R. (eds). Springer, Heidelberg.

Wang, W., Jungk, B., Wälde, J., Deng, S., Gupta, N., Szefer, J., Niederhagen, R. (2019). XMSS and embedded systems. In *SAC 2019: 26th Annual International Workshop on Selected Areas in Cryptography*, Paterson, K.G. and Stebila, D. (eds). Springer, Heidelberg.

PART 3

Hardware Security

12

Hardware Reverse Engineering and Invasive Attacks

Sergei SKOROBOGATOV

Cambridge Research and Engineering, United Kingdom

12.1. Introduction

Security in many modern systems rely on the underlying hardware when it comes to authentication, secrecy and integrity. This became especially important for modern IoT devices. Most of these are based on semiconductor devices fabricated on a single piece of silicon. It is important that these devices are designed in a way that even if their software is compromised, it should not be possible to overtake their control. To achieve that, both authentication and key management should be performed deeply inside their hardware. Examples of such devices include microcontrollers, FPGAs, SoCs and smartcards. In rare cases, custom designed hardware is built to further improve the hardware security. However, even in that case, it is likely to be based on a standard family of existing devices. Ultimately, in order to understand the security of the hardware features implemented inside silicon, at least partial reverse engineering of the internal structure is required.

12.2. Preparation for hardware attacks

Physical attacks require direct access to the device of interest. That assumes either access to the PCB components for establishing an electrical contact, opening

Embedded Cryptography 2,
coordinated by Emmanuel PROUFF, Guénaël RENAULT,
Matthieu RIVAIN and Colin O'FLYNN.

IC packages for accessing silicon die or removing the components from the PCB for placing them into a specialized environment. The latter could be a custom test board, special harness for microscopy or dedicated holder for mechanical polishing.

12.2.1. *Preparation at PCB level*

Some devices built with physical security in mind, for example, certified to FIPS 140-2 Level 3 standard will most likely be encapsulated into epoxy compound and placed inside a robust metal case to prevent physical access to their internal parts. In order to access those electronic components, the metal case must be first mechanically removed before the PCB can be cleaned from the epoxy. If plastic cases could be easily opened with a knife or a screwdriver, then metal cases require cutting blades, edge drill bits or a CNC machine. The example of FIPS140-2 certified device, Kingston IronKey D300 and its PCB encapsulated in the epoxy compound are presented in Figure 12.1.

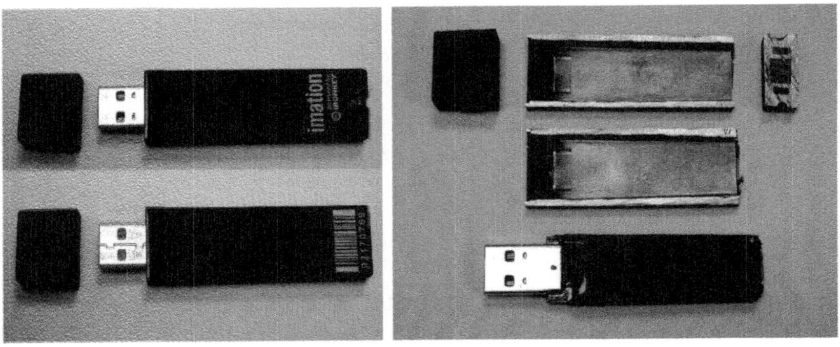

Figure 12.1. *IronKey device before and after opening its metal case*

There are several ways how the cured epoxy compound could be removed from the surface:

– Mechanical methods involve applying a force, for example, using pliers, vice or awl. Very often, it will break off at the PCB surface or from the IC package. However, in case of small SMD packages, there is a high chance that some PCB components will stick to the epoxy and go off the PCB. It might be easier to control the amount of material being removed using engraving tools or a CNC machine. There is still a danger of damaging PCB components or copper tracks.

– Structural strength of cured epoxy deteriorates quickly at temperatures above 150°C (302°F). Some compounds become soft like a rubber and could be easily removed with a toothpick or needle. That way, the epoxy can be easily peeled off plastic packages of the PCB components. However, some epoxy compounds do not soften even at 300°C (572°F), though their mechanical strength deteriorates and they become very brittle. Hence, the epoxy could be easily removed using a needle or blade. The danger of heating up the epoxy above 250°C (482°F) is associated with displacing PCB components since the solder melts at this temperature. If the epoxy is heated above 400°C (752°F), the components and PCB itself could be damaged as they both contain epoxy inside. For precise removal of small amounts of epoxy, we could use a soldering iron with a copper tip. By choosing the right tip size, applying certain force and controlling the temperature, the removal process could be easily adjusted.

– Cured epoxy could be softened by various chemicals such as acids, alkalines and organic solvents. After a certain time, it could be scraped off or easily removed with a blade, toothpick or needle. The best chemical for removing cured epoxy is nitric acid; however, it also corrodes PCB especially copper tracks and solder mask. Strong alkaline such as hot sodium hydroxide solution will corrode cured epoxy but at a much slower rate. It will also affect PCB material and IC packages. Organic solvents could work quite well and they are usually used in the industry for stripping off old paint. Some solvents could pose a significant health risk and can only be used under a controlled environment.

– Other methods for removing cured epoxy involve laser ablation and microwave induced plasma, which is widely used in the failure analysis industry. By combining different methods, the epoxy compound can be removed very efficiently without affecting functionality of a device. The result of the epoxy removal from encapsulated PCB is presented in Figure 12.2.

Figure 12.2. *IronKey device before and after epoxy removal. For a color version of this figure, see www.iste.co.uk/prouff/cryptography2.zip*

Once PCB is clear from any epoxy compound, its electronic components could be identified. This enables us to locate major components like microcontroller or FPGA, smaller ICs like USB controller and power regulators, and small components like capacitors, resistors, diodes and transistors.

Passive components such as resistors (white ceramic base with black top paint), capacitors (gray or brown ceramic package) and inductors (dark brown ceramic package) could be easily spotted. It is not always easy to distinguish between capacitors and inductors, but any digital multimeter can help. Inductors have resistance close to zero and capacitors have almost infinite resistance. The actual values of the components such as resistors, capacitors and inductors could be measured with an LCR meter.

Most 2-pin, 3-pin or even 4-pin devices are likely to be diodes and transistors. Small packages will be marked with SMD/SMT (surface-mount device/technology) codes because their full name will not fit within a small area. Their markings could be checked against SMD marking tables available from various providers. In some cases, the real name of a component could be found by a simple search on the Internet. Larger components are usually marked with a manufacturer's logo and real name of the device under which they could be found on the manufacturer's website.

Identification becomes more challenging if the IC has custom marking. There could be two outcomes – either the manufacturer decided to disguise the real name of the device or it is actually a custom made IC chip. The former could be bypassed by IC decapsulation and looking at the silicon die markings under an optical microscope. In most cases, the real name of the device will be clearly marked there. However, in small number of cases, there could still be factory custom markings even on standard chips. In this case, the device could be identified by its functionality and pinout. In a worst case scenario, some possible candidates could be ordered from distributors, decapsulated and compared with the chip in question. Usual places to look for SMD codes of the components are manufacturers' websites and SMD books.

The final step with the PCB analysis is creating a schematic of the device. In order to reconstruct the circuit diagram of the device, we need to trace all the wires on the PCB that connect all the components together. In the case of PCBs with only two layers, this process is tedious, but relatively straightforward. First, all the electronic components must be removed by desoldering them using a hot air gun at about 300°C and removing with tweezers or a blade. Then the remaining solder needs to be removed with a hot desoldering braid. Finally, the PCB has to be cleaned with a solvent and dried up. All the connection wires become clearly visible and easily traceable (Figure 12.3). In case of PCBs with four or more layers, each layer will need to be separated, for example, through a polishing process, then individually photographed before the overall picture is created (Figure 12.4). An alternative way of creating a 3D structure of the PCB that does not even require desoldering of components is an X-ray CT (computerized tomography) scan. It takes multiple images at different angles around the device and uses computer processing to reconstruct its 3D structure. Once the 3D image is created, each PCB layer could be individually focused at making wire tracing much easier (Figure 12.5). Then, the circuit diagram can be manually created from those PCB images using one of the CAD layout software tools, for example, Eagle from Autodesk.

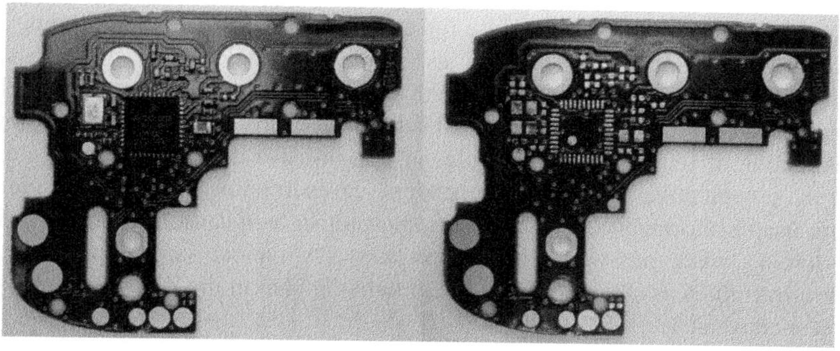

Figure 12.3. *Omnipod PCB before and after components removal. For a color version of this figure, see www.iste.co.uk/prouff/cryptography2.zip*

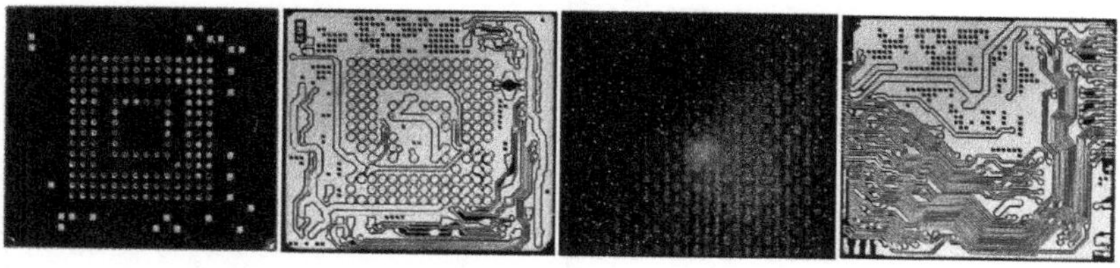

Figure 12.4. *eMMC package carrier at different depth of polishing. For a color version of this figure, see www.iste.co.uk/prouff/cryptography2.zip*

The circuit diagram or schematic of the device could help in identifying interconnections between ICs and spot any debug ports. The former could be useful for eavesdropping on communication protocols, while the latter might become useful for reverse engineering and firmware extraction. Some PCBs could contain dedicated test pads, leading to standard debug interfaces such as JTAG and SWD. Standard components like microcontrollers and FPGAs are likely to have well-documented debug pins. Those are likely to be the usual points of interest on the way to reverse engineering and better understanding the device functionality.

12.2.2. *Preparation at component level*

Sample preparation depends on the subsequent attack methods. Desoldering components and placing them on a test board is sufficient for most non-invasive attacks. These attacks are low cost as only moderately sophisticated equipment is required. In addition, they usually do not leave any tamper evidence as there is no physical harm to the device made during these attacks. The examples of non-invasive attacks include playing around with the supply voltage and clock signal in the form of power and clock glitching as this, for example, could affect the decoding and execution of individual CPU instructions. Another example is power analysis, in which we measure the fluctuations in the current consumed by the device. This allows various instructions and processed data to be clearly distinguished, leading to the extraction of secrets. Other examples of non-invasive attacks are timing attacks when the computation time is data dependent, eavesdropping on communication to acquire useful information, data injection into protocols to cause certain disruption, brute-forcing weak passwords and secret keys. A typical sample prepared for non-invasive attack is shown in Figure 12.6 with the chip in the ZIF socket on a test board for convenience.

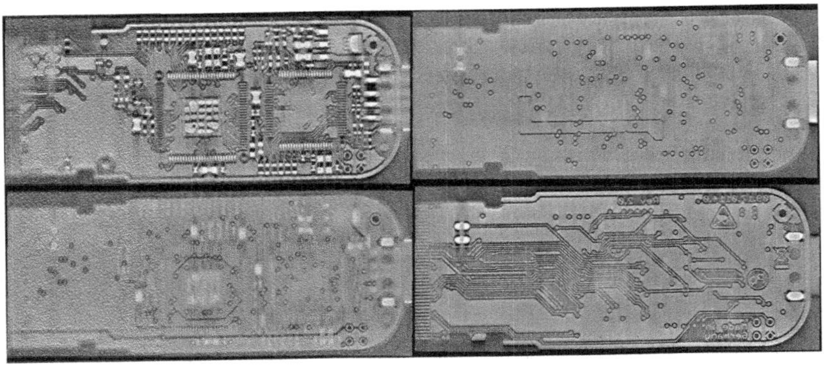

Figure 12.5. *Four PCB layers extracted with X-ray CT of Infineon Trust B evaluation kit*

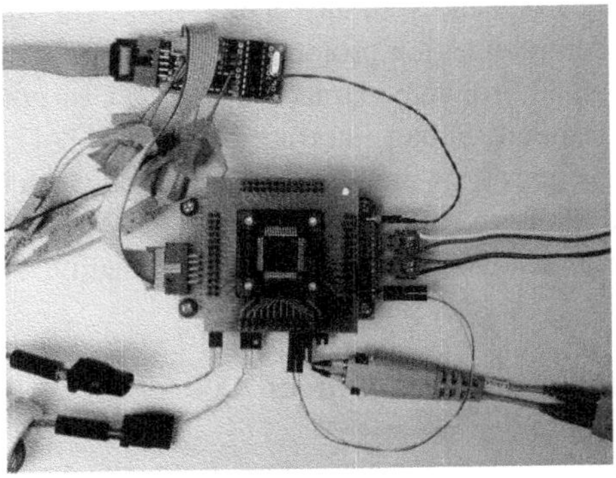

Figure 12.6. *Device prepared for non-invasive attack. For a color version of this figure, see www.iste.co.uk/prouff/cryptography2.zip*

Invasive and semi-invasive attacks start with the removal of a chip package to access its silicon die. Once the chip is opened, it is possible to perform probing or modification attacks. The most important tool for invasive attacks is a microprobing workstation. We have to remove at least part of the passivation layer before probes can establish contact. This could be done by etching, milling or by using a laser cutter. Plastic package material could be removed using chemical methods, typically with hot fuming nitric acid, or mechanically using precision CNC machines. Laser ablation can also be used for precise removal of plastic material, while preserving delicate bonding wires. However, its combination with microwave-induced plasma (MIP) decapsulation gives the best result in terms of speed and cleanliness of the surface.

Although chemical methods allow partial removal of the package material while preserving the device functionality, special attention must be paid to chips which use copper and silver for bonding wires. Unlike aluminum and gold wires (Figure 12.7), they will be quickly dissolved in fuming nitric acid. However, when a mixture of nitric and sulfuric acids is used, the wires will be preserved from dissolving (Figure 12.8). The alternative to chemical methods could be in using mechanical polishing followed by restoring the bonding wires with conductive paint, or in some cases the die of interest could require new connections to be established, which can be accomplished by soldering (Figure 12.9). For more sophisticated tasks, the new bonding wires could be established using wire bonding machines.

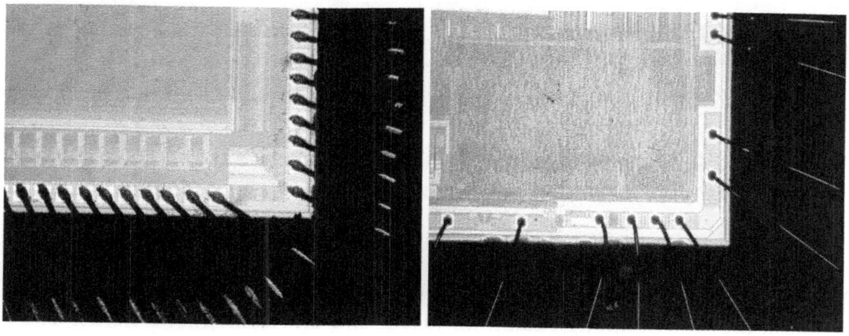

Figure 12.7. *Decapsulated dies with Aluminum and gold wires. For a color version of this figure, see www.iste.co.uk/prouff/cryptography2.zip*

All invasive attacks are quite complicated. They require hours or weeks in a specialized laboratory and, in the process, they destroy the package or even the device. In addition, invasive attacks require highly qualified specialists and a proper budget.

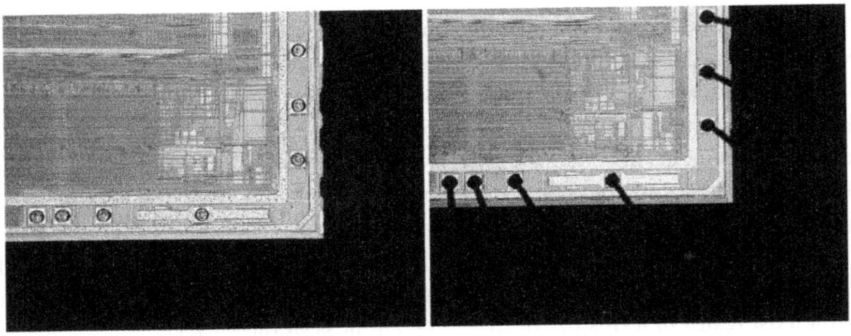

Figure 12.8. *Decapsulated die with copper wires. For a color version of this figure, see www.iste.co.uk/prouff/cryptography2.zip*

Figure 12.9. *Decapsulated dies bonded after invasive preparation. For a color version of this figure, see www.iste.co.uk/prouff/cryptography2.zip*

Semi-invasive attacks could be performed using such tools as UV light, X-rays and other sources of ionizing radiation, lasers and electromagnetic fields. They can be used individually or in conjunction with each other. Modern deep sub-micron semiconductor chips have multiple metal layers. Therefore, it is easier to approach their active area from the rear side of the bulk silicon substrate. For that, only part of the package that covers the bulk silicon needs to be mechanically removed, for example, using inexpensive engraving tools. Then, the laser could be directly focused through the silicon at the logic area or memory array. Electromagnetic pulses could also be applied from the rear side, thus injecting controllable faults. Although semi-invasive attacks are harder to implement as they require depackaging of the chip, very much less expensive equipment is needed than for invasive attacks. Also, these attacks can be performed in a reasonably short time. An example of the chip prepared for laser fault injection is presented in Figure 12.10.

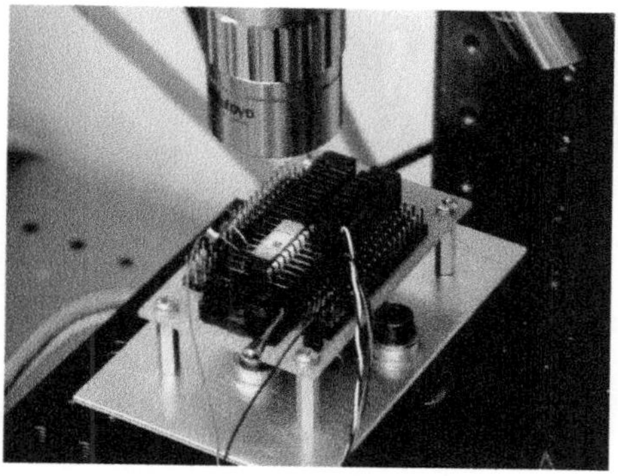

Figure 12.10. *Device prepared for semi-invasive attack. For a color version of this figure, see www.iste.co.uk/prouff/cryptography2.zip*

12.2.3. *Preparation at silicon level*

Most invasive attacks will require manipulations with the silicon die. This could be partial decapsulation for subsequent probing attacks or full decapsulation for subsequent reverse engineering. This is normally achieved with a pre-heated fuming nitric acid applied to a device through an aperture or stencil. For improving efficiency of laser fault injection attacks, the bulk silicon substrate of the die could be thinned from the usual 300 μm down to 20 μm or even less. For some packages, like flip-chip, this can be achieved by thinning the substrate on a lapping machine (Figure 12.11). The remaining thickness of the silicon must be controlled to avoid removing excessive material and permanently damaging the device. However, thinning silicon substrate down to approximately 2 μm is relatively safe for most modern CMOS devices. The most challenging packages for substrate thinning are BGA and QFN, where polishing will result in the removal of balls or pins within the package. For such packages, the substrate material must be selectively removed using specialized precision CNC machines. More precise polishing is required for deprocessing by removal of a specific number of internal layers inside the silicon die. For that more expensive lapping and CMP (chemical-mechanical polishing), machines should be used.

In silicon chips, the top-layer aluminum interconnect lines are covered by a passivation layer which needs to be removed before the probes can establish contact. The most convenient and easy-to-use passivation layer removing technique involves a laser cutting system. The system consists of the laser head mounted on the camera port of a microscope and the submicron-precision stage to move the sample. Such laser cutters can be bought second-hand at affordable cost.

Figure 12.11. *Thinning substrate on lapping machine. For a color version of this figure, see www.iste.co.uk/prouff/cryptography2.zip*

For modern chips with more than three metal layers or smaller than 0.35 μm fabrication process, more sophisticated tools such as focused ion beam (FIB) workstation have to be used. Although such equipment is expensive and require a lot of maintenance, these systems are widely used by universities across the world in physics, material science and engineering.

12.3. Probing attacks

Probing is used not only for signal observation or eavesdropping, but also to inject faults and new data. In some cases, this could be performed at a PCB level by soldering directly to the tracks or to IC pins. For example, if the debug interface is not wired to any connector, it could be custom built (Figure 12.12).

Figure 12.12. *Debug interface wired to the microcontroller. For a color version of this figure, see www.iste.co.uk/prouff/cryptography2.zip*

Figure 12.13. *Probing station (a) and probing needles landed on the chip surface (b). For a color version of this figure, see www.iste.co.uk/prouff/cryptography2.zip*

A microprobing station is one of the most important tools for invasive attacks. It consists of five elements: a microscope, stage, device test socket, micro-manipulators and probe tips. The microscope must have long working distance objectives – sufficient enough to accommodate six to eight probe tips (Figure 12.13) between the sample and the objective lens. It should also have enough depth of focus to follow the probe tip movement. For simple applications, a manually controlled probing station is enough. Passive probe tips are very cheap (only a few dollars), but active probes are quite expensive (over a hundred dollars); however, they can easily be built from an operational amplifier and a passive tip soldered directly to its input.

Some chips have additional debug interfaces which are not connected to any pins. In this case, the decapsulated device can be placed on a probing station and then all the necessary connections to the debug port established with probing tips.

Usually, to extract the information such as memory contents or a secret key, microprobing is applied to the internal CPU data bus. It is difficult to observe the whole bus at a time in one go and various techniques can be used to overcome this. For instance, the same transaction or memory read operation can be repeated many times and then two to four probes are used to observe the signals, which are then combined into a complete bus trace.

In order to establish a contact with internal wires, the insulation above them must be removed. For that, a laser cutter can be used with 100× objective lens. However, it is only practical to remove the insulation layer above the top metal layer. Therefore, all data bus lines have to be traced to their presence in the top metal layer. Then, probing needles can be placed on all eight data bus lines using micropositioners of the probing station. The view on the chip surface under the probing station's microscope with the probing needles landed on the data bus is presented in Figure 12.14. By injecting certain data into the data bus and observing the response from CPU, it was possible to bypass data bus encryption and inject an arbitrary code for execution. Modern chips fabricated with deep sub-micron processes and multiple metal layers would require sophisticated tools like FIB to establish a contact with internal wires and bring a test point to the surface (Figure 12.15).

Figure 12.14. *Probing tips landed on the data bus of the chip. For a color version of this figure, see www.iste.co.uk/prouff/cryptography2.zip*

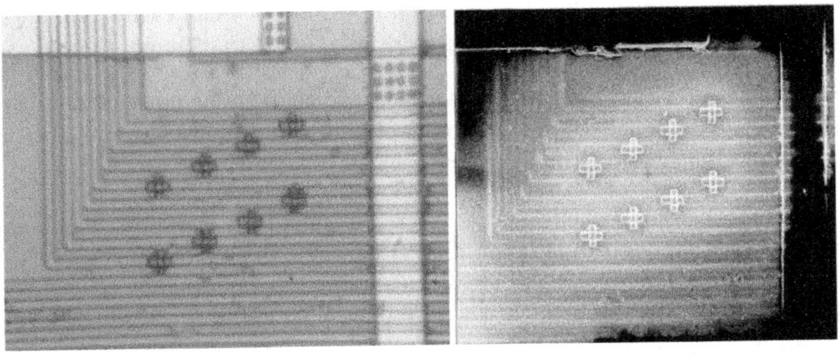

Figure 12.15. *Optical and SEM images of test points created under FIB. For a color version of this figure, see www.iste.co.uk/prouff/cryptography2.zip*

More sophisticated tools like FIB workstations can be used to perform attacks. FIB workstations simplify manual probing of deep metal and polysilicon lines. They can also be used for modification of the chip structure by cutting wires and creating new interconnect lines.

12.4. Delayering and reverse engineering

Another approach to understand how particular chip works is to reverse engineer it. The first step is to create a map of a new processor. It could be done by using a microscope to produce high-resolution photographs of the chip surface. The attacker has to be familiar with CMOS VLSI design techniques and chip architectures, but the necessary knowledge is easily available from numerous textbooks. Deeper layers can only be recognized in a second series of photographs after the metal layers have been stripped off, which can be achieved by chemical etching or by polishing the chip's die with a CMP machine.

There are two main applications of deprocessing. One is to remove the passivation layer, exposing the top metal layer for microprobing attacks. Another is to gain access to the deep layers and observe the internal structure of the chip. The best way to understand the functionality of a chip is to reverse engineer it. However, in practice, this process is very tedious and time consuming. Although all transistors, diodes and passive components inside the device are in the same planar layer, all interconnections between them are usually located in multiple metal layers and a polysilicon layer. In old chips, it was possible to see all the layers under an optical microscope as there were usually only one or two metal layers, while the fabrication process was above 0.5 μm. High-resolution optical microscopes allow each layer to be brought into focus while blurring out-of-focal-plane features. That way, the internal layers could be imaged without deprocessing. In modern chips with more than three metal layers, each layer must be individually exposed for imaging. The imaging itself is usually done with a scanning electron microscope (SEM) because optical microscopes cannot provide resolution better than 100 nm, while even entry level SEMs could offer 10 nm resolution. However, SEMs are not good for imaging structures well below the surface without seriously compromising on the resolution. Therefore, only a single metal layer exposed to the surface could be imaged under SEM with vias going to the next layer imaged at a higher acceleration voltage. As a result, each chip must be deprocessed to each metal layer, then to its polysilicon layer and finally to the transistor layer for taking high-resolution photographs under SEM. There are different deprocessing methods, each having their own pros and cons.

12.4.1. *Chemical deprocessing*

Conductive layers that form the signal wires inside the chip are made from aluminum or copper for top layers and polysilicon for the bottom layer. Interconnects between layers, called vias, could contain aluminum, copper, tungsten, titanium, silicides and nitrides. A passivation layer that protects the whole structure from moisture and air is at the very top and is usually made from silicon oxide or nitride. Inside plastic packages, the passivation layer is often covered with a polymer layer, usually polyimide, to protect against sharp grains in the compound during the package formation.

In wet chemical etching, each layer is removed by specific chemicals and this allows good selectivity over different materials. For example, a silicon dioxide insulation layer could be selectively removed without an etching metal layer. However, its downside is in the isotropic nature of the process that is uniformity in all directions. This produces unwanted undercutting. As a result, narrow metal lines will have a tendency to lift off the surface (Figure 12.16). Isotropic etching also leads to etching through holes such as vias, resulting in unwanted etching of underlying wires. In addition, some areas will be etched sooner than others due to the uneven distribution of chemicals in heterogeneous reactions, which happen between solid material and liquid solution. As a result, chemical etching is only used in specific cases such as removing top layers to expose transistors layer, removing bulk silicon, selective etching of metal or doped regions.

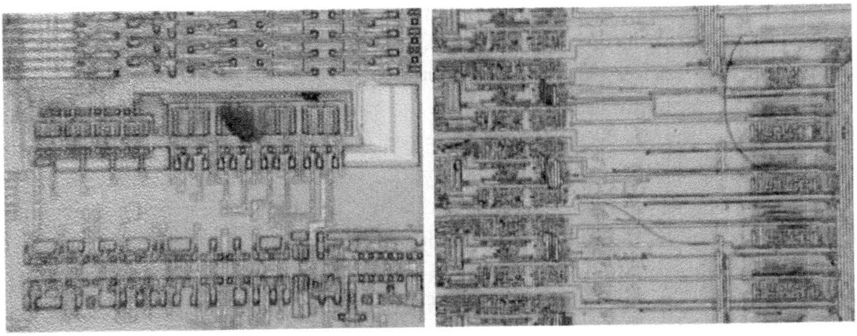

Figure 12.16. *1 μm (a) and 0.5 μm (b) chip after its top layer was chemically etched. For a color version of this figure, see www.iste.co.uk/prouff/cryptography2.zip*

12.4.2. *Mechanical deprocessing*

Mechanical polishing or lapping is performed with the use of abrasive materials. The process is time-consuming and requires special machines to maintain the planarity of the surface. From the inspection perspective, the advantages of using polishing over wet and dry etching techniques is the ability to remove layer by layer and view features in the area of interest within the same plane. It is especially useful on multi-layer interconnect processes fabricated with advanced planarization techniques. Polishing works well when it is necessary to remove a large amount of material. For example, when part of the plastic or ceramic package is needed to be removed, or for backside thinning. The major disadvantages of the lapping process are difficulty in maintaining flatness of the surface and inevitable scratches created by abrasive material embedded into polishing discs (Figure 12.17).

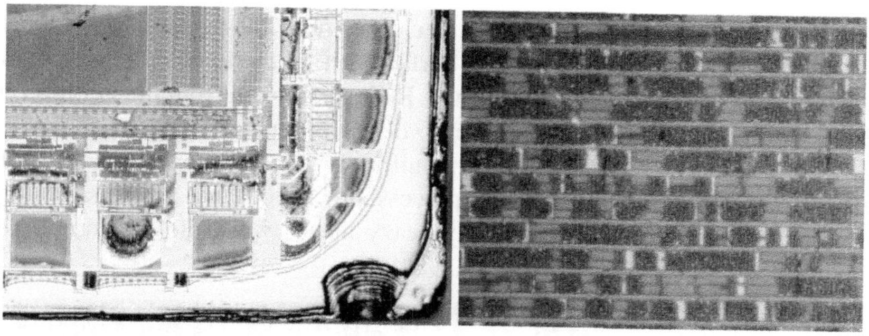

Figure 12.17. *Surface of the chip after lapping: (a) corner; (b) logic area. For a color version of this figure, see www.iste.co.uk/prouff/cryptography2.zip*

12.4.3. *Chemical–mechanical polishing (CMP) deprocessing*

CMP is the most widely used method. It combines fine mechanical removal with some chemicals helping in selective removal of certain material. However, it lacks the uniform removal of internal IC layers. Nevertheless, it gives very smooth surfaces and maintains flatness throughout the entire surface of the chip (Figure 12.18). The process requires special lapping machines equipped with felt discs and precision positioning of the sample, preferably with automatically controlled feeding of the slurry, which contains very fine abrasive particles suspended in a liquid with added chemicals.

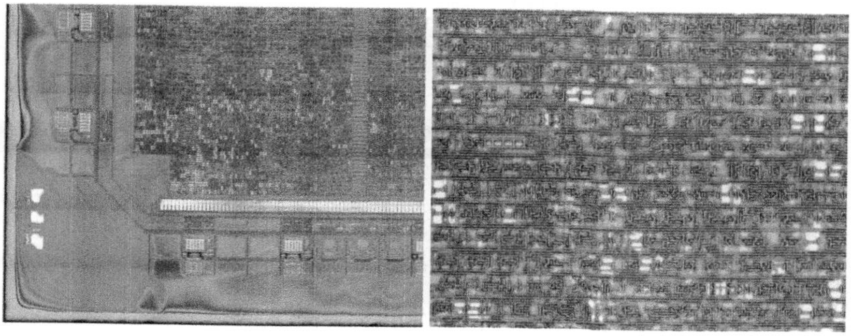

Figure 12.18. *Surface of the chip after CMP: (a) corner; (b) logic area. For a color version of this figure, see www.iste.co.uk/prouff/cryptography2.zip*

12.4.4. *Plasma, RIE and FIB deprocessing*

Both plasma and reactive-ion etching use radicals created from a gas inside a special chamber. However, in plasma etching, the gas molecules are ionized before reaching the sample's surface, while in RIE, the sample is placed directly on the RF electrode. As the ions are accelerated in an electric field, they usually hit the surface of the sample perpendicularly. Only the surfaces hit by the ions are removed; sides perpendicular to their paths are not touched. Radicals formed from the gas react with the material on the sample surface to form volatile products, which are pumped out of the chamber. This results in the layers uniformly removed across a large surface (Figure 12.19). Unfortunately, these deprocessing methods are not suitable for all types of material inside chips, especially heavy metals which do not form volatile compounds.

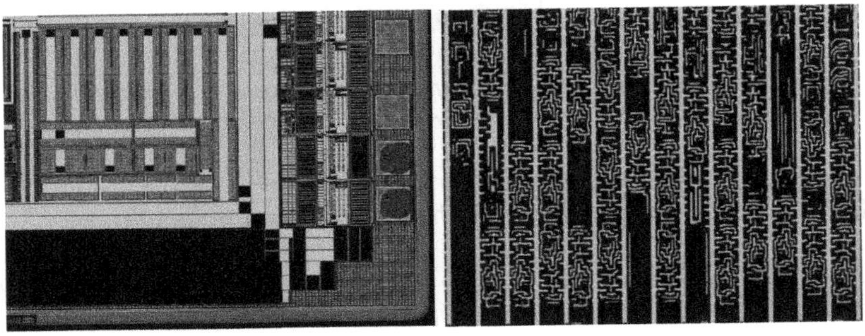

Figure 12.19. *Surface of the chip after RIE: (a) corner; (b) logic area. For a color version of this figure, see www.iste.co.uk/prouff/cryptography2.zip*

Some FIB machines are equipped with special gas injectors that allow fast and controlled etching of surface material. Although suitable for wide range of materials, they have limited size of the etching area. Table 12.1 outlines the discussed delayering methods with their pros and cons.

Method	Application	Advantages	Disadvantages
Grinding	Packaging and films	Fast, inexpensive	Rough surface, deep scratches
Lapping	Bonding wires, layers	Affordable	Uneven surface with scratches
CMP	Layers	Acceptable flatness	Uneven removal
Plasma and RIE	Layers	Good flatness	Not suitable for all materials
FIB etch	Layers	Uniform removal	Limited area of application

Table 12.1. *Sample preparation methods*

12.4.5. *Staining techniques*

Dash etching can help in distinguishing between p- and n-doped regions in the transistor layer. This helps in identification of CMOS library elements (Figure 12.20). That way, secure library elements can be spotted and Mask ROM content from some secure ICs could be extracted. Recipes for selective etching of different material are described in Beck (1998).

Figure 12.20. *Optical and SEM images of the logic area after selective dash etching*

12.4.6. *From images to netlist*

Once the samples are prepared and delayered, the next step is imaging. For structures down to 120 nm, optical microscopes can be used. For deep sub-micron structures present in modern chips, electron microscopes must be used. Modern microscopes are usually equipped with motorized stages and their software is capable of acquiring images automatically and storing them on a hard drive. Hence, imaging of a large area is only a question of properly configuring the software and the time required to take thousands of shots.

The next step is stitching the frames within the same layer. There are two approaches to this process: the images can be merged into a very large picture, or a database that holds coordinates of multiple tiles can be created. Given the high resolution of the images, there could be some performance issues when a large graphic file is processed. For example, a 1×1 mm^2 area imaged with 10 nm per pixel resolution will result in $100{,}000\times100{,}000$ pixels image. In the meantime, the database can be established by first merging the neighboring frames together before splitting them into tiles of fixed sizes. As a result, the alignment and processing of the layers could be done much faster.

For further processing, the final pictures of each layer must be aligned such that the same structural elements appear at the same coordinates. That way, it would become easier to trace the wires which usually go multiple times from one layer to another. Images can be merged, aligned and processed using various image editor software tools. For example, open source graphic editor GIMP allows various image manipulations, merging, and can handle multiple layers. Figure 12.21 shows the images of the same area after deprocessing and alignment: three metal layers, polysilicon layer and diffusion layer.

If in old chips everything was built from discrete transistors, then in modern devices, functionality is created by connecting standard logic cells with wires. Hence, it is wise to identify those standard cells and find their representations across the device. This is normally done in the image of the transistor layer, which is the very bottom layer exposed after deprocessing. This layer is also called diffusion layer or active layer. Each type of the element or gate such as flip-flop, NAND, NOR and XOR must be identified and named. The same applies to discrete components such as resistors, capacitors, individual diodes and transistors.

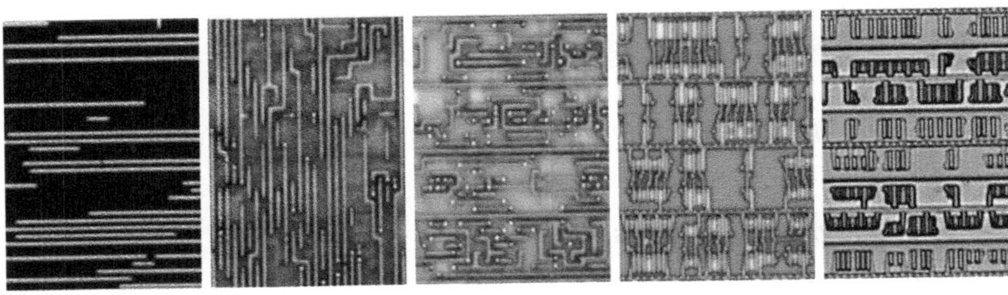

Figure 12.21. *Layers in 0.35 μm chip: (a) metal 3; (b) metal 2; (c) metal 1; (d) polysilicon; (e) diffusion. For a color version of this figure, see www.iste.co.uk/prouff/cryptography2.zip*

Finally, the connections between all the identified cells and components must be traced, thus creating the large schematic of the chip. The tracing is performed by following the wires from the input and output of the cells. Those wires could go in multiple layers and wires in different layers are connected together using vias – tiny metal links between metals, polysilicon and diffusion layers. After that, the netlist can be created. This represents description of all the elements and their interconnections. It can be viewed as a schematic image which is similar to a circuit diagram in electronics. Figure 12.22 shows different steps in the reverse engineering process from obtaining the SEM images and overlaying them to digitizing, selecting certain layers, extracting schematics for part of the circuit and Verilog simulation.

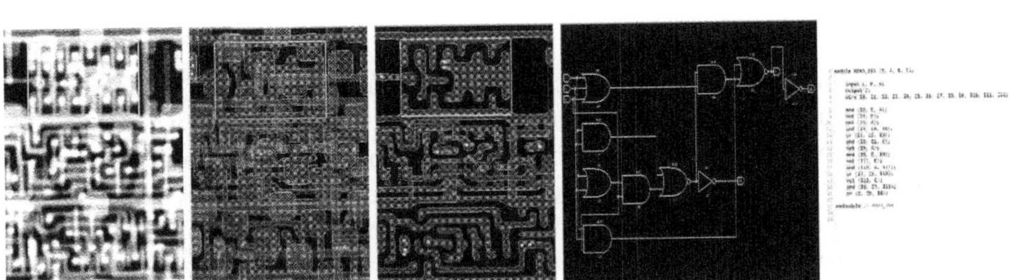

Figure 12.22. *Reverse engineering phases: (a) SEM overlay image; (b) digitized area overlay; (c) tracing specific layers; (d) schematic image; (e) Verilog description. For a color version of this figure, see www.iste.co.uk/prouff/cryptography2.zip*

The overall process and the outcome is very similar to that for PCB reverse engineering. The differences are in types of components, materials and dimensions. There are specialized software tools which could make the reverse engineering process less tedious. Among them, the most known ones are several commercial software tools: Pix2Net from MicroNet Solutions, Hierux from Cellixsoft and ChipJuice from Texplained, as well as an open source tool called Degate. Those tools assist in IC reverse engineering process offering automation and assistance for some steps such as stitching, cells identification, wire tracing and netlist extraction. Some of those tools can also help in the analysis of the netlist in order to identify hardware blocks, modules and functions. However, many standard chip designing tools such as Cadence from Cadence Design Systems can accept netlist and use it for simulation and design observation.

Reverse engineering helps in understanding the hardware and spotting weaknesses otherwise not visible during the normal design process. This way, a developer could look at the device as a black box and independently evaluate its security protection.

12.5. Memory dump and hardware cloning

Hardware cloning is the process of creating a component without investment into its design. Functional cloning could be done by observing the behavior of a device. This is only suitable for relatively simple devices where enough information could be collected with eavesdropping on its communication. Brute-forcing can be used to clone PLD and CPLD devices, which have a limited number of internal states. Modern systems are usually based on CPUs, microcontrollers, FPGAs and SoCs. Therefore, their cloning could be accomplished by copying their embedded memory, either the user data or bitstream. For security sensitive applications, developers tend to use devices with embedded memory, thus making any access to the code and data more problematic. In addition, some devices offer hardware encryption of the on-chip memory to make such access even more challenging, but not impossible.

For most custom-designed devices, the only practical way to understand their functionality is via reverse engineering of their silicon. However, the majority of systems around us are based on standard devices programmed with user code and data. Their analysis could be performed through disassembling and decompilation of the code stored in their embedded memory. In that respect, the attempt to extract and analyze the code becomes the first step in the hardware security evaluation of many devices.

If a device has a well documented debugging interface (JTAG or similar) that had been disabled by the developer, then most attacks will be aimed at bypassing this protection. However, for many devices there will be the lack of detailed documentation on their debugging interface or other means of access to the embedded memory. In this case there could be several options to obtain such knowledge. If the device has on-chip Mask ROM then most likely it would contain a factory test code or bootloader for uploading programmable memory such as EEPROM, Flash or SRAM. Information inside a Mask ROM array is usually stored in the form of present and absent transistors which is then turned into 0s and 1s by the memory control logic. The actual encoding could therefore be present inside a metal layer, a polysilicon layer, a diffusion layer or in a via layer. As a result, different deprocessing techniques must be used to make these encodings visible (Figure 12.23). When the encoding is done via different levels of doping concentration inside memory cell transistors, special staining techniques must be used after all top layers are stripped off the chip surface (Figure 12.24).

Figure 12.23. *Examples of deprocessed mask ROMs: (a) wet etching to metal 1; (b) wet etching to diffusion; (c) plasma etching to diffusion. For a color version of this figure, see www.iste.co.uk/prouff/cryptography2.zip*

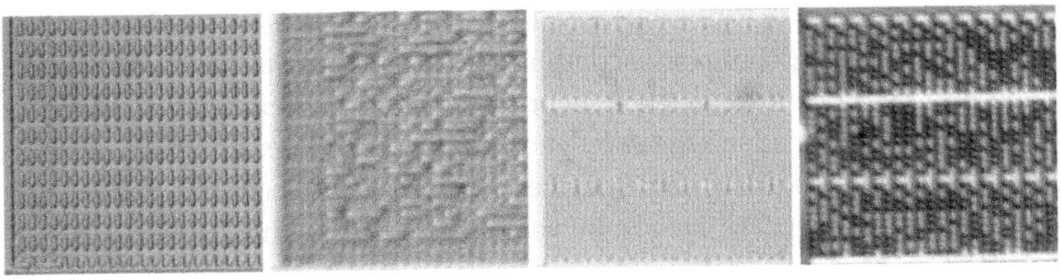

Figure 12.24. *Examples of stained mask ROMs: (a) deprocessed NOR ROM; (b) stained NOR ROM; (c) deprocessed NAND ROM; (d) stained NAND ROM. For a color version of this figure, see www.iste.co.uk/prouff/cryptography2.zip*

For data extraction from EEPROM and Flash, more sophisticated methods must be used. Some chips might have hidden backdoors that allow such access; however, finding those interfaces and exploiting them could be an extremely challenging task that often requires some level of reverse engineering to learn more about the device features. Microprobing could also help with data extraction when other methods fail; however, it is a more expensive approach. Ultimately, special tools such as atomic force microscopes and SEMs could directly image the state of memory cell transistors. However, this kind of approach requires sophisticated sample preparation methods and much slower than through electrical interfaces. Figure 12.25 shows conventional and advanced images of the Flash array in a modern chip using SEM. For some custom silicon devices, direct extraction using SEM imaging could be the most practical way of data extraction and analysis.

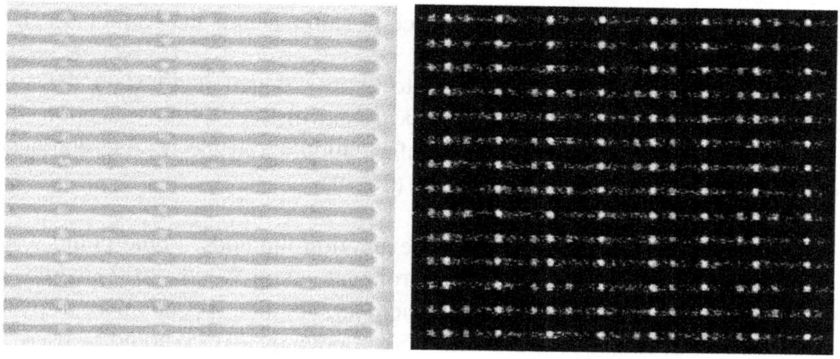

Figure 12.25. *Flash area SEM imaging in 90-nm chip: (a) conventional image; (b) advanced contrast image*

12.6. Conclusion

The methods discussed in this chapter can be used for attacking the devices. However, they can also be used for analyzing the existing security protection features and improving them. By finding weak spots in the hardware security and improving them, both the cost and time of possible attacks could be increased.

12.7. Notes and further references

– Section 12.2.1. The physical protection at PCB level is discussed. National Institute of Standards and Technology published FIPS 140-2 standard in Lee et al. (2001), which outlines requirements for physical protection of devices. Kingston Technology Company, Inc. (2018) is an example of a FIPS 140-2 Level 3 certified device. Microwave-induced plasma (Tang et al. 2017) could be used as an alternative to chemical decapsulation of various devices and careful removal of epoxy. Identification of SMD components present on PCBs could become easier with the use of SMD books (Turuta 2019).

– Section 12.2.2. Some examples of the initial preparation at the components level are given. Power and clock glitching was discussed in Anderson and Kuhn (1996).

Power analysis attacks were introduced in Kocher et al. (1999). Various kinds of semi-invasive and invasive attacks are described in Skorobogatov (2005).

– Section 12.3. Introduces probing attacks. Active probes could be made from relatively inexpensive components as described in Skorobogatov (2005). By placing a probing needle on the CPU bus, it is possible to inject an arbitrary code even into encrypted data bus (Skorobogatov 2017b). Chip modification could be used to bypass sophisticated security protections as described in Kömmerling and Kuhn (1999).

– Section 12.4.5. Staining techniques to expose doped regions on the silicon substrate are introduced. The recipes can be found in Beck (1998). Section 12.4.6 discusses netlist creation methods. More information about the reverse engineering process can be found in Torrance and James (2009).

– Section 12.5. This outlines memory extraction methods. Some could rely on undocumented features and backdoors (Skorobogatov and Woods 2012), while other methods require direct access to embedded memory. For that, special microscopy tools such as AFM (Nardi et al. 2006) and SEM (Skorobogatov 2017a) could be used.

12.8. References

Anderson, R.J. and Kuhn, M. (1996). Tamper resistance: A cautionary note. In *WOEC'96: Proceedings of the 2nd Conference on Proceedings of the Second USENIX Workshop on Electronic Commerce – Volume 2*. ACM, New York.

Beck, F. (1998). *Integrated Circuit Failure Analysis: A Guide to Preparation Techniques*. Wiley, Hoboken.

Kingston Technology Company, Inc. (2018). FIPS 140-2 non-proprietary security policy: Ironkey d300 series usb flash drive. Kingston Technology Company, Inc.

Kocher, P.C., Jaffe, J., Jun, B. (1999). Differential power analysis. In *Advances in Cryptology – CRYPTO' 99*. Springer, Heidelberg.

Kömmerling, O. and Kuhn, M.G. (1999). Design principles for tamper-resistant smartcard processors. In *USENIX Workshop on Smartcard Technology (Smartcard 99)*. Chicago.

Lee, A., Smid, M.E., Snouffer, S.R. (2001). Security requirements for cryptographic modules. NIST, FIPS PUB 140-2.

Nardi, C.D., Desplats, R., Perdu, P., Guérin, C., Gauffier, J.L., Amundsen, T.B. (2006). Direct measurements of charge in floating gate transistor channels of flash memories using scanning capacitance microscopy. In *ISTFA 2006: Conference Proceedings from the 32nd International Symposium for Testing and Failure Analysis*. Electronic Device Failure Analysis Society and ASM International, Austin.

Skorobogatov, S. (2005). Semi-invasive attacks – A new approach to hardware security analysis. Technical Report, University of Cambridge, UCAM-CL-TR-630.

Skorobogatov, S. (2017a). Deep dip teardown of tubeless insulin pump. *arXiv:1709.06026*.

Skorobogatov, S. (2017b). How microprobing can attack encrypted memory. In *2017 Euromicro Conference on Digital System Design (DSD)*. IEEE, Vienna.

Skorobogatov, S. and Woods, C. (2012). Breakthrough silicon scanning discovers backdoor in military chip. In *Cryptographic Hardware and Embedded Systems – CHES 2012*, Prouff, E. and Schaumont, P. (eds). Springer, Heidelberg.

Tang, J., Wang, B., Liu, C., Wang, J., Beenakker, C.I.M. (2017). Unique failure analysis capabilities enabled by the mip decapsulation technique. In *2017 IEEE 24th International Symposium on the Physical and Failure Analysis of Integrated Circuits (IPFA)*. Chengdu.

Torrance, R. and James, D. (2009). The state-of-the-art in IC reverse engineering. In *Cryptographic Hardware and Embedded Systems – CHES 2009*, Clavier, C. and Gaj, K. (eds). Springer, Heidelberg.

Turuta (2019). Active SMD semiconductor components marking codes. SMD-Codes Databook [Online]. Available at: http://www.turuta.md.

13

Gate-Level Protection

Sylvain GUILLEY[1] and Jean-Luc DANGER[2]

[1]*Secure-IC S.A.S., Cesson-Sévigné, France*

[2]*Télécom Paris, Institut Polytechnique de Paris, France*

13.1. Introduction

Many modern cryptographic algorithms are theoretically robust and immune from practical cryptanalysis in the "black box" model. However, some methods can be deployed to break the security by attacking the physical implementation of virtually any algorithm. These attacks can be mounted by merely observing or perturbing the targeted system. Observing the activity of the system and its correlation with potential guesses can yield sensitive information. Such attacks are better known as side-channel attacks (SCAs). When a device is perturbed such that it yields a non-nominal output, this together with expected output can lead to the secret key. Such attacks are called differential fault analyses (DFAs).

From the attacker point of view, the advantage of SCAs is that they can be perpetrated while the target system operates in its comfort zone. In such conditions, from the defense perspective, it is difficult to detect that the activity of the target is being observed. To defeat SCA efficiently, the countermeasures have to at least be submitted at the logic level.

Dual-rail with precharge logic (DPL) is a class of countermeasures which aims to make the device activity constant and independent of the data processed. DPL operates at the gate level: therefore, any single Boolean operation is protected against information leakage. It consists of balancing the side-channel leakage by activating

Embedded Cryptography 2,
coordinated by Emmanuel PROUFF, Guénaël RENAULT,
Matthieu RIVAIN and Colin O'FLYNN.

either one part of the gate, or its complement, depending on the value to be generated. Owing to this redundant representation, such gates can also be used to detect errors, and hence offer DFA resistance as a by-product.

The gates obeying DPL are fairly large in terms of silicon area: overheads of factors 3–5 are to be expected, depending on the security level. Security indeed comes at a cost. However, it is interesting to note that the societal and technological trends indeed make this apparent drawback acceptable. Embedded devices are becoming widespread and manipulate data that are more and more precious. Thus, the asset of an integrated circuit (IC) is expected to protect sensitive information which increases every day in quantity and in value. In the meantime, the fabrication of ICs is becoming more and more efficient, allowing for an exponential increase in integration capacity (tendency known as Moore's law). Thus, for those two reasons, it is interesting to trade silicon area for an increased security level conveyed by DPL: achieving the greatest security is more and more economically relevant as security needs are increasing and the silicon area is getting cheaper.

In this chapter, we propose an overview of the main gate-level styles, with a focus on their vulnerabilities against both side-channel and fault attacks.

The rest of the chapter is organized as follows. Section 13.2 presents the DPL countermeasure at the logical level and the major vulnerabilities incurred by the backend. Then, section 13.3 describes how the vulnerabilities are addressed by the already evaluated logic styles in either FPGA or ASIC. Section 13.4 explains how some optimizations and original solutions can be found using specific technologies. A synoptic comparison between the known logic styles is drawn in section 13.5. Finally, conclusions and perspectives are discussed in section 13.6.

13.2. DPL principle, built-in DFA resistance, and latent side-channel vulnerabilities

13.2.1. *Information hiding rationale*

The aim of DPL is to hide the internal circuit's activity from a prospective attacker. If any sensitive variable update occurs with a constant activity, it is likely that all side-channels are also updated. Therefore, the measurable quantity from an attacker's point of view is independent from any secret value. The protocol of the DPL consists of two phases: precharge and evaluation. The precharge phase allows new computations from a known electrical state to start. It thus prevents unexpected transitions between two computation steps. The dual-rail signalization of the data is conveyed by two wires for each Boolean variable: NULL $= (0,0)$ or $(1,1)$ while in precharge and

$\texttt{VALID} \in \{(0,1),(1,0)\}$ while in evaluation. Therefore, every evaluation consists of the transition of exactly one wire:

$$(0,0) \rightarrow (0,1) \qquad \text{or} \qquad (0,0) \rightarrow (1,0).$$

If the design is adequately balanced, an attacker will be unable to discern which transition actually occurred.

13.2.2. *DPL built-in DFA resistance*

Single bit faults are inefficient against DPL because they turn a VALID data into a NULL token that propagates and leads to a non-exploitable error since it hides the faulted value. This is the typical scenario described in the seminal paper by Selmane et al. (2009), introducing the intrinsic immunity of DPL against some classes of DFA.

Highly multiple faults ($(1,0) \leftrightarrow (0,1)$) randomly generate a large quantity of NULL values along with some more unlikely but devastating bit-flips. However, as NULL values are systematically propagated, they proliferate very quickly after some combinatorial logic layers traversal. And as they have the nice property to contaminate VALID values, the risky coherent bit-flips (simultaneous $0 \xrightarrow{*} 1$ and $1 \xrightarrow{*} 0$ in one dual-rail couple) have a great chance of being jammed through the propagation toward the algorithm output. This absorption property is all the more efficient as the number of NULL generated by the multiple faults is high. Therefore, the only way to inject a poisonous fault is to stress the circuit sufficiently enough to have multiple faults, without nonetheless creating too many faults so as to leave a chance for them not to be absorbed during their percolation towards the outputs.

13.2.3. *Vulnerabilities with respect to side-channel attacks*

Although perfectly sound at the logical level, DPL ends up being concretely implemented in physical devices. Now, the logical description of DPL ignores any timing and capacitance's notions.

Regarding the timing, three unbalanced behaviors can occur. On the way from the precharge to the evaluation, and vice-versa, the following can exist:

1) spurious transitions, referred to as glitches, that negate the hypothesis of activity invariability;

2) early evaluation (EE) effects: take place if the gate switching depends on the difference between the arrival time of the inputs;

3) technological bias: this flaw comes from the imbalance between the dual signals. It can be caused by the manufacturing dispersion, the place-and-route stage or merely the types of gate driving the true and false networks. This could be exploited by an attacker who measures the signal emanating from one wire of a pair.

The cross-coupling is another issue endangering the security of DPL designs.

Section 13.3 explains how these latent flaws have been addressed by some existing DPL logics, whereas section 13.4 illustrates technology-dependent optimizations and innovative solutions.

13.3. DPL families based on standard cells

13.3.1. *WDDL*

Wave dynamic differential logic (WDDL) meets all of the logical constraints of a DPL. The initial state is propagated by a wave of $(0,0)$ couples through the netlist thanks to the use solely of positive gates. The fact that exactly one half of the gates evaluate results from the duality between the true and false networks. In addition, the positivity of WDDL ensures the absence of glitches in the complete netlist. Note that WDDL with gates propagating the NULL spacer, but without being positive, is easily broken in practice. However,WDDL is prone to EE and early precharge. The early evaluation (EE) effect comes from the difference of delay between two variables of a same gate. Figure 13.1 illustrates the EE flaw when variable a is in advance to variable b. In this case, the output does not switch at the same time.

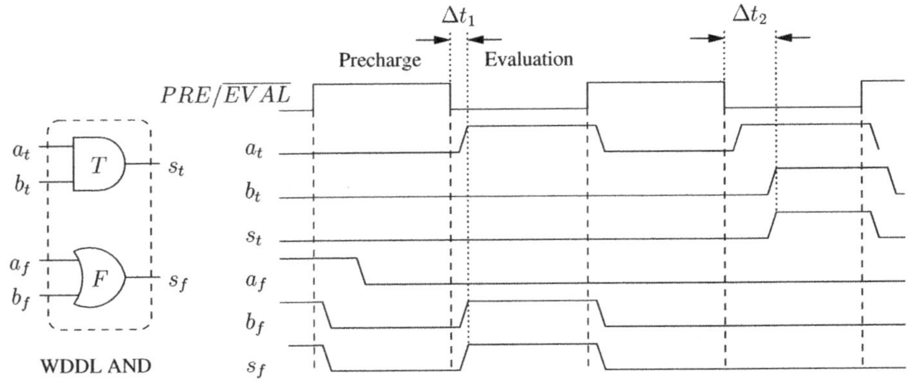

Figure 13.1. *WDDL AND gate with the early evaluation flaw*

Moreover, the dual networks are not necessarily balanced, since the transistor structures of $x \mapsto f(x)$ and $x \mapsto \overline{f(\overline{x})}$ differ. Therefore, either incremental improvements or radically novel strategies have shown up.

13.3.2. *MDPL*

Masked dual-rail with precharge logic (MDPL) is an attempt to fix the otherwise imbalance of WDDL. The assumption is that, in some conditions, it can be difficult to constrain a router to balance the differential interconnect. The fat wire and duplication methods allow the ASIC designer to balance the dual routing in ASIC. The transposition to FPGA is possible, albeit with less fine-grain control over the result. For this reason, MDPL proposes to swap the true and false routes randomly, so as to emancipate from the fatal routing unbalance. By the same token, it makes up for the structural unbalance of the dual pair of gates. The only gates involved in the logic are majority functions, both for the true and the false networks. Nonetheless, MDPL fails to provide a solution to the EE and precharge of WDDL. A fix is proposed under the name iMDPL.

13.3.3. *DRSL*

The primary focus of dual-rail random switching logic (DRSL) is to make the evaluation and the precharge gates data independent. For this reason, one pairwise unanimity gate[1] computes the validity of all inputs prior to allowing the gate to deliver any result, thus avoiding the EE flaw. On the contrary, the unanimity makes it possible for the overall DRSL logic to always anticipate the precharge. However, in the original design of DRSL, the functions are not required to be positive. The example of the AND function is sketched in Figure 13.2(a). Hence, the presence of data-dependent glitches in the return to precharge phase.

An extensive simulation of the DRSL AND gate has been carried out when it returns to precharge. Table 13.1 shows the situation where the mask is the fastest to return to NULL. More precisely, we assume that m returns to precharge first, followed by a and b in this order, which we abbreviate as $t_{m \to \text{NULL}} < t_{a \to \text{NULL}} < t_{b \to \text{NULL}}$. It happens that the DRSL AND gate glitches iff $a \oplus b = 1$, irrespective of the mask value.

Notice that it could have been anticipated that the glitching property does not depend on m if the mask is particular (e.g. the fastest signal) and a and b are equivalent. Indeed, when $m = 0$, there will be a glitching pattern for the DRSL AND

1 The pairwise unanimity Boolean gate performs the following computation: $(x_T, x_F, y_T, y_F, \ldots, z_T, z_F) \mapsto (x_T + x_F) \cdot (y_T + y_F) \cdot \ldots \cdot (z_T + z_F)$.

gate computing in the direct convention, whereas when $m = 1$, the glitching pattern will correspond to a complemented interpretation for the functional signals a and b. As, by design of DRSL, the attacker cannot make the difference between a transition occurring on a true or a false wire, and the glitches will be observed without any distinction for each value of m. As a return to NULL with a glitch consists of three transitions (one functional plus two non-functional), whereas a return to NULL without a glitch consists of a single transition, a correlation of the traces with the value $a \oplus b$ will yield a peak. Assuming that $a \oplus b$ is sensitive and predictable, this correlation is a means to test hypotheses.

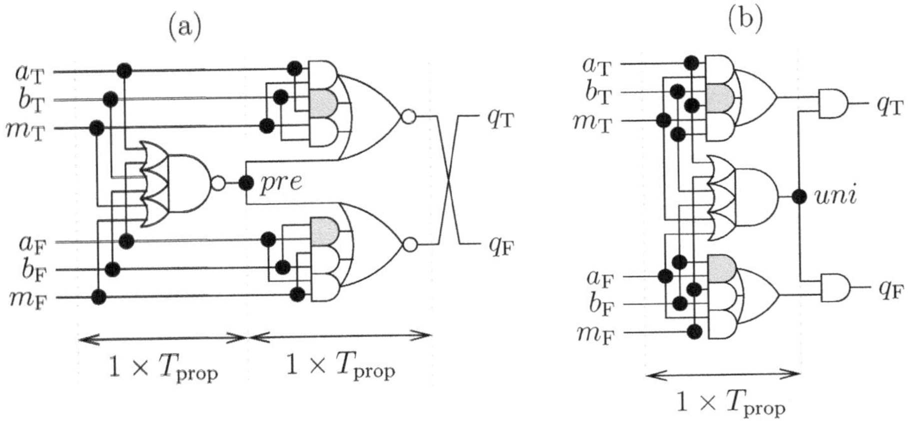

Figure 13.2. *(a) Genuine DRSL AND gate and (b) a glitch-free variant*

Other types of transitions ordering have been studied. In the cases where $t_{a \to \text{NULL}} < t_{m \to \text{NULL}} < t_{b \to \text{NULL}}$ or $t_{a \to \text{NULL}} < t_{b \to \text{NULL}} < t_{m \to \text{NULL}}$, the DRSL gate also features glitches, when $b \oplus m = 1$, irrespective of the value of variable a. But given that m is an unknown quantity, these glitches do not convey any information about the value of b. The glitches are thus innocuous in these cases. There is, however, a possible flaw if b is known (e.g. it is a primary input, such as one bit of the plaintext). In this case, the value of the cryptoprocessor-wide mask bit (i.e. only one bit of entropy is used for the routing randomness) can be estimated by classifying the traces according to their intensity.

However, the situation where the mask is the fastest to return to zero is the most likely, for at least two compelling reasons:

1) As the mask is global (shared by all the protected gates), it is amplified and therefore propagates very fast, in a similar way as a clock signal.

2) Also, the mask is directly available at one register's output, whereas the data signals can traverse many other DRSL instances prior to arriving at the gate's inputs.

Mask = 0: Direct function									Mask = 1: Dual function								
$a=0$		$b=0$		$m=0$		pre	q		$a=0$		$b=0$		$m=1$		pre	q	
0	1	0	1	0	1	0	0	1	0	1	0	1	1	0	0	0	1
0	1	0	1	0	0	0	0	1	0	1	0	1	0	0	0	0	1
0	1	0	1	0	0	1	0	1	0	1	0	1	0	0	1	0	1
0	0	0	1	0	0	1	0	0	0	0	0	1	0	0	1	0	0
0	0	0	0	0	0	1	0	0	0	0	0	0	0	0	1	0	0
$a=0$		$b=1$		$m=0$		pre	q		$a=0$		$b=1$		$m=1$		pre	q	
0	1	1	0	0	1	0	0	1	0	1	1	0	1	0	0	1	0
0	1	1	0	0	0	0	1	1	0	1	1	0	0	0	0	1	1
0	1	1	0	0	0	1	1	1	0	1	1	0	0	0	1	1	1
0	0	1	0	0	0	1	0	0	0	0	1	0	0	0	1	0	0
0	0	0	0	0	0	1	0	0	0	0	0	0	0	0	1	0	0
$a=1$		$b=0$		$m=0$		pre	q		$a=1$		$b=0$		$m=1$		pre	q	
1	0	0	1	0	1	0	0	1	1	0	0	1	1	0	0	1	0
1	0	0	1	0	0	0	1	1	1	0	0	1	0	0	0	1	1
1	0	0	1	0	0	1	1	1	1	0	0	1	0	0	1	1	1
0	0	0	1	0	0	1	0	0	0	0	0	1	0	0	1	0	0
0	0	0	0	0	0	1	0	0	0	0	0	0	0	0	1	0	0
$a=1$		$b=1$		$m=0$		pre	q		$a=1$		$b=1$		$m=1$		pre	q	
1	0	1	0	0	1	0	1	0	1	0	1	0	1	0	0	1	0
1	0	1	0	0	0	0	1	0	1	0	1	0	0	0	0	1	0
1	0	1	0	0	0	1	1	0	1	0	1	0	0	0	1	1	0
0	0	1	0	0	0	1	0	0	0	0	1	0	0	0	1	0	0
0	0	0	0	0	0	1	0	0	0	0	0	0	0	0	1	0	0

Table 13.1. *Exhaustive simulation of all the return to NULL cases in the DRSL NAND gate when the mask signal m is faster than the functional inputs a and b. The events unfold from top to bottom for the eight configurations of the triple (m, a, b). Dual-rail signals X are ordered as $X_T X_F$. Glitches are indicated in* **red boldface font**. *For a color version of this table, see www.iste.co.uk/prouff/cryptography2.zip*

The DRSL AND gate has been simulated in STMicroelectronics 130 nm technology with the BSIM3V3 MOS transistors model. The testbench consisted of the case of the return to precharge from the evaluation of $(a = 0, b = 0 \text{ or } 1, m = 0)$, where the dual-rail signal return to NULL in this order: first m, then a and finally b. We confirm that there is a glitch on the output, due to the race between the two gates "OAI222" (driving pre) and "AOI2221" (driving q_T and q_F), connected via the precharge signal pre. However, as it can be seen in Figure 13.3, the glitch on the output (more specifically on QT, the true wire of q) reaches only $vdd/2 = 0.6$ V, hence it is not likely to propagate through the next gates. At least, this conclusion holds in this simulation, but may differ in other technologies or setups (with different signals shape, power voltage, etc.). Thus, from the experiment, the leakage due to the glitch does not lead to 1 transition (on QF) versus 1 + 2 (on QT).

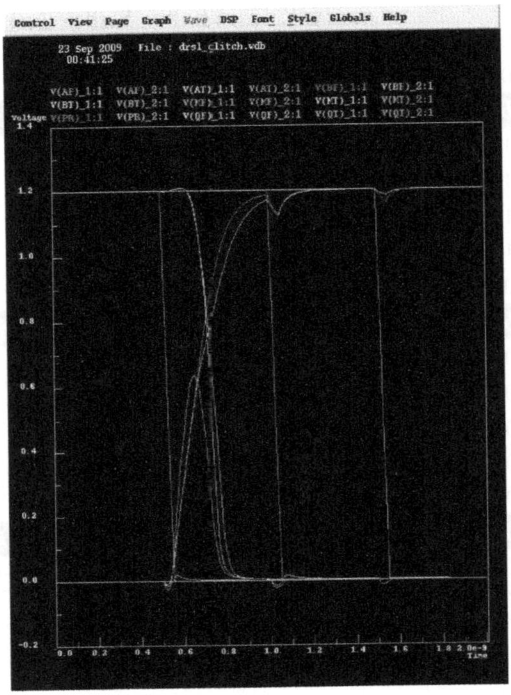

Figure 13.3. *Signal levels in a DRSL AND gate while it returns to precharge in a configuration that generates internal glitches. For a color version of this figure, see www.iste.co.uk/prouff/cryptography2.zip*

Two solutions can be imagined to patch the glitching problem of DRSL. The first one consists of adding buffers to delay the signals so as to balance the paths within the DRSL gate. This solution is however technology dependent. Another option consists of implementing DRSL in positive logic, as shown in Figure 13.2(b). This solution has a cost in CMOS logic, because inverting gates are smaller than non-inverting ones. However, this is not constraining in FPGA. A loss in area is nonetheless expected, as the functionality can only consist of positive gates, thereby limiting the degree of freedom of the logic synthesizers. In this case, the new logic, that we name DRSL+, consists of MDPL augmented with a synchronization by an unanimity cell.

Another attack against DRSL puts forward a vulnerability that is common to all masked DPL styles. The idea is that the masking of the gates allows us to make up for the routing unbalance. However, the mask signal is itself differential and therefore unbalanced. As it is not balanced (since this is the hypothesis when resorting to masked DPL), it paradoxically opens the door to an attack on itself.

13.3.4. *STTL*

Secure triple track logic (STTL) eludes any glitching risk by waiting to evaluate and precharge until all the inputs are either valid or NULL. This incurs useless delays in the return to precharge phase, which is however only detrimental to performance, not to security. The main drawback of STTL is the requirement to route one synchronization signal slower than the dual-rail, while granting a balanced routing within the dual-rail pair. However, the known methods to balance signals (fat wire and backend duplication) operate on a full netlist, and are therefore difficult to adapt on heterogeneous netlists, in which single-ended and dual-rail signals are mixed up.

13.3.5. *BCDL*

Balanced cell-based differential logic (BCDL) improves on STTL by accelerating the precharge phase due to a global signal. As BCDL design allows us to squeeze the precharge step, BCDL can compute about 80% faster than DRSL because the precharge is global. This possibility is depicted in Figure 13.4.

Furthermore, as the global signal is, by design, faster than data signals, BCDL is free from the flaw identified in DRSL. Additionally, BDCL is a truly differential logic. BCDL and STTL can be seen as equivalent at the netlist level: input synchronization logic (either C-elements or unanimity gates) can be factored in STTL to the detriment of the systematic addition of a third routing resource.

13.3.6. *WDDL variants*

Some variants of WDDL have also been devised to ease the balance of the WDDL networks. However, as already explained in the section devoted to MDPL, it is known that balancing the WDDL interconnect does not solve the EE inherent to this logic. Nevertheless, we introduce them here because some of these logics have unexpected positive side-effects on their security with respect to the EE.

13.3.6.1. *DWDDL*

Double WDDL (DWDDL) is a WDDL variant introduced to counterbalance one unbalanced network with a dummy dual one. Although this solution is sound in theory, other efforts have been deployed to reduce the overhead associated with the further duplication of hardware in DWDDL. For instance, the design of a WDDL substitution box (S-box) in BDD-style allows for a separation between the true and false halves by a copy-and-paste of the two halves, and guarantees the same backend.

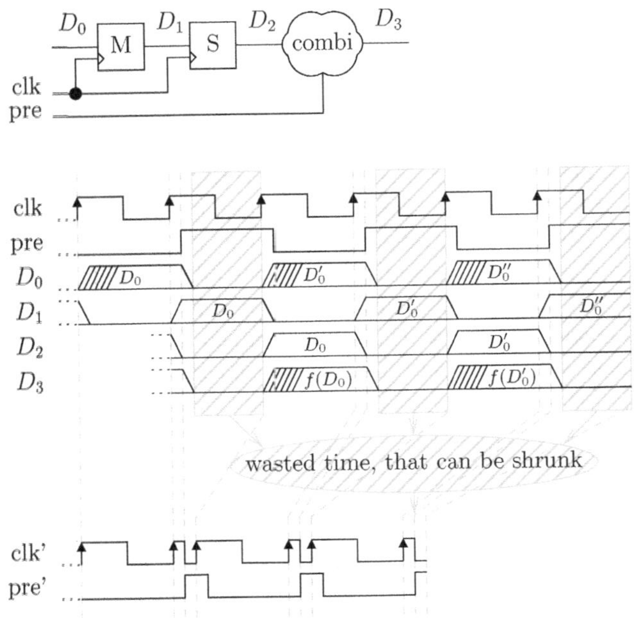

Figure 13.4. *Timing optimization in DPL protocol when the precharge is anticipated, illustrated on one half of a DPL circuit consisting of one two-stage register followed by one combinatorial function f*

13.3.6.2. *WDDL with divided backend duplication*

The "divided backend duplication" technique (Baddam and Zwolinski 2008) is an attempt to separate WDDL into two halves that do not communicate with each other. This way, the design can be placed-and-route for one half, and then copied and pasted for the second half, where gates are replaced by their dual function. For this purpose, the inverters are not replaced by wire-crossings, but by controlled inverters; such gates are:

– inverters in the evaluation phase;

– buffers in the pre-charge phase.

On the one hand, the functionality is preserved during the evaluation, and the two halves of the circuits remain dual. On the other hand, the functionality is changed during the precharge; however, the modified functionality is such that:

– the complete function is positive, thus propagating the null token;

– all of the nets are reached by the null token.

Thus, the netlist is properly precharged. For this behavior to be implementable, a global phase signal is required. It is called EVAL and must be faster than all the data changes. Indeed, its role is to cadence the DPL protocol. It is equal to 1 in the evaluation phase and to 0 in the precharge phase. The inverter $y_t = \overline{a_t}$ is thus replaced by a gate that computes a_t when EVAL $= 0$ and $\overline{a_t}$ when EVAL $= 1$. This gate is thus an exclusive or gate: $y_t = a_t \cdot \text{EVAL} + \overline{a_t} \cdot \text{EVAL} = a_t \oplus \text{EVAL}$. The transformation of an unprotected function into a WDDL and a divided backend duplication function is illustrated in Figure 13.5, for the example of the mapping $y = a \cdot \overline{(b + c)}$.

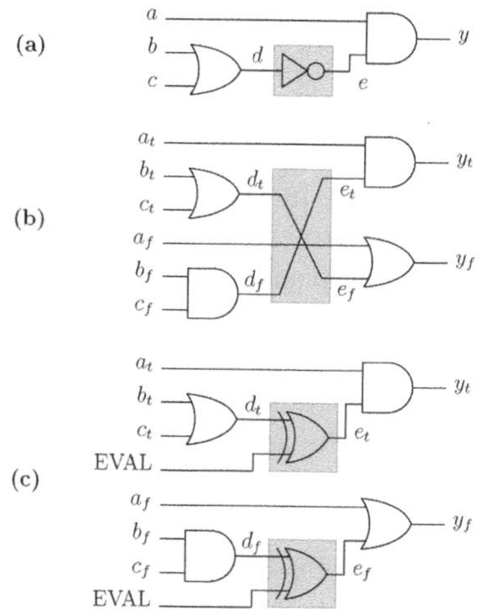

Figure 13.5. *Combinatorial function $y = a \cdot \overline{(b + c)}$ in (a) unprotected standard cell synthesis, (b) WDDL and (c) divided backend duplication. The inverters are highlighted in a gray box*

Nonetheless, this strategy is not secure, since the fundamental hypothesis of constant activity logics is violated. We illustrate this on the previous example, where (a, b, c) evaluates to either $(0, 1, 1)$ or $(1, 1, 1)$. In other words, the toggling count of this small netlist depends on the sensitive variable a, which permits, in principle, a side-channel attack.

As shown in the simulation depicted in Figure 13.6 on the left side:

– the net y_t has a non-functional $0 \to 1 \to 0$ transition (i.e. glitch) if and only if $a = 1$ in precharge (event noted (a));

– it has the same bias in precharge (event noted (b)), with, in addition, an early (respectively, late) transition if and only if $a = 1$ (*respectively* $a = 0$) (event noted (c)).

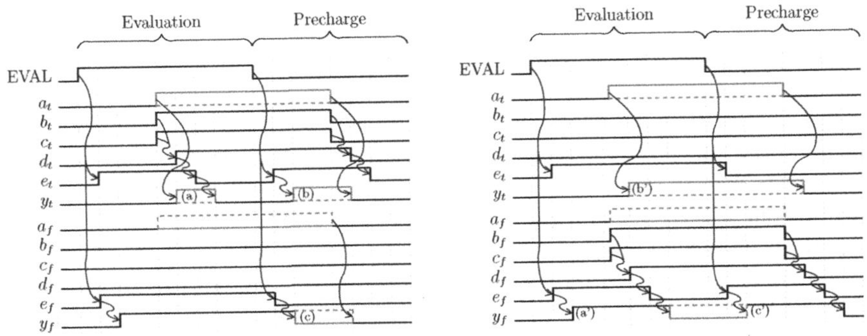

Figure 13.6. *Chronogram of execution of the netlist depicted in Figure 13.5(c) for* $(a, b, c) = (0/1, 1, 1)$ *(left) and for* $(a, b, c) = (0/1, 0, 0)$ *(right)*

Thus, this example shows that some configurations of some netlists leak more than an unprotected implementation. Indeed, the difference in the toggling count is $|1 - 0| = 1$ when the netlist is unprotected, whereas it is $|(1 + 2) - (1 + 0)| = 2$ otherwise. Furthermore, the early propagation effect is still present in this netlist. All in one, the security of the netlist is degraded, since it has conditional glitches. Regarding the data-dependent delays, the divided backend duplication method has helped fix the second-order issue of true/false pairs routing balancing, while nonetheless keeping the first-order flaw related to the early propagation effect.

Similar flaws can be observed when the netlist evaluates to $(0, 0, 0)$ or $(1, 0, 0)$. As shown in the chronogram on the right side of Figure 13.6:

– when $a = 1$, there is a glitch on y_f during evaluation (event denoted as (a')) and an EE of y_t (event denoted as (b'));

– the same happens in return to precharge: when $a = 1$, there is a glitch on y_f (event denoted as (c')) and an EE of y_t (event denoted as (b')).

In order to properly balance the delays, two conditions should be fulfilled:

1) Along the interconnection network, when the true and false signals are synchronized at the beginning, they should remain synchronized at the end of the path. This condition is made explicit in Figure 13.7.

2) The true and false values should be outputted at the same date for different input data, which is all the more important as the dual-rail inputs do not arrive simultaneously at the gate entrance. This requirement is illustrated in Figure 13.8.

The first condition is definitely enhanced by the divided backend balancing logic. However, the second condition is definitely not respected, as it inherits from the EPE issue of WDDL. The non-respect of this condition is more dramatic than the

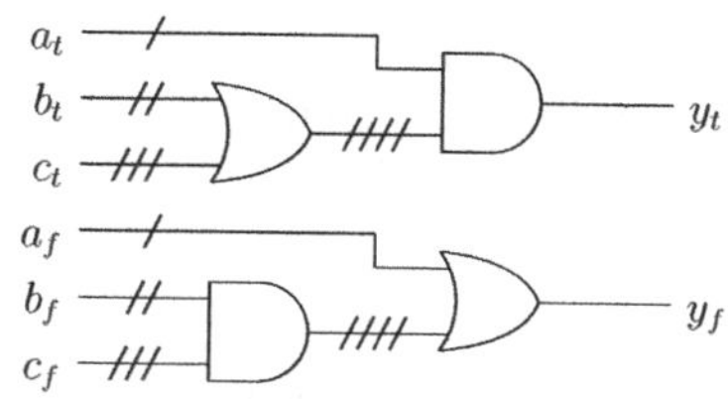

Figure 13.7. *Pairwise balance of dual-rail pairs in a DPL netlist*

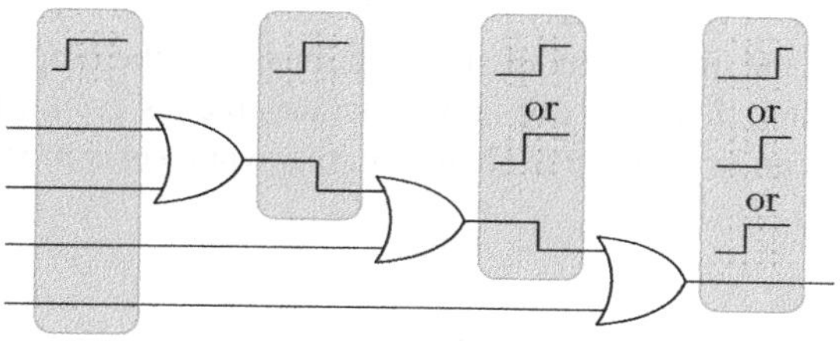

Figure 13.8. *Example of netlist (e.g. one half of a WDDL netlist) prone to the early evaluation effect. A netlist free from the early evaluation effect would have a constant evaluation time for all the intermediate nodes*

non-respect of the first condition, because it induces a bias that gets worse and worse as the gate is deep in the datapath.

13.3.6.3. *IWDDL*

Isolated WDDL (IWDDL) is a different strategy to separate a WDDL netlist into two unconnected halves. Here, inverters are kept, but potential glitches are stopped by systematically inserting one register after it. This strategy is expensive in terms of area and requires a redesign of the controller. Additionally, the design becomes much more pipelined, which requires much higher clock frequencies to maintain an acceptable throughput. However, the benefit of this approach is to stop the propagation of the EE wave. Apart from the very poor performance of IWDDL, this method is however very strong from a pure security standpoint. Only one point is questionable: the complete separation of the netlist opening the door to well-located EMA attacks that can selectively record the activity from only one half of the netlist, thus defeating the activity invariability property. This issue is all the more stringent as the netlist is much larger in IWDDL than in WDDL, because of the large quantity of registers added for the pipeline.

13.3.6.4. *WDDL w/o EE*

WDDL w/o EE is a logic style dedicated to FPGA that removes the EE without computing a rendezvous. Instead, each functional half gate receives the true and false inputs, and decides to output the VALID value only when all the inputs are VALID. This behavior can be achieved by a purely combinatorial gate. The detailed rationale behind the "WDDL w/o EE" style is as follows:

– The gate outputs NULL{0,1} when the inputs are NULL{0,1} or transitional from this value.

– The gate outputs VALID only when all the inputs are VALID.

– In case of inconsistent values with respect to the DPL convention, the gate outputs an arbitrary NULL value.

This logic does not evaluate early by design and propagates errors: if any input is stuck to NULL or if the input is out of specifications, then the output always remains NULL too. In addition, this logic does not generate glitches even if the functionality is not positive, and can be inverting. Therefore, the synthesis is more optimized than for plain WDDL.

13.4. Technological specific DPL styles

13.4.1. *Full custom optimizations*

The "sense amplifier-based logic" (SABL) style is one of the first full custom DPLs, which aims to make power consumption independent of both the logic values and the sequence of the data. Its principle consists of combining differential and dynamic logic (DDL), like in the "dynamic cascode voltage switch logic" (DCVSL) style, while fixing second-order asymmetry in the gate (especially for complex logic functions), due to parasitic capacitance. This allows us to decorrelate the power consumption from the inputs. Dynamic current mode logic (DyCML) is an improvement of SABL, as only one of the output nodes is discharged during the precharge phase. This leads to better performances, such as a reduction by 80% of the power delay product and by 50% of the power consumption. In addition, DyCML is assessed to be more resistant to DPA than SABL.

The ternary DPL (TDPL) tries to balance the DPL gates by adding a systematic discharge after the evaluation. The resulting computations are thus based on a ternary pace: (1) pre-charge, (2) evaluation and (3) post-discharge. When compared to SABL, TDPL simulations reveal that a gain of two-orders of magnitude is obtained in terms of balance.

SecLib is a full-custom logic style depicted in Figure 13.9. This logic is based on quasi-delay insensitive asynchronous primitives that are balanced to provide constant evaluation, precharge time and dissipation. Specially crafted transistor-level symmetry grants SecLib a higher resistance level to attacks than WDDL, albeit at a high cost in terms of silicon area.

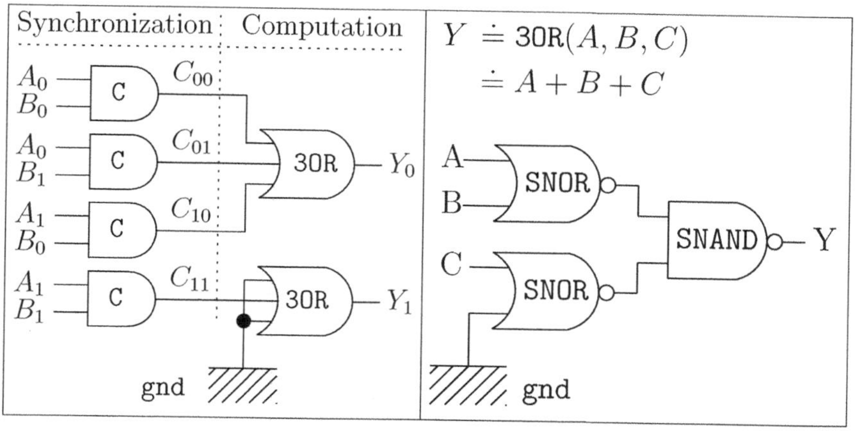

Figure 13.9. *Schematic of the QDI secured (aka SecLib) AND gate (left) and its internal 3OR architecture (right)*

"MOS current mode logic" (MCML) is a differential gate that offers reduced voltage swing thanks to differential operation. In addition, power consumption is independent of the operating frequency. It has been shown that it is also efficient to reduce the leakage.

The LUT-based dual-rail logic (LBDL) is a full-custom version of FPGA LUT relying on a tree of multiplexers. It uses an N-MOS look-up table (LUT) architecture for the computation, and P-MOS pull-ups at every internal node for the precharge. The LUT is implemented as a binary tree, where each node is controlled by one input (a_f, a_t). The net computes:

- 1 .... if $(a_f, a_t) = (0, 0)$,
- in_f .... if $(a_f, a_t) = (1, 0)$,
- in_t .... if $(a_f, a_t) = (0, 1)$,
- a short-circuit $(a_f, a_t) = (1, 1)$; this last situation should thus be avoided.

The example of the true half of an AND gate in given in Figure 13.10.

In this figure, the binary nets are highlighted in grey boxes. The use of pass-transistors instead of transmission gates for the look-up makes the propagation time dependant on the result. Indeed, N-MOS transistors propagate the zeroes more quickly than the ones; therefore, LBDL exhibits an asymmetric when it evaluates and when it precharges.

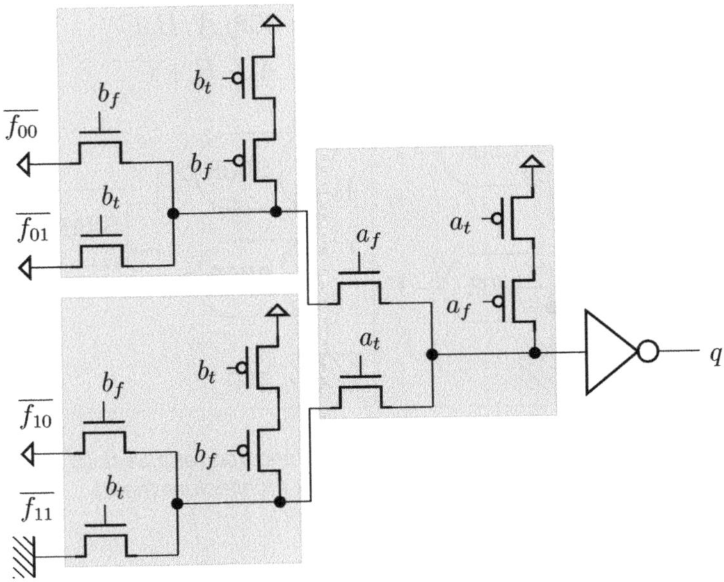

Figure 13.10. *True half of the AND gate in LBDL*

13.4.2. *Asynchronous logic*

Some asynchronous logic styles operate in a DPL mode. Their dual rail encoding and synchronization stage makes it intrinsically robust against side-channel attacks. If the netlist and their layout is additionally balanced, asynchronous styles can be a candidate for secure computing. In addition, asynchronous logics are also more tolerant to the environmental variations, which makes them inherently more difficult to attack with faults injections.

13.4.3. *Reversible differential logic*

Reversible logic is a means to compute without loosing energy at any step. This implies that at any moment of the computation, the operations may be reversed. Two precursors in this field of research were Tommaso Toffoli and Edward Fredkin, who proved that the concept of reversible computing was indeed realizable physically, provided that the function to implement is logically reversible. Basically, they demonstrated that any bijection can be mapped onto a reversible physical system. However, two difficult issues were left uncovered by their work:

1) A generic synthesis method for arbitrary bijections, and also an algorithm to provide the most compact netlist, is still be found.

2) An integrable electronic system suitable for the implementation of reversible logic is lacking. Indeed, the only concrete example illustrating Toffoli and Fredkin's work was the famous albeit unpractical "Billiard Ball" model, which cannot extend to thousands of interactions, as required by our modern computational needs.

13.5. DPL styles comparison

Table 13.2 draws up a comparison of the main DPL styles, in terms of principles, design constraints and performance, highlighting most of the known advantages (masking, synchronization) and drawbacks (primitives and back-end constraints, and technological bias) of such countermeasures.

Masking allows us to greatly reduce the technological bias, but also results in a significant increase in area. As a matter of fact, it requires at least a transformation of two-input operations into three-input majority functions (MDPL), or into a four-input RSL gates (DRSL).

Synchronization on both precharge and evaluation is mandatory to avoid glitches and early propagation effects.

Primitive constraints induce a higher complexity by reducing the panel of usable functions (like in WDDL, where only positive functions are allowed), or by binding the designer to use specific functions that can be more area-consuming or slower than basic ones (SecLib, MDPL and DRSL).

Back-end constraints generate extra design work, as the P/R stage has to meet specific requirements to achieve a good balance between the T and F networks. It can also cause a loss of performance, like in STTL where the synchronization signal must be manually made slower than the others, by adding delay elements between each of the gates in order to ensure that it always switches last.

Technological bias corresponds to the imbalance between the true and false networks. It encompasses the load, interconnect and CMOS structure differences. This is a significant source of information leakage, and must therefore be as low as possible to ensure a perfectly secure countermeasure.

13.6. Conclusion

In this chapter, we presented the different DPL logic styles that aim to hide the cryptoprocessors activity to thwart side-channel attacks. Although the DPL logic is based on an elegant manner to obtain secure implementations, flaws exist at the logical and physical levels. The different logic styles are more or less able to counteract these negative effects, but often with an higher complexity or back-end design. This chapter permits the understanding of the main DPL style and draws a comparison between them in order to help the pros and the cons analysis. Research on new DPL styles is still active to improve the robustness and keep a good compromise with complexity and performance requirements.

Logic	Mask	Synchro		Constraints		Tech	Speed
		Pre	Eval	Primitives	Back-end	Bias	
WDDL	no	✗	✗	positive funct only	balanced place&route	high	$< 1/2$
MDPL	yes	✗	✗	$MAJ^{\dagger}$	no	no	$< 1/2$
STTL	no	✓	✓	no	delay on sync signal	very low	$< 1/4$
DRSL	yes	✓	✗	no	no	no	$< 1/2$
LBDL	no	✓	✓	specific lib	back-end duplication	high	$< 1/2$
SecLib	no	✓	✓	specific lib	back-end duplication	very low	$< 1/2$
IWDDL	no	✓	✓	no	netlist post-processing	low	$< \frac{1}{2 \cdot n_i}$ ‡
BCDL	no	✓	✓	no	balanced place&route	low	$> 1/2$

† MAJ stands for the majority gate: $MAJ(a, b, c) \doteq a \cdot b + b \cdot c + c \cdot a$.

‡ n_i is the maximum number of inverters amongst all combinatorial paths.

Table 13.2. *DPL performance and security features overview*

13.7. Notes and further references

The seminal paper by Selmane et al. (2009) introduces the intrinsic immunity of DPL against some classes of DFA.

DPL families based on standard cells

DPL to thwart DFA:

– *WDDL* has been presented in Tiri and Verbauwhede (2004a). The flaws of WDDL, like the non-positiveness and the early evaluation, are discussed in Guilley et al. (2008d) and Suzuki and Saeki (2006, 2008), respectively. Some attacks exploiting the imbalance between the two WDDL networks are described in ASIC by Tiri et al. (2005) or in an FPGA by Sauvage et al. (2009).

– *MDPL* is a logic style that has been introduced in Popp and Mangard (2005). Balancing in ASIC can be done either by the fat wire (Tiri and Verbauwhede 2004b) or backend duplication (Guilley et al. 2005) methods. This can be transposed in FPGA with less accuracy (Guilley et al. 2008a).

– *iMDPL* is an improvement of MDPL in terms of elimination of the early precharge and evaluation issue (Popp et al. 2007, p. 90).

– *DRSL* has been presented in Chen and Zhou (2006). An attack on the mask is described in Tiri and Schaumont (2006). A more generic attack exploiting the imbalance of the dual nets of the mask is presented in Saeki and Suzuki (2008).

– *STTL* is introduced in Soares et al. (2008) and *BCDL* in Nassar et al. (2010).

– *WDDL variant double WDDL* (DWDDL) is introduced in Yu and Schaumont (2007). S-box implemented in BDD style is presented in Guilley et al. (2008a) and Akishita et al. (2008). The "divided backend duplication" technique to balance WDDL is introduced in Baddam and Zwolinski (2008). The *IWDDL* style is presented in McEvoy et al. (2009), and slight unbalances that are exploitable are shown in Moradi et al. (2012). *WDDL w/o early evaluation* is studied in Bhasin et al. (2009).

Technological specific DPL styles

Full custom implementations have been proposed in Tiri et al. (2002) and Verbauwhede and Tiri (2008). An improvement of SABL, the "Dynamic Current Mode Logic" *DyCML* is presented in Allam and Elmasry (2000) and Macé et al. (2004). The ternary DPL *TDPL* is described in Bucci et al. (2006).

– *SecLib* is a delay-independent logic style introduced in Guilley et al. (2004, 2007, 2008c) and Guilley et al. (2008b).

– *MCML* has been assessed in Regazzoni et al. (2007, 2009a, 2009b).

– *LBDL*, the LUT-Based Dual-rail Logic, has been presented in Yue et al. (2009).

– *Asynchronous logic* used for side-channel resistance is studied in Bouesse et al. (2004, 2005) and Hassoune et al. (2007). It is reminiscent of SecLib.

– *Reversible Differential Logic* arises originally as a solution for low-power constraints. Two precursors in this field of research were Tommaso Toffoli and Edward Fredkin (Toffoli 1980; Fredkin and Toffoli 1982). The question of the synthesis of the reversible logic has received some answers in Kerntopf (2004) and Wille and Große (2007). Regarding the implementation feasibility, it has been covered in Vos and Rentergem (2005), where the authors describe some implementations in CMOS.

13.8. References

Akishita, T., Katagi, M., Miyato, Y., Mizuno, A., Shibutani, K. (2008). A practical DPA countermeasure with BDD architecture. In *CARDIS*. Springer, Berlin, Heidelberg.

Allam, M. and Elmasry, M. (2000). Dynamic current mode logic (DyCML), a new low-power high-performance logic family. In *Proceedings of the IEEE 2000 Custom Integrated Circuits Conference (Cat. No. 00CH37044)*, Orlando.

Baddam, K. and Zwolinski, M. (2008). Divided backend duplication methodology for balanced dual rail routing. In *CHES*. Springer, Washington, DC. doi: 10.1007/978-3-540-85053-3_25.

Bhasin, S., Danger, J.-L., Flament, F., Graba, T., Guilley, S., Mathieu, Y., Nassar, M., Sauvage, L., Selmane, N. (2009). Combined SCA and DFA countermeasures integrable in a FPGA design flow. In *ReConFig*. IEEE, Cancun. doi: 10.1109/ReConFig.2009.50.

Bouesse, G.F., Renaudin, M., Robisson, B., Beigné, E., Liardet, P.-Y., Prevosto, S., Sonzogni, J. (2004). DPA on quasi delay insensitive asynchronous circuits: Concrete results. In *XIX Conference on Design of Circuits and Integrated Systems, Proceedings of DCIS'04)*, November, Bordeaux [Online]. Available at: http://tima.imag.fr/cis/publi/2004/DCIS04DPA.pdfPDF.

Bouesse, G.F., Renaudin, M., Dumont, S., Germain, F. (2005). DPA on quasi delay insensitive asynchronous circuits: Formalization and improvement. In *Proceedings of DATE'05*. IEEE Computer Society.

Bucci, M., Giancane, L., Luzzi, R., Trifiletti, A. (2006). Three-phase dual-rail pre-charge logic. In *CHES 2006*. Springer, Berlin, Heidelberg. doi: 10.1007/11894063.

Chen, Z. and Zhou, Y. (2006). Dual-rail random switching logic: A countermeasure to reduce side channel leakage. In *CHES 2006*. Springer, Berlin, Heidelberg.

Fredkin, E. and Toffoli, T. (1982). Conservative logic. *International Journal of Theoretical Physics*, 21(3/4), 219–253. doi: 10.1007/BF01857727.

Guilley, S., Hoogvorst, P., Mathieu, Y., Pacalet, R., Provost, J. (2004). CMOS structures suitable for secured hardware. In *DATE'04*. IEEE Computer Society. doi: 10.1109/DATE.2004.1269113

Guilley, S., Hoogvorst, P., Mathieu, Y., Pacalet, R. (2005). The "backend duplication" method. In *CHES 2005*. Springer, Berlin, Heidelberg.

Guilley, S., Flament, F., Hoogvorst, P., Pacalet, R., Mathieu, Y. (2007). Secured CAD back-end flow for power-analysis-resistant cryptoprocessors. *IEEE Des. Test Comput.*, 24(6), 546–555. doi: 10.1109/MDT.2007.202.

Guilley, S., Chaudhuri, S., Sauvage, L., Graba, T., Danger, J.-L., Hoogvorst, P., Vong, V.-N., Nassar, M. (2008a). Place-and-route impact on the security of DPL designs in FPGAs. In *HOST (Hardware Oriented Security and Trust)*. IEEE.

Guilley, S., Chaudhuri, S., Sauvage, L., Hoogvorst, P., Pacalet, R., Bertoni, G.M. (2008b). Security evaluation of WDDL and SecLib countermeasures against power attacks. *IEEE Transactions on Computers*, 57(11), 1482–1497.

Guilley, S., Flament, F., Pacalet, R., Hoogvorst, P., Mathieu, Y. (2008c). Security evaluation of a balanced quasi-delay insensitive library. In *DCIS*. IEEE [Online]. Available at: http://www.dcis.org/.

Guilley, S., Sauvage, L., Danger, J.-L., Graba, T., Mathieu, Y. (2008d). Evaluation of power-constant dual-rail logic as a protection of cryptographic applications in FPGAs. In *SSIRI*. IEEE Computer Society. doi: 10.1109/SSIRI.2008.31.

Hassoune, I., Macé, F., Flandre, D., Legat, J.-D. (2007). Dynamic differential self-timed logic families for robust and low-power security ICs. *Integration, the VLSI Journal*, 40(3), 355–364. doi: 10.1016/j.vlsi.2006.04.001.

Kerntopf, P. (2004). A new heuristic algorithm for reversible logic synthesis. In *DAC'04: Proceedings of the 41st Annual Design Automation Conference*. ACM, New York.

Macé, F., Standaert, F.-X., Hassoune, I., Quisquater, J.-J., Legat, J.-D. (2004). A dynamic current mode logic to counteract power analysis attacks. In *DCIS 2004 – 19th Conference on Design of Circuits and Integrated Systems*. DIAL, Bordeaux.

McEvoy, R.P., Murphy, C.C., Marnane, W.P., Tunstall, M. (2009). Isolated WDDL: A hiding countermeasure for differential power analysis on FPGAs. *ACM Trans. Reconfigurable Technol. Syst.*, 2(1), 1–23.

Moradi, A., Kirschbaum, M., Eisenbarth, T., Paar, C. (2012). Masked dual-rail precharge logic encounters state-of-the-art power analysis methods. *IEEE Trans. VLSI Syst.*, 20(9), 1578–1589. doi: 10.1109/TVLSI.2011.2160375.

Nassar, M., Bhasin, S., Danger, J.-L., Duc, G., Guilley, S. (2010). BCDL: A high performance balanced DPL with global precharge and without early-evaluation. In *DATE'10*. IEEE Computer Society.

Popp, T. and Mangard, S. (2005). Masked dual-rail pre-charge logic: DPA-resistance without routing constraints. In *Proceedings of CHES'05*. Springer, Berlin, Heidelberg.

Popp, T., Kirschbaum, M., Zefferer, T., Mangard, S. (2007). Evaluation of the masked logic style MDPL on a prototype chip. In *Cryptographic Hardware and Embedded Systems – CHES 2007*. Springer, Berlin, Heidelberg. doi: 10.1007/978-3-540-74735-2_6.

Regazzoni, F., Badel, S., Eisenbarth, T., Großschädl, J., Poschmann, A., Toprak, Z., Macchetti, M., Pozzi, L., Paar, C., Leblebici, Y., Ienne, P. (2007). A simulation-based methodology for evaluating DPA-resistance of cryptographic functional units with application to CMOS and MCML technologies. In *International Conference on Embedded Computer Systems: Architectures, Modeling, and Simulation (SAMOS IC 07)*. IEEE, Samos.

Regazzoni, F., Cevrero, A., Standaert, F.-X., Badel, S., Kluter, T., Brisk, P., Leblebici, Y., Ienne, P. (2009a). A design flow and evaluation framework for DPA-resistant instruction set extensions. In *CHES 2009*. Springer, Berlin, Heidelberg.

Regazzoni, F., Eisenbarth, T., Poschmann, A., Großschädl, J., Gürkaynak, F.K., Macchetti, M., Deniz, Z.T., Pozzi, L., Paar, C., Leblebici, Y. et al. (2009b). Evaluating resistance of MCML technology to power analysis attacks using a simulation-based methodology. *Transactions on Computational Science*, 4, 230–243.

Saeki, M. and Suzuki, D. (2008). Security evaluations of MRSL and DRSL considering signal delays. *IEICE Transactions on Fundamentals of Electronics, Communications and Computer Sciences*, E91-A(1), 176–183. doi: 10.1093/ietfec/e91-a.1.176.

Sauvage, L., Guilley, S., Danger, J.-L., Mathieu, Y., Nassar, M. (2009). Successful attack on an FPGA-based WDDL DES cryptoprocessor without place and route constraints. In *DATE*. IEEE Computer Society.

Selmane, N., Bhasin, S., Guilley, S., Graba, T., Danger, J.-L. (2009). WDDL is protected against setup time violation attacks. In *FDTC*. IEEE Computer Society. doi: 10.1109/FDTC.2009.40.

Soares, R., Calazans, N., Lomné, V., Maurine, P., Torres, L., Robert, M. (2008). Evaluating the robustness of secure triple track logic through prototyping. In *SBCCI'08: Proceedings of the 21st Annual Symposium on Integrated Circuits and System Design*. ACM, New York.

Suzuki, D. and Saeki, M. (2006). Security evaluation of DPA countermeasures using dual-rail pre-charge logic style. In *CHES 2006*. Springer, Berlin, Heidelberg.

Suzuki, D. and Saeki, M. (2008). An analysis of leakage factors for dual-rail pre-charge logic style. *IEICE Transactions on Fundamentals of Electronics, Communications and Computer Sciences*, E91-A(1), 184–192. doi: 10.1093/ietfec/e91-a.1.184.

Tiri, K. and Schaumont, P. (2006). Changing the odds against masked logic. In *13th Annual Workshop on Selected Areas in Cryptography*. Springer, Berlin, Heidelberg.

Tiri, K. and Verbauwhede, I. (2004a). A logic level design methodology for a secure DPA resistant ASIC or FPGA implementation. In *DATE'04. IEEE Computer Society*. doi: 10.1109/DATE.2004.1268856.

Tiri, K. and Verbauwhede, I. (2004b). Place and route for secure standard cell design. In *Proceedings of WCC/CARDIS*. Kluwer.

Tiri, K., Akmal, M., Verbauwhede, I. (2002). A dynamic and differential CMOS logic with signal independent power consumption to withstand differential power analysis on smart cards. In *European Solid-State Circuits Conference (ESSCIRC)*. IEEE, Florence [Online]. Available at: http://citeseer.ist.psu.edu/tiri02dynamic.html.

Tiri, K., Hwang, D., Hodjat, A., Lai, B.-C., Yang, S., Schaumont, P., Verbauwhede, I. (2005). Prototype IC with WDDL and differential routing – DPA resistance assessment. In *Proceedings of CHES'05*. Springer, Berlin, Heidelberg.

Toffoli, T. (1980). Reversible computing. In *Proceedings of the 7th Colloquium on Automata, Languages and Programming*. Springer-Verlag, London.

Verbauwhede, I. and Tiri, K. (2008). A dynamic and differential CMOS logic with signal-independent power consumption to withstand differential power analysis. US Patent 7,417,468 [Online]. Available at: http://www.wipo.int/pctdb/en/wo.jsp?wo=2005029704.

Vos, A.D. and Rentergem, Y. (2005). Reversible computing: From mathematical group theory to electronical circuit experiment. In *CF (Computing Frontiers)*. ACM, New York.

Wille, R. and Große, D. (2007). Fast exact Toffoli network synthesis of reversible logic. In *ICCAD'07: Proceedings of the 2007 IEEE/ACM International Conference on Computer-Aided Design*. IEEE Press, Piscataway. doi: 10.1109/ICCAD.2007.4397244.

Yu, P. and Schaumont, P. (2007). Secure FPGA circuits using controlled placement and routing. In *CODES+ISSS'07: Proceedings of the 5th IEEE/ACM International Conference on Hardware/Software Codesign and System Synthesis*. ACM, New York.

Yue, D., Sun, Y., Zhang, M., Li, S., Dai, Y. (2009). A look-up-table based differential logic to counteract DPA attacks. In *ASICON*. IEEE Computer Society. doi: 10.1109/ASICON.2009.5351561.

14

Physically Unclonable Functions

Jean-Luc DANGER[1], Sylvain GUILLEY[2], Debdeep MUKHOPADHYAY[3] and Ulrich RUHRMAIR[4]

[1]*Télécom Paris, Institut Polytechnique de Paris, France*
[2]*Secure-IC S.A.S., Cesson-Sévigné, France*
[3]*Indian Institute of Technology, Kharagpur, India*
[4]*LMU Physics Department, Ludwig Maximilian University of Munich, Germany*

14.1. Introduction

14.1.1. *Principle*

In the living world, we have organisms who share the same deoxyribonucleic acid (DNA) and yet are distinct via biometric traits, such as fingerprints. A classic example in this context (which we can connect easily) are twins. Although what distinguishes them and yet makes them so similar can be attributed to the wonders of nature, it emphasizes the importance of identity in a set of similar objects. Interestingly, in the modern world of mass production, where products are designed once and replicated from the initial template, it is also imperative to be capable of differentiating among the entities pertaining to the same class. This becomes all the more important in the world of cyber physical systems (CPS) when we consider billions of devices, which are aimed to be connected and communicating. In such situations, it is of absolute necessity to be able to identify the devices to carefully allow or disallow the power of control and command. The big question is, can the intrinsic device properties be used to generate distinct fingerprints much akin to the world of living creatures? Physically unclonable functions (abridged as PUFs) are electronic structures innate

Embedded Cryptography 2,
coordinated by Emmanuel PROUFF, Guénaël RENAULT,
Matthieu RIVAIN and Colin O'FLYNN.

to each chip instance, which generate unique per chip bit sequences. As humans are unable to have complete control on the chip design process, due to its inherent complexity and often approximated device models, many slight uncertainties creep in the circuits. These aberrations often arise due to process variations and are the center piece of PUF designs. It offers a native tamper-resistance compared to conventional cryptosystems, which need to store the secret keys in non-volatile memories. PUFs are a unique and promising hardware security primitive owing to the fact that the device's intrinsic nature generates a secret keying information, which is not explicitly stored in a memory or register. Instead, the key is rebuilt (alike) upon each power-up.

The fabrication concept is illustrated in Figure 14.1. The PUF blueprint is provided to the semiconductor foundry in a GDSII format, and the slight differences between the produced devices are expressed by their PUF instance.

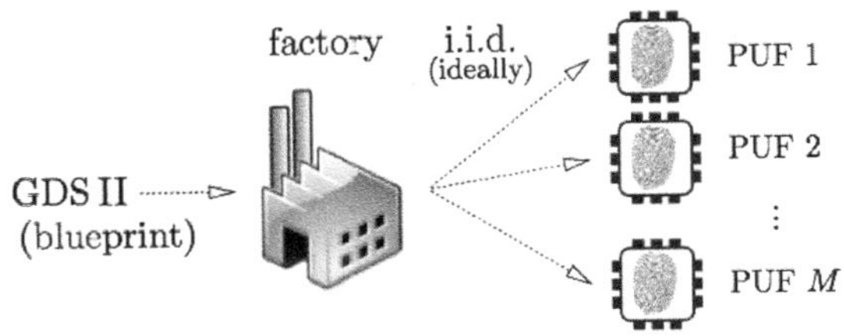

Figure 14.1. *PUF concept, from design to fabrication. For a color version of this figure, see www.iste.co.uk/prouff/cryptography2.zip*

For digital silicon PUF, the process variation that impacts the fabrication of every MOSFET transistor allows us to build a unique PUF for each device.

The threshold voltage V_{th} of the transistor is particularly impacted by the process variation. As it expresses the gate-source voltage that allows the drain-source channel to conduct, it can be used to differentiate two transistors. The reasons that underlie the variability in MOSFET transistors are threefold:

1) the density of dopants in the depletion area;

2) the thickness of the insulator below the gate;

3) the line edge roughness.

For specific fabrication processes, some additional factors can exist, such as the body thickness in the case of Fully Depleted Silicon On Insulator (FD-SOI). Figure 14.2 illustrates the variance of density of dopants and the silicon oxide thickness on a MOSFET transistor. These variations are increasing with recent thinner technologies.

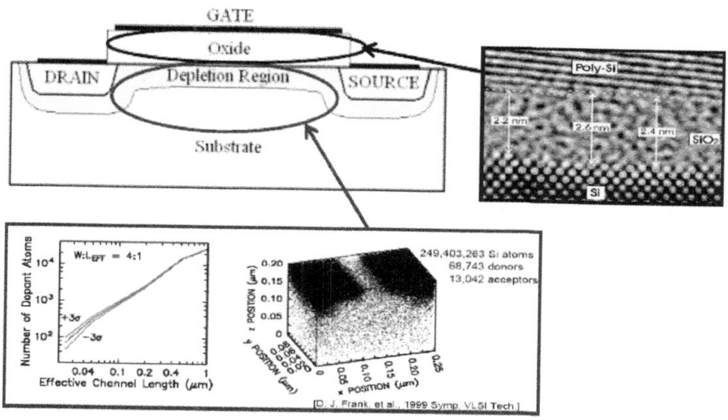

Figure 14.2. *Process variation in MOSFET transistor. For a color version of this figure, see www.iste.co.uk/prouff/cryptography2.zip*

14.1.2. *The twin nature of PUFs*

PUFs have a twin nature. On the one hand, the primitive can be abstracted as a Boolean function, mapping its inputs called *challenges*, to outputs that are referred to as *responses*. On the other hand, this challenge–response mapping should not be expressible as a closed form mathematical functions, or should not be amenable to be modeled by a computer program. This twin nature, is the most fascinating idea of a PUF, which potentially allows an easy way of obtaining challenge–response pairs (CRPs), which can be used to define a given hardware device, while the CRPs do not reveal any mathematical function which can be used to *compute* the unknown responses. In other words, the only way to obtain the responses is to have physical possession of the device and apply the input challenge. It is expected that because of the intrinsic properties of the device, the CRP mapping is unique for every device. The relationship between the challenge and the responses is thus dependent on complex properties of the underlying platform and is a manifestation of the physics of the phenomenon, which generates the output. It is believed that this physical function (as opposed to mathematical function) cannot be imitated and is unclonable. Informally, this implies that if we take two devices hosting a given PUF in it and apply the same challenge to both, their responses should be statistically independent. This means the knowledge of the response from one device should not reveal information of the response from another device. Subsequently, we discuss two broad classifications of PUFs that define two diverse design families of PUFs owing to their different applications and design principles. More formally, a PUF maps a set of digital input vectors, known as *challenges C*, to a corresponding set of outputs, known as *responses*

$\mathcal{R}$ for use as a unique fingerprint after the required amount of post processing. The mapping can be represented as:

$$\Gamma : C \rightarrow \mathcal{R} : \Gamma(c) = r \qquad [14.1]$$

Figure 14.3 illustrates the basic PUF block.

Figure 14.3. *Block diagram of a PUF circuit*

As the base of the PUF is physical, the architecture requires a quantization step to provide a digital response. This physical behavior is associated with addition of noise before digitization. This could create faults at the quantization step and a post-processing block should be added for correction. Figure 14.4 illustrates the generic PUF architecture.

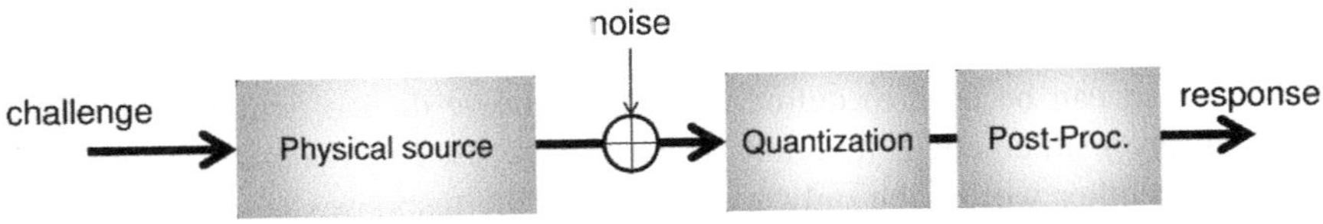

Figure 14.4. *Generic architecture of PUF. For a color version of this figure, see www.iste.co.uk/prouff/cryptography2.zip*

14.1.3. *Properties*

A PUF exhibits certain properties that are defined below using the above-mentioned mapping:

1) *Evaluable*: given Γ and c, it is easy to evaluate $r = \Gamma(c)$.

2) *Unique*: $\Gamma(c)$ contains some information about the identity of the physical entity embedding $\Gamma(c)$.

3) *Reproducible*: $y = \Gamma(c)$ is reproducible up to small (possibly correctable) error.

4) *Unclonable*: given $\Gamma(c)$, it is hard to construct a procedure $\Delta \neq \Gamma$ such that $\forall c \in C : \Delta(c) \approx \Gamma(c)$ up to a small error.

5) *Unpredictable*: given only a set $Q = \{(c_i, r_i = \Gamma(c_i))\}$, it is hard to predict $r_u = \Gamma(c_u)$ where $c_u \neq (Q)$.

6) *One-way*: given only r and Γ, it is hard to find c such that $\Gamma(c) = r$.

7) *Tamper evident*: altering the physical entity embedding Γ transforms to $\Gamma \rightarrow \Gamma'$ such that with high probability $\exists c \in C \neq \Gamma'(c)$, not even up to a small error.

Figure 14.5 illustrates the generic PUF architecture in its real environment, which makes it difficult to meet all these properties. As the architecture of PUF is natively physical, it is very sensitive to the bias introduced at the design stage and by volatile environmental variables such as temperature, voltage, aging and more importantly dynamic noise. It also offers many vulnerabilities to both physical attacks and mathematical attacks, simply by observing the CRPs.

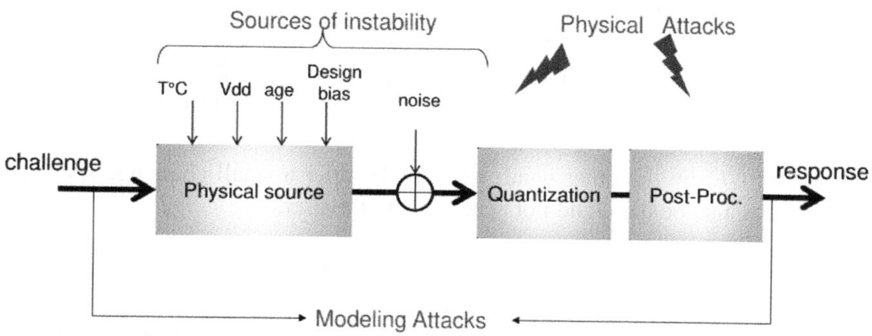

Figure 14.5. *Architecture of a PUF circuit in its real environment. For a color version of this figure, see www.iste.co.uk/prouff/cryptography2.zip*

We can clearly deduce that the PUF may not be a panacea as security primitive, as it can be impacted by the environment and attacks. This needs much attention to respect these properties:

– The *unicity* can be impacted by a bias in the PUF design. This can be compared with the real entropy of the PUF and requires specific care at design and inference stage.

– The *reproducibility* is dependent on its reliability to face the environmental noise. Indeed, the PUF relies on the extraction of physical sources that are very sensitive to noise. Current PUF technologies have a raw bit error rate (BER) between 2% and 15%. Some reliability enhancement, like the error correction mechanisms, have to be considered as post-processing blocks.

– The *unpredictability* can be compromised by a design bias or by the capability of modeling the PUF by an adversary. The PUF model should be very complex to thwart such modeling attacks (MAs).

– *Tampering* is a powerful threat by using physical means targeting the PUF. These threats also consider passive attacks such as side-channel analysis (SCA) able to read the PUF behavior and its response. Efficient countermeasures have to be devised to meet this property.

An international standardization ISO/IEC 20897-1/-2 (see section 14.7.1) addresses the properties and the requirements of PUFs, while being agnostic to the PUF particular implementation.

14.1.4. *Two broad classification of PUFs*

PUFs can be broadly classified into two broad classes based on the nature of security assurance they provide, catering to different type of applications:

1) *Strong PUF*: a strong PUF must have a large number of CRPs, often exponential with respect to some design parameters, for example, number of primitive constituents used in the design.

2) *Weak PUF*: on the other hand, weak PUFs offer a small challenge space and sometimes can also be fixed and not accessible to the user.

There is another key distinction between the two types of PUFs: in strong PUFs, the adversary can apply multiple challenges and has access to the responses, while in weak PUFs, the responses are secret and hidden from the adversary. Figure 14.6 illustrates the differences between the two types of PUF.

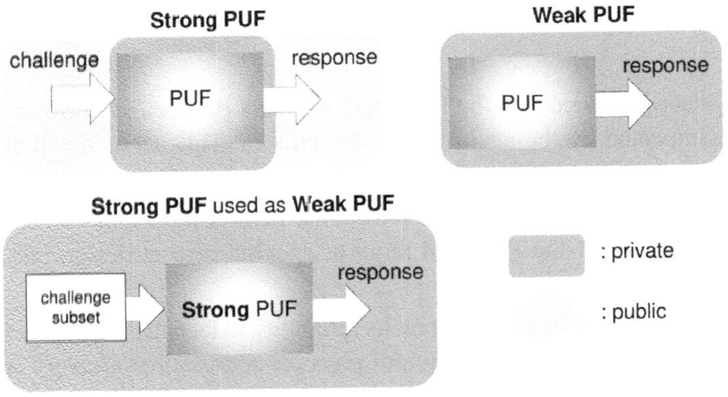

Figure 14.6. *Strong versus weak PUF. For a color version of this figure, see www.iste.co.uk/prouff/cryptography2.zip*

What makes design of strong PUFs trickier is the additional guarantee that the adversary who does not have physical possession of the PUF should not be able to predict the response for a challenge, which it has not applied before and observed the response. It may be emphasized that in literature there is a debate on the usage of the adjectives, *strong* and *weak*, in the sense they do not really compare security of the two categories of PUFs. It is indeed true that in cryptography, the usage of the words *strong* and *weak* is quite distinct, where it qualifies the ability of the primitive to satisfy certain security definitions in the face of adaptive adversaries in the former case, which is relaxed in the case of the weaker versions. In the literature of PUFs, strong and weak largely defines two widely different class of PUFs, which are also used in different applications. Strong PUFs are largely used for building lightweight authentication systems by using CRPs, while weak PUFs are used as key-derivation hardware security modules to take advantage of cryptographic functions. Strong PUF can also be used as weak PUFs to derivate a key. In this case, only a subset of challenges is used and remain private as shown in Figure 14.6.

14.1.5. *Necessity of enrollment*

14.1.5.1. *Purpose*

A PUF has two main types of output or "identifier": a list of CRPs, for a *strong PUF*, or a constant word for a *weak PUF*, which can be used as a cryptographic key. The enrollment phase is done just after fabrication, and it is mandatory to store the identifier in a trusted server and to help recovering it in a safe and secure way when the PUF is used (or reconstructed). The enrollment is executed only once. A very important stage at the end of enrollment is the *locking* of the PUF access in order to avoid an attacker performing the enrollment themselves to retrieve the secret identifier. It is more tricky for the strong PUF as the challenges and responses are public. The locking operation can be done by the use of a specific technology like anti-fuse, or by using a specific protocol to access the PUF. For a strong PUF, the list of CRPs is so large that a huge memory is necessary. It is preferable to model the PUF function as expressed in equation [14.1] and store it.

Ideally, the mathematical function of the PUF may be very complicated, thus not easy to model. Hence, some machine learning (ML) algorithms can be used. This modeling capability is contrary to the security requirement, as the modeling can be executed by an attacker as the challenges and responses are public words. Consequently, the complexity of the model has to be such that an ML attack (MA) is not possible in reasonable time. Even if the model is complex, modeling at the enrollment stage can be made possible by accessing some sub-parts of the PUF separately. This makes sense when the PUF is a composition of functions. These accesses have to be locked at the end of the enrollment phase.

14.1.5.2. *Enrollment of helper data*

The PUF is very sensitive to noise and has natively a high BER. This is particularly annoying for weak PUFs, which generate a cryptographic key and thus require a very steady response. To help correcting the errors, the enrollment phase registers a specific word to help the reconstruction: the *helper data* (HD). The use of helper data is explained in Chapter 3 of Volume 1 dedicated to the enhancement of the reliability property.

14.1.5.3. *Inference or reconstruction*

The inference of the PUF corresponds to the PUF usage. The identifier is extracted by running the PUF function without the necessity of a storage, thus providing a high level of security compared to secret stored in memories. During the reconstruction potential errors can be corrected by taking advantage of the HD to build a steady PUF. Figure 14.7 illustrates the two phases of enrollment and inference for a weak PUF, which generates a device identifier.

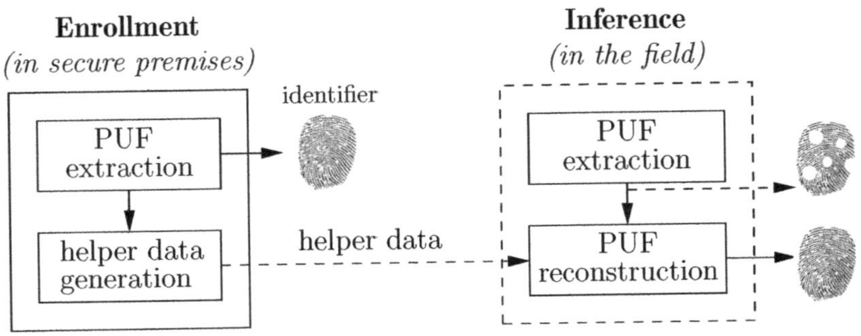

Figure 14.7. *The two phases of the weak PUF lifecycle. For a color version of this figure, see www.iste.co.uk/prouff/cryptography2.zip*

14.1.6. *Use-cases*

PUFs can be used to fulfill different needs where non-tamperability is a strong requirement. They are used to generate non-stored security parameters. The use-cases can be classified in three main categories: confidentiality, identification and authentication.

– *Confidentiality*: the PUF identifier is used as a cryptographic key for ciphering/deciphering. As the key is known neither by the designer nor by the firmware developer, such a solution solves the problem of key management, as each device handles its own key. There are many related use-cases. One specific to digital circuits is the protection of hardware intellectual properties by using logic locking.

– *Identification*: the PUF identifier is read to know the identity of the device. One typical use-case is the protection against counterfeiting using illegal overproduced devices. Only the recognized identifiers are considered genuine.

– *Authentication*: the PUF identification is made robust against man-in-the-middle attacks. Pure cryptographic protocols can be used with the key spawn from a PUF. The strong PUFs offers the possibility to use CRP protocols which are non-cryptographic, thus, they are well suited for low-cost solutions. However, this protocol can be the target of powerful attacks like replay attacks and MAs (refer to section 14.5), and should be protected.

14.2. PUF architectures

There are numerous architectures of PUF in digital electronics in CMOS and/or emerging technologies. They can easily be integrated in high-end or embedded systems like Internet of Things (IoT) or low-cost products. The sources from which the mismatch is extracted are electrical variables, depending on a small physical quantity, which has to be leveraged. As these sources are physical, it is necessary to convert them into the digital world. This generally requires a simple 1-bit quantizer. For instance, the digitization can be the comparison between two voltages, or the binary state of a cell, or a wire which is open or closed.

The architectures of PUFs closely depends on their category: either *weak* PUFs that are characterized by their small number of challenges or *strong* PUFs that have a multiplicity of CRPs.

14.2.1. *Weak PUFs*

Weak PUFs are structured with a set of elementary cells independent of each other. The memory PUF is a popular type of weak PUF as it does not require a specific design and the memory exists in all digital systems. It is more precisely described below. Another type of weak PUF is the contact PUF, as represented in Figure 14.8. It relies on vias between two metal layers. As the via is at the limit of connection, the noise during the fabrication process either creates a junction or leaves the via open.

Emerging Non Volatile memory, as resistive RAM, are good candidates to provide robust weak PUFs. Some other methods rely on the stress of the silicon oxide below the transistor gate. All these emerging PUFs require a specific process.

This chapter mainly focuses on the memory PUF that is the most used weak PUF. Its main drawback its native lack of reliability. Hence, there is a need to add processing to reduce the bit errors. This block is particularly important when the response is used for cryptographic use. A classical example of memory PUFs are the SRAM PUFs, one of the prominent PUFs that are commercially deployed. The startup values an SRAM cell that is otherwise used for storing data serves as a PUF response. As shown in Figure 14.9, the relative strength of the two inverters determine the power-up state of the SRAM cell. The address of the SRAM cell serves as the challenge for the PUF, which indicates the location of the SRAM cell activated to retrieve the response.

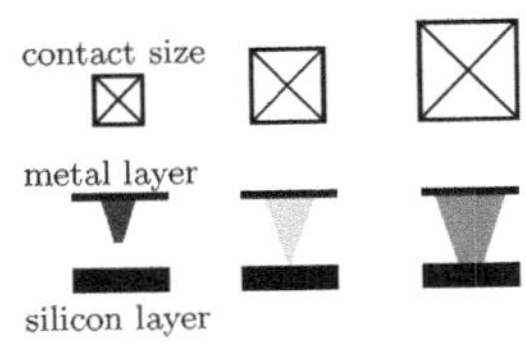

Figure 14.8. *Contact PUF. For a color version of this figure, see www.iste.co.uk/prouff/cryptography2.zip*

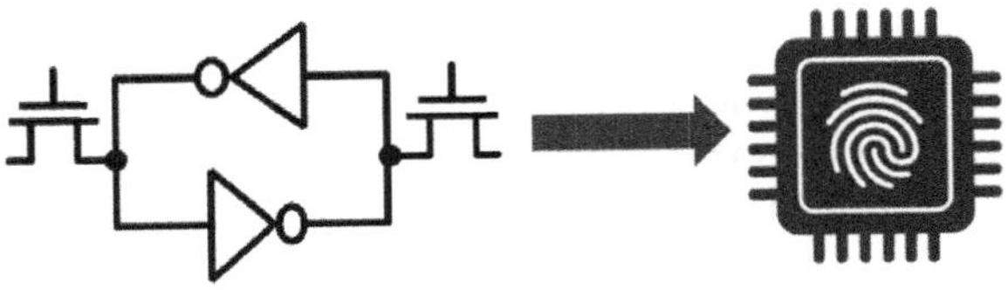

Figure 14.9. *SRAM cell with cross-coupled inverters and device fingerprinting using SRAM PUFs. For a color version of this figure, see www.iste.co.uk/prouff/cryptography2.zip*

SRAM PUFs are typically used for device intrinsic key generation as it can ideally generate unique response per device. It is to be noted that the response of an SRAM PUF is 0-skewed or 1-skewed or neutral, that is, it can either be 0 or 1. An error correcting code (ECC) is required to get a reliable response from SRAM PUFs. An ECC-enabled SRAM PUF can be used for reliable key generation for cryptographic applications.

However, all devices like FPGAs may not have such SRAM structures. In these situations, butterfly PUFs were proposed as candidate weak PUFs exploiting the basic underlying principles of SRAM PUFs. The basic building blocks for SRAM based PUFs are cross-couple circuits, which store a specific bit in the loop, owing to its positive feedback (Figure 14.10).

The latch has two stable operating points and one unstable operating point. The circuits are designed as symmetrically as possible, ensuring that the small differences are due to the slight wiring delay differences in the feedback paths and the voltage-transfer characteristics of the feedback elements. Thus, while the circuit is usually in the unstable operating region, it moves to one of the stable regions. However, the final stable operating point, which corresponds to a response of 0 or 1 is hard for an external person to predict due to the uncertainty of the disorder, which causes the circuit to stabilize. Hence, while for the same device the circuit produces a repeatable response, the response from one device does not provide any information of the response expected from another device, thus providing the much needed uniqueness property of PUFs. The concept of a butterfly PUF is based on using FPGA structures to realize the basic idea of cross-coupling as in an SRAM PUF. In this case (Figure 14.11), as combinatorial feedbacks are hard to design in an FPGA, there are two latches in a cross-coupled loop.

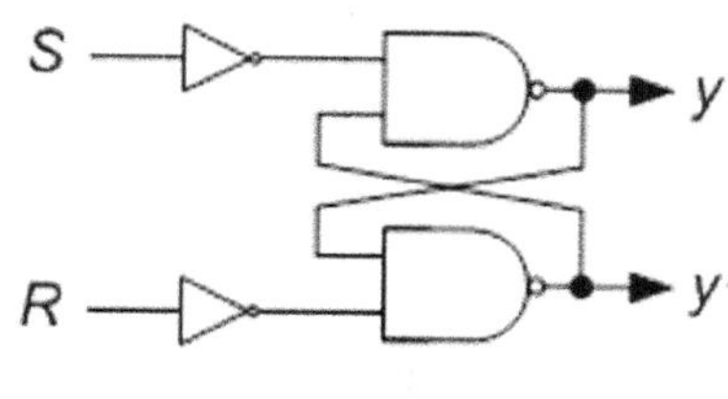

Figure 14.10. *Cross-couple latch: A basic building block for memory-based PUFs*

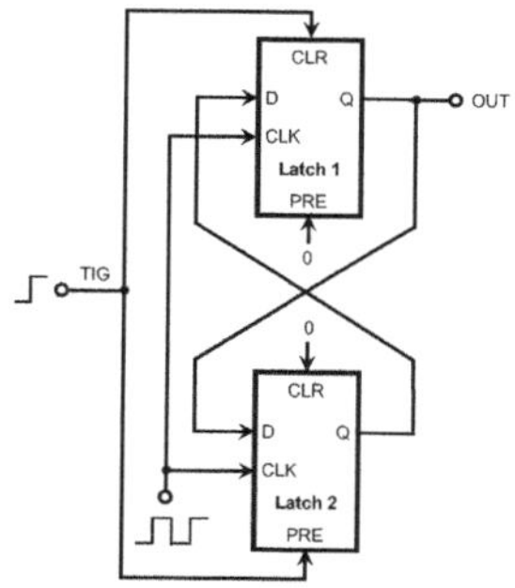

Figure 14.11. *Butterfly PUF*

The latch elements have a PRE signal, which when set high, drives the state Q of the corresponding latch to logic 1, while there is a CLR signal which when set high, drives Q to logic 0. The PRE signal and the CLR signal of the latches are set to logic 0, and the latch propagates the input D to Q when the clock signal (CLK) goes high. When we want the device to operate as a PUF, the input signal TIG is used to excite the circuit by assigning TIG to logic 1. This sets the two latches in conflicting modes, latch1 trying to go to logic 0, while latch2 tending to go logic 1. After few clock cycles, the TIG is brought low, thus allowing the circuit to settle down to either logic 0 or 1, depending on the wire delays. The wire delays are ensured almost equal lengths by careful manual placement or by suitably guiding the FPGA design processes through constraints, thus making the tendency toward 0 or 1 a function of the intrinsic properties of the device. This provides the circuit PUF like properties, where for the same device the response would be repeatable and reliable, even when the temperature or other operating conditions are varied, but for a new device, an external agent's guess on the stable state of the design would be as good as a random guess.

14.2.2. *Strong PUFs*

The strong PUF requires an architecture which accepts many CRPs and has a high complexity to make it difficult to model by an attacker. The delay-PUF is the most popular class of strong PUFs. It relies on the propagation time of logic gates along a delay chain.

The archetype of delay PUF in electronics is the arbiter PUF as illustrated in Figure 14.12.

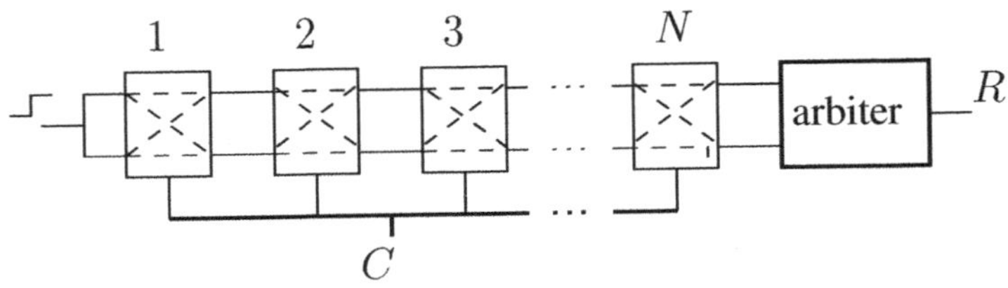

Figure 14.12. *Arbiter PUF*

The N-bit challenge C drives two delay paths feeding by the same signal. An edge of the input signal triggers a race between the top and the bottom path. The two paths are determined by N delay elements, which can swap the paths according to the challenge bit. The winner of the race is given by the arbiter (as an SR-latch) at the end of the chain. The decision is the 1-bit response R, who can be modeled as in equation [14.2].

$$R = sign(\sum_{i=1}^{N}(2^{C_i} - 1)(d_i^1 - d_i^0)) \qquad [14.2]$$

With C_i being the challenge bit of delay element i , d_i^1 being the delay difference between the top path and the bottom path when C_i is at '1', and d_i^0 is when C_i is at "0".

The design of the delay element is not obvious as the two lines must cross each other, which makes the element difficult to balance. As seen in the chapter related to entropy, the imbalance creates a bias that decreases the randomness of the response. It is preferable to design by using two identical delay chains as shown in Figure 14.13. The only design constraint is to duplicate the placement and routing of the two delay chains.

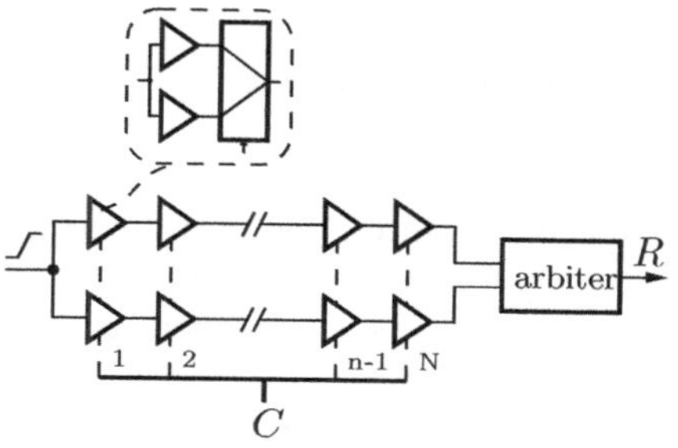

Figure 14.13. *Arbiter PUF with identical delay chain*

Rather than comparing two identical delay chains in one shot, the delay chain can be compared if they are looped by an inverter, thus forming a ring oscillator (RO). One interest of this approach providing ring-based PUFs is that the response can be quantified on more than one bit. However, the response latency is increased. The RO-PUF is the most popular ring-based PUF, as illustrated in Figure 14.14.

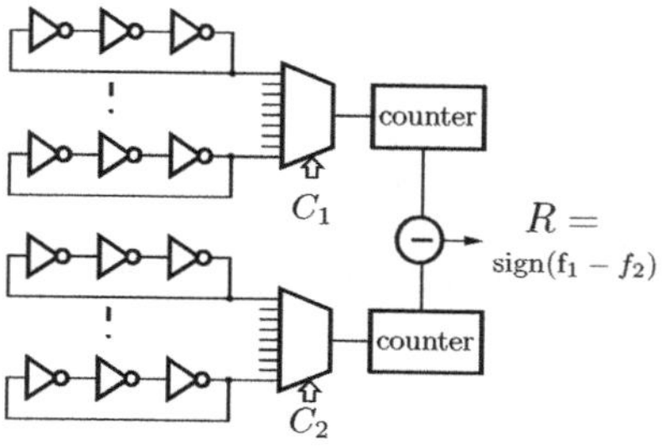

Figure 14.14. *RO- PUF*

The RO-PUF architecture relies on a set of identical ROs, where two of them are considered for a comparison of oscillation frequencies. The challenge bit is to select the pair of the two ROs to compare and the response is extracted from the frequency difference.

The loop-PUF is a ring-based structure that requires only one RO with controllable delay elements, as shown in Figure 14.15.

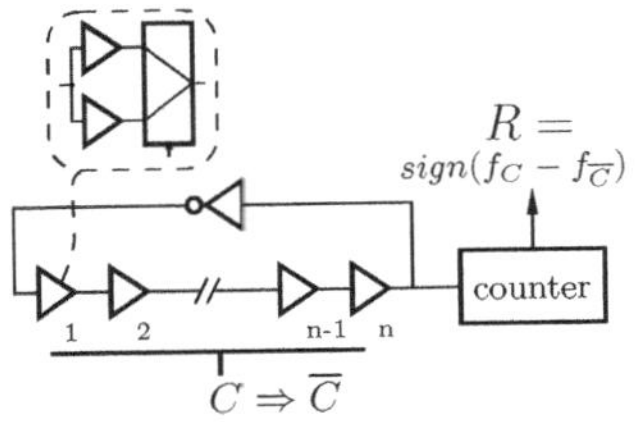

Figure 14.15. *Loop-PUF*

This PUF requires a specific protocol: the measurement of frequency with the challenge C must be followed by the measurement with the complementary challenge $\overline{C}$. The response is extracted from the frequency difference.

Concerning the ring-based PUF, like the RO-PUF and loop-PUF, it is interesting to note that the quantization of the response that may be not only the sign (or MSB). It can be on more MSB bits, giving rise to multi-bin response, whereas the arbiter-PUF has only a dual-bit response. This specificity can be helpful to optimize the reliability and entropy properties at the expense of a greater latency.

PUF	W/S	Physical source	Design type	Members
Delay-PUF	S	Difference of delays in delay chains	Standard	Arbiter-PUF, XOR-arbiter PUF, interpose-PUF, RO-PUF, RO-sum PUF, Loop-PUF
Memory-PUF	W	Difference of threshold voltage of two looped inverting gates	Standard or no design	SRAM-PUF, DFF-PUF, latch-PUF, buskeeper-PUF, MECCA-PUF, TERO-PUF
Metal-PUF	W	Conductivity of wires and vias	Custom	Contact-PUF, Litho-PUF
Oxide-breakdown-PUF	W	Gate oxide rupture when stressed	Custom	SOFT-BD-PUF
Emerging NVM-PUF	W	Cell resistivity after initialisation	Custom, hybrid technology	RRAM-PUF, MRAM-PUF

Table 14.1. *List of the main PUF types in digital circuits*

14.2.3. *Big picture of PUF architectures*

Table 14.1 shows a classification of the main representative PUF families in digital devices according to the physical sources. It indicates if they are natively strong or weak (W/S) and the main physical principle.

This table also shows the design effort for a given family. The delay and memory PUFs are easy to design in current CMOS technology like standard-cell ASICs or FPGAs, without the use of full custom technologies. As they are very sensitive to noise, other types of PUF families have been proposed to reduce this weakness. This table is not exhaustive as the literarure is rich of original and astute PUFs. It considers the most representative PUFs, which give rise to many studies, and for some of them, technological transfers to the industry.

14.3. Reliability enhancement

The steadiness, or reliability, is a key property as the generation of the PUF response can be corrupted by environmental noise and aging. For delay and memory PUFs, the experiments show that the BER is around 2–15%. It turns out that reliability enhancement techniques are necessary, especially when the PUF is used to generate a response which might be steady, as for a key generation. The main techniques to enhance reliability are as follows:

– correction with ECC, allowing us to build a "fuzzy extractor" of the key;

– proactive selection of challenges where unreliable CRPs or response bits are discarded;

– use of a technology that provides native stability. Some emerging technologies are proposed to be natively very reliable, such as metal-PUF, software-breakdown-PUFs and RRAM or MRAM PUFs. They require a significant design effort or an hybridization with CMOS technology.

The choice of ECC and the threshold to filter out unreliable challenges must integrate the environmental noise, that is, the change in temperature and power supply voltage in addition to local noise. The aging has also to be taken into account. The most impactful aging phenomenon is the negative bias temperature instability (NBTI), which is manifested by an increase of the threshold voltage of transistors, and is particularly evident in switched-on PMOS. This effect can be reduced by using burn-in stages to bypass the first period of usage where the aging is predominant.

Other solutions are to build architectures or protocols to make sure the P-MOS transistors are switch-off when the PUF is not used.

14.3.1. *Use of error correcting codes*

For ECC and challenge selection, HD is necessary to help reconstructing the PUF. Figure 14.16 illustrates the way to construct and use the HD when an ECC is used in a "code-offset" mode. The HD, called "secure sketch", is a linear addition of an ECC codeword and a set of response bits r. A key can be derived by the fuzzy extraction method based on a hash function of the set of corrected responses and a public word p.

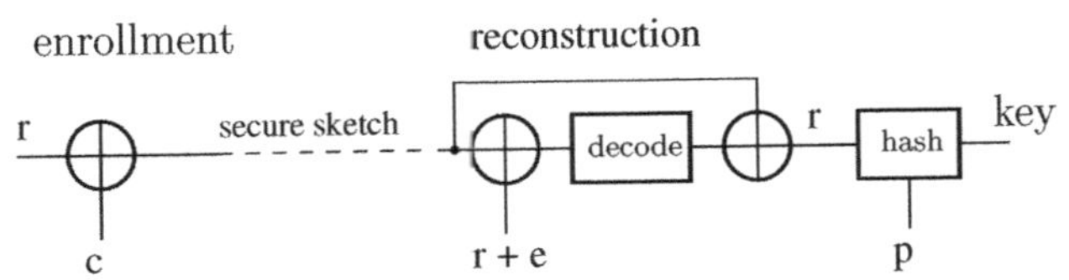

Figure 14.16. *PUF fuzzy extraction of a key by means of ECC and secure sketch*

With a high error rate of a few percentage, it is necessary to use concateneted ECC codes, that is, two ECC in cascade, to go down to very BEC-like 10^{-9}.

Some of the popular ECC schemes used to get a reliable PUF response include Bose–Chaudhuri–Hocquenghem (BCH) codes, Reed–Muller (RM) codes and repetition (C_{Rep}) codes. Hence, an ECC-enabled SRAM PUF can be used for reliable key generation for cryptographic applications. The ECC circuit is used to generate a helper information which is registered at the time of enrollment. Subsequently, the noisy PUF responses are corrected using the helper information. However, before discussing in detail the techniques of generating and using helper information, we present a brief background on the coding theory.

14.3.1.1. *Coding theory*

Coding theory explores the bijective mapping of a message space $\mathcal{M}$ into a codeword space $\mathcal{V}$. A linear block code (C) is typically defined using the parameters $[n, k, d]$ with message length $k = log_2(|\mathcal{M}|)$, n being the length of each codeword (v) and d being the minimum number of bits in which two unique codewords should differ. A code C is capable of decoding up to $t = \lfloor (d-1)/2 \rfloor$ errors. There exists 2^k valid codewords ($v \in \mathcal{V}$) and there are $(2^n - 2^k)$ invalid words (v'') such that $v'' \notin \mathcal{V}$. Further, the minimum weight among non-zero codewords in C is also d.

The translation $\mathcal{M} \rightarrow \mathcal{V}$ or the encoding process in C, utilizes generalized vectors which can be mapped into a $(k \times n)$ *generator matrix* (**G**), such that the following equation holds true:

$$v = \bigoplus_{i=0}^{k-1} m_i \cdot g_i \qquad [14.3]$$

Here, m_i denotes individual message bits of a message $\mathcal{M}$, wherein $m_i \in \{0, 1\}, \forall\, 0 \leq i \leq k-1$. Also, we use $g_i, 0 \leq i \leq k-1$ to denote the k-rows of the generator matrix, $\mathbf{G}$. $\mathbf{G} = [\mathbf{P}||\mathbf{I}_k]$, where $||$ is used to denote augmentation of two matrices $\mathbf{P}$ and $\mathbf{I}_k$, where $\mathbf{P}$ is the parity bit matrix and $\mathbf{I}_k$ is the $(k \times k)$ identity matrix. The *parity check matrix* ($\mathbf{H}$) is a crucial matrix utilized in the decoding process in C. $\mathbf{H}$ consists of an $(n-k) \times (n-k)$ identity matrix followed by the transpose of the parity bits in $\mathbf{G}$ $(= \mathbf{P}^T)$. Formally, $\mathbf{H} = [\mathbf{I}_{n-k}\mathbf{P}^T]$. During the decoding phase, v can potentially get corrupted and transformed to v', such that $v' = v \oplus e$, where v is the original codeword and e is the error vector introduced through the channel. Now, $e_i = 1$ for $v'_i \neq v_i$, otherwise $e_i = 0$ for $v'_i = v_i$, where $0 \leq i \leq n-1$. Let r be the received word such that $r \in \{v, v'\}$. The decoder computes an $(n-k)$-tuple, known as the *Syndrome* (Syn) of r. Mathematically, Syn can be defined as follows:

$$Syn = r \cdot \mathbf{H}^T = (v \oplus e)\mathbf{H}^T = v \cdot \mathbf{H}^T \oplus e \cdot \mathbf{H}^T \qquad [14.4]$$

For valid codewords, $Syn = 0$ implying $r = v$; otherwise, $Syn = e \cdot \mathbf{H}^T$ for $r = v'$. A special array consisting of the 2^n words (r) partitioned into 2^k disjoint subsets (D_i), such that each subset D_i has a one-to-one correspondence with a unique codeword (v), is called the *standard array*. Hence, the standard array highlights a decoding methodology for r. For *perfect codes*, r always differs at t-bits from a codeword v, that is, the Hamming distance between r and v denoted as $\mathbf{HD}(r, v) = t$. Words with $\mathbf{HD}(r, v) > t$ are not guaranteed to be decodable. For *cyclic codes*, any number of circular shifts in its codeword (v_x) configuration bits results in another codeword (v_y). The standard array has $2^n/2^k = 2^{n-k}$ disjoint rows, which are called the *cosets* of C. The first n-tuple error vector e_0 in a coset is called the *coset leader* or coset representative of each coset. However, any member of a particular coset can be its coset leader. The coset in which r belongs gives the introduced e in r, utilizing which the corresponding codeword v can be decoded. There exists 2^{n-k} coset leaders, including the all zero vectors. They form the *correctable error vectors*.

14.3.1.2. *Helper data algorithms*

Next, we discuss the importance and working principles of HD generation algorithms for PUF-based key generation. First, PUF responses are typically *noisy*. Hence, it cannot be used directly as a key in a cryptographic primitive. Secondly, even if the regenerated responses are not noisy, the PUF responses cannot form a cryptographically secure key because they are *not uniformly distributed*. This is where the secure sketch algorithm for HD generation comes to aid.

The secure sketch consists of a couple of procedures, namely, the generation procedure (GEN) that takes the input of the PUF response (x) and publishes the HD

(w_1). Formally, $w_1 \leftarrow GEN(x)$. The second procedure is the reconstruction procedure (REP) that utilizes the publicly known information p and the noisy version of the PUF response ($\tilde{x}$) to recover ($\hat{x}$). If $\mathbf{HD}(x, \hat{x}) < t$, the recovery is successful. Otherwise, there is no guarantee of the same. Here, t is the error correcting capability of the underlying block code in the secure sketch. Most secure sketches rely on binary block codes for the recovery procedure. Formally, $\hat{x} \leftarrow REP(\tilde{x}, w_1)$.

A fuzzy extractor slightly modifies the concept of a secure sketch. The first fuzzy extractor was initially aimed at biometric applications. It follows the same procedures as that of the secure sketch, however, with a slight modification. The GEN procedure now requires two inputs: the PUF response x and a set ($\mathcal{H}$) of the universal hash functions to publish the HD set W, such that $W = (w_1, w_2)$. Here, w_1 is generated in the same way as that of a secure sketch, hence it is synonymous to Y, but w_2 stores the index of the hash function chosen as randomness extractor to generate the secret key. Henceforth, the REP procedure recovers the key using HD set W and the noisy PUF response ($\tilde{x}$) to regenerate the secret key (K). Like a secure sketch, the fuzzy extractor relies on binary block codes (C) for the GEN and REP procedures. Exploring elaborately into the GEN procedure, the PUF response (x) is XORed with a randomly chosen word C_s from C. The secret key is generated from the response by utilizing a *hash* function. Figure 14.17 lists the fuzzy extractor's GEN and REP procedures. The error correcting capability of the fuzzy extractor depends on the efficacy of the underlying block code utilized in its construction. One important aspect is the fact that as the HD depends on the PUF response, it does leak some information of the secret response. Entropy bounds have been developed to measure this leakage.

$(K, W) \leftarrow GEN(x, h)$	$K \leftarrow REP(W, \tilde{x})$
$K \leftarrow h_i(x)$	$C'_s \leftarrow w_1 \oplus \tilde{x}$
$W(w_1, w_2)$	$C_s \leftarrow C'_s$
$random\ C_s \in C$	$x \leftarrow w_1 \oplus C_s$
$w_1 \leftarrow C_s \oplus x$ and $w_2 \leftarrow h_i$	$K \leftarrow w_2(x)$

Figure 14.17. *The fuzzy extractor for key generation*

14.3.2. *Discarding unreliable bits*

In case of challenge filtering, the unreliable response bits, sometimes called dark bits, are marked and discarded. The HD can be used to point out these bits. They will be discarded during the reconstruction phase. This filtering operation requires a reliability threshold to adjust the BER. This directly impacts the entropy as less responses are available.

14.3.3. *Stochastic model of reliability*

Stochastic models are build to express the PUF properties according to the architecture, the technological dispersion and the environment including dynamic noise, temperature and aging. Reliability and entropy are the main properties, which can be formalized by stochastic models.

The stochastic model is expressed with the error probability, or BER, where a bit of response is considered erroneous if it differs from the reference enrollment value. The knowledge of the stochastic model greatly helps the designer to add correction mechanisms. A parameter that directly impacts the reliability is the ratio of the variance of the process mismatch to the noise variance, often called signal-to-noise ratio (SNR). The process and noise distributions are normally distributed which is verified by the experiments on many PUFs. As the delay and memory PUFs in CMOS are natively unreliable, with a BER of a few percentage, their stochastic model allows the designer to dimension the effort to make the PUF steady.

14.3.3.1. *Weak PUFs*

The responses of weak PUFs have a two-bins distribution. Their stochastic model is validated by multiple measurements and relies on the distribution of the error probability. Weak PUFs are dependent to their spatial position and layout, especially if they are organized in matricial architectures like SRAM PUFs. It turns out that the error probability is specific to each memory cell. An accurate stochastic model has to take into account the position of each cell, along with the environmental noise and aging.

14.3.3.2. *Strong PUFs*

If we consider Delay-PUFs, their response is the result of a threshold function which is generally the sign of the delay difference: $\operatorname{sgn}\left(\sum_{i=1}^{n} c_i \Delta_i\right)$, where $c_i \in \{\pm 1\}$ are the challenges bits (being equal to either -1 or $+1$), and where Δ_i is the random process variation associated with element $1 \leq i \leq n$ in an n-bit delay PUF. It has been shown that the *BER* model is expressed by: $\widehat{\text{BER}} = \frac{1}{\pi} \arctan(\frac{1}{\sqrt{\text{SNR}}})$. The correction capacity of the *ECC* is then applied to refine the model. Multi-bin strong PUFs facilitates the correction as the reliability is internally known in the module of the response. For instance, the *ECC* correction can take advantage of a soft-decision for decoding. Also, when filtering out unreliable challenges with multi-bin delay-PUFs, a response is considered unreliable if its reliability value is within $W.\sigma$ with σ being the noise standard deviation. The stochastic model in this case is closed to:

$$\text{BER} = \frac{2}{\operatorname{erfc}(\frac{W}{\sqrt{2}\sqrt{\text{SNR}}})} \left(T(W, \frac{1}{\sqrt{\text{SNR}}}) + \frac{1}{4} \operatorname{erf}(\frac{W}{\sqrt{2} \cdot \sqrt{\text{SNR}}})(\operatorname{erf}(\frac{W}{\sqrt{2}}) - 1) \right).$$

with T being the Owen's T function. Figure 14.18 illustrates the *BER* curves according to the SNR for different levels of filtering. Another method with the multi-bin PUFs is to use two metrics rather than the sign (or 0 threshold), thus allowing us to choose the best metrics for a maximal reliability, the HD indicating which is the best metrics.

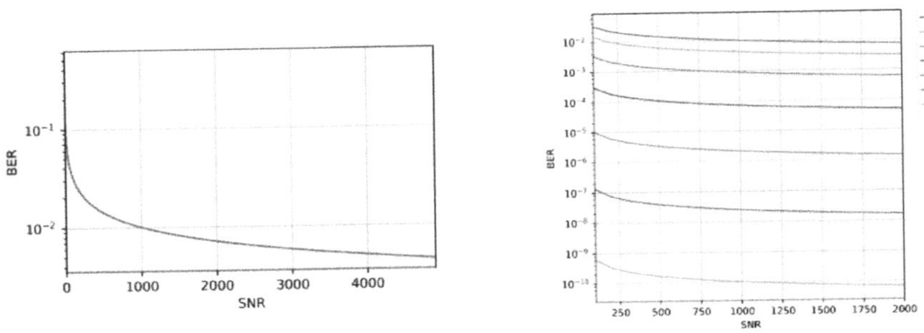

Figure 14.18. *BER with and without challenges filtering. For a color version of this figure, see www.iste.co.uk/prouff/cryptography2.zip*

14.4. Entropy assessment

The PUF entropy is also of utmost importance as it expresses the unpredictability and uniformity of the PUF responses in a same device (intra-die) or between devices (inter-die). The entropy inter-die corresponds to the "uniqueness" property. It is fundamental to get a trusted identification and authentication of devices. The entropy intra-die is particularly important to know when the PUF generates a cryptographic key, as it must be exactly equal to the key length. The uniformity is one characteristic to express the quality of randomnsess. It corresponds to the 1-bit intra-die entropy and allows us to point out a bias in the PUF architecture.

The uniqueness and randomness properties can be assessed by statistical tests such as the ones proposed in the ISO/IEC 20897-1/-2 international standards (see section 14.7.1), or the true random number generator (TRNG) tests. As the uniqueness requires many devices, the tests can be leveraged by a stochastic model formalizing the entropy versus the architecture, environment and noise. It can also formalize the n-bit entropy, which is crucial for a key generation.

14.4.1. *Stochastic model of the entropy*

The entropy is greatly impacted by the reliability, the PUF architecture and the PUF layout, which can generate bias. Unbiased weak PUFs have a very simple expression of their entropy: it is equal to the number of elements which are reliable. The estimation of the entropy for strong PUFs is more complex: The number of challenges is *exponential* in the size of the PUF, but the entropy is not scaling as fast. For instance, a one-bit difference in challenges of a delay-PUF involves a very small increase in entropy. It has been shown that an n-bit delay PUF, as the arbiter-PUF or Loop-PUF, has an entropy which is equal to n for n-bit challenges if they are reliable and belong to Hadamard codes, that is, having a minimum Hamming distance of $n/2$. This property enables us to use strong PUFs as weak PUFs to generate a key. Beyond the entropy of n, the Shannon entropy scales about *quadratic* in the challenges space size as shown in Figure 14.19 with other types of entropy.

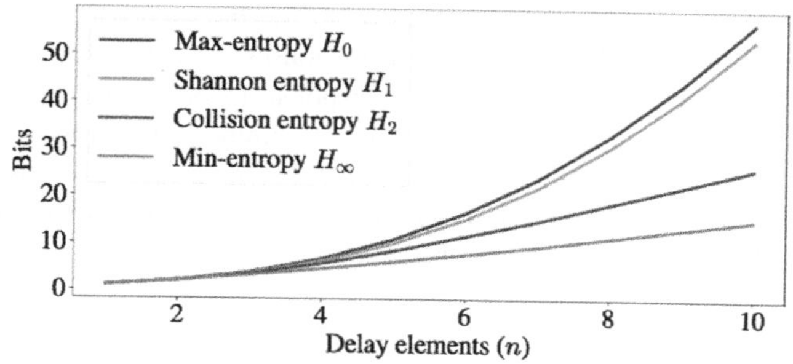

Figure 14.19. *Different entropy types for a delay PUF with $n \leq 10$ bits. For a color version of this figure, see www.iste.co.uk/prouff/cryptography2.zip*

14.4.2. *Entropy loss due to helper data*

Entropy is the measure of randomness. The min-entropy is a conservative measure of the randomness of an outcome. The min-entropy of a random variable X can be defined using equation [14.5].

The conditional min-entropy of a random variable X, given another random variable Y, is determined using equation [14.6], where X and Y may or may not be correlated.

$$\mathbb{H}_\infty(X) = -\log_2(\max_{x \in X} \mathbb{P}(X = x)) \qquad [14.5]$$

$$\tilde{\mathbb{H}}_\infty(X|Y) = -\log_2\left(\mathbb{E}_{y \leftarrow Y}[\max_{x \in X} \mathbb{P}((X = x)|(Y = y))]\right) \qquad [14.6]$$

Analyzing the entropy leakage of the PUF response, denoted using X, due to the exposure of the helper information, denoted as Y, thus amounts to bound the value of $\tilde{\mathbb{H}}_\infty(X|Y)$. Assume that the HD is generated by a linear block code C with parameters $[n, k, d]$. The residual conditional min-entropy of the PUF response (X), given the HD (Y), is always less than the min-entropy of the original PUF response. According to the HD algorithms, the simple reason is that whenever the HD is published, there is an information leakage that might lead to the successful recovery of the secret PUF response. Thus, it is easy to infer that the min-entropy loss should be minimized to achieve desired security.

The min-entropy loss, or the information leakage, is bounded by the well-established $(n - k)$ bound. However, subsequently researchers have proposed tighter bounds corresponding to the min-entropy loss utilizing a coset-based graphical approach. They have used a subset-partitioning of the PUF responses that consider realistic distributions in the PUF responses. One such partitioning could be based on the Hamming weights of the PUF responses; based on the intuition for a given Hamming class, the probability of a response to occur is similar. Thus, the subset-partitioning partitions X into a finite number of subsets φ_j, where $j \in \{1, (n + 1)\}$ such that all the elements belonging to a subset (φ_j) has the same probability (f_j) of occurrence. Here, f_j would denote the probability that the Hamming weight of a response x, is a chosen $(j - 1)$.

The residual min-entropy, $\tilde{\mathbb{H}}_\infty(X|Y)$, can be estimated using equation [14.6] and applying Bayes theorem. Thus, we have:

$$\tilde{\mathbb{H}}_\infty(X|Y) = -\log_2\left(\sum_{y\in\mathcal{Y}} \mathbb{P}(Y = y) \max_{x\in X} \frac{\mathbb{P}(X = x)\mathbb{P}(Y = y|X = x)}{\mathbb{P}(Y = y)}\right) \quad [14.7]$$

$$= -\log_2\left(\frac{1}{|\mathcal{M}|}\sum_{x\in X} \mathbb{P}(Y = y|X = x)\right) \quad [14.8]$$

Here, $\mathcal{M}$ denotes the message space. To obtain $\tilde{\mathbb{H}}_\infty(X|Y)$, a coset-based graphical approach, as illustrated in Figure 14.20, is utilized. The HD elements are mapped to the coset elements (represented as black squares), and the white squares are un-mapped coset elements. Figure 14.20 illustrates the case where 2^n PUF responses are uniformly distributed across all 2^{n-k} cosets. This provides an upper bound of the estimate for $\tilde{\mathbb{H}}_\infty(X|Y)$. On the other hand, a non-uniform and skewed distribution would provide the lower bound estimate.

However, equation [14.7] can now be rewritten as equation [14.9] to estimate $\tilde{\mathbb{H}}_\infty(X|Y)$ for any distribution of the PUF responses.

$$\tilde{\mathbb{H}}_\infty(X|Y) = -\log_2\left(\frac{1}{|\mathcal{M}|}\sum_{j=1}^{J} s_j^P f_j\right) \quad [14.9]$$

Here, s_j^P is the number of standard array elements assigned to the jth subset (φ_j) of the PUF response. Equation [14.9] proposes to estimate the residual min-entropy by iterating over all x. It assigns a HD $y \in Y$ to it through $x \oplus v$ until the set Y, the entire HD set, which is the standard array of size 2^n of the underlying linear block code, is exhausted.

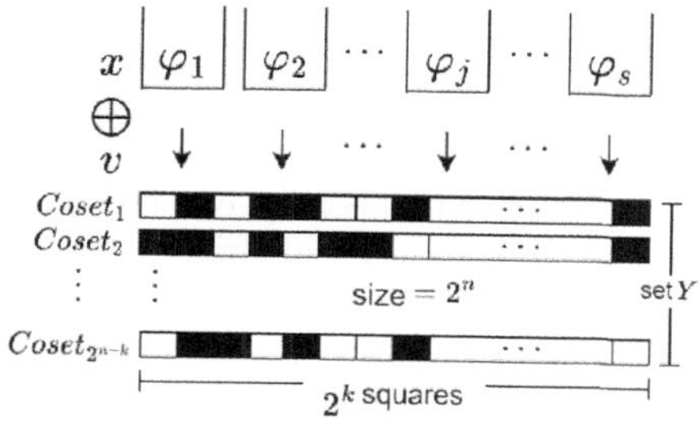

Figure 14.20. *Distribution of 2^n PUF responses into the set Y of size 2^n. Black squares denote the (decodable) terms in set Y that contribute to the calculation of residual min-entropy. The white squares do not contribute to $\tilde{\mathrm{H}}_\infty(X|Y)$*

14.5. Resistance to attacks

The resistance to attacks, whether mathematical or physical, is also imperative to keep the high level of security provided by the PUF.

The attacker's goal is to get the PUF response, and in case of strong PUFs the model in order to derive the response from any challenge. Attacks can be sorted according to their level of intrusion, or the type of channel used to extract information:

1) non-invasive attacks, which use functional channels from which the attacker manipulates inputs/outputs. One powerful non-invasive attack is the MA, which aims at finding the PUF model. It is particularly efficient when using ML algorithms;

2) semi-invasive attacks, using side-channels to observe or disturb the PUF activity. It can be used to extract the PUF response when not available on the functional channel; it can also be a support to MAs or used as profiling attacks;

3) invasive attacks, where the PUF blueprint is copied and cloned by physical means. This attack type tries to jeopardize the native unclonability property of PUFs.

The attacks on PUF can be mathematical, physical or both. Mathematical attacks are non-invasive and perpetrated by using functional channels. Physical attacks can be either semi-invasive or fully invasive by using side-channels or accessing the internal PUF structure.

14.5.1. *Non-invasive attacks*

The attack changes the inputs at will and accesses the outputs. The main attack type is to get the PUF model, also called PUF MA, by collecting many CRPs. As the weak PUF has no challenges, it is not concerned by this type of attack. The exploitation of the public HD is another type of powerful non-invasive attack.

14.5.1.1. *Modeling attacks*

The MA exploits the publicly available CRPs to find the model of a strong PUF. The resistance of a PUF to MA can be quantified with its representation as a Boolean function. The more this Boolean function is diffusive and non-linear, the more difficult it is to fit a model on the PUF. This property of strict avalanche criterion (SAC) is not met by strong PUFs, which have linear additive delay models, thus are easy to model. The ML algorithms are particularly efficient to build the model, which can be learned in a few thousand pairs of challenge-responses in an arbiter-PUF. Moreover, an ML attack can be greatly helped by side-channel observations. In order to be resistant against MA, the addition of nonlinearity is to combine PUFs, or to cipher the challenge and/or the response, or to use a specific protocol between the trusted server and the PUF.

PUF combination: the combination relies on using different PUFs either in parallel, or by composing them sequentially, or both. A popular combination of PUFs relies on XORing different strong PUF outputs. XORing many arbiter PUFs, seriously increases the robustness against MA, but at the expense of a loss of reliability. However, this type of combination remains vulnerable asymptotically. For instance, one of the most robust PUF is the interpose PUF, which turns out to be more robust than the XOR-PUF with the same complexity. However, it has been attacked by powerful ML using a divide-and-conquer approach and millions of CRPs in the training dataset.

Ciphering the challenge-response: the PUF is "controlled" or surrounded by cryptographic blocks like a hash function to thwart the ML attacks. The response requires necessarily an error correction block as a single bit error generates an avalanche of errors at the cryptographic block output. This solution is efficient against ML attacks but involves the use of a cryptographic functions which may not meet the low-cost requirement. This raises the question of using the PUF with CRPs as the protection against MA involves a significant increase in complexity compared to the PUF generating a cryptographic key and a priori unsensitive to MA.

PUF protocol: if the authentication server and the PUF agree on a specific protocol, the response is not directly obtained from the challenge, thus thwarting the MA. Many protocols have been proposed. Recent studies have shown that no protocol is perfectly immune to these attacks

14.5.1.2. *Attacks exploiting the helper data*

When the PUF generates a cryptographic key or is used as controlled PUF in an unreliable technology, the HD is absolutely necessary. However, it is a public word which can be used or manipulated to give rise to powerful attacks. As the response is not known, the attacker tries to find the dependency between the HD and the PUF behavior or directly use the modified key. For instance, in the code-offset method when using ECC, the HD, or secure sketch, can be simply Xored with another codeword to change the key and perpetrate related key attacks. The HD can also be used without manipulation: as the codeword provides redundancy of the PUF, the knowledge of the code family, the HD and the challenge leaks the PUF model which can be found by ML. Another simple example is to manipulate the bits of HD pointed to reliable challenges. If two consecutive bits (only one being reliable), are swapped in the HD and the PUF behavior is the same, it can be deduced that the bits are the same. Extending this 2-bit comparison to all the bits allows the attacker to find the whole response. Protection against such attacks is crucial. One solution is to store the HD in a non-writable memory to avoid manipulation, another is to hash it and combine with the generated key.

14.5.2. *Semi-invasive attacks*

Side-channel attacks (SCA) are the main class of semi-invasive attacks. A side-channel can be the power, the electromagnetic radiation, the execution time or an error probability. They can be used to support the MA, to extract the response of PUF or to do a profiling attack by SCA. Only strong PUFs are targeted in both cases. They are generally passive, but some of them can be active to disturb the internal behavior of the PUF.

Modeling attacks supported by side-channel: the side-channel leakage is a strong support to MA, especially to target the intermediate results of a compositions of PUFs where a divide and conquer approach is used. The error probability is a particularly efficient side-channel as it gives accurate value of the delay accumulation near the decision threshold of the response bit. For instance, it has been shown that the XOR arbiter PUF can be attacked linearly with the number of XORs by taking advantage of the reliability information. Also, by changing the environment conditions, like increasing the temperature and thermal noise, the MA based on low reliability is facilitated.

Direct attack by side-channel: the response of a PUF can directly leak in its side-channels. This attack is powerful when the response is not directly accessible like for controlled PUFs or PUFs generating a key. For instance, the RO-PUF and loop-PUF are prone to EM analysis which can extract the oscillation frequency, thus the response. An EM probe can also inject harmonics to lock the internal RO oscillations of PUFs like TRNG based on ROs. Attacking an arbiter PUF is more difficult as the SNR is very small as it is a one-shot arbitration, but it can be leveraged by multiple tries.

Profiling attack by side-channel: if the adversary has access to a reference arbiter-PUF, they can use the storage Flip-Flop for distinguishing the response and perform a non-invasive "profiling" attacks. They create from the power traces a reference PUF whose responses can be learned by ML. Then, ML is used to infer the response of other unknown PUFs, thus giving rise to *Cross-PUF* attacks. Profiling attacks can also target associated PUF processing as ECC, where the code redundancy amplifies the leakage.

Protections against SCA: the protection against MA using power side-channel can be inspired by those devised for cryptographic implementations, which could be either hiding or masking the leakage. The masking method can be temporal to randomize the frequency of ROs, or spatial, as for instance the use of threshold implementation. Hiding can be the use of dual-rail logic that makes the power constant. However, the process mismatch which is the good property to get a PUF can harm the balance required by the dual-rail logic.

14.5.3. *Invasive attacks*

The invasive attacks allow the attacker to copy the PUF from the observation and/or modification of its layout. It requires a preparation phase to access the PUF and can be destructive. A priori it seems very difficult to extract the static physical information from PUFs as the technological dispersion is hardy observable, thus involving the unclonability property. However, it has been shown that cloning a memory cell can be planned with sophisticated failure analysis setup. Typically, if the circuit is still operational, SRAM PUFs are vulnerable to the readout operation by laser which stimulates the cells. Then, a cloning can be done by using a "Focus Ion Beam", which can edit silicon structures. As this attack is sensitive to noise and is efficient at startup, a countermeasure is to use a reset signal on SRAM that would be triggered only by the user.

14.6. Characterizations

In this section, some public datasets of measurements are provided for the reader to have the opportunity to exercise themselves.

14.6.1. *Reliability–aging*

Reliability and aging estimation requires some datasets where the PUF outputs a physical quantity, before turning it into bits. Some papers of the literature provide studies relying on public dataset, along with some python scripts for further analysis and graphical representations. One method of reliability analysis for the delay-PUFs is to characterize through repeated measurements of preselected challenges for a full range of temperatures and voltages.

14.6.2. *Machine learning attacks on challenge–response protocol*

The software `pypuf` is a toolbox for simulation, testing and attacking PUFs. It contains datasets (obtained from simulations) and attack codes for the following strong PUFs:

– arbiter PUF-based designs utilizing the additive delay model, including simulations of the arbiter PUF, XOR arbiter PUF, lightweight secure PUF, permutation PUF and interpose PUF;

– feed-forward arbiter PUFs and XORs;

– PUF designs based on bistable rings;

– integrated optical PUFs.

14.7. Standardization

14.7.1. *International standards*

ISO/IEC 20897-1 specifies the security requirements for PUFs. They concern the output properties, tamper-resistance and unclonability of a single and a batch of PUFs. It also describes the typical use cases of a PUF.

ISO/IEC DIS 20897-2 specifies the test and evaluation methods for PUFs. They consist of inspection of the design rationale of the PUF and comparison between statistical analyses of the responses from a batch of PUFs or a unique PUF versus specified thresholds.

These standards present a way to categorize the PUFs. The responses from PUFs and their repetitive calls are arranged into a cube as Figure 14.21 shows. The single small cube describes a 1-bit response from a PUF. The three axes of the cube and the time are described hereafter as directions:

– *Direction B*: "#bit" shows the bit length of the response obtained from a single challenge. In a 1-bit response PUF, for example, arbiter PUF, the dimension B collapses.

– *Direction C*: "#challenge" shows the number of different challenges given to a PUF. In a no-challenge PUF (or, more rigorously, a one-challenge PUF like in SRAM PUF), the dimension C collapses.

– *Direction D*: "#PUF" shows the number of different PUF devices under test.

– *Direction T*: "#query" shows the number of query iterations under the fixed PUF device and challenge.

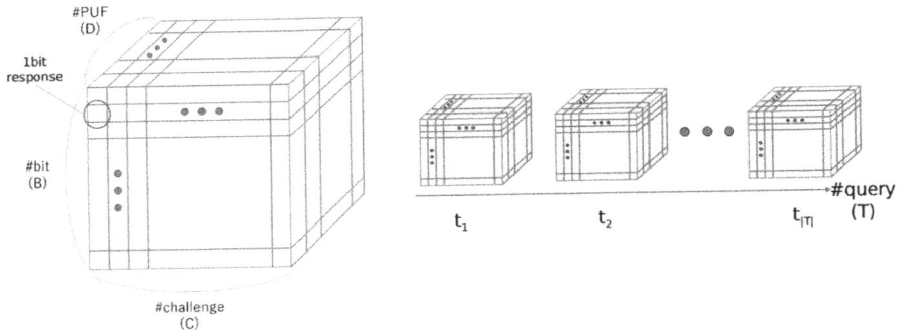

Figure 14.21. *The four dimensions involved in the PUFs metrics. For a color version of this figure, see www.iste.co.uk/prouff/cryptography2.zip*

14.7.2. *Standards requiring PUF*

Some market-oriented standards prescribe the use of PUFs. For instance, EVITA is specifying the requirements for security in automotive applications. The key security component in an automotive chip is its "Hardware Security Module" (HSM). Requirements are set on the HSM, which can be either *low*, *medium* and *high*, depending on the criticality of the ECU to be protected. It is mandated for EVITA high profile that a PUF is used for the master key.

14.8. Notes and further references

History: the concept dates back from early 1980s, by the pioneering work of Bauder (1983) and Simmons (1984, 1991). Naccache and Frémanteau (1992) provided an authentication scheme in 1992 for memory cards. The terms POWF (physical one-way function) and PUF (physical unclonable function) were coined by Pappu (2001) and Gassend et al. (2002a); the latter publication described the first integrated PUF where, unlike PUFs based on optics, the measurement circuitry and the PUF are integrated onto the same electrical circuit (and fabricated on silicon).

PUF types: there have been numerous PUF variants reported so far (Böhm and Hofer 2012; Basel 2018). Here is an excerpt of technologies taken from a selection of published academic papers: optical PUF by Pappu (2001), coating PUF by Tuyls et al. (2007), SRAM PUF by Holcomb et al. (2009), glitch PUF by Suzuki and Shimizu (2010), arbiter PUF by Pappu et al. (2002) and Gassend et al. (2002a), ring-oscillator PUF by Suh and Devadas (2007), loop-PUF by Cherif et al. (2012), memory in logic PUF (MeLPUF) by Vega et al. (2020), memory contention PUF by Güneysu (2012), oxide rupture PUF by Wu et al (2018b), transistor voltage threshold by Su et al.

(2008), Via-PUF by ICTK (2021), resistive RAM by Mazady et al. (2015), TERO by Marchand et al. (2016), etc.

Use cases: a tutorial about PUFs is given in Herder et al. (2014). An example of key generation is in Maes et al. (2012) and an application to logic locking in Roy et al. (2008).

Reasons for variability of PUFs: the three main reasons in CMOS are the density of dopants in the depletion area (Asenov et al. 2001), the thickness of the insulator below the gate (Asenov et al. 2002) and the line edge roughness (Asenov et al. 2003).

Properties: desirable properties have been explored since 2012 Maes (2012). Some of these notions have been analyzed theoretically by Armknecht et al. (2016). Since then, those properties have made their way to practical implementations (Danger et al. 2016). It is expected that the reliability remains good enough, across PVTA (process voltage temperature aging) corners of the PUF (Anik et al. 2021). Experiments can be carried out to quantify the reliability (Katzenbeisser et al. 2012). Besides, aging can also be taken into account (Karimi et al. 2016, 2017, 2018). Postprocessing with error correction codes (ECC) to build a fuzzy extraction is proposed by Dodis et al. (2004). Some implementation examples are given in Bösch et al. (2008); Maes et al. (2009, 2012). Proactive selection of challenges are presented in Hofer and Böhm (2010); Suh and Devadas (2007), where unreliable changes are discarded; some technologies that provides native stability can be found in Wu et al. (2018a); Liu et al. (2016); Chuang et al. (2019).

Architectures: a comprehensive list of VLSI PUFs is maintained by the National University of Singapore (National University of Singapore – Department of Electrical & Computer Engineering, Faculty of Engineering (Massimo Alioto 2021). This database contains performance indications and also security information.

Reliability: the work from Maes (2013) introduces a model of reliability in memory PUF. The reliability of RO-PUFs and loop-PUFs is studied by Schaub et al. (2018, 2020a). The two-metrics approach to enhance reliability in multi-bin PUFs is presented in Danger et al. (2019).

Entropy: the entropy of a PUF can be modeled as a function of the technological dispersion as shown in Pelgrom et al. (1989). PUF are biased already at their architecture as shown in Sahoo et al. (2016). The number of challenges is *exponential* in the size of the PUF, but the entropy is not scaling as fast (Ganji et al. 2016). Such exercise is carried out in the study by Schaub et al. (2020b). The min-entropy is assessed for some PUFs in Delvaux et al. (2016). The underlying question is the relationship between the number of challenges and the obtained entropy as discussed in Schaub et al. (2020b).

Attacks: in Rührmair et al. (2010), modeling attacks have been carried out on many PUF types. A study about composed PUFs is given in Sahoo et al. (2014). The ML attack on Interpose-PUF is presented in Wisiol et al. (2020). Attacks on helper data are presented in Delvaux (2017). The controlled PUF is introduced in Gassend et al. (2002b). Delvaux et al. (2015) gives a survey of PUF protocols. A recent attack by using helper data without manipulation and MA is presented in Strieder et al. (2021). Modeling attacks using physical side-channel are presented in Delvaux and Verbauwhede (2013); Becker and Kumar (2014); Rührmair et al. (2014); Becker (2015). Direct side-channel attacks with EM analysis is presented in Merli et al. (2011); Tebelmann et al. (2020, 2021). The cross-PUF profiling attack is presented in Kroeger et al. (2020a). Template side-channel attacks exploiting the ECC block is described in Karakoyunlu and Sunar (2010). Readout attacks of logic states with a laser are accounted for in Nedospasov et al. (2013).

Characterizations: the dataset corresponding to Schaub et al. (2018) allows us to characterize the reliability of the PUF through repeated measurements. The simulations used to support the study of aging on arbiter PUF in Kroeger et al. (2020b) are available as a public dataset. The toolbox `pypuf` (Wisiol et al. 2021) allows the simulation and test of security against modeling attacks. An overview of tests for PUFs with multi-bin responses is presented in Anik et al. (2023).

Standardization ISO/IEC 20897-1 (ISO/IEC 2020) specifies the security requirements for PUFs along with the description of typical use cases. *ISO/IEC DIS 20897-2* (ISO/IEC 2022) specifies the test and evaluation methods for PUFs. EVITA (FP7 European Project 2020) is a standard for automotive applications that prescribes the use of PUF for security.

14.9. References

Alioto, M. (2021). Physically Unclonable Function database. Thesis, National University of Singapore [Online]. Available at: http://www.green-ic.org/hwsecdb.

Anik, M.T.H., Danger, J., Diankha, O., Ebrahimabadi, M., Frisch, C., Guilley, S., Karimi, N., Pehl, M., Takarabt, S. (2021). Testing and reliability enhancement of security primitives. In *36th IEEE International Symposium on Defect and Fault Tolerance in VLSI and Nanotechnology Systems, DFT 2021*, Dilillo, L., Cassano, L., Papadimitriou, A. (eds). IEEE, Athens. doi: 10.1109/DFT52944.2021.9568297.

Anik, M.T.H., Danger, J.-L., Diankha, O., Ebrahimabadi, M., Frisch, C., Guilley, S., Karimi, N., Pehl, M., Takarabt, S. (2023). Testing and reliability enhancement of security primitives: Methodology and experimental validation. *Microelectronics Reliability*, 147, 115055.

Armknecht, F., Moriyama, D., Sadeghi, A., Yung, M. (2016). Towards a unified security model for physically unclonable functions. In *Topics in Cryptology – CT-RSA 2016 – The Cryptographers' Track at the RSA Conference 2016*, Sako, K. (ed.). Springer, Heidelberg. doi: 10.1007/978-3-319-29485-8_16.

Asenov, A., Slavcheva, G., Brown, A.R., Davies, J.H., Saini, S. (2001). Increase in the random dopant induced threshold fluctuations and lowering in sub-100 nm MOSFETs due to quantum effects: A 3-D density-gradient simulation study. *IEEE Transactions on Electron Devices*, 48(4), 722–729.

Asenov, A., Kaya, S., Davies, J.H. (2002). Intrinsic threshold voltage fluctuations in decanano MOSFETs due to local oxide thickness variations. *IEEE Transactions on Electron Devices*, 49(1), 112–119.

Asenov, A., Kaya, S., Brown, A.R. (2003). Intrinsic parameter fluctuations in decananometer MOSFETs introduced by gate line edge roughness. *IEEE Transactions on Electron Devices*, 50(5), 1254–1260.

Basel, H. (2018). *Physically Unclonable Functions – From Basic Design Principles to Advanced Hardware Security Applications*. Springer, Heidelberg. doi: 10.1007/978-3-319-76804-5.

Bauder, D. (1983). An anti-counterfeiting concept for currency systems. Research Report PTK-11990, Sandia National Labs, Albuquerque.

Becker, G.T. (2015). The gap between promise and reality: On the insecurity of xor arbiter pufs. In *International Workshop on Cryptographic Hardware and Embedded Systems*. Springer, Heidelberg.

Becker, G.T. and Kumar, R. (2014). Active and passive side-channel attacks on delay based PUF designs. *IACR Cryptology Archive*, 287 [Online]. Available at: https://eprint.iacr.org/2014/287.

Böhm, C. and Hofer, M. (2012). *Physical Unclonable Functions in Theory and Practice*. Springer, Heidelberg.

Bösch, C., Guajardo, J., Sadeghi, A.-R., Shokrollahi, J., Tuyls, P. (2008). Efficient helper data key extractor on FPGAs. In *International Workshop on Cryptographic Hardware and Embedded Systems*. Springer, Heidelberg.

Cherif, Z., Danger, J.-L., Guilley, S., Bossuet, L. (2012). An easy-to-design PUF based on a single oscillator: The loop PUF. In *Digital System Design (DSD)*, Izmir. IEEE.

Chuang, K.-H., Bury, E., Degraeve, R., Kaczer, B., Linten, D., Verbauwhede, I. (2019). A physically unclonable function using soft oxide breakdown featuring 0% native BER and 51.8 fJ/bit in 40-nm CMOS. *IEEE Journal of Solid-State Circuits*, 54(10), 2765–2776.

Danger, J.-L., Guilley, S., Nguyen, P., Rioul, O. (2016). PUFs: Standardization and evaluation. In *Proc. 2nd IEEE Workshop on Mobile System Technologies*. Milan.

Danger, J.-L., Guilley, S., Schaub, A. (2019). Two-metric helper data for highly robust and secure delay PUFs. In *IEEE 8th International Workshop on Advances in Sensors and Interfaces, IWASI 2019*. Otranto. doi: 10.1109/IWASI.2019.8791249.

Delvaux, J. (2017). Security analysis of PUF-based key generation and entity authentication. PhD Thesis, KU Leuven, Leuven.

Delvaux, J. and Verbauwhede, I. (2013). Side channel modeling attacks on 65nm arbiter PUFs exploiting CMOS device noise. In *2013 IEEE International Symposium on Hardware-Oriented Security and Trust, HOST 2013*. Austin. doi: 10.1109/HST.2013.6581579.

Delvaux, J., Peeters, R., Gu, D., Verbauwhede, I. (2015). A survey on lightweight entity authentication with strong PUFs. *ACM Comput. Surv.*, 48(2), 26. doi: 10.1145/2818186.

Delvaux, J., Gu, D., Verbauwhede, I. (2016). Upper bounds on the min-entropy of RO Sum, Arbiter, Feed-forward arbiter, and S-ArbRO PUFs. In *Asian Hardware Oriented Security and Trust Symposium*. IEEE.

Dodis, Y., Reyzin, L., Smith, A. (2004). Fuzzy extractors: How to generate strong keys from biometrics and other noisy data. In *EUROCRYPT*. Springer, Heidelberg.

FP7 European Project (2020). E-safety vehicle intrusion protecTed applications (EVITA) [Online]. Available at: https://www.evita-project.org/.

Ganji, F., Tajik, S., Seifert, J. (2016). PAC learning of arbiter PUFs. *J. Cryptographic Engineering*, 6(3), 249–258. doi: 10.1007/s13389-016-0119-4.

Gassend, B., Clarke, D.E., van Dijk, M., Devadas, S. (2002a). Silicon physical random functions. In *Proceedings of the 9th, CCS 2002*, Atluri, V. (ed.). ACM, Washington, D.C. doi: 10.1145/586110.586132.

Gassend, B., Clarke, D., van Dijk, M., Devadas, S. (2002b). Controlled physical random functions. In *Proceedings 18th Annual Computer Security Applications Conference, 2002*. IEEE, Las Vegas.

Güneysu, T. (2012). Using data contention in dual-ported memories for security applications. *Signal Processing Systems*, 67(1), 15–29.

Herder, C., Yu, M., Koushanfar, F., Devadas, S. (2014). Physical unclonable functions and applications: A tutorial. *Proceedings of the IEEE*, 102(8), 1126–1141.

Hofer, M. and Böhm, C. (2010). An alternative to error correction for SRAM-Like PUFs. In *CHES 2010*, Mangard, S. and Standaert, F.-X. (eds). Springer, Santa Barbara. doi: 10.1007/978-3-642-15031-9_23.

Holcomb, D.E., Burleson, W.P., Fu, K. (2009). Power-up SRAM state as an identifying fingerprint and source of true random numbers. *IEEE Trans. Computers*, 58(9), 1198–1210. doi: 10.1109/TC.2008.212.

ICTK (2021). VIA PUF [Online]. Available at: https://ictk.com/VIAPUFIP.

ISO/IEC (2020). ISO/IEC 20897-1. Information security, cybersecurity and privacy protection – Physically unclonable functions – Part 1: Security requirements [Online]. Available at: https://www.iso.org/standard/76353.html.

ISO/IEC (2022). ISO/IEC 20897-2. Information security, cybersecurity and privacy protection – Physically unclonable functions – Part 2: Test and evaluation methods [Online]. Available at: https://www.iso.org/standard/76354.html.

Karakoyunlu, D. and Sunar, B. (2010). Differential template attacks on PUF enabled cryptographic devices. In *2010 IEEE International Workshop on Information Forensics and Security*. Seattle.

Karimi, N., Danger, J.-L., Lozach, F., Guilley, S. (2016). Predictive aging of reliability of two delay PUFs. In *Security, Privacy, and Applied Cryptography Engineering – 6th International Conference, SPACE 2016*, Carlet, C., Hasan, M.A., Saraswat, V. (eds). Springer, Heidelberg. doi: 10.1007/978-3-319-49445-6_12.

Karimi, N., Danger, J.-L., Slimani, M., Guilley, S. (2017). Impact of the switching activity on the aging of delay-PUFs. In *22nd IEEE European Test Symposium, ETS 2017*. Limassol. doi: 10.1109/ETS.2017.7968223.

Karimi, N., Danger, J.-L., Guilley, S. (2018). Impact of aging on the reliability of delay PUFs. *J. Electronic Testing*, 34(5), 571–586. doi: 10.1007/s10836-018-5745-6.

Katzenbeisser, S., Kocabaş, U., Rožić, V., Sadeghi, A.-R., Verbauwhede, I., Wachsmann, C. (2012). PUFs: Myth, fact or busted? A security evaluation of physically unclonable functions (PUFs) cast in silicon. In *CHES 2012*. Springer, Heidelberg. doi: 10.1007/978-3-642-33027-8_17.

Kroeger, T., Cheng, W., Guilley, S., Danger, J.-L., Karimi, N. (2020a). Cross-PUF attacks on arbiter-PUFs through their power side-channel. In *IEEE International Test Conference, ITC 2020*. Washington, D.C. doi: 10.1109/ITC44778.2020.9325241.

Kroeger, T., Cheng, W., Guilley, S., Danger, J.-L., Karimi, N. (2020b). Effect of aging on PUF modeling attacks based on power side-channel observations. In *2020 Design, Automation & Test in Europe Conference & Exhibition, DATE 2020*. IEEE, Grenoble. doi: 10.23919/DATE48585.2020.9116428.

Liu, R., Wu, H., Pang, Y., Qian, H., Yu, S. (2016). A highly reliable and tamper-resistant RRAM PUF: Design and experimental validation. In *2016 IEEE International Symposium on Hardware Oriented Security and Trust (HOST)*.

Maes, R. (2012). Physically unclonable functions: Constructions, properties and applications. PhD Thesis, KU Leuven.

Maes, R. (2013). An accurate probabilistic reliability model for silicon PUFs. In *International Conference on Cryptographic Hardware and Embedded Systems*. Springer, Heidelberg.

Maes, R., Tuyls, P., Verbauwhede, I. (2009). A soft decision helper data algorithm for SRAM PUFs. In *2009 IEEE International Symposium on Information Theory*.

Maes, R., Van Herrewege, A., Verbauwhede, I. (2012). PUFKY: A fully functional PUF-based cryptographic key generator. In *Proceedings of the 14th International Conference on Cryptographic Hardware and Embedded Systems, CHES'12*. Springer-Verlag, Heidelberg. doi: 10.1007/978-3-642-33027-8_18.

Marchand, C., Bossuet, L., Cherkaoui, A. (2016). Design and characterization of the TERO-PUF on SRAM FPGAs. In *IEEE Computer Society Annual Symposium on VLSI, ISVLSI 2016*. Pittsburgh. doi: 10.1109/ISVLSI.2016.18.

Mazady, A., Rahman, M.T., Forte, D., Anwar, M. (2015). Memristor PUF – A security primitive: Theory and experiment. *IEEE J. Emerg. Sel. Topics Circuits Syst.*, 5(2), 222–229. doi: 10.1109/JETCAS.2015.2435532.

Merli, D., Schuster, D., Stumpf, F., Sigl, G. (2011). Semi-invasive EM attack on FPGA RO PUFs and countermeasures. In *Proceedings of the Workshop on Embedded Systems Security*. ACM, New York.

Naccache, D. and Frémanteau, P. (1992). Unforgeable identification device, identification device reader and method of identification. Patent, European Patent Office, EP0583709B1.

National University of Singapore – Department of Electrical & Computer Engineering, Faculty of Engineering (Massimo Alioto) (2021). Physically unclonable function database. Green IC [Online]. Available at: http://www.green-ic.org/hwsecdb.

Nedospasov, D., Seifert, J., Helfmeier, C., Boit, C. (2013). Invasive PUF analysis. In *2013 Workshop on Fault Diagnosis and Tolerance in Cryptography*, Fischer, W. and Schmidt, J.-M. (eds). IEEE, Los Alamitos. doi: 10.1109/FDTC.2013.19.

Pappu, R.S. (2001). Physical one-way functions. PhD Thesis, Massachusetts Institute of Technology.

Pappu, R.S., Recht, B., Taylor, J., Gershenfeld, N. (2002). Physical one-way functions. *Science*, 297(5589), 2026–2030. doi: 10.1126/science.1074376.

Pelgrom, M.J., Duinmaijer, A.C., Welbers, A.P. (1989). Matching properties of MOS transistors. *IEEE Journal of Solid State Circuits*, 24(5), 1433–1439. doi: 10.1109/JSSC.1989.572629.

Roy, J.A., Koushanfar, F., Markov, I.L. (2008). EPIC: Ending piracy of integrated circuits. In *DATE*. IEEE.

Rührmair, U., Sehnke, F., Sölter, J., Dror, G., Devadas, S., Schmidhuber, J. (2010). Modeling attacks on physical unclonable functions. In *Proceedings of the 17th ACM Conference on Computer and Communications Security*. ACM, New York.

Rührmair, U., Xu, X., Sölter, J., Mahmoud, A., Majzoobi, M., Koushanfar, F., Burleson, W.P. (2014). Efficient power and timing side channels for physical unclonable functions. In *Cryptographic Hardware and Embedded Systems – CHES 2014 – 16th International Workshop*, Batina L. and Robshaw, M. (eds). Springer, Busan. doi: 10.1007/978-3-662-44709-3_26.

Sahoo, D.P., Saha, S., Mukhopadhyay, D., Chakraborty, R.S., Kapoor, H. (2014). Composite PUF: A new design paradigm for physically unclonable functions on FPGA. In *2014 IEEE International Symposium on Hardware-Oriented Security and Trust*. Arlington. doi: 10.1109/HST.2014.6855567.

Sahoo, D.P., Nguyen, P.H., Chakraborty, R.S., Mukhopadhyay, D. (2016). Architectural bias: A novel statistical metric to evaluate arbiter PUF variants. Report 2016/057, Cryptology ePrint Archive [Online]. Available at: http://eprint.iacr.org/2016/057.

Schaub, A., Danger, J.-L., Guilley, S., Rioul, O. (2018). An improved analysis of reliability and entropy for delay PUFs. In *21st Euromicro Conference on Digital System Design, DSD 2018*, Novotný, M., Konofaos, N., Skavhaug, A. (eds). IEEE Computer Society, Prague. doi: 10.1109/DSD.2018.00096.

Schaub, A., Danger, J.-L., Rioul, O., Guilley, S. (2020a). The big picture of delay-PUF dependability. In *European Conference on Circuit Theory and Design, ECCTD 2020*. IEEE, Sofia. doi: 10.1109/ECCTD49232.2020.9218396.

Schaub, A., Rioul, O., Danger, J.-L., Guilley, S., Boutros, J. (2020b). Challenge codes for physically unclonable functions with Gaussian delays: A maximum entropy problem. *Adv. Math. Commun.*, 14(3), 491–505. doi: 10.3934/amc.2020060.

Simmons, G. (1984). A system for verifying user identity and authorization at the point-of-sale or access. *Cryptologia*, 8, 1–21.

Simmons, G. (1991). Identification of data, devices, documents and individuals. In *IEEE International Carnahan Conference on Security Technology*. Taipei.

Strieder, E., Frisch, C., Pehl, M. (2021). Machine learning of physical unclonable functions using helper data: Revealing a pitfall in the fuzzy commitment scheme. *IACR Transactions on Cryptographic Hardware and Embedded Systems*, 2021(2), 1–36.

Su, Y., Holleman, J., Otis, B.P. (2008). A digital 1.6 pJ/bit chip identification circuit using process variations. *IEEE Journal of Solid-State Circuits*, 43(1), 69–77.

Suh, G.E. and Devadas, S. (2007). Physical unclonable functions for device authentication and secret key generation. In *Proceedings of the 44th Design Automation Conference, DAC 2007*. IEEE, San Diego. doi: 10.1145/1278480.1278484.

Suzuki, D. and Shimizu, K. (2010). The glitch PUF: A new delay-PUF architecture exploiting glitch shapes. In *CHES*. Springer, Heidelberg.

Tebelmann, L., Danger, J.-L., Pehl, M. (2020). Self-secured PUF: Protecting the loop PUF by masking. In *Constructive Side-Channel Analysis and Secure Design – 11th International Workshop, COSADE 2020*, Bertoni, G.M. and Regazzoni, F. (eds). Springer, Lugano. doi: 10.1007/978-3-030-68773-1_14.

Tebelmann, L., Kühne, U., Danger, J., Pehl, M. (2021). Analysis and protection of the two-metric helper data scheme. In *Constructive Side-Channel Analysis and Secure Design – 12th International Workshop, COSADE 2021*, Bhasin, S. and Santis, F.D. (eds). Springer, Lugano. doi: 10.1007/978-3-030-89915-8_13.

Tuyls, P., Skoric, B., Kevenaar, T. (2007). *Security with Noisy Data: Private Biometrics, Secure Key Storage and Anti-Counterfeiting*, 1st edition. Springer, London.

Vega, C., SLPSK, P., Paul, S.D., Bhunia, S. (2020). MeLPUF: Memory in logic PUF. *arXiv* [Online]. Available at: https://arxiv.org/pdf/2012.03162v1.

Wisiol, N., Mühl, C., Pirnay, N., Nguyen, P.H., Margraf, M., Seifert, J., van Dijk, M., Rührmair, U. (2020). Splitting the interpose PUF: A novel modeling attack strategy. *IACR Trans. Cryptogr. Hardw. Embed. Syst.*, 2020(3), 97–120. doi: 10.13154/tches.v2020.i3.97-120.

Wisiol, N., Gräbnitz, C., Mühl, C., Zengin, B., Soroceanu, T., Pirnay, N., Mursi, K.T. (2021). pypuf: Cryptanalysis of physically unclonable functions. *GitHub*. doi: 10.5281/zenodo.3901410.

Wu, M.-Y., Yang, T.-H., Chen, L.-C., Lin, C.-C., Hu, H.-C., Su, F.-Y., Wang, C.-M., Huang, J.P.-H., Chen, H.-M., Lu, C.C.-H. et al. (2018a). A PUF scheme using competing oxide rupture with bit error rate approaching zero. In *2018 IEEE International Solid-State Circuits Conference-(ISSCC)*.

Wu, M., Yang, T., Chen, L., Lin, C., Hu, H., Su, F., Wang, C., Huang, J.P., Chen, H., Lu, C.C. et al. (2018b). A PUF scheme using competing oxide rupture with bit error rate approaching zero. In *2018 IEEE International Solid-State Circuits Conference, ISSCC 2018*. San Francisco. doi: 10.1109/ISSCC.2018.8310218.

List of Authors

Lejla BATINA
Radboud University
Nijmegen
Netherlands

Sonia BELAÏD
CryptoExperts
Paris
France

Begül BILGIN
Rambus Cryptography Research
Rotterdam
Netherlands

Łukasz CHMIELEWSKI
Radboud University
Nijmegen
Netherlands
and
Masaryk University
Czechia

Jean-Sébastien CORON
University of Luxembourg
Luxembourg

Pedro Maat COSTA MASSOLINO
PQShield
Oxford
United Kingdom

Jean-Luc DANGER
Télécom Paris
Institut Polytechnique de Paris
France

Sylvain GUILLEY
Secure-IC S.A.S.
Cesson-Sévigné
France

Matthias J. KANNWISCHER
Chelpis Quantum Corp
Taipei
Taiwan

Ange MARTINELLI
Agence nationale de la sécurité des systèmes d'information
Paris
France

Nele MENTENS
Leiden University
Netherlands
and
KU Leuven
Belgium

Lauren DE MEYER
Rambus Cryptography Research
San Francisco
USA

Debdeep MUKHOPADHYAY
Indian Institute of Technology
Kharagpur
India

Ruben NIEDERHAGEN
Academia Sinica
Taipei
Taiwan
and
University of Southern Denmark
Odense
Denmark

Colin O'FLYNN
Dalhousie University
and
NewAE Technology Inc
Halifax
Canada

Louiza PAPACHRISTODOULOU
Fontys University of Applied Sciences
Eindhoven
Netherlands

Thomas PORNIN
NCC Group
Canada

Emmanuel PROUFF
LIP6
Sorbonne Université
Paris
France

Guénaël RENAULT
Agence nationale de la sécurité des systèmes d'information
Paris
France

Matthieu RIVAIN
CryptoExperts
Paris
France

Francisco RODRÍGUEZ-HENRÍQUEZ
Cryptography Research Center
Technology Innovation Institute
Abu Dhabi
United Arab Emirates

Franck RONDEPIERRE
Agence nationale de la sécurité des systèmes d'information
Paris
France

Mélissa ROSSI
Agence nationale de la sécurité des systèmes d'information
Paris
France

Mylène ROUSSELLET
Thales DIS
France

Ulrich RUHRMAIR
LMU Physics Department
Ludwig Maximilian
University of Munich
Germany

Peter SCHWABE
Max Planck Institute for
Security and Privacy
Bochum
Germany
and
Radboud University
Nijmegen
Netherlands

Sergei SKOROBOGATOV
Cambridge Research and Engineering
United Kingdom

Abdul Rahman TALEB
CryptoExperts
Paris
France

Yannick TEGLIA
Thales DIS
France

David VIGILANT
Thales DIS
France

Rina ZEITOUN
Cryptography & Security Labs
IDEMIA
Courbevoie
France

Index

C, D

E, F

G, H

P

Q, R

S, T

U, W

X

Summary of Volume 1

Chapter 4. Supervised Attacks
Eleonora CAGLI and Loïc MASURE

Chapter 5. Unsupervised Attacks
Cécile DUMAS

Chapter 8. Mode-Level Side-Channel Countermeasures
Olivier PEREIRA, Thomas PETERS and François-Xavier STANDAERT

Part 3. Fault Injection Attacks

Chapter 9. An Introduction to Fault Injection Attacks
Jean-Max DUTERTRE and Jessy CLEDIERE

Chapter 10. Fault Attacks on Symmetric Cryptography

Debdeep MUKHOPADHYAY and Sayandeep SAHA

Chapter 11. Fault Attacks on Public-key Cryptographic Algorithms

Michael TUNSTALL and Guillaume BARBU

Chapter 12. Fault Countermeasures
Patrick SCHAUMONT and Richa SINGH

Summary of Volume 3

Chapter 4. Code Obfuscation

Sebastian SCHRITTWIESER and Stefan KATZENBEISSER

Part 2. Randomness and Key Generation

Chapter 5. True Random Number Generation

Viktor FISCHER, Florent BERNARD and Patrick HADDAD

Chapter 8. Nonce Generation for Discrete Logarithm-Based Signatures

Akira TAKAHASHI and Mehdi TIBOUCHI

Chapter 9. Random Error Distributions in Post-Quantum Schemes

Thomas PREST